READINGS IN MANAGEMENT

READINGS IN MANAGEMENT

Harold Koontz

GRADUATE SCHOOL OF BUSINESS ADMINISTRATION
UNIVERSITY OF CALIFORNIA
LOS ANGELES

Cyril O'Donnell

GRADUATE SCHOOL OF BUSINESS ADMINISTRATION
UNIVERSITY OF CALIFORNIA
LOS ANGELES

McGRAW-HILL BOOK COMPANY, INC.

New York   Toronto   London

1959

READINGS IN MANAGEMENT

v

PREFACE

One of the difficulties faced by all who read or teach in the area of management theory and policy is the fact that much of the best thought and experience in the field are found in widely scattered sources. Moreover, the great interest in management in recent years has led to a deluge of materials on the subject. Even if a reader wades through this mass of information, he finds difficulty in selecting the most pertinent and representative writings. And even guided by a well-selected bibliography, he is faced by the limitations of libraries and his understandable desire to have the material conveniently at hand. One cannot readily expect students and others interested in management to search libraries and rely on them for their reading even though multiple copies of periodicals and books may be available.

Particularly for students, but for the practicing manager as well, who would like to have some of this writing readily available, a book of selected readings in management has seemed to us to be especially worthwhile. None of the books devoted to an analysis of managerial functions can do much more than to refer to some of the more significant literature of management. The tendency for such books to be rather narrow in approach and to deal summarily, rather than broadly, with the subject matter is unavoidable. These characteristics are not, by choice, the fault of those who write such books; rather, they naturally result from the restrictions of space imposed by the publishers and the size limitations of such a book from the standpoint of the reader.

This situation appears to be especially serious as far as the area of general management is concerned. It is compounded because the source material is not only widely scattered, but because it is also found in books and journals devoted to the social sciences, in business and management association publications, and in journals concerned with functional activities in business.

In attempting to collect in one place some of the significant writings on general management, the problem of selecting appropriate material from several hundred sources is monumental. Uppermost in our minds was the purpose of choosing excerpts from the recognized classics in the field and significant contributions, of both a theoretical and technical nature, to specific phases of general management. These materials have been grouped in a manner that can easily be identified with the organization of our *Principles of Management*.

In choosing the selections, we have been dominated by the desire to reprint a representative sample of the significant literature of management while maintaining a book of relatively limited size and cost. In doing so, we have been forced to leave out many articles and other contributions of a stature and interest equal to those included. Had we chosen to take shorter excerpts of items we could have included many more articles. But we have preferred, in general, to incorporate enough of each item to cover the subject as adequately as the author has intended. While, in some cases, we have omitted unnecessary paragraphs and sentences, we have undertaken to present the material essentially as it was originally presented.

We are indebted to the authors of the selected readings and to their publishers for permission to reprint this material. Their cooperation has been both prompt and helpful.

Harold Koontz
Cyril O'Donnell

CONTENTS

PART SIX. CONTROL

Part One

THE BASIS OF A
THEORY OF MANAGEMENT

The Need for and Possibility of Management Teaching*

Henri Fayol

The real reason for the absence of management teaching in our vocational schools is absence of theory; without theory no teaching is possible. Now there exists no generally accepted theory of management emanating from general discussion. There is no shortage of personal theorizing, but failing any accepted theory each one thinks that he has the best methods and everywhere there may be observed—in industry, the army, the home, the State—the most contradictory practices under the aegis of the same principle. Whereas in the technical sphere a head would not dare to infringe certain established rules without risking total loss of prestige, in the managerial one the most undesirable practices may be indulged in with impunity. The methods used are judged not on their own merits but on their results, which often are very remote and mostly difficult to relate to their causes. The situation might be quite otherwise were there an accepted theory, that is to say, a collection of principles, rules, methods, procedures, tried and checked by general experience. It is not principles which are lacking: were it sufficient to proclaim them to have them prevail we should enjoy the best possible management everywhere. Who has not heard proclaimed a hundred times the need for the grand principles of authority, discipline, subordination of individual interest to the common good, unity of direction, co-ordination of effort, foresight, etc.? It must be admitted that proclamation is not enough. The fact is that the light of principles, like that of lighthouses, guides only those who already know the way into port, and a principle bereft of the means of putting it into practice is of no avail.

Nor is there any lack of methods: their name is legion, but good and bad are to be found side by side at the same time in the home, workshop and State, with a persistence only to be explained by lack of theory. The general public is not in a position to pass judgment on managerial activ-

* Reprinted by permission of the publisher from *General and Industrial Management* (New York: Pitman Publishing Corporation, 1949), pp. 14–16. Mr. Fayol was a highly successful French industrialist who perceived the universality of management and the need for management principles. This excerpt was originally published in 1916 and was based, in part, on lectures delivered in 1908.

ity, hence the importance of establishing a theory of management as soon as possible. It would be neither lengthy nor difficult if a few industrial leaders decided to set forth their personal views on the general principles which they consider most calculated to promote smooth running and on the means most conducive to the realization of such principles. Light would soon be thrown on the subject as the result of comparison and discussion. But the majority of higher managers have neither time nor inclination for writing and most often depart without leaving either doctrine or disciples. Hence too much reliance must not be placed on help from this quarter.

Fortunately there is no need to be concerned with the running of a large-scale undertaking or to proffer a masterly treatise in order to make useful contribution to the building up of theory. The slightest comment appropriately made is of value, and since there is no limit to the possible number of commentators it is to be hoped that once the stream has started to flow it will not be stemmed. It is a case of setting it going, starting general discussion—that is what I am trying to do by publishing this survey, and I hope that a theory will emanate from it. This done, there is the question of teaching to be solved. Everyone needs some concepts of management; in the home, in affairs of State, the need for managerial ability is in keeping with the importance of the undertaking, and for individual people the need is everywhere greater in accordance with the position occupied. Hence there should be some generalized teaching of management; elementary in the primary schools, somewhat wider in the post-primary schools, and quite advanced in higher educational establishments. This teaching will no more make good managers out of all its pupils than technical teaching makes excellent technicians out of its trainees. All that would be asked of it would be services analogous to those rendered by technical education. And why not? It is chiefly a matter of putting young people in the way of understanding and using the lessons of experience. At present the beginner has neither management theory nor method, and in this respect some remain beginners all their lives. Hence an effort must be made to spread management ideas throughout all ranks of the population. Obviously school has a large part to play in this teaching. In establishments for higher education teachers will be well able to work out their courses the day when management forms part of their teaching. It is more difficult to conceive what primary school teaching of management should be. On this point I have made an attempt which I shall set out, without claiming anything for it, in the conviction that a good primary teacher will be better able than I am to select from theory and put within his pupils' reach what is suitable to teach them.

The General Nature and Functions of Systematic Theory *

Talcott Parsons

It is scarcely too much to say that the most important single index of the state of maturity of a science is the state of its systematic theory. This includes the character of the generalized conceptual scheme in use in the field, the kinds and degrees of logical integration of the different elements which make it up, and the ways in which it is actually being used in empirical research. On this basis the thesis may be advanced that sociology is just in the process of emerging into the status of a mature science. Heretofore it has not enjoyed the kind of integration and directed activity which only the availability and common acceptance and employment of a well-articulated generalized theoretical system can give to a science. The main framework of such a system is, however, now available, though this fact is not as yet very generally appreciated and much in the way of development and refinement remains to be done on the purely theoretical level, as well as its systematic use and revision in actual research. It may therefore be held that we stand on the threshold of a definitely new era in sociology and the neighboring social science fields.

"Theory" is a term which covers a wide variety of different things which have in common only the element of generalized conceptualization. The theory of concern to the present paper in the first place constitutes a "system" and thereby differs from discrete "theories," that is, particular generalizations about particular phenomena or classes of them. A theoretical system in the present sense is a body of logically interdependent generalized concepts of empirical reference. Such a system tends, ideally, to become "logically closed," to reach such a state of logical integration that every logical implication of any combination of propositions in the system is explicitly stated in some other proposition in the same system.[1]

In a highly developed system of theory there may be a wide variety of different types of generalized concepts and functions which they may

* Reprinted by permission of the publisher from *Essays in Sociological Theory* (Glencoe, Ill.: Free Press, 1954), pp. 212–219. Mr. Parsons is Professor of Sociology, Harvard University.

[1] For a fuller development of this view of theory, see the author's *The Structure of Social Action* (New York: McGraw-Hill, 1937), especially Chaps. I and XIX.

serve. A thorough discussion of the possibilities cannot be undertaken here, so attention will be confined to those most vital to the general status of the scientific field. The two most general functions of theory are the facilitation of description and analysis. The two are most intimately connected since it is only when the essential facts about a phenomenon have been described in a carefully systematic and orderly manner that accurate analysis becomes possible at all.

The basic category of all scientific description seems to be that of empirical system. The empirical references of statements of fact cannot be isolated from each other, but each describes one aspect or feature of an interconnected whole which, taken as a whole, has some measure of independent significance as an entity. Apart from theoretical conceptualization there would appear to be no method of selecting among the indefinite number of varying kinds of factual observation which can be made about a concrete phenomenon or field so that the various descriptive statements about it articulate into a coherent whole, which constitutes an "adequate," a "determinate" description. Adequacy in description is secured in so far as determinate and verifiable answers can be given to all the scientifically *important* questions involved. What questions are important is largely determined by the logical structure of the generalized conceptual scheme which, implicitly or explicitly, is employed.

Specific descriptive propositions often refer to particular aspects or properties of an empirically existent set of phenomena. Such propositions are, however, empirically meaningless unless the "what" which they qualify is clearly and determinately conceived and defined. This "what," the interconnected empirically existent phenomena which constitute the field of description and analysis for a scientific investigation, is what is meant by an empirical "system." It is that which can, for scientific purposes, be treated at the same time as a body of phenomena sufficiently extensive, complex and diversified so that the results of their study are significant and not merely truistic, and sufficiently limited and simplified so that the problems involved are manageable and the investigator does not get lost in the maze.

The functions of a generalized conceptual scheme on the descriptive level seem to be performed mainly in terms of two types of conceptual elements. The first consists in what is called the "frame of reference." This is the most general framework of categories in terms of which empirical scientific work "makes sense." Thus, in classical mechanics, three-dimensional rectilinear space, time, mass, location, motion are the essential elements of the frame of reference. Every descriptive statement, to be applicable to a mechanical system must be referable to one or more "particles" each with a given mass, capable of location in space, changing its location in time through motion, etc. Besides providing the specific categories in terms of which a system is described, the function of the frame of reference is above all to provide a test of the determinacy of the description of a system. It is a logical implication of the structure of the conceptual system that there is a limited number of essential categories, specific values for which must be obtained before the description can be determinate. Its use is the only way of locating the important gaps in available knowledge.

The second level is that of the structure of systems as such. Phenomena which are significantly interrelated, which constitute a system, are intrinsically interrelated on the structural level. This fact seems to be inherent in the most general frame of reference of empirical knowledge itself, which implies the fundamental significance of the concept of system as that is taken for granted here. Structure is the "static" aspect of the descriptive mode of treatment of a system. From the structural point of view a system is composed of "units," of subsystems which potentially exist independently, and their structural interrelations. Thus a system in mechanics is "made up" of particles as its units. The structure of the system consists in the number of particles, their properties, such as mass, and their interrelations, such as relative locations, velocities and directions of motion.

The functions of the frame of reference and of structural categories in their descriptive use are to state the necessary facts, and the setting for solving problems of dynamic analysis, the ultimate goal of scientific investigation. Besides the immense possibilities of variation in the scope of analysis, there are two aspects of the goal itself; first the "causal explanation" of past specific phenomena or processes and the prediction of future events; second, the attainment of generalized analytical knowledge, of "laws" which can be applied to an indefinite number of specific cases with the use of the appropriate factual data. The attainment of the two goals, or aspects of the same goal, go hand in hand. On the one hand specific causal explanation is attainable only through the application of some generalized analytical knowledge; on the other, the extension of analytical generalization is only possible by generalization from empirical cases and verification in terms of them.

The Coordinative Principle*

James D. Mooney

Organization begins when people combine their efforts for a given purpose. We have shown this by the simple illustration of two people uniting their efforts to lift and move some weighty object. This combination, however, is not the first principle of organization. It is only an illustration of organization itself.

To find the first principle, let us carry the illustration a step further. The efforts of these two lifters must be coordinated, which means that they must act together. If first one lifted, and then the other, there would be no unity of action, and hence no true organization of effort. Coordination first appeared in organization when one of those hairy slow-witted ancestors of ours assumed authority and gave the guttural equivalent of "heave ho!" *Here, then, we find the first principle of organization.*

Coordination, therefore, is the orderly arrangement of group effort, to provide unity of action in the pursuit of a common purpose.

When we call *coordination* the first principle, we mean that this term expresses the principles of organization *in toto;* nothing less. This does not mean that there are no subordinated principles; it simply means that all the others are contained in this one of coordination. The others are simply the principles through which coordination operates and thus becomes effective.

As coordination contains all the principles of organization, it likewise expresses all the purposes of organization, in so far as these purposes relate to its internal structure. To avoid confusion we must keep in mind that there are always two objectives of organization, the *internal* and the *external.* The latter may be anything, according to the purpose or interest that calls the group together, but the internal objective is coordinative always.

AUTHORITY

In some spheres of organization the external objective is not continuous. This is true of army organizations in peacetime, when all external

* Reprinted by permission of the publisher from *The Principles of Organization* (New York: Harper & Brothers, 1947), pp. 5–13. Mr. Mooney was an industrialist and a director on numerous corporate boards.

7

objectives are in abeyance, and the army merely waits for mobilization day, for the day of action. In every form of organization, however, the internal objective must be constant. This internal objective is organized efficiency, and everything that is essential to such efficiency is expressed in the single word "coordination." There can be no waiting for "M-day" in coordination. It is a constant necessity in organization, essential to the existence of the organization itself.

As coordination is the all-inclusive principle of organization, it must have its own principle and foundation in *authority,* or the supreme coordinating power. Always, in every form of organization, this supreme authority must rest somewhere, else there would be no directive for any coordinated effort.

The term "authority," as here used, need not imply autocracy. Where true democracy prevails, this authority rests with the group as a whole, as it rests in our government with the people of the United States. In the simplest and most compact forms of democractic organization it is represented in the entire group, assembled at one time, in one place. Examples in secular government are separated as widely in time as the ecclesia of ancient Athens and the present New England town meeting.

In whatever form it may appear, this supreme coordinating authority must be conceived simply as the source of all coordination, and not necessarily as the coordinating directive that runs through the entire organization. In a democracy like our own this authority rests with the people, who exercise it through the leaders of their choice.

The distinction between authority and leadership is such a vital one that it will in due course be considered at greater length. It is sufficient here to observe that the supreme coordinating authority must be prior to leadership in logical order, for it is this coordinating force that makes the organization. Leadership, on the other hand, always presupposes the organization. There can be no leader without something to lead. Leadership, of course, must exercise a derived authority. In absolutist forms of government the supreme coordinating authority usually exercises its own leadership, but this fact does not alter their essential difference.

Just as vital as the distinction between authority and leadership is that between authority and power, two terms so often confused. Power in the psychic sense—that is ability to do things—is distinctly an individual possession. When we speak of the power of an organization we mean that this power has become collective through coordinated effort.

Authority, on the other hand, is a right. Hence we use the expression "moral authority," and may say of some great teacher, as was said of Jesus, the greatest of all teachers, that he speaks "as one having authority," which means that he has a moral right to speak as he does. In organization, authority is likewise a right, because it inheres legitimately in the structure of the organization. The distinction in the political sphere between de jure and de facto governments is based on the difference between the right of authority, acquired through some procedure recognized as legitimate, and the mere possession of power, however obtained.

The same observations apply to the exercise of authority, a truth that is not altered by the fact that authority rests on *moral right*. Rights cannot be divorced from duties, and if authority does not use its rights with due solicitude relative to these duties, it is sooner or later bound to fall. No organization has any prospect of stability if moral factors are not its basis.

→ MUTUAL SERVICE

Community of interest is the legitimate basis of every organization. In searching for its psychic fundaments we find that it can mean only *mutuality of interest*. This in turn implies mutual duties, which means the obligation to *mutual service*. This obligation is universal, transcending, therefore, the sphere of organization. As expressed in the ancient Roman juridical maxim *do ut des* (I give that thou mayest give), it is the manifest basis of all human relations.

In a special sense, however, it has an application within the sphere of organization. Here it is the moral phase of the principle of coordination. It is for this reason that organizations of all kinds, whether governmental, religious, military, or industrial, furnish our best human examples of the spirit of mutual service.

Although the formal technique of organization has, until recent years, received but scant attention, the humanistic phases of organization have an extensive literature. In this literature the obligation to mutual service is called by various names, among them cooperation, integration, functional relating, and integrated functioning. All these terms suggest the formal as well as the human side of coordination, which shows how impossible it is to separate them. We must keep in mind that organizations are the creations of people, and hence that everything that is formal in organized forms must rest on psychic fundaments.

A true coordination must be based on a real community of interest in the attainment of the desired object. It is equally true that a community of interest that is real, not only in the objective sense but likewise in everybody's consciousness, can come only through a real community of understanding. This means not merely that administration and members must understand each other, but that each and all must understand what the real purpose is and, furthermore, that every group represented in the organization must understand how and why the attainment of this purpose is essential to the welfare of all.

The reason, we think, is obvious. Mutuality of interest or, let us say, a common interest, does not, so far as human consciousness is concerned, constitute an *identity* of interest. The only conceivable means of attaining a true integration of all group interests in organization is through administrative policies that will make this community of interest a more tangible reality to every member of the group.

It is evident that every element of psychic coordination is a necessity in the establishment of harmony in all internal relations. Even this statement, however, does not include everything necessary in a truly coordinated efficiency. Before we leave this subject of coordination, therefore, let us consider one more element, especially conspicuous in church and military organization, which has its lessons for organizers in every sphere.

Doctrine

how is objective going to be accomplished.

Coordination implies an aim or objective. But it does not follow, even where there is a true mutual interest, a mutual understanding, and a degree of mutual participation, that each and every member of the organization does in fact carry in his mind a deep understanding of the objective and how it may be attained. Among the higher officials, those who are responsible for results, this understanding should be ever present. They should know, furthermore, that the more this understanding seeps down through all ranks and grades, until all are permeated with it, the greater will be the coordinated effort and the greater the strength of the organization for the accomplishment of its purpose. It is the necessary means to this end that brings us in contact with the significant word "doctrine."

To most people this word has a religious flavor, and well it may, for, of all forms of organization, religious associations are the ones that are most deeply imbued with its spirit. But the word itself has a broader meaning. We see this illustrated in the various applications of the title "doctor," which means simply the teacher, representative, or practitioner of a doctrine. There is, indeed, a doctrine for every conceivable form of collective human effort.

Doctrine in the primary sense means the *definition of the objective*. In religious associations this doctrine is based on faith, as formally stated in the *creed*. In industrial organizations it is the attainment of a *surplus through service*. In governmental organization we find different and constantly changing doctrines, but always a doctrine of some sort, however varied its interpretations by the leaders and statesmen of history. In this primary sense doctrine is synonymous with the objective.

When we consider, however, the *procedure necessary to attain the objective* we encounter the secondary meaning of the word, which it seems a misnomer to call secondary, for it often transcends the primary meaning in practical importance. This fact the following examples will show.

With a physician or surgeon the doctrine of the objective is obvious. It is to make the patient well. But the doctrine of procedure and its application call for a thorough training and wide experience. Likewise, the doctrine of the military objective is simple. According to the school of Foch and Napoleon, it is the forcing of a decision through the overthrow of the adversary. The necessary procedure, however, constitutes a highly technical art, in which all the principles of military strategy and tactics are involved.

This point is vital in all forms of coordinated effort. Always there is sure to be a doctrine of procedure of some kind, but it is not enough to have such a doctrine, nor is it sufficient for the doctrine to be a sound one. Above all, it is essential that this doctrine shall, in the popular phrase, be "sold" to everyone concerned. Every member of an organization should not only know its doctrine, but he should feel it and absorb it until he lives in its atmosphere and makes it the guide of all his acts.

A doctrine of procedure does not mean a body of set rules that must be accepted as though they were articles of faith. We shall presently discuss more broadly the distinction between rules and principles in organization. "Indoctrination" in the military sense means simply the inculcation of those principles which serve as the guide of the military man, whatever the situation he is compelled to face.

To find a simpler illustration of unity of doctrine, and its necessity in the attainment of any group objective, we may turn to the field of sports, such as our national games of baseball and football, where groups are competing and where success in the attainment of the purpose depends on coordinated effort. In these sports there is a real functional differentiation of duties. In the formal sense, however, the problems of organization are all predetermined by the rules of the game. The primary objection also is so simple that the shortest word will state it. It is to *win*.

When we come, however, to procedure, in other words, to the means necessary to win, we find emerging in each case a real doctrine which accounts for the high importance of the baseball manager and the football coach. Tracing each doctrine through all the intricacies of baseball and football strategy we find that it rests, as it must, on the first principle of organization, namely, coordination of effort. This coordination, so essential to victory in any sport where a number of players combine their efforts for a common purpose, has given us the splendid word "teamwork."

Another illustration in a different sphere is the coordination of a symphony orchestra. Here the purpose is the production of a collective harmony, not as a means to an end but as an end in itself. To attain this end each individual musician merges himself in the common purpose. Functionalism in an orchestra is as varied as the nature of the different instruments. In the orchestra these individual functions derive their importance solely from their contribution to the common purpose, and the relation of each musician's function to this purpose is ever present in the instant result. This fact of the objective resulting instantly from the initial coordination makes the orchestra the supreme symbol and the simplest illustration of a coordinated effort.

DISCIPLINE

One other factor essential to organized efficiency must not be overlooked. Organized efficiency in the pursuit of any objective demands a doctrine, but the efficient application, even of the soundest doctrine, demands in turn an organized *discipline.* By this we mean something more vital than the discipline imposed by command. That is essential, but even more vital is the discipline which command must impose on itself, for such is the first necessity to ensure a truly organized efficiency. Without such self-discipline at the top it would be useless to expect it anywhere else down the line. The commander of a battleship is subjected to a greater degree of discipline than a bluejacket. Even the pope must every year wash the feet of a beggar and must go to confession twice a week. Discipline by example we may call it, but such examples are essential to the discipline of any organization.

The sum of these observations is that the strength of an organization is determined by its spirit, that the spirit must be determined by the purpose and the means necessary to its attainment, and that these means imply a doctrine out of which the spirit of an organization grows and on which it lives. On the other hand, no organization can live on its spirit alone. Coordination must have its formalism, which means its technique or method by which its power is directed to the attainment of the purpose.

The Pressure for Principles: A Challenge to Management Professors *

Leon C. Megginson

The thesis of this paper is very simple; its defense is more difficult; and its implementation will be even more difficult.

My thesis is this: There exists a systematic body of knowledge that constitutes a core of principles of management that are true in all managerial situations; these principles are applicable whether it is a business organization, a government organization, a religious organization, a social or any other type of organization; these principles are also true of all levels of management from the foreman to the top executive.

As a first corollary of this thesis is the belief that if a manager knows these principles and *knows how to apply* them to a given situation, he will perform the managerial functions most efficiently and effectively; also, if the teacher of management knows and understands these principles, he should be able to apply them in teaching the more advanced management courses. This latter statement is true whether the teacher uses the lecture, discussion, case, or any other method of presentation.

Before attempting to defend this thesis, I should perhaps first discuss it briefly and suggest *a* way of implementing it.

To me, there are differences between laws, principles, and fundamentals. First, a *law* is defined as "a statement of an order or relation of phenomena which, so far as known, is invariable under the given conditions." [1] A *principle* is "a general proposition sufficiently applicable to the series of phenomena under consideration to provide a guide to thought." [2] A *fundamental* is a statement that serves as the basis of action.

As is true in the other social sciences and in the natural sciences, there are few laws of management; and there are relatively few principles of management; but there are many fundamentals of management. It is my contention that the long lists of so-called principles found in most management text books today are not, in reality, principles but are, instead,

* Reprinted by permission of the publisher from *The Journal of the Academy of Management,* vol. 1, no. 2 (August, 1958), pp. 7–12. Mr. Megginson is Professor of Business Administration, Louisiana State University.

[1] *Webster's Collegiate Dictionary,* 1943.

[2] L. P. Alford and H. R. Beatty, *Principles of Industrial Management* (New York, The Ronald Press Company, 1951), p. 30.

fundamentals or truisms. If there is to be a true principle of management, there must exist a general proposition that applies sufficiently well to a series of phenomena to provide a guide to thought or action; that is, there must be a statement of probability of cause and effect to guide a person's judgment in the process of decision making, which is the essence of the managerial functions.

Now, I shall try to defend my thesis. Several years ago, Dr. Ronald Shuman in an address before a group at Louisiana State University made the statement that "management is a universal." In his presentation, he emphasized the fact that experience had shown, particularly during World War II, when there was such mass conversion from civilian to war production, and, conversely, following the War, that an effective manager could transfer from one type of industry to another without an appreciable loss of efficiency. This statement implied to me that there must be a unique body of knowledge that formed a set of principles that these managers followed, regardless of the industry in which they were operating. This possibility was so intriguing to me that it led me into an investigation that has progressed intermittently since that time.

The history of management literature is an implication of, and a groping for, this body of knowledge or set of principles. As early as 1644 B.C. the Chinese applied the principle of division of labor.[3] In 1832 Charles Babbage wrote about the principle of specialization, which is another statement of division of labor.[4] All of us realize that Taylor believed there was such a thing as a science of management, and he and his followers attempted to explain and further develop these and other principles which comprise this science. Taylor himself recognized, though, that the development of a set of principles was an evolutionary process. This was evident when he said, "Scientific management at every step has been an evolution, not a theory. In all cases the practice has preceded the theory, not succeeded it. There is nothing in scientific management that is fixed."[5]

As further evidence of this evolutionary development of management it must be recognized that the great progress in manufacturing in this country is most satisfactorily explained on the grounds that managers of industrial concerns unconsciously applied a body of fundamentals which have brought improvements and increased success. One fact that stands out above all else in the writings, autobiographies, and biographies of outstanding managers is that they applied principles in performing the managerial function.

[3] Alford and Beatty, loc. cit.
[4] Charles Babbage, On the Economy of Machinery and Manufacturers (London, Charles Knight, 1832), p. 137.
[5] Scientific Management in American Industry (The Taylor Society, New York, Harper and Brothers, 1929), p. 42.

L. P. Alford attempted to reduce the "laws" of management as they apply to manufacturing into a codified body of knowledge. He said that amid the complexities of present-day manufacturing, the maze of systems, and the innumerable variations of methods, ". . . what executive has not wished for some formulation of the underlying fundamentals which have been developed through the long process of thought and experience? . . . In the very nature of things, such basic principles must exist." [6] Although not agreeing with him that there were some fifty fundamental laws, I must agree with him that there is this body of principles that serves as the foundation for the practice of the management profession.

Adding his voice to the others was Henri Fayol, who said,

The managerial function finds its only outlet through the members of the organization (the body corporate). . . . The soundness and good working order of the body corporate depends on a certain number of conditions termed indiscriminately principles, laws, rules. For preference I shall adopt the term principles whilst dissociating it from any suggestion of rigidity, for there is nothing rigid or absolute in management affairs; it is all a question of proportion.[7]

At the present time there is much controversy raging over the content and methods of teaching management courses. There seem to be three different and distinct groups sharing different opinions. These groups are those that believe that management can be taught as a set of principles that will pervade thinking and application in other areas; those who think of management in terms of policy; and those who believe management should be included in all business courses.[8] Included in the first group and bearing out my thesis is William H. Newman, who says that there exists such a body of knowledge, which he terms basic principles:

A considerable body of knowledge exists about successful techniques for administering an enterprise. This knowledge, however, is in scattered places, often consisting of intangible know-how that is passed from one executive to his subordinates without any clear-cut formulation. Moreover, *basic principles* of administration are frequently so incumbered with a specific application that their key features are not apparent.[9]

In 1955, before a meeting of the American Association of Collegiate Schools of Business, Dr. Robert D. Calkins implied that there was such a body of knowledge when he said,

[6] L. P. Alford, *Laws of Management Applied to Manufacturing* (New York, The Ronald Press Company, 1928), p. iii.

[7] Henri Fayol, *General and Industrial Management* (London, Pitman Publishing Corporation, 1949), p. 19.

[8] Alfred Bornemann, "The Development of Economics and Administration in the School of Business," *The Journal of Business of the University of Chicago*, Vol. XXX, April, 1957, p. 139.

[9] William H. Newman, *Administrative Action* (New York, Prentice-Hall, Inc., 1951), pp. vii and viii. (Italics are Newman's.)

Administration is fundamentally the direction of affairs. It is purposive action and to an increasing degree it is informed, rational, and deliberate action. It draws upon the knowledge of the physical sciences and the practical arts; it employs the knowledge and techniques of the social sciences; but it is overwhelmingly concerned with the choice of ends, ways, and means for the attainment of desired results. It is curbed by moral codes and ethical principles; and it is driven by springs of ambition and devotion that largely escape analysis.[10]

Finally, the same conclusion was reached by Charles E. Summer, Jr., in the study sponsored by the Academy of Management concerning the factors in effective administration. His conclusions are:

The term "field of administration" is used here in a special sense. Traditionally, a *field* implies a systematic body of knowledge. It is an important thesis of this report that the *field of administration* includes not only a cluster of knowledge factors, but an equally or more important cluster of attitudes and abilities. . . .

There is some weight of opinion to the effect that administration is also applicable to all organizations in which people work together toward a purpose—business, government, and nonprofit organizations of all types.

And, . . . there is almost complete agreement that at least parts of administration are applicable to all levels within the organization, from foreman and supervisor to president, from police captain to police commissioner.[11]

It should be emphasized at this point that I am not saying that management is a science. I cannot agree with Taylor that it is a mechanical application of certain principles. Instead, I agree with Sheldon when he says that the exercise of human faculties in combination makes essential the exercise of the human faculty of management, and being the exercise of a special human faculty,

. . . management is an art. The present emphasis is laid upon the science of management. Undoubtedly, there is a science of management, but it is to be sharply distinguished from the art which employs that science. *A profound knowledge of the ascertained and codified facts of management does not necessarily entail a capacity for management.* Scientific knowledge is an essential preliminary to the practice of an art, but it is not the art itself. The science of management has not as yet been reduced to an acceptable form.[12]

It is my contention that it is not a question of management being either *an art or a science,* but that management is a combination of both and that *this combination is not a fixed proportion* but is found in *varying* proportions. I cannot agree with Dean Stanley F. Teele of the Harvard Business School, who says that business management is mixture of art and

[10] American Association of Collegiate Schools of Business, *Faculty Requirements and Standards in Collegiate Schools of Business* (New York, 1955), p. 151.

[11] Charles E. Summer, Jr., *Factors in Effective Administration* (New York, Columbia University, 1956), pp. 113–114.

[12] Oliver Sheldon, *The Philosophy of Management* (London, Sir Isaac Pitman & Sons, Ltd., 1930), pp. 33 and 34. (Italics are Sheldon's.)

science; and although there is plenty of disagreement about the relative proportions,

. . . the present ratio is about 90% art and 10% science. Though a very great variety of developments are presently increasing that proportion which can properly be called science, I am willing to venture a guess that by the end of another generation, the ratio will still be 80% art and perhaps 20% science.[13]

The development of a codified body of knowledge such as I am advocating will tend to increase the proportion of the management function that is scientific and will tend to lower the proportion that is artistic; however, it can never eliminate the latter. This opinion is shared by Clarence Randall, former Chairman of the Board of Inland Steel Corporation, who said, "A lesson of my own business experience is that . . . the art of management, even in an industry that rests for its success on the achievements of the scientist and engineer, requires a broadly cultivated mind." [14]

Just as the medical doctor uses an art in practicing medicine, but bases his skill upon the sciences of biology, chemistry, zoology, and other disciplines; just as the art of painting is based on the science of the mixing of colors; just as the composition of music is based, among other things, upon the science of mathematics (as witnessed by the fact that an electronic computer recently composed a piece of music using mathematical logic), just so is the art of management based upon the other social and natural sciences and the body of principles that go to make up scientific management.

Also, many of the principles of the other fields of knowledge are used by management. For example, two laws of physics apply equally well in managing people. These are Newton's Third Law of Motion, which says that "for every action there is an equal but opposite reaction," and the Law of Inertia, which says, "A body at rest tends to remain at rest; a body in motion tends to remain in motion." Both these principles hold equally true in dealing with employees. Also, many principles of economics are used by management, for example, the Law of Diminishing Returns, the Principle of Marginal Utility, and so on.

The science, or scientific part of management, is that body of principles that I am suggesting exists: the art of management is the application of these principles in dealing with the factors of production of land, labor, and capital; or, from the managerial point of view, men, materials, money, machines, and methods—for everyone who knows *how* does not know how *to do*.

[13] Dean Stanley F. Teele, Harvard Business School, "Knowledge and Wisdom in Education for Business," Dedication of Copland Hall, Ohio University, College of Commerce, April 1, 1957.

[14] *Ibid.*

Now, for the implementation of this idea. This is left up to us—the professors of management. It cannot be done by the National Association of Manufacturers, the American Management Association, the American Institute of Management, or any other group of professional managers; it must come from some esoteric group such as a group of management academicians. It may come from an organization such as the Academy of Management. More likely, this codification of a body of knowledge will come from a professor or scholar who will devote his lifetime to such an undertaking. For, although the practical businessman may notice these phenomena, he is too involved with the daily press of decision making to evolve the necessary principles. A mid-Victorian educator expressed this thought in these words:

He who learns from one occupied in learning, drinks of a running stream. He who learns from one who has learned all he has to teach, drinks "the green mantle of the stagnant pool." [15]

In summary, I believe there is some inherent quality found in good managers that permits them to move from one managerial situation to another and still operate effectively. This quality must be an abstract one and is connected with an individual combination of senses of values that allows an insight into the nature of men, machines, and materials. It must be abstract; otherwise, it could not be transferred from one situation to another, or from one organization to another, without losing its effectiveness.

[15] A mid-Victorian educator as quoted by Mary E. Murphy, *Accounting Review,* October, 1957, p. 637.

Major Processes of Organization and Management *

Catheryn Seckler-Hudson

It may be said that the study of organization and management is essentially a matter of analyzing large enterprises from the point of view of "division" and "synthesis." Division of large establishments is necessary so that manageable units can be agreed upon, and assigned work. This assumes specialization of one or more kinds and therefore calls for coordination or synthesis of the efforts of the specialized persons or units into one whole entity.

In dividing the organization, the leader arranges for proper *distribution* of policies, programs, responsibilities, authority, resources, various kinds of information and instructions, etc. In synthesizing, the leader produces coordination of results and sees to it that there is proper accountability concerning the things which were distributed.

This matter of division and synthesis establishes a two-fold function for the administrator. First, he has the function of organizing—that is, arranging and piloting his enterprise so that each person and each unit within it will be enabled to perform effectively and contribute to the whole. But he also has the function of assembling the individual and group performances within the organization and so combining and relating them as to cause the organizational policy to be achieved. This is the coordinative function. *Both of these functions are continuous and changing.*

If the leader of a large organization is to perform the two functions well, it is essential that he be aided by subordinate leaders who are themselves coordinators. The subordinate leaders may assist in the proper subdivision of the organization and in the synthesis of effort, but their primary responsibility is within the subdivisions which they head, and wherein they do the coordinating. Thus, when the total effort reaches higher levels, and eventually the top, the chief administrator should devote himself to coordinating the already coordinated parts. This kind of an

* Reprinted by permission of the publisher from *Organization and Management: Theory and Practice* (Washington: The American University Press, 1955), pp. 59–66. Catheryn Seckler-Hudson is Chairman of the Department of Government and Public Administration, The American University, Washington, D.C.

arrangement will greatly help the chief administrator and enable him to operate at his proper level. Care must be taken, of course, in the selection and placing of the subordinate leaders. In this connection Paul Appleby has written:

There is more inadequacy in government because of the inability of officials to operate on their proper levels than from any other single cause. But such inadequacy is not inevitable; it is not something that cannot be improved; it is not something predetermined by the limits of the human mind. It stems chiefly from a failure to realize the importance of taking careful note of the qualities of mind, temperament, and personality required for a position on a given level and then searching for those qualities in the person to be appointed.[1]

Implicit in the executive function at the top of the organization and at every level of responsibility down the line are certain matters that have to get done. These have been variously defined and classified. Henri Fayol has analyzed these as functions and listed them under these heads: to plan, to organize, to command, to coordinate, and to control.[2] Luther Gulick had contributed his famous POSDCORB, a word coined to call attention to the various elements of the work of the executive. POSDCORB is made up of the initials which stand for certain processes:

Planning, that is working out in broad outline the things that need to be done and the methods for doing them to accomplish the purpose set for the enterprise;

Organizing, that is the establishment of the formal structure of authority through which work subdivisions are arranged, defined and coordinated for the defined objective;

Staffing, that is the whole personnel function of bringing in and training the staff and maintaining favorable conditions of work;

Directing, that is the continuous task of making decisions and embodying them in specific and general orders and instructions and serving as the leader of the enterprise;

Co-ordinating, that is the all important duty of interrelating the various parts of the work;

Reporting, that is keeping those to whom the executive is responsible informed as to what is going on, which thus includes keeping himself and his subordinates informed through records, research and inspection;

Budgeting, with all that goes with budgeting in the form of fiscal planning, accounting and control.[3]

This is indeed a helpful pattern and useful in many kinds of endeavors.

[1] Paul H. Appleby, *Big Democracy* (New York: Alfred A. Knopf, Inc., 1945), p. 70.

[2] Henri Fayol, *Industrial and General Administration,* English translation by Constance Storrs, with a foreword by L. Urwick, Sir Isaac Pitman and Sons, Ltd., London, 1949.

[3] In *Papers on the Science of Administration* (New York: Institute of Public Administration, 1937), p. 13. [Italics are supplied.]

This writer believes that for each of the principles of organization and management . . . , there are accompanying *processes,* or activities. In government and elsewhere these processes are carried on at every level of responsibility from the top to the bottom of the organization, wherever leadership is found. They go on continuously and are carried forward

FIGURE 12

MAJOR PROCESSES OF ORGANIZATION AND MANAGEMENT AT ALL LEVELS OF OPERATION

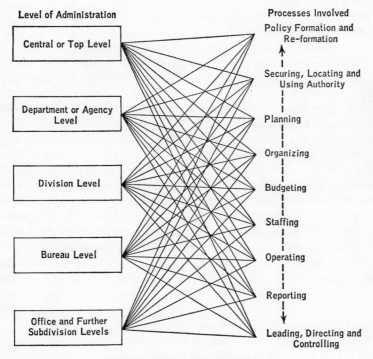

Level of Administration

Central or Top Level

Department or Agency Level

Division Level

Bureau Level

Office and Further Subdivision Levels

Processes Involved

Policy Formation and Re-formation

Securing, Locating and Using Authority

Planning

Organizing

Budgeting

Staffing

Operating

Reporting

Leading, Directing and Controlling

Permeating factors of all the processes
1. Time
2. Place
3. Quality
4. Quantity

Each and all the processes interact horizontally and vertically

well or poorly. If neglected, there is still the impact of neglect, for the processes interweave and interpenetrate each other and condition every level of performance. Each level of performance conditions each process and the totality of this conditioning and reconditioning provides the internal environment for administration (see Figure 12).

In many respects it is unfortunate to discuss the processes separately, for in any actual sense of coordinated effort they cannot be separated.[4] But for purposes of discussion and analysis they are listed below.

The major processes of organization and management include:

1. The process of policy formation and re-formation.
2. The process of securing, locating, and utilizing authority.
3. The process of planning.
4. The process of organizing.
5. The process of budgeting.
6. The process of staffing.
7. The process of operating.
8. The process of reporting.
9. The process of leading, directing, and controlling.

Two additional points are necessary to understand: First, the interlacing and interweaving of the several parts of the organization should be regarded as conditioning each of the processes. Secondly, the permeating factors of *time, place, quality,* and *quantity* pertain to and condition all of the processes at each and all levels of the administrative hierarchy.

The position that there are subordinate principles governing each of the processes might be validated. However at the present stage of development in administrative matters, it is doubtful whether these "practices" can actually be classified as "principles." It would seem sounder to project criteria or *check lists,* in the form of questions, that may be useful in the checking of the application of the principles. Again, the projection of check lists leaves open the matter of whether, in all cases, the particular criterion *should* apply, and invites the reader to question the validity of the criterion in terms of his specific situation. Many of the criteria . . . may seem obvious, but experience indicates that it is frequently the obvious that is most neglected or overlooked. Many of the check lists have been put to practical use, especially in governmental agencies in Washington, D.C., since the writer began preparing them in 1938.

In 1947 the United States Bureau of the Budget prepared a document entitled "The Tasks of Management" which was used in connection with the Bureau's conferences on Organization and Methods. Because it parallels and supplements the "processses" indicated above, it is presented here as modified since its original preparation. It follows: [5]

Although the term "management" is not susceptible to precise definition, management's total job can be broken down into a number of specific "tasks" or duties which are common to the management function no matter where it is carried out. The time and sequence in which management (or the manager) carries out these tasks cannot be specified: neither is it feasible to determine

[4] See Leon C. Marshall and Catheryn Seckler-Hudson, *Forming, Maintaining, and Governing Groups,* mimeographed, Washington, D.C., 1940.

[5] Presented with the permission of the United States Bureau of the Budget.

their relative importance in the total job. Since management is dynamic, it should be recognized that in nearly all cases the tasks listed below are carried on simultaneously and that they represent a continuous and changing process.

This list does not presume to answer the "where," "how," or "who," in the performance of these tasks; it merely specifies "what" tasks must be carried out by management if an enterprise is to function effectively and efficiently.

In order to manage, then, the manager or executive must either carry out the following tasks, or see that they are carried out.

1. Define objectives for the enterprise (policy planning):
   a. Determine the broad objectives in terms of desired results.
   b. Set priorities for these objectives.
   c. Decide the general method of reaching these objectives, e.g., enforcement through education or prosecution.
   d. Establish broad time, cost and quality limits for these objectives.
2. Plan programs to carry out these stated objectives (program planning):
   a. Determine activities necessary to reach objectives.
   b. Set priorities for these activities.
   c. Translate these activities into specific programs by:
      (1) Forecasting work volume by activity and location, clientele group, organization unit, etc.
      (2) Determining available resources; i.e., time, funds, skills, etc.
      (3) Identifying, through analysis and research, special factors or situations which will condition the program.
      (4) Preparing a detailed work plan for the program.
      (5) Setting schedules (both partial and final completion dates) for both the program as a whole and its component parts.
3. Plan and build organization structure to carry out programs:
   a. Examine and compare all basic work processes involved in carrying out the agency's program activities.
   b. Develop structure for line organization to integrate these processes and activities.
   c. Develop staff facilities required to serve each echelon and develop a plan for staff activities.
4. Plan and install procedures and methods for activities:
   a. Develop detailed routines, procedures and systems for substantive, staff, and service activities which give proper attention to:
      (1) Distribution and sequence of work.
      (2) Scheduling and control of work.
      (3) Worker methods.
      (4) Skill utilization.
      (5) Forms, space, equipment, etc.
5. Procure funds and administer finances:
   a. Translate estimates of staff, equipment and supplies into funds by time periods.
   b. Estimate revenues and appropriations required.
   c. Make allotments.

6. Staff the organization:
   a. Define individual positions and the number required.
   b. Determine and schedule staffing priorities.
   c. Recruit and place individuals.
   d. Train the staff.
7. Provide the necessary information for controlling:
   a. Determine what information various echelons of management will require:
      (1) To evaluate performance.
      (2) To relate progress to program schedules.
      (3) To see status of funds (i.e., maintain accounts), staff, plant, equipment and material.
   b. Establish a work measurement system to yield required data.
   c. Develop, where possible, standards of cost, quality, and production for individual work operations.
   d. Set up a system of control records and reports to collect and summarize this information for management's use.
   e. Develop a system of operational audits as a continuing control device.
   f. Determine what information is required about the program's effect on the community and provide for its collection.
   g. Provide for the collection of intelligence and information necessary for planning.
8. Analyze the information provided for control:
   a. Program operations:
      (1) Analyze information on performance provided by reports and surveys to determine:
         (a) Deviation from standards.
         (b) Amount of progress in meeting program schedules.
         (c) Realization of schedules for staffing, expenditures, and procurement.
      (2) Authorize special investigations and surveys to determine causes of poor performance and necessary corrective action.
   b. Program objectives:
      (1) Review information on effect of program on community.
      (2) Analyze outside survey and intelligence data.
      (3) Evaluate correctness of objectives and means in the light of this information.
9. Adjust and improve program operations and objectives:
   a. Revise and improve organizations, procedures, and methods.
   b. Provide more adequate staff facilities.
   c. Improve the quality of personnel and supervision.
   d. Alter program objectives and activities to meet external conditions.
10. Motivate the organization:
   a. Measure the reaction of organization members to policies and objectives.
   b. Analyze external forces and conditions affecting attitude.
   c. Indoctrinate in organization policies.
   d. Interpret and communicate changes in goals promptly.

e. Develop economic, social and other types of incentives.

f. Develop and promote staff according to a systematic plan.

g. Promote the two-way flow of experience and opinion by stimulating communication and the interchange of information.

h. Develop responsible participation and initiative among workers.

i. Utilize performance data to inform worker of his progress.

11. Provide facilities and supplies:

a. Plan the establishment, maintenance and use of plant.

b. Procure and maintain supplies and equipment.

12. Maintain external relationships with:

a. Congress.

b. Administrative superiors.

c. Related agencies.

d. Agency clientele.

e. General public.

13. Issue orders to carry out decisions and policies and develop a system for the control and distribution of issuances.

The Source of Managerial Authority *

Cyril J. O'Donnell

At a time when the subject of enterprise management is just beginning to receive the systematic attention which it has long deserved, there is a serious possibility that the energies of theorists may be diverted from promising research to a barren argument about the source of authority. Business men may be surprised to learn that their right to command is being questioned. For these many centuries they have operated on the assumption that their orders must be obeyed. In relatively recent years it has been asserted that they have no authority except in so far as their subordinates choose to confer upon them the right to issue commands. Perhaps an inquiry into the source of managerial authority will eliminate the basis for disagreement.

Indeed, success in this venture may do much more. It is not only important but extremely urgent that management theory develop a generally accepted explanation of the source of authority. To continue in the present maze of conflict is both unproductive and undignified. Until the matter is settled there is really little merit in talking about what managers do. We must know by virtue of what authority they act at all. The urgency of this issue will be best understood if we realize that the present world conflict in ideologies rests upon diverse theories of authority.[1]

I. THE HISTORIC POSITION

For four decades none of the writers in the management field inquired into the nature of authority, not even into its source. This is not strange, of course, when one considers that their main interest was in the specialization of enterprise tasks. But it is significant that none seemed to think that the right of managers to give orders would be questioned. Seeing all about them that business men, in fact, did give orders and that they were generally obeyed, that the state promulgated laws and that these were generally obeyed also—seeing these things, the facts seemed to point to

* Reprinted by permission of the publisher from the *Political Science Quarterly*, vol. 67, no. 4 (December, 1952), pp. 573–588. Mr. O'Donnell is Professor of Business Organization and Policy, University of California at Los Angeles.

[1] E. L. Allen, "Authority and Freedom in East and West," *The London Quarterly and Holborn Review* (April 1948).

acceptance of the idea that the right to issue orders must certainly rest with the business managers. Indeed, if the question had been put to them they probably would have agreed with Petersen and Plowman, who state that

Under our democratic form of government the right upon which managerial authority is based has its source in the Constitution of the United States through the guaranty of private property. Since the Constitution is the creature of the people, subject to amendment and modification by the will of the people, it follows that society, through government, is the source from which authority flows to ownership and thence to management.[2]

It is more than probable that business men past and present would subscribe to this statement as it stands. They would be surprised to find out that the source of authority is a very contentious subject of political theory.

II. THE DISSENTIENTS

First among the writers in the field of management theory to question this accepted doctrine was Chester I. Barnard, Harvard graduate, successful top manager of large-scale enterprises, and the author of *The Functions of the Executive*.[3] Apparently reading widely in the fields of philosophy and psychology, and being much impressed by the political theory of Harold Laski, Barnard postulates that a correct theory of authority must be consistent with the facts and then proceeds to enumerate several instances wherein the members of an organization have refused to obey persons in authority. On the basis of these "facts" he states that "which specific laws will be obeyed or disobeyed by the individual citizen are decided by him." His approximate definition of authority is "the character of a communication (order) in a formal organization by virtue of which it is accepted by a contributor or 'member' of the organization as governing the action he contributes. . . ." And again, "the decision as to whether an order has authority or not lies with the persons to whom it is addressed, and does not reside in 'persons of authority' or those who issue these orders." This concept means, if anything, that the source of authority lies in the members of an organization, that they confer authority upon their superior by deigning to accept and act upon commands, that they may, if they wish, decide to accept orders seriatim, and that they may withdraw conferred authority at any time by refusing to obey the commands of their superiors.

Barnard does appear to be somewhat disturbed by the obvious conflict between the widely held legal conception of authority and his own, but he proceeds to show that there *really* is no cause for alarm if one merely

[2] Elmore Petersen and E. Grosvenor Plowman, *Business Organization and Management* (Chicago, 1949), p. 62. This is a very restricted view of the source of authority.

[3] Cambridge, 1950. Succeeding quotations from Barnard are from his chapter xii.

sprinkles the discussion with such words as "usually," "greater part," "most of," "considerable," and "essentially"—words which scientists have long since plucked from their lexicon.

The fact of the matter is that Barnard leaves the reader with a distinctly queasy feeling. He does cite two sources which are presumably included to buttress the position which he takes on authority. He has two sentences from Roberto Michels' article in the *Encyclopaedia of the Social Sciences* and three sentences from General Harbord's *The American Army in France*. But even these sources, doubtful as they are for the purposes in hand, are dismissed by the cavalier statement, "We must not rest our definition, however, on general opinion." Overlooking the fact that two opinions certainly do not make "general opinion," Barnard proceeds with his entire discussion of authority on the basis of personal musings.

Mr. Barnard is not alone in his ideas about the source of a manager's authority. Robert Tannenbaum [4] dubs as "formal" the authority of a manager when it is viewed as "originating at the top of an organization hierarchy and flowing downward therein through the process of delegation." He thinks of "informal" authority as a right conferred upon a manager by his subordinates. Thus, informal authority is equated with Barnard's complete concept. But Tannenbaum, as a practical matter, does not actually differ from Barnard because he says,

The real source of the authority possessed by an individual lies in the acceptance of its exercise by those who are subject to it. It is the subordinates of an individual who determine the authority which he may wield. Formal authority is, in effect, nominal authority. It becomes real only when it is accepted.

In order to substantiate this conception of authority, Tannenbaum quotes approvingly from Barnard, Kardiner, Benne and Simon. The citation attributed to Kardiner does not appear to me to be particularly applicable because he is, in that place, concerned with parental authority, and even in this respect is generalizing from a report of one case which illustrates a relationship between a mother and a very dependent child. Benne has written a thoughtful book in which his interest is to develop a theory of authority from a psychological approach. But even Benne says, "Certainly no one could be more aware than I am that the conceptual analysis of authority which I have sought to carry through is in need of further testing, clarification, and correction." [5] Perhaps unnoticed, the quotation from Simon does not support the position taken by either Barnard or Tannenbaum, although it may be said parenthetically that this source could be used to support either the historical position or that

[4] Robert Tannenbaum, "Managerial Decision-Making," *The Journal of Business,* XXIII, 1 (January 1950).

[5] Kenneth D. Benne, *A Conception of Authority* (New York, 1943), p. 157.

of the dissentients. And I may add that Selekman [6] simply cannot make up his mind on the subject so he says:

It is true enough that the management executive must, directly or indirectly, obtain consent to his decisions from the men under him; the importance of such consent now receives ever-increasing recognition. Nonetheless, the manager still wields authority over his workers as of right—a right delegated to him by the owners of the business.

Thus the pendulum has swung from the theory that the source of authority rests with property owners to the theory that it lies with the subordinate members of an organization. It is now moving back from the latter extreme to a position where it points in both directions. This is not an eclectic theory: authority is merely thought of as bifurcated.

III. The Implications of Dissent

At this point I believe that it is pertinent to comment upon certain assumptions underlying the theory of authority which is supported by Barnard and Tannenbaum, and upon the implication of this theory. Mr. Barnard is greatly impressed by his citation of instances wherein members of an organization refuse to obey the commands of their superiors. His cases are rather meagre. He should look into the discussion of this matter by Charles Merriam.[7] Of course, it is generally recognized that there are many instances of refusal to obey. Who has not heard of Tolstoy and his boycott of government, Gandhi and his passive resistance, Americans and their Eighteenth Amendment, and our own revolution which brought us independence? But to generalize from this behavior that the source of authority *therefore* rests with the subordinates, the ordered, the workers, the individual citizens is assuredly a *non sequitur*. These instances merely tell us that sometimes (and, indeed, not very often) subordinates do refuse to obey. An acceptable theory of authority would have to include these phenomena within its framework but not to the exclusion of the much more important patterns of obedience.

In describing how subordinates confer authority upon their superiors, these writers leave the distinct impression that such is the procedure within each organization. Now if this were the actual case, every organization would be in the hands of subordinates. The dream of Sorel and the Syndicalists would be realized.[8] Owners would be quickly deprived of all of their rights. Trade and industrial unions would be triumphant in the destruction of enterprise. Do these writers realize the implications of

[6] Benjamin M. Selekman, *Labor Relations and Human Relations* (New York, 1947), pp. 175–76.

[7] *Political Power* (New York, 1943), pp. 156 *et seq.*

[8] For a synopsis see J. Ramsay Macdonald, *Syndicalism* (Chicago, *circa* 1913).

their doctrine? It is exceedingly doubtful, although neither raises the question.

Authority is the right to command or to act. It implies the possession of the power to coerce, for obviously if there were no way to enforce an order the enterprise would become disorganized and unable to achieve its purpose. To realize how clear this is, the reader should imagine what would happen in a business if workers failed to adhere to the opening and closing hours of work; if individual players on a football team decided to engage their opposites in competition at any time; if the local government could not punish the violators of traffic regulations; and what actually did happen under the Articles of Confederation when the central government taxed the states.

Now, if subordinates do confer authority on their superiors, they must also confer the right to levy sanctions, even to coerce.[9] Neither Barnard nor his followers deal with this aspect. Tannenbaum does get close when he has the subordinate include the disadvantage of coercion in his hedonistic calculus to determine whether or not to obey. But does this mean that such subordinate did in fact confer upon his superior the right to levy sanctions? It seems most unrealistic so to assume.

In the last two decades so much propaganda has poured forth from the trade unions and nonbusiness enterprises that the business manager may be forgiven if he has begun to think that for him there may be, indeed, no rights. He is warned about the political power of the organized workers; he sees that many enterprises are engaged in illegal activities without repression; he is instructed by psychologists on the danger of creating a "block" in the attitudes of his employees; he is taught that the productivity of labor would rise phenomenally if he would only quaff deeply of the milk of human kindness; and, lastly, he is told in a convincing manner that *really* he has no authority except that which his subordinates give to him.

It is anarchistic to imagine that subordinates confer authority on their superiors. This teaching is perilous because it provides a philosophical basis for the direct action of subordinates, for unilateral action, for the complete control of the enterprise by organized workers, for power without responsibility.

IV. A Theory of Authority

A search of the literature on the source of authority reveals that it is the political theorist who has been most concerned with this problem. Inquiry into the source of authority has been made at least since the Greek city-states flourished. As the symbol of power seemed to sway from emperors

[9] Coercion includes sanctions and the compulsion of obedience despite the lack of approval of a majority.

to churchmen to victorious generals to divine-right kings to parliaments, there were always writers at hand with a theory about the origin of authority. Sometimes they were mere time-servers catering to a sovereign, sometimes they were churchmen intent upon the aggrandizement of ecclesiastical power, sometimes they were mere propagandists who wanted to provide an apparently reasonable basis for a "movement," and some-times they were learned men who were genuinely interested in trying to find a satisfactory explanation.

A generally acceptable theory of the source of authority would have to begin with a clear understanding of the natural rights of man. With-out arguing the question, it may reasonably be assumed that there is a human nature, that it is the same for all men, and that man is gifted with intelligence as a result of which he acts with understanding and with the power to determine for himself the ends for which he strives. The natural rights of man are summarized in the law of mankind and in the natural law.[10] These consist of what man "ought" to do, as we understand by the duty-right identity, and of what man "may" do. The sum of these natural rights is the sum of our liberties. It is "law" in the older sense. As a community changes its characteristics, these rights may increase in num-ber, complexity, nature and content—indeed, become such a problem that for mnemonic purposes attempts are frequently made to codify them.

Somehow the moral sense of mankind has developed along with the process of becoming civilized. True it is that our moral unity had a

[10] According to Radin (see *infra* note 12), there have been three rather distinct legal traditions. Aristotle, noting the dichotomy, taught that there was a law by nature and a law by convention. (The Stoics and the Churchmen felt that the latter was no law at all.) A second tradition conceived the law as of two parts, the civil law, that is, the law of a particular community, and the *ius gentium* which was based on the nature of man. The third tradition conceived of a law as a triple transmission, namely, the civil law, the *ius gentium*, and natural law. The second and third comprised the Roman legal tradition.

The *ius gentium* was discoverable by observation—an innately scientific approach because what men do is natural and it can be observed. Now it so happens that the early writers and travelers were more interested in the differences between peoples than in the similarities. Consequently, the reports of how men lived seldom contained infor-mation which we would consider vital from the point of view of the moral unity of mankind. The critics of natural law have seized upon this omission, emphasized the divergencies, and concluded that there really was no *ius gentium*. But careful research does note many similarities which have become the root of the regulation of property, family life and penology. Its modern fruit may be observed in the law of commerce and, since the Dark Ages, in the universal punishment of acts of aggression against man which includes such matters as the security of life, property, person, and family relations.

The concept of natural law was considerably different. It was held that law was derived from reason, that right reason would command what was good and forbid what was bad. Thus the Stoics, arguing from suppressed premises of accepted moral standards, pointed out that slavery was quite proper according to the *ius gentium*, but was irrational since it violated natural law.

precarious beginning in the right of a man to protection should he be cast upon strange shores. The principle was well understood in Homeric times that the rights of man did not arise from a political authority or from a tradition in any one country. In the course of a few millennia the rights of man have increased manyfold and have now found their best expression in the Declaration of Human Rights.[11] "More men than ever before would think it impossible to deny that men as men have rights, and by admitting that they have, they would be asserting the kind of law for which 'natural law' is a bad name, but still a name." [12] The measure of our civilization is the continuous expansion of these rights.

It profits little to speculate about natural rights as they may have existed in the "original state of nature." Anthropological evidence reflects the universal existence of relatively large social units from the earliest times of which there is a record. This means that everywhere man has developed an organized behavior. He has naturally chosen to live a community life.

Now, the *order* in organized behavior implies authority—the right to command coupled with the right to coerce. Malinowski is emphatic in saying that "submission to laws as well as the power to enforce laws and rules are indispensable in human behavior." [13] Otherwise, there will only be anarchy. West is of the opinion that

The prime requisite and firm creator of any community life is a law of order maintained by force. For human nature is such that, in all its most necessary social relationships, it is subject to the permanent threat of the self-assertive impulse, which misinterprets facts, misjudges events, and then, through consequent self-justificatory passion, breaks the social bond, unless it be externally restrained. We may claim this as adequately confirmed. Nursery studies and family life confirm it. Social and natural history confirm it. Modern psychology confirms it. And finally, our common sense tends to confirm it—for all others except ourselves, which is in itself a final confirmation. Individual, group or nation-state, we cannot judge our own cause. And if we try to do so, we shall be reduced again and again to fighting for a supposed "right" against a supposed "wrong," for one set of illusions against another.[14]

Thus man, as an intelligent and sentient being, has chosen to establish an authoritative institution which we have called a tribe, a clan, or a state —the highest expression of the institutional side of secular life—as the best means of furthering the enjoyment of his natural rights.

Quite clearly, then, the state is a mechanism or tool for achieving

[11] Myres S. MacDougal and Gertrude C. K. Leighton, "The Rights of Man in the World Community: Constitutional Illusions Versus Rational Action," *The Yale Law Review,* vol. 59, No. 1 (December 1949).

[12] Max Radin, "Natural Law and Natural Rights," *The Yale Law Review,* vol. 59, No. 2 (January 1950), p. 232.

[13] Bronislaw Malinowski, *Freedom and Civilization* (New York, 1944), p. 27.

[14] Ranyard West, *Conscience and Society* (London, 1942), p. 240.

certain purposes willed collectively by the citizens. The latter, as a group, evaluate their civilization in terms of "what to do next," or, negatively, in terms of the limiting factors. If the state appears to offer better means of achieving their objectives than individual action, the right to act in the area of the limiting factor(s) will be granted in the basic constitution or an amendment thereto. It is obviously unrealistic to think of the peoples of the various states in the world evaluating their objectives in the same way or in the same order of importance. The pursuit of happiness to a Russian may very well be visualized in terms of higher living standards and, until some degree of satiety is achieved in this area, he may not feel at all that free speech or private property is important. Other people may evaluate peace most highly, and be quite willing to overlook incursions upon free enterprise as long as they are protected—a situation that seems to exist today in China and certain Latin-American countries. Thus, it appears reasonable to look upon a people as having a scale of values relative to the development of its civilization; this scale may change with changes in environment, and so on; it is the strategic or limiting or obstructing factor which stands in the way of achieving its purposes, and consequently it is this factor that must first be removed. In the course of time, successive limiting factors are gradually overcome until a people may, ideally, develop a noble civilization in fullest measure.

It is not implied that there is a necessary positive growth factor in the extent to which the objectives of a people are achieved. Should the environmental factors move adversely to the growth of culture, a new evaluation of objectives would be required. For instance, it is conceivable that external forces may combine with internal elements to bring about the loss of a free press in the United States. After a time the citizens may be persuaded that their greatest danger is foreign invasion; that to fend off this threat, free speech, private property, and so on, are really unimportant. A large share of the national product would be devoted to building a "defense." Such a development would, quite clearly, result in a cultural regression similar to that experienced by the great empires which pass in review before the historian.

Neither should it be assumed that because a group is not presently allowed to enjoy certain natural rights it is thereby forever deprived of them. Governments, exercising coercive power, can and frequently do deprive a people of many liberties. This may be done by overemphasizing other objectives the accomplishment of which saps the attention and the substance of a people to a point where the natural rights which it enjoys are disparagingly evaluated. ". . . the people is never corrupted, but it is often deceived, and on such occasions only does it seem to will what is bad." [15]

[15] Jean-Jacques Rousseau, *The Social Contract and Discourses* (New York, 1950), p. 26.

Thus, in considering the degree to which natural rights are enjoyed by a people it makes little difference whether its government uses sanctions or coercion. In the former case, a majority of the people approve of the actions taken, and in the latter case government is by minority. A governing group simply uses different means to keep people from reëvaluating objectives in such a way as to seek actively greater liberties than are presently enjoyed. The period over which success will attend these official efforts is a more or less short run. We know that it took many decades for a people to demand and get a Magna Carta, a monkish thesis tacked to a church door in Wittenberg, and a Declaration of Independence. But eventually freedom from certain types of political and religious repression was obtained. With the passage of time the periods of long struggle seem to grow shorter because the world itself is smaller: communication is swift, a higher level of education is achieved, the lessons of foreign struggles are fresh, and the power of foreign help is imminent. Those who yearn for liberty can now have the bright hope of achievement within their lifetime. Note how quickly the nations of Europe have freed themselves from the necessity of supporting a "royal" family; how rapidly has come the disintegration of British, French and Dutch imperialism; and how quickly spreads around the world the consensus of the United Nations.

And, finally, it should be noted that no social contract is implied. As is well known, Rousseau gave the greatest currency to such an idea. It was his view that there existed in fact a contract between the state and its people whereby in return for civil liberty and the proprietorship of all he possesses, man gives up his natural liberty. This contract was thought of as inviolable without destruction of the state; man could not retrieve his bargain. Jefferson, on the other hand, unequivocally takes the position that the ultimate authority lay in the national will.[16] If the state fails to meet the expectations of the people, there is no reason why the grant of authority could not be modified, restricted, or retrieved. I look upon the state as a mechanism by which a people achieves certain purposes. It has no life of its own beyond that conferred by the national will and it must always be amenable to this will.

Upon its establishment, government proceeds to carry out the purposes of the people by the passage of laws and by providing for their interpretation through a legal system. A law is a rule of conduct approved and promulgated by government authority and enforced by sanctions. Morally, a law may not be enacted which is *ultra vires* of the governing authority. It must be within the areas of authority which the people have delegated to government. The subject matter of the laws may be derived from the generally accepted practices of a people as determined by the courts, it

[16] Charles M. Wiltse, *The Jeffersonian Tradition in American Democracy* (Chapel Hill, 1935), p. 93.

may be directly derived from the provisions of the basic constitution, and it may be conceived by legislators as a rule which will enhance the opportunity of the people to improve the hope of fulfillment of their human nature.

Now, part of the subject matter of legal systems is the well-established law of contract. This is the proximate source of a manager's authority. The relationship between the entrepreneur and employee is one of right-duty in which the manager has the *right to command* and the managed the *duty to obey*. While the employee has the *power* to disobey, and thus he may do so, he is subject to whatever penalties the law provides. Note carefully that *the exercise of the power to disobey does not deprive the manager of his authority*.

But, it may be asked, of what avail is authority when employees exercise their power of disobedience? The manager has recourse to the broad penalties of the law. These have proved generally effective in securing obedience in our society, for, be it remembered, man behaves in an organized way. If this recourse is insufficient, and disobedience spreads to universal proportions, the society is undergoing a revolution which may or may not be morally justified. But the end result will always be a new legal system and, possibly, a new set of managers and managed in which the former derive their authority from the same source as always—the collective will of the people.

As long as the legislative activity of the government and the interpretive activity of the courts are confined to the areas set forth in the basic constitution of the people, the obedience of the latter can be taken for granted. It is a case of prior acceptance. If the trend of law or its interpretation appear to infringe upon the achievement of a people's objectives in a way which has not been foreseen, such a law or such interpretation of its meaning can be clarified by statute whenever the people as a whole so desire. A good case in point was the developing relationships between managers and labor just prior to the passage of the Taft-Hartley Act. It was the general sense of the people that the Wagner Act was being interpreted in such a way as to infringe upon the rights of both property owners and consumers. An attempt to protect these rights was made by the passage of a new statute.

But supposing, it may be said, that the government in question uses its police powers immorally by requiring obedience to laws which are not only *ultra vires* but are an infringement upon natural rights. For example, we are faced in the United States with a strong tendency among the people to approve of legislation which infringes upon the right of free speech and free press—a tendency which John Stuart Mill foresaw [17] and which was deplored by Justice Holmes in *Abrams v. United States.* When a government takes such action, it is a usurper. The people as a group

[17] John Stuart Mill, *On Liberty* (New York, 1885), chapter iv.

have not granted authority to it in this area, but they will obey individually (sometimes) in the same way that we would deliver up our goods
to a highwayman who has the "drop" on us. Force creates no right. But,
of course, this is not the end of the matter. Education and other means
of propaganda may ultimately be successful in reversing the legal interpretation, repealing the statute, or causing a new constitution to be
written. Failing this, there is always the right of revolution which was
invoked by George Washington and the Founding Fathers.

V. APPLICATIONS OF THE THEORY

In order to test this theory of the source of authority, various circumstances may be considered, especially those occasions when it appears that
"man is born free, but everywhere he is in chains":[18] the parent-child
relationships; the operation of a government enterprise; and the managerial authority relationships in business enterprise.

Perhaps enough has already been written about the circumstances in
Spain, Argentina, Russia, China—in fact, all areas that now seem to be
outside the pale of democratic Western European culture—to indicate
that there, indeed, the people appear to be in chains. But the essential
point is that what appears to be a chain, as viewed from the vantage
point of America, need not be and, indeed, probably is not so viewed by
the majority of the inhabitants of those nations. They may consider that
peace or economic welfare is the great desideratum. But we may look
forward confidently to the time when, their present greatest desires having been achieved, they will reëvaluate their objectives and modify the
authority of their governments in such a way as to permit the further
development of their civilization.

Sometimes the relationship between parent and child is cited for the
purpose of illustrating the delegation of authority by the child to the parent. The point is made that very early, and in progressive degree, the
parent is defied and consequently deprived of authority. Now in most
societies the patriarchal conception of the relationship between parent
and child is very strong. We do not choose our parents. Neither do we
"hold a quinquennial inquiry into the manner in which they have dis-
charged their duties and decide, in the light of this, whether we shall
continue to accept them or shall engage others."[19] Our marriage laws
confer on a couple authority over their prospective children. They have
this "anticipatory" authority in the same sense as the sheriff has authority
to incarcerate a criminal before there is a crime. The asserted "rebellion"
of the child should be viewed in the light of the anticipated adjustments
by which parents gradually recede from particular relationships as the

[18] Rousseau, *op. cit.*, p. 3.
[19] Allen, *op. cit.*, p. 141.

child's capacity to act in his own interest develops. Despite frequent poor timing, it is all "according to plan."

We in America have been conditioned during the past twenty years to view with approval the spectacle of our government engaging in the ownership and operation of a few yardstick enterprises. The TVA is a good example. What is the authority relationship of managers and subordinates in this activity? All subordinates have a duty to obey the lawful commands of their superior managers because the right to issue such orders descends from the people as a whole through the Constitution to the federal government which has approved the project. The use of coercive methods to secure acceptance of orders is the manager's right. The recalcitrant subordinate can and should be deprived of employment in this enterprise if he disobeys commands, for he not only endangers the success of the firm in achieving its objectives but he may not, as an individual, decide issues which are the prerogative of the collective will.

In the case of private business enterprise the authority relationships operate in much the same way. Americans have not deprived themselves of their common-law freedom to engage in business activity. It is true that elaborate safeguards for the rights of others have been spelled out in ordinance, rule, law and constitution, but within this framework anyone can engage in business as an individual proprietorship or on a partnership basis without special permission. Since corporations are legal persons created by law, their managers exercise authority which has reached them through the chain of delegation from the people to their constitution and thence through government to its creature. But whether a manager is operating an incorporated enterprise or not, his subordinates are obliged to obey his lawful orders, as long as the employer-employee relationship exists, because the right to command issues ultimately from the collective will of the people. Neither the individual subordinate nor the trade union to which he may belong is in a position to disobey those commands. If there is doubt of their pertinency, the courts may adjudicate the matter. If both the right to command and its interpretation by the courts are unacceptable to individual or union, the proper procedure is to begin political action designed to bring about favorable legislation or an amendment to the constitution. A well-known recent instance of such action resulted in the passage of the Wagner Act.

VI. SUMMARY

Writers in the field of management have either neglected to consider the source of a manager's authority, or they have made the bland assumption that it derives from the right of private property. These positions left them open to vigorous criticism, especially by those who assert that the manager derives authority from his employees. Neither of these positions appears tenable to the present writer. My thesis is that: (1) man as man has natural rights derived from the law of mankind and from the natural law; (2) somehow, man has developed a moral sense; (3) man has always behaved in an organized way and thus submits to laws and the power to enforce them; (4) the tool created for the purpose of developing statute law and confirming natural law is the state; (5) part of the legal system is the law of contract which establishes the right of a manager to command and the duty of the managed to obey; (6) the managed have the power to disobey but the broad penalties of the law generally prove sufficient, along with the natural behavior of man, to achieve obedience; and (7) at the extreme, universal disobedience results in revolution which is succeeded by another legal system embodying status or contract law which is approved by the collective will of the people. The source of managerial authority cannot be conferred upon a manager by an employee; nor is it derived from property rights. It rests ultimately in the nature of man.

Part Two

ORGANIZATION

A. THE SPAN OF MANAGEMENT

The Manager's Span of Control *

Lyndall F. Urwick

There is no question that in the last quarter century the work load of the executive has greatly increased. The top management man has new functions that he cannot possibly delegate completely; take, for instance, his new responsibilities in public relations and industrial relations. Businesses have grown in size, in complexity, and in geographical coverage; the duties and problems of the top executive have increased commensurately.

For this reason, one of the biggest tasks confronting the manager is that of reducing his overload of less important daily duties, thus giving himself time for reflection as well as for the personal contacts with his organization which are the mainspring of leadership—the "personal touch" which makes the executive a business *leader*.

It is in connection with this organizational problem that the "span of control" concept has received so much attention. As the first writer to apply this principle formally to business, I propose here to re-examine the concept, to analyze the main criticisms that have been levied against it, and to demonstrate why and how a restricted span of control can improve executive effectiveness, reduce pressure, inefficiency and incompetence, produce better employee cooperation, and build morale and a sense of unity within the organization.

THE PRINCIPLE

As far as I know, the first person to direct public attention to the principle of span of control was a soldier—the late General Sir Ian Hamilton. His statement (which, of course, reflects his military association) is the basis for subsequent interpretations of the concept oriented to business:

The average human brain finds its effective scope in handling from three to six other brains. If a man divides the whole of his work into two branches and delegates his responsibility, freely and properly, to two experienced heads of

* Reprinted by permission of the publisher from *Harvard Business Review*, vol. 34, no. 3 (May–June, 1956), pp. 39–47. Colonel Urwick is Chairman of Urwick, Orr and Partners, Ltd., Consulting Specialists in Organization and Management. He is also an internationally known scholar, lecturer, and author on management.

branches he will not have enough to do. The occasions when they would refer to him would be too few to keep him fully occupied. If he delegates to three heads he will be kept fairly busy whilst six heads of branches will give most bosses a ten hours' day. Those data are the results of centuries of the experiences of soldiers, which are greater, where organization is in question, than those of politicians, business men or any other class of men. . . .

Of all the ways of waste there is none so vicious as that of your clever politician trying to run a business concern without having any notion of self-organization. One of them who took over munitions [1] for a time had so little idea of organizing his own energy that he nearly died of overwork *through holding up the work of others*; i.e., by delegating responsibility coupled with *direct access to himself* to seventeen sub-chiefs! Now it will be understood why a Battalion has four companies (and not seventeen); why a Brigade has three or four battalions (and not seventeen).

Organizations are run by rule then; a rule whereby from three to six "hands" are shepherded by one "head," each "head" in turn being member of a superior group of from three to six who are being wheeled into line one by one. . . .

As to whether the groups are three, four, five or six it is useful to bear in mind a by-law: the smaller the responsibility of the group member, the larger may be the number of the group and vice versa. That is to say, one N.C.O. in charge of three private soldiers would be too idle; one lieutenant general in charge of six divisional generals would be too busy. The nearer we approach the supreme head of the whole organization, the more we ought to work towards groups of six.[2]

I came across General Hamilton's organizational rule in the early 1920's and called it to the attention of friends interested in management problems. The principle made its initial and rather informal appearance in management literature in 1922. H. P. Kendall of Boston, addressing a meeting of the Taylor Society, stated:

At a dinner the other evening, I heard the President of the General Electric Company asked how many people should report directly to the President of a large industrial company. He said that eight or nine were reporting at present, but that it was too many, and he was reorganizing his functions so that only four or five would report directly to himself; and I imagine that four or five is enough. Not that a chief executive should not have contact with others; but that is about as many general functions as should regularly and directly lead up to him.[3]

Some eight years later I was walking in Paris with a friend, A. V. Graicunas,[4] and he said, "Can you come back to my flat for a good talk?

[1] The British Ministry of Munitions in World War I.

[2] Sir Ian Hamilton, *The Soul & Body of an Army* (London, Edward Arnold & Company, 1921), p. 229.

[3] H. P. Kendall, "The Problem of the Chief Executive," *Bulletin of the Taylor Society*, Vol. 7, No. 2, April 1922.

[4] Believed dead. He was in Lithuania, his native country, when it was occupied by the Russians.

You know you're always stating that the number of subordinates reporting to an executive should be limited; I think there is mathematical proof of it. I shall want your help in presenting the idea."

Group Relationships

The result of our discussion was Graicunas' article "Relationship in Organization," which appeared originally in the *Bulletin of the International Management Institute* in 1933.[5]

Graicunas' idea was basically very simple. The superior, in dealing with his subordinates, must keep in mind not only the direct relationships between himself and each subordinate as an individual but also his relationships with different groupings of the subordinates and the cross relationships between all the subordinates. These relationships vary considerably with the size of the subordinate group. While the supervisor's own direct relationships with individuals increase in proportion to the addition of subordinates, the group and cross relationships increase much more than proportionately. To illustrate:

If A supervises two persons, B and C, he can deal with them individually or as a pair. The behavior of B in the presence of C and of C in the presence of B will differ from their behavior when each is with A alone. Furthermore, what B thinks of C and what C thinks of B constitute two cross relationships which A must keep in mind when delegating work on which B and C must collaborate in A's absence. In other words, even in this extremely simple unit of organization, with two subordinates, a superior must keep up to six relationships constantly in mind.

Then, when a third subordinate, D, is added, A's direct relationships with individuals increase by only 1 (A-D), but the various groupings he may have to deal with increase by 7 (A-B-D, A-D-B, A-C-D, A-D-C, A-B-CD, A-C-BD, and A-D-BC), and the various cross relationships he may have to reckon with increase by 4 (B-D, D-B, C-D, D-C), making a total of 18.

A fourth subordinate brings the total up to 44. The situation really gets complex when a fifth subordinate is added—even granting that many of the relationships will never need explicit attention. The superior again increases his direct relationship with individuals by 1—representing a 25% gain in his *power to delegate*. But the number of group and cross relationships he may have to deal with has gone up from 44 to 100—more than a 100% increase in the burden of *supervision and coordination*.

If a sixth man is added, the group and cross relationships jump to about 200. A seventh subordinate puts the figure at between 450 and 500. And so on.

Graicunas, had he expanded on his principle, would probably have agreed that no executive should have to deal directly with more than a half-dozen men. Actually, because of the psychological concept known

[5] Reprinted in Luther Gulick and Lyndall E. Urwick, editors, *Papers on the Science of Administration* (New York, Institute of Public Administration, 1937), p. 183.

as "the span of attention," which limits the number of items that the human brain can keep within its grasp simultaneously, it seems doubtful if any individual can keep track of and understand the large number of group relationships involved with more than five subordinates.

Graicunas did qualify his observations to some degree. He noted that since it is the cross relationships between subordinates which render the task of supervision more complex, this difficulty will not occur to the same degree where the work is of such a nature as to require few working contacts between the subordinates concerned. This is the same premise which General Hamilton had stated earlier in his bylaw: "The smaller the responsibility of the group member, the larger may be the group. . . ."

In reducing Graicunas' work to a definite statement of principle a few years later, I was careful to include his exception to the rule, and the wording of the concept now stands as:

No superior can supervise directly the work of more than five or, at the most, six subordinates *whose work interlocks*.[6] [Italics added.]

CRITICISM OF CONCEPT

The "span of control" is not a rigid rule to be applied woodenly in all situations. But it is a very useful general principle and a valuable diagnostic instrument in cases where organizational weakness exists. However, the concept has met with substantial opposition, encountering objections both on theoretical and on practical grounds.

Theoretical Attack

Herbert A. Simon has questioned the validity of the span of control in terms of theoretical soundness. He writes:

. . . A contradictory proverb of administration can be stated which, though it is not so familiar as the principle of the span of control, can be supported by arguments of equal plausibility. The proverb in question is the following:

"Administrative efficiency is enhanced by keeping at a minimum the number of organizational levels through which a matter must pass before it is acted on."

In many situations the results to which this principle leads are in direct contradiction to the requirements of the span of control.[7]

Mr. Simon finds further fault with the span of control, which inevitably produces, he thinks, excessive red tape. As he sees it, each contact

[6] Lyndall F. Urwick, *Scientific Principles and Organization* (New York, American Management Association, Institute of Management Series No. 19, 1938), p. 8.

[7] Herbert A. Simon, *Administrative Behavior* (New York, The Macmillan Company, 1947), pp. 26–28.

between organization members must be carried upward until a common superior is found, thus involving needless waste of time and energy.

In general, industry is now tending to pay more attention to the inefficiencies of extended levels of organization than it is to those of the span of control. The International Business Machines Corporation, for example, recently cut one entire level of middle management from its organization and increased the span of control of the remaining executives. One organization expert, commenting on this type of action, has said, "You have a place in which good people can grow rather than stagnate when you discard this traditional idea of the span of authority." [8]

The drive to shorten the chain of command, which in effect denies the importance of careful limitations on the span of control, is an attempt to improve communications, as well as to force some authority and responsibility down into the organization structure. Both these objectives are commendable; nevertheless, the limits of the span of control are real and important restrictions. It is clear that a careful balancing of the inefficiencies of levels against those of spans is necessary—and this is entirely possible, as I shall try to point out later.

Concern for Democracy

Other people object to the idea of a limited span of authority on the ground that it prohibits democratic participation within the organization. According to Burleigh B. Gardner of Social Research, Inc.:

> There is good reason to believe that the gain in productivity achieved by overspecialization and its twin brother, overcentralization of authority, has been lost in the debilitating and enervating effects they have had on employee morale and willingness to cooperate.[9]

In current organization practice and experience, there seems to be a general concern with the relative merits of the highly centralized, pyramidal system with a tight span of control and the flat, more decentralized system. At present, there are many in favor of the flat setup. Proponents of this form of organization argue that it makes for a minimum of social and administrative "distance," and that although the great number of subordinates creates a certain looseness of supervision, this same looseness promotes initiative in a way that no bonus system can match.

In fact, there appears to be a practical dilemma overshadowing management organization—a dilemma between morale and efficiency. In this connection, psychologist Alex Bavelas and a group at M.I.T. have staged

---

[8] Harold Koontz and Cyril O'Donnell, *Principles of Management* (New York, McGraw-Hill Book Company, Inc., 1955), p. 98.

[9] William H. Whyte, Jr., and the Editors of Fortune, *Is Anybody Listening?* (New York, Simon and Schuster, 1952), p. 129.

some interesting experiments with different types of communication networks in order to measure effects on performance:

Bavelas arranged one group of five people so that they communicated with each other in a circular pattern—this would be representative of the flat, democratic organizational structure. He set up another group of five in a hierarchical pattern—this representing the stricter, chain-of-command organization. Both groups were given the same problem and were instructed to solve it by exchanging messages.

Bavelas found that the group in the circular pattern was very happy—but not very efficient; and that the hierarchical group got much more efficient results—but was not very content or satisfied with the manner in which its decisions had been reached. This experiment did seem to prove that morale is very closely tied in with the degree of participation; it is understandable that many managements feel "there is a potential choice to be made. Which is to be emphasized—morale or efficiency?" [10]

Actually, I do not think that efficiency is incompatible with organizational morale. In fact, I feel that one of the strongest arguments for the span of control is that it can, if used intelligently, combine these two vital elements.

Denial of Concept

In addition to the criticisms based on size of organization and lack of democracy, there is the type of criticism which merely states that a given organization is efficient despite apparent infraction of the span of control and that, therefore, the principle is incorrect. For instance, here is a statement describing a wartime administrative situation:

With three squadrons on the station the C.O. had as many as eleven officers under his immediate control (the total strength being about 2500 men and women). Senior R.A.F. officers handle such concerns efficiently, thus denying the oft-repeated statements of leading businessmen that the span of control of one man should be a maximum of six. The Captain of a large battleship has the same wide span of control and can fight his ship just as well. Either the theory of the limited span of control [Graicunas'] is false, or the businessmen who make such statements would do well to learn from the Navy and the R.A.F.[11]

I have found, after 20 years' experience as a management consultant, that the span of control is a principle which is very frequently broken in practice at all levels of business. The fact is, however, that neglect of the concept often underlies the severest management difficulties. When the principle is recognized as valid, it can point the way to simple changes in structure in organizations that are suffering from malmanagement. Such changes have, it is true, added to the number of administrative levels in the instances I have observed. But they have also proved most valuable

[10] *Ibid.*, p. 134.

[11] T. F. Paterson, *Morale in War and Work* (London, Max Parrish, 1955), p. 23 (note).

in improving effectiveness and in rescuing individuals from misdirected charges of personal incompetence.

In some such situations, the manager or foreman concerned had simply been overstraining his capacity by trying to deal with too many subordinates directly. Once this was realized, and the stress was reduced by grouping a certain number of subordinates under an appropriate intermediate control, the effect was marked and almost instantaneous. In many such instances the individual who had previously been under criticism proved more than equal to his responsibilities after the change.

Human Failings

There are, of course, some very strong human temptations to ignore this principle of span of control in business:

(1) Business has so far failed to distinguish rank or status from function, and today we attach an exaggerated importance to unofficial symbols of status. To report directly to the chief rather than to some intermediate authority is such a symbol; subordinates feel they can enhance their status by doing this. Here is one reason why the span of control is not widely accepted in business circles.

(2) Businessmen have always been and always will be cost-conscious. There is sometimes pressure on management to avoid making new appointments, however necessary from the standpoint of better organization, because additional personnel will increase the company's overhead cost.

(3) Sometimes there is the higher level manager who cherishes a misleading stereotype of the "efficient executive." He sees his value as a businessman measured by his busyness; he feels that the number of individuals reporting to him directly is an index of his value to the organization. He likes the sense of power and self-importance generated by a queue on his doormat. Personal ambition sometimes finds an outlet in acquiring additional responsibilities, without too nice a regard for organizational refinements. This tendency, usually described as "empire-building," is universal in all forms of human organization.

Of course, the top executive cannot always take all the blame for the confusion. It is hard for him, as a human being, to resist pressure from his subordinates who want to be directly accountable to him, especially when these men are individuals of weight and value to the company. They may be creative men, whose new ideas and fresh departures need the personal attention of the boss if they are to be introduced successfully.

If, in addition to these pressures, the practical validity of the span of control is itself called into question and those who are tempted to ignore it can defend themselves as being more "democratic" and avoiding administrative and social "distance," the moral courage to enforce the principle sufficiently—and this often requires real moral courage—will be lacking. Business organization will suffer accordingly.

UTILIZING THE CONCEPT

At this point, I should like to examine the criticisms of the principle more closely and show how it may and should be applied in organizational situations.

Taking first the apparent dilemma between managerial efficiency and democratic participation, this "practical" objection to the span of control is not really valid. There is no greater stimulant of morale than a collective consciousness of efficiency. There is nothing which rots morale more quickly and more completely than poor communication and indecisiveness—the feeling that those in authority do not know their own minds. And there is no condition which more quickly produces a sense of indecision among subordinates or more effectively hampers communication than being responsible to a superior who has too wide a span of control.

Needed: A Leader

The choice in managerial practice should not be between the executive who wants to overcentralize—i.e., the man who cannot delegate properly and therefore demands a tight span of control so that he can pass on every subordinate decision, important or not—and the executive who is prepared to trust his subordinates and therefore wishes to see little of them. The first type of manager is simply one who does not know how to *lead* and hence tries to *dominate*. The latter type is one who does not realize that leadership calls for as much constant personal contact as circumstances permit.

However much responsibility may be delegated, subordinates like to have fairly frequent opportunities of ensuring that their chief's mind is in step with their own and vice versa. They need a chance to cement confidence between themselves and the boss, even though at such interviews they may not discuss actual administrative detail at all.

The chief with too wide a span of control tends to frustrate this very proper wish to cultivate mutuality; here is where the argument for "democratic participation" falls flat. In a loosely organized business with no strict limits on the executive's span of authority, subordinates will line up in his secretary's office and will be constantly frustrated when they want a word with him. They will feel that he is too absorbed in business to take time to get to know his men and try to understand and appreciate their problems.

Both the man who cannot delegate and the man who neglects to make a point of meeting frequently with his subordinates have failed in exercising their leadership duties, and consequently confusion and inefficiency are rife. This situation occurs often in organization structures which, in principle, are quite satisfactory and should work well. The trouble can usually be traced to an insufficient appreciation on the part of the chief that leadership has other functions besides administration—functions of representation, initiation, and interpretation.

Above all, the difficulty is due to an inability to see the business enterprise as a social group—rather than only an organization with an economic purpose. This in turn is the reason for neglect of one of the major responsibilities of leadership, as expressed by an official regulation of the British Army in World War II: "The first duty of an officer is to care for, that is to know, his men."

Actually, the problem of morale is largely one of giving the business executive time to be a business *leader,* and this can only be accomplished through cutting down some of the other demands on him.

Misconceptions

Moreover, it is not true that a correct span of control necessarily results in "administrative distance"; that assumption is based on two unfortunately widespread misconceptions:

(1) "That a superior should never have direct contact with individuals at lower levels except through or in the presence of their immediate superior." This is nonsense, and is a clear indication of poor morale within the organization. It shows that the lower-level manager concerned is doubtful of the good sense and loyalty of both his subordinates and the higher executive. The intermediate manager may feel that his own authority is being bypassed by the superior; he has visions of his subordinates using this opportunity to criticize him and advance their own interests with the boss. All this indicates that the lower-level manager is sadly out of touch with his chief—that there has been no chance for confidence and trust to be established—and this condition is particularly apt to occur where the top manager's span of control is too wide.

(2) "That 'the official channels' should be the only avenues of communication." Official channels should, of course, be the only avenue of *official* communication which goes "on the record." But the individual who thinks they are the *only* means of communication has little notion of business as a social activity. He is probably preoccupied with the economic purpose of the undertaking and its formal structure; he doesn't recognize the importance of the unofficial and informal relationships which occur at all levels of any organized activity and which are usually far more important to morale and effectiveness than the official relationships. In any organization where morale is high, most of the important work is done by verbal contacts between men who trust each other, talk the same language, and share the same doctrine. The "record" comes later.

There must, of course, be official records, but the recording procedure is a secondary one. It is the tendency to regard it as all-important which makes so many of our large businesses excessively bureaucratic, and it is because some chiefs elevate paper work to a position of significance which it should not occupy that they are overworked. Many managers spend too large a proportion of their time mulling over documents and too small a proportion cultivating good individual relations with their subordinates. The resulting lack of confidence between people forces them into an elaborate machinery of committees which further restricts their time for personal contacts.

Problem of Levels

Once businessmen have overcome their misconceptions about the span of control, the need for limiting the number of levels in an organization can be appraised in a clearer light.

Herbert Simon has said that the principle of minimizing organizational levels directly contradicts the requirements of the span of control. But the cure for "administrative distance" is not to extend the executive's span of authority beyond what he can reasonably handle in order to reduce the number of levels. Rather, the method is to ensure (a) that at each level the executive has a pattern of organization which enables him to devote ample time to getting to know and understand his immediate subordinates, and (b) that he regards maintaining such personal contacts as one of his principal duties—in other words, that he is a leader before he is an administrator.

Subject to these two limitations it is, of course, desirable to restrict the number of levels as much as possible. Any level which is not vital is an organizational complication which should be eliminated. But in determining the number of levels which are necessary, prime regard should be paid to the span of control, not vice versa. Forcing managers to exceed their feasible span of control merely in order to reduce the number of levels will *increase* administrative and social distance. In effect, the executives will no longer have time to meet with their subordinates and find out what is going on in the organization.

One good way of reducing the difficulties connected with structural divisions is to encourage lower-level personnel in developing cross relationships and communication to the maximum. There are many matters which never need come to the attention of a top executive, many problems which could be solved quickly and satisfactorily at the subordinate level if the habit of communication and cooperation is accepted and promoted. For example:

An employee at the third level of responsibility in Department A (let us call him A3) who has business with an employee at the same level of responsibility in Department B (B3) should not have to climb wearily up the hierarchy to the head of Department A, across to the head of Department B, and down that chain of command until he finally arrives at his destination—his opposite number in Department B's third level. He should go to him direct.

"Excessive red tape" is easily avoided if cross communication is fostered within an organization. Of course if either A3 or B3 thinks the matter is sufficiently important to interest an immediate superior—A2 or B2—the superior should be informed and/or consulted. But action should not have to wait on an extended communication process justified only by the fact that the two department heads distrust each other or have no confidence in their subordinates.

Apparent Exception

At this point I might emphasize again the qualification to Graicunas' span of control principle—that a superior's authority should extend over no more than six subordinates *whose work interlocks.*

In cases where there does not happen to be any interlocking of the work of subordinate units, there is most certainly less need for extensive subdivisions or levels of control. This can be demonstrated by a look at the organizational setup of Sears, Roebuck and Co.—ostensibly a "flat" arrangement.

The chart of the organization of Sears' buying department (the company keeps such charts for the information of visitors) shows close to 100 buyers reporting directly to one manager. However, when the organization is examined more closely, we find that:

¶ Each of these buyers purchases a clearly defined range of articles; there is no reason why the men should encroach on each other's bailiwick.

¶ Where the buyers have common problems or use common services (transport facilities, for example), the manager of the buying department has the aid of four assistants, each of whom specializes in one of these problems or services.

Thus, since there are five people dividing between them the work of supervising the buyers, the real span of control is nearer 20 than 100. And, since the buyers are each responsible for a clearly defined unit of goods, their areas of responsibility only touch occasionally and then just at the circumference. Provided that the buyers have been properly selected and trained, there is not too much for the supervisor to do except to make sure that predetermined standards are being maintained and to deal with casualties.

Similar situations characterize most stores and departments within one store. There is no reason why 20 stores situated in different towns and operating on a more or less standardized pattern should not be controlled effectively by a single chief. These are isolated units with few working contacts with each other. Their departments sell different kinds of goods. Once appropriate personnel have been found and trained, there is little occasion for the type of interdepartmental or interbranch connections and conflicts which would occur in a manufacturing business set up along functional lines. This latter type of organization does demand authoritative supervision if failures in coordination are to be avoided.

I know of a case in Great Britain where the director of a parent company was controlling quite successfully some 30 or more subsidiary companies. Considerable autonomy was allowed to the boards of the subsidiary companies—which were all in different countries. The top manager in this case had only to satisfy himself that each subsidiary was developing "according to plan"; he had none of the daily stresses found in the unified manufacturing concern organized on a functional basis.

THE GENERAL STAFF

The one criticism of the span of control which I have not yet touched on concerns the military experiences which seem to deny the need for any limitations on the top officer's scope of command. T. F. Paterson stated that an officer commanding an air force station in World War II had eleven immediate subordinates and that the captain commanding a battleship had just as many.

I could not agree more with Mr. Paterson that "businessmen . . . would do well to learn from the Navy and the R.A.F." But what businessmen should learn from the military services is how to organize so that the chief executive of a functionally arranged business can handle directly a larger number of specialized subordinates, all of whom have the right of direct access to him, without overstraining his span of control. The answer to this problem lies in the correct use of *general,* as opposed to *special,* staff officers—a form of organization which business has, as yet, rarely understood or applied successfully. This form of relationship, though not necessarily with the title "general staff," is found in an air force station such as T. F. Paterson has described and also in the British Navy.

"Commanding Machine"

During 1917–1918 I had the opportunity to observe at firsthand the organization of a British infantry division. There were 18 persons directly responsible to our Divisional Commander—a dozen more than we have said the ordinary business executive can effectively handle. And yet the Commander seldom spent more than a couple of hours a day in his office, and he maintained very close contact with all his subordinates. How had this apparently successful neglect of the principle of span of control been made to work?

First of all, a clear distinction was drawn between the *nominal* right of direct access to the Commander and the *frequent use* of that right. Normally heads of specialized branches, and indeed all subordinates, were expected to take up all *routine* business through the appropriate general staff officer in the first instance. Only if they regarded the matter as one of outstanding importance which justified them in approaching the Commander—and this only *after* they had failed to secure a satisfactory settlement with one of his general staff officers—would the Commander accept a direct discussion. However, the subordinates' *right* to require direct access to the top officer was clearly recognized, and this safeguarded their independent responsibility in the exercise of their functions as well as their professional or organizational "status."

The Commander had thus only six immediate subordinates who usually approached him directly—the three Brigadiers General in charge of infantry brigades, the Brigadier General of Artillery, and his two principal general staff officers. The latter were able to relieve the Commander of all the routine work of coordinating line and specialist activities. They did virtually all the paper work, drafting operational and routine orders, conducting correspondence, etc. However, the responsibility for every word they wrote was the Commander's; they had no personal authority.

The Commander utilized much of the time saved him from office routine in visiting personally all 18 of his subordinates. The object of his visits was to give them the feeling that he was interested in their problems, that he was concerned with their progress. He did not encourage them to discuss routine business at these meetings. Indeed, if a subordinate did raise a routine question, the Commander almost invariably replied: "Well, you know, I keep out of administrative detail. I'll have to look into it, but I'll see you tomorrow."

Then he would put the paper into his pocket and, when he got back to headquarters, would ask the general staff officer concerned for an explanation of the situation. The Commander would see the subordinate the next day and do his best to satisfy him that the matter had been dealt with correctly, and he would keep tabs on the situation to make sure that everything turned out well.

Thus, at one and the same time the Commander protected his general staff officers from resentment and unjust accusations and satisfied all his subordinates that they had constant access to him and that anything which went wrong would be taken care of promptly. The effect of this system was that while the Commander's nominal span of control was 18 persons, his actual span of control—the number of people with whom he had constant personal contact on *business* matters—was only 6.

Also, the problem of the multiplication of levels was avoided. The general staff officers did not constitute a separate level between the chief and the chief's immediate subordinates. The whole general staff setup was regarded as an extension of the Commander's personality, a "commanding machine" rather than an individual. Communications took place directly between the subordinate units and the Commander; the fact that a letter might be opened and answered by some general staff officer and that the Commander might never see it had no bearing on this principle or on the way in which the communications channel was regarded by subordinate units. All acts of Headquarters were the Commander's acts and no one else's.

Implications for Business

The principle that a chief may delegate a great deal of the daily business of commanding and of coordinating to subordinate officers whose formal communications carry his authority is clearly understood in the combat services. Unfortunately, it is not so commonly appreciated in business circles.

What appears to have happened in business, particularly in the United States, is that, with the growth of industrial specialization, second-line positions in an organization have become increasingly functional or specialist positions. Different functions do have different orientations and interests which sometimes conflict—take manufacturing and marketing, for example—and these conflicts of interest have thrown a very much increased burden of coordination on chief executives. This fact is responsible for much of the pressure on the chief and on higher executives to enlarge their spans of control.

Also, the number of specializations which business must use is always growing, and this means that more and more line units want to have direct access to the top manager. If specialized ideas and methods, particularly when they are new and untried, do not have the chief's interest and support, they cannot gain the recognition they need for successful entry into the field, and the criticisms of the limited span of control cited in this article are probably, in part, a reflection of this "pressure of specialization."

It seems to me that there is only one possible answer to the dilemma. Business should not weaken on the principle of the span of control in a vain attempt to induce already strained executives to stretch a little farther. Rather, it should re-examine its assumptions about organization, and it should give special attention to the use of general staff officers. As I have pointed out, military experience suggests a solution which, while not denying to the specialist his status and final right of access to the chief, allows the top executive to reduce his effective span of control.

The chief will then have time to consider important problems and proposed improvements. He will have the opportunity to see personally and talk with those subordinates who need his help and his approval. The result should be more "democratic participation," greater efficiency, and substantially improved organizational morale.

Parkinson's Law*

It is a commonplace observation that work expands so as to fill the time available for its completion. Thus, an elderly lady of leisure can spend an entire day in writing and despatching a postcard to her niece at Bognor Regis. An hour will be spent in finding the postcard, another in hunting for spectacles, half-an-hour in a search for the address, an hour and a quarter in composition, and twenty minutes in deciding whether or not to take an umbrella when going to the pillar-box in the next street. The total effort which would occupy a busy man for three minutes all told may in this fashion leave another person prostrate after a day of doubt, anxiety and toil.

Granted that work (and especially paper work) is thus elastic in its demands on time, it is manifest that there need be little or no relationship between the work to be done and the size of the staff to which it may be assigned. Before the discovery of a new scientific law—herewith presented to the public for the first time, and to be called Parkinson's Law [1]—there has, however, been insufficient recognition of the implication of this fact in the field of public administration. Politicians and taxpayers have assumed (with occasional phases of doubt) that a rising total in the number of civil servants must reflect a growing volume of work to be done. Cynics, in questioning this belief, have imagined that the multiplication of officials must have left some of them idle or all of them able to work for shorter hours. But this is a matter in which faith and doubt seem equally misplaced. The fact is that the number of the officials and the quantity of the work to be done are not related to each other at all. The rise in the total of those employed is governed by Parkinson's Law, and would be much the same whether the volume of the work were to increase, diminish or even disappear. The importance of Parkinson's Law lies in the fact that it is a law of growth based upon an analysis of the factors by which the growth is controlled.

The validity of this recently discovered law must rely mainly on statistical proofs, which will follow. Of more interest to the general reader is

* Reprinted by special permission of the *Economist*, vol. 188 (Nov. 19, 1955), pp. 635–637, in which this unsigned article (but later ascribed to Professor C. Northcote Parkinson, Raffles Professor of History at the University of Singapore in Malaya) first appeared; and by Houghton Mifflin Company, Boston, publishers of *Parkinson's Law* (1957) in which this article was reprinted.

[1] Why? Why not?—Editor.

the explanation of the factors that underlie the general tendency to which this law gives definition. Omitting technicalities (which are numerous) we may distinguish, at the outset, two motive forces. They can be represented for the present purpose by two almost axiomatic statements, thus:

Factor I. An official wants to multiply subordinates, not rivals; and

Factor II. Officials make work for each other. We must now examine these motive forces in turn.

THE LAW OF MULTIPLICATION OF SUBORDINATES

To comprehend Factor I, we must picture a civil servant called A who finds himself overworked. Whether this overwork is real or imaginary is immaterial; but we should observe, in passing, that A's sensation (or illusion) might easily result from his own decreasing energy—a normal symptom of middle-age. For this real or imagined overwork there are, broadly speaking, three possible remedies:

(1) He may resign.

(2) He may ask to halve the work with a colleague called B.

(3) He may demand the assistance of two subordinates to be called C and D.

There is probably no instance in civil service history of A choosing any but the third alternative. By resignation he would lose his pension rights. By having B appointed, on his own level in the hierarchy, he would merely bring in a rival for promotion to W's vacancy when W (at long last) retires. So A would rather have C and D, junior men, below him. They will add to his consequence; and, by dividing the work into two categories, as between C and D, he will have the merit of being the only man who comprehends them both.

It is essential to realize, at this point, that C and D are, as it were, inseparable. To appoint C alone would have been impossible. Why? Because C, if by himself, would divide the work with A and so assume almost the equal status which has been refused in the first instance to B; a status the more emphasized if C is A's only possible successor. Subordinates must thus number two or more, each being kept in order by fear of the other's promotion. When C complains in turn of being overworked (as he certainly will) A will, with the concurrence of C, advise the appointment of two assistants to help C. But he can then avert internal friction only by advising the appointment of two more assistants to help D, whose position is much the same. With this recruitment of E, F, G and H, the promotion of A is now practically certain.

The Law of Multiplication of Work

Seven officials are now doing what one did before. This is where Factor II comes into operation. For these seven make so much work for each other that all are fully occupied and A is actually working harder than ever. An incoming document may well come before each of them in turn. Official E decides that it falls within the province of F, who places a draft reply before C, who amends it drastically before consulting D, who asks G to deal with it. But G goes on leave at this point, handing the file over to H, who drafts a minute, which is signed by D and returned to C, who revises his draft accordingly and lays the new version before A.

What does A do? He would have every excuse for signing the thing unread, for he has many other matters on his mind. Knowing now that he is to succeed W next year, he has to decide whether C or D should succeed to his own office. He had to agree to G going on leave, although not yet strictly entitled to it. He is worried whether H should not have gone instead, for reasons of health. He has looked pale recently—partly but not solely because of his domestic troubles. Then there is the business of F's special increment of salary for the period of the conference, and E's application for transfer to the Ministry of Pensions. A has heard that D is in love with a married typist and that G and F are no longer on speaking terms—no one seems to know why. So A might be tempted to sign C's draft and have done with it.

But A is a conscientious man. Beset as he is with problems created by his colleagues for themselves and for him—created by the mere fact of these officials' existence—he is not the man to shirk his duty. He reads through the draft with care, deletes the fussy paragraphs added by C and H and restores the thing back to the form preferred in the first instance by the able (if quarrelsome) F. He corrects the English—none of these young men can write grammatically—and finally produces the same reply he would have written if officials C to H had never been born. Far more people have taken far longer to produce the same result. No one has been idle. All have done their best. And it is late in the evening before A finally quits his office and begins the return journey to Ealing. The last of the office lights are being turned off in the gathering dusk which marks the end of another day's administrative toil. Among the last to leave, A reflects, with bowed shoulders and a wry smile, that late hours, like grey hairs, are among the penalties of success.

The Scientific Proofs

From this description of the factors at work the student of political science will recognize that administrators are more or less bound to

multiply. Nothing has yet been said, however, about the period of time
likely to elapse between the date of A's appointment and the date from
which we can calculate the pensionable service of H. Vast masses of
statistical evidence have been collected and it is from a study of this data
that Parkinson's Law has been deduced. Space will not allow of detailed
analysis, but research began in the British Navy Estimates. These were
chosen because the Admiralty's responsibilities are more easily measurable
than those of (say) the Board of Trade.

The accompanying table is derived from Admiralty statistics for 1914
and 1928. The criticism voiced at the time centred on the comparison
between the sharp fall in numbers of those available for fighting and the
sharp rise in those available only for administration, the creation, it was
said, of "a magnificent Navy on land." But that comparison is not to the
present purpose. What we have to note is that the 2,000 Admiralty officials of 1914 had become the 3,569 of 1928; and that this growth was
unrelated to any possible increase in their work. The Navy during that
period had diminished, in point of fact, by a third in men and two-thirds
in ships. Nor, from 1922 onwards, was its strength even expected to
increase, for its total of ships (unlike its total of officials) was limited by
the Washington Naval Agreement of that year. Yet in these circumstances
we had a 78.45 per cent increase in Admiralty officials over a period of
fourteen years; an average increase of 5.6 per cent a year on the earlier
total. In fact, as we shall see, the rate of increase was not as regular as
that. All we have to consider, at this stage, is the percentage rise over a
given period.

ADMIRALTY STATISTICS

	1914	1928	Percentage increase or decrease
Capital ships in commission..............	62	20	−67.74
Officers and men in Royal Navy..........	146,000	100,000	−31.50
Dockyard workers.......................	57,000	62,439	+ 9.54
Dockyard officials and clerks.............	3,249	4,558	+40.28
Admiralty officials......................	2,000	3,569	+78.45

*

Can this rise in the total number of civil servants be accounted for
except on the assumption that such a total must always rise by a law
governing its growth? It might be urged, at this point, that the period
under discussion was one of rapid development in naval technique. The
use of the flying machine was no longer confined to the eccentric. Sub-
marines were tolerated if not approved. Engineer officers were beginning
to be regarded as almost human. In so revolutionary an age we might

expect the storekeepers would have more elaborate inventories to compile. We might not wonder to see more draughtsmen on the pay-roll, more designers, more technicians and scientists. But these, the dockyard officials, increased only by 40 per cent in number, while the men of Whitehall increased by nearly 80 per cent. For every new foreman or electrical engineer at Portsmouth there had to be two or more clerks at Charing Cross. From this we might be tempted to conclude, provisionally, that the rate of increase in administrative staff is likely to be double that of the technical staff at a time when the actually useful strength (in this case, of seamen) is being reduced by 31.5 per cent. It has been proved, however, statistically, that this last percentage is irrelevant. *The Officials would have multiplied at the same rate had there been no actual seamen at all.*

It would be interesting to follow the further progress by which the 8,118 Admiralty staff of 1935 came to number 33,788 by 1954. But the staff of the Colonial Office affords a better field of study during a period of Imperial decline. The relevant statistics are set down below. Before showing what the rate of increase is, we must observe that the extent of this department's responsibilities was far from constant during these twenty years. The colonial territories were not much altered in area or population between 1935 and 1939. They were considerably diminished by 1943, certain areas being in enemy hands. They were increased again in 1947, but have since then shrunk steadily from year to year as successive colonies achieve self-government.

COLONIAL OFFICE OFFICIALS

1935	1939	1943	1947	1954
372	450	817	1,139	1,661

It would be rational, prior to the discovery of Parkinson's Law, to suppose that these changes in the scope of Empire would be reflected in the size of its central administration. But a glance at the figures shows that the staff totals represent automatic stages in an inevitable increase. And this increase, while related to that observed in other departments, has nothing to do with the size—or even the existence—of the Empire. What are the percentages of increase? We must ignore, for this purpose, the rapid increase in staff which accompanied the diminution of responsibility during World War II. We should note rather the peacetime rates of increase over 5.24 per cent between 1935 and 1939, and 6.55 per cent between 1947 and 1954. This gives an average increase of 5.89 per cent each year, a percentage markedly similar to that already found in the Admiralty staff increase between 1914 and 1928.

*

Further and detailed statistical analysis of departmental staffs would be inappropriate in such an article as this. It is hoped, however, to reach a tentative conclusion regarding the time likely to elapse between a given official's first appointment and the later appointment of his two or more assistants. Dealing with the problem of pure staff accumulation, all the researches so far completed point to an average increase of about 5¾ per cent per year. This fact established, it now becomes possible to state Parkinson's Law in mathematical form, thus:

In any public administrative department not actually at war the staff increase may be expected to follow this formula:

$$x = \frac{2k^m + p}{n}$$

where k is the number of staff seeking promotion through the appointment of subordinates; p represents the difference between the ages of appointment and retirement; m is the number of man-hours devoted to answering minutes within the department; and n is the number of effective units being administered. Then x will be the number of new staff required each year.

Mathematicians will, of course, realize that to find the percentage increase they must multiply x by 100 and divide by the total of the previous year, thus:

$$\frac{100 \, (2k^m + p)}{yn} \, \%$$

where y represents the total original staff. And this figure will invariably prove to be between 5.17 per cent and 6.56 per cent, irrespective of any variation in the amount of work (if any) to be done.

The discovery of this formula and of the general principles upon which it is based has, of course, no emotive value. No attempt has been made to inquire whether departments ought to grow in size. Those who hold that this growth is essential to gain full employment are fully entitled to their opinion. Those who doubt the stability of an economy based upon reading each other's minutes are equally entitled to theirs. Parkinson's Law is a purely scientific discovery, inapplicable except in theory to the politics of the day. It is not the business of the botanist to eradicate the weeds. Enough for him if he can tell us just how fast they grow.

B. DEPARTMENTATION

The Division of Basic Company Activities*

Ernest Dale

The alternative methods for dividing the work of a company toward the accomplishment of its objectives are numerous. They include, traditionally, function, product, location, customers, process, equipment, and time. It should be noted that in many companies these various bases of division are combined, and coordinated by checks and balances. But there is usually one predominant type of subdivision of the major company activities, made by the chief executive officer himself, called "basic subdivision," "basic delegation," or "departmentation."

The first step in the division of work is the determination of the primary responsibilities of the enterprise—that is, the purpose of the enterprise, and the major functions necessary to accomplish it. Thus, in a manufacturing enterprise, production is one basic responsibility; in merchandising, it may be advertising; in public utilities, the maintenance of equipment; in the liquor business, the determination of credit risk; in flour milling, the purchase of flour.

The principal or primary subdivision of the activities of an enterprise may then be divided on the following bases:

1. *Function.* Major subdivision by function, subject-matter or principal activities is found in many enterprises where actual control throughout all hierarchies and over all locations is exercised by the heads of managerial functions—such as finance; production (including plant design, construction and maintenance, purchasing); manufacture; engineering (product design or research, possibly quality control); law (claims, tax laws, corporate affairs); human relations (relations to stockholders, employees, community, government); sales (marketing, advertising). Many companies are so subdivided at the top. This arrangement has the advantages of specialization. More importantly, it should make possible adequate time for basic long-run planning and major decision-making and consultation for those in charge of the major management functions. But

* Reprinted by permission of the publisher from *Planning and Developing the Company Organization Structure*, Research Report, no. 20 (New York: American Management Association, 1952), pp. 25–38. Mr. Dale is Professor of Management at Cornell University and senior partner of Ernest Dale and Associates, Management Consultants.

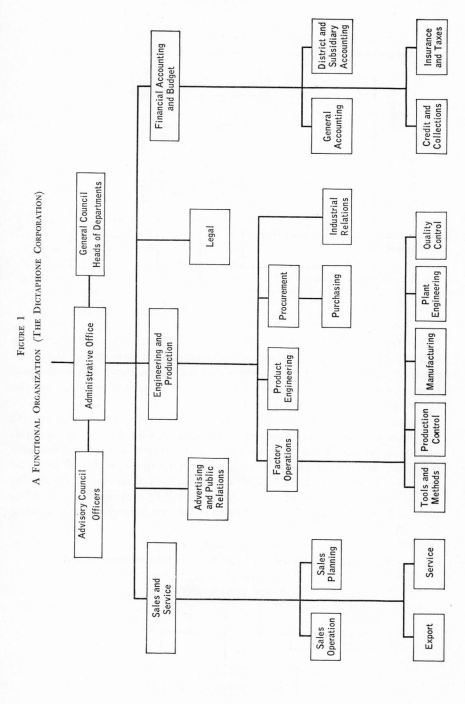

FIGURE 1

A FUNCTIONAL ORGANIZATION (THE DICTAPHONE CORPORATION)

FIGURE 2

ABBREVIATED ORGANIZATION CHART (STANDARD OIL COMPANY OF CALIFORNIA)

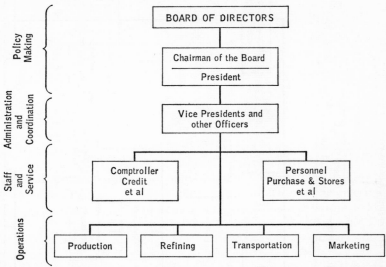

it may result in inter-departmental jealousies and conflicts over the limits of authority. It is also subject to considerable conflict among the local plant managers in multi-plant organizations. An example of a functional type of organization setup is shown in the organization chart of the Dictaphone Corporation (Figure 1).

There appears to be a certain degree of uniformity in basic managerial functions of the top organization structure, at least in very large companies, as is shown in the accompanying illustrations of abbreviated organization charts (Figures 2–4). Of particular interest is the abbreviated organization chart of Standard Oil Company of California (Figure 2), which employs the use of the conventional line and staff organization plan and, in addition, identifies in vertical arrangement the following

FIGURE 3

ABBREVIATED ORGANIZATION CHART (GENERAL MOTORS CORPORATION)

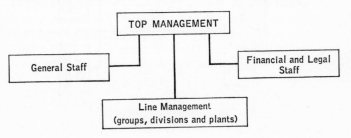

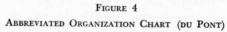

FIGURE 4

ABBREVIATED ORGANIZATION CHART (DU PONT)

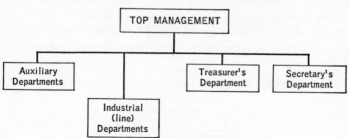

basic functional groups: Policy Making, Administration and Coordination, Staff and Service, and Operations.

2. *Product.* Management activities may be grouped on the basis of the major types of products or services marketed, and sold separately. This kind of grouping is used by some large companies manufacturing a diverse product line.

At General Foods Corporation and International Harvester Company, the major subdivisions of work are on a product basis. Other examples are found in merchandising, automobile, chemicals and meat packing. Grouping by product has the advantage of bringing together and coordinating in one place major activities required to make a particular product (purchasing, engineering, production, distribution, etc.). Such an arrangement provides a particularly sound basis for decentralization. It may also make possible close control and accounting comparability through central staff agencies.

Even in the "mono-product plants" (as General R. Johnson, President of Johnson & Johnson, describes them) it may be wise to make "little ones out of big ones." For example, at the General Electric Company the refrigerator cabinet is made separately from refrigerator compressor units. Or in the production of locomotives, the cabs and running gear are made in separate sections, erected and assembled in another section; the rotating units are made in another shop; and control gadgets in still another. In making control gadgets of infinite variety, the necessity for a multi-product plant really arises.

Figure 5 shows the product organization at The Kendall Company, a medium-sized company which is famous for its work in scientific management. It shows a basic organization built about three major products. It also shows in an interesting way the provision of staff services to these line divisions, the operation of which is decentralized, while coordination and control are centralized.

3. *Location* (also called territorial or geographical division or departmentation). Under this type of arrangement, all activities performed in a

particular area are brought together. It is found in companies serving customers on a national or international scale—e.g., the liquor business, railroads, chain stores, life insurance companies, the overseas branches of motor car and oil companies. The product and locational principles may be combined, with different factories in different locations devoted to the production of different types of products (e.g., General Motors).

FIGURE 5

PRODUCT ORGANIZATION (KENDALL COMPANY)

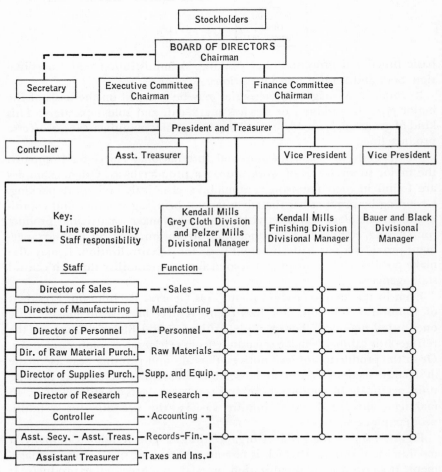

The major subdivisions of oil companies are often on a regional basis, since the natural unit of work centers around the major oil-producing fields. Production and selling or the selling function alone may often be subdivided on a regional basis. The advantage of such a division is that the power of decision-making is concentrated near the source of origin and is all-inclusive, with functional central control. It prevents the losses of efficiency that arise when a company spreads out too thinly. It ensures that careful account is taken of local conditions—an important factor, since the problems of selling may be different in different parts of the country. It makes it possible to take advantage immediately of favorable opportunities arising on the spot. It permits coordination on a manageable scale. It facilitates operation in times of emergency or war. Finally, it provides opportunity for training of lower executives in a wide range of activities so that qualified men will be available to fill vacancies in higher jobs.

Figure 6 illustrates territorial or geographical division of company activities.

FIGURE 6

TERRITORIAL DIVISION OF ACTIVITIES (AMERICAN FELT COMPANY)

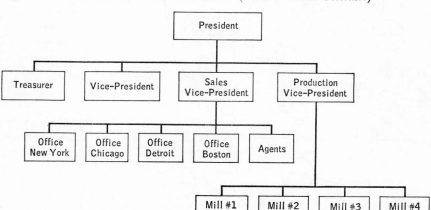

4. *Customers.* Major subdivision on a customer basis occurs in certain fields—radio and television, for example. Here emphasis is principally on selling programs to individual clients, such as a cigarette company, a soap manufacturer, etc. Lower level subdivisions on a customer basis are found, for example, on railroads (Pullman and Coach travellers), and insurance companies (type of policy-holders, sometimes divided by groups of serial numbers).

In a broader sense, not only customers, but other parties connected with the enterprise may be represented on the organization chart. Figure 7 shows such a division of functions in terms of management communications to its own people at all levels—stockholders, suppliers, financiers, the consumer audience and the general audience. While the usual organization chart shows the structure of the management hierarchy, this chart shows the inter-relationships (and their absence) between the various "publics" connected with the enterprise. It shows the functions which fall into natural groupings and the combinations of functions which are possible in various managerial activities. For instance, in preparing the company annual report, its uses and the varying interests of the different groups may be indicated by such a chart. (This chart was prepared by A. F. Arnold, designer and management consultant to industry.)

FIGURE 7

DIVISION OF FUNCTIONS SHOWN IN TERMS OF MANAGEMENT COMMUNICATION

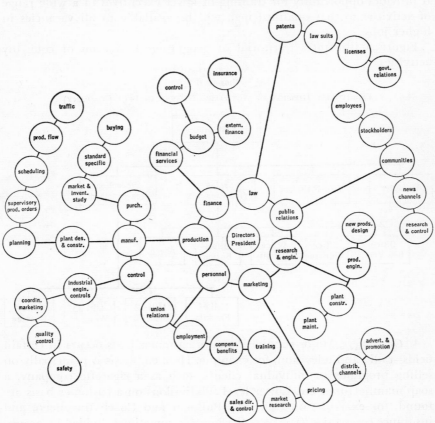

5. *Process.* In integrated textile concerns, major divisions may be made on the basis of operational sequence—e.g., spinning, weaving, bleaching, dyeing, inspection, boxing, shipping. In steel and men's and women's clothing subdividing is often based on the process.

6. *Equipment.* In certain fields, equipment determines major subdivisions. In a secretarial school, for example, the subdivisions may be determined by the chief instruments whose operation is taught, such as the typewriter, the stenotyping machine, the comptometer, etc. (often identical with process).

7. *Time.* Division of work may be based on time sequences, with the work broken down under the categories of planning, execution and control. Thus the first major business division would be devoted to the formulation of objectives, methods of accomplishing them, forecasts and budgets. The second major division would be devoted to the execution of the plans, and would correspond roughly to the major operating group in a business. The third major division is devoted to the control of the results of execution in the light of the objectives and plans of the business.

To present an illustration, at one prominent company the general manager has three principal assistants, each of whom is responsible to him for one of the three main aspects of management, i.e., planning, execution, and control. There are three aspects of planning. In order to do a job one must analyze it carefully and study the available resources. Next, one must balance resources against the job, and design the job to fit the resources. The program must be scheduled on a time basis, and must meet certain set standards of quality and quantity. All these activities are found under the First Vice President. In another corporation this might be a continuing function of the secretariat of a general policy or planning committee. Although the committee may be made up of certain heads of subordinate departments, the permanent secretariat is in fact the Office of the Vice President. Second, general management is supplied with a Vice President for Operations, charged with the execution of the company's program. He is responsible for the day-to-day coordination, direction and supervision of the company's affairs. To his desk come the thousand and one issues which demand prompt decisions to expedite the efficient execution of any large and complex program. And, finally, in the jurisdiction of the Third Vice President is the function of controllership. His is the job of keeping the progress of the company under scrutiny, comparing it constantly with its program. One might say that this Third Vice President serves the other two. He serves the planner by making prognosticative analyses, and by analysis of past performance which can serve as the basis for future program activities. Obviously, he is a most valuable aid to the General Manager, because he is able to make decisions on the basis of *all* the facts—not merely those which happen to come to him in connection with specific problems.

8. *The "harmonious overlap."* Another method of work division may be useful, particularly in research work which must be speedily completed to meet competition or fulfill an urgent customer requirement. It can sometimes be applied to a variety of rush jobs.

This method of work division may be best explained by recounting Dr. Alexander Sachs' conference with the late President F. D. Roosevelt in 1939 on dividing the work on the atomic bomb construction:

F.D.R. was worried whether an atomic weapon could be ready in time to decide the outcome of the war. Dr. Sachs had estimated the project might cost two billions, and honestly told the President that, ordinarily, it would take 25 years to do the job. He explained to F.D.R. that he had searched the history of human thought for an example of how time could be telescoped.

He found the example in music, he says. The composer of music had ways of making time three-layered. Remember the old round you used to sing: "Are you sleeping, etc.?" Three tunes going at once, harmoniously overlapping each other. This, he advised, was what must be done with the atomic project.

"When you start one part of the project, assume you have finished it success- fully, and start the next as if you had." That is exactly what was done, probably for the first time with such a huge undertaking. It worked.[1]

9. *Coordination and balance.* An attempt has been made to bring to- gether the various factors of organizational planning in such a way that each acts as a check or balance on the others. In his *Design for Industrial Co-ordination,*[2] Robert W. Porter set out a technique for coordinating the basic functions in the field of industrial organization. He set up seven major categories for classifying industrial activities, with three subsidiary classifications for each:

1. The problems of policy, performance and compensation, identified as tech- nical problems.
2. The problems of planning, production and inspection, identified as func- tional problems.
3. The problems of administration, management and operation, identified as jurisdictional problems.
4. The problems of communication, cooperation and control, identified as organizational problems.
5. The problems of executive capacity dealing with intellect, volition and ethics, identified as leadership problems.
6. The problems of employee stimulation, application and discipline, identi- fied as institutional problems.
7. The problems of expectancy, efficiency and economy, identified as measure- ment problems.

The author attempts, on the basis of wide practical experience, to bring out the inter-operation and relationships of the 21 elements of performance, so that staff needs can be reduced, while the coordination process is improved. It is claimed that this plan of division has the advan- tages of economizing staff services, improving communication, cutting down jurisdictional problems, and providing better balance in general.

The foregoing are some general guides for determining how the work of the organization may be subdivided, and what consequences may follow. Their specific application will depend upon the special needs of the enterprise. There is no indication from this list that any one way of

---

[1] From "How F.D.R. Planned to Use the A-Bomb," by Nat S. Finney, *Look Magazine,* March 14, 1950, page 25, copyright 1950 by Cowles Magazines, Inc.
[2] Harper & Brothers, New York, 1941.

grouping activities is better than another. If one basis is adopted, then other bases will have to be intermixed. Even when a proper primary basis of dividing work has been decided on, its specific limits must be determined. For example, suppose it has been decided that it will be best to divide sales activities on a territorial basis. This still leaves open the question as to how the territories are to be split up. It is not always practical to determine sales territories by geographical boundaries. The problem must be solved in terms of selling a particular article in a particular situation.

For these reasons it is necessary to develop criteria which are helpful in deciding which method of grouping to use. That method should then be chosen which satisfies best the criteria under consideration, and is best adapted to individual needs.

CRITERIA FOR DETERMINING THE DIVISION OF BASIC ACTIVITIES

In general, the various functions which must be performed to accomplish the objectives of the enterprise should be so assigned as to obtain the greatest possible advantage from the division of labor:

1. Work should be so divided that the incumbent of a position should be able to become a specialist and increase his knowledge on the particular job assigned to him.

2. Special abilities should be used to the full.

3. Groups of people (divisions, departments) should comprise a workable, homogeneous and separate field of activity. The nature of their work should be similar or complementary (the former is probably more important in the lower executive ranks, the latter more important in the upper ranks).

Three major criteria may be distinguished for dividing work—economic and non-economic criteria and the size of the company.

Economic Efficiency

Economic criteria relate to business efficiency. These in turn may be evaluated in terms of saving money, contributing more to the company's revenue, in the speed or accuracy of transacting business.

That particular grouping of activities should be chosen which will make the greatest contribution to the profitability of the enterprise. This may take many different forms, some of which are discussed below:

1. *Major Contributions to Survival and Profitability.* In the early stages of a company's growth the fundamental problem is that of economic survival. This may require improvement of the production process so that goods will be turned out on time and within the proper cost limits. It may require successful acquisition of sources of raw materials, as in the timber industry and mining. Or, most commonly, it may require acqui-

sition of cash through sales to meet current expenses and to build up a reserve of working capital. These basic objectives tend to become the major function in the business, with the executive in charge becoming in fact the most important official in the business.

Once production or sales have reached satisfactory levels and have become more or less stabilized, they may well lapse into secondary activities, while research and control become dominant. The primary aim at this point may be technical superiority. If this is under pressure by competitors, or the company itself is forging ahead, this very instability will greatly increase the importance of the technical function—especially if the firm's competitive superiority rests on it. The development by the research or style department of innovations which will accelerate the growth of the company are likely to be primary functions. Or the primary activity, from the standpoint of profits, may be that of integration, consolidation and establishment of central control. Once the firm has reached its final stage of growth and is at the point of defending its share of the market, sales may again become predominant.

2. The company may wish to take full advantage of *specialization* and therefore may group together similar functions or specialties. Thus the selling function is often divided into groups of closely related products— in a food company, confectionery products, for example, may be grouped together so that salesmen can devote themselves to selling one product group well rather than dissipate their efforts over many products. Similarly, activities which serve the same purpose may be most efficiently grouped together—e.g., recruitment, interviewing, testing, hiring and induction may be handled by the employment department, while the employee benefit activities are handled separately by a welfare department.

3. *Lines of communication* may be shortened by a particular type of grouping. Thus specific functions in subsidiary plants may communicate directly with the corresponding headquarters function without going through the local plant manager—e.g., control and auditing.

4. *Duplication* may be reduced or abolished by consolidating a particular function which was previously widely scattered, e.g., the consolidation of the personnel function into a headquarters department.

5. *Balance* may be improved and better operating results attained by combining different parts of a job under several men into one complete job under one man. Joseph B. Hall, President of The Kroger Company, describes such a change in operations as follows:

Until the past few years, we operated on a functional basis with one man responsible for buying and another man responsible for selling. Sometimes there was friction between these men. If, for instance, merchandise failed to sell, the sales promotion man claimed that the merchandise was inferior; whereupon the buyer would intimate that the sales promotion man had missed his true vocation and should be farming or cleaning the streets. The situation was somewhat like that between the meat managers and the grocery managers; in both cases it was difficult to hold men responsible when each man handled only a part of the complete job.

Railroads have experienced similar cleavages between different parts of the system.

6. The extent of delegated authority may be widened so that lower executives have a greater *power of decision-making*. This has the advantage that people on the spot who are most familiar with the problems can make better and speedier decisions.

7. *Uniformity and consistency* of policy may be brought about. For example, if a personnel department is set up, there is likely to result greater uniformity in pay for similar jobs, more consistent policies with regard to merit rating and promotion, hiring and training.

8. *Control* may be improved. Work may be so divided that similar units are created so that there is better comparability of selling and production efforts. On the other hand, control may be improved by separating inspection activities from the group—e.g., separation of the financial or auditing function from a subsidiary plant, separating credit from sales for fear salesmen will be too easy on the creditors.

9. Activities may be grouped in the department which makes the *most effective use* of them. For example, a company might consider having the production department take over the training function from the personnel department if this is the best way to gain acceptance from foremen and hourly-rated employees.

10. *Competition* may be the criterion for dividing activities. Accordingly, the work may be split up into different departments or factories so that the results are fairly comparable. For example, in cement companies the work is distributed to different plants which are usually highly comparable. Sometimes it may be necessary to proceed on the opposite line of reasoning and join two types of work in order to suppress competition which hurts the total effort of the company.

11. *Job interest* may be severely impaired by over-specialization of individual jobs as well as of whole departments. Where work is divided too finely, with little variation or change, the monotony may obscure the meaning of the job and its relation to the end product, and give rise to job dissatisfaction and quits. Over-specialization is likely to require extra supervision (to deal with the resulting discontent) and an elaborate system of formal controls.

Non-economic Factors

There may be important *non-economic* factors to consider in the division of work. These frequently make for *autonomy* in a particular activity. Thus a special division may be set up to look after special interests connected with the enterprise, e.g., a division on stockholder relations or local community relations. Or the division is created to arouse *attention* to the particular activity—defense work, governmental relationships, safety (Central Maine Power Company), executive health, or salary evaluation. At the National Biscuit Company, for example, the head of the Sanitation Department reports directly to the president because the company attaches primary importance to the maintenance of sanitary conditions. Or a special division may be created for a *particular man*—to feather his ego, to "kick him upstairs," to take account of reduced abilities, or to retain some of his services on retirement (e.g., the position of Honorary Chairman of the Board). Division of work may have to be fitted to traditional arrangements within the company. For example, both the production and sales manager may have equal standing in a subsidiary and be given equal powers, but there may be no plant manager. Or the office manager may take over personnel work because there may not be enough of it to justify a full-time division. Or a particular division may continue to occupy an important position within the company simply because it has existed for a long time—e.g., in one company the engineer in charge of bridge-building (the oldest activity in the company) headed up a major division and reported to the president long after bridge-building had become a minor activity. *Preconceived ideas* and principles, and excessive reliance on formality may also be powerful factors in structuring a business enterprise.

Finally, the *personal interests* or hobbies of the chief executive may play a role. For example, Mac Fisheries were originally added to the Lever soap business in order to facilitate sale of the catch of fishermen of some islands on the West Coast of Scotland in whose development the first Lord Leverhulme took a private interest.

Obviously, not all the factors mentioned above are either rational or desirable determinants of the division of work within an enterprise. However, their existence should be taken into account and the reasons for their existence understood before any attempt is made to change the status quo.

Size of Company

The final major criterion for dividing the work of the organization is the size of the company. The importance of the chief problems faced by the top management varies as the company grows. Hence the major functions exercised and supervised by the chief executive are likely to change also. This may be illustrated by the Work Table which the great French industrialist, Henri Fayol, drew up: [3]

[3] From Henri Fayol, *General and Industrial Management*, Sir Isaac Pitman & Sons, London, 1949, pp. 10–11. Translator Constance Storrs.

RELATIVE IMPORTANCE OF REQUISITE ABILITIES OF PERSONNEL IN INDUSTRIAL CONCERNS

	Requisite abilities						
	Man-agerial, %	Tech-nical, %	Com-mercial, %	Finan-cial, %	Se-curity,* %	Account-ing, %	Total evalua-tion, %
One-man business	15	40	20	10	5	10	100
Small firm	25	30	15	10	10	10	100
Medium-sized firm	30	25	15	10	10	10	100
Large firm	40	15	15	10	10	10	100
Very large firm	50	10	10	10	10	10	100
State enterprise	60	8	8	8	8	8	100

* Safeguarding property, avoiding social disturbances in the broad sense and any influence endangering the life of the business.

From this table the following conclusions may be drawn:

1. The most important ability of the head of the small industrial company is technical ability.

2. As one goes up the chain of command, the relative importance of managerial ability increases and that of technical ability declines. Equilibrium between these two obtains in medium-sized companies.

3. The most important ability on the part of the heads of large companies is managerial ability or skills, and the more important the company the greater the place occupied by this ability.

4. Commercial and financial ability play a relatively more important part in the case of heads of small and middle-sized companies than they do in the case of larger companies.

5. As one goes up the scale of industrial concerns the managerial co-efficient increases at the expense of the rest, which tend to even out, approximating up to one-tenth of the total evaluation.

It is clear that the larger the size of the business the greater the emphasis on broad managerial functions, such as planning, forecasting, organizing, commanding, coordinating and controlling.

CONCLUSION

The most important criterion for the division of work is that of economic efficiency. This should lead to specialization, full utilization of abilities and homogeneity between groups.

Where this criterion is paramount, the basic functions (i.e., those supervised by the chief executive) are those which make the greatest contribution toward profitability. However, the economic criterion, it should be remembered, must usually be modified in the light of non-economic needs. Both need to be fitted to the particular stage of the growth and the special requirements of the company.

Business Organization and Guides for Grouping Activities*

L. C. Sorrell

BUSINESS ORGANIZATION FOR MANAGEMENT

Like many other business expressions, the term, "organization," is loosely used. Often it simply means the business entity or company. Accompanied by the adjective, "legal," it means the corporate versus the partnership or single proprietorship methods of adjusting the legal rights and duties of owners and creditors. Preceded by the word, "financial," it refers to the capital or capital stock structure of the business—for example, the amounts of bonded indebtedness as compared with descriptions of assets and liabilities. Its derivative, "reorganization," has even wider usage. Thus, a business is said to undergo reorganization when its policies are revised, its operating methods and practices are changed, as well as when its financial structure is altered, the personnel replaced, and the allocation of authority and responsibility among the executive personnel is under investigation. In a stricter sense it means the authority relationships between the personnel employed in the enterprise, and it is this last meaning that will be employed in this discussion.

To organize involves doing—precisely what? Say that any given task is one of some complexity and requires the cooperation of several human beings, the process of organizing requires, first, that it shall be analyzed, or split up into more elementary ones; next that these shall be so grouped that they may be assigned to an individual for performance; then that particular individuals shall be obtained who will perform them. The requirement must not be forgotten that these individuals must all work together. Analysis, specialization, delegation of authority, and coordination of specialists are associated phases of this organizing process. Stated differently, organizing is the process of determining the kind and extent of the specialization to be employed in performing tasks. The same is true even though a single individual only is involved; he must

* Reprinted by permission of the publisher from "Organization of Traffic and Transportation Activities," *Traffic World*, vol. 46 (December, 1930), pp. 1505–1507, 1569–1571. Mr. Sorrell is retired from his former position of Professor of Transportation in the Graduate School of Business at the University of Chicago.

allocate his energy at different times to different parts of the task. He may likewise be said to be planning his work.

But our present concern does not lie with the planning of all kinds of business tasks. It is commonly recognized that two general classes of personnel are encountered in any large business—those who perform various tasks and those who manage those who perform. A distinction exists between managers and those who are managed. This simply means that a specialized kind of work—managerial—is assigned to specialists, called managers, or executives, and the organization of this type of work, termed management, is an important phase of business organization. Indeed, it is this phase that especially concerns us in this series of articles.

Another view of the management organization is often helpful. As already stated, a group of activities may be assigned to a single individual for performance. Similarly, a group of individuals may be assigned to a subordinate executive to manage, the same constituting a section or bureau. Then several bureaus may be combined to form a department and the several departments form the business as a whole. This combination of sections, bureaus, divisions, districts, and departments forms what may be termed the mechanical framework of the organization. In order to visualize the scheme better, many firms draw up an organization chart that shows someone's idea of the organization at a given time. If correctly drawn, it should show the result of the process of organizing and reorganizing the business activities.

Business Departmentation

This process of sub-division and grouping of activities under specialized managers results in departmentation. It is a familiar fact that business enterprises of any considerable size are divided into departments and sub-departments, each supposedly in the charge of a single executive. As soon as the business passes beyond the capacity of a single controlling head to supervise each individual worker, the need for departmentation is realized. For departmentation essentially is a grouping of workers for the purpose of direction and control. An alternative method of organizing the work of management does, indeed, exist. For example, without grouping the workers themselves, it is possible to assign specialist managers to different phases of the work performed by each worker. Thus, one manager might supervise the training of each worker, another the condition of his machines and tools, still another the inspection of his output, and so on—a scheme of organization associated with the late Frederick W. Taylor and oftentimes called "functional control." Difficulties inherent in this method have prevented any widespread use of it. Most business organization thought contemplates a grouping of workers under a single executive who is responsible for their efforts. This grouping of workers is departmentation.

Now, different methods or bases for departmentation exist.[1] It is possible, for example, to assign all the workers located in a given place to a single executive; this may be regarded as a territorial grouping of workers for the purpose of management. It is commonly encountered in railroads, chain retail stores, and the field organizations of sales forces. Thus, under prevalent practices of American railroads, the operating and maintenance forces employed on a certain section of the road are placed under the authority of a division superintendent; and, if the property is of great extent, division superintendents are grouped under district superintendents and the latter under regional managers. Or a number of chain stores located within a specified district of a salesman supervisor whose jurisdiction is confined to that territory.

Again, it is possible to assign to a given executive all or a defined part of the workers engaged in the production and selling of a given commodity or group of commodities. This basis of grouping is commonly encountered in department stores, wholesale companies, and also in manufacturing enterprises. Thus, the merchandising function of department stores, which is a combination of buying and selling activities, is commonly so organized; buyers are specialized in terms of commodities; groups of buyers are placed under assistant merchandise managers who, in turn, respond to a general merchandise manager. In such cases only the merchandise function is so organized. Other activities, such as store operation, are differently grouped.

A third basis of grouping is commonly called functional. This word is variously used but, fundamentally, it means an activity or group of activities. Thus, when we speak of the sales department, we are speaking of a functional group of activities: It includes those who engaged in the activity of selling. Likewise, the terms production, purchasing, accounting, finance, and traffic more or less accurately indicate a functional classification of activities.

Now, territorial departments group together activities performed within a prescribed area; commodity departments bring together those affecting certain commodities; but what is the basis of functional departmentation? Since this method of analysis must be employed in further discussion of traffic organization, a more careful examination is warranted.

FUNCTIONAL DEPARTMENTATION

"Functionalization may be defined as that fundamental of organization which requires that all the proper functions of a business be recognized, granted existence, combined where similar or complementary, and

[1] American Management Association, Production Executives Series No. 83, p. 9. Mr. Thomas R. Jones, of the Cincinnati Milling Machine Company, enumerates as possible bases for grouping, the following: product, process, equipment, geography, function, and combinations of the foregoing. In my opinion equipment and process merge into product and function.

placed under the direction, supervision, and control of properly qualified executives who have only one, or at the most but a few, similar functions to perform." [2]

"We have, therefore, to determine the functions of management in such a way that, firstly, each function forms a compact group of intimately associated activities; secondly, each function is clearly distinguishable from other functions; thirdly, each function is suitable for single control." [3]

In spite of the awkwardness of these formulations, two ideas seem to emerge. One is that a functional departmentation requires the grouping of activities that are similar to each other, and the other is that it may also require the grouping of activities that are intimately associated with each other.

What constitutes likeness or similarity of activities to warrant grouping as a function? Presumably, not identical or repetitive activities, such as are encountered in a machine drilling operation. Presumably, the concept means likeness from the point of view of interest, aptitude, attitude, training and education, personality, and physique required for performing given tasks. Approaching it negatively, sales activities are commonly regarded as unlike production ones. Clearly, a salesman requires personality, attitude (like to meet people), knowledge, capacity for expression, tenacity (not easily discouraged); an operator of a machine drill requires some skill, strength, quickness, and a capacity for enduring monotonous repeat operations. In these cases the contrast is quite clear, the activities are quite unlike, and it would be difficult for the same individual to perform both effectively. And it is assumed that it would also be difficult for the same individual to manage such unlike activities.

Take another problem. Advertising, too, is quite unlike selling by personal effort. It deals with humanity in the mass, whereas the latter deals with it as individuals. Advertising employs the written or pictured idea, salesmanship the spoken word. The techniques and attitudes required appear strikingly different. And yet, unlike as these activities are, save in purpose, they are often placed in the same major department and under the control of the same departmental executive. Here the second idea of functional grouping comes into play; they are so disposed of because they are very intimately associated in purpose. That purpose is selling goods. Advertising is one method and personal salesmanship is another. They must both operate closely. Advertising is but the initial part of the selling process, completed by personal effort.

Observe another illustration. In department stores, the buying and selling functions are commonly committed to merchandise managers

[2] Webster Robinson, *Fundamentals of Business Organization* (New York: McGraw-Hill Book Company, Inc., 1925), p. 36.

[3] Oliver Sheldon, *The Philosophy of Management* (New York: Pitman Publishing Corporation, 1923), pp. 51–52.

who are responsible for both types of activity—an organization arrangement that generally does not prevail in manufacturing establishments. One reason that may be assigned for this practice is that responsibility could not readily be obtained if these two activities were placed under separate and coordinate authorities, for then selling would be prone to explain its failure to make sales on the ground that the goods were not properly bought, and buying would rejoin that the goods were all right, but that poor salesmanship was the cause. This situation suggests that the two activities are so closely associated that they may properly be treated as a single function for organization purposes. The presence of style goods naturally renders this problem more acute than where staples are purchased or where purchasing buys for factory consumption rather than for sale.

Hence, the functional grouping seems to require, in some cases, similarity of the activities and in others, inquiry concerning the intimacy of their association. The justification of functional departmentation rests on the assumption that an executive can better manage activities so grouped than when some other principle is chosen. In part, it is a protest against illogical methods of allocation, such as the accidental interest of an executive in some subject, or an assignment to a certain executive in order that he may have a more imposing array of activities under his control, or because no one else cares to adopt the orphan, or because of the incapacity of an executive to surrender any subject that has ever been under his authority. In part, its justification depends on an assumption that, in many situations, functional grouping is superior to commodity or territorial departmentation. All three are types of managerial specialization. If functional departmentation may properly be regarded as more economical in the employment of high-grade managerial ability, railroad experience, at least, suggests that territorial specialization may produce better all-around managers.

Where complexity results from the presence of very diverse products or extensive territories, usually some combination of these methods is necessary. The combinations may be simultaneous or successive and may actually overlap. They are simultaneous if they occur at the same organization level. For example, the United States Bureau of Foreign and Domestic Commerce has an assistant director in charge of foreign offices, another in charge of domestic offices, and another in charge of the commodity divisions. In the latter the gathering of information is organized along commodity lines. Here territorial and commodity organizations parallel each other. Or an organization may be functionally departmented at the top and territorially organized farther down. A sales department is a functional grouping; the next order of grouping may be territorial; and then a branch house, as a territorial unit, may itself be organized functionally. Here a successive application of these methods is observed. Once more, suppose a business, like meat packing, is functionally departmented, but, at the same time, one executive has general supervisory power over all pork operations, another over all cattle operations, and so on. In this case an overlapping of the methods of grouping is evident. . . .

SOME INSTANCES OF VARIATION IN ASSOCIATION OF ACTIVITIES

The organization of manufacturing and mercantile companies, as well as railroads, reveals a large amount of variation in the association of specific groups of activities.

We shall mention a few examples only. Purchasing may be treated as part of the production function, or it may be linked to selling as in department stores, or it may be considered a major function, coordinate with both production and sales. Similarly, engineering is commonly found within the production field. Sometimes it is associated with selling and occasionally it is a major department. Railroad freight claims may be domiciled in the operating, traffic, legal, or accounting department. Sometimes overcharge claims are assigned to accounting and loss and damage claims go to the legal division. Commercial research wavers between an independent status and that of a subordinate division of sales. Accounting is often allied with finance, but probably more frequently these two activities are segregated. Commercial invoicing may belong to sales or to accounting. Office management may be construed to include accounting or may be separated therefrom. Industrial traffic departments often include shipping, receiving, and trucking activities; often the latter are assigned to the production department. Freight claim activities of industries sometimes are concentrated in the accounting division, and, on the other hand, some phases of freight accounting may be found within the traffic department itself. A similar question exists concerning the wisdom of assigning the store's function to the control of the purchasing department. Industrial traffic departments themselves are assigned to sales, purchasing, production, office management, or may have coordinate rank. Production and general accounting dispute control over cost accounting activities. What is true concerning these larger groups of activities also applies to the narrower ones—much diversity exists.

Most business concerns are organized for the purposes of buying or producing goods and services and selling them. Production and sales, thus, appear as distinct groups of services. Finance, accounting, and personnel are involved in each of them. Establishing these activities as coordinate departments necessarily removes some activities that otherwise would be embraced within sales and production. It is not surprising that conflict arises. Furthermore, it appears that some activities may be quite closely associated with several other groups and this fact occasions variation in practice. It is desirable to inquire briefly concerning the bases on which allocation is predicted.

BASES FOR THE ASSOCIATION OF ACTIVITIES

Generalizing from a number of cases of variation and the arguments advanced to support some particular association or dissociation of activities, certain theories appear to be accepted.

First may be mentioned the theory that a given activity may properly be associated with the group of activities (i.e., department) that can make most of it. Call this the principle of use. It is well stated by Donaldson Brown, Vice-President of General Motors Corporation,[4] in discussing the organization of that company:

> Where any given plant produces a component entering into the finished product of just one of our divisions, it is deemed proper, unless the manufacture is of a highly specialized character, that the investment in that plant and its operation be placed under the jurisdiction of the consuming division. Generally speaking, where the product of a given plant enters into the product of two or more of our divisions, it is deemed desirable to place the investment in such plant and the full responsibility for its operation under the jurisdiction of a separately organized division.

The same reasoning may apply to a service as well as to a product. Thus, if industrial traffic activities are performed chiefly in connection with outbound shipments, this theory might, in the absence of other considerations, warrant assignment of traffic to sales. If commercial research or engineering is mainly employed in selling, a similar allocation might be made. On the other hand, should these activities be extensively utilized by several departments, segregation might be the solution.

A second theory holds that an activity may properly be assigned to that department whose executive is interested and capable of giving intelligent direction to the same. Thus, one encounters the argument that the training and conduct of the sales people in a department store should be assigned to the personnel division of the store operating department, rather than to the merchandise (buying) department, because the buyers, although responsible for sales, generally speaking, are not interested in or capable of administering this activity. It is also argued that commercial research should not be assigned to the selling department, especially if the latter is managed by a salesman manager type, rather than a real director of sales, and that production managers, by reason of training and bias, are often incapable of inadequately supervising the purchasing function. This theory may merge into the first, because the executive who uses the services of a given bureau may be more in-

[4] *Decentralized Operations and Responsibilities with Coordinated Control*, Annual Convention Series No. 57, American Management Association.

terested in its administration than anyone else. This theory, however, does not justify assignment simply on the basis of accidental interest.

THE COMPETITIVE THEORY

A third theory of association or dissociation may be termed the competitive one; that is, certain groups of activities may be segregated rather than associated, in order to permit the fullest possible development of each and to prevent domination of one by the other. This basis has been used, sometimes, to justify a foreign sales department completely divorced from the domestic sales department and involving coordination only at the level of the chief executive. With a sales manager more interested in domestic than foreign sales, the latter probably would languish, and the opposite result might accrue if the sales manager were more interested in foreign sales. Give each an independent status and let them develop competitively. It has also been used to justify the maintenance of parallel organizations of salesmen, selling different products, or competing brands of the same product. In the field of transportation it has seemed to warrant the exercise of governmental authority to prevent railways from absorbing waterway and highway transportation agencies. While conceding that some loss may follow the duplication of services that accompanies competition, some believe that it serves as a spur to each of the agencies to improve service and reduce cost. The sailing vessel reached the highest pitch of success under the stress of competition with steam; railways have reached their greatest efficiency in the period of growing highway competition. This theory seems to be more vital to the newer instrumentalities because, if they are grouped in operation with the older, men trained in the older and, therefore, possessing the viewpoint of the dominant methods, are likely to give less vigor to the development of the new. In this aspect it resembles somewhat the second theory—that of interest and capacity.

A variant of this idea is encountered in the practice of attempting to place certain activities on their own feet and practically conduct them as though they were independent business units. Thus, the foreign department of a bank may be considered simply as a service bureau for domestic operations and little consideration may be given to the profit aspect of foreign exchange. Or, that department may have a capital and personnel of its own and be required to show profits as well as the rest of the banking operations. The trust functions of a commercial bank may be treated in a similar fashion and so might the trucking activities of a mercantile firm. The discussion of General Motors, cited above, affords another example of a conscious application of this theory:

If the advantages of such a type of organization are to be enjoyed fully, it is absolutely essential that each unit be constituted so that it represents a self-contained business enterprise. The capital placed under its jurisdiction must be identified definitely with its own business and no other; and prices at which its products are sold must be based upon actual competitive values. Otherwise there is no tangible basis upon which the general effectiveness of the direct management can be gauged reliably.

COORDINATION OF ACTIVITIES

A fourth theory is the opposite of the third. Activities may be associated so that competitive development may be diminished or prevented and so that coordination may be obtained, in the sense that each facility may be used to perform the tasks for which it is best fitted. This may be effected simply by means of joint ownership, affecting policy, but not the management organization; or it may go the length of changing the latter. Thus, a transportation company may own railways, waterways, and trucks, but may leave each to a separate department. Or, it might give its division superintendents authority over all transport instrumentalities. The latter, of course, would be a closer form of coordination. Unified ownership and/or operation would not eliminate all competition between them, but it is likely that it would be held within narrower bounds. Say that an industrial concern has intra-plant transport facilities consisting of standard gauge electric, narrow gauge electric, highway trucks, and small industrial tractors and trailers. These may be organized competitively or they may be welded into a unified operating organization.

Fifth, a bureau may be assigned to a given department because of a supposed necessity of controlling the policy of the former in the interest of the latter, or, conversely, it may be withheld from a certain department because of the fear that the latter would contribute too much bias to the administration of the bureau.

Railroad claims seem to be a good illustration of this line of reasoning. This activity might be assigned to operation on the ground that operation causes loss and damage claims, at least, and should be charged with that responsibility so that it will have an incentive to prevent them. Traffic might allege that it is much interested in the maintenance of the shipper's good-will—that claims constitute a prolific source of ill-will and can be administered so as to maintain good-will, if correct policies prevail. Law, of course, can point to the fact that claims of all kinds involve questions of law, and accounting, too, can point to the accounting aspects of claims, particularly over-charge claims. The association with operation is predicated on responsibility and prevention; with traffic, on good-will; with accounting and law, on the basis of technical matters. The policy in the settlement of claims may be strict or lenient; it may range all the way from a tendency to evade all responsibility to a tendency to regard the customer as being always right. Operation possibly might tend

toward strictness, because claims are a reflection on their own performance. Traffic might be too lenient, because of a disposition to pacify the
customer. Law or accounting might be more balanced between these two
viewpoints—more neutralized. Moreover, with railroads, the anti-rebating
provisions must not be overlooked. A non-public utility, per contra,
might readily reason that commercial claims should be assigned to sales,
in order that the latter might control the policy of the former.

SOME ACTIVITIES NOT EASILY SEGREGATED

Sixth, the fact is encountered that some activities are not easily separated from others; the break is not "clean"; they must be kept together,
if responsibility is to be obtained. This seems to be the theory that underlies the association of buying and selling goods in department stores. That
goods well bought are more than half-sold is a maxim that seems to
incorporate the idea. It is probably less omnipresent where staples are
being sold and where manufacturing is involved. Again, it may happen
that one bureau or division cannot effectively perform its function unless
some other bureau will faithfully carry out instructions. To some extent
this pervades all business organizations, but it does seem that the functioning of certain departments is more inter-related than is that between
others. Charge traffic with the responsibility of effecting the most economical purchase of transportation; this cannot be achieved unless shipping and receiving will faithfully carry out instructions. Traffic might
thus argue that these activities are so inter-dependent that they should be
associated in management. Cooperation may be gained otherwise, but
association under the same manager, at least, removes one possible barrier.
Some activities are so integrated physically that separation for organization purposes seems impossible—for instance, conveyor systems that feed
machine or assembly operations. And if a personnel department can force
an employee on an unwilling foreman, the latter's authority and capacity to maintain discipline will probably be diminished.

Seventh, a negative principle is often encountered—that an activity may
not properly be associated in organization with activities that it should
check. Thus, some accountants argue that that function may not properly
be combined with treasury, first, because it should operate as a check
on financial activities as well as on other departmental functions and,
second, because it is likely to reflect too much of the financial point of
view. In discussing the authority of the controller over cost accounting
and accounts receivable ledgers, as compared with the authority of
manufacturing and credit departments, respectively, J. P. Jordan[5]
presents a similar argument:

As a blanket argument, however, the guiding thought in respect to the controller's department is that of its being a check upon all operations of the

[5] 1929 Yearbook, National Association of Cost Accountants, p. 18.

business in order that such a check will be entirely separated from either the line or staff departments which may be too vitally concerned whether with covering up or overlooking laxity in some form or other.

This principle may establish what associations should not exist; it does not say what should be done.

GROUPING DEPENDS ON NECESSITIES OF COORDINATION

Finally, it should be observed that the grouping of activities into departments depends on the necessities of effecting some type of coordination. For example, take a branch house organization. Within a branch house are several functions—selling, storing, shipping, receiving, accounting, collections and credits, trucking. In a large branch house a considerable personnel may be found in each activity. The manager will probably be someone with sales experience, because that is the main function of a non-manufacturing branch. Definitely, he belongs to the sales organization. But not all the branch house activities may be so classified. It may, nevertheless, be desirable to give the branch house manager authority over all of the branch house activities and employees, because he is so situated that he can supervise them, whereas the specialists in each of these functions can exercise only absentee supervision. The necessities of coordination at that selling point and the maintenance of discipline seem to require this grouping of associated activities.

Railroad transportation in the United States offers another illustration of the same point in the long standing argument concerning the merits of the divisional and departmental methods of organization. As traffic men know, this relates wholly to the operating and maintenance activities. Under the departmental system, if completely carried out, engineering, mechanical, and operating appear as major sub-departments within the operating and maintenance department. The chief engineer has direct authority over the division engineer, the chief mechanical officer over the master mechanics on the division, and the superintendent of transportation over the division superintendents. But the division superintendents have no authority over division engineers and master mechanics. But, under the divisional system, though these same departments exist, the division superintendent does have direct authority over division engineers and master mechanics. So far as the organization plan itself goes, the pure departmental system makes no provision for coordination among these three activities short of the general manager, whereas the divisional system ties them together at the level of the division superintendent. The question, of course, is at which point in the organization scheme it is most necessary to obtain that coordination. Exponents of the departmental system emphasize the economy of man power and uniformity of standards secured. Adherents of the divisional system point to the necessity of obtaining cooperation quickly for dealing with emergencies, such as floods and wrecks, and affirm that this method develops better all-around managers. It hardly needs to be emphasized that neither method exists in pure form and that personalities and devices quite outside the organization plan may modify the actual working of both schemes.

C. DECENTRALIZATION OF AUTHORITY

General Motors Organization Philosophy and Structure*

Harlow H. Curtice

I. FOUR BASIC REASONS UNDERLYING OUR GROWTH

May I first make the point that the growth of General Motors has taken place principally over the past 35 years. This period coincides with that in which the policies and business of the corporation have functioned under the existing management organization.

In my opinion there are four principal reasons for our success. These are, first, the dynamic growth of our country; second, the even more rapid growth of the automobile industry; third, our management structure; and, fourth, our approach to problems.

It is obvious that our country has grown tremendously since the early 1920's. To cite just one measure of growth, our gross national product has increased three-fold on a constant dollar basis. Actually, in terms of current dollars the increase has been from about 80 billion to a current rate of 395 billion. The country has grown and businesses of all kinds have grown.

General Motors would have grown substantially over the past 35 years had it done no more than keep pace with the growth of the country.

However, the automobile industry, and with it General Motors, has grown faster than has the country. Over the years our industry has become an increasingly important factor in the economy, supplying the vital needs of transportation of goods and people. Its contributions to the nation's expanding output of useful goods and services have become increasingly significant.

General Motors has grown faster than has the automobile industry as a whole. Quite obviously, we have made things that people wanted, and people in increasing numbers have bought them. We have built up customer satisfaction in our products and, equally important, the constant improvement in our cars has created customer desire for the new model by making him dissatisfied with the old. As one newspaper expressed it,

* Reprinted from "The Development and Growth of General Motors," a Statement before the Subcommittee on Anti-Trust and Monopoly of the United States Senate Committee on the Judiciary, Dec. 2, 1955, pp. 5–12. Mr. Curtice was formerly President of the General Motors Corporation.

to find the reason for General Motors' success it is necessary to "get out of the hearing room and into the show room. The reason GM is big is because people want to buy its products. The reason people want to buy its products is that they are good and they are priced right."

General Motors has been able to offer greater dollar values in its products, and at the same time it has been able to operate efficiently to provide dividends for its shareholders and substantial sums for reinvestment in the business.

But, one may well ask why and how; and this brings me to what to my mind are the two fundamental reasons for the success of General Motors.

Both fall under the heading of what might be termed management philosophy. When this General Motors philosophy was formulated in the early 1920's—and I might add that the credit for its formulation largely goes to one man, Alfred P. Sloan, Jr.—it was unique as applied to industry. That it is no longer unique is in itself evidence of its soundness.

The first element of this philosophy has to do with organizational structure, the second with our approach to problems. Both, of course, concern people—in fact, can only be put into practice by people.

It is in this sense that in General Motors we often speak of the importance of people, and stress the fact that it is people that make the difference between one organization and another. In a more fundamental sense, however, the people of one organization are more effective than those of another because the organizational structure enables them to work as a more effective team and because the organization's philosophy gives them a better approach to problems. . . .

II. UNIQUE ORGANIZATIONAL STRUCTURE

To fully appreciate the revolutionary nature of the organizational structure developed by Mr. Sloan in the early 1920's, it is necessary to appraise it in the light of conditions as they existed at that time. The business enterprise which the present management took charge of in 1921 had been put together, beginning in 1908, by W. C. Durant, and it largely bore the stamp of his personality. Durant had genius as a creator and super-salesman. He was not an administrator and did not develop an effective organization. Twice under his administration the Corporation was in serious financial difficulties—first in 1910 and again in 1920.

Prior to 1921 there existed no real concept of sound management in General Motors. Operations were neither integrated nor coordinated. There was no consistent policy with respect to product programs. Frequently poor judgment was exercised in making capital expenditures and establishing production schedules. The Corporation did not have a properly developed research and engineering staff nor any sound concept of budgetary control. The central administration did not exercise adequate control over the operations of the individual divisions. There were wide variations in the competence of divisional managements. In short, the Corporation was unorganized and the individual units largely out of control.

CHART I

GENERAL MOTORS PER CENT OF INDUSTRY VEHICLE SALES FOR THE YEAR 1921

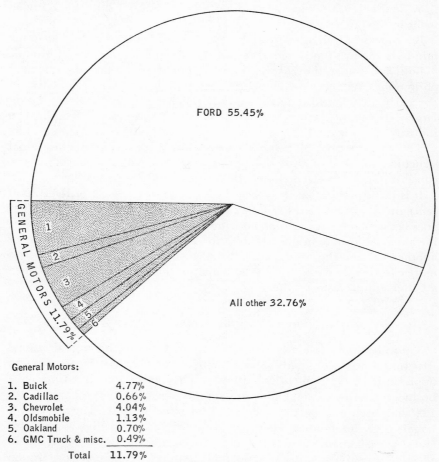

General Motors:

1.	Buick	4.77%
2.	Cadillac	0.66%
3.	Chevrolet	4.04%
4.	Oldsmobile	1.13%
5.	Oakland	0.70%
6.	GMC Truck & misc.	0.49%
	Total	11.79%

SOURCE: F.T.C. "Report on Motor Vehicle Industry," page 27.

It is not surprising, therefore, that this (see Chart I) was the competitive picture in 1921 when the management changed and Mr. Sloan began to put into effect the policies with respect to organizational structure which I will now outline.

Even before the crisis of 1920 materialized, Mr. Sloan was very conscious of the need in General Motors for a new and clearly defined concept of management philosophy. He had observed that much time was being consumed in solving detailed administrative problems and in meeting the critical situations which were constantly arising. He recognized that too great a concentration of problems upon a small number of executives limited initiative, caused delay, increased expense, reduced efficiency and retarded development.

He realized that centralization, properly established, makes possible directional control, coordination, specialization, and resulting economies. He also realized that decentralization, properly established, develops initiative and responsibility; it makes possible a proper distribution of decisions at all levels of management, including the foreman—with resulting flexibility and cooperative effort, so necessary to a large-scale enterprise. His objective was to obtain the proper balance between these two apparently conflicting principles of centralization and decentralization in order to obtain the best elements of each in the combination. He concluded that, to achieve this balance so necessary for flexibility of operation, General Motors management should be established on a foundation of centralized policy and decentralized administration.

Mr. Sloan's concept of the management of a great industrial organization, expressed in his own words as he finally evolved it, is "to divide it into as many parts as consistently as can be done, place in charge of each part the most capable executive that can be found, develop a system of coordination so that each part may strengthen and support each other part; thus not only welding all parts together in the common interests of a joint enterprise, but importantly developing ability and initiative through the instrumentalities of responsibility and ambition—developing men and giving them an opportunity to exercise their talents, both in their own interests as well as in that of the business."

In pursuance of that plan (Chart II) each of the various operations was established as an integral unit under a General Manager. Then, those operations which had a common relationship were grouped under a Group Executive for coordinating purposes. These Group Executives reported to the President who was the Chief Executive Officer.

To perform those functional activities that could be accomplished more effectively by one activity in the interest of the whole and to coordinate similar functional activities of the different operating units and promote their effectiveness, a General Staff, and in addition, Financial and Legal Staffs, were established to operate on a functional basis.

Over a period of years, the functions of the General Staff have varied and have been expanded with business experience and changed conditions but within the framework of the general concept. Today, the General Staff concerns itself with the following functions: distribution, engineering, manufacturing, personnel, public relations, research and styling.

Since the adoption of the foregoing plan of organization, each staff

Chart II

Organization Chart, General Motors Corporation

Chart II. Organization Chart, General Motors Corporation

SHAREHOLDERS

BOARD OF DIRECTORS

Audit Committee

Bonus and Salary Committee

Financial Policy Committee

Operations Policy Committee

Administration Committee

Defense Plans Committee

Policy Groups
Canadian
General Engine
Household
Appliance
Overseas

Policy Groups
Distribution
Engineering
Manufacturing
Personnel
Public Relations
Research

PRESIDENT

Executive Vice President

Executive Vice President

General Staff

Distribution
Vice President

Motors Holding Division
General Manager

Business Research
Executive in Charge

Engineering
Vice President

Research
Vice President

Personnel
Vice President

Styling
Vice President

Manufacturing
Vice President

Public Relations
Vice President

Financial and Legal Staffs

Financial
Vice President

Treasurer

Comptroller

Legal
Vice President
General Counsel

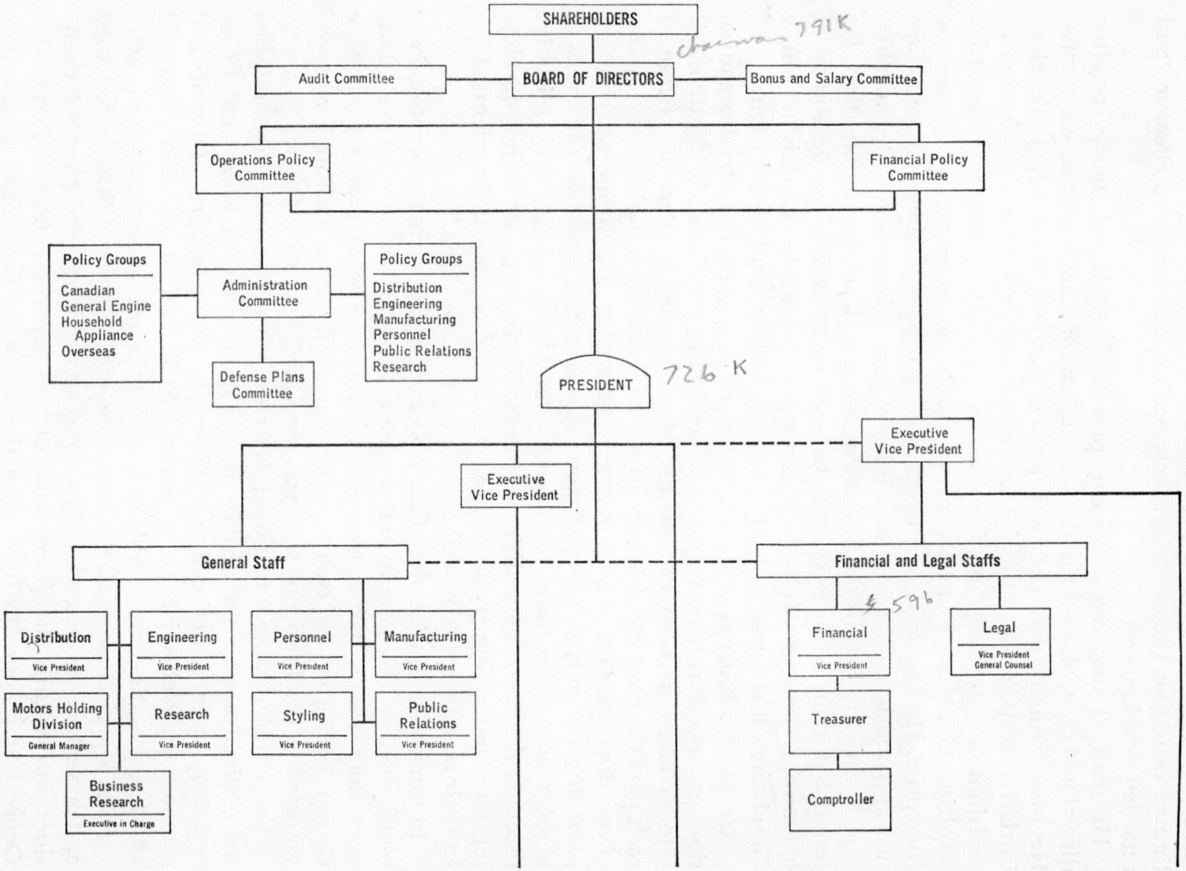

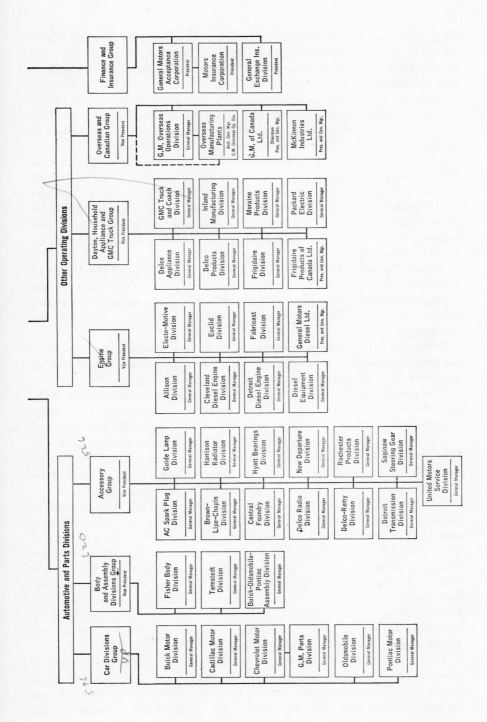

Vice President has been a coordinating executive and has no direct authority over the operating units or their departments. With his staff he contributes to the development of better and more advanced policies and programs within his functional area through research and study. Certain of these staffs cooperate directly with those departments of the operating units whose activities are in the same functional areas. This provides coordination for the divisional operations, which are subject to local leadership and have local responsibility for functioning.

These decentralized operations function under the overall jurisdiction of the Board of Directors and committees of the Board of Directors which operate within the authority granted to them by the Board of Directors in the establishment of financial and operating policies. In addition, there were during the early period and subsequently, certain advisory committees or groups, the membership and functions of which have varied from time to time.

Today, General Motors has two principal committees of the Board of Directors—the Financial Policy Committee, which is concerned with the financial and legal affairs of the Corporation, and the Operations Policy Committee, which deals primarily with the operating affairs of the business.

There are two additional committees of the Board of Directors, namely, an Audit Committee and a Bonus and Salary Committee, consisting of directors who are not members of management.

The membership of the Financial Policy Committee includes, in addition to three members of the management, representatives of large stockholder interests, and men with broad experience in business and finance. This representation provides a diversification of viewpoint and opinion. The Operations Policy Committee is made up entirely of members of the management of General Motors Corporation. Three of its members are also members of the Financial Policy Committee.

In addition, for several years past the Corporation has had an Administration Committee that functioned under the jurisdiction of the Operations Policy Committee. Its membership includes all of the members of the Operations Policy Committee and the General Managers of representative divisions of the Corporation. The Administration Committee reports on the manufacturing and selling activities of the Corporation and makes recommendations with respect to such operations. Assisting the Administration Committee are certain policy groups headed up by staff Vice Presidents and Group Executives which consider and recommend policies within their respective areas.

In the structure and function of a decentralized organization such as General Motors, no part can properly be understood and appraised separately from the whole, if that part is to be properly evaluated in relation to performance and efficiency. The major parts of the General Motors operations are its Central Office Staff coordination and its decentralized divisional operations. Necessarily, there must be continuing cooperation and exchange of ideas between these two groups and among the divisions. In the final analysis, it is this cooperative effort, properly stimulated and developed, which makes for maximum efficiency.

The balance between decentralized operations, on the one hand, and coordinated control, on the other, varies according to areas. It also varies according to the temperaments and talents of executives, and the way in which they work. While the relationships of physical things are inherent in the business, it is men who establish and govern these relationships. The relationship between the Central Office Staff and the Divisional line operations may vary according to conditions and circumstances.

In summary, the organization of General Motors Corporation under the Board of Directors consists of the Financial Policy Committee and the Operations Policy Committee, supported by other committees and policy groups; staff operations; component product divisions; end product divisions; and service operations; all headed up by staff executives or general line officers who report to the Chief Executive Officer, except for the executives in charge of the financial and legal activities who report to the Chairman of the Financial Policy Committee.

The two principal committees of the Board pass on all major issues in the field of policy and administration. As already stated, the other committees or groups make reports and recommendations, serving as a channel for the flow of information and advice through the central management, to and from the committees and the operations in the field.

The Group Executive, through discussion, counsel and advice, directs and coordinates the activities of his divisions. However, within the established policies of the Corporation and under the Chief Executive Officer, the Group Executive has complete administrative authority over these divisions. Under the Group Executive, and within the framework of uniform policies and procedures, the General Manager has full administrative authority over the operations of his divisions.

The Central Staffs operate in more or less specialized areas. The Distribution Staff concerns itself with policies and problems in the sales and distribution area and cooperates with the divisions in the development of effective merchandising and service procedures. It collects, evaluates and distributes information, makes reports and recommendations and generally guides the operations within its policy area. It concerns itself with broad problems which I will deal with more specifically later.

The Engineering Staff works on forward engineering policies and coordinates the product programs of divisions. It also concerns itself with long-range engineering projects and developments. The day-to-day engineering work and the short-term engineering problems are handled by the engineering staffs of the manufacturing divisions, although they also undertake special long-range projects both in their own interests and in the interests of the Corporation as a whole. The Engineering Staff is also available to any division for advice and assistance.

The Development Groups of the Engineering Staff carry out engineering studies of new products and of new engineering developments of existing products which are beyond the basic research stage, but are not sufficiently close to production to warrant test or final development by divisional engineering staffs.

The Engineering Staff also operates the General Motors Proving Ground. Here comparative tests are made of products of General Motors and competitors to keep management informed about our engineering progress and to assist the divisions in the fulfillment of their responsibility for the development and quality of General Motors products.

The Manufacturing Staff undertakes technical studies and experimental projects for the improvement of manufacturing methods and facilities; the development of new processes for greater efficiency of operations; and the continuing quality improvement of General Motors products. In addition it has the vital function of planning ahead for the coordination and balanced in-flow of basic materials so necessary to the efficient operation of the Corporation's facilities. In this connection, during the postwar period, this staff has searched for and located materials in short supply for the divisions.

The Personnel Staff assists in the development of policy in the area of employee relationships for all employees. It develops and recommends employee benefit plans, including safety, health and insurance programs of all types. This Staff negotiates and is responsible for the administration of national collective bargaining agreements with international labor unions. It also assists in the negotiation of local labor agreements. At present, the Corporation has several national agreements and a large number of local agreements.

The Public Relations Staff assists in the development of policies and activities insofar as public relations aspects are concerned. It keeps Management informed of public attitudes and interprets General Motors policies and actions to the public. It helps build good relations in the various communities in which General Motors operates. Divisions frequently consult with this staff operation and utilize its services in connection with their own public relations activities.

Two of the Central Office staffs operate in an area in which there is no staff or departmental activity, as such, in the divisions. They are the Research and the Styling staffs.

The Research Staff directs its efforts primarily to the more fundamental studies which are the basis for long-range programs beyond the immediate scope of divisional operations. Fundamental research in this activity has developed new methods and new products. The Staff also provides advice and assistance to the divisions on current problems.

The Styling Staff has the responsibility of creating and developing advanced styling for all products. It works with the divisions in presenting to management the product styling to be considered, not only for the next model year, but for many model years ahead. All of our consumer products are re-styled annually. The leadership which General Motors enjoys in the market is due in a very large degree to the contributions made by the Styling Staff.

The Financial and Legal Staffs report to the Financial Policy Committee. There is no departmental area, as such, in the divisional operations in connection with legal activities. Similarly, the Financial Staff is responsible for taxes, insurance, and banking relationships for the Corporation as a whole. The Financial Staff also assists the divisional operations and coordinates their activities in the financial area, and it furnishes, supervises and audits a general accounting system which is the guide and control for all operations in reflecting and reporting their costs, expenses, reserves and profits.

Such a management concept provides a continuous flow of ideas and information upward and downward through the management organization, by means of reports, meetings and conferences of both staff executives and line executives at all appropriate levels. This results in mutual education and understanding with respect to the authority, responsibility, objectives and purposes of management at all levels from the foreman to the Chief Executive Officer. It provides interpretation and understanding of policy and procedure as it is or may be established or changed. It produces an upward flow of information with respect to situations arising in operations, full knowledge of which is necessary if appropriate changes in policy or procedure are to be accomplished intelligently and promptly. It provides maximum initiative at every managerial level and at every point requiring administrative judgment, by the men closest to all the facts of the situation having full responsibility for their decisions. Finally, it makes possible accurate and prompt appraisal and evaluation of the contribution of the individual executive at every level of management, and of the contribution as well of every divisional organization and staff operation.

Although for many years this form of decentralized industrial management was identified primarily with General Motors, in more recent years decentralized management has been adopted by other large industrial companies.

The success of General Motors is the proof of the soundness of this management philosophy and its effectiveness in its application to a large industrial organization. Testifying to this has been a growing consumer preference expressed in the purchase of General Motors products.

Decentralization at General Electric *

Ralph J. Cordiner

Every company should be managed in accordance with some workable, ethically responsible philosophy of management. That is, the managers of the company should be in general agreement on a set of underlying principles that will guide their work in providing leadership for the company.

For some companies, the set of principles that guide the managers may be tacitly understood, without ever being presented systematically. They may be part of the company's tradition or may even reflect the personal philosophy of the chief executive.

While General Electric's present philosophy of management has had a long evolution in Company tradition and reflects the personalities of its great leaders in years gone by, considerable effort has been devoted in the past ten years to "thinking through" and presenting this managerial philosophy in a systematic way.

In this lecture, I should like to discuss the results of these studies: the philosophy of decentralization, and how it has been applied by General Electric in building an organization structure to meet the challenges of an expanding economy.

At the very outset, let me make clear that I am not selling our particular approach to organizing and managing as a solution for the problems of other companies. If I have any thesis, it is that each company should study, for itself, the particular conditions that will determine its future, and out of such detailed study should evolve a philosophy and structure that is fully appropriate for an individual company. The patterns of organization with which I shall deal are General Electric's solutions to General Electric's problems, and may or may not be applicable elsewhere.

REVIEWING THE CHARACTERISTICS
OF GENERAL ELECTRIC

The General Electric Company faces certain opportunities and challenges that are natural results of its own particular characteristics. At

* Reprinted with permission of the publisher from *New Frontiers for Professional Managers* (New York: McGraw-Hill Book Company, Inc., 1956), pp. 40–79. Mr. Cordiner is Chairman of the Board and Chief Executive Officer of the General Electric Company.

the risk of being repetitious, let me summarize these characteristics here:

1. General Electric is the leading manufacturer in the electrical industry, which is probably the most sustained and dynamic growth industry of the twentieth century.

2. General Electric is owned by 358,000 share owners, one of the most widely owned companies in the world. Approximately one half of the Company's quarter million employees are now or are becoming share owners in the Company.

3. General Electric is managed by professional managers, who are not the owners of the business but employees hired by the share owners through their elected directors and the Company Officers, to manage their business in the balanced best interests of all concerned. Seventeen of the nineteen directors are non-officers, or "outside" directors.

4. The Company has a long tradition of public responsibility and integrity, as demonstrated by its participation in national, community, and educational affairs, and its services in the national defense.

5. General Electric is a customer-focused Company. Through this emphasis on serving the customer, it has also provided great benefits for share owners, employees, suppliers, retailers, and others who share in the work of serving these customers.

6. This is a Company with outstanding technical skills and facilities, where one out of every thirteen employees is a scientist or engineer.

7. General Electric has the capacity—and the inclination—to take large, long-term risks in introducing new products, new businesses, and ultimately new industries.

8. General Electric grows from within. It is expanding not by merger or purchase of other companies, but by developing new products and markets—and hence new businesses.

9. General Electric is one of the most diversified companies in the world, with some 350 distinct product lines and about 3 million catalog items. These products have an original basis in the technologies involved in producing equipment to generate, transmit, distribute, and utilize electric power.

10. General Electric is a large company that has grown in service to the nation and the world. Its sales volume in 1955 was more than $3 billion, and its net earnings were $201 million. It provides rewarding opportunities for 252,000 employees in the United States and 29,000 employees in foreign lands, for 40,000 suppliers, and for 400,000 distributive-type businesses which derive all or part of their income from selling and servicing General Electric products.

11. General Electric needs to be managed with a long-range point of view, which is natural for a company in the business of innovation.

Out of these eleven characteristics of the General Electric Company arise its particular challenges and opportunities, and the particular forms of management and organization that are practiced in the Company.

EXPLOSIVE GROWTH RAISES ORGANIZATIONAL QUESTIONS

Up until 1939, the Company was able to operate efficiently under a highly centralized form of management. During World War II, however, General Electric began a period of almost explosive growth which caused its managers to question whether it might not be necessary to evolve new techniques to be used in organizing and managing the Company.

From 1920 to 1939, the Company's sales volume had risen slowly from $200 million to $342 million a year. By 1943, under the pressure of war production, it rose suddenly to $1,370,000,000 a year—over a four-fold increase in four years. Postwar experience and forecasts indicated that this was only the beginning of an opportunity for continuing, rapid growth in serving the nation's demands for electrical and related products. The Company produced over $3 billion worth of goods and services last year; and if we do the job we should do of satisfying customers, this figure may well rise—as the Company has publicly stated many times— to $6 billion early in the 1960's.

It is obvious that a Company with such growth characteristics, and operating on such a scale, requires a different managerial approach than the Company of the 1920's and '30's. This was, of course, recognized by Gerard Swope, who served as president during those decades when the foundations for future growth were carefully laid, and by Charles Wilson, the Company's president during the hectic, war-torn '40's. Under their leadership, I was asked to study the new problems of organizing and managing such a rapidly growing enterprise.

From the beginning of the study, it was apparent that the Company was going to require increasingly better planning, greater flexibility, and faster, more informed decisions than was possible under the highly centralized organization structure, which was suited for earlier and different conditions. Unless we could put the responsibility and authority for decision making closer in each case to the scene of the problem, where complete understanding and prompt action are possible, the Company would not be able to compete with the hundreds of nimble competitors who were, as they say, able to turn on a dime.

In addition, General Electric faced the need to develop capable leaders for the future; the need for more friendly and cooperative relationships between managers and other employees; the need to stay ahead of competition in serving the customers; and the very human need to make the work of a manager at all echelons of the organization more manageable. The work had to be made more manageable so that it could be understood and carried out by people of normally available energy and intelligence, thus leaving no requirement for the so-called indispensable man.

The Solution: Decentralization

To these and many other challenges which were described in my previous lecture, the philosophy of decentralization seemed to provide useful solutions.

Now, decentralization has different meanings for different people. The decision to decentralize General Electric did not mean that it was decided to "break up the Company" into smaller pieces. This would be self-defeating, because it would lose to the public and to the Company those advantages that are the distinctive contribution of large enterprises: the ability to serve as a source of major innovations in the nation's economic life, creating new products, new industries, new employment, and new outlets for smaller businesses; the ability to energize the flow of mass production and mass distribution; and the ability to provide a broad range of advanced technical capacity in order to produce the more complex products and systems of our times.

In General Electric, decentralization is a way of preserving and enhancing these contributions of the large enterprise, and at the same time achieving the flexibility and the "human touch" that are popularly associated with—though not always attained by—small organizations.

Under this concept, we have undertaken decentralization not only according to products, geography, and functional types of work. The most important aspect of the Company's philosophy is thorough decentralization of the responsibility and authority for making business decisions.

Here is the underlying logic. The share owners, through their Board of Directors, delegate to the President responsibility for the conduct of the whole business. The responsibility carries with it all the authority required to get the work done, except such authorities as are specifically withheld by the Board and the share owners. The total responsibility also carries with it full accountability for results. General Electric may be unique in that the Board of Directors has issued a position guide for the President, stating in detail his responsibility, authority, and accountability.

Now, the President is of course unable to do all the work himself, and so he delegates the responsibility for portions of the total work through organization channels to individuals who have the talents and knowledge required to do it. This is done by planning and building the work of the Company into an organization structure which consists of all the necessary positions and components required to do all the work in the most effective and efficient manner.

Each employee thus takes on responsibility for some part of the over-all Company work. Along with this responsibility, each position naturally carries with it full accountability for measured results, and all the necessary authority required for the position except those authorities that are specifically stated as withheld. Therefore each employee of the Company has, in his position, full responsibility, authority, and accountability for a certain defined body of work and teamwork. Through teamwork he recognizes his relationships to the other employees who perform a share of the total work of the Company.

With this philosophy, General Electric achieves a community of purpose between leaders and their associates, and is able to attain that voluntary integration which is the hallmark of a free and decentralized enterprise.

In such compressed statement, this management philosophy may sound somewhat obscure, but its practical result is to put the responsibility for making business decisions not with a few top executives, but with the individual managerial and functional employees who have the most immediately applicable information required to make sound decisions and take prompt action. When such responsibility—along with commensurate authority and accountability—has been delegated according to a carefully planned organization of work, then each individual in the Company has a challenging and dignified position which will bring out his full resources and enthusiastic cooperation.

TEN GUIDING PRINCIPLES

Since philosophy is, by definition, a system of first principles, I should like to list for you ten principles which express General Electric's philosophy of decentralization.

1. Decentralization places authority to make decisions at points as near as possible to where actions take place.

2. Decentralization is likely to get best over-all results by getting greatest and most directly applicable knowledge and most timely understanding actually into play on the greatest number of decisions.

3. Decentralization will work if real authority is delegated; and not if details then have to be reported, or, worse yet, if they have to be "checked" first.

4. Decentralization requires confidence that associates in decentralized positions will have the capacity to make sound decisions in the majority of cases; and such confidence starts at the executive level. Unless the President and all the other Officers have a deep personal conviction and an active desire to decentralize full decision-making responsibility and authority, actual decentralization will never take place. The Officers must set an example in the art of full delegation.

5. Decentralization requires understanding that the main role of staff or services is the rendering of assistance and advice to line operators through a relatively few experienced people, so that those making decisions can themselves make them correctly.

6. Decentralization requires realization that the natural aggregate of many individually sound decisions will be better for the business and for the public than centrally planned and controlled decisions.

7. Decentralization rests on the need to have general business objectives, organization structure, relationships, policies, and measurements known, understood, and followed; but realizing that definition of policies does not necessarily mean uniformity of methods of executing such policies in decentralized operations.

8. Decentralization can be achieved only when higher executives realize that authority genuinely delegated to lower echelons cannot, in fact, also be retained by them. We have, today, Officers and Managers who still believe in decentralization down to themselves and no further. By paying lip-service to decentralization, but actually reviewing detailed work and decisions and continually "second-guessing" their associates, such Officers keep their organization in confusion and prevent the growth of self-reliant men.

9. Decentralization will work only if responsibility commensurate with decision-making authority is truly accepted and exercised at all levels.

10. Decentralization requires personnel policies based on measured performance, enforced standards, rewards for good performance, and removal for incapacity or poor performance.

DESIGNING ORGANIZATIONAL STRUCTURE

Now, given this philosophy, how can it be expressed in an organization structure suitable to the General Electric Company? In our experience, the following work must be done to attain a sound, flexible, and dynamic organization structure:

1. Determine the objectives, and the policies, programs, plans, and schedules that will best achieve those objectives; for the Company as a whole and in turn, for each component of the business.

2. Determine the work to be done to achieve these objectives, under such guiding policies.

3. Divide and classify or group related work into a simple, logical, understandable, and comprehensive organization structure.

4. Assign essential work clearly and definitely to the various components and positions in the organization structure.

5. Determine the requirements and qualifications of personnel to occupy such positions.

6. Staff the organization with persons who meet these qualifications.

7. Establish methods and procedures which will help to achieve the objectives of the organization.

This is the procedure which has been followed in carrying out General Electric's current decentralization program, which had its beginnings in studies started in 1943, and went into the actual application phase in February, 1951. As you can imagine, the entire process involves a tremendous amount of self-analysis and education throughout the organization. Not only new ideas, but new attitudes need to be developed and accepted. Many former positions and organizations need to be discontinued, and many new and responsible positions and components are created. Persons may feel, under such changing circumstances, that their careers and livelihoods are threatened, so that they may be inclined to be suspicious, or at least over-cautious, until the new philosophy has been thoroughly assimilated, refined, and established. Timing is of the utmost importance, and I personally felt in 1951 that five years would be required to evolve the new structure and have it implemented with understanding and enthusiasm. The program appears to be just about on schedule.

Through all these difficult conditions, the General Electric men and women have performed with admirable wisdom and maturity, maintaining the momentum of progress in serving their customers while absorbing this latest phase in the Company's evolution. The work of organization is never done and the structure has to be continuously adapted to new and anticipated conditions. Nevertheless, it is safe to say that the new type of decentralized organization structure has been substantially established and manned, with outstanding personnel, products, and facilities to make it effective. The results, in terms of better values for customers and better earnings for share owners and employees, are reflected in the Company's statement for the first quarter of 1956, which shows an increase of 14% in sales and 30% in orders, over the first quarter of 1955.

GENERAL ELECTRIC'S OBJECTIVES

I indicated that the first step in organization is to sharpen up the objectives of the Company as a whole, to provide a framework for the objectives of each organization component and each position in the Company.

These Company objectives have been subjected to deep study, and are still undergoing review by managers throughout the organization. At present, they are ten in number and broad in character, and they are reflected in the Company's organization structure. Briefly summarized, General Electric's objectives are as follows:

1. To carry on a diversified, growing, and profitable worldwide manu-

facturing business in electrical apparatus, appliances, and supplies, and in related materials, products, systems, and services for industry, commerce, agriculture, government, the community, and the home.

2. To lead in research in all fields of science and all areas of work relating to the business in order to assure a constant flow of new knowledge that will make real the Company theme, "Progress Is Our Most Important Product."

3. To operate each decentralized business venture to achieve its own customer acceptance and profitable results, by taking the appropriate business risks.

4. To design, make, and market all Company products and services with good quality and with inherent customer value, at fair, competitive prices.

5. To build public confidence and friendly feeling for products and services bearing the Company's name and brands.

6. To provide good jobs, wages, working conditions, work satisfactions, stability of employment, and opportunities for advancement for employees, in return for their loyalty, initiative, skill, care, effort, attendance, and teamwork.

7. To manage the human and material resources of the enterprise for continuity and flow of progress, growth, profit, and public service in accordance with the principles of decentralization, sound organization structure, and professional management.

8. To attract and retain investor capital through attractive returns as a continuing incentive for wide investor participation and support.

9. To cooperate with suppliers, distributors, retailers, contractors, and others who facilitate the production, distribution, installation, and servicing of Company products and systems.

10. To meet the Company's social, civic, and economic responsibilities with imagination and with voluntary action which will merit the understanding and support of all concerned among the public.

To the casual reader or listener, these broad objectives may sound vague and obvious, but thoughtful study will reveal that each of them represents a number of deliberate and important managerial decisions. They provide a direct expression of the Company's ethical standards, its managerial philosophy, and its continuing purposes—in a form which makes them understandable and acceptable, after study, to every member of the organization.

GENERAL ELECTRIC'S ORGANIZATION STRUCTURE

In order to achieve these objectives on a continuing and profitable basis, an improved organization structure was devised in accordance with the principles of decentralization. This structure and the reasons for it are outlined in considerable detail in a paper I presented before the American Management Association in June, 1952, but here we shall sketch only the main outline of the structure.

The organization of General Electric is essentially a three-part structure which carefully distinguishes between Operating work, Services work, and Executive work.

The Operating Components

First let us consider the Operating work. Today, General Electric's products are engineered, manufactured, and marketed by nearly a hundred decentralized Operating Departments, each of them bearing full operating responsibility and authority for the Company's success and profitability in a particular product or service field. The special skills and knowledge required for each operating business are thus brought to bear by a local business managerial team which can concentrate on the opportunities of a specific product or marketing area. Through these integrated managerial teams, each with a specific profit-and-loss responsibility for the operation of a defined business, we achieve the flexibility, drive, and the "human touch" that comes from direct participation in the daily problems of a business.

To demonstrate that the responsibility, authority, and accountability of these Operating Departments is real, not window dressing, consider their pricing authority. The price of a product can be raised or lowered by the managers of the Department producing it, with only voluntary responsibility on their part to give sensible consideration to the impact of such price changes on other Company products. In one area of General Electric products, the major appliances such as refrigerators, ranges, and home laundry equipment, there are two Divisions competing directly with each other. The Hotpoint Division in Chicago and the Major Appliance and Television Receiver Division in Louisville have different facilities, different product designs, different distribution, and different prices. They compete at the market place very aggressively, and, incidentally, very profitably. Other Departments compete with each other by presenting different types of products that perform essentially the same function. For example there is the competition between electronic tubes and transistors, or between room air conditioners and central air conditioning.

As further evidence of the freedom provided by decentralization to the Operating Departments, consider the fact that the operating budget of the General Electric Company is not a document prepared by the Executive Offices in New York. It is an addition of the budgets prepared by the Operating Department General Managers, with the concurrence of the Division General Managers and Group Executives. These budgets include planned sales volume, product development plans, expenditures for plant and equipment, market targets, turnover of investment, net earnings, projected organization structure, and other related items.

In the days when the Company had a centralized organization, it was the custom for Operating components to submit budgets which were promptly blue-penciled, modified, expanded or contracted, and "second-guessed" by the headquarters Executives. As a result, Operating people did not usually take their budgeting too seriously.

Now they are taking it seriously because they know they will be measured on their ability to achieve the budgeted results which they, themselves, have established as proper goals for their organizations.

We are frequently asked how these Operating Departments can do accurate forecasting and budgeting, and how the Executives can delegate this difficult function to persons less broadly experienced than themselves. The Operating Departments can do better forecasting and budgeting because they are intimately informed as to the conditions which prevail and will prevail in their line of business.

Since they are better informed, they are authorized to make whatever prudent commitments they should on materials, and we have recently increased the approval authority of the Operating Department General Managers over capital expenditures so that they can, by their own decision, make commitments up to $500,000.[1]

In such a diversified company as General Electric, it is impossible for the Executives in New York to have detailed knowledge of such a variety of businesses and markets. Executives can help by supplying some general aiming areas for the Company as a whole, and information as to the probable general trends of business. But this information is to be factored in, and not to dominate the budgeting of the Operating Departments, nor does it do so.

The fact is that the Operating Departments are now doing better budgeting than was done by headquarters in years gone by. Last year the Company as a whole was within 1% of its budgeted sales results, although some individual Departments were off by substantially greater percentages one way or another.

The Operating Departments are now making plans and budgets which are firm commitments for five years and estimates for ten years. This is not on the Soviet model of the so-called "Five Year Plan" which regards each plan as a separate batch of work, to be succeeded by the next plan. Instead, a General Electric operating plan is a continuous and dynamic structure based on a rolling forecast, always ten years ahead of current

---

[1] I believe that too much of a fetish has been made in the past of capital expenditures. A manager can lose a lot more money on inventory, foolish pricing policy, careless personnel staffing, or poor production scheduling. Let me illustrate. In General Electric, capital expenditures in 1955 amounted to $153 millions, but we bought $1,400 millions of materials and had a payroll of $1,200 millions.

operations. Frequent reviews and annual adjustments keep the plans realistically attuned to new conditions and competitive developments. Thus each is a dynamic business plan, not a rigid strait jacket of the "planned economy" type.

It is important to emphasize the voluntary nature of a position in General Electric. For every position in the Company, including these Operating General Managers, a man has the personal right to accept or refuse the position—along with accountability for the results expected, and the risks involved in accepting such responsibilities. If for personal or other reasons he decides not to accept a particular position, there is no prejudice against him. He will receive other offers for which he is qualified as such positions become available. Voluntary and whole-hearted acceptance is of course a necessary condition if a man is to be held accountable for results in risk-taking ventures.

At the present time the Company has nearly 100 manufacturing Operating Departments, plus a number of sales and service business departments. For purposes of management, these departments are grouped into 21 Operating Divisions. Each division must be described as a family of businesses; for example, the Turbine Division consists of the Gas Turbine Department, the Large Steam Turbine–Generator Department, the Medium Steam Turbine, Generator, and Gear Department, the Small Turbine Department, and the Foundry Department.

After he has proven his capacity to be an Officer, the General Manager of a Division is usually elected a Vice President of the Company. Most of the Division General Manager's time is devoted to long-range planning for the Division as a part of the over-all Company, while operating responsibilities for the specific businesses are clearly delegated to the Department General Managers.

To assure that the Operating Departments and their customers will receive the full benefit of the Company's broad resources in knowledge and risk-taking capacity, two other types of work are provided for in the Company's over-all organization structure: Services work and Executive work.

The Services

The functional services are components at the corporate level, staffed with the Company's most experienced personnel in the major business functions: accounting, engineering, legal and corporate, management consultation, manufacturing, marketing, public and employee relations, treasury, and research. It is important to note that, in contrast with the powerful Operating authority wielded by headquarters functional Executives under the earlier centralized structure, these Services people have no authority whatsoever over the Operating Departments and Divisions, except the authority of knowledge. They have, instead, two Company-wide responsibilities: to do research, teaching, and long-range guidance in personnel development in their functional field; and to do such functional operating work for the Company as a whole as can best be done at the corporate level.

First, let us consider the research and teaching—what we call "Services functional work." In each business function, such as accounting or marketing, General Electric is trying to apply the same principles of fundamental research and creative study that have long kept it ahead in the area of science and technology. The Services have been deliberately freed of Operating responsibility so that they can think ahead, developing through research the most advanced knowledge, principles, and techniques in their functional field, as well as keeping abreast of current knowledge developed elsewhere.

Services also have the responsibility to convert this new knowledge into usable forms and patterns, and to make it available through advice and teaching, to the Operating Departments and Divisions. Services also help to formulate Company policies appropriate to their function, and maintain a "clearinghouse" of current practices and standards within the Company to help facilitate a free flow of functional knowledge across the entire organization.

Of course, communications should never bog down in channels. If a Section Manager in steam turbine engineering at Schenectady, for example, wants some information pertaining to the engineering of aircraft gas turbines in another section, in Evendale, he does not have to go all the way up through channels to a Group Executive and down the other channel. He is expected to get the information straight across the Company just by picking up the telephone and talking to the fellow in Evendale who has the information.

The duties of Services also include long-range personnel development planning, to assure a continuing supply of outstanding people with the required changing functional skills.

Thus the emphasis in Service functional work is on the future: anticipating future opportunities and future problems, so that when they arrive General Electric will have the personnel and knowledge ready to meet them unsurprised.

The other important duty of the Services is to perform such operating work as can best be done at the corporate level, for the Company as a whole.

This includes, for example, the work of Treasury Services in handling corporate financing and investment activities on an efficient basis. There would be great confusion if the 21 Operating Divisions or 100 Operating Departments were to deal with the banks entirely separately. It should be remembered, however, that the authority to deny the use of capital from the Company's treasury to Operating General Managers who wish pru-dently to invest is not part of the Treasurer's responsibilities.

Another example of Operating work in the Services is the conduct of public relations programs such as institutional advertising and television, preparation of the annual report, and similar informational activities that deal with the Company as a whole. It is important that Services perform such corporate operating work with great distinction, to serve as a high standard for functional work throughout the Company.

The Executives

Leadership and long-range planning for the Company as a whole con-stitute the Executive classification of work in the Company structure. To understand this Executive aspect of the General Electric organization, it is important to understand two unusual organizational devices: The President's Office and the Executive Office.

The President's Office is a group of Executives who share the work of the President. In addition to the President, it includes the Chairman of the Board, and five Executive Vice Presidents. The Chairman of the Board, in addition to the duties assigned him directly by the Board, represents the President in such areas as financial affairs, public and governmental liaison, and international matters, and each of the Execu-tive Vice Presidents represents the President in relationships with a specific group of Operating Divisions. This unique organizational device was created in recognition of the fact that no one man would have the time and knowledge required to provide effective Executive leadership for the variety of businesses in a Company as large and as diversified as General Electric. Thus each Executive Vice President serves as the Presi-dent in a defined Operating area, without in any sense relieving the President of the ultimate responsibility placed upon him by the Board of Directors for the success of the enterprise as a whole.

The Executive Vice Presidents, in General Electric, are true Executives. That is, they have been freed of Operating responsibility and adminis-trative details so that they can devote their time to long-range planning, appraisal of current performance, bringing divisional objectives and plans into a working pattern with over-all Company needs, and making sure of the needed continuity of competent managerial and other personnel in the decentralized businesses.

These seven members of the President's Office, together with the nine Company Officers in charge of the Services, form what is known as the Executive Office. These Senior Officers deliberately set aside about 20% of their time to serve, not as Executives for their particular area of Operations or Services, but as a well-balanced group of general Executives who advise the President on matters that concern all functions and all operations—in other words, the Company as a whole. In this way, the Executive Office provides a melding of extensive business judgment and advanced functional knowledge to help the President plan the Company's management, growth, and course ten or more years ahead.

There you have the organizational structure of the General Electric Company: a three-part structure consisting of the Executives, who provide leadership and long-range planning for the Company as a whole; the Services, which provide leadership and advanced research in each functional field; and the Operating components, which have decentralized responsibility for the success, growth, and competitive profitability of the Company's diverse Operating businesses.

A significant feature of this organization is that it has no place for assistants, "assistants-to," or "administrative assistants." It is our firm belief that such titles or positions create confusion as to responsibility, authority, and accountability, and tend to retard the growth of men and the Company. If a position is too big for one person and appears to require assistants, then the work should be divided up and reorganized into as many positions as are required to do the work efficiently. Each position in the Company should be able to "stand on its own," with a specifically defined area of responsibility, of authority, and of accountability.

Likewise, General Electric structure has no place for committees as decision-making bodies. It is my feeling that a committee moves at the speed of its least informed member, and too often is used as a way of sharing irresponsibility. Before decentralization, an official tried to get on a great number of committees. He would lead a very calm, safe, orderly life. Not much would happen, but nothing would ever happen to him.

Today, a committee may be helpful as an advisory group, and indeed the Executive Office of the General Electric Company meets twice monthly as an Advisory Council for the President. In any such arrangement, however, it must be made abundantly clear that the authority for any particular decision lies with the responsible individual, even if he makes it while sitting with the other Council members.

Such a deliberate avoidance of assistants and decision-making committees is directly in keeping with the decentralization philosophy, which requires full delegation of responsibility, authority, and accountability to the person who is best qualified to make the decisions for a certain area of work.

CHALLENGES OF DECENTRALIZATION

Bringing this decentralized organization structure to full effectiveness poses a number of immediate challenges to every member of the organization, and particularly to the managers. These include:

The development of men.

Leadership by persuasion rather than command.

The achievement of teamwork, integration, and balance.

The measurement of results.

Proper use of all types of compensation.

Criteria for determining the scope of a business at Department and Division levels, and for the Company as a whole.

We can touch on only a few of these challenging topics, but in the next lecture I will take up in greater detail these and other frontier areas for professional managers.

Development of Men

First, consider the development of men. Our studies indicate that this challenge will be met by applying four concepts:

The first concept is self-development. The Company has a policy of equal opportunity for every employee to develop and advance just as far and as rapidly as he can. It is part of each manager's work to challenge and guide those who report to him, in their self-development planning. But the initiative, the spark, must be provided by the man himself.

The second concept is "climate for growth." The Company's research into the processes of manpower development indicates that the growth— or lack of growth—of strong leaders and self-reliant individuals depends a great deal on what we call "managerial climate." This "tone" or "atmosphere" in an organization can be subjected to analysis and a certain degree of measurement. Furthermore, the manager and the individuals in the component can do specific things to improve the climate, so that men will develop faster and work will be done more effectively and enthusiastically.

The third concept is manpower planning. This is the manager's work. He needs to plan ahead specifically for his future requirements and then begin to develop people who will be qualified for future openings in his own component and throughout the Company.

The fourth concept for manpower development is increased education. The complexities of modern business demand ever higher levels of education among employees. Industry is therefore obliged to step up its own adult educational activities, and to utilize more fully the resources of the nation's educational institutions. In General Electric, one out of eight General Electric employees at all levels of the organization takes advantage of Company-conducted courses, in an average year. The cost of this educational and training activity in General Electric is on the order of $35 to $40 million a year.

Such activities range all the way from factory courses to retrain employees for changes in assignments, to advanced educational courses for professional employees in every function, including the function of management. By the end of the year 1956, about 4,000 General Electric men will be taking the Professional Business Management Course in decentralized components across the country.

Within three years it is expected that 25,000 employees will have completed this course of study.

Just this year, General Electric completed construction and began operation of a Management Research and Development Institute at Crotonville, New York. In addition to training leaders for the Professional Business Management Course, the Institute conducts an Advanced Management Course for classes of 80 carefully selected employees who spend 13 weeks at the Institute, away from their regular duties. The Institute is thus serving as a focal point for a major Company-wide effort in manager education.

Leading by Persuasion

Another major challenge posed by the decentralization philosophy is the challenge to lead by persuasion rather than command. This is inherent in the very idea of decentralization. I do not think that I exaggerate when I say that about 20% of the time of the Officers is spent talking to employees at all levels, exploring and answering questions to arrive at a common understanding of what the Company is and what it is trying to do.

A centralized organization implies control from a central point, with close supervision and issuance of orders and mandatory courses of action, so that the centralized control can be effective. Decentralization, on the other hand, implies freedom for individuals everywhere in the organization to act on the basis of their own knowledge of the particular conditions that apply to the particular problem at hand. This does not mean that a decentralized organization should be loose-jointed or uncoordinated. On the contrary, even more effective and flexible integration can be achieved through the formulation and communication of common objectives and policies, and common means for measurement, so that the man in the decentralized components of the organization will voluntarily and responsibly make sound decisions beneficial to the entire enterprise.

In this situation, the manager's work is to lead others by drawing out their ideas, their special knowledge, and their efforts. Since self-discipline rather than boss-discipline is the hallmark of a decentralized organization, the manager resorts to command only in emergencies where he must admit temporary failure to make the situation and the necessary course of action self-evident. To the degree that the contributions of every individual are made voluntary and are self-disciplined, the manager is leading by persuasion rather than command.

Integration, Teamwork, and Balance

A third challenge of decentralization is the challenge of integration, teamwork, and balance. There is no question but that decentralization can set up powerful centrifugal forces that could pull a company apart. We have had to discourage managers from pre-empting, through squatters' rights everything they could see. They had been suppressed by strong hands, and the power and authority given to them under decentralization was raw meat. Maybe they were "overtrained" because they sometimes became so independent that they wanted neither advice nor restrictions in the interests of the whole Company. I am greatly concerned when a man talks about "my organization," "my Division," or "my men," for all of us are just passing by.

There is a need for some practical instruments to assure that local decisions will recognize and advance the interests of the Company as a whole, rather than work at cross-purposes with the rest of the organization.

One basic instrument is the formulation and communication of clear objectives for the Company as a whole. Then each component can establish its own objectives to help attain, rather than contradict, the objectives of the whole enterprise. This is why it is important that a company's objectives be studied and understood by everyone in the organization.

Another need is for policies which clearly express the common interests and the common purposes of all members of the enterprise. It is important that the number of policies be kept to a minimum, and my opinion is that about 50 policies should suffice to spell out the policy considerations of the General Electric Company. In most situations, the policy merely requires that conscious and orderly thought be given to the over-all business enterprise before important local decisions are made. Only in a very few fields is use made of directive policies which prescribe a mandatory course of action based on a corporate rather than a local decision.

Yet another instrument of integration is a system of common nomenclature, a common language in describing the work classifications, and positions, and the organizational components of the Company.

However, beyond such formal means as common objectives, policies, and nomenclature, the integration of a decentralized company requires an active understanding and acceptance of the concept of deliberate and voluntary teamwork. The concepts of teamwork, integration, and balanced effort need to prevail or the company can drift inevitably toward recentralization. Hence the Company's managers, in order to preserve their freedom of decision-making, need deeply to learn the habits of voluntary teamwork in the interests of the enterprise as a whole.

A Philosophy of Freedom

What I have said of decentralization as a philosophy applies with equal force to any large organization of free human beings, whether it be a government, a university, a union, or a business. Decentralization is a creative response to the challenges of our time, a way of preserving and enhancing the competitive enterprise system as it evolves into the new forms that have been so aptly named the "people's capitalism."

The economy of the United States, and its position as a world power, make large enterprises both an irreversible fact and an actual necessity for economic and national security reasons. Any attendant perils lie not in bigness itself, but in the way the energies of large organizations are organized and managed. Centralized administration of large institutions of any kind can lead to irresponsibility, short-sightedness, inefficiency, and the abuse of power—but this need not happen under wise and self-disciplined guidance. Responsible decentralization—as a philosophy—makes it possible to provide at once the big results that come from big enterprises, with the human freedom that comes from respecting the competence and dignity of every individual in the enterprise.

General Electric's particular form of decentralization may or may not be applicable elsewhere, but it is built firmly on the chosen philosophy that recognizes the dignity and capacity of the individual human being, and recognizes his responsibility and authority for making the decisions that count. This philosophy, I deeply urge, must prevail if freedom is to survive in the world.

D. LINE AND STAFF

The Nature of Line and Staff *

Lyndall F. Urwick

The number of informal and personal relationships found in any undertaking are, of course, very numerous. The number of formal organization relationships usually found are, in fact, only three. The fact that there are three is, however, very seldom realized. It has been obscured by a general misunderstanding that there are only *two* such relations as implied in the widespread use of the phrase "staff and line." This error is due to a curious verbal confusion. In the Army of the United States the word *staff* has tended to be used in two different meanings—of specialists who assist the "line" in its duties by the contribution of special skills and services and also of officers who assist the commander in carrying out his functions of command.

General staff officers assist the commander by performing such duties pertaining to the functions of command as may be delegated to them by regulations or given them by the commander. Technical and administrative staff officers assist the commander and his general staff in an advisory capacity in matters pertaining to their special branches. The staff does not form a link in the Chain of Command, or in any other way take from or add to the authority and responsibility of commanders. ["Command, Staff and Tactics" prepared by the General Service Schools, Fort Leavenworth, Kansas, quoted by H. S. Dennison, *Organization Engineering* (New York: McGraw-Hill Book Company, Inc., 1931), p. 146.]

But, by whatever name they may be called, there is a difference between the activities of assisting a commander or executive in carrying out *his* functions of command and providing advice and assistance to such a commander or executive and his subordinates *on some specialized subject*. In modern American military and naval organization this distinction is recognized.

The staff is provided to assist the commander in the performance of his four functional duties, which are as follows: (1) Personnel (2) Military Intelligence (3) Operations and Training and (4) Logistics. . . . In addition to the general

* Reprinted with permission of the publisher from *Notes on the Theory of Organization* (New York: American Management Association, 1952), pp. 67–74. Colonel Urwick is Chairman of Urwick, Orr and Partners, Ltd., Consulting Specialists in Organization and Management. He is also an internationally known scholar, lecturer, and author on management.

staff or unit staff, all units have a special staff . . . which may include all or some of the following: chaplain, surgeon, munitions officer, reconnaissance officer, communications officer, etc., etc. ("The Officer's Guide," Military Service Publishing Company, Sept. 1951, p. 373.)

Most Naval Staffs . . . are composed of a Personal Staff, a Coordinating Staff and a Special Staff. . . . The Personal Staff consists of those officers ordered as aides to the admiral (Chief of Staff, Flag Secretary, Flag Lieutenant). . . . The Coordinating Staff is divided into four or five standard military staff sections [Administration Section, Intelligence Section, Operations Section, Logistics Section, Communications Section. A footnote (p. 403) reads "Communication Officer in some staffs is a member of special staff."] . . .

The Special Staff consists of those officers with special training whose duties do not fall logically within the sphere of responsibility of the Personal Staff or of any Section of the Coordinating Staff. (Air Officer, Gunnery Officer, Legal Officer, Medical Officer, Chaplain.) ("The Naval Officer's Guide," Arthur A. Ageton, McGraw-Hill Book Company, 1951, pp. 402–410.)

But in transferring the term *staff* to business, writers on management have failed to distinguish between the duties and relationships of the general staff (Army) or personal and coordinating staffs (Navy) on the one hand, and of the special staffs on the other. And this failure is of importance, because the two groups of duties are in one respect incompatible. One of the main duties of an officer who is assisting his chief in "carrying out his functions of command" is to relieve him of the growing burden of coordination already emphasized. If he is a specialist he is, by definition, unable to do this. Indeed he must add to his chief's burden of coordination, since necessarily he brings to bear a further specialist point of view in addition to those which his chief has to coordinate already Secondly the relations of the specialist (a supply or medical officer for instance) to his chief and to his chief's "line" subordinates are necessarily somewhat different from those of a general or coordinating staff officer. The former carries the authority of his special knowledge and training: he renders a specialized service, the need for which is generally accepted. The latter merely represents his chief's authority, relieving him of much of the detail of actual command. This representative function is a very delicate one. And owing to the confusion between the two uses of the term *staff* in civil life the complex series of regulations and conventions which the fighting services have built up to govern this "difficult" relationship have never been correctly worked out in business.

In consequence, many executives, and particularly chief executives, are grossly overworked. In many cases their lives are abbreviated drastically and unnecessarily. Specialization is the way of more exact knowledge and more exact knowledge spells efficiency. Its evolution and extension are inevitable. But specialization unaccompanied by the organization devices necessary to relieve leaders at all levels of the increased burden of coordination which it imposes, must mean jurisdictional disputes and other frictions which dissipate much of its advantage in personal disunity. Chiefs who should expend the major proportion of their time in leading their units or undertakings become incurably desk-bound. The magnificent training opportunities offered by true "staff" positions (general or coordinating staff posts) do not exist. Not only is the present generation of leadership frustrated and exhausted before its time. Its successors perpetuate its errors because they come to overall responsibilities without the irreplaceable experience of looking at the undertaking intellectually from an overall angle while their minds are still fresh and comparatively flexible.

THE THREE RELATIONSHIPS

It is therefore of great importance that business men should learn to understand that there are not *two* relationships in formal organization, but *three*. There are not only *line* relationships and *staff* relationships: there are *line* relationships, *specialist* relationships and *general staff* relationships.

The differences between the three can be defined very simply by indicating the kinds of authority and responsibility involved in each of them. *Line Relations* everyone understands. They are the normal relations between superior and direct subordinate. What is not so generally appreciated is that they persist whatever the function of the superior or of the the subordinate. A subordinate may be a general staff officer ("Assistant to" an executive) or he may be a specialist of some kind. The superior may be a "line" superior or a specialist or a senior general staff officer. The relations between the two are always "line" relations. Broadly, the superior is responsible to the undertaking for the subordinate: his authority is direct. And the subordinate has to do whatever his superior directs him to do: his responsibility is general.

A second difficulty is encountered because men are doubtful which activities in any undertaking should be regarded as "line." The working rule here is "without which not." "Line" activities are those in the absence of which it is impossible to imagine the undertaking continuing even for a brief period. In a manufacturing business they are usually making and selling. All other activities are ancillary to these: they are not the basic things which the undertaking exists to do. Generally the Principle of Authority should always be expressed through the "line" activities of an undertaking: the Chain of Command, the central skeleton of authority and responsibility should be built up round the delegation of responsibility for the "line" activities of that particular enterprise. But, as already emphasized, the relations between superior and direct subordinate remain "line" relations whatever the function either is discharging.

Specialized or "Functional" Relations arise wherever an individual is charged with authority for a particular subject and in relation to an equal discharging another function or to a subordinate directly responsible to somebody else. Here the "functional" officer can have no direct authority. An equal in another function or the subordinate in a "line" relation to somebody else already have a chief and "no man can serve two masters." Hence the authority of the specialist is necessarily indirect. Theoretically it is always exercised *through* the other individual's "line" superior. In practice in any healthy situation, once the "line" authority of the direct superior is fully acknowledged by the specialist and he is not afraid that it will be infringed, the specialist can do 95% of his work direct. "Official channels" are not the way to do business. They are there "for the record" in case good personal relations break down or there is a sudden change of personalities. But the real work of the world is always done by individuals who trust each other and whose good relations are informal. The formal procedure is necessary—as necessary as are drains in a house. In fact it performs exactly the same function as drains in a house: it carries off the waste matter of bad human relations. But to imagine that effective collaboration can be secured by the formal procedure alone is lunatic, as eccentric as if a householder decided to live in his drains.

The responsibility of the subordinate towards the specialist is strictly limited to the specialist's subject. That is obvious, since by definition the subordinate is in a "line" relation to someone else. The specialist who goes outside the strict limits of his subject is "asking for trouble."

GENERAL OR COORDINATING STAFF RELATIONS

It is this relationship which is most usually misunderstood. The true "staff" officer, the "Assistant to" an executive, should never have or be allowed to imagine that he has any authority of his own. He is merely an extension of his chief's personality, expressing his chief's authority. This does not mean that he may not do a great deal of work for his chief. He may draft and issue over his own signature almost every instruction which emanates from his chief's headquarters. But he does so as the representative of his chief's authority. The instructions are his chief's instructions, not his. And since they have been issued in writing his chief's direct subordinates are "covered": they can point to the written order as the justification to the chief for any action they have taken in accordance with it. One of the conventions developed to safeguard this position in the British Army is that no "staff" officer should ever give a verbal order to any of his chief's direct subordinates or to their subordinates.

Another is that he should not offer them advice unless it is requested. And vis-a-vis the chief no direct subordinate can quote verbal advice offered by a "staff" officer: the responsibility remains wholly his. This follows logically from the fact that the "staff" officer has no authority of his own: applying the Principle of Correspondence, since he has no authority he cannot relieve his chief's direct subordinates of any of their responsibility. His responsibility is purely advisory.

A second convention by which true "staff" relations overcome the limitations imposed by The Span of Control is that chiefs of specialist branches, while retaining their nominal right of direct access to the commander, normally always approach the appropriate "staff" officer in the first instance. He is thus enabled to relieve his chief of a very large proportion of the detailed work of coordination, to forestall friction between specialists and "the line," and generally to see that the day by day housekeeping of the undertaking proceeds without constant reference of minor disputes to higher authority. A British divisional commander in 1917 had nominally some 16 or 18 direct subordinates. Actually the vast majority of his work of command was confined to two principal staff officers, an artillery commander and three commanders of infantry brigades. Since the last three did not interlock, this was in practice a span of control of four. Because he was relieved of an enormous mass of office work and daily details he was able to keep in constant personal contact with his specialist chiefs. Because they understood the convention they did not take up administrative detail with him and he was thus able to exercise his true function of leadership.

Developing Sound Line and Staff Relationships*

Louis A. Allen

In many companies, there is no clear recognition of the proper role of line and staff. In addition to misunderstanding, there is frequently rivalry and even animosity. Where these exist, the unfavorable repercussions are clearly evident.

EVIDENCES OF STAFF-LINE FRICTION

One evidence of the inability of staff and line to get along is delay and disagreement in decision-making. For example, in one case, a multiplant company in New Jersey built a new plant in the South. This plant required phenol as a raw material in one of its basic processes. The phenol was produced in another company plant located in the Midwest. The new Southern plant was geared to start operations on the first of April. However, a disagreement developed between the division manager, who was responsible for the new plant and the central staff traffic manager, who handled interplant shipments. Should the phenol go by rail or by water? The argument was carried back and forth for several days. Finally it reached the president for arbitration. The net result was late shipment. The start-up date for the new plant had to be delayed for three days with attendant losses in time, money, and patience.

This loss of money brought the whole issue into the open and led to a careful examination of the proper role of line and staff and the relationships necessary for effective teamwork.

In another case, a manufacturer of electrical products developed a new type of unit heater. The company spent large sums on development and tried to get the model into production as quickly as possible. However, many delays intervened. A competitor finally captured the market by coming out first with a similar product. This led to a personal investigation by the company president. At first, material and design delays pointed to technical inefficiency. After continued probing, however, the president found that there had been a good deal of disagreement behind

* Reprinted by the permission of the publisher from *Improving Staff and Line Relationships*, Studies in Personnel Policy, no. 153 (New York: National Industrial Conference Board, Inc., 1956), pp. 70–80. Mr. Allen is President of Louis A. Allen Associates, Management Consultants.

the scenes between the director of engineering and the vice-president of the manufacturing division. This, in turn, was reflected by pulling and hauling between individual engineering and manufacturing people further down the line, who were directly involved in the design and development of the new product.

In a midwestern company, both the staff personnel department and the line sales division placed "blind" advertisements in local newspapers for field salesmen, without one knowing what the other had done. In a multi-plant metal fabricating company, the staff production department in central headquarters completed part of a detailed analysis of the cost of installing an intricate conveyor system in one of the plants, before it found out that the division manager had already placed a consultant on retainer to do the same job.

There is often running warfare between line managers and their staff counterparts. This is sometimes apparent even to casual observation. In other instances, it is camouflaged, but none the less menacing to company productivity. This antagonism may exist in the lower echelons of the organization as well as at the top. Foremen frequently resent the services of specialists from staff departments. For example, in one company the production superintendent complained to the plant manager, "That training director keeps my department in an uproar. He pulls my fore-man off the floor to attend his conferences and gives them ideas I don't agree with." In another company, the manager of an operating division sent a letter to the president telling him that he had ordered the public relations director off the lot and that he didn't want to see him back. The reason: "He talks big about the company to local people and says things I can't live up to."

Both line and staff managers sometimes come to regard their opposite numbers as natural opponents and often present a common front in their attempts to justify their own actions and discredit or outwit the "opposition." In a large Eastern chain store operation, for example, the inventory control unit in the central headquarters was responsible for maintaining the company policy of bringing inventories to a specified level by January 1 of each year. Store managers developed their own methods for protection from this "staff" policy. Immediately after Christ-mas each year, a procession of trucks paraded from one store to another within each city in which stores of the chain were situated. The store managers were making sure that their inventories were at requisite levels before the staff people came "snooping around."

There is another side to the picture, however. In some companies line and staff mesh smoothly together. They work as a coordinated team, attacking problems with great effectiveness. In these cases, staff finds it hard to keep up with demands for its services by the line. For example, the training manager of an Eastern manufacturing company saw his department grow from one to seven persons and from a budget of $10,000 to $145,000 within three years. The reasons for this growth is obvious in the training director's concept of his relationship with the line organization. As he expressed it: "The only reason we're here is to help the line. We count our success in terms of the number of calls for help we get. I feel that if we can't offer something that the operating people need, we don't belong in the plant at all."

The experience of companies that have arrived at satisfactory solutions to this problem indicates that there is no simple, and certainly no standard, answer. The part played by staff and line differs among companies as widely as do methods of doing business, objectives, and personalities.

CAUSES OF CONFLICT

What is at the root of the difficulty? In most cases, the causes of staff-line conflict can readily be identified. Questioning of a large number of both line and staff managers brings out two viewpoints with considerable consistency.

The Line Viewpoint

Line managers most often have these complaints about the staff organization:

Staff tends to assume line authority.
Staff does not give sound advice.
Staff steals credit.
Staff fails to keep the line informed.
Staff fails to see the whole picture.

Staff Tends to Assume Line Authority. Many line managers feel that a basic cause of friction is the failure of staff to recognize its place. Line managers are generally keenly aware that they are accountable for results, including profits. While they may recognize that the staff specialist is a necessary and valuable part of the business scenery, they frequently resent what he does, or what they think he is trying to do, because they feel it encroaches upon their duties and prerogatives. Where there is friction, line managers often feel that the ready solution is to "put staff in its place."

As one production manager said, "After all, we have the headaches of getting the stuff out the back door. We worry about scheduling and costs and customer returns. Staff people want authority, but they are not held for results the way we are. They should realize that their job is to help us, not to be telling us what to do."

According to some line managers, this usurpation of authority may extend to actual encroachment on the work being done. A number of instances were cited in which personnel people assigned new employees to production departments without first consulting with or getting the agreement of the foreman concerned. In a candy company, the sales manager pointed to a small sticker advertising a statewide charitable appeal. "These go on every box of candy we sell in this state during the next two weeks," he said. "The public relations manager talked the president into it without consulting me. It might be a good idea from a public relations viewpoint, but I think I should make this kind of decision, not a staff man."

Staff Does Not Give Sound Advice. Many managers complain that while staff is supposed to give counsel and advice, the ideas they come up with are not always fully considered, well-balanced, and soundly tested. In some companies, staff is considered "academic," "ivory tower," "unrealistic," and "too theoretical."

The reasons for this attitude on the part of line are clear. For one thing, since staff is not held to account for ultimate results, some staff managers show a tendency to propose new ideas without thinking through or testing them. One common reason for this is the tendency to take over a program bodily because some other company has used it successfully. The fact that the idea is not adapted to the particular conditions which exist locally does not become evident until after a good deal of time and effort have been devoted to trying to make it work.

Another reason for this attitude of line is that the staff specialist often neglects to explain to and consult with the line man. And even if he does both of these, he frequently neglects to give the line man time to absorb and "catch up" with the specialist's thinking and knowledge. As one plant manager said, "Central Staff came down here and put up some racks and started to give away comic books and manuals by the truckload on how to grow a garden and how to wave your own hair. I figure we have to sell a couple hundred units of our product a day just to pay for this. Personnel says it will make people appreciate free enterprise, but I think that's wishful thinking."

The tendency of staff to use technical or "professional" jargon also contributes to this line attitude. "That psychologist we have for a personnel manager is always talking about 'motivation' and 'correlation' and 'personality traits,' " said one supervisor. "I wish he would talk plain English so I would know what he was getting at."

Staff Steals Credit. Another common complaint centers about the tendency of staff to assume credit for programs when they are successful and to lay the blame on the line when they are not. In one company, a new program of statistical quality control was developed and installed under staff auspices. The first year the program was in operation several flaws showed up, resulting in an unusually high percentage of customer returns. The staff quality control department wrote a lengthy memo which tended to prove that the fault was the foremen's because they allowed drilling and reaming operations to get out of specification limits. An intensive training program was instituted, with the result that both re-work and returns went down to record lows. Both the quality control and training departments then prepared reports showing that their efforts were responsible for the considerable savings in factory costs that resulted.

The Conference Board found that members of line management are particularly vocal about this. "We take the rap until we get the bugs ironed out," one superintendent said, "then every staff man in the shop rushes in to grab the credit."

Staff Fails to Keep the Line Informed. Many line managers complain bitterly about cases in which the staff works with the line manager's subordinates but does not let the boss himself know about it. In a chemical company, for example, the training department installed a job training program in three production departments before letting the production superintendent know what they were doing. In the superin-tendent's eyes, the fact that they had gained his consent to introduce a general training program did not warrant their starting this new activity without informing him. "I first knew that I was doing job training when the plant manager complimented me on it," said the production super-intendent. "I realize the training people are doing a good job for me, but I'd like them to let *me* know about it too."

Staff Fails to See the Whole Picture. Line executives frequently point out that staff people tend to operate in terms only of the limited objec-tives of their own specialty, rather than in the interests of the business as a whole. The difficulty here seems to be that the staff man becomes so involved in his own area that he fails to relate it fully to the task of the line and to the over-all objectives of the company.

The personnel administration manager may be more concerned with building up a large central personnel group and increasing the technical proficiency of his own unit rather than with the development of effective personnel people in the operating divisions of the company. The indus-trial engineer may carry the investment in a methods improvement pro-gram past the point of profitability because he is over-concerned with perfecting the system.

A manufacturing vice-president in a large, multi-unit company cites what he feels is a classic example. "The personnel department has spent a great deal of money developing psychological tests for the selection of executives," he said. "It has reached the point now that you have to pass a whole battery of tests before you are favorably considered for promo-tion. Some of the men who have built up fine records of performance on the job have done poorly in the tests. Several have left us. Many are frustrated and discouraged because they feel they are up against some-thing that is arbitrary and inaccurate. The personnel people simply do

not realize that it takes all kinds of people to make a good team. If we
have too many star performers, we won't have teamwork. What we need
is balance. The personnel people don't know enough about running
the business as a whole to see that. If they'd put more time and effort
on helping us develop the people we now have, instead of figuring out
reasons why they're no good, we'd all be better off."

The Staff Viewpoint

Complaints in the staff-line relationship are not entirely one-sided.
Many staff men have strong opinions as to their treatment at the hands of
the line. Their views usually center about these specific points:

Line Does Not Make Proper Use of Staff. "I feel about as useful as an
appendix around here," said one personnel manager. "The production
vice-president I report to figures he is an expert on human relations and
personnel administration. Instead of my advising and counseling him,
he calls me in once a week and lays out detailed instructions that I'm
supposed to follow to the letter."

Some line managers have strong and dominant personalities and are
intelligent and well-enough informed to feel that they do not need
advice. When this is true, the line manager probably needs only a personnel staff assistant and not a full staff complement.

In other instances, however, the line manager requires the help of
staff specialists, but either because of personal inability to accept advice,
or distrust of his advisors, he rejects the suggestions he receives.

Staff specialists point out that when this situation exists, they cannot
possibly do a good staff job. "I can't come up with a good proposal if the
old man just tells me he wants 'a program for forecasting the economic
picture,' " said the sales manager of a metal goods manufacturer. "He and
the board of directors talked all afternoon about that one, but he is very
reluctant about giving me the details I need to do a job. He says the
information is confidential, but if he doesn't trust me, he should get a
new man."

In still other cases, staff people say that some line executives who most
need their specialized help rarely invite the specialist into the picture.
The staff people say the line man either is "afraid" of interference or
he fails to appreciate the help that is available for the asking. (In rebut-
tal, some line people say that the staff people whom they "overlook"
inviting into the picture are too weak and ineffectual to be of real
assistance.)

Line Resists New Ideas. Many staff men feel that line management
tends to be shortsighted and resistant to new ideas. In one company, the
personnel manager pulled out copies of memoranda which he had for-
warded to the president. They dated back to 1946. All reiterated the
need for a program of management development to provide a continuing

supply of management replacements. The company had recently expanded its basic product line, and several key management positions were open.

The personnel manager was bitter. "We had to go outside and hire people at fancy prices. It knocked our whole salary structure out of line," he said. "Yet I recommended a program nine years ago that would have prevented this."

Line Does Not Give Staff Enough Authority. A common theme in the staff manager's complaints is lack of authority. "We're paid to be experts. Most of us know a lot more about our specialty than the line people. But we haven't got the authority to make it stick," said one purchasing agent.

When questioned, many staff managers express themselves strongly that, if they have what they feel is the best solution to a problem they should be able to enforce action on the line man involved. In one instance, a personnel manager mentioned that a general foreman had turned down four people consecutively who had been referred to him for an opening in his department. "He wants us to agree to his hiring a fellow-member of the military society to which he belongs," the personnel manager explained. "But we tested the man and he simply doesn't have the intelligence or aptitudes that are needed on this job. We should be able to ring the curtain down ourselves without making all these false passes."

SOLUTIONS

What is the answer to the problem of staff and line? How can better teamwork be developed? The answer seems to lie first in better understanding of the basic relationship between line and staff. Many companies which have investigated the problem find that neither line nor staff is very clear as to what the other is supposed to do. Improved cooperation usually follows clear definition of the role of each, and thorough indoctrination and education of both line and staff people.

The Basic Line-Staff Relationship

The basic relationship which exists between line and staff in many companies may be summarized as follows:

1. The units that are designated as line have ultimate responsibility for successful operation of the company. Therefore, the line must also be responsible for operating decisions.

2. Staff elements contribute by providing advice and service to the line in accomplishing the objectives of the enterprise.

3. Staff is responsible for providing advice and service to appropriate line elements when requested to do so. However, staff also has the respon-

sibility of proffering advice and service where it is not requested, but where it believes it is needed.

4. The solicitation of advice and the acceptance of suggestions and counsel is usually at the option of the line organization. However, in some cases, it must be recognized that only the top level of the line organization has this option and that its decision on the use of staff advice or service is binding throughout lower levels. In these cases, subordinate levels in the line may have no option in the use of specialized staff services, but may be required to use them.

For example, the engineering department may analyze the use of machines, tools, jigs, and fixtures and present recommendations to the line. The operating line organization does not ask for this advisory service. Higher management provides it as a means of improving operations by bringing to the problem the most highly skilled and best informed specialists.

In this case, it is the line manager's responsibility to make most effective use of this advice. If he disagrees with it, he should have the opportunity to appeal to higher authority.

The same holds true with certain services. Because the line manager cannot possibly equip himself to perform highly specialized parts of his job, staff units may perform this service for him. For example, the services of the cost accountant are provided to help the line manager determine his costs. If the line manager disagrees with the methods of collecting this data or with the figures themselves, he may appeal to higher authority. But since he is not equipped to gather and analyze this data himself, and since cost standards are necessary to effective operation, he must use the services of the accountant.

5. Line should give serious consideration to offers of advice and service made by staff units and should follow it if it is to the company's best interest to do so. However, except in those cases where the use of staff advice and service is compulsory and subject only to appeal to higher authority, it is not mandatory that the advice of staff should be followed unfailingly. Except as noted above, line managers have the authority to modify, reject, or accept such advice.

6. Both line and staff should have the right of appeal to higher authority in case of disagreement as to whether staff recommendation should be followed. However, this right to appeal should not be permitted to supersede the line's responsibility for making immediate decisions when required by the operating situation.

How Staff Can Do a Better Job

In spite of the widespread difficulties arising from poor staff-line relationships there is abundant evidence that staff specialists can improve their relationships with line. Many companies find that if staff observes the following points, it can increase both the acceptance and the over-all value of the work it does.

Operate in Terms of the Objectives of the Company as a Whole. Staff exists to help the line organization accomplish the objectives of the company. It follows that to operate effectively, staff should know what the company is trying to accomplish in terms of operations, costs, and sales. The purchasing agent who does not know how the end products of the company are made, sold, and used is operating as blindly as the personnel manager who does not know the trend of total labor costs to sales or to what extent indirect labor costs are increasing over direct labor.

Operating people are generally concerned with day-to-day operating goals. Many operating managers rely upon staff specialists to think ahead for them. As the president of a large processing company in Philadelphia said: "If the personnel department does not think ahead and anticipate personnel needs ten years from now, who is going to do it? I expect the personnel staff to tell me what our objectives related to people should be, but I expect them to find out what the rest of the company is doing and plans to do before they come up with their own recommendations."

Encourage and Educate Line Components to Use Staff Effectively. This requires education of line personnel to the point where they know what the staff specialty is concerned with and what it can do for them. In some companies, this is accomplished through meetings, talks and discussions, in which staff people describe their specialties to line managers. In other cases, position descriptions of staff jobs are prepared and distributed to line managers. Brochures and booklets of various kinds may also be used to outline staff duties. In some instances, where the company has no prepared program for acquainting line with staff duties, the individual staff managers make it a point to talk informally with line managers about their operation, using this opportunity to outline their own activities and how they can be useful to the line man. (Yet, the staff activities that seem to be overburdened with requests from line executives for help, service and advice also appear to be manned with unusually competent and alert people. This may indicate that a good job by the staff department is an effective method of encouraging and educating line components to use staff.)

Prerequisite to this approach, of course, is the need for the staff man to brief himself thoroughly on the line man's operation. In fact, the more he knows about the operating picture, the quicker his own ideas will be accepted and the more effective he will be.

Many successful staff specialists point out that certain personal qualities are necessary if the staff man is to secure acceptance. Because of his specialized knowledge, the staff manager frequently is tempted to "expert."

This usually arouses antagonism and resistance. Most staff managers find that a humble attitude, the use of many questions, and a *sincere* desire to be of help are likely to be more productive.

The staff manager also must be able to satisfy his need for personal recognition from satisfaction with a job well done and the favorable remarks of his own superior, rather than with public identification with the success of the program which he may have personally sponsored and developed. Staff managers usually find that it is best to give full credit to the line organization for the results that are accomplished.

Recognize and Overcome Resistance to Change. One of the important reasons for line opposition to ideas presented by staff is the psychological factor of resistance to change. People automatically tend to resist ideas that threaten to change the way they have been doing things. The fact that a change is suggested is in itself an implied criticism that the old way was not good enough.

People resist changes in the way they do their work or in the work itself. But it is not commonly recognized that they are even more set against changes that threaten disturbance or alteration in personal relationships. For example, a maintenance supervisor may be offered a change in his job responsibilities. Perhaps he has always been responsible for the installation of new equipment and he does not want to give it up, even though he is being given responsibility for the lubrication program in its place. It is to be expected that he would be opposed to this change unless he saw some immediate personal gain in it for himself. His opposition would be intensified if he saw any threat to himself in the change. Under the same conditions the supervisor's resistance would be still greater if the change meant that he would also have to move to another part of the plant and work with another group of people. Here the gains to himself would also have to be even greater to offset this threatened disruption of his social pattern of group relationships.

Resistance is to be expected any time a change is proposed. This fact is of particular importance to specialized staff people, who continually deal in change and proposals for change.

Staff specialists can anticipate and overcome this natural resistance to change. Many companies have found these points helpful:

A. Determine to what extent the change proposed will affect the personal relationships of the people involved. Is the staff man advocating a major, sweeping change which will affect the social patterns established in the group he is working with? Can the change be broken down into smaller, more numerous moves which will have less negative impact?

B. When major changes are involved, which will modify the relationships between a line manager and the people who work for him, opposition from the manager will be minimized if he participates from the early planning stages. When announcement of the change is to be made, the line manager can make it as a working partner, and not as an unwilling associate. In effect, the line manager has an opportunity to make the idea his own.

C. The people who will be affected by the change will accept it better if:

¶ They realize it will benefit them personally—that it will make their work easier, faster or safer. The change should be tied in as closely as possible with the individual's personal goals and interests—his job, family, future.

¶ They have an opportunity to offer suggestions, ideas, and comments concerning the change as it affects them—provided these suggestions are sincerely wanted and are given serious consideration.

¶ They are kept informed of the results of the change.

¶ They are able to check up on how well they are doing in terms of the change.

Acquire Technical Proficiency. A primary reason for the existence of staff is that it is highly informed and expert in a specialized field. It follows that the staff specialist needs to have a detailed and extensive knowledge of his field. To be most effective, the staff man also needs a breadth of knowledge concerning the whole company and its operations. The more familiar he is with the problems and operations of line and of other staff specialities, the better he can develop effective recommendations in his own area. The director of personnel administration, for example, is not entitled to a hearing for his ideas unless he is able to orient and evaluate them in terms of the other problems of his company's management. He must, in other words, appreciate the problems of finance, production, procurement, sales, profits, costs, product research, planning, and so forth. Line managers tend to distrust the staff manager who operates in a vacuum, even if he is well informed about his own specialty. Glib recital of "text book" solutions, failure to recognize practical operating conditions, and adherence to a strictly theoretical point of view, quickly alienate line executives.

Technical proficiency, for a staff man, means more than subject knowledge. Since his value lies in how well he can apply and communicate this knowledge, he requires training and education in the techniques of creative and logical thinking. More than this, the staff man also needs to develop the basic skills of writing and speaking so that he can convey his ideas clearly and succinctly.

How Line Can Make Better Use of Staff

It is important for line to learn how to use specialized staff assistance effectively because the value of the line manager to the organization depends to a large extent upon the use he makes of staff services. This, in turn, depends to a large extent on his ability to secure the interested help of the individuals supplying and performing these services.

In spite of this, staff advice and services are relegated to a secondary position by many line managers, even when the staff people are highly competent executives. These line managers call upon staff only as a last resort—and then only after they have exhausted every other available resource. One widespread reason is that there is a carefully camouflaged rivalry between the line and staff manager. The line manager wants to demonstrate that he can do it "on his own." The staff man wants an ample share of credit if the results are good, and he is constantly striving to maneuver himself into a protected position where he can also say, "I-told-you-so," if the project goes to pieces.

This credit-grabbing, "I-told-you-so," attitude often stems from the staff man's sense of insecurity. But, regardless of the reason, the more he displays this attitude, the more the line manager displays resentment and lack of confidence in the staff man. The vicious circle is completed as the staff man thus grows increasingly insecure from the fear that the line manager will eventually try to dispense with his services and eliminate his job.

Make Maximum Use of Staff. Specialized skills are made available in the staff departments so that the line manager can use them to help him perform his job more effectively. The more the line man calls upon and makes use of staff, the better acquainted the specialist will become with the line manager's problems and his way of working. Highly successful line executives find that it is only common sense to make habitual use of staff. They have learned that this enables them to bring to bear on their problems special abilities and a fresh viewpoint. Where competent staff is available, the line manager has, in effect, a consultant or retainer who can help him to do his job better.

As one large company points out, when advice or service is volunteered by a specialized staff department, the line man should accord it the same recognition and careful consideration that he would if he had requested it. Otherwise, he is spurning the specialized advice and assistance made available to him by the corporation.

Make Proper Use of Staff. It is to be expected that qualified staff specialists want to put their abilities and experience to work on problems of real importance. They become annoyed and frustrated, however, when a line manager asks them to help and they later find out that their time was wasted because he had incorrectly identified his problem. In one case, a plant manager asked the purchasing agent to secure some data on the costs of a pusher-bar conveyor installation as compared with those of the existing crane and magnet operation. After the purchasing agent had completed his study at considerable time and effort, the plant manager told him, "We haven't got the money for new equipment. I guess what I really wanted to know was how to operate that crane with two men instead of three." He then called in the industrial engineer to make the new study for him.

In another case, the production superintendent in a processing plant was having difficulty getting acceptance of the methods improvement program he had recently installed. He felt that the training director, who had been teaching management courses in the plant, would be able to help him. The production superintendent outlined the program, but left the impression that the program was lagging because the foremen did not understand it. The training director came up with a suggested communications program for helping employees to understand the details of methods improvement. He was greatly confused when the production superintendent declared that this was not what was needed. It was only after prolonged discussion that the staff man found that the production manager's introduction of the program had been arbitrary and had antagonized the foremen. What he needed was a retake of the whole program to secure maximum participation and a sound basis for motivating people to make suggestions for improving of operations.

The line manager saves his own time and that of his specialized staff associates if he thinks through his problem until he can identify the key factor that is causing his difficulty. It is not until he has defined the real problem that the staff man can proceed with assurance.[1]

There is another important way in which staff is improperly used by line. Some line managers frequently encourage staff to give orders by asking them to make final decisions that are line prerogatives. For example, a line manager who gives the personnel manager authority to hire employees and to place them without consent of the foreman or supervisor involved needs to recognize in advance that he is giving away his line prerogative. The president who asks the labor relations manager to travel to a distant plant, negotiate the union contract for the plant manager, and to sign it himself, needs to recognize the hazards of asking the staff man to exceed his proper scope.

Keep Staff Informed. Line managers at the corporate level frequently fail to keep their staff managers fully informed of decisions which affect them. For example, an executive vice-president and a division manager decided to install a fully automatic assembly line in one plant of the company. This necessitated the use of many more maintenance and technical people over a period of years, together with several additional engineers. The personnel manager found this out only when a request for additional personnel came through when the work was completed. Instead of having an opportunity to train and upgrade people from within the company over a period of months, he was forced to hire people from the outside.

[1] Many executives have also found it desirable (where the cause of a problem is not clearcut) to call in the staff specialist and ask him not only to suggest a solution but also to start out by identifying the real problem.

Fitting in the Specialist without Antagonizing the Line *

Lyndall F. Urwick

Unfortunately there is a tide in the affairs of men which, in this context, seems to be always at the ebb. And my object in writing this paper is to examine briefly why this is so and to suggest, if I can, means by which the specialist can avoid what often appears to be the inevitable friction and contretemps which so frequently accompany his introduction. The facts, indeed, suggest that there is some fatal obstacle which insures, almost without exception, that the arrival of some new form of specialization in any business is the signal, as it were, for loud assertions of competence or less loud, but even more deadly, whispers of incompetence, both of which are unmistakable symptoms of bad personal relations or lowered morale in the whole or part of the executive team.

What is this obstacle, if it exists? Why do specialists suffer from a special form of disability to "get on with" existing "line" officials, or don't they? It is perhaps not pushing my analogy too far to suggest that they seldom, if ever, seem to have a natural taste for "two-seaters" or native skill in their construction. So that the two parties eye each other uneasily and then make a concerted rush for the same accommodation which ends in a collision on the doorstep—of some higher executive. If we admit an obstacle, it would not be inappropriate to describe my modest contribution as "Hints and Tips on Building Two-seaters" or, to borrow the title of a much more famous contribution to management literature, "Handicrafts for the Handicapped."

LABOR UNDER HANDICAP

For the specialist does labor under a handicap. Being a specialist he usually talks a jargon of his own. Ordinary folk are suspicious of him. There is the old crack about "the specialist who knows more and more about less and less till eventually he knows everything about nothing."

*Reprinted by permission of the publisher from *Advanced Management*, vol. 17 (January, 1952), pp. 13–16. Col. Urwick is Chairman of Orr, Urwick and Partners, Ltd., Consulting Specialists in Organization and Management. He is also an internationally known scholar, lecturer, and author on management.

The late Sir Arthur Quiller-Couch has put the same thought in more literary form:

Against knowledge I have, as the light cynic observed of a certain lady's past, only one complaint, that there is so much of it. If you crave for knowledge, the banquet of knowledge grows and groans on the board till the finer appetite sickens. If, still placing all your trust in knowledge, you try to dodge the difficulty by specializing you produce a brain bulging out inordinately on one side and, on the other cut down flat and mostly paralytic at that. And, in short, I hold that so long as the Creator has an idea of a man, no uneven specialist realizes it.

SUSPICION NOTHING NEW

Nor is this suspicion of the specialist anything new. Almost exactly a century ago, a brilliant woman, Florence Nightingale, suggested that the function of military nursing which had previously been performed by untrained male orderlies under the command of the Army Medical Corps should be specialized and—horror piled on horror!—that it should be entrusted to women. Today that seems an ordinary idea enough which everyone accepts as a matter of course. But, at the time, the leaders of the Army Medical Corps were loud in their contempt for such a fantastic notion and, when it appeared that there were fools and traitors in London who were prepared to take it seriously, savage in their denunciation. . . .

Lytton Strachey has a brilliant description of one incident. Thousands of men in the hospitals at Scutari were dying of cold. A consignment of warm shirts arrived from England. The Purveyor, who controlled issues, said that it was impossible to unpack the shirts till a Board of Audit had passed the consignment. A Board of Audit which must include a General Officer would take three weeks to assemble. Florence Nightingale who could always do what she liked with rank and file, called up a Corporal's guard and opened the bales forcibly with a hatchet while the Purveyor stood by "wringing his hands in departmental agony."

What is the reason for this age-old suspicion of new form of specialization? One reason is the fact that the specialization is new. Man is a creature of habit; he is hag-ridden by custom and established patterns of behavior. Novelty of procedure, probably even still more novelty of ideas, are always suspect. That is why I have put the onus of proof, as it were, the main responsibility for avoiding trouble, on the specialist and not on the "line" man. In all forms of human society, not only in business, the newcomer has to "pay his footing"; initiation rites can be extremely painful. So, when in any business organization some subject—personnel work or time-study or planning or what you will—which has previously been part of the responsibility of the "line" supervisors is taken out of their hands and specialized they are very apt to be "cagey" and suspicious about the new departure.

DIFFERENT CREATURE

The "specialist" too is apt to be rather a different kind of creature not easily understood by his "line" colleagues. All through the last half of the nineteenth century, much of the work of the skilled engineering craftsman on the shop floor was being gradually taken away from him and concentrated in drawing offices and research laboratories. His workmanlike judgment and discretion were progressively restricted. He had to do his part of the job to more and more detailed drawings, to finer and finer tolerances, to more and more exact instructions. He did not like it one little bit and he said so on occasions with a pungency which seemed unnecessary to those who worked on tasks which enabled them to keep their hands clean.

But on the whole his craftsmanlike good sense approved the greater accuracy of the new methods. His foreman, a craftsman like himself, was satisfied and he could explain the changes as they took place so that they "made sense" to the worker. There was very little trouble under that head of which the echo has come down to us. On the other hand, when Taylor started to study the actual processes and methods of working on the machines under laboratory conditions, when he and his imitators tried to introduce "the one best way" of doing actual operations in the shops, there was a flaming row which has been going on more or less ever since. Organized labor bitterly resented the ideas of Scientific Management.

LABOR'S RECEPTION

This difference in the temperature of the reception given by labor to what were in fact, two halves of the same inevitable progression—one of its strongest critics observed that "Scientific Management is inherently in line with the march of events"—has often puzzled observers. It can be explained logically on the "one last straw" basis; the workers felt that despite the detailed drawings, they still had their skill; scientific management seemed to be taking that last refuge away from them, to be transferring even their skill into the hands of management. But the reaction of the men on the shop-floor was not of a logical character; it was non-logical and often highly emotional. And it is always dangerous to try to explain the non-logical sentiments of one social group by logical concepts which happen to make sense to another social group.

The one practical difference in the two situations was that the men who staffed the drawing-offices and research laboratories did not come down onto the shop floor very much. And when they came, they came as visitors, not as residents. Thus, while the engineering craftsman was aware that they were a strange breed—bright young men who had been at universities and who spoke a different language, who were apt to be at The Drama League or a musical when he was at a ball game—they did not obtrude too much on his social living. They left the pattern undisturbed. He only met them through his foreman who was usually, and quite justly, satisfied with his own ability to deal with any eccentricities they might attempt.

COMES THE INVASION

But with the coming of time-study and methods engineering the bright young men began to invade the shop-floor. And they pitched their tents. Offices began to spring up in odd corners where the worker had been accustomed to withdraw for a tolerated, if illegitimate, smoke. It looked to him as if they were becoming, as they were, a permanent part of the community of the shop-floor. And that did disturb him because it altered the social pattern. It is one thing to entertain a foreigner as an occasional visitor and quite another to make him a member of one's family. Moreover, the foremen, the men who were there to give the worker a lead, were just as worried by this new development as he was, though for a different reason. The bright young men had the support of their bosses and often the foreman found himself in trouble because he was not as quickly receptive to what seemed to him their crazy ideas as the bosses thought he should be. He was less certain of his authority than he had been. He felt that he was no longer master in his own house. He was not in the mood to explain these new changes so that they "made sense" to the men.

This last point is probably the most important of all in the analysis of the difficulties which face the new kind of specialist. If he is a *new* kind of specialist he is by definition going to do a job of work which was formerly done, however badly, by the "line" executive as part of his overall task of supervision. Moreover, the responsibility of the specialist, again by definition, is not for a particular process or group of machines, something which can be delimited physically even if it is only by a white line on the floor of the shop. It is for a particular subject, a kind of work, something which can only be delimited by a verbal definition; and words are a very inexact and imprecise instrument of communication. They leave all kinds of loopholes for "interpretation." If they did not there would be no work to occupy the time of the legal profession.

This fact hits the "line" executive in a number of different places. He asks himself why the hell the specialist should know more than he does about a job he's doing for half a lifetime? And when he gets through that one and is prepared to admit that the man who specializes on one bit of his whole task may be better at that one bit than he is, he begins to worry about "his authority" over "his" men. And even when he has that one settled to his satisfaction and the authority and responsibility have been defined in terms which seem to him reasonable, a new and ambitious young man turns up in the specialist job and he finds that the definition can mean very different things to different people.

Now "his authority" over "his" men, his responsibility for results, is the only ground that the "line" executive has to stand on. The specialist may have, often must have, a professional qualification. He has a "ticket" which will earn him his living anywhere. But the departmental manager or foreman has only his personal record, which is almost exclusively a question of his ability to deliver the goods, to get results. Nine tenths of the difficulty in introducing new kinds of specialists is just plain fear. The "line" men are afraid of something which everyone is afraid of when it comes down to cases, that they are going to be asked to manage a particular area of activity, be held responsible, that is accountable for getting results within the area, without having the necessary authority. There is nothing more uncomfortable than being held accountable for anything when you haven't the authority to control all the factors in the situation.

Two Points

If the specialist can learn to overcome two things:
1. The feeling that he is new and strange.
2. The suspicion that he is going to take away some of the "line" man's necessary authority over "his" men, we can eliminate an enormous amount of friction and misunderstanding in plants all over the world.

To deal with the second point first, if trouble for this reason is to be avoided the difference between specialized authority and direct authority must be more clearly recognized. The difficulty cannot be dodged by describing the specialist's authority as "purely advisory." This phrase is a nonsense, a classic in wishful thinking. It was invented to mollify infuriated "line" managers, like nurses make clucking noises at babies. Chief Executives do not appoint, and Boards of Directors do not allow them to appoint extensive specialists in order that "line" managers may please themselves as to whether they listen to them or not. They are appointed, or should be appointed, as the result of a definite development of corporation policy. That new policy is both their charter and their authority. They are there in order that the whole undertaking may have the benefit of their specialized knowledge whenever and wherever matters arise within the field in which they are specially knowledgeable.

On the other hand it is clear that they must not interfere with their "line" colleagues' *direct* authority over "their" subordinates. The chain of command must be left intact. No man should be asked "to serve two masters."

INDIRECT AUTHORITY

The logic of that situation is sufficiently obvious. The specialist must recognize that his authority over anyone who is a "line" subordinate to any other executive is *indirect*. Officially speaking, it must only be exercised *through* that "line" superior, that is, with his approval and agreement. This does not mean, however, that all action must climb wearily up one chain of command, across the top and down the other chain. Once a specialist has won the confidence of a "line" executive that he understands and recognizes that executive's "line" authority over his subordinates and has no idea or intention of infringing it, he can do 90% of his work direct, provided he is meticulous in observing two precautions:

a. He should *always* have the common courtesy to inform a "line" executive of any action he has taken affecting any of that executive's subordinates.

b. If there is the least chance of dispute or disagreement about any action, he should go *through* the "line" superior first, either personally or officially.

On the second point it should be noted that dispute can start, and usually does start, from the subordinate. A "line" executive may be wholly reasonable and genuinely anxious to live at peace with his specialist brethren. But if a subordinate comes to him with a sad, possibly a garbled, story about what that adjectival planning clerk or personnel assistant has told him to do, the "line" executive has to be something more than human if he is not sometimes to "fly off the handle." As the late C. E. Montague remarked shortly after the close of World War I, "There may be laid up in heaven a pattern of staff which are beloved by the man in the line, but such love is not in the nature of man."

TRY TRUSTING

It may be thought that this careful observance of "the official channels" must necessarily slow down business. But this conclusion really rests on a misunderstanding of what "the official channels," paper work, are for. They are "for the record," a safeguard in case personal relations break down, *not, repeat not,* a primary means of getting work down. All the real work of the world in good organizations is done by men who trust each other. They agree to decisions on the telephone, using first names and get on with it, merely telling their secretaries "to file the confirmation when it comes through." If there is the least chance of misunderstanding or disagreement they try to meet each other face to face; if you can't see the other fellow's eyes, you can't really tell "what's biting him."

Of course you must have the confirmation, the record. Because officers change, human relations do sometimes go wrong, men forget, sometimes when a decision has had an unfortunate result they "forget" their part in it. "Official channels" are as necessary in large organizations as are drains in a house; and they fulfill exactly the same functions as drains— they get rid of the waste matter. But the people who try to use them as a primary method of getting work done are not executives; they are bureaucrats. They are in fact citizens who, referring to the last speaker, "have a pathosis" for living in their drains.

But when he is new, when his colleagues don't yet know him well personally and are unaccustomed to the idea of specializing his particular function, the specialist should fall over backwards to observe the protocol, to stick precisely to the official channels. Because his first job is to convince them, beyond the per-adventure of a doubt, that he does recognize and accept their direct, their "line" authority over their own subordinates. Until they feel that, as a matter of course which they don't have to think about, they are apt to be suspicious and watchful of his every step.

That leads back into the first point—the newness of the specialist and man's instinctive distrust of what is novel. That is more difficult because it is not entirely under the specialist's control. Higher management too often appoints new specialists in a fit of enthusiasm, perhaps without having worked out the policy and the organizational arrangements which the policy demands or having taken the trouble to "sell" them to those concerned. It then tells some equally enthusiastic new specialist that it expects quick results from his appointment.

There can be no more fatal requirement. Because the one thing which is essential if human beings are to accustom themselves to new ideas is *time*. It is one of the paradoxes of the history of management that, despite the bitter attacks made by organized labor on the very idea of Scientific Management, there never was a strike in any plant in which F. W. Taylor was operating personally. That was due to his sensitive appreciation of the importance of the time factor. When he became the first management consultant, he refused to operate for any client who would not take a three years' view of the project. He always emphasized the importance of not attempting to alter the conditions of a single worker until *everything* that could be done to make management conditions effective has been seen to. Even then he would not apply the new methods to more than one worker at the beginning. He always demanded opportunity for time to work, for the force of example, of something they could see, to convince the workers: he knew that argument was futile. He said repeatedly that in introducing Scientific Management convincing the workers was comparatively easy if the job was tackled in the right way.

In the context of this argument three years is an excessive period for the introduction of a new specialist. But *some time* to allow his "line" colleagues to get used to him is essential. Broadly speaking, no new specialist should ever be asked to get or try to get positive results for *at least six months* after he has been appointed. He should be encouraged to devote that six months to getting to know his "line" colleagues personally, persuading them to talk and *listening*. In making these contacts he should have two purposes:

1. To use the opportunity to convince every "line" manager and supervisor in the place that he recognizes and accepts their direct authority over their own subordinates and that he would never dream of trying to cut across it.

2. To try to discover some point which is worrying his "line" colleagues, something which is a headache to them, which he can use in his new specialized and central position to clear up. The man who can start something new by being helpful in a practical way is already far along the road to being accepted as a member of the family.

Six months may seem a long time to many executives during which they should employ an expensive specialist without looking for results. But few businesses think anything of devoting two or more years to developing a new model or a fresh product. A new model of organization which challenges the patterns of behavior, the social structure, of any human society—and a business is after all a society—cannot be introduced overnight. If attempts are made to do so they must almost inevitably end, as do attempts to rush out new patterns or products, in frustration, disappointment and excess cost.

Let the new specialist *start* by making himself and his specialization acceptable to those on whose collaboration its utility to the undertaking must depend and all things else will be added unto him.

E. COMMITTEES

Management by Executive Committee *

W. H. Mylander

¶ What are the advantages, and the disadvantages, of committee management for the modern American business corporation?

¶ At what point in a company's growth, or product diversification, should consideration be given to committee management?

¶ How does committee management work, and what kind of people are required to make it work successfully?

Questions of this kind were put to 12 of the top executives of E. I. du Pont de Nemours & Company, which has pioneered in using the executive committee form of organization, and this article represents a composite of their replies—their expressions of judgment based on the test of experience.

FORM OF ORGANIZATION

Du Pont, now in its 153rd year, began as a manufacturer of powder on the banks of the Brandywine Creek near Wilmington, Delaware. Its 72 plants in 26 states produce some 1,200 chemical product lines with a sales volume of close to $1.7 billion in 1954.

Until 1921, du Pont was operated with the customary line organization headed by a president assisted by vice presidents in charge of specialized functions such as finance, production, and sales. Then, under the far-sighted presidency of Irénée du Pont, now honorary chairman of the board, the company adopted a committee-line system regarded as unique in American industry.

At the top is an executive committee of the board of directors consisting of President Crawford H. Greenewalt and nine vice presidents. These men devote full time to the company's affairs, although relieved of day-by-day functional responsibilities. As a committee, they meet each Wednesday, and oftener if necessary. The bylaws provide that between the monthly meetings of the board the executive committee:

* Reprinted by permission of the publisher from *Harvard Business Review*, vol. 33, no. 3 (May, 1955), pp. 51–58. Mr. Mylander is an administrative assistant of E. I. du Pont de Nemours & Company.

. . . shall possess and may exercise all the powers of the Board of Directors in the management and direction of all the business and affairs of the company . . . in such a manner as the Executive Committee shall deem best for the interest of the company in all cases in which specific directions shall not have been given by the Board of Directors.

The only other limitation on the executive committee's powers involves certain financial decisions which are reserved for the board's committees on finance, audit, and bonus and salary. The executive committee constitutes about one-third of the board's membership, and is, in effect, a daily "working board."

Strangers in Wilmington sometimes are told that "the executive committee runs the company and the general managers run the business." This is because du Pont operations are decentralized below the committee level into ten manufacturing departments headed by general managers with full authority to run their businesses as they please—so long, as they observe over-all company policies and earn a satisfactory return on the investment of plant and working capital entrusted to them. At present these departments are electrochemicals, explosives, fabrics and finishes, film, Grasselli chemicals, organic chemicals, photo products, pigments, polychemicals, and textile fibers.

Du Pont also has fourteen staff or auxiliary departments. Twelve of these—advertising, chemical, development, employee relations, engineering, foreign relations, general services, legal, public relations, purchasing, traffic, and economist—are headed by directors who are appointed by and report to the executive committee. The other two are the departments of the secretary and the treasurer, who are elected by the board and report to the president and the finance committee.

The company principle that "authority must be commensurate with responsibility" extends to the staff groups. The directors organize and run their own departments. In serving the manufacturing departments, their relations by and large are similar to those of outside agencies selling specialized services. There is no rule that requires a manufacturing department to utilize du Pont's staff facilities, but it is rare when a general manager prefers outside counsel. The staff departments also provide institutional services for the company as a whole.

The general managers and directors hire their own personnel. Each selects an assistant who must be approved by the executive committee since he should be capable of taking over in event of illness or disability of the general manager or director. "It makes you a little more careful in your choice," said one general manager.

While careful to preserve the independence of the departments in personnel matters, the committee keeps a watchful eye on the training of managerial talent. Potential executives are noted usually when they are in the early thirties and have been with du Pont from five to ten years. Those who show ability are given the opportunity to round out their experience by taking a hand in all aspects of the business. They are moved across functional fields, such as from research to production or sales, and are even transferred from one manufacturing department to another, in order that their development may be furthered.

The general managers have their own technical, production, and sales divisions, and such others as they deem advisable. They, along with the directors of staff departments, report regularly to the executive committee on their operations. "Our general managers," said one vice president, "have substantially as much power as the average company president."

ORIGIN OF THE SYSTEM

When Irénée du Pont and his associates conceived the executive committee-line system of management under which the company has grown and prospered for 34 years, they were seeking a better way to deal with the problems presented by product diversification. The old line organization had been adequate when the company was just making and selling explosives, but by 1921 a deliberate program of expansion into the broad field of chemical products was well under way.

Product Diversification

As early as the turn of the century came the modest beginning of du Pont's now famed program of research. Pending the time when its own laboratories would create the present steady flow of new and improved products, the company had bought chemical concerns with know-how and experience in various lines here in this country and had purchased patents and scientific knowledge abroad. Consequently du Pont, with a sales volume in 1921 of $55 million, was suffering growing pains with the new products.

It was one thing to make and sell explosives and quite another to make and sell paint, as du Pont's centralized sales and production divisions soon discovered. The salesmen who knew explosives and how to sell them knew little about paint. Unfamiliar sales and production problems also stemmed from other new products, such as plastic-coated fabrics, dyes, pigments, and the "fibersilk" now known as rayon.

Most chemicals are sold to other industries rather than directly to the consumer (consumer purchases today account for less than 9% of du Pont's production). The successful chemical salesman, therefore, not only must know his own wares, but must be familiar with the needs and problems of the industries to which he sells. He must be able to demonstrate how a chemical can be used to improve the end product manufactured by his customer. Obviously it was demanding too much to expect the sales expert in explosives to be equally expert in dyestuffs.

The centralized manufacturing department encountered the same troubles as the centralized sales department. But unfamiliarity with new products was not the only headache. A veteran of those days recalls an instance when the manager of a paint plant insisted on turning out all the white paint he could make because he knew how to make it at a good profit. The salesmen, however, discovered that the public wanted colored paint. They reported the demand for colors to their manager, who passed the word up the line to the vice president in charge of sales. This vice president in turn took the matter up with the vice president in charge of manufacturing, who sent the word back down the line to the plant manager. But by the time it reached the plant manager and production had been geared to sales, the inventory tanks contained an appalling amount of white paint.

"Our principal difficulty," recalls Walter S. Carpenter, Jr., now chairman of the board, "was that when trouble occurred anywhere in the organization, it had to filter all the way up to the top and all the way back down again before it was corrected."

Company Growth

All the executives interviewed felt that the need for the new organization stemmed primarily from diversification and complexity of products, although company growth in itself was a factor.

¶ "There would be far less need for an executive committee," said one, "if a company had only one product line regardless of its size. But even then, the committee might be valuable in considering broad trends and developments without having to be tied down with live issues."

¶ "It would be impossible," said another, "for any one person to administer such diversified operations as we are engaged in. It is necessary always to think in terms of what is best for the company as a whole, rather than for any one of the various components."

¶ "When a company is big enough," said a third, "complex enough or diverse enough to need more than one man to see the sum of the whole, the committee system should be given consideration."

¶ A fourth simply observed, "Ten heads are better than one."

How the Committee Operates

The vice presidents sometimes tell the general managers: "You are the bosses, and we are the philosophers." No one in du Pont, however, and least of all a general manager, would make the mistake of attributing top company authority anywhere but to the executive committee.

Responsibilities

Fundamentally, the committee exercises three important responsibilities:

(1) It determines the broad, basic policies for the operations of the company.

(2) It selects the men to carry out these operations.

(3) It maintains a continuous review, and seeks to make an honest and objective appraisal of the conduct of the business to make sure that the men selected are doing a good job.

The opinions of the committee members command the respect of general managers and other executives down the line. Each member is recognized as an expert in specific fields, which gives to the committee as a whole a prestige seldom possible for a single individual to attain. If a weakness appears in a department, the committee is quick to assist the general manager in determining whether the trouble is in sales, research, or production. When the weak spot is located, committee experts in that field help the general manager to find a solution.

The Wednesday Meetings. Each manufacturing department presents a monthly operating report, which the committee usually considers on the first and last Wednesdays of each month. In addition, the committee averages one meeting a month in a chart room, where the performance and forecasts of sales and earnings for each department are reviewed with the general manager. (A series of departments is considered each time, with every department averaging about four reviews a year.) If there is a slump in either performance or forecast, the general manager is expected to provide a satisfactory explanation and to discuss with the committee the steps which should be taken to bring operations up to standard.

Capital expenditures or long-range commitments of the departments which are above certain amounts must go to the committee for approval, and those above higher limits must be approved by the finance committee as well. This insures committee scrutiny of projects such as new plant construction, plant expansion, or new commercial ventures. The projects, however, are initiated by the general managers.

The committee passes on agreements and contracts proposed by the departments. The staff departments present annual budgets for approval. The operating departments and the chemical and engineering departments present their own research budgets. Construction forecasts are presented four times a year by the engineering department.

Decisions on operating schedules, prices, individual salary raises, and other day-by-day operating problems are left to the general managers, but are subject to the policy framework established over the years by the executive committee. However, if a department gets out of line in these respects with the rest of the company, the committee quickly calls in the general manager for a talk. It should be noted that such talks are rarely necessary.

"The heart of our operation is the Wednesday meeting," said President Greenewalt. "We spend the rest of the week directly or indirectly preparing for it."

Each Friday afternoon, committee members find on their desks a stack of reports two inches high which they are expected to read and digest prior to the next Wednesday. "We are supposed to have time to think," said one vice president indicating the stack. The members, however, do find it helpful to study a proposal in writing before taking it up in oral discussion with the officials concerned.

In the Wednesday meetings, each member of the committee has one vote, including the president, who usually votes only to make or break a tie. Split decisions are uncommon. Five members constitute a quorum, and four affirmative votes are required for the adoption of any resolution. Occasionally the members of the minority ask to have their opposition recorded. Otherwise the action is simply noted as taken, or as taken unanimously.

The practice in some companies of requiring unanimity for committee action finds no support at du Pont. Each member pays careful attention to the views of the others when a question is debated, and minds have been changed by debate. The members feel, however, that it would be stultifying to have to go along with a decision if they sincerely believe it to be wrong, and they pride themselves on being "rugged individualists." A showdown on important questions usually is postponed until all members are present, although, as stated above, five constitute a quorum for ordinary business.

As chairman of the meetings, President Greenewalt has the usual presiding officer's responsibility to see that there is opportunity for full debate, to narrow the issues to their essence, and to call for a decision after adequate discussion. Other members praise his objectivity as chairman, although they know he does not hesitate to speak his mind and express his own views when they differ from others. When fuller explanation of a decision than the customary "advice of action" is warranted, he calls the general managers together and does the explaining.

The agenda for an executive committee meeting averages at least 12 items. The regular required reports from the manufacturing departments provide the framework, and either the departments or members of the committee can initiate additions. "In a live organization, the agenda will take care of itself," was one comment. (See Exhibit 1 for a sample agenda —typical in breadth and variety though not necessarily in specific subject matter.)

"Court of Appeals." Since the manufacturing departments compete

with each other as well as with outside rivals, and the staff departments have their own differences of opinion, the executive committee is available as a court of last resort to settle intracompany disputes. The committee does not like to be placed in this role, however, and this fact is emphatically made known to the disputants. When all consultation and mediation fails, the committee if called upon will step in and resolve the issue—and the disputants will resolve never again to let it go as far as the committee.

EXHIBIT 1

AGENDA FOR A WEDNESDAY MEETING

Chart room

1. Fabrics and Finishes Department regular report for January.
2. Grasselli Chemicals Department regular report for January.
3. Photo Products Department regular report for January.
4. Pigments Department regular report for January.
5. Foreign Relations Department — annual report and operating budget.

Committee room
Unfinished business

6. Engineering Department—operating budget.
7. Motion picture program based on the Company's programs re "How Our Business System Operates." Joint report from Advertising, Employee Relations, and Public Relations Departments.

New business

8. Organic Chemicals Department regular report for January.
9. Appropriation project covering partial design, procurement of long delivery equipment, and preparation of construction cost estimate New River Pump House, ash and waste retention facilities, Old Hickory Rayon and Cellophane Plants.
10. Appropriation project—replacement of worn-out pirns, Waynesboro Plant.
11. Credit appropriation—additional power facilities, Spruance Rayon Plant.
12. Appropriation—project for synthesis gas via coal partial combustion—Step #1, Belle Works.
13. Adjustment of permanent investment—QY catalyst facilities, Arlington Works.
14. Supplemental report on accomplishment—second year's operation—continuous polyvinyl alcohol and monomer process, Niagara Falls Plant.
15. History, present status, and future prospects of the "Elvanol" polyvinyl alcohol business. Report from Electrochemicals Department.
16. Miscellaneous items.

Review of Department Projects. Members of the committee believe that the system functions at its best when they are able to stimulate and encourage the initiation of ideas and projects from down the line. They do not hesitate, however, to inject their own proposals when they believe them to be for the best interests of the company:

¶ "It is rare when a general manager is turned down on a project," said a vice president. "He knows his proposal will be reviewed by experts; and since our general managers are able men, they don't bring anything to us unless they are pretty sure."

¶ "Sometimes we don't agree with a general manager," said another, "but it is better to let a mistake be made than to order a general manager to act against his judgment—unless too many people would be hurt."

¶ "We err on the side of letting the general managers run their businesses according to their own lights," said a third. "When I was a general manager, they let me spend half a million dollars playing around with superpressures without getting any results."

There is a readiness among the vice presidents to concede that du Pont has made mistakes—"some of them beauts"—but they do point out that the initiation of projects by the departments, followed by executive committee review, provides a built-in weeding-out process which disposes of most ill-considered proposals before they ever reach the action stage.

Long-range Considerations. The committee feels strongly its obligation to look into the future for national trends, and in 1939, for example, it anticipated a country-wide pattern of wage increases. The general managers were called in and encouraged to grant increases promptly in the interest of sound employee relations. It took some convincing in certain departments where general managers were reluctant to curtail department earnings, but the result was regarded as worthwhile.

Operating officials in their planning, too, are encouraged by the committee to take into account long-range considerations of the public interest. For example, du Pont is the sole supplier of neoprene rubber for the free world. When expanded production of this product seemed advisable, the general manager proposed and the committee approved the construction of a second plant rather than enlargement of existing facilities. Among other reasons given in support of this proposal was that a second plant would guarantee an alternate source of neoprene for defense and commercial use in case one plant should be shut down by fire or disaster. As far as the company itself was concerned, the enlargement of the single plant, obviously, would have meant a greater return on investment over the near term.

One of the ways in which the committee seeks answers to its own questions, and stimulates thinking in the departments, is by requesting "whither" reports. These are so named because they ask "whither nylon?" or "whither titanium?" The studies involved in preparation of these documents dealing with the future of specified products are enlightening to the general managers as well as to the committee.

Study and consultation constitute a continuous process at du Pont. In fact, most decisions of the committee are reached only after careful examination of all available facts and opinions and consultation with everyone in a position to make some contribution.

Advisory Duties

In a secondary role, members of the committee serve as individual advisers in areas where they are best qualified by skill, training, and experience. But in contrast to formal committee decisions in which they have a vote, as advisers their influence is indirect, and they are quick to say that they can't give orders as individuals "to anybody but my secretary."

Although committee members advise, rather than dictate, it takes a strong-willed general manager or staff department director, who is sure of his ground, to take counteraction after soliciting counsel. This is not because the committee members seek to impose their will upon management down the line, but because everyone in the company looks up to them as experts in specialized areas. Thus:

Vice President Walter J. Beadle, a former treasurer, advises on foreign relations and legal matters. Another former treasurer, Vice President T. C. Davis, is adviser to the treasurer's department. Vice President Charles A. Cary, up from assistant general manager of the old rayon department, advises on traffic, purchasing, and general services. Vice President J. Warren Kinsman, up from general manager of fabrics and finishes, the company's largest direct sales area, is adviser on advertising and sales. Vice President Henry B. du Pont, who came up from engineering research, advises on engineering. Vice President William H. Ward, a former general manager of explosives, advises on personnel, salaries, and employee relations.

Vice President Walter Dannenbaum, up from general manager of the old ammonia department, advises on manufacturing. Vice President Roger Williams, who was chemical director of the ammonia department and later was in charge of the Hanford atomic energy project as assistant manager of explosives, advises on chemical research and development. President Greenewalt is the adviser on public relations, and is also consulted along with Mr. Williams on technical and scientific problems. Vice President Robert L. Richards, promoted last fall from general manager of textile fibers, awaits his advisership assignment.

Executive committee members also serve on other committees. Messrs. Beadle, Ward, and Williams are members of the company's subcommittee on "B" bonus, while Mr. Dannenbaum is chairman of the "A" bonus committee. Messrs. du Pont, Kinsman, and Dannenbaum are members of a subcommittee on purchases and sales, while Messrs. Beadle, Cary, and du Pont are members of a subcommittee on construction forecasts. In addition, some members of the executive committee are directors of certain subsidiary corporations.

¶ "We give advice, solicited or volunteered," explained one. "There is no compulsion to follow it, although we sometimes resort to tactful **persuasion.**"

¶ "It is cooperation, contact, the development of a common understanding, and talking out problems," said another. "The key to the company's success is how the general managers run the business. Our task is to create an environment which will help them do a better job."

¶ "We should never attempt to exercise too much power for that would destroy the autonomy of the departments," said a third.

¶ "It is always desirable to avoid sending down pronouncements from on high," observed a fourth. "We try to get the viewpoints of others involved and work out a mutually satisfactory answer."

While individual members of the committee are frequently consulted in advance for their views on special aspects of a project—for example, Mr. Williams on the technical end, Mr. Kinsman on sales, or Mr. Dannenbaum on manufacturing—they are not expected to commit themselves on the project as a whole. The project, as a *project,* is considered on its merits when the general manager formally presents it to the committee, even though the financial, legal, technical, sales, and manufacturing problems connected with it may have already been discussed individually with the special advisers in these fields.

QUALIFICATIONS FOR MEMBERSHIP

In selecting the executive committee, the board of directors, in the words of one director, "tries to create a superman by combining the great breadth of experience represented by the various members, so each can contribute his own viewpoint for the benefit of the others and the group as a whole." Specifically, the following qualifications are looked for:

Basic experience and expertness in one or more fields, especially research, production, sales, finance, or engineering, constitute a primary qualification.

A well-rounded background is desirable because, as another put it, "when a man goes on the committee, he is not supposed to look at an issue from the standpoint of his old department or activity, but in the interest of the company as a whole."

Sound judgment, objectivity, breadth of vision, and a willingness to cooperate are essential qualities.

The prospective committee member should be well read, versed in industrial problems, and aware of what's going on in the nation and the world.

He should enjoy good health, and be of an age which will permit him to serve at least 10 years before compulsory retirement at 65.

Other specifications as they were expressed by the board members interviewed include:

"His head should be screwed on right."

"He should be an individualist—we don't want go-alongers."

"He should balance independence of opinion with the grace to submit to the will of the majority."

"He should have ideas but be willing to see them turned down without waiting for an opportunity later to say 'I told you so.' "

"He should have a specialty and as much else as he can bring with him."

"He should be a self-starter willing to be an adviser—with all that the term implies and all that it doesn't imply."

"We want men who won't be earth-bound by logic but have the instinct or intuition to do the right thing whether logical or not."

"He should have forbearance, and recognize that the other fellow has strong convictions, too."

"He should have profound tolerance, and avoid getting provoked."

"He needs personality, a fine mind, and a quick wit."

Two members of the committee separately mentioned "dedication" as a qualification. One defined this quality as "a will to devote all your time and interest to the company's affairs," while the other remarked, "I told a general manager the other day that coming on the committee is like joining a monastery—you work 16 hours a day and get your fun out of the job. You must be dedicated."

It is acknowledged that fate has a hand in the selections. A man with all of the qualifications may miss promotion to the committee because there are no suitable vacancies while he is in the proper age bracket. One of the vice presidents also suggested that "an individual might be an excellent general manager and a poor vice president, or vice versa."

The size of the committee has varied from time to time. Asked why it numbers ten, instead of five or fifteen, a member explained that it was essential to have technical, financial, manufacturing, sales, and engineering experience represented. Then, he continued, it is better to have two from each field, both to insure a quorum for the weekly meetings, despite illnesses, vacations, or business trips, and to make available the judgment of two experts, rather than one, on specialized issues. Also, he felt that ten could function as a committee without the loss of individualism, but twice that number might lead to "herd thinking" or the development of cliques.

"We need a good, wide spectrum," said another, "but not so many as to become unmanageable."

All present members of the committee have come up through the ranks of du Pont, which practices a policy of promotion from within. They absorbed the spirit and became familiar with the theory and practice of the company before assuming their present posts. Committee members believe that outsiders could be brought in if necessary and would soon become accustomed to the system, but they concede it might take time and result in some dissatisfaction.

ADVANTAGES OF THE SYSTEM

When questioned concerning the advantages of the committee-line system, the executives interviewed stressed the following:

1. *The strength and security of group decisions—*

"We are less likely to go to extremes, since the committee assures a balanced viewpoint on every issue."

"If one individual could always come up with the right answer, we would not need a committee."

"When seven men out of ten—all intellectually honest—can reach agreement, the chances are that it is sound."

"It may take longer to get action, but this pays off handsomely in better decisions and ability to follow through on long-range policies."

"We reap the benefit of diversified experience. One of the ten will think of some important angle that may be a blank to everyone else."

2. *Objectivity in decision making—*

"The system permits discussion and consideration of policy by men relieved of day-to-day decisions. This means more than 'time to think.' It means that nobody on the committee will be influenced consciously or unconsciously by the effect of the decision on an operation for which he is responsible, because we aren't responsible for operations."

"We all have more to do than we can get done, but we do have time to concern ourselves with things we couldn't do if we had line responsibilities."

"The discipline of having to work out an agreement with nine others promotes objectivity and thorough analysis of the problems."

"There is some duplication of effort, but we get a combined judgment based on all considerations and weighed without bias."

3. *Continuity of administration—*

"The committee changes so gradually that our management is always on an even keel, whereas, when a dictator dies, there is no successor."

"The committee assures the company of an averaging-out of temperament and ability in top management."

4. *Development of personnel—*

"The system accommodates a greater diversity of executive talent. There is a place for the man who sings solo, and also for the man who sings best in the chorus."

"General guidance by suggestion through the adviserships encourages initiative throughout the organization."

"Our advice always is so worded that a general manager is free to disregard it if he wishes."

"Where there is decentralization at the top, there is initiative down the line."

Other advantages briefly mentioned included: increasing the stature of departmental manager, relieving part of the burden which usually falls upon the president or chief executive officer, encouraging the resolution of problems at lower management levels, and flexibility.

DISADVANTAGES OF THE SYSTEM

The executives were at a loss for a ready answer when asked to list the disadvantages of the system. After some thought the following were brought out:

(1) A few who had come up through departmental management mentioned a certain sense of frustration.

"On the committee you feel inhibited. You move up to it from an active to an ethereal field, and have to get things done by advice and suggestion."

"Men who have been on the firing line, making day-to-day decisions, suddenly find when they move up to the committee that they can't give orders as individuals to anybody but their secretaries."

"There is difficulty in making the transition from line management to the committee, with the danger that departmental allegiances will stay in the picture."

"Compromise isn't always easy, and expediency must be paid for."

(2) Some of the others cited as a minor disadvantage the fact that outsiders frequently are unaware of the division of responsibilities at du Pont, and expect the president and the vice presidents to make decisions on sales or other matters which lie within the province of the general managers.

(3) One of the more individualistic members pointed out that ten people had to read every report, but added that there is compensation in the fact that one of the ten occasionally spots something the other nine miss.

(4) It was also suggested that in a small company an executive committee might not have enough to do, that autonomy of the departments would be weakened if the committee set up too many rules, and that there might be room even at du Pont for "something to fall between the slats of responsibility."

On the whole, however, the members of the committee were unable to cite serious disadvantages, and two of them suggested that the question be put to one of the general managers.

After some thought the general manager consulted answered that with his title he did find it a little difficult to compete for customers' attention against the head of a competing company, who had the title of president, even though his own department's total output is five times larger than that of the competitor.

"But I just can't think of any other disadvantages of our system," he said. "I would much rather go to ten men with a project than take my chances on one."

In conclusion, the 12 top executives stressed that (1) they are not urging other companies to adopt their committee-line system, (2) they believe unanimously it has been successful for du Pont, and (3) they feel it should work for any other large producer of diversified lines.

Part Three
STAFFING

Developing the Executive of Tomorrow *

Myles L. Mace

In my judgment, the executive of tomorrow will not be a walking digital computer, complete with high-speed input and output devices but no judgment. I am equally sure that tomorrow's executive will not have a Ph.D. in mathematics in order to fulfill his functions.

Fanciful pictures have been drawn by some scientists of management. They would lead us to believe that tomorrow's management decisions will be made by a coldly calculating monster of logic, available on a rental basis of $35,000 a month, and capable of performing the work of 182 managers. However I doubt very much whether this fictional technological unemployment of management people will come about.

Dr. Harold Luxenberg, head of the Litton Industries Computation Center, facetiously formulated the job of tomorrow's executive. The executive of tomorrow, he said, will need a psychologist, a mathematician, and a programmer on his staff. The psychologist, through the use of tests, will measure the parameters of the executive from which the mathematician will construct a mathematical model. The corporate programmer will then program the mathematical model into the general-purpose computer, thereby simulating the actions and decision-making processes of the executive. When this is accomplished, technological unemployment of the executive will result, leaving the psychologist, the mathematician, and the programmer to run the enterprise. Perhaps not even the psychologist and the mathematician will be needed.

This is not to say that computers will not have a dramatic impact on business operational methods. Great improvements have been accomplished through the use of the computer as a tool, but it is merely a tool and not a business judgment exerciser. Data-processing equipment can provide more quantitative, accurate, economical, and up-to-date information on which to base decisions. The computational methods can cope with hundreds of variables and thus permit intellectual consideration of various alternatives. However, it is still the responsibility of the

* Reprinted by permission of the publisher from *Improving Managerial Performance*, General Management Series, no. 186 (New York: American Management Association, 1957), pp. 19–24. Mr. Mace was Vice President and Director, Litton Industries, Inc., Beverly Hills, California, and is now Professor of Business Administration at the Harvard Business School.

executive to apply judgment. It is interesting to conjecture about living with a machine equipped to cope with the daily vicissitudes of human behaviour. Whenever the results turned out to be attractive, we could praise the sound premises which were cranked into the electronic brain; and, if it turned out that the judgment solutions of the machine were wrong, it would be comforting to be able to blame the inanimate machine for its fallacious decisions.

However, I strongly suspect that tomorrow's executive will bear a marked resemblance to the executive of today. I also suspect that, unless we reach the science-fiction stage of complete mechanization, the skills of administration are here to stay. The executive's job of getting things done on a cooperative basis through people and with a profit will continue to be his role in the future.

Learning by Doing

How, then, do we prepare members of the organization to perform the jobs of the future? How do we help them to become more able and more responsible administrators of men? How do we help them to develop the judgments required for responsible jobs?

Several years ago, I made a study of the policies, formal programs, informal approaches, and practices of manufacturing companies known or believed to have an effective method of developing men for responsible management positions. It was not a statistical study but, rather, an attempt to determine by selective inquiry what seemed to be the main elements of a constructive approach for the growth and development of men in business.

One conclusion of the study—though it may not appear very profound —was that the most effective way of developing administrators is through the performance of the day-to-day requirements of the job. Essentially and simply, people learn by doing. The process of administration does not consist of dealing with static units of matter with fixed, known, and predictable reactions. If this were the case, anyone who had read a book or memorized a series of rules on administration presumably would qualify as an executive. In practice, it was found that few reliable rules or dependable guideposts existed for the automatic solution of administrative problems. Each administrator, therefore, must have opportunities to practice his skills and to exercise his capacities if he is to occupy a position of responsibility.

The Superior as a Coach

People do learn by doing, but the extent of their learning and the speed with which they learn depend largely on the immediate superior to whom they are responsible. The superior controls the working environment, and it is he who has such an important role in contributing to the growth of his subordinates.

Strategically, the superior is in the best possible position to help subordinates grow because:

1. He knows—or he ought to know—his subordinates better than anyone else in the organization. To use their abilities and capacities on the job, he must know their strengths and weaknesses.

2. He has the opportunity to assign tasks to subordinates which strengthen their weaknesses or shortcomings. When the job is completed, the superior can discuss the subordinate's performance with him and the learning process is thereby re-related to a concrete working situation which is part of the environment in which the subordinate hopes to grow and progress.

The job of the superior can be described as coaching, and coaching is also the basis of the process of administration—in other words, getting things done through people on a cooperative basis. Coaching is not a new technique; it is going on all the time on the job. We coach, teach, and administer our subordinates every day on the job, and the real challenge of management development is to do a "more better" job of what we are doing already.

FIVE ELEMENTS OF GOOD COACHING AND ADMINISTRATION

Let us briefly consider the five elements of coaching and administration for possible evaluation against our own administrative experience.

1. *Delegation of Authority.* If people learn by doing, then subordinates must be given opportunities, and this means that superiors must delegate.

As I worked on my survey, I chatted with many executives who indicated that, in theory, they accepted the idea of delegation; however, in practice, they found it difficult to divest themselves of their authority. A typical comment was: "I had this job before I moved into my present job, and nobody can do it as well as I can. I want to continue doing it myself." It is relatively easy to accept the *concept* of delegation intellectually and logically, but the *practice* of delegation is very difficult—especially for those superiors who have had years of experience as "doers."

The National Audubon Society, in an effort to encourage the identification of business birds, might consider admitting to membership a new collection known as "Delegatos Americanum." These birds are found only in the business community, and a few species may be listed as follows:

1. The White-Shirted Hoverer. (He gives a subordinate a job to do, then perches above his shoulder.)

2. The Pin-Striped Whoopster. (Related to the Hoverer, but can be very raucous when the subordinate deviates from the way *he* thinks the job should be done.)

3. The Pussy-Footed Mouse Trapper. (He doesn't actually hover, but is likely to swoop down at any moment.)

4. The Bald-Headed Perforator. (He leans over the subordinate's shoulder and goes, "Pst! Pst!")

5. The Grey-Thatched String Holder. (Thrives in a nest of red tape.)

6. The Yellow-Bellied Credit Snatcher. (A very highly regarded bird.)

7. The Lesser White-Crested Cuckoo. (The fair-haired prince who, by habit, lays the egg in the other fellow's nest.)

The concept of delegation requires judgment to determine when and what to delegate to each subordinate for his individual growth and development. The objective, as L. F. Urwick has so concisely said, "to break the chaps loose by giving them opportunities."

2. *Counseling.* When subordinates are given opportunities to perform on the job, the occasion is provided for affirmative counseling by the superior. The primary emphasis should be on helping the subordinate to learn the techniques of administration. This may involve job knowledge, managerial skills, or personality adjustments. However, if superiors relate the counseling to the jobs done in the work situation, they can contribute most effectively to the growth of their subordinates.

A division sales manager in a major oil company's overseas operating unit stated recently: "During the 20 years I was in India not one person from the higher echelons of management ever discussed with me how I, as an individual, could do a more effective job. Today, our main job is to help the young men who will be the managers in a few years."

However, some people still resist the idea of counseling. "We are getting soft!" they claim. Certainly, it is not soft-minded or sentimental to help subordinates do a better job. Rather, it is soft-minded to neglect these opportunities.

3. *Creating a Team.* Much of what has been said and written about creating a team sounds wishy-washy and namby-pamby, yet the concept itself has deep administrative meaning. But what are the characteristics of a *good* team?

First, the superior must know his people—and their strengths and weaknesses—if he is to use them properly and if he is to concentrate his coaching attention on individuals. Second, the superior must let subordinates know what their jobs are, where they fit in the organization, and what others in the organization do. A company president reported that, when he had been made controller several years before, the monthly profit and loss statement was top secret. "Even my department heads never saw the whole document. I changed all that," he said. "They were part of the controller team and therefore ought to know." Third, in creating a team, the superior must let his subordinates participate. Letting them only "feel" that they participate is an administrative fraud, which any subordinate will quickly perceive.

Sometimes the autocratic organization attitude is "I'm the boss. I'll make the decisions and you had better fall in line." However, participation does not mean the abrogation of authority and respect. It means a larger input of information on which wiser and better decisions can be based. I have never seen a solution to a business problem which was not better because of the addition of other points of view.

Finally, another characteristic of a good team is fair treatment: Subordinates must know that they will be judged and administered fairly.

4. *Mutual Confidence.* This should be the basis of the whole relationship between the superior and subordinate, and this confidence must be manifested by actions. As an executive of General Mills commented: "If you as administrator want results from a subordinate, your success is in direct proportion to the subordinate's belief of your belief in him." In other words, the subordinate must believe that you believe in him, and this belief can't be artificial or superficial; it must be real, genuine, and sincere.

5. *Standards of Performance.* The superior must set personal and business standards as examples that his subordinates may follow. In order to establish mutual confidence, a superior doesn't approve everything his subordinates do. The approval must have meaning, and this meaning should evolve from a reasonable set of operating standards.

Conclusions

It is difficult to envison the kinds of problems that subordinates will face in the next 10, 20, or 30 years. Therefore, it seems to me that—in addition to insuring that our employees have sound, substantive business knowledge—the best thing we can do to assist them in meeting the problems of tomorrow is to contribute to their understanding of the importance of integrity, honesty, sincerity, and character.

More important than the intellectual acceptance of the concepts of coaching is the adoption of these concepts as part of our day-to-day behavior on the job. Education has meaning only insofar as it is reflected in behavior. Each administrator, I am sure, can do something to contribute to the growth and development of his subordinates, who are destined to be the executives of tomorrow.

Management Development at Boeing
The Formal Educational Program *

Philip B. Swain

A large and important part of the individual development needs which the appraisal and coaching process emphasizes are needs which are best met by an individualized, on-the-job approach. It may become apparent, for example, that the individual lacks familiarity with an activity closely related to his work and that his position performance suffers as a result. Or he may be devoting a disproportionate amount of his time to relatively unimportant aspects of his assignment. Or perhaps there are scheduling problems which, once clearly recognized, can be worked out by the individual with the counsel and assistance of his superior. Many, many other examples could be cited to illustrate our thesis: that a large and important part of the aggregate developmental needs existing throughout our organization lends itself most effectively to cooperative action on the part of a man and his superior.

FOUR FORMAL METHODS OF DEVELOPING MANAGERS

What, then, of the more formalized measures—such as courses and other organized activities—that comprise our Management Education program? Briefly, it is their purpose to complement the developmental job done by the individual manager in four ways:

1. We provide managerial skills courses when needs in these subject matter areas are found to be common to a number of individuals in various components of the company. These courses are particularly intended to be of assistance in carrying out individual improvement plans.

2. We also offer courses and seminars that are aimed at special situations or at particular levels of management. Instead of being geared to individually identified development needs, these courses and seminars may result from over-all needs perceived by our top management, or they may anticipate foreseeable changes and problems. Examples here would

* Reprinted by permission of the publisher from *Assuring Adequate Reserves of Key Personnel*, Personnel Series, no. 169 (New York: American Management Association, 1956), pp. 18–22. Mr. Swain is Management Education Chief, Boeing Airplane Company, Seattle, Washington.

include a six-session course with the descriptive title "A Manager's Survey of Data Processing"; a management seminar on "The Administration of Change," related to the major re-organization through which our company is concurrently going; and "Fundamentals of Management," an internal course which endeavors to bring to our middle management group many of the benefits which our top managers obtain from participation in the advanced management programs of the various universities and other institutions. Another important and continuing program of this type is a four-day course for all newly appointed supervisors, which helps them to bridge the gap from their former status by providing information on company organization, functions, and procedures, as well as discussion of the responsibilities and problems of the first-line manager.

3. As a company, we also participate in "outside" courses, and maintain and furnish current information and evaluations on them so that line management can make the most effective use of them. Related to this activity is the extensive use of worth-while seminars and conferences for development because of the opportunity they provide for outside exposure and interchange of experience. We also find that community projects and professional societies—although less explicitly pointed in this direction—offer special development opportunities, and our managers are encouraged to participate in them.

4. Finally, we endeavor to make available to each manager promptly the complete information which he needs in order to relate the work of his component to over-all goals and in order to interpret the company properly to both subordinates and the community. A major vehicle for accomplishing this is our management newsletter, of which special issues are distributed when and as needed. In addition, special informational and discussion meetings are held for all managers on such topics as the company's annual report to stockholders. Furthermore, we have a management library, which is, in itself, a way of making available to the individual manager a wealth of information on the managerial profession. We are convinced that one of the most effective, and at the same time most economical, media for self-development is the reading of worthwhile business literature. From a central library location we periodically circulate reviews of newly acquired management books, and we have just recently furnished each member of management with an up-to-date, annotated library catalogue. Some 150 to 200 books are circulated monthly in this manner, with the details handled by a secretary.

THE COMPANY COURSE PROGRAM

In Boeing, we firmly believe that management education or training is not an end in itself, but is, rather, a justifiable activity only if directly addressed to specific needs of the organization and the people in it. We apply this criterion to our program of management skills courses. In doing so, we are aided immeasurably by the fact that, each time a member of management is appraised, the central Management Development office receives a copy (an *anonymous* copy) of the development plan which is worked out jointly by the man and his superior. Each plan shows the one or two needs that the two men together have agreed upon as being most important. From study of the total of such individually reported needs, we who are responsible for the course program are in a position to determine which ones lend themselves to the course approach and which ones are most important.

ANALYSIS OF INDIVIDUAL DEVELOPMENT PLANS

What do we find as a result of our study of these individual improvement plans? In a recent analysis of 500 of these plans, we classified reported needs under three major headings:

1. *Needs for improved social skills,* under which we used such subheadings as communications skills, human relations skills, and needs even more distinctly personal (for example: attitude, aggressiveness).

2. *Needs for improved skill in certain managerial functions,* under which we used such subheadings as planning, delegation, coordination, control, training, evaluation, and methods.

3. *Needs for more knowledge,* under which we used subheadings to distinguish between technical knowledge, knowledge of company policies and procedures, and knowledge of the work of other company units.

COMMUNICATIONS SKILLS NEEDED

When we study the 500 carefully prepared analyses of individual development needs, we find a stress on the need to improve the communications skills of individual managers. Perhaps this is not so surprising if we think of the very prevalent and apt definition of the manager as one who gets things done through other people. To do this, he must be able to get objectives, procedures, and ideas clearly understood and accepted and must himself be a good receiver and able to tap the thinking of others.

To us, this means that our need-oriented management skills courses must provide help in the acquiring of improved communications skills. Specifically, we have written communication courses at two separate levels; we have a reading improvement course, an oral communication course, a conference leadership course, and an "effective meetings" course that approaches better utilization of the meeting situation from the standpoint of both the leader and the participant.

EMPHASIS ON SOCIAL SKILLS

In the subcategory of social skills (needs of a more personal nature) it is our experience that the appraisal and coaching course has a major contribution to make to the individual manager's day-to-day, on-the-job approach to his subordinates' needs in this area.

In our analysis of individually reported needs—still within the "social skills" category—a need for improved skill in human relations is also reported with substantial frequency. Here, too, we have oriented our program of management skills courses to this perceived need, and have made available a variety of courses grouped together under the designation of "human factors in management."

In these courses we do not presume to give the participant definitive answers to all his "people problems," but endeavor instead to increase his understanding of people, both as individuals and as members of the work group, by dealing with (1) basic concepts of human behavior, (2) approaches to gaining greater understanding of particular human relations situations, and (3) methods of taking action on human relations problems encountered on the job.

COURSE ADMINISTRATION AND OBJECTIVES

Boeing's course program does *not* require an oversized instructional staff; we have a basic program into which we can fit resource personnel from other parts of the company, community resources, university instructors, and so forth, as well as our own instructional staff.

We're also continually thinking about the program and working to refine it. This means dropping courses that have reached the end of their usefulness and adding those that have promise of filling identified organizational needs. In the fall of 1956, for example, we have started a few sections of a creative thinking course, under carefully controlled conditions, with the intent of evaluating its usefulness and continuing to offer it only if it fulfills this criterion of need satisfaction.

One other important characteristic of our courses is that participation in them is voluntary, and the individual attends on his own time. In the case of some other Boeing educational activities, men are scheduled to attend during regular working hours. But, basically, we are convinced that without self-development there is no true development at all, and so the initiative for participation in the management skills courses rests with the individual. This individual initiative in enrolling results in a commitment to learning and change that we feel would not exist in many cases if participation were required. The objectives are explained in the foreword to the current course catalogue: "To assist *you* as individual members of management in *your* task of self-development, and to assist in carrying out improvement plans prepared jointly by individual managers and their supervisors, Management Development offers a group of courses designed especially for Boeing managers." In the first eight months of 1956 alone, over 1,300 managers in our Seattle area divisions have accepted the challenge which is implicit in this philosophy of the individual's responsibility for his own development, and have voluntarily participated in one of these off-hours management skills courses.

In formulating our plan of management education, we at Boeing are responsive to individual needs, recognizing that the process never ends—that it must be progressively adapted to the requirements of the individual as he advances in the organization. The plan itself, of course, has to be in a continual state of evolution and adaptation to reflect changes that have been found necessary and worth while in our organization.

Appraising the Performance of
Management Personnel *

M. S. Kellogg

Few problems that confront industry are as challenging and rewarding as the difficult task of evaluating performance. Whether a company relies upon the "huddle and muddle" technique or measures performance through a formal program, it is constantly evaluating a man's abilities in relation to his present job and future growth possibilities. This is a day-to-day activity whether it is recognized as such or not. Thousands of manhours are spent by industry annually in an effort to make formal rating techniques as sensitive and as precise as possible. Despite these continued efforts, subjective considerations are often major influencing factors in assessing individual performance. While it is not suggested that personal judgment should be eliminated in appraising men, the reliability and validity of personnel evaluation can undoubtedly be increased by sharper individual judgment and the encouragement of more critical thinking. . . .

THE EARLIER SYSTEM

Our old personnel evaluation system was based on two different trait-rating forms. The first, used for all professional and supervisory personnel, listed 11 traits or personal characteristics, such as analytical ability, industry, judgment, initiative, leadership, and so forth. In evaluating the employee on each count, the rater could choose one of six ratings ranging from outstanding to unacceptable. The rating form also was designed to give information on the employee's value in his present work and his capacity for future growth. Raters were encouraged to discuss the rating with employees, but there were rather frequent instances when this was not done.

The second trait-rating form was used primarily for salary administration. This form listed six of the same traits as appeared on the first form and provided similar choices which were used to establish a numerical

* Reprinted by permission of the publisher from *Personnel*, vol. 31, no. 5 (New York: American Management Association, March, 1955), pp. 442–455. Mr. Kellogg is Manager of Employee Relations, Aircraft Gas Turbine Development Department, General Electric Company.

index of performance. Since the information was confidential, the engineer usually did not know what his numerical index was.

We decided to change the dual trait-rating system described above because we found it unsatisfactory in the following respects:

1. The two ratings did not have to be made simultaneously and seldom were. There was often a lack of agreement between the rating a supervisor made on a "confidential" basis and the one he discussed with the employee. This frequently made it difficult to explain to an employee why he did not get a raise after he had been told that his performance was good.

2. Supervisors found it difficult to differentiate between such terms as "initiative" and "leadership." It was also difficult to get common understanding of specific traits.

3. Since ratings were not always discussed, many employees never knew where they stood.

4. The difficulty of the job was not a major determining factor in fixing compensation. Consequently, two engineers carrying out similar duties at the same level of performance were sometimes paid different salaries because of the emphasis placed on technical experience.

5. To be effective any personnel development program must possess a reasonably objective measure of an employee's on-the-job performance and a realistic estimate of his growth potential. Our merit-rating plan was not sufficiently critical in these areas.

We believed that our trait-rating plan could be improved upon in all these respects. However, before considering the merits of alternative measurement techniques we began by clearly defining our objectives.

OBJECTIVES OF THE NEW PLAN

Our objectives were determined by our two-fold aim of fostering our employees' personal development and providing a guide to their equitable compensation. Accordingly, we decided that our plan should incorporate the following basic features:

1. *Require supervisors to consider, at regular intervals, the relative strengths and weaknesses of each subordinate and to measure the effectiveness of his performance in relation to his assigned responsibilities.*

This objective is fundamental to the adoption of a formal periodic performance appraisal plan. While valuation of performance is a continuous activity, which is independent of a formal program, there are many advantages to formalizing supervisory judgments and making them a matter of record. Both the administration of merit increases and personnel development activities are without factual foundation if no evaluation program exists. Before effective coaching or counseling can be done, it is necessary to define the areas of strength and weakness and to select those which can be modified by the ratee. This presupposes the critical evaluation of personnel through the medium of a formal appraisal program. In common with industry as a whole, therefore, our decision was not whether to appraise but, rather, how to appraise most effectively.

2. *Provide the opportunity for periodic discussion of performance, (a) to let the employee know where he stood, and (b) to improve on-the-job performance.*

This aimed at overcoming one of the basic deficiencies of our old rating system—the fact that it did not assure that every employee knew where he stood. We felt that, to be truly effective, a personnel measurement plan must provide for discussion of performance between the supervisor and the employee. Most of the personnel development benefits to be gained from an effective appraisal program are dependent upon frank and full discussion between supervisor and employee. In this way, the employee learns what is expected of him, how far he measures up to the requirements of his job, and what he must do in order to advance. This provides a basis for self-appraisal and spurs him on to improved performance and self-development. It also makes for better and closer working relationships because of the opportunity to air misunderstandings and misgivings, as well as the coaching and counseling to improve on-the-job performance which generally result from such discussions.

3. *Serve as a guide to supervisors in observing and evaluating employee performance for the purpose of salary adjustment, and place responsibility for merit increases closer to the immediate supervisor.*

There is a significant change of emphasis here. In view of our experience with the earlier trait-rating form, we wanted to relate performance and merit increases more closely; but we also wanted to place more responsibility for recommending merit increases in the hands of the immediate supervisor. Hence, we departed from a system that aimed at measuring general ability and potential to one that placed more emphasis on how well a specific job is performed.

4. *Provide supervisors with information that would be helpful in the promotion, transfer, or discharge of personnel, and that would serve as a measure of an employee's performance over a period of time.*

To be of real value, an appraisal system must provide accurate data, not only as a help in making decisions involving promotions, transfers, or discharges, but also to throw light upon organizational weaknesses and deficiencies. While the trait-rating form provided some valuable information, and has therefore become a useful part of the record of employees with longer service, we felt that it could be improved upon in a number of respects.

5. *Encourage the rater and ratee to consider together and formulate plans helpful to individual improvement.*

This was adopted to stimulate individual development. Our personnel development program is founded on the basic premise that development is primarily the responsibility of the individual. Our efforts are therefore directed toward: (a) helping the individual do his present job better, and (b) giving him the opportunity to acquire new skills that will fit him for positions of greater technical and managerial responsibility.

To achieve these aims, the employee must not only be willing to help himself, but must also recognize that some improvement is necessary. This is why we felt it important that the employee should evaluate his own performance and set his own objectives. Since every supervisor is responsible for the development of his men, we felt that he should share in this task.

6. *Assist supervisors and employee relations personnel to identify personal development and training needs.*

This objective reflects the importance of slanting personnel development and training programs to individual needs. We recognize that learning by doing is more important and more effective than learning by study and formal education; but we do not minimize the importance of courses to increase technical knowledge and managerial ability. Consequently, we sought to incorporate into our plan an accurate means of identifying the employee's individual needs for training and development.

After considerable study, we finally decided that the "responsibility appraisal method" would best meet the objectives of our new personnel measurement plan. In putting this method into effect, we had the assistance of a consultant.

The Existing Organization and "Climate"

To appreciate the magnitude of the problems that confronted us, it is necessary to know something of the organization of the Aircraft Gas Turbine Division of the General Electric Company. This division is composed of five departments, one of which—the Aircraft Gas Turbine Development Department—assumed responsibility for the preliminary work before the performance appraisal plan was established on a divisional basis. Of the 2,400 management personnel of the Aircraft Gas Turbine Division, roughly 400 were employees of the Aircraft Gas Turbine Development Department. However, while the following account of the plan's initiation applies more specifically to the Aircraft Gas Turbine Development Department, the same general procedure was followed in the rest of the division.

In passing, it should be emphasized that a fundamental requirement for the success of a performance appraisal plan is an organizational climate in which management is both able and willing to provide good performance information and to make wise use of it. (This is also one of the best measures of a plan's effectiveness.) The top management of the

Aircraft Gas Turbine Division was fully aware of the need for an appraisal plan that would measure performance more accurately, because the company's proposed new salary plan depended upon a systematic method of appraisal to provide a basis for establishing merit increases.

A pilot study was launched to test the rating plan and procedures, and the experience gained from it helped us to make further refinements in the plan.

INITIATION OF THE PLAN

Following the pilot study, the appraisal plan was initiated on a divisional basis. Our first step was to inaugurate a series of two-hour training and orientation sessions for raters, explaining the philosophy underlying the performance appraisal plan. In the training sessions, appraisal techniques were thoroughly discussed and attractively illustrated booklets entitled "How to Appraise the Performance of Management Personnel," were distributed. At the close of the sessions, rating forms were handed out for completion and target dates were set for their return.

The forms were returned to designated Employee Relations personnel in each department, who acted as a central control to enable the General Managers to guard against rater errors. It was thus easy to identify raters who were either too lenient or too critical, or who were disposed to rate centrally. Chats with these raters proved beneficial in stimulating critical evaluations. The accompanying graph shows how the Aircraft Gas Turbine Development Department fared in the distribution of ratings.

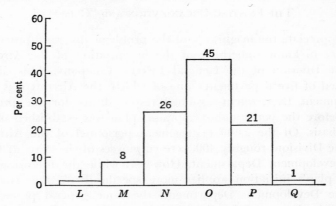

The letters in the graph refer to the rating scale which is part of the over-all evaluation summary on the performance appraisal form. These are defined as follows:

L —Fails to meet requirements.
M—Meets minimum requirements.

N —With a few exceptions meets normal requirements.

O —Without exception meets normal requirements.

P —Exceeds normal requirements.

Q —Far exceeds normal requirements.

On the initial "go-around" of the new plan, discussions of performance were deferred until the appraisals were approved and a short training course could be conducted. Two-hour training sessions for raters were held, pointing out the most effective way to conduct performance discussions. As a further aid to raters a discussion check list was distributed as well as copies of a booklet giving hints on how to improve discussions of performance with management personnel.

The discussion of performance and the preparation of a long-range individual improvement plan concluded the appraisal cycle.

FEATURES OF THE PLAN

Before enumerating the conclusions we reached from our first year's experience with the performance appraisal plan, it is appropriate to consider the answers to the following basic questions:

1. *Who is appraised?* The new appraisal plan is used for all management personnel. This includes engineers, supervisors, specialists, and administrative staff.

2. *When is the appraisal made?* When the new performance appraisal plan was installed, all appraisals were scheduled for the same time period and it was initially planned to schedule subsequent annual appraisals in the same way. Special appraisals were provided for, should the growth and pace of the individual warrant them. In the event of a transfer before the close of the normal appraisal period, provision was also made for an appraisal before the employee took up his new duties.

3. *What is appraised?* Demonstrated performance of the items listed in the "responsibility summary."

4. *What is the responsibility summary?* The responsibility summary consists of the ten to fifteen responsibilities which are most important for fulfilling the job. By way of illustration, three of the Performance Appraisal Administrator's responsibility summary statements follow:

The performance of the Performance Appraisal Administrator is measured by:

(a) The quality of the performance appraisal plan, forms, and booklets as measured by the degree of uniformity of interpretation by raters, usefulness of appraisal information obtained and acceptance of recommended changes in the plan by supervision, as appraised by supervisory judgment.

(b) The degree to which established schedules for appraising performance are maintained as appraised by supervisory judgment.

(c) The quality of instruction provided in appraisal and discussion courses as measured by the extent to which such training is reflected in the quality of class members' appraisals and discussions before and after the course and the reaction of individuals trained as appraised by supervisory judgment.

Each specific responsibility is numerically weighted to reflect the relative importance the immediate supervisor attaches to it. The numerical weights distributed throughout the responsibility statements total 100. The summary provides the basis for evaluating each person's accomplishments in relation to the most important features of his position and insures a distinctive appraisal sheet for each position, but not necessarily for each person rated.

5. *Who prepares the responsibility summary?* The responsibility summary is jointly prepared at three levels: by the person to be appraised, his supervisor, and the latter's immediate superior. It is developed for the most part by the person to be appraised. For this purpose he is provided with a copy of his job description and a Responsibility Summary Preparation Check List (Figure 1).

FIGURE 1

RESPONSIBILITY SUMMARY PREPARATION CHECK LIST
(For the person to be rated)

........Read your position analysis.

........List the 10–15 most important responsibilities of your position, based on your position analysis. These may be specific items under any Factor in the position analysis or a combination of two or more items that make up a major responsibility.

........Begin each with an action verb.

........Avoid overlap.

........Place more important items nearer the top of the list.

........Submit to your supervisor no later than....................................
....

........(Suggestion) Mentally rate yourself.

(The reverse of this form, the Responsibility Summary Work Sheet, consists of a blank sheet, ruled off for completion in accordance with the instructions shown above.)

The immediate supervisor looks over the responsibility summary with the employee, weighs the statements and approves or alters it as appropriate; in turn, his superior reviews and exercises final approval of its content and weighing.

6. *Who makes the appraisal?* The immediate supervisor is the primary rater but he may ask one or more supplementary raters to help him. . . . The primary rater has final responsibility for preparing the performance appraisal, subject to the review and approval of his superior. Therefore,

he has the option of accepting, modifying, or rejecting the comments of the supplementary raters. The latter are selected from management personnel at approximately the same level as the primary rater and have knowledge of the ratee's performance.

7. *How is the appraisal made?* The appraisal is made by evaluating employee performance against the specific statements of the responsibility summary. Raters are encouraged to request employees to submit evidence of accomplishments at periodic intervals. This gives a factual basis for the rater and assures the employee that his achievements are fully considered. The rater considers the ratee's performance and records the objective basis or critical incidents that support his choice of one out of six alternative points on a performance scale ranging from "fails to meet requirements" to "far exceeds normal requirements." The appraisal form shows the points on the scale and how the evidence supporting the appraisal is recorded. It will be noted that provision is made for an over-all evaluation. Though this is often an average of the individual ratings on specific responsibilities, it need not be. For instance, a man might be rated as "fails to meet requirements" on one or two responsibilities because priority for other projects, or factors beyond his control prevented him from doing his best in these particular instances. The over-all evaluation is not mathematically determined and therefore need not necessarily be lowered because of such ratings.

8. *What is the personal improvement plan?* The personal improvement plan is one of the most valuable products of the performance appraisal discussion. This enables the supervisor and the subordinate to discuss the latter's relative strengths and weaknesses and determine a course of action to help him fulfill the requirements of his job and prepare him for greater responsibilities. On the form used for this purpose, the rater can comment on the ratee's reaction to the discussion. The discussion itself is particularly fruitful if the employee is encouraged to appraise his own performance before the supervisor makes his appraisal and the personal improvement plan has been jointly formulated. A copy of the personal improvement plan, but without the rater's comments on the ratee's reaction, is given to the subordinate. . . .

Conclusions

Our past year's experience has led us to conclude that certain modifications in the performance appraisal plan are desirable. A research study which evaluated such factors as acceptance of the plan, the use and quality of the data obtained, and procedural aspects proved helpful in singling out certain merits and defects. The conclusions we have reached are summarized below:

1. The performance appraisal plan provides supervisors with an orderly

and systematic method of recording their considered judgment of the effectiveness with which an employee performs the duties that have been assigned to him.

2. The information obtained provides a useful tool for personnel development and a guide for the equitable administration of merit increases.

3. The plan does not provide sufficient information about the employee's potential for future advancement. While considerable information can be derived by inference, it would appear that the questions about promotability on the back page of the appraisal form should be revised to elicit specific data on this score.

4. Our experience suggests that a system of staggered yearly appraisals is better than department-wide appraisals held annually over a short period. We are therefore adopting an individually scheduled appraisal plan to apportion the workload on supervision throughout the year and meet the objections of some supervisors who felt that rating all employees simultaneously created too much of a burden. Further, this system emphasizes that appraisal is a continuous and individual process, not an annual mass affair; it also points up the fundamental thesis that performance "pays off." The plan also provides for a salary review at the same time, thus enabling the supervisor to include the question of compensation in the performance discussion.

5. It was found that the rating scale on our appraisal form caused some confusion to supervisors, owing to the fact that there was no established median rating among the alternative choices on the rating scale. While each supervisor has a concept of "average," this concept is not necessarily the same for all supervisors. For instance, some supervisors thought that "With few exceptions—meets normal requirements" was an average rating whereas others took the view that this was expressed by "Without exception—meets normal requirements." Accordingly, we are considering changing the latter rating to "Meets normal requirements" and the former to "Exceeds minimum, below normal," and propose to establish "Meets normal requirements" as average.

6. The value of the personal improvement plan may be improved by emphasizing to supervisors the importance of their role in helping to formulate realistic and worthwhile objectives. To promote this end we intend to offer a course in "How to Discuss Performance Appraisals with Management Personnel" which will make use of role-playing and lectures to increase skill and knowledge in this area.

7. A real hazard to the integrity of the performance appraisal plan comes from the fact that the over-all evaluation is used as a guide to compensation. Because supervisors may let this factor influence their rating judgment, there is a danger that some appraisals may not be truly critical. It is necessary, therefore, to continually impress supervisors with

the vital importance of making critical appraisals. Consequently, the Performance Appraisal Administrator has an important function to perform in reviewing appraisals and discussing them with supervisors.

REACTIONS OF PERSONNEL

An attitude survey conducted in May, 1954 showed that 91 per cent of management personnel in the Aircraft Gas Turbine Development Department liked the periodic performance appraisal and the accompanying discussions. Random interview samples since that date show that this same feeling still prevails. We are particularly encouraged by the frequently expressed sentiment that the new performance appraisal plan provides a fair and just means of evaluating performance and assuring equitable rewards. We feel the same way.

While we are satisfied with our progress to date and the results achieved by the performance appraisal plan, the comments summarized above reflect our view that considerable improvement can still be made both in the quality of appraisals and in the measurement technique. Though the responsibility summary provides a good point of departure it can undoubtedly be improved upon by establishing more objective standards of performance and better indices of success. We intend to work toward this end.

Management Appraisal—Key to Building Executives*

Booz, Allen & Hamilton

Business leaders know that building a successful enterprise depends upon people—their proper selection, development and use. The discovery of executive talent and its development emerges constantly in discussions with business leaders as an abiding and central concern. The search for management talent is unceasing, not only to get today's job done better but also to provide for expansion and to build for the future.

The president of a corporation, therefore, spends a large part of his time trying to find able people and to use their talents to best advantage. To do this, he must identify and appraise ability. Appraisal is the key. Many techniques for measuring management ability have been devised to help a president with his vital task, but the shortcomings of any individual measure have often left him uncertain as to the reliability of the result.

The search for greater reliability in executive evaluation has led us to review appraisal practices in prominent companies and our own experience, for the purpose of developing a program that is valid and practical for management to use. The results of our research convince us, more than ever, that reliability can be substantially improved by the use of several differing methods of appraisal, all integrated into a single, final evaluation on a carefully planned basis. Such a multiple method looks at a man from all sides and pulls together results that can be cross-checked and confirmed. It is this integration, this accumulation of evidence behind every conclusion, that provides reliability.

As a first step in our research to make evaluation more dependable, current practices of prominent companies were reviewed. These findings are given below. Following this and drawing on our own long experience in executive appraisal, the report (1) shows by case history how a practical evaluation can be carried out, (2) lists the standards for a reliable program, and (3) demonstrates the use of appraisal results.

PRESENT APPRAISAL PRACTICES

A survey of management appraisal programs in 50 prominent companies was undertaken as background research for this report. One half

* A brochure published in 1955 by Booz, Allen & Hamilton, Management Consultants, and reprinted with their permission.

of these companies relied solely on a single supervisor's opinion for appraisal, and results appeared inadequate. Another 15 companies, or 30%, had persons in addition to the supervisor make appraisals, usually the supervisor's supervisor or a rating committee. Improved appraisals and better records for manpower planning resulted. Ten companies, or only 20%, had gone beyond the usual evaluation practices. Even here the appraisal records kept for manpower planning were far less complete than plans for manufacturing, sales or distribution in the same companies.

These are the research findings for the most prominent companies having organized programs. If all companies are considered, appraisal appears to be largely unplanned and sometimes amounts to little more than impressions of key supervisors. Human resources are then not inventoried or well known. The range of ability and the total value of a man may be overlooked. This creates a tendency for management to judge men by the things they do wrong, rather than by their entire ability. Under these conditions, a company's primary asset—management talent—is not used as well as it could be.

Despite shortcomings in present practice, the benefits from adequate appraisal are clear to most executives. People will be better placed, more capable backer-ups will be chosen, and development of talent will be more effective. The general quality of management will improve.

A Case History of a Practical Appraisal Program

To realize these benefits, management needs a practical, as well as a reliable, appraisal program. In our experience four appraisal methods can be successfully woven into such an evaluation. Less than this number enlarges the margin of error; and more than four makes the program costly and difficult to carry out. Each of the four methods serves as an independent measure, and they are later integrated to confirm appraisal findings.

The four elements in the appraisal program are:
1. Analysis of experience
2. Appraisal by associates
3. Personnel tests
4. Planned interviews

Perhaps the best way to demonstrate how an appraisal program is carried out, and how the integration is made, is to follow through the appraisal of one individual. The case history will have to be shortened greatly because the actual forms and appraisal facts are too lengthy to discuss in detail here. However, the essentials of the appraisal program and integration may be shown in the case of James Smith, age 34, an assistant controller in a medium-sized company.

Analysis of Experience

An analysis of Mr. Smith's background was undertaken to determine his past pattern of accomplishment, or its lack. Successful work performance and rapid advancement in the past are important indications of promotional potential. The assumption of responsibility, both on the job and in civic and social life, reflects leadership ability. A comparison of such background with that of fellow workers, on a planned basis, is the first step to find men who can develop into leadership positions.

In the case of Mr. Smith, an analysis of his background showed that his work experience had been narrow and confined to accounting. Salary increases had been rapid, and internal company ratings had been high. His promotions in position level had been faster than usual. Mr. Smith was a member of two professional associations. The experience analysis showed that he had not taken part in other professional organizations or in civic activity. He had held no leadership positions outside his company.

Appraisal by Associates

Five business associates were used to appraise Mr. Smith in order to achieve objectivity and accuracy. Each business associate made an independent and confidential evaluation. These appraisers were chosen for their knowledge of Mr. Smith from positions above and beside him in the controller's department and from positions in other departments with which he worked. The objective was to look at Mr. Smith from every angle and eliminate "blind spots." The appraisers were forced to make a choice on Smith's strong points and weaknesses. Mr. Smith was rated by his associates on position, performance, mental qualities and human relations. Mental qualities and human relations were included because these qualities are increasingly important at higher management levels.

The five business associates who appraised Mr. Smith were in substantial agreement that the strong points of his position performance were his job knowledge and his drive. Turning to his weak points, they questioned the work accomplishment in his section and his ability to delegate and control the activity under him.

As to mental ability, his business associates felt that he was exceptionally alert and flexible, but there was doubt about his creativeness.

On human relations, his associates felt that his attitude was good, but they agreed that he was weak on supervision, the training of subordinates and self-control.

Overall, his business associates thought that he probably had a promotion potential to the departmental or vice presidential level in the accounting field. They felt his main training needs were in the handling of people and a broader outlook on the company's activity.

Personnel Tests

Tests were used in four areas—basic mental ability, interests, personal characteristics and knowledge of supervisory principles. The tests were chosen to integrate with other parts of the program. Test results were compared with company norms, or the scores made by other individuals within the organization. The tests were used to confirm and explain other appraisal findings. In short, tests were used only in a supporting role and not as a sole evaluation technique.

The test profile confirmed Mr. Smith's high mental ability. It showed that he had a strong accounting interest and maintained a rapid work pace. The tests indicated that he tended to assume responsibility readily. Test results confirmed the appraisal of his business associates on his weakness in handling people. He had poor knowledge of proper supervisory principles. He lacked the basic desire to help others, was deficient in self-control and tended to work things out alone. It is interesting to note that Mr. Smith's tendency to work individually rather than in a team effort is confirmed by the tests, by associates' appraisal and by his experience record.

Planned Interviews

A planned appraisal interview was arranged with Mr. Smith to pick up the loose ends and balance out the total appraisal. The interview was intended to provide facts not obtained elsewhere, such as personal appearance, poise, personality, mental organization and fluency, as well as to clear up queries raised by other findings. It played an important part in the integration process, by probing, resolving and confirming results.

The interview with Mr. Smith indicated that he had a very pleasing personal appearance, a high verbal facility and demonstrated good mental organization. His job knowledge was outstanding. The weak points indicated by the interview were a narrowness of interests, irritability and poor self-control, and lack of interest in or knowledge on how to deal with people.

Appraisal Summary

The most important thing to note about this appraisal case history is that the four parts—experience analysis, associate appraisal, personnel tests and planned interview—are consciously designed and applied to yield related results. It thus becomes possible to accumulate appraisal findings. Confirmed facts are assembled; isolated findings are dropped from consideration. Each accepted appraisal fact is backed by accumulated evidence.

In combining the appraisal findings on Mr. Smith, it was concluded that he was strong in mental qualities, job knowledge and performance but that he possessed deficits in administration, supervision and training. Each of these points could be substantiated in the accumulated evidence from each section of the program. The evaluation of Mr. Smith further indicated that he probably could advance ultimately to the vice presidential level. This would be his ceiling, unless he broadened very considerably under a development program.

At the time of the appraisal, Mr. Smith did not seem to possess the background, training, interest, administrative facility or human relations skill needed to become president. Still he could be very valuable to the company, ultimately, as vice president in charge of accounting and finance. However, for this position he needed additional training and development. He needed a better knowledge of treasurer functions, training in administration and personnel management, personal counsel on his deficits and a better understanding of company operating problems.

The appraisal results on Mr. Smith, therefore, gave management a list of his strengths and weaknesses, his advancement potential, the position that he seemed most eligible to fill, and the training and development necessary to qualify for that position. The appraisal provided the basic material needed for Mr. Smith's placement, promotion and development. Taken together with similar appraisal findings on all management personnel within the organization, appraisal thus proves to be an effective tool for manpower planning, utilization and development.

STANDARDS FOR RELIABLE APPRAISAL

Although the case history of Mr. Smith has been given as a narrative of appraisal results, the evaluation actually took place on a carefully planned basis. The appraisal was planned to meet ten specifications that have been derived from our consulting experience with a wide range of companies. These specifications may be regarded as the bylaws of good appraisal, for they are the means by which reliability can be obtained. They have been tested in use and their practicality has been proved. A soundly constructive program should include the following elements.

1. The appraisal factors and methods should be selected to key in with a company's needs. The program must, therefore, have individuality and conform to the practical requirements of a company's operation.

2. Several appraisal methods should be used, and these methods should differ. Diverse methods provide a balanced appraisal that eliminates "blind spots."

3. An appraisal system should be integrated in such a way that findings from one part of the program can be cross-checked with those from others. Real appraisal accuracy is the outgrowth of confirmed findings and accumulated evidence.

4. A direct evaluation of an individual's performance on the job, and

a comparative measure of the man against other jobs and other people, should be made. This provides a practical test of whether a man can meet new job requirements and whether he is the best man for the job.

5. An appraisal program must be operated on a periodic basis to discover individuals who may have been missed on the first appraisal and to measure the development of those who are striving to get ahead.

6. A careful written appraisal is essential to permit the step-by-step course of evaluation to be followed and the accumulation of evidence to be observed.

7. An appraisal program should be flexible enough to be applied to all management levels because there is a constant transition in management staff as promotions, replacements and transfers are made.

8. Management appraisal should be applied to all executive personnel because everyone in a management position is part of the reservoir of future talent.

9. The appraisal program must be easy to understand to gain management confidence and to provide ease of administration.

10. Appraisal records must be kept confidential to prevent lowering of morale and to insure honest evaluation.

The planning and carrying out of an appraisal program that meets these standards requires experience and objectivity as well as full company participation. This combination of qualities can be obtained by using experienced consultants who help plan an appraisal program and who then take company personnel through the appraisal skills. This enables the company staff to carry on the program and to assume their responsibility to develop better management personnel.

USING APPRAISAL RESULTS

The case history of Mr. Smith also suggests how appraisal findings help in the development and use of executive talent. Given appraisal results of demonstrated reliability, management can use these conclusions for counseling, planning of replacements, improved executive selection and setting up of training schedules to meet individual needs.

Using Appraisal Results to Build Men

The first use of appraisal results is to counsel with each employee about his future development. This can be accomplished when the supervisor reports on the evaluation and tells each individual how he is doing and how he can improve.

Admittedly, this counseling and coaching procedure is difficult. It is hard to talk to a man about his weaknesses and to do it in such a way that he is motivated to try to improve himself. This is certainly one of the primary responsibilities of the executive today and promises to be even more so in the future.

By the manner in which the executive carries out this vital function, he sets up a gauge of his own effectiveness.[1]

Counseling is a difficult art not born of textbooks and manuals. For the supervisor, as for the subordinate, it is a point of self-improvement and growth.

When the evaluation is thoroughly discussed in a friendly, private conference, the immediate superior has an opportunity to:
Recognize the individual's outstanding accomplishments.
Tell him exactly where he stands.
Show him in what areas it is felt he can improve.
Explain why it is to his advantage to undertake this improvement.[2]

This counseling step should help the management person improve his present job performance, point the way for qualification to higher jobs and help him develop those broad characteristics important in a top management position.

Planning Replacements

Management is not a permanent thing—replacement needs are always impending. ". . . we find that American business needs enough men to do the work of today, to replace losses through illness, old age, and death, and to meet the requirements of expansion." [3] To this must be added replacements for those whose performance is unsatisfactory.

One way that future executive needs can be soundly planned is through the use of a replacement table. This is a top management report giving a view of the road ahead. It lists each key position and indicates the approximate time when the position may be vacated. It also lists the most likely candidates for each position and shows when they will be ready for promotion. In addition, positions are indicated for which a qualified replacement cannot be found or developed in the present organization.

The replacement table may also be translated into a replacement *chart*. The organizational chart is coded to show present position incumbents and the most qualified backer-ups, together with each person's present and ultimate promotion potential. One form of replacement chart, frequently employed, is shown in the figure below. The coding of this chart has been simplified in this illustration to show only the broad gradations of a man's ultimate potential. Red [the hatched space] indicates that the

---

[1] Louis A. Allen, "Building Executives for the Future," *Advanced Management*, November 1952, p. 20.

[2] William F. Wrightnour, "Management Development: A Practical Application," *Personnel*, January 1952, p. 288.

[3] Earl G. Planty and Carlos A. Efferson, "Developing Leadership for Tomorrow's Tasks," *Dun's Review*, February 1952, p. 32.

man has the potential ability to be president, white that he has potential for vice president, gray [dotted] that he can be promoted one position level, and black that the man is at his ceiling. The timing of advancement appears alongside the man's name and age. It shows whether he can be promoted now, soon or later.

This excerpt from a replacement chart indicates its advantages as an administrative tool. Three positions are shown in the sales organization.

FORWARD PLANNING AND REPLACEMENT CHART

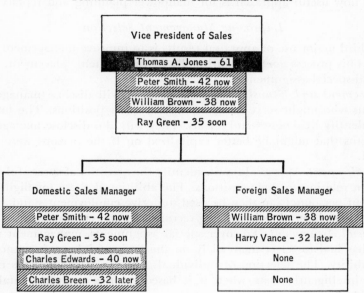

The top position is that of a vice president of sales. The present incumbent is Thomas A. Jones, 61 years of age, who is satisfactory in the position but possesses no promotional possibilities beyond it, indicated by the black color. Mr. Jones will retire in four years; hence plans should be made shortly to fill the position.

There are two candidates, Peter Smith and William Brown, both of whom are ready to be vice president of sales now and both of whom have the ability, as shown by the red, ultimately to become president of the company. Mr. Smith has a good replacement in Ray Green, who could be readied for the domestic sales manager's position soon. Charles Edwards is also an adequate replacement and is ready for promotion now but has less long-range potential than Mr. Green. The chart suggests that the decision rests on whether immediate replacement is more impor- tant than ultimate potential.

Now look at the foreign sales manager's position. The good candidate is Harry Vance, who is rather young (32) and could be readied for the position only after a considerable time. Moreover, no further candidates seem available for the foreign sales manager's job. William Brown has a job left to do, to develop backer-ups for the foreign sales manager's position.

Under these circumstances, if something were to happen to Vice President Jones today, Peter Smith is the logical choice because replacements are available. If the position is not to be filled until Mr. Jones retires, then William Brown is aware that he must develop proper backer-ups if he wants to be a strong vice presidential candidate. This example shows how useful appraisal is for manpower planning and replacement.

Improving Management Selection

A third major use of appraisal results is to improve management selection. This process goes on continually in employment, placement, transfer and special assignment.

Placement and Transfer. Appraisal results will disclose management persons who might serve more capably in other positions. The findings will identify weaknesses and misfits. They will also disclose management strengths that might be better capitalized on if the persons were transferred.

Employment. Appraisal results identify the qualities of successful executives in relation to their positions. The abilities of these top-flight management personnel can then be used to derive employment standards for each key position, thus improving recruitment and employment.

Special Assignment. To cover special assignments, management in the past has had to select men solely on the basis of job performance and availability. The selection of individuals for special assignments can be more intelligently done when it is based upon a complete catalog of individual abilities.

Wherever management personnel are to be selected, the appraisal process yields an inventory of management strengths, weaknesses, abilities and personal characteristics that provides an excellent base for intelligent decisions.

Providing a Base for Management Development

The fourth major use of appraisal results is to provide a base for management development. This can be approached by the construction of a development guide for each management person. This guide includes an identification of the individual, the positions for which he seems best qualified, the limitations or training needs derived from a comparison of appraisal results with position requirements, and recommendations for training to fill out the person's competence. A schedule showing the timing of the development program should also be provided. This schedule will disclose when the candidate can be promoted to the next higher position with promise of successfully carrying out its duties.

Hence the entire training program for each management employee can be developed from appraisal results. Group development programs can be devised to meet the "clusters" of needs appearing in the various individual records. The appraisal results therefore provide a basis for tailoring a sound development program to company needs.

CONCLUSION

Business has grown rapidly in recent years, and the number of management employees has multiplied. This has compounded executive personnel problems. Business has had some difficulty improving its techniques for handling management people in keeping with business expansion. Objective inventorying of executive talent has become more urgent as size and complexity have increased. Yet some companies still rely on supervisory opinion for personnel decisions, and this type of evaluation is falling short of the present task.

The pressure of events is likely to bring an improvement in present company practices, for evaluation deals with the most important asset of a business—its manpower talent. The need for more executives in growing organizations, for one thing, is focusing attention upon effective means to develop management talent from within. As long ago as 1936, a prominent personage put his finger on this need when he stated, "To me the crux of the situation (finding business leaders) is not so much the need for men, nor the scarcity of proven leaders, as it is the failure of American business management generally to introduce an orderly and methodical system for the discovery, development and assignment of executive personnel." [4]

A second reason for expecting more attention to be devoted to executive appraisal and manpower planning is that orderly evaluation is now practical. The principles and methods presented here embody a form of appraisal developed from programs installed in a wide range of companies. The principles are tested and their reliability proved.

Third, the return of rigorous competition is forcing the improved use of executives. In many instances the margin of competitive success or failure is locked up in the quality of management talent. Experience indicates that the right personnel organized into an effective management team is essential to the continuing success of an enterprise. This is the reason that we foresee growing emphasis on organized appraisal—the key to building better management.

[4] In an address by the late Edward R. Stettinius, Jr., before the 1936 graduating class of Harvard University.

Management Development at Boeing
The Appraisal and Coaching Program *

Norman Allen

The Boeing Airplane Company is a young company, only 40 years old in July, 1956. As might be expected, our management is also young. In fact, the average age of all our upper- and middle-level management is only 43. A high percentage of our managers at all levels have spent their entire management career with Boeing and were promoted from the ranks.

Particularly in recent years, the company has grown rapidly; we now have 72,000 employees, 5,000 management people, and about a billion dollars in annual sales. Because of this rapid growth, many of our management people reached positions of high responsibility at an early age. They had to meet a tremendous challenge with a minimum of preparation. On the other hand, their very youth has been a source of considerable strength. It has provided the company with vigor, courage, creativity, imagination, and an open-minded attitude. Our founder, Bill Boeing, made the statement: "We should never let any new idea pass us by." This has been a continuing management credo.

Another major factor which affects our management needs is the nature of the airplane business and, in particular, the extremely rapid advancement of the aeronautical art. The one constant in our business is change. And, with each step forward to faster, more complex airplanes, our engineering, production, and management problems increase in an exponential ratio. Yesterday we were training production employees in relatively simple skills like rivet bucking; today we are training electronics technicians. Ours is a research and development-minded organization with a marked creative flair, and our engineering organization is one of the largest in the world.

Because of these factors—rapid growth, continuous change, and rapid technological progress—we need management people who are versatile,

* Reprinted by permission of the publisher from *Assuring Adequate Reserves of Key Personnel*, Personnel Series, no. 169 (New York: American Management Association, 1956), pp. 11–18. Mr. Allen is Assistant to the President in Charge of Management Development, Boeing Airplane Company, Seattle, Washington.

well informed, and fast on their feet. For this reason, it may be that our need for management development may be greater than it is in other industries.

BASIC CONVICTIONS OF MANAGEMENT DEVELOPMENT

At Boeing, we have seven principal convictions on which we base our management development efforts.

1. *Able, high-quality management is our most valuable resource.* To put it another way, the judgment and ability of a management to reach sound decisions, its courage in making them, and its administrative skill in carrying them out, are primarily the factors which determine the success of a company.

For example: In 1952, our management decided to build a jet transport prototype airplane. At that time, there were no orders on the books for either the commercial or military versions of this aircraft, and it involved an expenditure of many millions of dollars. Today, our commercial orders for this vehicle alone exceed half a billion dollars. Able, sound, and courageous management personnel are necessary to make this kind of decision and carry it to successful fruition. Because of the importance of management, we believe that it is good business sense to do everything possible to develop the best possible management for today and tomorrow.

2. *Management development is one of the most important responsibilities of a manager.* First, a manager is responsible for his own continuing self-development and should avail himself of opportunities for this development. Second, he should stimulate, guide, and counsel his subordinates, and provide them with development opportunities available within the framework of his organization. He should provide them with broadening work experiences and give them opportunities for resolving real problems of progressively greater magnitude.

3. *Each manager has the right and duty to manage*—in the fullest sense of the word. To do this, he must accept his responsibilities, be given commensurate authority, and be held accountable for results. Increasingly, we have been trying to give more meaning to this conviction, and have taken many steps to assure that it is a reality.

4. *Management is a separate art or activity and can be learned by able people.* Our management development efforts are concerned solely with this area; and it is our purpose to make available to all members of management the encouragement, the opportunities, the tools, and the techniques they may need for their continuing education in the art.

I have a growing personal conviction that a competent top-level manager can transfer his talents of planning, organizing, leading, and so on, from one field to an area foreign to his profession or specialty with good results. Growing evidence of this fact has been furnished by the leadership of competent managers in the fields of government, civic affairs, social service, and church work.

5. *Management development will result when managers believe sufficiently in its importance.* If they believe it is important, managers will seek and avail themselves of development opportunities and will provide the necessary stimulation and inspiration to their subordinates, so that they, too, will want to avail themselves of development opportunities. We further believe that the key to this motivation is a sound relationship between the superior and his subordinate—a relationship based on mutual trust and understanding. In line with this belief, we believe that periodic appraisal, followed by a constructive coaching interview, is one of the best ways of improving the relationship between a superior and his subordinates.

6. *Indoctrination in sound management principles, philosophies, tools, and practices should begin at the earliest possible date in a manager's career, preferably when he begins his pre-management training.*

7. *Sound methods of selection and recruitment are necessary at the beginning levels of management.* We need to have a sufficient supply of able, high-quality young men coming in, so that we will have competent men from whom to choose for our management positions in the years ahead.

Organization of Management Development

With these principles as a frame of reference, Management Development at Boeing is organized into a unit reporting directly to the president at the headquarters level. Each division vice president and general manager has on his staff a Management Development assistant who reports directly to him. As a staff agency, Management Development never encroaches on nor assumes any of line management's responsibilities. Our job is primarily one of technical assistance. We research needs; design and recommend processes; do some over-all monitoring; and provide counsel, encouragement, and evaluation. It is our job to create an awareness on the part of our managers that management development is an important responsibility and do everything we can to help them become expert practitioners. If we are successful in this, we will then have 5,000 management developers in our company.

The company's long-range goal for management development is to help every manager become more proficient in the art of management; and, to reach that goal, we have placed our efforts wherever there is an opportunity to achieve a part of that long-range objective. We are trying to proceed in an orderly fashion, and we utilize every opportunity to promote the principles of sound management.

THE FORMULATION OF AN APPRAISAL PROGRAM

The appraisal process is the core of our whole management development effort, and it exemplifies the convictions we follow. In 1953, Boeing's president, William Allen, became interested in developing a more formal process of appraising executive performance. As a result of this interest, we were asked to make a recommendation as to whether a periodic process of executive appraisal should be adopted and also recommendations on the method to be used. Accordingly, we studied a great many plans and methods and made a recommendation to the president's Management Development Committee that we adopt a process for executive appraisal. We also made certain policy and procedural recommendations.

An important part of this recommendation was that a course of instruction be designed and given to our executives, for the purpose of developing appraisers with a good grounding in the principles and techniques involved and, in addition, giving them experience in conducting coaching interviews before they made their appraisals. (A consulting firm was retained to help design the course.)

Our recommendation was approved, but on an experimental basis. The president said: "Let us go slowly. Let us first give this course to ourselves and our immediate subordinates. We'll try it and see what we think of it." A group consisting of the president and eight vice presidents were given the prepared course of instruction and gained experience in coaching interviews. They then made appraisals of their subordinates and held interviews with them.

After this experimental test, the course was approved for adoption on a continuing basis, not only for the executive group, but for all members of management including first-line foremen and supervisors. We were directed to provide instruction first to top-level management and then to the other managers in the organization, level by level. At the present time, 2,500 management people from all divisions of the company have completed this course. Illustrative of the enthusiasm with which the process has been received is the fact that we were recently asked to speed up appraisal instruction and to complete it by February, 1957, a year earlier than the original target date.

Our appraisal plan is in accordance with the conviction that a manager has the right and duty to manage, and that the Management Development staff is there to help him become more proficient in the process. We hope and expect, as time goes on, that our managers will become more and more able to appraise fairly, accurately, and objectively. Of course, providing our entire management group with the necessary knowledge and skills to carry out the appraisal and coaching program in their organization has necessitated a comprehensive training program of no small proportion.

The Training Program in Appraisal and Coaching

The time devoted to the course is approximately 20 hours, although there are variances based on a division's requirements and desires. It is usually divided into three lecture-discussion sessions of about 2½ hours each, followed by four practice sessions of about 3 hours each. We normally schedule 24 people for the lecture-discussion sessions; the session is later divided into three groups of eight for the practice session.

The training program is centered around three activities:

1. The presentation and discussion of certain basic principles of effective appraisal and coaching.

2. The presentation, explanation, and discussion of the operating tools used in the appraisal and coaching process.

3. Practice sessions designed to provide practical application of the principles and experience in working with these tools.

In introducing the course, we emphasize that we are dealing with the two most difficult problems in the entire developmental process: effective appraising and effective coaching. We also emphasize that there is no rule or formula which will insure a solution to these problems and that in the course we have put together a combination of certain basic principles and operating tools that will help them accomplish the objective.

We then describe our basic principles: career dynamics, effective coaching, and behavior principles.

Career Dynamics. This principle concerns the dynamic nature of an individual's career with the company. Obviously, an individual's opinion of his performance and potential for advancement may, and frequently does, differ from the opinion of his superior. Sometimes there is a considerable variance, which can be very costly if not recognized early and dealt with realistically. Without a realistic approach we frequently find discouragement, frustration, anxiety, tension, shock, unrealistic ambitions, less than peak performance, and sometimes even a loss of good men. The need for realism in this area effectively demonstrates the desirability of a systematic appraisal and coaching program.

Effective Coaching. In discussing effective coaching, we define it as a process by which a superior endeavors to get a subordinate to change or modify his way of discharging responsibilities. In other words, coaching is helping a man to help himself. We discuss the different types of coaching: the daily unscheduled kinds, and the regularly scheduled annual coaching interview which includes a review of the individual's performance based on the appraisal plan. We believe that effective performance of scheduled coaching will also improve an individual's ability with the informal types of coaching. Five requisites for effective coaching are also discussed: (1) setting performance goals, (2) permitting individuals to perform, (3) observing and judging performance, (4) taking action to get results, and (5) developing enthusiastic team action. Finally, we discuss development principles or what is needed for a subordinate to develop. The five principles suggested as basic are: (1) Subordinates need to know what is expected of them; (2) they need opportunities for development; (3) they need to know how well they are doing; (4) they should be provided with assistance when necessary; and (5) they should receive adequate recognition for the results of their efforts.

Behavior Principles. Numerous textbooks have been written about the broad areas of behavior principles, and we can do no more than touch the high points in our course. A good management coach should get results on a "how to" basis, but he should also have an understanding of the basic principles underlying the recommended techniques. For this reason, we discuss three selected principles of behavior: motivation, perception, and learning. Motivation can be thought of as the will to do; perception refers to the way people look at things; and learning is finding out "how to do" or the process of improvement.

We also describe the use of the three basic operating tools: the position description, the performance appraisal, and the coaching interview.

The Position Description. We use position descriptions as a systematic method of defining what is expected of a man on a job. They enable the superior to be more precise in defining his performance expectations from those in his group. Our position descriptions include a brief summary statement of the major functions of a position, a statement of the major responsibilities, and an indication of the key relationships. Since the position description is the standard tool used in making the appraisal, supervisors are given instruction in its preparation.

The Performance Appraisal. In the performance appraisal section, we discuss the appraisal form and its use, emphasizing that the major benefit sought is the improved performance of each individual in his current job. Six requisites for a sound appraisal program are covered: (1) A specific purpose or purposes must be established; (2) good performance information must be obtained; (3) wise use must be made of performance information; (4) managers must be both able and willing to appraise accurately; (5) managers must be both able and willing to use the information, particularly in coaching systematically and regularly; and (6) it is necessary that continuous improvement be made in complying with the other five requisites. Some stumbling blocks in appraising management performance are reviewed, and the major pitfalls or bias tendencies in evaluating performance are considered. Our appraisal form is carefully examined and the participants are instructed in its use.

The Coaching Interview. We then discuss various types of effective coaching interviews, and a practical pattern or plan is suggested and demonstrated. We believe that the ability to conduct a constructive interview has been the most neglected factor in many appraisal and coaching courses. In preparing for an interview, a supervisor must (1) make the appraisal (we recommend self-appraisal by subordinates), (2) prepare a balance sheet as a guide for his discussion, (3) consider probable causes for unsatisfactory performance, (4) consider action that might be taken to remedy the causes, (5) determine what he wants the individual to do differently as a result of the interview, and (6) consider the personality of the individual and the kind of a person he is. At this point, we recommend that he review the appraisal with his immediate superior. Following such a review, he schedules the interview.

About 60 per cent of the time spent in training is devoted to the practice sessions in which each course participant gets actual practice in conducting an interview, in the role of both a superior and a subordinate. Each practice interview is accompanied by evaluations made by the group and the instructor. Needless to say, these practice sessions constitute the heart of the training program.

After completing the course, every manager is expected to appraise and coach each of his subordinates annually and to prepare a mutually agreed upon improvement plan for the development of the individual. Copies of the improvement plans, signed by the superior but not bearing the name of the subordinate, are turned over to Management Development. The original copy remains the confidential property of the appraiser. These improvement plans are our prime instrument for the determination of development needs and for designing media to satisfy those needs, both on and off the job.

Job Rotation*

James R. Morris

I

The development of top-level executives and managers has become increasingly important to business and industry since the end of World War II. The shortage of executives is attributable to minimal advancement programs during the depression of the 1930's and during the war period itself and to the great expansion of business and industry requirements in the postwar years. In recent years job rotation has come to be considered one of the most important means of encouraging executive development.

Job rotation is the planned movement of men from one position to another for the basic purpose of encouraging and stimulating the growth of the individual. Rotation may include shifts of the manager to and from staff and line positions. It may be intrafunctional or interfunctional. Generally, intrafunctional rotation is to train the executive for better performance on the job within the scope of a specialized function. Interfunctional rotation, however, emphasizes breadth of growth and is primarily for the purpose of preparing the executive for advancement as well as for better performance in positions which require, or would benefit from, more generalized abilities and understanding.

A large number of assumed effects of rotation have been advanced by those concerned with executive development. This is a preliminary report on selected aspects of a case study which is still in progress. The study represents an attempt to learn from the rotated men themselves how they have been affected by rotation. The company concerned is a public utility company which has several thousand employees. Managers are rotated at all levels in the company, including the vice-presidential level. The rotation is of a long-term and continuing nature. Positions may be held for several months or several years, depending on the man, the job, and company requirements. A total of fifty-two executives, middle managers, and staff assistants were interviewed for the study. The sample

* Reprinted by permission of the publisher from "Human Aspects of Management," *Journal of Business,* vol. 29, no. 4 (October, 1956), pp. 268–273. Copyright, 1956, University of Chicago. Mr. Morris is an instructor in economics, University of Illinois, Chicago, Illinois.

was weighted with high-level personnel and included rotatees from middle management through top-level management. Thirty-nine rotatees were interviewed, the average length of the interview being approximately two hours. In addition, thirteen non-rotated men were interviewed to check on some of the findings. The latter interviews averaged approximately one hour in length. Some of the findings of the study are discussed, as well as some suggestions which some of the rotatees thought would make job rotation more effective.

II

One of the commonly expected results of rotation is that the limitations of narrow specialist training can be overcome, thus preparing the executive for higher-level, general management positions. That this does occur seems to be borne out by the interviews. Interestingly, those interviewed felt, for the most part, that knowledge of their own fields was increased and broadened by rotation, while a number pointed out (sometimes regretfully!) that specialization on their part had been prevented by rotation. The belief was unanimous that rotation had materially increased their knowledge and understanding of general management problems. Thus one rotated engineer attributed to rotation an awareness and knowledge which he had not had before of legal problems, costs, relations with government, and the financing problems of the company.

The belief also was general that knowledge and understanding of technical problems in other departments were greater as a result of rotation. It was pointed out that in a new position related problems in other departments became apparent and that this "helps you put a sense of values on things that come up in your own field." This greater understanding is probably a natural concomitant of the increased knowledge.

Over three-fourths of the interviewees reported having had assignments or positions where knowledge and skills were required in which they did not feel well qualified. The most common methods of coping with the situation were (1) hard work to learn the job, which included learning from the others in the department, and (2) reliance upon the organization and men in it for the details of the job. Thus one interviewee remarked: "I think that rotation business teaches you that you don't have to have all the answers yourself. It makes you depend on the organization more." Techniques of learning included studying the files, listening, taking company courses, and questioning others about the handling of problems. It seemed evident that rotation had the effect of forcing men to grapple with problems in such a way as to develop or strengthen themselves in areas where their performance had previously been weak.

Rotation had a pronounced effect in increasing the interest of the rotatees in their work. Thus one said, representatively: "It presents new challenges. There is a high interest factor because it's a new field. It introduces you to new people and to new problems." Generally, the men felt that the new challenge served as a strong stimulus to "get on top of the job." One interviewee said it affected interest "adversely" because it prevented intense specialization, but he said that "it doesn't let you go to seed, even if you want to."

A preponderance of the interviewees found that they had changed their methods of meeting and handling new problems. They developed wider perspectives on how to go about solving problems because of having worked under a variety of superiors and also, as one said: "I more quickly find someone who is working for me or with me to help. I devote more time to thinking about the problem and deciding who to hand it to. Before, I used to try to solve the basic features of it before giving it to someone else." This suggests a substantial improvement in problem-solving techniques, since one of the great executive arts is that of selecting quickly and wisely someone else to carry through with the actual performance, leaving the executive free to think, to plan, and to evaluate.

Rotation apparently had a substantial effect on the rotatees' methods of dealing with people. A few felt that it had had no effect, but most believed their ability to deal with people was much improved. One pointed out that as a result of his experience as a staff man without line authority he had "learned to get people to do things because they want to rather than because you tell them to. And that makes it easier when you get back into a job where you have people working for you." That is not an unimportant principle in the motivation of personnel to have learned to appreciate as a result of rotation.

The rotatees agreed that rotation had given them a much better understanding of the various external and internal forces which affect the company. They were particularly impressed by their greater understanding of public relations, including customer, stockholder, and supplier relations, and relationships with village boards and city councils.

A majority of the rotatees thought that they received more coaching as a result of rotation. Some attributed this simply to having had different superiors who made it a point to impart their views and methods of handling things. Another common view was expressed as follows: "Your superior knows that you don't have background in the job, therefore he puts himself out to help you get that background, which is highly beneficial." Apparently, one of the greatest values with respect to coaching was the fact of having had a variety of superiors; this provided a breadth of perspective otherwise unobtainable. A few felt that they received less coaching because they thought their superiors regarded it as hardly worthwhile to coach them.

Internal communication—one of the most important problems of large organizations—was improved very greatly as a result of rotation. Terminology tended to become more uniform, and there was a wider knowledge of specialized departmental jargon. Thus one executive reported: "It has brought us all a little closer. It has tended to wipe out departmental variations, or it has made them more widespread, so that the same terms are employed with respect to a particular association. It tends to wipe out localism in terminology and provincialism generally." Another indicated that it contributed to interdepartmental co-operation, saying: "Rotation indicates to a person the necessity for knowledge and information being given to other departments. You learn how others have a need for certain information."

Rotatees were in agreement that interdepartmental relationships had been much improved. They felt that co-operation was greater because of more understanding and because of personal contacts within departments. Thus one reported: "You know the people in the other departments, and they know you too. You get an appreciation of the other fellow's problem. You can't help but develop a closely knit team by that." Another reported: "They sort of lose this sense of not understanding what others are doing. There is more of a sense of respect for each other."

Closely related to the broadened viewpoint which gave rise to better interdepartmental relationships was the growth of a recognition that decisions should be evaluated not only on the basis of their effect on the department but also on the basis of their effect upon the company as a whole. Loyalties were broadened as men became increasingly conscious that departmental decisions were rarely merely of departmental concern. A typical statement was: "I have a better background for making decisions favorable to the company as a whole rather than for the individual department." And in a similar vein, one stated: "Rotation has taught me to consider carefully before making any decision or changing any procedure or order—to consider what the effect is going to be on the other parts of the company." Rotation evidently had a pronounced effect in broadening the perspective and loyalty of the rotatee. Those with little rotation seemed more inclined to identify or equate departmental welfare with company welfare.

Over three-fourths of the rotatees thought they were better off financially as a consequence of having been rotated. About one-fourth of the interviewees pointed out that at given times they were temporarily worse off financially. In most instances this was the result of geographical moves which necessitated the relocation of the family. All costs incident to moving were not paid by the company. Thus there would be the costs of damaged furniture, new draperies and carpeting, and so on. There also was the real cost of time lost searching for new housing, a particularly onerous and time-consuming problem during the postwar years.

One of the most outstanding results of rotation was to be seen in the profound effects upon the social and family life of the rotatees. Although about one-third of the men reported no significant effect, among the others the effects ranged from increasing to decreasing social life, with some reporting both social and family life substantially disrupted. The greatest impact was felt by those who had to make geographical moves. Thus one who had made no geographical moves reported simply that his social life had "decreased" because he spent more time in "study in handling a new assignment." But another reported that his child had attended several different high schools and at times had substantial difficulty gaining entree to the new groups encountered. In one community this man found some friction because of a general belief that he was getting someone else's job. Others reported disruption of church, school, bridge groups, and other associations and ties. Roots were dislodged, and the rotatee and his family made transients, as it were. For rotatees who were moved fairly frequently, it appeared that entering deeply into the community activities and life was most difficult. On the positive side, acquaintanceships in the areas served by the company were broadened, and the constant readjustments may have contributed to the development of self-reliance and confidence of both rotatees and their families. In some instances rotation led to an introduction to civic activities and fostered a continuing interest in such affairs.

A majority reported that subordinates in new positions were co-operative for the most part with the new superior. A very few said they were regarded as the fair-haired boys. There was evidence of some tension, with occasional hostility toward the new man, in a good many instances. One stated: "Initially at least you find a feeling of jealousy—resentfulness sometimes—in the people there who might have been picked for the spot. It takes time and selling yourself to those people before they respect you and confide in you. Some of those people you never can win over, others will gradually come around." Nevertheless, most of the rotatees found the majority of the subordinates co-operative, and some reported them to be quite friendly.

The personal disadvantages reported by rotatees varied according to their personalities and the particular experiences they had undergone. Reactions ranged from strong feelings of insecurity ("of being lost—feeling of not knowing anyone") to annoyance at not concentrating on any one specialty. The major disadvantages mentioned included personal and family readjustments, relocation of housing, and fear or insecurity in varying degrees.

Rotation might seem to expose the company to substantial costs incurred because of erroneous decisions made by the rotatees. A small proportion said they had known of such losses. The vast majority reported, however, that they knew of nothing more than a few relatively minor errors at most. This was borne out by one executive who was in a position to know; and he stated: "No one person is too much on his own. He has a hell of a lot of help—whether he knows it or not." The emphasis on group action and decisions which has gained currency in recent years serves to minimize the possibility that major costs may be incurred as a result of an unilateral decision by a rotatee.

Rotatees generally believed that rotation had the long-run effect of increasing both departmental efficiency and departmental teamwork. There is a temporary loss of efficiency because of the disruption, the natural concern as to what will happen, and also because the rotatee lacks knowledge of many things at first and "subordinates tend to shelve or hold back some matters" out of consideration for the man rotated. Efficiency picks up as morale is built and as re-evaluation of established practices takes place; apparently emphasis on integrating the department with the company plays a part in this. Rotatees felt teamwork improved substantially. One observed: "My own experience is that it improves it. You rotate a new individual in, and the team forms behind him to get the job done. That brings the group together as a team to carry the load of the department better than if the department is static. I think rotation brings the objectives of the department to the foreground." Of course, too frequent rotation may be merely disruptive.

More than 60 per cent of the rotatees reported knowing men not included in rotation who felt resentful, unhappy, or slighted. More than a third reported that others were indifferent or happy about not being rotated. A representative statement was: "Some are very disappointed—sour. Some are damn happy; especially some technical people don't want it and would be very unhappy." Another stated: "I could say there were people who were disappointed, who were angry, and who didn't give a damn—as many reactions as you can name." Among those who did not want rotation were those who wanted to concentrate on one field of specialization and those who did not want the added work and responsibility. A few rotatees said that some non-rotated men became discouraged, lost interest in their work, and felt less loyalty to the company.

One final aspect of the study may be reported. An overwhelming preponderance of the rotatees reported that they felt more confidence in themselves as a result of the rotation program. The very fact that they were being rotated added to the confidence of some, while the mastery of the new jobs and wider knowledge and perspectives added much to their confidence. A very few said that it decreased confidence because of the uncertainty involved in rotation.

III

The rotatees advanced many suggestions which they thought would contribute to the effectiveness of the program. The following were suggested by various individuals among the rotatees. Among other things it was suggested that rotation should be planned and managed through a central company agency. This central agency would be responsible for long-range planning of rotation, with careful consideration given to the selection of the men to be rotated, the positions to which they are rotated, and the timing of the moves. It was suggested that men to be rotated should be selected with very great care, with safeguards against favoritism in the choice of rotatees. It was pointed out that rotation should not be employed as a device to achieve other than developmental purposes. Thus, for example, a rotated man should not be "used," in the invidious sense, to solve local personnel problems; nor should rotation serve as a cloak for the shelving, sidetracking, or deadending of men.

Some rotatees felt that more should be done in the way of preparation of men for rotation. It was suggested that they should know more about why they were being rotated, what the major objectives and plans of the company were, and that they should receive at least some counseling as to how they were expected to fit into the over-all picture. A good many felt that there should be a careful discussion with the man about proposed moves and about his likes and dislikes and that there should be more real free choice—to turn down a proposed move or to select a move among alternatives. Some thought that contact with a central guiding agency, coupled with some coaching and counseling through it, would add a desirable degree of stability and certainty which might be helpful. Several rotatees thought that men should have their performance rated annually and, in addition, that ratings should be made at the end of each job upon transfers to another position. One suggestion was that job descriptions be made available in order to help a man gain quickly an understanding of what the new job is; however, it was recognized that this might have a stultifying effect on some rotatees. In lieu of a job description, the previous incumbent as well as the new superior might give the newcomer an oral briefing as to the general character of the new job.

The preceding suggestions, selected at random from many made by the rotatees, also, of course, may be regarded as indicative of some of the reactions to the rotation program itself.

The Assistant-To: The Man in Motley *

Thomas L. Whisler

The chief executive of the modern business firm sits at the center of a management web—the frontiers of which have moved farther from him as the firm has grown. The frontiers have also expanded in a second dimension with the increase in technical knowledge. With these developments, the decision-maker's need for information has increased enormously. However, until recent years no responsive change in management structure has been observable save for persistent (and generally abortive) efforts to decentralize—to create whole and essentially separate webs as part of the large web. Now in many companies a new face has appeared at the decision-making center (and in large corporations at subcenters). The face belongs to the "assistant-to"—Sloan Wilson's man in the gray flannel suit.[1] In Wilson's novel the hero, as part of finding himself, gave up the role of assistant-to. That role is the subject of this paper, which will attempt to analyze organization structure through analysis of a role that apparently reflects a common organizational need. It is part of a broader attempt that is being made "to flesh out present skeleton theories on management organization with information on what really goes on . . . through behavioral research on how people and business groups interact."[2]

There appear to be two general uses of the title "assistant-to": (*a*) What might be called the "limbo" function. Under this title the incompetent but senior executive can be turned out to pasture. Or temporary supernumeraries, to be retired or promoted, can be stored here for some time, presumably with benefit to themselves and no harm to others. In this function there is a cage around the individual which permits him to observe and perhaps to be consulted but not to range out and define his own job. (*b*) The free-lance function. This is an active, operating function in which the individual is not caged or withdrawn from the main stream

* Reprinted by permission of the publisher from "Human Aspects of Management," *Journal of Business*, vol. 29, no. 4 (October, 1956), pp. 274–279. Copyright, 1956, University of Chicago. Mr. Whisler is Assistant Professor, School of Business, University of Chicago.

[1] *The Man in the Gray Flannel Suit* (New York: Simon & Schuster, 1955).

[2] From a speech by Mason Haire before the 1956 General Management Conference of the American Management Association in New York (quoted in *Business Week*, No. 1396 [June 2, 1956], p. 162).

of management activity. The man is expected to make a contribution to the successful operation of his company. The way in which he does this becomes the focal point of our research.

The Assistant-To, as He Sees Himself

Through a series of intensive interviews with men holding the assistant-to title, we have been able to get some picture of the common dimensions of the role this man plays in the modern management organization. The men themselves have in their minds no such clear picture as we are about to draw. They emphasize the fact that one of their great problems is to learn what it is they are supposed to do. The formal explanation for creating the assistant-to position usually has to do with "special projects." The president who creates such a position, for example, announces that certain sorts of important activities cannot be delegated and, at the same time, that they take too much time for him to handle personally. The personal assistant is presented as the solution. Whatever the truth of this rationale, the role seems inevitably to pass beyond the bounds of simple execution of special projects.

What does the assistant-to do that is significant organizationally? Men in the position tell us that three functions are of prime importance: (1) to aid the boss in interpreting the information he receives from his subordinates (this inevitably involves appraising and interpreting the subordinates); (2) to interpret the boss to others below him—especially those several levels below him; and (3) to initiate a flow of information about organizational needs to the executive that he would otherwise not receive. We can elaborate on these functions sufficiently to show that they logically tie together. Before doing so, it is well to say again that, while these are the important functions, they are likely not to be the official functions of the assistant-to. They are, however, the kind of activities that the assistant-to cites as most crucial in determining the kind of evaluation his boss makes of him.

Interpreter of Others to the Executive

The subjects of our research most clearly perceive interpretation of others to the executive as important to the boss. The busy executive (say the subjects) has a limited amount of time available to give audience to any one of his line subordinates. Such audience time must serve the needs of the subordinate as an individual as well as the needs of the organization and its chief decision-maker. Under these circumstances the executive is frequently treated to a dramatic presentation which leaves him with the problem of guessing how much of the presentation is true and what of organizational importance may not have been presented. The executive is unable to make sufficient firsthand observations of events to judge his subordinates adequately.

In this situation the assistant-to serves the executive's needs by fully informing him of the "true" state of affairs, thus serving as an effective interpreter. Should the assistant-to not be adequately informed on some particularly puzzling communication from below, he may then find that he has a "special project" cut out for him.

It is necessary to remember that the assistant-to has exceptional mobility. He is not restricted to any department or activity but may move wherever his boss might, had he (the boss) time enough.

This, then, is one important function reported by the subjects. Just why the executive should place such a high degree of trust in his assistant-to remains to be explained. A clue may lie in the nature of the assistant-boss relationships, to be discussed later.

Interpreter of the Executive to Others

The function of interpreting the executive to others is not so clearly seen by all subjects as is the first. Those aware of its existence believe it to be a most valuable contribution to the executive's effectiveness, although not one which is likely to produce specific commendation from the boss.

Those most likely to be treated to an interpretation of executive actions and directives are managers several levels below the executive rather than his immediate subordinates. The reason is a simple one— these interpretations are the coin with which the assistant-to repays those who keep him informed of developments at lower operating levels and with which he "buys" a general willingness to co-operate with him. People several levels away from the executive, although affected by his actions, are unlikely to have personal contact with him. They are motivated by curiosity about his motives and by concern that he, in turn, be aware of what is taking place at lower levels. These lower-level managers recognize the game-playing activities of the chief executive's subordinates (who are their superiors) just as he does and use the assistant-to to offset them.

Organizational Watchdog

It is as an observer and careful diagnostician of organizational needs that the assistant-to may win the highest praise of his boss. In this activity he initiates reports instead of waiting to be asked for judgments and interpretations. This function parallels the first one described. There the assistant-to acted as interpreter and verifier of information coming from the executive's subordinates. Here he supplements this flow of information with other information which he judges to be important to the chief executive. Such things as serious morale problems, egregious deviation from company policy, and unusually able performance at some lower level are examples of such information.

Subjects emphasize the necessity for being absolutely certain that their judgment is correct before initiating these reports. One gets a strong impression that the rewards and the risks are considerably higher in this initiatory function than in the others.

His Relationship with the Boss

The subjects emphasize the necessity for being honest without exception in talking to the boss. They believe this to be of the highest importance. As one phrases it, "If he [the boss] found out that I was not leveling with him, I'd be dead."

Usually the assistant-to is in the presence of his boss much more than is any line subordinate. After-hours conferences are quite common—a Saturday morning at the office, a weekday dinner at the boss's house, etc.

The typical assistant-to tends to make a complicated evaluation of his boss. The predominant attitude is one of strong, almost worshipful, regard. But the boss's basic weaknesses are usually remarked. Most often they are weaknesses in his relations with others, the correction of these weaknesses being the assistant's clearly perceived and self-appointed task. Occasionally they are weaknesses in the area of technical knowledge which the assistant may offset with his own particular training.

The assistant-to worries about the relationship with his boss. His deepest concern is about the boss's evaluation of his performance. The vagueness of the title and the lack of task content are clearly evident to the subjects. Knowledge of the boss's reaction becomes crucial as a guide to their activities.

His Future

Most subjects are deeply concerned about the future. The younger men, particularly, feel that they have made a wise decision in taking the job because of the great opportunity to observe events at the decision-making center. But many are frank to admit that they have no notion of the best way to capitalize on this—to what sort of job they should move; whether they should stay in the company; when they should move on.

Most subjects seem eager to take on any sort of activity which gives them the security of a task-related title (as contrasted to the person-related title they hold). It is our impression that this reaching out for a more substantial status begins soon after the assistant-to takes on his new job.

THE ASSISTANT-TO AS PART OF THE MANAGEMENT STRUCTURE

The Executive–Assistant-To Relationship

The dominant feature of the relationship between the executive and the assistant-to seems to be the high degree of dependence of assistant upon boss. Strong dependency seems to be a feature of hierarchical authoritarian structures, but this situation is unusual. The assistant-to's title holds the clue. By virtue of his not being in charge of anything but, instead, being assistant-to to another person, the organization (and the rest of the world) must rely completely upon his boss for an appraisal of him. No provision is made for him to demonstrate ability through performance of organizationally important and observable tasks.

Some questions arise: What kind of personality functions with the least personal conflict as the assistant in this situation? Is this personality the most effective from the executive's point of view? Does the top executive who insists upon a personal assistant always do so in order to satisfy a need for complete dominance of another individual? [3] Does the assistant-to with a "healthy" personality seek early escape from this dependency strait jacket? Does the "infantile" personality, on the other hand, tend to move from one assistant-to job to another?

These questions and others like them might be answered by a clinician. At present this has not been done, since the problems of entree into top-management circles for this purpose present difficulties. We do have the hypothesis that the executive who utilizes an assistant-to is likely to be highly authoritarian as a leader in the business situation as well as outside—more so, at least, than those executives who prefer not to use an assistant. It may be that this hypothesis can be generalized somewhat more. Considering the problem-solving committee as an example of the use of "nonauthoritarian" leadership, it would seem, naïvely, a likely hypothesis that any executive who looks favorably upon the use of an assistant-to would be unfavorably disposed toward use of such committees. We are attempting to test this hypothesis. Measurement is difficult. Our hypothesis, for example, concerns people at the extreme of the scale (authoritarian-permissive) in comparison with others who probably lie at the same end of the scale.

It is important that examination of personality factors not obscure the fact that these two men work in an organizational framework. It does not seem sensible to try to explain the existence of the assistant-to solely in terms of the psyches of the persons immediately involved. We might more sensibly say that executives in business firms face certain fundamental common problems of decision-making. These problems relate directly to the fact that decisions must be made in an organizational context. Alternative ways of dealing with these problems, such as use of a personal assistant, are open to these executives. It is a tenable hypothesis, then, that personal needs become prime determinants of the choice made. More specific hypotheses tend to be made as answers to the questions raised in our earlier paragraph.

Let us now consider the nature of the general problem for which the assistant-to may be one solution.

[3] Wilson's hero decided that his boss was seeking a son (Wilson, *op. cit.*, pp. 249–52).

Communications in the Management Hierarchy

The management hierarchy of a business firm is a centralized, asymmetrical communications network. The communications flow might be diagrammed as in Figure 1. The arrows indicate the *net* flow of messages (and, possibly, information) between positions in the management structure. The structure is represented as a wheel rather than as a traditional pyramidal form. Representation of the communication structure as an interconnected series of two-men groups is the model most closely corresponding to the traditional organizational concepts guiding managers in their activities.

FIGURE 1

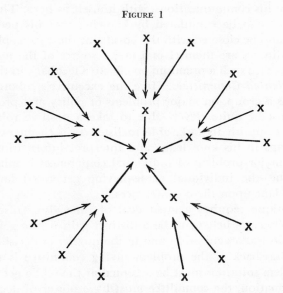

The mechanism of feedback, common to a communications system, is utilized in this one in an effort to interpret the messages received at the center. But feedback would tend, logically, to become increasingly inadequate as one approaches the center of the network, for the following reasons: (1) more decision-making power exists—hence a greater need for information; (2) the message flow gets increasingly heavy, with proportionally less feedback time available per message (each executive has about the same length workday available, regardless of his location); (3) the percentage of coded messages gets higher, as does the percentage of messages that are codings of codings (this is another way of saying that the briefed-down communications received by superiors require interpretation via the feedback process; interpretation itself becomes quite time-consuming); and (4) a greater variety of codings must be interpreted because of a greater number and variety of message sources. So the closer to the center of this system one is, the greater the need for effective feedback mechanisms. It is true that condensed and timely standardized reports help to reduce coding complexity. But these reports are, typically, devoid of feedback provisions. The alternatives apparently open to the central executive are as follows:

1. *Extensive Face-to-face Contact with Individual Subordinates.* A skilful executive will find this quite effective. But it has serious limitations. It is an enormously time-consuming technique—probably too much so, given more than a certain number of subordinates.

More important, it has a self-defeating feature. It spurs the game-playing activities of the subordinate—the efforts to make a dramatic production of his communications, with himself as hero. The impulse to dramatize seems to be stimulated by knowing that his peers and competitors will also be closeted with the boss.[4] But these game-playing efforts of the subordinates are themselves a major source of the noise and confusion which place such a premium on effective feedback in the first place.

2. *Task-oriented Committees.* Here the executive's subordinates regularly work, as a group, on major problems of policy and procedure. The executive must be quite clever—able to take a positive role in helping the group accomplish its task, able to listen to such an extent that he can fill in gaps in his knowledge and interpret information he has received. One major problem of individual conferences is minimized with this technique—the individual game-playing generated largely by the secrecy attendant upon these conferences.

This technique requires a great deal of time also. Offsetting this is what some observers believe to be a distinct gain in the general flow of information in the organization and in the quality of decisions resulting.

Another drawback of the problem-solving committee is the fact that "poor" problem solutions must be accepted at times. To get any effective flow of information, the committee must have power of decision. Otherwise it tends to become an obedient echo of the executive's beliefs—a non-learning situation from his standpoint. Whether such committees produce a larger or smaller percentage of poor solutions than the chief executive does alone is conjectural.

3. *Adopting a Personal Assistant to Himself.* Feedback needs are served here by the personal interpretation of the behavior of others that the assistant can give. In addition, he can originate information. His high depend-

---

[4] The individual subordinate goes into these private conferences knowing that he has a limited time at his disposal in which he must appear to be on top of his job and that others will be doing the same in their turns. Unfortunately, he does not know what information others may divulge at these meetings. His best play is try to steer the session on to topics about which he has superior knowledge. The executive may also face a tacit conspiracy among the subordinates. They will avoid any appearance of telling tales on one another for fear of retaliation in kind.

ency on his boss minimizes the gamesman tactics which line subordinates are prone to practice. In addition, if the assistant has a background and value system quite similar to that of his boss, his communications are that much easier to interpret. (We have found that, in practice, the assistant's training background replicates that of the boss far more often than it complements it.)

This alternative requires that the executive find a very perceptive person, willing to serve in a highly dependent role *indefinitely*. When this person disappears (as he is likely to), the communications void may seem intolerable.

Viewed in these terms, it looks as though the assistant-to represents one of various organizational mechanisms which might provide the "feedback" so strongly needed by the central executive in the large management group in his efforts to make intelligent decisions.

Part Four
DIRECTION

A New Look at Management Communication *

Frank E. Fischer

Over a decade ago Alvin Dodd, then President of the American Management Association, said, "The No. 1 management problem today is communication." Offhand, we seem to have come a long way since those benighted times. A number of colleges are now offering seminars and courses for executives in some phase of communication. Management books and periodicals are full of information about new communication devices and techniques. Lecturers by the score have spread the gospel of communication throughout the business world. Many companies have installed specialists in newly created "Communications" Departments. Consultants in communication have sprouted all over the land. The International Council of Industrial Editors estimates that management spends over $112,000,000 a year in publications designed to influence the thinking of employees, stockholders, and customers.

And yet . . . the editors of *Fortune* and Peter Drucker have charged that all this communicating is not worth a damn. All the talk, the activity, the gimmicks, and the prescriptions have failed to build a bridge between labor and management, between superior and subordinate. "We have been inept," says A. S. Igleheart, formerly Chairman of the Board and President of General Foods, "in communicating the ideas and information which create understanding among people who work together in an enterprise."

Why Communication Fails

Is this true? Has management lost its way? Not really, but many are foundering for one or more of the following reasons: First, many executives have mistaken the form of communication for its substance. They have paid too much attention to media and devices, too little to purpose and content. It is this phenomenon that led *Fortune's* W. H. Whyte, Jr. to conclude that "the great enemy of communication is the illusion of it."

Second, executives have gone astray because they have considered communication a simple, isolated problem instead of a complex and dynamic

---

* Reprinted by permission of the publisher from *Personnel*, vol. 31, no. 6 (New York: American Management Association, May, 1955), pp. 487–495. Mr. Fischer is Director of Seminars and Courses, American Management Association.

process. They have overemphasized one form of communication—the employee magazine, personnel counseling, good reading racks, economic indoctrination—at the expense of other equally important elements.

Third, they have talked too much and listened too little. They have sought to extinguish the fire of discontent by dousing employees with information on every subject from taxes to taxidermy. But, as an industrial psychologist, Charles Flory, has warned, "We can't assume that all communication is done through words . . . that people behave in uniform ways, and that any failure to understand an executive pronouncement lies with the receiver and not with the initiator." The real problem is more often lack of understanding than lack of information.

The fact of the matter is that many executives still do not understand what communication is and what it can do. They underestimate its complexity, its power, and its importance. Too few appreciate that communication is at the heart of all business operations, that it encompasses all those activities by which we influence others. Actually, communication is the most important tool we have for getting things done. It is the basis for understanding, for cooperation, and for action.

The Cost of Miscommunication

Many of management's problems are traceable to failures in communication: Someone neglects to tell the production manager that a critical material will be in short supply for the next few weeks; someone forgets to notify the advertising agency that the new product will not reach the market as scheduled; a promising junior executive accepts an attractive offer from a competitor because his boss gave him no indication how his work was appreciated; a grievance is filed because the foreman paid no attention to a worker's grumbling about the need for a safety guard on his machine; a department head's 50-page report goes unread because his superior wanted only a brief summary of the problem.

The cost of miscommunication of this sort is beyond calculation—not only in terms of time and money but in misunderstanding, inefficiency, and hostility. John Kusik, Vice-President of Chesapeake and Ohio Railroad, states that his company handles at least a billion written messages a year and many times that number of oral communications. Two-thirds of the payroll, he estimates, is spent for the sending, transmitting, and receiving of messages. Beyond question, a great deal could be saved by eliminating, combining, and condensing the simple routine messages that pulsate through a modern business. The first step in this direction is to improve the executive's *personal* skill as a sender and receiver of communications. This would require greater sensitivity to language and attention to the emotional content of messages. It demands awareness of communication barriers and how to overcome them, and the ability to tap the ideas and experiences of others.

THE COMMUNICATION PROCESS

As Lawrence Appley has pointed out, skill in communicating depends upon mastery of the basic communication process and involves the following steps:
1. Clarifying the idea or problem.
2. Getting participation in developing a solution to the problem.
3. Transmitting ideas or decisions.
4. Motivating others to take action agreed upon.
5. Measuring the effectiveness of communications.

1. Clarification

Communications often misfire because one or more of these steps are omitted or mishandled. Customarily, the busy executive limits his attention to the third phase of the process: transmitting ideas. Of course, messages must get through if communication is to be complete. But, as Clarence Randall has said, "The beginning of all communication is an idea." Unless the idea is first clearly formulated in the mind of the transmitter, the message is likely to be misunderstood by the receiver. You can't make a clear print from a blurred negative. The study of communication, therefore, must begin with a careful and precise identification of the problem that requires action. It helps to try to reduce the problem to a simple statement for, as John Dewey has observed, "A problem well stated is half solved."

The executive's next task is to gather from all available sources data that bear upon the problem. After collecting this information he must evaluate it. He selects what is important and relevant to the problem, then proceeds to develop alternate solutions. He examines assumptions, weighs precedents, and anticipates consequences. He chooses finally what appears to him to be the best alternative and outlines this solution to test its logic and completeness.

2. Participation

At this point he draws others into the problem. He does this primarily for three purposes:

(a) To clarify and test his *own* thinking by sharing his ideas with others.

(b) To gather the ideas and suggestions of others in a position to contribute to the solution of the problem.

(c) By inviting their participation, to motivate those responsible for carrying out the decision.

There are few problems so simple, few answers so obvious, that an executive's thinking cannot be sharpened by consulting with others. Some executives who can create or plan most brilliantly are inept in stirring the interest or gaining the cooperation of other people. Productive participation demands careful preparation, a permissive climate, sensitive listening, and the willingness to credit others for their contributions. In addition it requires skill in leading conferences, meetings, and committees where people can speak freely and responsibly. And most important, it requires confidence in the ability of people to make effective decisions. If you don't *expect* people to act responsibly, the chances are they will justify your expectations. Sensibly handled, participation is *not* a device for evading responsibility or syndicating the risk of making decisions.

3. *Transmission*

Having arrived at a solution or a decision, the executive's next step is to communicate it to those who will carry it out or who will be affected by it. Here he must plan carefully what to communicate, to whom to communicate, and how best to do it. Whether the communication is written or oral, the same care must be taken that he says what he has to say simply and clearly. He has to consider the nature of the person or group with whom he is communicating, the organizational and psychological barriers that may get in his way. He must remember that language that is clear to him may be obscure to others. Words that seem neutral to him may create feelings of suspicion or hostility in those who read or hear them.

4. *Motivation*

Clarity alone, then, is not enough. Most communications require not only that they be understood, but that they be accepted and acted upon. This leads directly into the fourth phase of the communication process, namely, motivation. If the communication not only states clearly what is to be done but inspires the recipient to want to do it, then we have truly communicated. This is basic in every situation requiring coordination and teamwork. It is particularly important when the communication threatens the established ways of doing things or thinking about things.

Evidence is accumulating that the morale of an organization and in large degree its productivity are related directly to the communication process. Employees who know what is expected of them, who know how their work ties in with the objectives of the company, who learn about changes before they take place, will obviously work with heightened interest and enthusiasm. Likewise, their motivation is better if they feel free to discuss problems with their supervisor and contribute to decisions that affect their work.

This factor was demonstrated long ago in the famous Hawthorne experiments of the Western Electric Company. It is confirmed by more recent surveys conducted by the University of Michigan in industries like steel, railroading, and insurance. Evidence from many sources points to the fact that free communication between the parts of a business generally results in improved morale and productivity. In each of these studies one major point keeps coming to the fore: Improvement in communication depends not so much on lavish investment in mass media, but on the daily work relations between superior and subordinate.

The National Industrial Conference Board surveyed the production employees of two plants operated by the same company.[1] The two groups were matched except that Plant "B" had participated in an active communication program for a number of years. Plant "A" had not been influenced by any such program. The following highlights from the survey's findings underline the intimate relation that seemingly exists everywhere between morale and the freedom to communicate:

1. Q. *Does your company do a good job of telling you what's going on and what's being planned?*

A. Answer	Plant A	Plant B
Very good job.....................................	18%	55%
Doesn't do much..................................	22%	14%

2. Q. *Does your foreman ask your advice before deciding things that affect you?*

A. Answer	Plant A	Plant B
Hardly ever	65%	40%
Almost always	11%	26%

3. Q. *Can you talk things over with your foreman when you want to?*

A. Answer	Plant A	Plant B
Yes, I always can..................................	34%	56%
Hardly ever	5%	0%

4. Q. *Do you feel a part of your company?*

A. Answer	Plant A	Plant B
I feel I really belong..............................	29%	62%
I feel I just work here.............................	42%	14%

5. Q. *How does your company compare as a company to work for with other companies?*

A. Answer	Plant A	Plant B
Worse than average...............................	4%	3%
Just average.......................................	35%	19%
One of the very best..............................	20%	45%

5. *Evaluation*

Just as communications often suffer from lack of planning, so they suffer from failure to evaluate their effectiveness. Much has been learned about why some conferences succeed and others don't, why some memos

[1] See "Communicating with Employees," *Studies in Personnel Policy No. 129.* National Industrial Conference Board, Inc., New York, pp. 36–40.

are clearer than others, why some talks get results and others produce indifference, why counseling in one instance results in improved performance and in another produces only resistance. It is possible also to trace the impact of communications from attitude surveys, from records of productiveness, absenteeism, turnover, and the like.

How to Achieve Effective Communication

There is little need today for special pleading in the cause of communication. Progressive managers everywhere recognize it as the basic skill of management. They know that it is not an independent activity but an essential part of everything the manager does. Executives have become painfully aware how often carefully laid plans and programs have foundered on the rocks of faulty communication. That's why so many executives are asking, "What can be done throughout the company to establish and maintain a sound system of communication? What can I personally do to help my managers become better communicators?"

The Essentials

A volume could be written in answer to such questions. However, two fundamental recommendations can be outlined. First of all the executive must set an example that will announce to all of management his belief in the importance of communication. "Every organization," says Douglas Lynch, Executive Vice-President of Brush Electronics, "is colored by the man at the top to a degree that very few of us would like to admit." By his precepts, his policies, his actions—in short, by the leadership he exercises—he can nourish or stifle the communication in his organization. In defining the responsibility of his executives, in setting standards for their performance, and in rewarding them for their efforts, he must consider skill in communication as one of the main attributes of leadership. If this seems obvious, glance through the descriptions and standards for executive positions in your company. Is there any mention of the communication responsibilities of the executive? Think also of the basis on which you last promoted an executive. Without question, you considered his record as a planner and producer. But did you review his ability to coordinate others into a well-informed, highly motivated team?

Secondly, most executives, regardless of natural endowment, can improve their abilities to communicate—*if* they are properly guided and encouraged. How much is being done in your company to help the executive clarify his thinking, secure the participation of others, transmit ideas clearly and persuasively, motivate others to act affirmatively, or to evaluate the effectiveness of their communications? Recently, AMA made a survey of companies with formal management development programs. Only 10 to 20 per cent offered training in communication.

Other Requirements of an Effective Program

In addition to these broad fundamentals, a survey of industrial practices, both good and bad, indicates that, to be effective, a communication
program must meet the following requirements:

1. *Express the needs and character of the organization.* It makes a
difference whether the company is small or large, old or new, manufacturing or retail, centralized or decentralized, union or non-union. It
makes a very great difference whether the company has a tradition of
secrecy or freedom of information, of authoritarianism or democracy.
Every communication is judged in the context of a company's traditions
and practices. That is why it is so risky to copy someone else's communication program—no matter how successful it was. You may remember
how the March Hare in *Alice in Wonderland* tried to fix the Mad Hatter's
watch with butter. When it failed, he could only say, in pained surprise:
"And it was the *best* butter, the *best* butter."

2. *Communication grows best in a climate of trust and confidence.*
Managements that have a record of keeping faith with their employees,
reporting the facts honestly, and listening sincerely don't have to depend
upon high-pressure indoctrination or slick handouts. An employee's
knowledge that he has free access to information is more important than
any specific information we can give him. Paul Arnold, President of
Arnold Bakeries, recently said in this connection: "If your employee relations program is a sound one, if your intent is true, if your people believe
in that intent, and in that truth, then and only then are you successfully
communicating."

3. *Communication should form an integral part of each executive's
job.* Though personnel specialists can advise the line and administer a
program of formal communication, each executive is responsible for
maintaining clear and consistent communication with his associates. This
is one responsibility that he cannot delegate.

4. *Communication must be a continuing program, not a brief campaign.* It is not a panacea for sudden ills, but a day-in, day-out way of
managing people. We must not, like the famous blind men who recon-
structed the whole of an elephant from a single part, identify the whole
of communication with one of its devices. Exploitation of one particular
medium will often create more problems than it will solve. This is a lesson
some companies have learned when, after a long history of indifference
to employees' interests, they have begun an all-out drive to indoctrinate
them on some particular subject. The fanciest annual report, the fattest
pay insert, the busiest reading rack, or the loudest public address system
in and of themselves win few friends and influence few people.

5. *Communication must be stimulated.* Management must show what
Alexander Heron, Vice President of Crown Zellerbach Company, has

called "an *aggressive* willingness to share information with its employees." Stonewall Jackson is said to have been so secretive that he often misled his own staff more than he did the enemy. In their fear of competitors too many executives do likewise. It is not enough to correct misinformation or even to tell employees only what they *have* to know or what *management* thinks they should know. The proper starting point is to find out *what employees are interested in hearing.*

6. *Communication must be directed to a purpose and a person.* It is not, as Lawrence Appley has warned, an end in itself. Its true end is "effective management." Perhaps executives think too much about *how* to communicate and too little about *why* they are communicating. "I don't advise you," says Clarence Randall, "to start talking until you have begun thinking. It's no good opening the tap if there is nothing in the tank." It is equally risky to communicate without taking into account the individual or group you are dealing with. Every individual brings to the communication process certain personal equipment—experiences, attitudes, feelings, expectations—that must be considered if we are to achieve understanding with him. Alexander Heron has expressed this idea very forcibly:

The foundation for any program for understanding between us and our employees is a complete respect on our part for the personality and individuality of the employee. While there may be a hundred or a hundred thousand employees on our payroll, and while we may bargain collectively with them through their chosen representatives, our relations are not with a mass of men; our relations are with each one of a hundred or a hundred thousand individual persons. We cannot share information with an abstract, imaginary entity such as "the public," "labor" or "the union," or "the rank and file." We can share information with Al Adams and Bill Brown and Carl Casey and Dan Davis, who work with us and receive their income in wages which we deliver to them.

7. *Communication must move freely in both directions.* It is commonplace today to emphasize that communication is a two-way street. In actual practice, however, management devotes far more attention to telling, informing, and commanding than it does to listening, asking, and interpreting. Only 4 per cent of the 160 executives polled by the Bureau of National Affairs disagreed with *Fortune's* recent article on management's failure to listen to its people. One way to learn what people want to know about is to encourage them to communicate upward in the organization. To find out whether its story is understood and accepted by employees, management must stimulate them to express their ideas and questions—and then management must *do* something about the problems that are raised.

8. *Communication must consider the supervisor's role.* In building a bridge between top management and employees, we must never forget

that the prime communicator is the supervisor. He is in the most critical position to interpret—or misinterpret—top management thinking for the employees. H. J. Ruttenberg, the well-known labor leader, has said that in his experience the unionization of almost every plant has been preceded by the distortion of top management's attitudes and policies by minor functionaries. Useful as they are, such devices as president's letters, suggestion boxes, employee counselors, attitude surveys, and company magazines all represent detours. They route the employee's thinking and his problems around the supervisor. "First-line supervisors and foremen," said L. W. Tate, Vice President of Dallas Railway and Terminal Company, "are in the best position to feel the pulse of the workers in their day-to-day contacts on the job." Management must do everything in its power to keep the supervisor continually informed and to tap his knowledge of what employees are doing and thinking.

9. *The lines of communication should be as clear and direct as possible.* Many communications become diluted or distorted as they pass

FIGURE 1

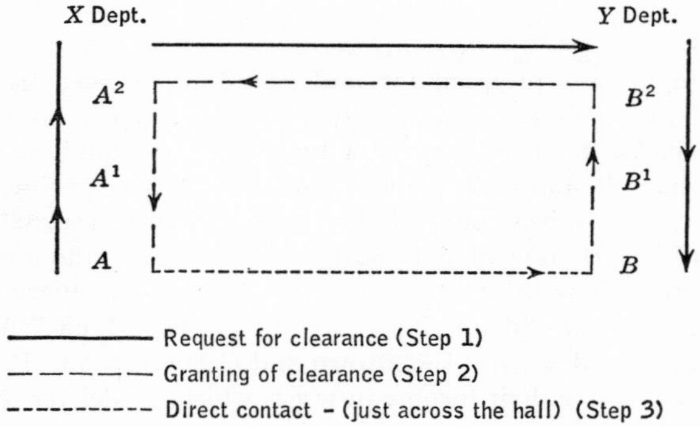

———————— Request for clearance (Step 1)
— — — — — Granting of clearance (Step 2)
- - - - - - - - - - Direct contact – (just across the hall) (Step 3)

through levels of management. Others lose their usefulness because of delays in their journey down the management hierarchy. In establishing policy in communication, top management is haunted by the dilemma of maintaining the formal organizational channels and the necessity for speed and timeliness. One company prescribed exactly the channels through which communications must flow. When executive "A" wished to make a contact with executive "B" not prescribed in the standard procedure, he had to submit a request to his own boss, "A^1," that started the labyrinthine process shown in Figure 1.

Contrast this with the sensible policy on communication developed by Jones and Laughlin: "The plan of organization should permit and require the exercise of common sense and good judgment at all levels in determining the best channels of contact to expedite the work." In other words, management is told to communicate in the most direct way consistent with good sense.

10. *Communication must reflect the everyday policies and practices of management.* The important word here is "practices." In the long run, employees are influenced not by what management says but by what it does. It is the context of behavior that gives words their meaning. Employees are not fooled when the boss says good morning or asks about an ailing wife because the manual tells him that this is good human relations. The boss who levels with his people, who listens to their problems, who is genuinely interested in them, can exercise effective leadership even though he may forget sometimes to say good morning. It is useless for an executive to announce an "open-door" policy if employees do not feel comfortable once they go through the door. The manager who tells a foreman that he is interested in his problems but ignores his requests for help or information is, in effect, really telling the foreman that he is *not* interested in him.

We must never forget that the most powerful communication isn't what you *say*, it's what you *do*. What counts, in the final analysis, is not what people are *told* but what they *accept*. It is this concept of the role of communication in industry that characterizes effective leadership. This is the key that will unlock the gates to higher morale and productivity. To use this key we must have the faith that induced Charles McCormick to launch his plan of multiple management. We must act on the belief, as he did, that people can do anything if (1) they want to do it, (2) they are trained to do it, and (3) they understand the reason for doing it.

Ten Commandments of Good Communication *

As a manager, your prime responsibility is to get things done through people. However sound your ideas or well-reasoned your decisions, they become effective only as they are transmitted to others and achieve the desired action—or reaction. Communication, therefore, is your most vital management tool. On the job you communicate not only with words but through your apparent attitudes and your actions. For communication encompasses all human behavior that results in an exchange of meaning. How well you manage depends upon how well you communicate in this broad sense. These ten commandments are designed to help you improve your skills as a manager by improving your skills of communication— with superiors, subordinates, and associates.

1. *Seek to clarify your ideas before communicating.*

 The more systematically we analyze the problem or idea to be communicated, the clearer it becomes. This is the first step toward effective communication. Many communications fail because of inadequate planning. Good planning must consider the goals and attitudes of those who will receive the communication and those who will be affected by it.

2. *Examine the true purpose of each communication.*

 Before you communicate, ask yourself what you *really* want to accomplish with your message—obtain information, initiate action, change another person's attitude? Identify your most important goal and then adapt your language, tone, and total approach to serve that specific objective. Don't try to accomplish too much with each communication. The sharper the focus of your message the greater its chances of success.

3. *Consider the total physical and human setting whenever you communicate.*

 Meaning and intent are conveyed by more than words alone. Many other factors influence the over-all impact of a communication, and the manager must be sensitive to the total setting in which he communicates. Consider, for example, your sense of timing—i.e., the circumstances under which you make an announcement or render a decision; the *physical setting*—whether you communicate in private, for example, or otherwise; the *social climate* that pervades work rela-

* Reprinted by permission of the *American Management Association*. Copyright, 1955.

tionships within the company or a department and sets the tone of its communications; *custom and past practice*—the degree to which your communication conforms to, or departs from, the expectations of your audience. Be constantly aware of the total setting in which you communicate. Like all living things, communication must be capable of adapting to its environment.

4. *Consult with others, where appropriate, in planning communications.*
Frequently it is desirable or necessary to seek the participation of others in planning a communication or developing the facts on which to base it. Such consultation often helps to lend additional insight and objectivity to your message. Moreover, those who have helped you plan your communication will give it their active support.

5. *Be mindful, while you communicate, of the overtones as well as the basic content of your message.*
Your tone of voice, your expression, your apparent receptiveness to the responses of others—all have tremendous impact on those you wish to reach. Frequently overlooked, these subtleties of communication often affect a listener's reaction to a message even more than its basic content. Similarly, your choice of language—particularly your awareness of the fine shades of meaning and emotion in the words you use—predetermines in large part the reactions of your listeners.

6. *Take the opportunity, when it arises, to convey something of help or value to the receiver.*
Consideration of the other person's interests and needs—the habit of trying to look at things from his point of view—will frequently point up opportunities to convey something of immediate benefit or long-range value to him. People on the job are most responsive to the manager whose messages take their own interests into account.

7. *Follow up your communication.*
Our best efforts at communication may be wasted, and we may never know whether we have succeeded in expressing our true meaning and intent, if we do not follow up to see how well we have put our message across. This you can do by asking questions, by encouraging the receiver to express his reactions, by follow-up contacts, by subsequent review of performance. Make certain that every important communication has a "feed-back" so that complete understanding and appropriate action result.

8. *Communicate for tomorrow as well as today.*
While communications may be aimed primarily at meeting the demands of an immediate situation, they must be planned with the past in mind if they are to maintain consistency in the receiver's view; but, most important of all, they must be consistent with long-range interests and goals. For example, it is not easy to communicate frankly on such matters as poor performance or the shortcomings of a loyal

subordinate—but postponing disagreeable communications makes them more difficult in the long run and is actually unfair to your subordinates and your company.

9. *Be sure your actions support your communications.*

In the final analysis, the most persuasive kind of communication is not what you say but what you *do*. When a man's actions or attitudes contradict his words, we tend to discount what he has said. For every manager this means that good supervisory practices—such as clear assignment of responsibility and authority, fair rewards for effort, and sound policy enforcement—serve to communicate more than all the gifts of oratory.

10. *Last, but by no means least: Seek not only to be understood but to understand—be a good listener.*

When we start talking we often cease to listen—in that larger sense of being attuned to the other person's unspoken reactions and attitudes. Even more serious is the fact that we are *all* guilty, at times, of inattentiveness when others are attempting to communicate to us. Listening is one of the most important, most difficult—and most neglected—skills in communication. It demands that we concentrate not only on the explicit meanings another person is expressing, but on the implicit meanings, unspoken words, and undertones that may be far more significant. Thus we must learn to listen with the inner ear if we are to know the inner man.

The Three Basic Methods of Leadership *

Auren Uris

"The earth is flat."

"The moon is made of green cheese."

"Leaders are born, not made."

Whether you're talking about the earth's shape or the origin of leaders, false theory hampers progress and practice.

That's why, for example, as long as men believed in the "spontaneous generation" of disease agents, they were helpless to combat them. But when Louis Pasteur demonstrated the existence of bacteria, our fight against disease surged forward.

One by one, we've cast our false ideas about leadership. Unfortunately, many still remain. Here are two cases that show the kind of ideas hamstringing present-day practices:

CASE I

Superintendent Hal Byrnes is trying to break a production bottleneck in one of his departments.

"Tom," he says to his departmental foreman, "don't you think what we're up against is basically a storage problem?"

"Could be, Mr. Byrnes. Guess we are a little crowded. But we've got to have every one of these items close at hand."

"Think it over, see if there's anything you can do," requests Byrnes.

Week follows week. From time to time Tom gets a corner cleared, moves a lot of cartons from one spot to another. But the storage jam lingers on—and so does the bottleneck.

CASE II

Here is a second business executive's approach to the same problem:

"Jim, I've been checking your storage setup. It's got to the point where clutter is actually slowing down production. I want you to get moving

* Reprinted by permission of the publisher from *How to Be a Successful Leader* (New York: McGraw-Hill Book Company, Inc., 1953), pp. 25–31. Copyright, 1953, by Auren Uris. Mr. Uris is the author of numerous books and articles in the area of human relations.

on it right away. By tonight I want every aisle cleared. By tomorrow night I want benches free of everything but tools and work in process. And by the end of the week I want every bit of scrap sorted and moved over to salvage, where it belongs. I'll be down to check first thing Monday."

"O.K., Mr. Brown," says Jim.

Brown's orders are carried out. The result? An unquestionable improvement in the department's appearance. Definitely, an easier flow of materials. And, in a few days, a gradual rise in output.

BEHIND THE FRONT

If we could tune in on the thought waves of these two executives, we'd be likely to get something like this:

Hal Byrnes: "Maybe I didn't get results. But at least I handled Tom in the right way. I treated him like a human being. I gave him a chance to use his initiative and to participate in a decision that affected his department."

Mr. Brown: "I guess I got results," he admits, "but in the worst possible way. I had to put my foot down hard—right on Jim's neck. I know that's not the way to build a good working relationship."

Note this strange fact: Hal Byrnes *defends* his *failure.* Brown *apologizes* for his *success.*

Here are some widely accepted ideas about leadership that explain the views of men like Byrnes and Brown:

It's not "right" to interfere in matters for which a subordinate is responsible. You take away his self-esteem.

It's not "right" to issue flat orders. The right way is to "consult" and "discuss."

It's not "right" to demand obedience from a subordinate. It destroys his initiative.

The two cases illustrate a major leadership dilemma:

The "right" way often fails to produce results. The "wrong" way is often successful.

HOW COME?

What accounts for this peculiar state of affairs?

The root of the difficulty springs largely from some misconceptions and misinterpretations arising from early experiments in the field of leadership.

In 1939, psychologists Kurt Lewin, Ronald Lippitt, and Ralph White, working at the University of Iowa, undertook to explore the nature of leadership.

Two sets of experimental groups were organized. One was dominated by a dictatorial leader, who determined policy;

decided what was to be done and how it was to be done;

assigned tasks to individuals and decided the work companions for each member;

was personal in his praise, criticism, and comments in general.

The second group was led by a so-called "democratic" leader, who brought up matters of policy for group discussion;

encouraged group members to participate in decisions;

permitted individuals to choose work companions;

was "objective" in his comments.

Then came an unplanned and unexpected development: one of the individuals playing the role of "democratic" leader was creating an atmosphere *different* from that achieved by other "democratic" leaders. He

exercised virtually no control over the group;

permitted group members to shift for themselves to a large extent;

had them tackle the problems that arose as best they could.

And the *group response to this technique differed* from the reactions of other democratic groups.

Lewin and his colleagues accordingly set up a third type of group to conform to this method, which they termed *laissez faire*.

RESULTS

Observers noted differences in atmosphere, behavior, feelings, and accomplishments among the three groups.

Dictator-led. Group members were quarrelsome and aggressive. Some individuals became completely dependent upon the leader. When the leader was absent, activity tended to stop altogether. Work progressed at only a fair rate.

"Democratic." The individuals got along with one another on a friendly basis. Relations with the leader were freer, more spontaneous. The work progressed smoothly, and continued *even when the leader was absent*.

Laissez Faire. Work progressed haphazardly and at a slow rate. Although there was considerable activity, much of it was unproductive. Considerable time was lost in arguments and discussions between group members on a purely personal basis.

EVALUATING THE RESULTS

The imagination and keen thinking of the experimenters, the epoch-making nature of their studies, cannot be over-estimated. Dr. Lewin and his associates made a major contribution to the study of group functioning.

But according to Dr. David Emery, an associate of Lewin's who conducted follow-up studies, many of the practical applications of Lewin's ideas have been misguided.

Take, for example, the very terms Lewin used. For purposes of his experiment, the words "autocratic," "democratic," and *"laissez faire"* were given specific and clear-cut meaning. But these words have general meanings and connotations. In many cases, these were substituted for Lewin's experimental definitions.

One result was the tendency to reject everything that smacked of autocratic and laissez-faire leadership.

For the term "autocratic," people supplied the connotations "dictator," "Hitler," "tough and unreasonable boss." For *"laissez faire,"* the substitutions were "wishy-washy," "irresponsible," "spineless."

Another result was the overselling of "democratic" leadership. This was not the fault of "democratic" leadership. The error lay *in the misunderstanding of its method and limitations.* It is these misconceptions, about democratic methods, for example, that lead to the unrealistic situations typified by the Byrnes and Brown examples—a "hands off" policy with nothing accomplished, or intervention with feelings that "it's wrong to intervene."

CLEARING THE WAY

As has been said, the Lewin-Lippitt-White studies were eye openers. Distortion of the results in some quarters does not make less valid the fact that the Lewin studies provide a sound starting point for an approach to leadership.

Actually, the three methods developed in the University of Iowa investigation provide an essential key. For the sake of clarity, let us define the three methods, under the names by which they'll be discussed in the following pages:

Autocratic Leadership. The leader mainly seeks obedience from his group. He determines policy and considers decision-making a one-man operation—he being the man.

Democratic Leadership. The leader draws ideas and suggestions from the group by discussion and consultation. Group members are encouraged to take part in setting policy. The leader's job is largely that of moderator.

Free-rein Leadership. (Lewin's laissez-faire method)—The leader is more or less an information booth. He plays down his role in the group's activity. He's on hand mainly to provide materials and information. He exercises a minimum of control.

Much of our present difficulty lies in the fact that psychologists and sociologists haven't been content to *describe* these three different methods; they have also compared and *evaluated* them. And they have generally decided that democratic leadership is *best*. But the fact is:

Autocratic leadership, *in certain situations,* will be effective and successful, when the democratic or free-rein approaches would fail.

Democratic leadership, *under the right conditions,* will give better results than any other method.

Free-rein leadership, also *under the right conditions,* will produce more successful results than either of the other methods. And this is true despite the fact that it is often written off as ineffective.

RECAP

It's worth repeating: the tools of the leader are the three basic methods —autocratic, democratic, and free-rein leadership. Contrary to common belief, these three approaches are *not* mutually exclusive.

No one has to choose between using autocratic, democratic, or free-rein methods, for example. That would be like telling a golf player he has to choose between using a driver and a putter. In the course of a game, he'll use *both*.

Note Mr. X, a successful plant manager:

He *directs* his secretary to make up a report, on all overtime worked on a special order, until the order is completed.

He *consults* with his five department heads on the best way to push a special order through their departments with a minimum of upset to regular production.

He *suggests* to his assistant that it would be a good idea to figure out ways in which they can handle special orders a little more smoothly in the future.

Note the different approaches Mr. X is using. He orders (autocratic) on one phase of the problem; he consults (democratic method) on another phase; and he suggests an objective (free rein) in planning for similar problems.

The skill of leadership lies largely in knowing *when* to use *which* method. Your problem, then, is to learn to vary techniques to fit the changing *conditions* and *people* you meet in your work.

The skill with which you apply the three basic tools of leadership— autocratic, democratic, and free-rein techniques—determines your personal success as a leader.

More about the Methods *

Auren Uris

A couple of young Italian farm hands were headed toward Naples for romance and adventure.

"If you get into trouble," cautioned Alberto, the more experienced of the two, "don't give your right name."

They met at an agreed-upon rendezvous when it was time to return home.

"Pietro," exclaimed Alberto, "what happened to you! The bandages, the blood!"

"I got into a little trouble with the police. They asked my name and I gave them a false one, as you suggested. And this is the result."

"How is that possible? What name did you give?"

"Benito Mussolini."

We can be fully aware of the importance of names, and still make a poor choice.

This is the case with the names of the three basic methods of leadership. The words "autocratic," "democratic," "free rein" are not the most desirable labels for the methods they signify. Still, they are used here because to change them to something else would cause even more confusion.

MEANING AND FEELING

As one semanticist puts it, "Words can make love and pick fights."

The process of twentieth-century education, for instance, is likely to have given many of us an unfavorable reaction to the word *autocratic*. In the same way, few of us reach maturity without having strong pro feelings for the word *democratic*. Even the term *free rein* has its emotional weight. But here individual reactions are likely to differ.

You can learn your own reaction by a brief word-association test. Go down the following list of cue words, one at a time, as rapidly as possible.

* Reprinted by permission of the publishers from *How to Be a Successful Leader* (New York: McGraw-Hill Book Company, Inc., 1953), pp. 32–39. Copyright, 1953, by Auren Uris. Mr. Uris is the author of numerous books and articles in the area of human relations.

Write down or make a mental note of the word you associate with each:

Cue	Response
1. black (example)	bad
2. neat	*o K*
3. industrious	*weather*
4. speed boat	*fast*
5. free rein	*loose*

The first four words have no special significance. Their function is to establish the pattern of response. It's your answer to the term *free rein* that's important. People taking the test generally show one of two reactions:

Favorable. For one group, the term free rein draws such associated words as *freedom, liberty, independence.*

Unfavorable. For the opposed group, free rein has such connotations as *loose, aimless, no place to go.*

Tool Descriptions

Remember the last time you looked through a mail-order catalogue? Do you recall how carefully each item, be it an article of clothing or an incubator, was described? The mailorder houses long ago learned that, for best selling results, merchandise has to be described as completely and accurately as possible.

It will make for smoother sailing in the pages ahead if at the outset, the three terms, the three tools of leadership, are described as carefully as possible. It's advisable not only because the words have everyday meanings that may differ from those given in this book; in addition, the terms as used by Lewin and other investigators came to have meanings which differed from one another and, in some respects, from the meanings intended here.

Let's begin by getting a couple of loose pebbles out of the road. Here are some of the things the terms *don't* mean—popular notions to the contrary notwithstanding.

Autocratic leadership does *not* mean dictatorship, or willful self-satisfaction of the leader at the expense of his followers.

Democratic leadership does *not* mean putting all decisions to a vote.

Free-rein leadership does *not* mean absence of leadership, a group left to lurch along without guidance or direction.

"Check Shooting Irons Here"

Let's try to do mentally what hosts of the Old West used to demand of their guests. Let's park our artillery—the preconceived ideas as to the meaning of these terms—at the door.

The fact is, it's important to shed any emotional associations you may have with the leadership terms in question. Your handling of these leadership tools is likely to be more expert if it is free of feelings irrelevant to the matters at hand.

Comparing the three methods shows that there are both similarities and differences. Note what they are in relation to some key points:

1. *Historical Background.* It may seem illogical to say, on the one hand, that the concepts with which we're dealing are unique and should be identified by new terms; and, on the other, to indicate that these concepts have histories which can be studied to good advantage. Actually there's no contradiction. No one quarrels with the anthropologist who seeks to understand more about modern man by studying the Neanderthal Man.

Two of the three concepts we're discussing do have roots in old ideas and practices. But the terms as we are going to use them do not coincide in meaning with their historical counterparts. Nevertheless, the basic ideas do have histories reaching back to antiquity. This background is of interest because it helps to some extent to explain present attitudes toward the terms.

Autocratic leadership, for example, is by far the oldest of the three concepts. Its origin and the first application of its methods were made by our half-brute prehistoric forebears.

Interestingly enough, in our individual history, the autocratic method is also the one we meet with first. The parent-child relationship, typified by the dependent child and the dominant parent, is one extreme form of the autocratic method.

The democratic idea has equally vague beginnings. But it was in ancient Greece that the term originated. And it was also in Greece that the governmental form described as "democratic" developed.

The free-rein approach, as a method of guiding the efforts of others, seems to have little historical precedent. Leaders of the past have undoubtedly used the method, but individual applications apparently never reached the stage of standardization, where the method was recognized as a usable approach to leadership.

2. *Relationships.* The main point of similarity among the three methods is that each can be used—under certain conditions—to guide the efforts of subordinates. They are not extensions of one another; that is, they are not different degrees of the same thing.

3. *Centrality.* Each method focuses on a different element; that is, the energy and ideas which advance the cause of the group originate from different sources in each case. The differences can be represented in this way:

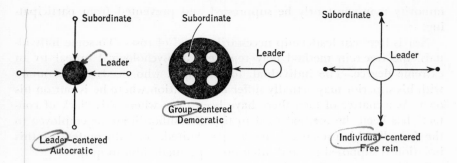

In the autocratic method, the *leader* is the spark plug. His ideas, his plans are the ones that are carried out.

In the democratic method, the *group* is the central element. The abilities, ideas, and energies of the entire group are a pool from which the leader gets the "materials" to build accomplishment.

In the free-rein method, there is a multiple focus. Each individual in the group tends to become a supplier of ideas, and so on.

4. *Leader Activity*. It is sometimes falsely assumed that an autocratic leader, for example, must be more active than a democratic one. Actually, the democratic leader may be as "busy" or even busier than an autocratic leader. But his activity is of a different *kind*. For the time spent by the autocratic leader in personal planning, the democratic one may be occupied in organizing a group of subordinates to do similar planning. And the free-rein leader may be equally active, again the difference being in kind, rather than amount, of activity.

5. *Responsibility*. There is no difference between the amount of responsibility shouldered by leaders using each of the three methods. In the final analysis, for example, each type of leader can fire a subordinate, or set in motion the purchase of necessary equipment, and so on.

6. *The Moral Angle*. It is sometimes thought that autocratic methods —and here the term "autocratic" is used in its general sense—are less desirable than democratic methods.

It is claimed, for example, that the individual under autocratic leadership is robbed of his natural dignity. Oppositely, the individual in a democratically led group is supposed to retain his individual dignity and self-importance.

These ideas frequently fail to pan out.

Under intelligent autocratic leadership, the rights of the individual may be *better* protected than under leadership which holds to the democratic method in form rather than spirit.

And observers have pointed out conditions under which the democratic method may become a tyranny. Where a majority rules, for example, the minority may constantly be suppressed and prevented from participating.

Nor is free-rein leadership necessarily a bed of roses. To some individuals, the free-rein method may represent a psychological ordeal to an extreme degree. The individual, for example, who needs close contact with his superior may actually suffer in a situation where he is put on his own. As a matter of fact, there have been cases where this "lack of contact" has been the method used to tip off a subordinate or employee to the fact that his presence is no longer desired. The discomfort of this isolation is supposed to—and often does—persuade him to quit.

7. *Effectiveness.* There is *no* difference in the effectiveness of each method. It cannot be said that the democratic method is *more* effective than the autocratic, or the autocratic *more* effective than the free-rein. In a given situation you will find that each method has particular advantages and disadvantages.

Selecting Your Approach

The next four chapters describe in detail the considerations you have to keep in mind to decide under what conditions each method is particularly suitable.

The four considerations—paralleled by the chapter headings—are:

the individual subordinate. No two people are alike. The ways they differ, the effect the differences have on your method of dealing with them, are explained.

the group. The make-up of your group exerts an influence on your method of handling it. The characteristics by which one group differs from another supply the key to your approach.

the leadership situation. The life of a group has ups and downs, peaks and low points of activity and pressure. The extent to which leadership must change with the situation is clarified.

your own personality. You yourself, the kind of person you are, often becomes the major factor in your methods of leading your people. Certain methods are better suited to certain personality types. The facts are provided which can help you make a decision along these lines.

At the outset, a basic question arises: does an approach that calls for a change of leadership method from one case to another, let us say, suffer from inconsistency? For example, how can you be an autocratic, democratic, and free-rein leader in turn, and not leave your subordinates completely up in the air? Doesn't such variation cause confusion?

The answer is a definite *no*—as long as the reasons for the change are understood by you. Consider the skipper of a sailing craft. He sets his sails and tightens his lines according to the prevailing winds and currents, changing them when necessary. He's not being inconsistent; he's being *flexible*. And it's the quality of flexibility—the suiting of leadership method to leadership needs—that is the supreme skill of the effective leader.

From Death to Life

We face the same problem in leadership that the biologist faces. In order to study the vital organs, for example, the biologist frequently must separate them individually from the living organism. As soon as he takes this step, he is studying, not a living dynamic organism, but a dead one.

You must make the same mental reservations as the biologist. You must keep in mind that in analyzing these factors, one by one, we are actually pulling apart—and therefore changing the nature of—the process. Yet there is enough to be learned by this method to justify the move. The biologist's technique has given us our major advances in our knowledge of the life process. In the same way, our analysis of the suspended process can give us insight into leadership in action.

Informal Organization*

Keith Davis

Beneath the cloak of formal relationships in a business there exists a more complex, complicated system of informal relationships. The informal organization is significant to management because it is a powerful influence upon productivity and job satisfaction. . . .

THE NATURE OF INFORMAL ORGANIZATION

Informal organization is that network of personal and social relations which is not established or required by formal organization. It arises from the social interaction of people, which means that it develops spontaneously as people associate with each other. The emphasis within informal organization is on people and their relationships, whereas formal organization emphasizes positions in terms of authority and functions. Informal authority, therefore, attaches to a *person,* while formal authority attaches to a *position* and a person wields it only by virtue of his position.

Characteristics of Informal Organization

Managers sometimes wish they could order the informal organization abolished with the stroke of a pen. Most of them would prefer to work with only the formal organization, because this would make their job simpler and involve less worry. From their point of view the informal organization is a "thorn in the side" which regularly offers resistance to their formal orders, or amends them, or accomplishes them by a procedure different from the intended one. Regardless of how helpful or harmful it is, managers soon learn its first characteristic—it cannot be absolutely abolished. A manager can rescind any formal organization which he has established, but he did not create the informal organization and he cannot rescind it. As long as there are people in business there will be informal groups.

Authority in informal organization is earned or given permissively,

---

* Reprinted by permission of the publisher from *Human Relations in Business* (New York: McGraw-Hill Book Company, Inc., 1957), pp. 98–118. Mr. Davis is Professor of Management, School of Business, Arizona State University.

rather than delegated. Informal authority comes from those who are the object of its control; but formal authority comes from "outsiders" who are "higher up the line," rather than from the people who are controlled by it. In contrast to the downward flow of formal authority, informal authority more often flows upward or horizontally. It is more of a privilege than a right. It is usually more unstable than formal authority, since it is subject to the sentiments of people. Because of its subjective nature, informal organization is not subject to management control in the way that formal organization is.

As a result of the differences between the two sources of authority, formal organization may grow to immense size, but informal organizations (at least the closely knit ones) tend to remain smaller in order to keep within the limits of personal relationships. There are, therefore, many different informal organizations within a large business. They exist at all levels. Some of them are wholly within the business; others are partially external to it.

Informal Leaders

The leaders of informal groups arise from various causes. Some of these causes are age, seniority, technical competence, work location, freedom to move around the work area, and a pleasant, responsive personality. The causes are actually as multitudinous as there are situations because each leader arises under slightly different circumstances. Informal groups overlap to the extent that one person may be a member of several different groups, which means that there is not just one leader but several of varying importance. The group may look to one employee on matters pertaining to wages and to another to lead recreational plans. In this way each person in a department may be some type of informal leader. Perhaps there is an "oldtimer" who is looked upon as the expert on job problems, a "listener" who serves as counselor, and a "spokesman" who is depended upon to convey key problems to the manager. In return for his services, each leader usually enjoys certain rewards and privileges. Perhaps the "oldtimer" is permitted to punch the clock first, and so on. One significant reward is the esteem in which the leader is held.

Although each person in a work group may be leader of some small informal organization, there is usually one primary leader who stands out above the rest. His influence is predominant. Each manager needs to learn who the informal leader of his subordinates is and to work with that person to assure that his leadership is furthering the company's objectives, rather than hindering them. When the informal leader is working against the company, his effect is far greater than his numerical proportion in the group. He is in a biological sense the "dominant gene" in his interaction with others. His influence is illustrated statistically in the following example. Assume that A is the informal leader in group

ABCDE. In this group there are 26 interpersonal combinations as follows: [1]

AB	ABC	ABCD
AC	ABD	ABDE
AD	ABE	ACDE
AE	ACD	ABCE
BC	ACE	BCDE
BD	ADE	ABCDE
BE	BCD	
CD	BCE	
CE	BDE	
DE	CDE	

Assuming that *A* is the leader and that each of the 26 combinations occurs as often as any other, it is seen that *A* (who is one-fifth of the group) is involved in approximately three-fifths (58 per cent) of the interactions. The result would be identical selecting *B, C, D,* or *E* as the informal leader. Since an anticompany informal leader "poisons" a majority of the interpersonal contacts, it is easy to see how one such person can quickly undermine a manager and ruin morale in a whole department. The informal leader in this instance is the one bad apple who ruins the barrel.

The informal organization is a good place for potential formal leaders to develop, but it should be remembered that an informal leader does not always make the best formal manager. Business history is replete with incidents of good informal leaders who became arrogant bosses once they received formal authority. Informal authority, since it comes from those acted upon, holds arrogance in check, but there is no such check on formal authority.

Some informal leaders fail as formal ones because they fear formal responsibility, something they do not have as informal leaders. They often criticize management for lacking initiative, not daring to be different, or being overcautious; but when they take a management job, they become even more conservative because they are afraid to make a mistake. Other informal leaders fail because the area of formal management responsibility is much broader than the tiny functional area in which they had informal authority. The fact that Joe is the leader in departmental social activities does not mean that he will be equally good as the departmental manager.

[1] The number of combinations for any group may be computed by the combinatorial formula $C \dfrac{N}{r} = \dfrac{N!}{r!(N-r)!}$ which indicates the number of ways in which *n* things can be combined *r* at a time. See Acheson J. Duncan, *Quality Control and Industrial Statistics,* Chicago: Richard D. Irwin, Inc., 1952, pp. 81–82.

Functions of Informal Groups

Informal groups arise and persist because they satisfy wants of their members. These wants are determined by the group members themselves. A want which seems to be felt by all groups is the necessity to perpetuate its culture, and this is an important function of any informal organization. A second informal group function is communication. In order to meet wants and to keep its members informed of what is taking place that may affect want satisfaction, the group develops systems and channels of communication.

A third function is social control by which the behavior of others is influenced and regulated. Social control is both internal and external. Internal control is directed toward making members of the group conform to its culture. In an accounting office an employee wore a bow tie to work. Comments and "razzing" from other workers soon convinced him that a bow tie was not an "accepted" style in the group, so thereafter he did not wear it. External control is directed toward those outside the group such as management, union leadership, or other informal groups. Pressures of external control can be quite strong, as when a walkout strike occurs.

Benefits of Informal Organization

Informal organization is sometimes looked upon as a negative force in the work group, but this is not necessarily so. If its interests and goals are integrated with the company's, it will then work for company objectives rather than against them. The manager's big responsibility is to do all he can to effect this integration so that the two groups will mesh instead of clash. This is effective management, and its over-all result is that the informal organization helps get the work done. Dubin, Shartle, and others recognize that this blending of the formal and informal is the most effective way to accomplish work. Formal plans and policies cannot meet *every* problem in a dynamic situation, because they are preestablished and partly inflexible. Some requirements can be met better by informal relations, which can be flexible and spontaneous. Dubin states, "Informal relations in the organization serve to preserve the organization from the self-destruction that would result from literal obedience to the formal policies, rules, regulations, and procedures." [2] Shartle, in reporting his field research on leadership, comments, "The informal structure is one index of the dynamics of getting work done, and it appears that for efficiency it will necessarily deviate from the formal structure." [3] This idea can be stated as the *principle of informal organization* as follows:

[2] Robert Dubin, *Human Relations in Administration*, Englewood Cliffs, N.J.: Prentice-Hall, Inc., 1951, p. 68.

[3] Carroll L. Shartle, "Leadership and Executive Performance," *Personnel*, March, 1949, p. 378.

an integration of the interests, goals, methods, and evaluation systems of formal and informal organizations tends to increase productivity and job satisfaction.

The over-all result of "helping get the work done" can be subdivided to show the different types of specific benefits which informal organization brings. First, it may act to lighten the work load of the formal manager. If employees know that their manager has the support of the existing informal organization, they are more likely to respond to his ideas, to be motivated to work efficiently, and to proceed with their assigned tasks without bothering their manager "just to be sure." The manager in this situation feels more free to delegate and decentralize because he is confident that his group will cooperate. This confidence in his people will also act to lighten the mental burden of his responsibility, but not the responsibility itself.

Informal organization acts to fill in gaps in formal orders or in the manager's abilities. If a manager is weak in planning ability, one of his employees may informally help with planning, either through suggestions or open action, so that the over-all result is the same as if the manager did good planning. Shartle reports that executives tend to choose principal assistants who complement their own abilities.[4] This may be because the situation has been ripe for that type of informal leader to arise within the group. As mentioned earlier, informal organization is a good place to develop leaders, although informal leaders are not always the best formal leaders.

A significant benefit of informal organization is that it gives satisfaction and stability to work groups. It is the means by which workers achieve a sense of belonging and security. It is a device to protect themselves from outside influences and to preserve their culture. The new employee joins a work group as an outsider, and he collides with this protective attitude of the group. Although his formal induction is achieved in a day, his social (informal) induction may take weeks or may never be achieved. He may remain an isolate or outsider. He does not *join* the group in the true sense of the word; he has to be accepted into it.

A well-known benefit of informal organization is that it can be a useful channel of employee communication. Management, in fact, often depends on the informal system to convey certain types of information. Another benefit is that it is a safety valve for the frustrations and other emotional problems of group work. If a man is unhappy and feels he cannot talk to his supervisor, perhaps he will talk to a friend. If a worker has leadership abilities, but the formal organization cannot use them, perhaps he will use his abilities by becoming an informal leader.

A benefit of informal organization which is seldom recognized is that its presence encourages a manager to plan and act more carefully than

4 *Ibid.,* p. 378.

he would otherwise. Any manager who recognizes its power knows that it is a check and balance on his unlimited use of authority. He will introduce changes into his group only after careful planning because he knows that the informal group could provide the impetus to undermine an ill-conceived and shaky project. He wants his projects to succeed because he will have to answer to *formal* authority if they fail.

Each of the benefits of informal organization can be reversed to become disadvantages under different circumstances. The informal group can lighten the load of the manager, but it can also cause him extra burdens when it works against him. Its communication system can carry useful information, or it may carry useless rumor and gossip. One of the worst effects of informal organization is its support of restriction-of-work practices in order, supposedly, to protect its members.

Types of Informal Groups

Sociologists have classified three types of informal groups: friendship-kinship groups, cliques, and subcliques.[5] In addition there is a fourth category "isolates," who are not a group but a number of individuals with negligible informal work-group ties. Their differences are illustrated in Figure 6-1. Friendship-kinship groups denote close personal ties as friends or relatives. They most frequently exist in pairs. This type of group in business is especially significant to the *spread* of influence or information. Two close friends or relatives may be members of two separate cliques and thereby carry from one clique to the other an idea or bit of news.

Cliques are composed of persons who commonly associate with each other and maintain certain social practices and standards. Acceptance of a person into the clique requires acceptance by the group, rather than by an individual in it. Subcliques are attached to a clique through having one or more members in it. Subclique members not in the main clique are given only partial acceptance by it.

Charting the Informal Organization

The diagram of group attraction in Figure 6-1 may be called a *sociogram*. This study and measurement of feelings of group members toward each other was pioneered by J. L. Moreno in the 1930s and is called *sociometry*. Moreno classed feelings as attraction, repulsion, and indifference. To learn these feelings in a work group he asked members to rank their choices of people with whom they would like to work or not to work. The person receiving the most votes is the star or sociometric leader. This person is the one liked the most, but is not necessarily the true informal leader who motivates the group to take action. The star can make or break a social fad, but he may be secondary to someone else in leading

[5] Delbert C. Miller and William H. Form, *Industrial Sociology*, New York: Harper & Brothers, 1951, pp. 282–283.

the group toward a work goal. When the patterns of feelings are charted, the result is a sociogram. Sociometric rankings have been used to build work teams to achieve better teamwork and efficiency. In one instance carpenters and bricklayers were organized into sociometrically selected

FIGURE 6-1

TYPES OF INFORMAL GROUPS

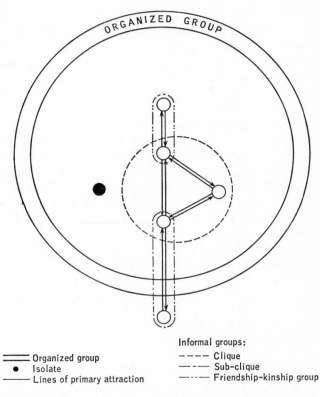

Informal groups:

═══ Organized group
● Isolate
─── Lines of primary attraction

─ ─ ─ Clique
─ ⋅─ Sub-clique
─ ⋅⋅─ Friendship-kinship group

teams, which reduced their labor cost index from 36.66 to 32.22 and the materials cost index from 33.00 to 31.00 during the eleven-month period after the teams were organized. The over-all result was a saving of five per cent in total production costs, plus more satisfied workers.[6]

Another charting approach is to diagram the actual informal interactions of people, such as with whom one spends the most time and with whom one checks when he does not check with his supervisor. Charts of these relationships are usually called interpersonal charts, interaction

───────────

[6] Raymond H. Van Zelst, "Sociometrically Selected Work Teams Increase Production," *Personnel Psychology,* Autumn, 1952, pp. 175–185. See also "Foremen by Popular Acclaim," *Business Week,* March 26, 1955, pp. 171–172.

charts, or informal organization charts. These interaction patterns can be superimposed on the formal organization chart in order to show variation between the two. This is illustrated in Figure 6-2, from a study made by the author. Superimposed on the formal chart are lines showing the patterns of contact which developed from an event known to the man-

FIGURE 6-2

PATTERNS OF CONTACT ABOUT AN EVENT KNOWN TO MANAGERS IN POSITIONS 27 AND 234

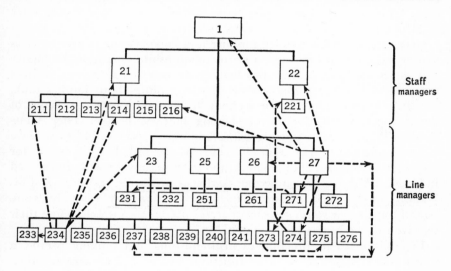

agers in positions 27 and 234. Most of these contacts were neither with a direct supervisor nor direct subordinates. Contacts were largely *outside* the direct chains of command. Some of these contacts were required by procedure and were consequently formal, but a large portion of them were informal.

Surveys of employees to determine their interpersonal contacts are called *contactual surveys*. These surveys show informal and procedural relationships and aid management in the following ways: [7]

1. Checking and charting the informal organization
2. Making plans to change organization or procedures
3. Setting up management controls
4. Solving communication problems
5. Locating people who are active communicators and/or facilitate action
6. Locating persons with leadership potential

[7] William B. Seiniger, "Charting the Informal Organization," *Advanced Management*, November, 1951, pp. 24–27.

STATUS

Status refers to the social rank of a person in comparison with others. There are two kinds of status, formal and informal. Formal status refers to the relation of supervisor and subordinate as designated by the chain of command in any organization. Informal status refers to the social rank which others accord to a person because of their feelings toward him. It is the position which one has in a social system. Since this chapter concerns informal organization, the term "status" used hereafter will refer to informal status unless the context implies otherwise.

Status relationships require ranking and comparison. It always takes two or more persons to make a status relationship. One must be higher and the other lower. Status also has certain external markings, such as fancy desks. These are the symbols of status. Since status implies rank, people in business are concerned about it. The desire for status is one of the strongest motivating factors among business people. They sometimes will make unreasonable effort and sacrifice in order to achieve slightly more status. The term "lose face" is often used as a synonym for loss of status in personal interaction, and its seriousnss is widely recognized in business. When a person becomes seriously upset over his status and his inability to change it, he is said to have *status anxiety*. Individuals are bound together in *status systems* or *status hierarchies*, which define their relative rank to others in the system.

In addition to its function of distinguishing and ranking people, a status system serves three other functions in the business organization. First, it provides a framework for communication and cooperation. Second, it is a basic means of giving people a sense of responsibility. Loss of status is more than loss of prestige. It seriously affects personality. People, therefore, become quite responsible in order to protect and develop their status. Barnard comments, "The desire for improvement of status and especially the desire to protect status appears to be the basis of a sense of general responsibility." [8] Third, and related to responsibility, is the incentive function of status. Since status is important to people, they will work hard to achieve it. Many will seek it for its own sake, even if it provides no additional pay, improved working conditions, or other tangible benefits. When status is attached to actions which further the company's goals, strong incentives are released toward their accomplishment.

By way of illustration, a laundry manager used to devote negative attention and reprimand (low status) to workers whom he found idle, even when they had

[8] Chester I. Barnard, "Functions and Pathology of Status Systems in Formal Organizations," in William F. Whyte, ed., *Industry and Society,* New York: McGraw-Hill Book Company, Inc., 1946, p. 69.

finished their work and were waiting for more from another operator. He wanted them to help other operators, but he found that his approach simply caused them to work slower. Upon reexamination of his approach, he decided to try to build the status of his "idle" employees who finished their work ahead of others. He visited with them in a friendly way as he walked through his shop. He permitted them to go to any other work station to talk and visit, or to get soft drinks for themselves or others. The slow workers began to work faster to achieve this status, and the fast workers improved in order to preserve their relative position. As the fast workers visited other work stations they developed friendships and did considerable informal training and helping of the slow workers. The manager later commented, "I am amazed by the changed attitudes of the workers and their increased productivity."

The importance of status requires management to give attention to how it arises and whether management actions affect it. The total causes of status probably stretch to infinity, because each situation is different. There are, however, several status causes generally found in most business situations, such as age, working conditions, and type of work done. A factor such as age cannot be changed by management, but its influence on status can be modified. Other factors such as working conditions can be somewhat changed.

In-company Causes of Status

Following are some of the status influences which occur within a company.

Organizational Level. A basic cause of informal status is the rank which a person has in the formal organization. Higher formal rank places him in a position to make decisions about others and to initiate action affecting them. It places one "closer to the top." If people with lamps on their desks originate action on people without desk lamps, then desk lamps eventually become symbols of status. A person who acquires a desk lamp augments his status at the same time, even though he does not initiate action on others. Consequently company desk lamps become sought after, and some persons may even offer to buy their own lamps if the company cannot supply them. Status of a particular level attaches also to those who closely assist that level. The secretary to a vice-president usually has more status than the secretary to a department head.

Type and Level of Skill. Society generally attaches more status to mental skills than to physical skills, but this relationship is further affected by the skill level which is applied. An unskilled machine operator tends to have less status than an unskilled clerk, but a skilled toolmaker will have more status than the unskilled clerk. The toolmaker acquires his status by virtue of his high skill, even though his work is considered to be largely physical by those who accord him status. Status is also

affected by the amount of formal education and effort which was required
to prepare for the job.

Sometimes an "insignificant" detail such as the material used affects
status. W. F. Whyte in his study of the restaurant industry discovered
that cooks who prepare chicken have higher status than those who prepare meat, and that within the zone of chicken preparation the informal
scale of jobs falls from white meat to dark meat! [9] These relationships tend
to exist even when the pay and working conditions are almost identical.

Working Conditions. Better working conditions generally accord higher
status to the person having them. This is one of the reasons white-collar
jobs throughout the world usually carry more status than blue-collar jobs
of equal skill. Most people seem to prefer such white-collar surroundings
as soft chairs, air conditioning, and clean hands. Because these things are
sought after and there is limited supply relative to demand for them,
they eventually achieve higher status. In this respect the status *value*
given to different conditions has a supply-and-demand relationship similar
to that in economics. When supply is small relative to demand, high
status value is attached. When the supply is adequate relative to demand,
status value will be less. To illustrate, in an office where a few people
are accorded desk pads they may become important status symbols, but
when everyone gets desk pads, they assume less status value and the group
starts looking for some other way to distinguish their members. As one
status symbol becomes generally available to everyone and therefore no
longer a mark of distinction, another status symbol will arise to take its
place, because the group exhibits a basic need to distinguish its members. The result is that status symbols vary somewhat from department
to department, company to company, and time to time.

Pay. Skill level, working conditions, and other factors determine pay,
which in itself becomes a symbol of status. In any work group, status
hierarchies are built around differences in pay, and any disturbance of
this hierarchy by job evaluation or incentives may produce major dis-
ruptions in the social system. When management revises wage scales, it
does not simply change a job rate, but it also changes the informal rank
of people.

Even the way that pay is computed has its status implications. It is a
real mark of distinction to graduate from time-clock punching to merely
signing a weekly time sheet. Even more status is achieved when a person
makes no time report at all. In a similar way, great prestige is attached
in some companies to a listing on the semimonthly payroll instead of the
weekly payroll, even though the pay check received is identical.

Seniority. Being an oldtimer in a company usually merits higher status
than do the newcomers. Having been there longer, the oldtimer "knows

[9] William F. Whyte, *Human Relations in the Restaurant Industry*, New York: Mc-
Graw-Hill Book Company, Inc., 1948, pp. 33–46.

the ropes" and is in position to assume informal leadership of the new-comers. His group has also secured certain seniority privileges, either through formal agreement with management or as a matter of custom. Some of these privileges seek to protect his job security, because he recognizes that older workers tend to have more difficulty finding employment. Other privileges are purely for personal convenience and status. Vacation dates, overtime, day-shift work, and other privileges are awarded by seniority. Management sometimes permits these practices to exist even when they are detrimental to the company.

Shift preferences were determined by seniority in one firm with the result that nearly all experienced personnel were on the first shift. The night shift suffered greatly from lack of technically qualified men, but management chose not to upset this long-established situation. Night-shift productivity was only 80 per cent of the day shift's. Even foremen and superintendents were assigned shifts by seniority, which gave the night shift young, inexperienced leadership.

External Status Causes

A worker's status is not wholly determined in the company. There are external cultural factors which affect the rank of people in the company social system.

Age. Though related to seniority, age has an influence all its own. Age is a physiological measurement, but it has its social significance. Younger workers often "look up" to older workers, partly as a carryover of the father-son relationship. Older workers tend to have mutual interests and associate closely.

Sex. Custom in each plant has decreed certain jobs for men and others for women. Especially in factory work, a woman sometimes is thought to be an intruder who is taking a job away from a man, and is consequently rejected and given secondary status. There is a secular trend toward equal work status for women, but differences still exist.

Racial and Cultural Status. Social status of a particular racial or cultural group outside the plant affects the status of that entire group in the informal organization. Many business units are located in a *plural community,* which is defined as one in which distinctly different racial or cultural groups coexist within one over-all political and economic unit without mingling in the other aspects of their daily lives.[10] One example is a community having native-born workers and immigrants who cling strongly to customs of the "old country." The group with lesser status in the community will tend to have lesser status in the plant.

In a plural community management must learn to interpret some of its in-plant problems in the light of existing social distinctions in the community. Each worker brings to the work situation a set of viewpoints

[10] Cyril Sofer, "Working Groups in a Plural Society," *Industrial and Labor Relations Review,* 1954, p. 68.

and feelings conditioned by the place his group occupies in the whole society. He reacts to his supervisors, subordinates, and co-workers partly as an individual and partly as representative of the different groups to which he belongs. They, in turn, react to him the same way. A business which enters a community with distinctly different racial or cultural groups will find that its human relations problems are made tougher by preexisting conditions. Though the firm did not cause these conditions, it may be blamed for permitting them to continue at work, because they are fundamentally not related to jobs. The firm is sometimes unrealistically blamed because, although it can ignore racial or cultural differences on the job, they still exist in the minds of men and will continue to influence the informal organization. Management's practical responsibility, therefore, is to make a precise compromise between recognizing differences and not recognizing them.

In one company, a certain culture of immigrants and their descendants had always held all of the foundry jobs. Other members of the community were just as capable of learning foundry work. At no time did management prohibit outsiders from taking foundry work because it felt that would open it to a charge of discrimination, but it did discourage others from taking foundry work to the extent that foundry work largely remained the special vocation of a certain cultural group.

Occupational Status. A job's status within a plant is partly affected by the general prestige rating of that occupation among the public. This general prestige rating is the one which a company should expect for its jobs, except where there are significant in-plant factors to cause variation. A study of 90 occupations based on 2,920 interviews with a representative sample of people, showed that the highest rankings were U.S. Supreme Court Justice, physician, and state governor, in that order. Lowest ranked jobs were garbage collector, street sweeper, and shoe shiner. The occupational status of selected business jobs, indicated by rank from the top, follows: member of the board of directors of a large corporation, 18; accountant for a large business, 29; official of an international labor union, 40.5; electrician or trained machinist, 45; carpenter, 58; local official of a labor union, 62; machine operator in a factory, 64.5; and janitor, 85.5. People were generally consistent in the ratings, except that they rated their own and related occupations higher than others did.[11]

Occupational status is significant to human relations in several ways. It often helps a counselor diagnose status problems and conflicts. It definitely influences the employee's reaction to promotion, transfer, and wage administration. In general, employees expect pay to be positively related to status, especially within each promotion hierarchy. A machine opera-

[11] Carroll L. Shartle, *Occupational Information,* 2d ed., Englewood Cliffs N.J.: Prentice-Hall, Inc., 1952, pp. 114–117.

tor, for example, expects each job on his promotional route to give him higher status as well as pay. If management's job-evaluation scheme gives higher pay to a lower-status job, he may not want to promote to it even though it pays more. Occupational status also helps determine who will be informal leader of a group composed of different occupations. It definitely serves as a motivation to those seeking to advance in the organization. Some persons are status seekers, wanting a job of high status regardless of its other conditions. These persons can be encouraged to qualify themselves for high-status jobs so that they can become better adjusted— or their level of aspiration must be lowered.

Status of an Industry. Just as occupations have status, so does any industry. People attach more status to one industry than to another, which tends to affect recruiting for that industry. It probably also affects job satisfaction because a worker tends to be sensitive about what his friends and neighbors think about the industry that employs him. A study by Brayfield shows that men and women college students generally agreed on the rank of an industry, which indicates that industry status is not materially influenced by sex. Each industry's status attached to all jobs of its employees, because it was largely unaffected by whether a respondent considered himself a manager or a laborer in the industry. This means, for example, that a vice-president in an industry ranked 4th would tend to have higher community social status than one in an industry ranked 7th or 13th. The same would be true for a laborer. The five industries with highest status were, in order of rank: medical services, banks, education, Federal government, and farming.[12]

Symbols of Status

The status system of business reaches the ultimate of observable evidence with its *status symbols*. These are the visible, external trappings which attach to a man's person or workplace and serve as evidence of his social rank. They exist in the office, shop, warehouse, refinery, or wherever work groups congregate. They are most in evidence among different levels of executives because each successive level usually has the authority to provide itself with surroundings just a little different from those lower in the structure.

In one office the size and type of wastebasket is a mark of distinction. In another, significant symbols are type of desk, stapling machines, and telephones. In the executive offices, such paraphernalia of rank as rugs, bookcases, curtains, and pictures on the wall are important.

All of this concern for symbols of status seems amusing, and at times it is, as illustrated by Figures 6-3 and 6-4. Managers enjoy poking fun at themselves, but at other times status symbols are a deadly serious prob-

[12] Arthur H. Brayfield, Carroll E. Kennedy, Jr., and William E. Kendall, "Social Status of Industries," *Journal of Applied Psychology*, August, 1954, pp. 213–215.

FIGURE 6-3

A READY GUIDE FOR EVALUATING EXECUTIVES, OR R-H-I-P. IN USE BY CHEMISTS, ENGINEERS, TRAINEES, AND STUDENTS THROUGHOUT THE GENERAL OFFICE—HUNDREDS OF SATISFIED USERS

Visible appurtenances	Top dogs	V.I.P.s	Brass	No. 2s	Eager beavers	Hoi polloi
Brief cases	None—they ask the questions	Use backs of envelopes	Someone goes along to carry theirs	Carry their own—empty	Daily—carry their own—filled with work	Too poor to own one
Desks, Office	Custom made (to order)	Executive Style (to order)	Type A "Director"	Type B "Manager"	Cast offs from No. 2s	Yellow Oak— or cast-offs from Eager Beavers
Tables, Office	Coffee tables	End tables or decorative wall tables	Matching tables Type A	Matching tables Type B	Plain work table	None—lucky to have own desk
Carpeting	Nylon— 1 inch pile	Nylon— 1 inch pile	Wool-Twist (with pad)	Wool-Twist (without pad)	Used wool pieces—sewed	Asphalt tile
Plant stands	Several—Kept filled with strange exotic plants		Two—repotted whenever they take a trip	One medium-sized Repotted annually during vacation	Small Repotted when plant dies	May have one in the department or bring their own from home
Vacuum water bottles	Silver	Silver	Chromium	Plain painted	Coke machine	Water fountains
Library	Private collection	Autographed or complimentary books and reports	Selected references	Impressive titles on covers	Books everywhere	Dictionary
Shoe Shine Service	Every morning at 10:00	Every morning at 10:15	Every day at 9:00 or 11:00	Every other day	Once a week	Shine their own
Parking space	Private, in front of office	In plant garage	In company garage— if enough seniority	In company properties— somewhere	On the parking lot	Anywhere they can find a space—if they can afford a car
Luncheon menu	Cream cheese on Whole Wheat Buttermilk and Indigestion Tablets	Cream of Celery Soup Chicken Sandwich (White Meat) Milk	Fruit Cup - Spinach Lamb Chop - Peas Ice Cream - Tea	Orange Juice Minute Steak French Fries - Salad Fruit Cup Coffee	Tomato Juice Chicken Croquettes Mashed Potatoes Peas - Bread Chocolate Cream Pie Coffee	Clam Chowder Frankfurter and Beans Rolls and Butter Raisin Pie A'la Mode Two Cups of Coffee

Used with permission of the author, K. B. Bernhardt.

FIGURE 6-4

A HUMOROUS DESCRIPTION OF OFFICE STATUS PROBLEMS

TOTEMISM AND PROTOCOL IN THE AMERICAN ENTERPRISE SYSTEM

This is the way it is in offices:

First you start at desks that are
huddled together back to back with
barely squeeze room between them

     Then you work

     at desks that

     all face the

     same way and

     are neatly spaced.

And if yours occupies a space by

        ITSELF

all know that you must be a
Senior whatever-it-is
till the rare day when you ascend
to the Supervisory or Middle Management level
and get a desk that is *catty-cornered.*

(If you never get another promotion, of course, in due time
you will even get
(*catty-cornered desk.*)
a fence around your
But if you are reasonably happy in your choice of adjectives
you may look forward to achieving
    AN OFFICE OF YOUR OWN
with your name on the frosted panes that extend to eye level,
all above being clear glass; for you will never get a solidly
walled-in office until you are in like Flynn and have become a

       w
    !   h
    l   e
     e

SOURCE: By I. H. E. Otto, Reproduced with permission of the American Management Association, *Management Review*, April, 1953, p. 186.

lem. They endanger morale because an executive who does not have a certain symbol and thinks he should, can become a gloomy, nervous man. They lead to conflict, because executives vie with each other to get particular symbols. And finally, symbols can affect the company budget if executives try to acquire too many of them. One writer comments: "If one vice-president hangs a few abstract oil paintings on his walls, and bills the company, what's to keep the other seven V.-P.'s from doing the same and turning the shop into an annex of the Museum of Modern Art?" [13]

Since symbols of status exist in every company, a manager needs to be alert to them. They will serve as a disruptive force or as positive motivation, depending on the skill with which management handles the problem. When, for example, an employee gives unreasonable attention to status symbols, this is evidence of status anxiety which requires management attention. Status symbols seem to be growing in importance in modern business. They are becoming a larger part of the over-all "compensation" which an executive receives. Income-tax structure prevents a company from giving an executive large increases in spendable income, but the trappings of status which it can provide are almost unlimited. Evidence already exists that executives, as well as workers, do respond to status motivation.

What should be management's policy toward status symbols? Some managers go so far as to deny the existence of status symbols in their firms, but this is hardly realistic. Others allow symbols to develop as a part of tradition. It is understood that when a corner office becomes vacant the next man in line gets it, and so on, but nothing is put in writing. This policy works under conditions of stability, but a move to a new office building may so upset relationships that there has to be some codifying of the rules. Codification reduces friction, is the most efficient way to allocate space, and gives positive budget control over symbol purchases, but it also smacks of regimentation. Regardless of which approach is used, the rule usually is that executives of equal rank in the same department receive approximately equal status symbols. There may be some variation between broad departments, such as production and sales, because work is distinctly different and rank is not so easily comparable. In any case, managers face the fact that status exists and must be dealt with. They do have the power to influence and control status relationships somewhat.

SOCIAL GROUPS IN INDUSTRY

Of all the influences on status, type and skill of work and level of work are probably the most important. They are the primary determinants of

[13] "The Big Puzzle: Who Gets How Much of What," *Business Week*, October 16, 1954, p. 66.

the five broad social groups typically found in any business large enough for these distinctions to be made. The groups are: [14]

Top managers
Middle managers and supervisors
Technical and professional workers
Office and clerical workers
Shop workers

Members of each group have common interests, possess similar status, tend to associate together, and so on. Their problems and relationships are discussed throughout this text.

The Wives of Management

In addition to the five company social groups, there is a sixth semi-company group—the wives of employees, especially of management. Although they are not employees, they are sometimes interviewed and screened when their husbands are employed or promoted.[15] They are increasingly being invited to orientation programs, and company parties are definitely swinging toward including wives. This is concrete evidence that companies consider them a significant part of the company informal organization. Their influence is felt in several ways:

1. They are a chain of communication to other managers through their wives.

2. They are a part of many company social functions for employees, executives, and customers.

3. Their attitudes will significantly affect the job performance of their husbands.

The wife's role is assumed to be that of helping her husband progress upward in the corporation. She is expected to be a gracious hostess and social agent. She should be gregarious and eager to make "constructive friendships" appropriate to her husband's place in the social structure at that time. As he moves upward in the corporation, she too should be easily mobile to new friends, new neighborhoods, and new modes of social life. She needs to be understanding of the stringent requirements, such as night work and travel, which the firm makes of her spouse.

Since the wife is not an employee, the corporate demands on her which have just been described can be easily overdone. It is evident that she should be motivated toward these requirements, rather than coerced. To do otherwise might result in an informal revolt and do more harm than good. Further, there are ethical questions concerning just how much the

[14] F. J. Roethlisberger, *Management and Morale*, Cambridge: Harvard University Press, 1941, pp. 35–36.

[15] "Roughly half the companies on which *Fortune* has data have made wife-screening a regular practice and many others seem ready to do so." William H. Whyte, Jr., "The Corporation and the Wife," *Fortune*, November, 1951, p. 109.

corporation should expect of one only informally related to it. Neither is the husband a twenty-four-hour servant of the firm, and his family life for the most part is beyond the scope of his employer's control. It is clear that too much control produces uniformity and regimentation, and tends to destroy the individualism and freedom which corporate leadership professes to support. It is quite true that management needs to be concerned about the wife because she affects the firm; but management cannot expect to control everything which affects its operations!

CONTROL OF INFORMAL ORGANIZATION

It has been noted that management did not put informal organization in business, and neither can management take it away. Nor would it want to do so. But management can exercise a measure of control. Since the informal organization operates during work as well as away, management exercises partial control over it by such means as what management communicates, what people are permitted to work close together, and how management recognizes informal leaders. Management's job is:

1. To let employees know that management accepts and understands informal organization

2. To influence it (exercise a measure of control over it)

3. To control it so that its interests and objectives are integrated with those of the formal organization

4. To keep formal activities from unnecessarily threatening or disrupting it

The formal organization has one set of values and system of evaluating people. The informal has another. If these two evaluation systems are far apart there will be conflict. Pace of work serves as an example. If the informal codes of behavior give high status to the low producer who restricts work and if formal management standards give high status and wages to high producers in accordance with an incentive plan, then the two evaluation systems are far apart and conflict is certain. If the two evaluation systems can be brought into closer agreement, there tends to be less conflict and better morale and productivity in accordance with the principle of informal organization. This is management's control objective with informal organization.

Management in order to maintain control is cautious to keep informal organization secondary to the formal organization. Arguments have been advanced that when formal management is incompetent an *overriding* informal organization is necessary and desirable in order to keep the group working effectively. The statement, "We get along here in spite of the boss, rather than because of him," is descriptive of actual situations. But is this desirable? Normally it is better to discover incompetent leadership early, because informal leadership will not forever keep the group on a course toward the formal objective. Sooner or later formal and informal interests will conflict and then formal authority is needed to resolve the conflict. This concept, which is widely accepted in management, may be stated as follows: *Considering all an organization's activities, formal organization should be the primary control, although certain single activities may be primarily controlled informally.*

THE PERSONALITY OF A BUSINESS

Formal and informal organization, as they are adapted to meet the changing environment, give to each business a personality, just like a person has. This personality is sometimes called *organizational charter.*[16] Each company has its own culture, traditions, and characteristic methods of action. Some companies are bustling and efficient, others are easygoing. Some are quite human, others are hard and cold. They change slowly, being influenced by their leaders and their environment. Like people, some are more susceptible to change than others. A company tends to attract and keep people who fit its personality so that its patterns are to some extent perpetuated. A certain manufacturing company serves as an illustration. Its management stresses seniority, centralized control, and cautious decisions. It has difficulty attracting and retaining young, educated men with promotion potential. What else could be expected? Men of this personality do not fit the company's pattern of living, *its personality*. In order to achieve maximum results, managers as they deal with human problems in a business need to know that firm's particular personality pattern, just as they need also to know an individual worker's personality.

SUMMARY

Informal organization exists permanently with business because it arises from the interaction of people. Along with formal controls, it influences human behavior at work and is consequently of concern to management. It is indirectly subject to some management control. The basic control objective in this instance is to integrate closely the long-run interests of the formal and informal systems so that they will operate to evaluate and reward people in about the same way.

Rank of people in informal organization is determined by their status. There are innumerable causes of status both within and without a business. Various physical surroundings become associated with a certain status and therefore become symbols of that status. Like magical herbs these symbols are much sought after because they distinguish one person

[16] E. W. Bakke, *The Fusion Process*, New Haven: Labor and Management Center, Yale University, 1955, p. 9.

from another and are supposed to accord status to their possessor. Groups with similar status constitute the broad social groups in industry: managers, supervisors, shop workers, office workers, and professional people. A semi-company group is the wives of employees.

Formal and informal organization together give a company its personality as it interacts with other influences. In many companies the major additional human relations influence is a second formal and informal organization—the union.

Motivation: The Core of Management*

Rensis Likert

It is widely recognized that there are large differences in the productive efficiency of different companies. Even within a company there are usually substantial differences in productivity among the different plants or departments. These differences in productivity are often due to differences in managerial policy and practice.

There is too little information on what a good management does that makes the difference between high and low productivity, between high and low employee morale. American business is spending millions of dollars every year applying the scientific method to product development and the improvement of production methods, but it is not similarly applying its resources to discover how the most effective managers and supervisors function and how their principles and practices can be applied more generally.

The Institute for Social Research of the University of Michigan is one of the few organizations conducting systematic research on this problem.[1] It is trying to find what makes an organization tick; trying to discover the principles of organizational structure and the principles and practices of leadership that are responsible for high productivity and high job satisfaction.

The Institute program is designed to provide a mirror for business so that it can see in its own operations and experience what works best and why. Studies have been conducted or are under way in a wide variety of organizations. These include public utilities, an insurance company, an automotive company, a heavy machinery factory, a railroad, an electric appliance factory, and some government agencies. The work of the organizations studied has varied from highly routine clerical and assembly operations to complex scientific research.

One of the basic concepts underlying this research is that no matter

* Reprinted by permission of the publisher from *Motivation: The Core of Management,* Personnel Series, no. 155 (New York: American Management Association, 1953), pp. 3–21. Mr. Likert is Director of the Institute for Social Research and Professor in both the Psychology and Sociology Departments at the University of Michigan.

[1] This program was started by a contract with the Office of Naval Research. Since its initiation, business organization and governmental agencies, as well as ONR, have contributed to its support.

how varied the task—whether in government, industry, or any part of the military organization—there are common fundamental principles applicable to the effective organization of human activity. In addition to these general principles, there may be specific principles that apply to particular types of work—such as selling, as opposed to office management. But the philosophy behind this whole program of research is that scientifically valid data can be obtained which will enable us to state general principles. Once we know the general principles, we must learn how to transfer them from one situation to another. We are doing this research at all levels of organization—not only at the employee level and the small-unit level but at the plant level and the company level. We expect that some principles will carry right on through; others will be specific, perhaps, for the different levels or parts of an organization.

In carrying forward this program of research, two major criteria have been used to evaluate administrative effectiveness:

1. Productivity per man-hour or some similar measure of the organization's success in achieving its productivity goals.

2. The job satisfaction and other satisfactions derived by employees or members of the group.

The results being obtained show that a consistent pattern of motivational principles and their application is associated with high productivity and high job satisfaction, irrespective of the particular company or industry in which the study is conducted. I shall present some of these results and briefly summarize some of the generalizations that are emerging from this research.

FACTORS IN HIGH AND LOW PRODUCTIVITY

There are some factors which are commonly assumed to increase productivity but which, when actual results are examined, are found not to be related to productivity or else to have a negligible relationship. Thus we are finding very little relationship, *within a company,* between employees' attitudes toward the company and their productivity. The more productive employees or sections do not have appreciably more favorable attitudes than do the less productive employees. Chart 1 illustrates the

CHART 1

RELATION OF ATTITUDE TOWARD COMPANY AND PRODUCTIVITY

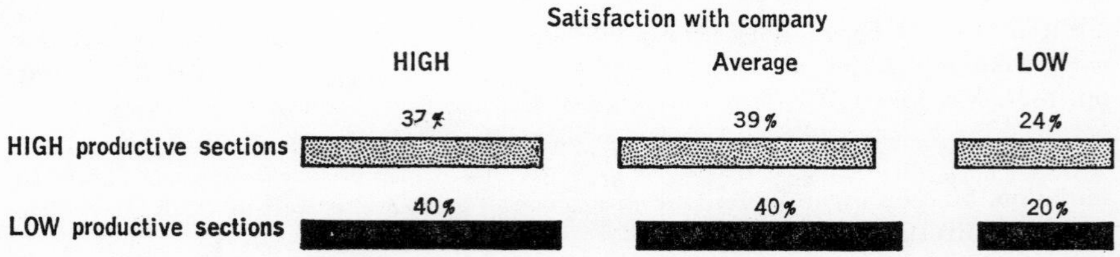

Satisfaction with company

	HIGH	Average	LOW
HIGH productive sections	37%	39%	24%
LOW productive sections	40%	40%	20%

pattern of relationship that we are finding. The common assumption that developing a favorable attitude among employees toward the company will result in increased productivity does not seem to be warranted.

A favorable over-all attitude toward one's company and job does result in less absence from the job. I suspect also that it may result in less turnover and may attract a better labor force in a tight labor market, but we do not yet have any data on these points.

Illustrative, again, of the kind of variables that show no relationship to productivity or even a negative relationship is the material in Chart 2.

CHART 2

PARTICIPATION IN COMPANY RECREATIONAL ACTIVITIES

	Frequently	Occasionally	Never
HIGH productive sections	8%	20%	72%
LOW productive sections	7%	34%	58%

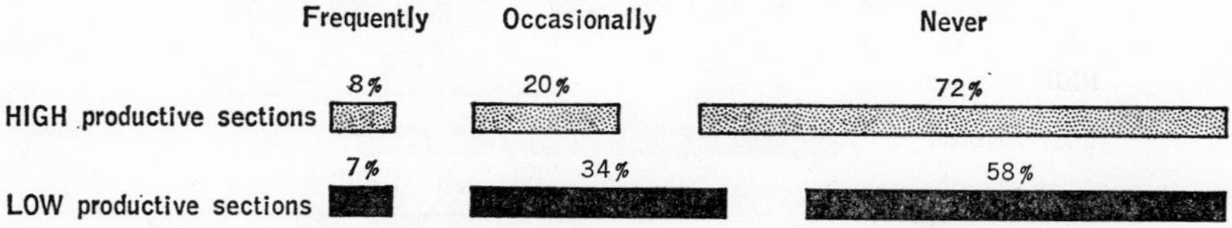

We are finding, in some situations at least, that there is a negative relationship between the extent to which employees participate in a recreational program and their productivity. The less productive sections participate in recreational activities more often than do those sections that are more productive.

THE SUPERVISOR: EMPLOYEE-CENTERED OR PRODUCTION-CENTERED

In contrast to these patterns involving factors of a nonpersonal nature, we are consistently finding that there is a marked relationship between the kind of supervision an employee receives and both his productivity and the satisfactions which he derives from his work. When the worker (or a person at any level in a hierarchy) feels that his boss sees him only as an instrument of production, as merely a cog in a machine, he is likely to be a poor producer. However, when he feels that his boss is genuinely interested in him, his problems, his future, and his well-being, he is more likely to be a high producer. Some typical results are shown in Chart 3.

The employee-centered supervisor not only trains people to do their present job well but tends to train them for the next higher job. He is interested in helping them with their problems on the job and off the job.

The following illustrations represent typical viewpoints of supervisors whom we have classified as employee-centered or production-centered:

Employee-centered supervisors are those who describe their work as did this one:

I've tried to help my girls in getting better jobs and to get advanced, but there're so few positions for them to go to. That's why I teach them how to supervise. A lot of my girls are assistant section heads today.

In spite of the fact that this supervisor has promoted many of her ablest girls to better positions, she still has a high-production section. By giving her girls supervisory experience or letting one of them supervise two or three others in small groups, she builds effective teamwork and a friendly, cooperative atmosphere.

CHART 3

"EMPLOYEE-CENTERED" SUPERVISORS ARE HIGHER PRODUCERS THAN "PRODUCTION-CENTERED" SUPERVISORS

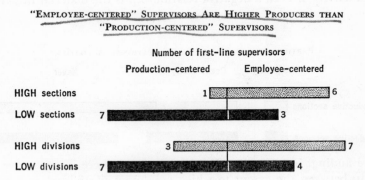

Another supervisor, also employee-centered, commented as follows:

I study the girls' work, find out who works together and put them together. The main thing is to keep the girls happy. I talk with them and learn what their peculiarities are so that if a girl gets excited, I know whether it is important or not. Your girls have to feel that you are one of them, not the boss. Some girls get sort of cranky, and you can't just say, "Do it." It is much better to ask them to do the work in other ways; that's only human nature.

Another employee-centered section head commented as follows:

I try to understand each girl. I remember I was one once and that I liked to be the kind that was known by my supervisor. Knowing the girls helps with handling the work here. You also have to know what happens outside to help them inside here at their work.

In contrast, this comment is illustrative of the attitude of a production-centered supervisor in charge of a low-production section:

I know we're doing what is supposed to be done in our section. Hit the work in and out—and hit it right—not slipshod.

Another production-oriented, low-producing section head commented as follows:

It is my job to get the employee to stay on the job and produce. I have to work up efficiency charts. My efficiency chart is my argument if I have to make any complaint. My biggest headache is to get the employees to do their best.

Still another production-centered supervisor commented as follows:

The girls sometimes stop work before the bell rings; I have been after them and I keep them overtime to do the work. You have to do something drastic and make examples of them.

PRODUCTIVITY AND CLOSENESS OF SUPERVISION

Related to pressing for production is the *closeness* of supervision that a person experiences. Close supervision tends to be associated with lower productivity and more general supervision with higher productivity. This relationship is shown in Chart 4.

CHART 4

LOW-PRODUCTION SECTION HEADS ARE MORE CLOSELY SUPERVISED
THAN ARE HIGH-PRODUCTION HEADS

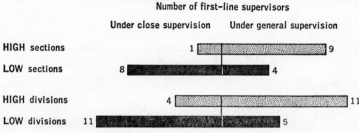

Low productivity may at times lead to closer supervision, but it is clear that it may also cause low productivity. In one of the companies involved in this research program it has been found that switching managers of high- and low-production division results in the high-production managers raising the productivity of the low-production divisions faster than the former high-production divisions slip under the low-production managers. Supervisors, as they are shifted from job to job, tend to carry with them and to maintain their habitual attitudes toward the supervisory process and toward their subordinates. This suggests that supervisory attitudes and habits tend to be the causal influence. For example, an assistant manager of a low-production department, in discussing his situation, said, "This interest-in-people approach is all right, but it is a luxury. I've got to keep pressure on for production, and when I get production up then I can afford to take time to show an interest in my employees and their problems." Being under pressure for increased production, and being primarily concerned with it, seem to cause supervisors to neglect important human dimensions of the supervisory process which in the long run determine the production of their groups.

Heads of low-producing sections seem to recognize that close supervision adversely affects their work. They show more dissatisfaction with the way their job is organized than do high-producing section heads and give as the reason for this dissatisfaction "too little delegation of authority."

In studying the results one gets the impression that persons who use general supervision tend more often to specify the goal or tasks to be accomplished and give subordinates some leeway in how it is accomplished. Persons using close supervision, however, are more likely to specify the precise activities of subordinates. Those using general supervision may, of course, make available to subordinates the resources of work simplification, etc., but do not specify in every detail precisely how they will be used.

When people are given general supervision, it is necessary to keep them well-informed. As shown in Chart 5, supervisors in charge of high-production groups report more often that they are kept informed about developments than do supervisors in charge of low-production groups.

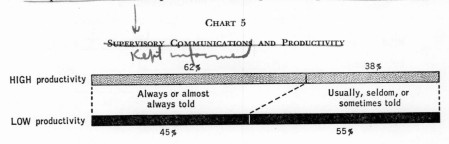

CHART 5

SUPERVISORY COMMUNICATIONS AND PRODUCTIVITY

We are finding conflicting patterns of relationship between morale and productivity. In some situations there is high morale and high productivity; in others we find high morale and low productivity or the converse. There are good reasons for these variations, and they are related to the kind of supervision that exists. But the significant finding for this discussion is that the kind of supervision which results in the highest productivity also results in the highest morale. Thus, for example, employee-centered supervision produces high levels of job satisfaction as well as high productivity.

Chart 6 illustrates the kind of findings being obtained. Where work groups with the highest and lowest morale were asked to describe what their supervisors did, the results were as shown in Chart 6. The workers in low-morale groups mentioned just as often as workers in high-morale groups that their supervisors performed such production-centered tasks as "enforces the rules," "arranges work and makes work assignments," and "supplies men with materials and tools." But the high-morale groups mentioned much more frequently than the low such employee-centered functions as "recommends promotions and pay increases," "informs men

CHART 6

PERCENTAGES OF HIGH AND LOW MORALE GROUPS DESCRIBING
WHAT THEIR SUPERVISORS DO

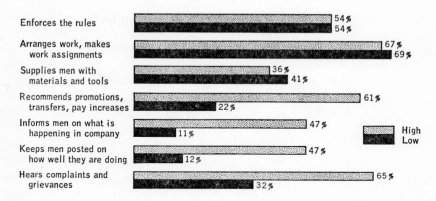

on what is happening in the company," "keeps men posted on how well they are doing," and "hears complaints and grievances." [2]

IMPORTANCE OF THE GROUP RELATIONSHIP

Books on management and administration tend to deal with the relationship between superior and subordinates, between supervisors and employees, as *individuals*. Research on management similarly has tended to focus on the relationship between the superior and the subordinates as individuals. We are encountering increasing evidence, however, that the superior's skill in supervising his subordinates *as a group* is an important variable affecting his success: the greater his skill in using group methods of supervision, the greater are the productivity and job satisfaction of the work group.

Chart 7 shows the relationship between the feeling that the "company is interested in employees' ideas and suggestions" and the level of employee morale. For both blue-collar and white-collar workers, there is a marked relationship between worker morale and how much employees feel that their boss is interested in discussing work problems with the work group.

Another important and striking relationship is shown in Chart 8. Foremen of high-production work groups report much more frequently than the foremen of low-production groups that their work groups perform well when they, the foremen, are absent. High-production supervisors,

[2] In this discussion the term "morale" is used as meaning the total satisfactions the individual derives from his work situation. It is not being used as synonymous with the degree to which the individual is motivated to do his work.

CHART 7

RELATIONS OF EMPLOYEE MORALE TO FEELING THAT COMPANY IS INTERESTED IN
EMPLOYEES' IDEAS AND SUGGESTIONS

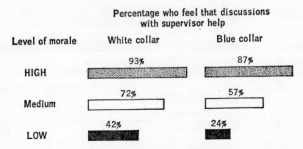

through group methods of supervision, apparently develop within the
work group the expectation and capacity to function effectively whether
the foreman is present or not. This ability to function well in the absence
of the supervisor is, no doubt, one of the reasons for the greater productivity of the high-production groups.

CHART 8

HIGH-PRODUCTIVITY WORK GROUPS PERFORM WELL WHEN FOREMAN IS ABSENT

Chart 9 shows the relationship between group pride (or loyalty) and
group productivity. The high-production groups show greater group
loyalty and greater group pride than do the low-production groups. We
are finding that this relationship holds for many kinds of groups and
many kinds of work. In Chart 9, for example, "Situation I" deals with
clerical workers and "Situation II" deals with maintenance-of-way crews
on a railroad.

In the study of the clerical operations, the workers and supervisors
who displayed pride in their work group would make such comments as:
"We have a good group," "We work together well," or "We help out each
other." One supervisor said about her group:

They all have definite assignments, and they're a nice cooperative

CHART 9

RELATION OF PRIDE IN WORK GROUP TO PRODUCTIVITY

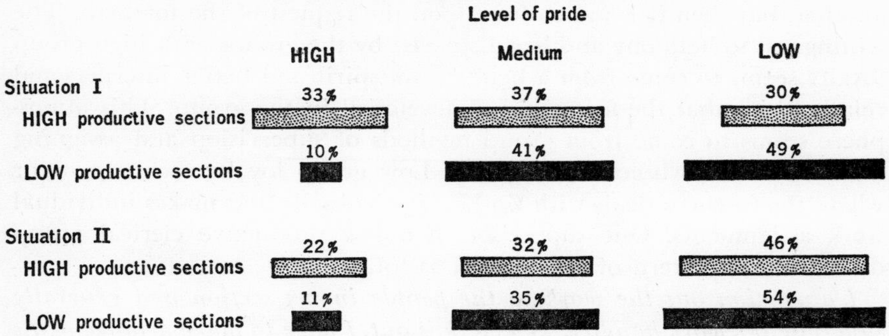

Level of pride

	HIGH	Medium	LOW
Situation I	33%	37%	30%
HIGH productive sections			
LOW productive sections	10%	41%	49%
Situation II	22%	32%	46%
HIGH productive sections			
LOW productive sections	11%	35%	54%

crowd. They just jump in and do things and never bother me. They have a responsibility toward the group.

How Group Pride and Group Loyalty Operate

There appear to be several reasons why work groups with high group pride and loyalty are the more productive. One reason is that the workers cooperate more and help one another in getting the work done. Work groups with high group loyalty show more teamwork and more willingness to help each other than do those with low group loyalty. In the high-loyalty groups there tends to be a flow of work back and forth between the workers depending upon the load. In groups with low group loyalty there tends to be more of a feeling that each worker is on his own and that how he gets along with his work is his own responsibility.

CHART 10

GROUP SOLIDARITY AND PRODUCTIVITY

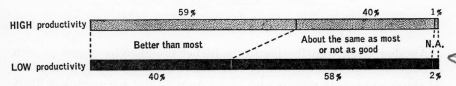

The effect upon productivity of workers helping one another is shown in Chart 10. When foremen were asked, "How does your section compare with other sections in the way the men help each other on the job?" the answers showed a marked relationship to group productivity. The foremen of high-production groups reported much more often than the foremen of low-production groups that their men helped one another in getting the work done.

The workers in the high-production work groups not only have greater group loyalty and help one another more but give this help on their own initiative. Workers in groups with low group loyalty at times help one another, but then it is more often upon the request of the foreman. The willingness to help one another displayed by the groups with high group loyalty seems to come from a better team spirit and better interpersonal relationships that the foreman has developed in the group. This atmosphere seems to come from group methods of supervision and assigning work tasks as a whole to the group. Low group loyalty seems to occur where the foreman deals with workers individually and makes individual work assignments. One supervisor of a low productive clerical group described his pattern of supervision as follows:

I apportion out the work to the people in my section and generally supervise the work handled. If a clerk is out, I have to make arrangements to have her work done. The work must go on even though there are absences. This involves getting work redistributed to those who are there.

CHART 11

GROUP SOLIDARITY, WHITE-COLLAR MEN

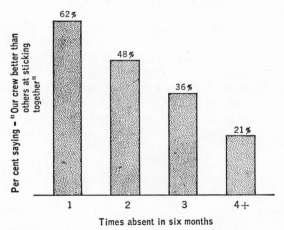

Another factor contributing to the higher productivity of groups with high group loyalty is their lower rate of absence from the job. As Chart 11 shows, persons in groups with high group loyalty are much less likely to be absent from work than persons in groups with lower group loyalty. This chart is based on data from white-collar workers. Similar results were obtained for blue-collar workers. Liking the work group clearly results, for all kinds of workers, in less absence from the job.

As might be expected, work groups with high group loyalty have more favorable attitudes toward production than do groups with low group loyalty. Thus we find that high-loyalty groups differ from groups of low group loyalty in having higher production goals. Their opinion as to what is reasonable production is higher and is more nearly the same as that of their foreman. Moreover, the high-loyalty groups have a more favorable attitude toward the high producer. This is shown in Chart 12.

CHART 12

THE RELATIONSHIP OF THE EMPLOYEE'S ATTITUDE TOWARD THE HIGHLY PRODUCTIVE
WORKER AND SECTIONAL PRIDE IN WORK GROUP

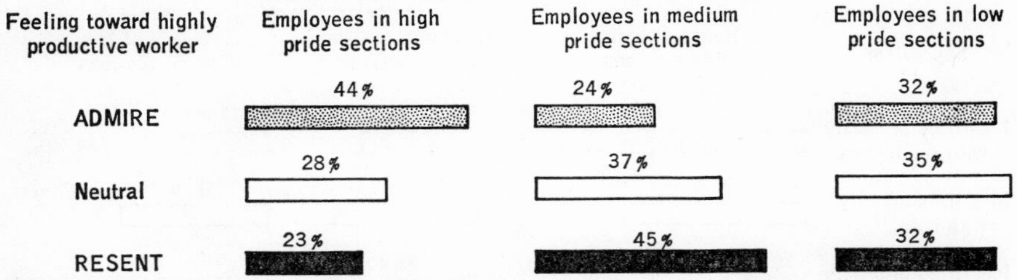

Feeling toward highly productive worker	Employees in high pride sections	Employees in medium pride sections	Employees in low pride sections
ADMIRE	44%	24%	32%
Neutral	28%	37%	35%
RESENT	23%	45%	32%

We are finding that the high-loyalty groups differ from the low in ways that form a consistent pattern. In addition to the differences already mentioned, the following characteristics have been found. The groups with greater group loyalty are more likely to

¶ Have greater identification with their group and a greater feeling of belonging to it.

¶ Have more friends in the group and in the company—rather than outside the company.

¶ Have better interpersonal relations among the members of the work group.

¶ Have a more favorable attitude toward their job and their company.

¶ Not only have higher production goals but produce more with less sense of strain or pressure.

There is evidence that whenever a supervisor (or manager) abdicates his leadership role and does not develop a good team spirit, other persons within the group will take over and develop some kind of group loyalty. Often the informal leadership which emerges establishes groups with goals counter to the goals of the over-all organization. Human nature is such that there seems to be no question as to whether or not groups will be formed. If constituted leadership lacks group skills and fails to establish group leadership, other leadership will emerge and take over.

DEVELOPING GROUP LOYALTY AND TEAM SPIRIT

Since high group loyalty and a good team spirit seem to result in greater production, greater job satisfaction, less absence, and, I suspect, less turnover, it is important to ask, "How can group loyalty be developed?" One factor which exercises an influence is shown in Chart 13.

When a superior treats subordinates as human beings, it results in greater group loyalty and pride. Moreover, as Chart 14 shows, when supervisors stay sufficiently close psychologically to their workers to be able to see the problems of the workers through the eyes of the workers, the supervisors are better able to develop good group loyalty.

CHART 13

THE RELATIONSHIP OF THE SUPERVISOR'S ATTITUDE TOWARD HIS EMPLOYEES AND THE EMPLOYEES' DEGREE OF PRIDE IN WORK GROUP

Supervisor	Heads of high pride sections	Heads of medium pride sections	Heads of low pride sections
Identifies primarily with employees	58%	25%	17%
Identifies equally with both	38%	31%	31%
Identifies primarily with the company	13%	33%	54%

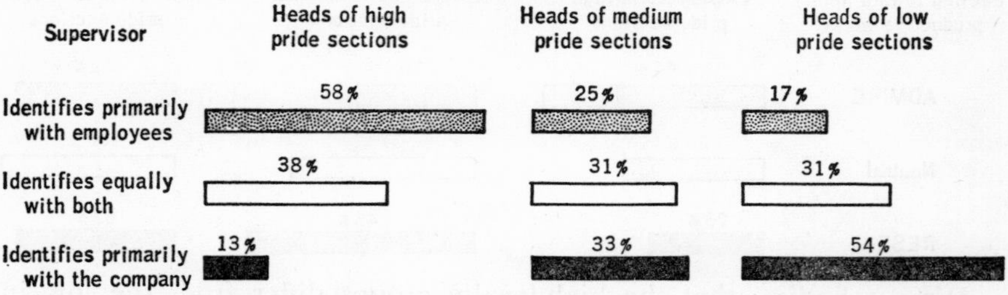

The good supervisor is able to identify with his employees and keep psychologically close to them. This seems to foster a good team spirit with open communication. It permits the supervisor to understand problems as employees see them and to interpret for top and middle management the employees' points of view. The supervisor who fails to identify with employees becomes psychologically far from them. This makes him incapable of seeing and dealing with problems as employees

CHART 14

THE RELATIONSHIP OF THE SUPERVISOR'S ATTITUDE TOWARD HIS EMPLOYEES AND THE EMPLOYEES' DEGREE OF PRIDE IN WORK GROUP

Supervisor	Heads of high pride sections	Heads of medium pride sections	Heads of low pride sections
Considers employees as human beings	47%	20%	33%
Considers employees primarily as people to get the work out	26%	35%	39%

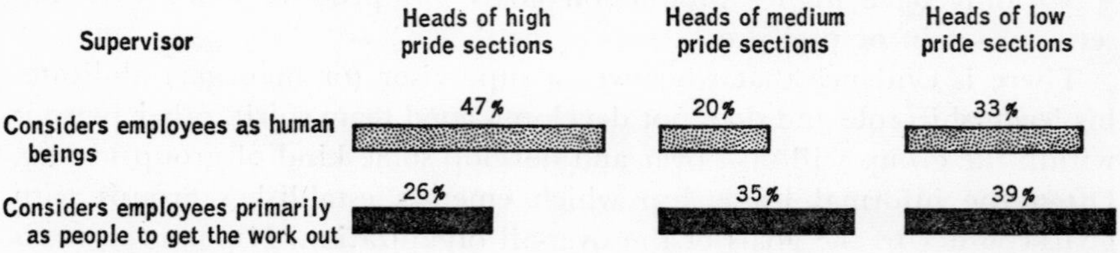

see them and hence unable to arrive at mutually satisfactory decisions. This supervisor is also unable to help middle and top management to see problems as employees see them and thereby to help management to arrive at policy decisions which will be mutually satisfactory.

Our research results indicate that it is important for supervisors to accept the goals of the over-all organization and to have a clear understanding of the role and function of their work group in achieving the over-all goals. When supervisors recognize and accept responsibility for performing the functions required of their work group and at the same time have the capacity to identify with their employees, effective results are obtained.

There are, of course, many other factors which are important in developing group loyalty and team spirit. Scattered research in industry and elsewhere indicates that commonly recognized methods of group leadership will yield good group loyalty when used. These methods and skills include those developed and taught by the National Training Laboratory in Group Development. Among the most important of these methods are those involving group participation in decisions affecting the group. There is evidence that group participation and involvement are beneficial at all levels in an organization. One of the best ways, for example, to have supervisors become aware of the job that needs to be done by their work group and to have them accept responsibility for it is to involve them in decisions where the functions and responsibilities of their work group are examined and reviewed.

Conclusion: Nature of Human Motivation

Some general conclusions have been stated here as the different results were presented. Additional conclusions emerge, however, as the results are looked at in an over-all manner. Thus these results suggest an important conclusion as to the nature of human motivation. An examination of the results presented here and of results from other research shows that every human being earnestly seeks a secure, friendly, and supportive relationship and one that gives him a sense of personal worth in the face-to-face groups most important to him. The most important face-to-face groups are almost always his immediate family group and his work group. If his formal face-to-face work group is hostile, he develops new friendly informal groups. Human nature seems to motivate each of us to establish and maintain these friendly supportive relationships in those face-to-face groups in which we spend most of our lives. Either we successfully establish these friendly and supportive relationships or we crack up.

It is not surprising, therefore, that we see people generally striving for a sense of dignity and personal worth. We all seem to seek recognition and a sense of importance in terms of the values and goals which we cherish and which our most important face-to-face groups also cherish.

To say that people seek friendly and supportive relationships does not mean that they seek to be coddled. Quite the contrary. People seek to achieve a sense of importance from doing difficult but important tasks which help to implement goals which they and their friends seek.

The Findings Applied

If there is anything of value in the results presented and the conclusions drawn, then when these findings are applied there should be an increase in productivity and in job satisfaction. We have been running several tests applying these results. These tests involve hundreds of employees in widely different kinds of industries. I shall report briefly the results obtained in one of these tests.

Chart 15 indicates the effect of participation upon productivity. This

CHART 15

THE EFFECT OF PARTICIPATION ON PRODUCTION

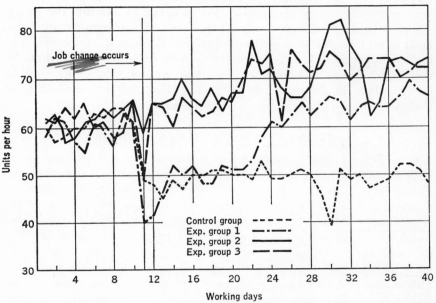

Working days

chart is based on the experiment by Coch and French [3] designed to employ three variations in participation procedure.

The first variation involved participation through representation of the workers in designing the changes to be made in the jobs. The second variation consisted of total participation by all members of the group in designing the changes. A third (control) group was also used. Two experimental groups received the total participation treatment. The (control) group went through the usual factory routine when they were changed. The production department modified the job, and a new piece rate was set. A group meeting was then held in which the control group was told that the change was necessary because of competitive conditions, and that a new piece rate had been set. The new piece rate was thoroughly explained by the time study man, questions were answered, and the meeting dismissed. Experimental group 1 was changed in a different manner. Before any changes took place, a group meeting was held with all the operators to be changed.

[3] Coch, Lester, and French, John R. P., Jr., "Overcoming Resistance to Change," *Human Relations*, Vol. I, No. 4 (1948).

The need for the change was presented as dramatically as possible, showing two identical garments produced in the factory; one was produced in 1946 and had sold for 100 per cent more than its fellow in 1947. The group was asked to identify the cheaper one and could not do it. This demonstration effectively shared with the group the entire problem of the necessity of cost reduction. A general agreement was reached that a savings could be effected by removing the "frills" and "fancy" work from the garment without affecting the folders' opportunity to achieve a high efficiency rating. Management then presented a plan to set the new job and piece rate:

(1) Make a check study of the job as it was being done.

(2) Eliminate all unnecessary work.

(3) Train several operators in the correct methods.

(4) Set the piece rate by time studies on these specially trained operators.

(5) Explain the new job and rate to all the operators.

(6) Train all operators in the new method so they can reach a high rate of production within a short time.

The group approved this plan (though no formal group decision was reached) and chose the operators to be specially trained. A sub-meeting with the "special" operators was held immediately following the meeting with the entire group. They displayed a cooperative and interested attitude and immediately presented many good suggestions. This attitude carried over into the working out of the details of the new job; and when the new job and piece rates were set, the "special" operators referred to the resultants as "our job," "our rate," etc. The new job and piece rates were presented at a second group meeting to all the operators involved. The "special" operators served to train the other operators on the new job. Experimental groups 2 and 3 went through much the same kind of change meetings. The groups were smaller than experimental group 1, and a more intimate atmosphere was established. The need for a change was once again made dramatically clear; the same general plan was presented by management. However, since the groups were small, all operators were chosen as "special" operators; that is, all operators were to participate directly in the designing of the new jobs, and all operators would be studied by the time study man. It is interesting to note that in the meetings with these two groups, suggestions were immediately made in such quantity that the stenographer had great difficulty in recording them. The group approved of the plans, but again no formal group decision was reached.

The results shown in Chart 15 clearly demonstrate the effectiveness of participation upon production. It is significant that the control group, when treated like experimental groups 2 and 3 in another change that occurred some months later, showed a productivity record identical to that shown by experimental groups 2 and 3. Chart 16 shows these curves.

The following, also taken from Coch and French, presents evidence on the power of group standards:

Probably the most important force affecting the recovery under the control procedure was a group standard, set by the group, restricting the level of produc- .

CHART 16

A COMPARISON OF THE EFFECT OF THE CONTROL PROCEDURE WITH THE TOTAL
PARTICIPATION PROCEDURE ON THE SAME GROUP

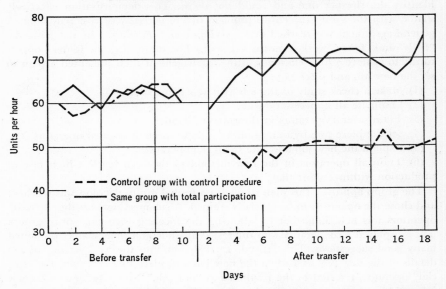

tion to 50 units per hour. Evidently this explicit agreement to restrict production
is related to the group's rejection of the change and of the new job as arbitrary
and unreasonable. Perhaps they had faint hopes of demonstrating that standard
production could not be attained and thereby obtain a more favorable piece
rate. In any case there was a definite group phenomenon which affected all the
members of the group. . . . An analysis was made for all groups of the individual
differences within the group in levels of production. In Experiment I the 40
days before change were compared with the 30 days after change; in Experiment
II the 10 days before change were compared to the 17 days after change. As a
measure of variability, the standard deviation was calculated each day for each
group. The average daily standard deviations before and after change were as
follows:

Group	Variability	
	Before change	After change
Experiment I:		
Control group	9.8	1.9
Experimental 1	9.7	3.8
Experimental 2	10.3	2.7
Experimental 3	9.9	2.4
Experiment II:		
Control group	12.7	2.9

There is indeed a marked decrease in individual differences with the control
group after their first transfer. In fact the restriction of production resulted in

a lower variability than in any other group. Thus we may conclude that the group standard at 50 units per hour set up strong group-induced forces. . . . The table of variability also shows that the experimental treatments markedly reduced variability in the other four groups after transfer.

This experiment by Coch and French shows that the results from research can be applied in the shop and can yield substantial improvements in production. This experiment also yields improvement in attitudes toward the job.

Personnel departments have a very large and important task to perform in helping the line organization to apply the results of human relations research. This includes helping the line organization to appreciate that employee-centered supervision yields better production and better job satisfaction than production-centered supervision. Chart 17, which shows

CHART 17

WHAT FOREMEN SAY ARE THE MOST IMPORTANT THINGS THEY HAVE TO DO

Production	78%
Human relations	7%
Both	15%

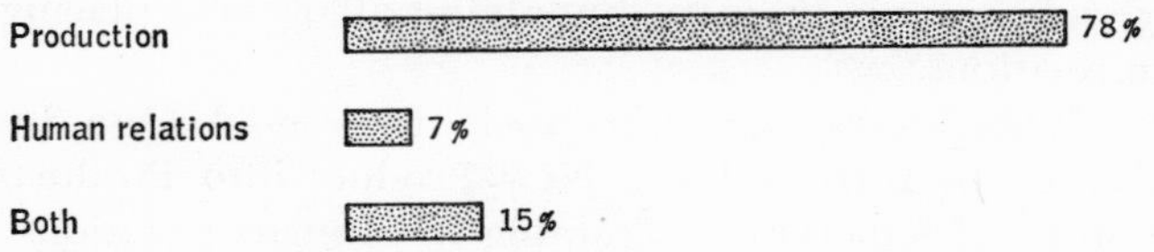

what the foremen in a very well-managed company say are the most important things they have to do, gives an indication of the magnitude of the job that personnel people face in helping the line organization to become employee-centered in its supervision. Over three-quarters of the foremen in that company state that pushing for production is the most important part of their job. The line organization, moreover, needs help in learning the skills required for using employee-centered supervision effectively. Research results pointing to effective ways to develop these skills are available, but that is a topic for other discussions.

Thinking Ahead: What Price Human Relations? *

Malcolm P. McNair

In 1956 the Inland Steel Company appointed a vice president of human relations. The Inland Steel Company, of course, is big business; but little business is not being neglected, for I note that the McGraw-Hill Book Company, Inc., is publishing a book on *Human Relations in Small Industry*. The Harvard Business School has had a chair of Human Relations since 1950; by now the number of courses in Human Relations in schools and colleges throughout the country has multiplied substantially. Even more marked is the rapid growth of executive development programs, some in schools, some in industry, but almost all of them placing emphasis on human relations.

Doctoral theses increasingly carry such titles as "A Case Study of the Human Aspects of Introducing a New Product into Production," "An Intensive Study of Supervisory Training in Human Relations and Foreman Behavior at Work," "A Case Study of the Administration of Change in the Large Modern Office," and "Emergence of Leadership in Manufacturing Work Groups." And recently the *Harvard Business Review* has reprinted a dozen articles on human relations, under the title "How Successful Executives Handle People, 12 Studies on Communications and Management Skills," which include such intriguing subjects as "Making Human Relations Work," "Barriers and Gateways to Communication," and "The Fateful Process of Mr. A Talking to Mr. B."

It is obvious that human relations is very much the fashion in business thinking today. And fashions in business thinking are not a novelty; there have been many others. I can well recall that when I first joined the Harvard Business School faculty, the reigning vogue in business thinking was scientific management. Only a few years later, however, the grandiose claims of scientific management were sharply debunked. What was of solid worth remained—but a considerable amount of froth had been blown off the top.

* Reprinted by permission of the publisher from *Harvard Business Review,* vol. 35, no. 2 (March-April, 1957), pp. 15–23. Mr. McNair is Lincoln Filene Professor of Retailing at the Harvard Business School and a director of Indian Head Mills, Inc., Allied Stores Corporation, the National Retail Dry Goods Association, and several large department stores.

Must we go through the same process—with all its waste and possible damage along the way—to get to what is worthwhile in human relations?

*

My quarrel is not with the solid substance of much that is comprehended by the phrase "human relations," but rather with the "cult" or "fad" aspects of human relations, which are assuming so much prominence.

There can be no doubt that people are of absorbing interest to other people. To verify this fact you have only to look at what makes headlines in the newspapers. There is a fascination for most of us in speculating about people and their behavior. So it is not surprising that human relations has assumed so much prominence as a fashionable mode of thinking. But, as with any kind of fashion, it can be carried to the point where people accept it without questioning—and certainly this can be dangerous when we are dealing with such an important segment of man's activity.

Therefore, just because the tide has gone so far, I must make my points in the most emphatic manner possible. Though I feel I have not distorted the picture, I do not care whether businessmen accept my interpretation in full, or even in large part, *so long as they get stirred up to do some critical thinking of their own.*

*

Before going any further let me try to indicate the things in this area of human relations which are really basic and with which there is no conceivable quarrel. In the first place, there can be no dispute with research in the social sciences, including the behavioral sciences. Obviously such research is highly important to business management and to business education. Business management and education must seek to understand the behavior of people as workers, the behavior of people as members of organizations, and, of course, the behavior of people as consumers. In all these areas we need more and better understanding of human behavior.

Neither is there any dispute in regard to the things that are important for a man's conduct in relation to his fellow men. The foundation is good Christian ethics, respect for the dignity of the individual human being, and integrity of character. On these we should stand fast. Personally I have always liked this paraphrase of what Theodore Roosevelt once said in a commencement address: "On the Ten Commandments and the Sermon on the Mount, uncompromising rigidity; on all else, the widest tolerance." [1] But between acceptance of high moral principles and the

[1] From the Introduction to *Theodore Roosevelt's America,* edited by Farida Wiley (New York, Devin-Adair Company, 1955), p. xxi.

exigencies of day-to-day conduct of affairs there can be, with the best intentions, a very wide gap. This is the gap which by better understanding of human motivation we should try to fill.

Also there can be little dispute about the observations on the behavior of people at work which Professor Fritz J. Roethlisberger, the leader of the human relations group at Harvard, summed up half a dozen years ago:

> People at work are not so different from people in other aspects of life. They are not entirely creatures of logic. They have feelings. They like to feel important and to have their work recognized as important. Although they are interested in the size of their pay envelopes, this is not a matter of their first concern. Sometimes they are more interested in having their pay reflect accurately the relative social importance to them of the different jobs they do. Sometimes even still more important to them than maintenance of socially accepted wage differentials is the way their superiors treat them.
>
> They like to work in an atmosphere of approval. They like to be praised rather than blamed. They do not like to have to admit their mistakes—at least, not publicly. They like to know what is expected of them and where they stand in relation to their boss's expectations. They like to have some warning of the changes that may affect them.
>
> They like to feel independent in their relations to their supervisors. They like to be able to express their feelings to them without being misunderstood. They like to be listened to and have their feelings and points of view taken into account. They like to be consulted about and participate in the actions that will personally affect them. In short, employees, like most people, want to be treated as belonging to and being an integral part of some group.[2]

In other words, "People behave like people." They have feelings. They don't always behave logically. The concept of the economic man can be a dangerous abstraction. Every individual wants to feel important, to have self-esteem, to have "face." Everybody likes to feel that he is "wanted." He likes to have a "sense of belonging." Group influences and group loyalties are important. The desire for psychological "security" is strong. People don't always reveal their feelings in words.

That all these human attitudes have important consequences for management is likewise not open to dispute. It is well accepted in management thinking today that leadership has to be earned, it cannot be conferred; that authority comes from below, not from above; that in any business unit there will be "social" groups which will cut across organization lines; that good communication involves both the willingness to listen and the ability to "get through" but not by shouting.

Dean Stanley F. Teele of the Harvard Business School recently made

[2] From a speech entitled "The Human Equation in Employee Productivity" before the Personnel Group of the National Retail Dry Goods Association, 1950.

the statement, "As we have learned more and more about a business organization as a social unit, we have become increasingly certain that the executive's skill with people—or the lack of it—is the determining element in his long-range success or failure." [3] Here we are down to the nub of the matter. What is this skill? Can it be taught? Are there dangers in the teaching of it? Is skill an appropriate concept?

Perhaps I can give a clue to the line of thought which I am developing when I say that I am essentially disturbed at the combination of *skill* with *human relations*. For me, "human relations skill" has a cold-blooded connotation of proficiency, technical expertness, calculated effect.

*

There is no gainsaying the fact that a need long existed in many businesses for a much greater awareness of human relations and that, in some, perhaps in a considerable number, the need still exists. The very avidity with which people prone to fashionable thinking in business have seized on the fad of human relations itself suggests the presence of a considerable guilt complex in the minds of businessmen in regard to their dealings with people. So it is not my intent to argue that there is no need for spreading greater awareness of the human relations point of view among many businessmen. Nevertheless it is my opinion that some very real dangers threaten.

The world's work has to be done, and people have to take responsibility for their own work and their own lives. Too much emphasis on human relations encourages people to feel sorry for themselves, makes it easier for them to slough off responsibility, to find excuses for failure, to act like children. When somebody falls down on a job, or does not behave in accordance with accepted codes, we look into his psychological background for factors that may be used as excuses. In these respects the cult of human relations is but part and parcel of the sloppy sentimentalism characterizing the world today.

Undue preoccupation with human relations saps individual responsibility, leads us not to think about the job any more and about getting it done but only about people and their relations. I contend that discipline has its uses in any organization for accomplishing tasks. And this is especially true of self-discipline. Will power, self-control, and personal responsibility are more than ever important in a world that is in danger of wallowing in self-pity and infantilism.

Most great advances are made by individuals. Devoting too much effort in business to trying to keep everybody happy results in conformity, in failure to build individuals. It has become the fashion to decry friction,

[3] From a speech entitled "The Harvard Business School and the Search for Ultimate Values" at the presentation to the *Harvard Business Review* of a citation from The Laymen's Movement for a Christian World, New York, October 25, 1955.

but friction has its uses; without friction there are no sparks, without friction it is possible to go too far in the direction of sweetness and light, harmony, and the avoidance of all irritation. The present-day emphasis on "bringing everybody along" can easily lead to a deadly level of mediocrity.

We can accept the first part of a statement by Peter Drucker: "The success and ultimately the survival of every business, large or small, depends in the last analysis on its ability to develop people. . . . This ability . . . is not measured by any of our conventional yardsticks of economic success; yet it is the final measurement." Drucker, however, goes on to add a further thought, which opens more opportunity for debate. He says, "Increasingly from here on this ability to develop people will have to be systematized by management as a major conscious activity and responsibility." In this concept there is the familiar danger of turning over to a program or a course or an educational director a responsibility that is a peculiarly personal one.

The responsibility for developing people belongs to every executive as an individual. No man is a good executive who is not a good teacher; and if Drucker's recommendation that executive development be "systematized by management as a major conscious activity" is interpreted as meaning that someone trained in the new mode of thinking should be appointed as director of executive development, then the probable outcome will be simply another company program in human relations. While this may be good for some of the executives, no long-run contribution to the development of good people will be made unless the good individuals personally take the responsibility for developing other individuals.

Please do not misunderstand me. I am not talking about old-fashioned rugged individualism or the law of the jungle, and I am not holding up as ideals the robber barons of the nineteenth century, or even some of the vigorous industrialists of the early twentieth century. But I ask you to consider whether some of today's business leaders, well known to all of us—Clarence Randall, Gardiner Symonds, Neil McElroy, Tex Colbert, Earl Puckett, Fred Lazarus, and so on—are not primarily products of a school of friction and competitive striving. We need more men like them, not fewer. It may be appropriate here to cite the recent observations of Dean Teele on "inner serenity" and "divine discontent":

Any realistic approach to the nature of top business management, and therefore to the problems of selection and development for top business management, makes abundantly clear that the balance between these two [attributes] is perhaps the most important determinant of success in top business management. Let me elaborate.

Psychiatrists, psychologists, and religious advisers join with ordinary lay observers in noting how often human efficiency is greatly reduced by sharp inner conflicts—conflicts which usually center around value judgments. That is to say, conflicts as to basic personal purposes and objectives, as to the values to be sought in life, are far more often the barriers to effective performance than intellectual incapacity or lack of necessary knowledge. The goal then from this point of view is the development of that inner serenity which comes from having struggled with and then resolved the basic questions of purpose and values.

On the other hand, in business as in the world generally, discontent is an element of the greatest importance. Dissatisfaction with oneself, with one's performance, is an essential for improvement. So important to the progress of the world is discontent on the part of the relatively few who feel it, that we have come to characterize it as divine discontent. Here . . . the need is for both inner serenity and divine discontent—a need for both in a balance between the two appropriate for the particular individuals.[4]

To keep that important balance of inner serenity and divine discontent in our future business leaders, we need to focus educational and training programs more sharply on the development of individuals than is the fashion today. What is important for the development of the individual? Obviously, many things; but one prime essential is the ability to think, and the nurturing of this ability must be a principal objective of all our educational effort.

In the field of business education this ability to think, to deal with situations, to go to the heart of things, to formulate problems and issues, is not an innate quality. It has to be cultivated, and it requires long and rigorous and often tedious practice in digging out significant facts in weighing evidence, foreseeing contingencies, developing alternatives, finding the right questions to ask. In all business education, whether at the college or graduate level or at the stage of so-called executive development, we must not omit the insistence on close analysis, on careful reasoning and deduction, on cultivation of the power to differentiate and discriminate.

There is a very real danger that undue preoccupation with human relations can easily give a wrong slant to the whole process of education for business leadership. For one thing, it tends to give a false concept of the executive job. Dealing with people is eminently important in the day's work of the business executive, but so are the processes of analysis, judgment, and decision making. It takes skill and persistence to dig out facts; it takes judgment and understanding to get at the real issues; it takes perspective and imagination to see the feasible alternatives; it takes logic and intuition to arrive at conclusions; it takes the habit of decision and a sense of timing to develop a plan of action.

On the letterhead of the general policy letters that are sent periodically

---

[4] "The Fourth Dimension in Management," an address to the American Management Association, New York, May 25, 1956.

to the managing directors of all 80-odd stores in the Allied Stores Corporation there is this slogan:

> To LOOK is one thing.
> To SEE what you look at is another.
> To UNDERSTAND what you see is a third.
> To LEARN from what you understand is still something else.
> But to ACT on what you learn is all that really matters, isn't it?

An executive's ability to see, to understand, to learn, and to act comprises much more than skill in human relations.

*

Awareness of human relations as one aspect of the executive's job is of course essential. But, in my view, *awareness of human relations* and the *conscious effort to practice human relations on other people* are two different things, and I think this is crucial.

As soon as a man consciously undertakes to practice human relations, one of several bad consequences is almost inevitable. Consciously trying to practice human relations is like consciously trying to be a gentleman. If you have to think about it, insincerity creeps in and personal integrity moves out. With some this leads by a short step to the somewhat cynical point of view which students in Administrative Practices courses have described by coining the verb "ad prac," meaning "to manipulate people for one's own ends."

A less deliberate but perhaps even more dangerous consequence may be the development of a yen for managing other people's lives, always, of course, with the most excellent intentions. In the same direction the conscious practice of human relations leads to amateur psychiatry and to the unwarranted invasions of the privacy of individuals.

Hence I am disturbed about the consequences to business management of human relations blown up into pseudoscience—with a special vocabulary and with special practitioners and experts. In fact, to my mind there is something almost sinister about the very term "human relations practitioner," though I am sure that all sincere devotees of human relations would vigorously disclaim any such imputation.

*

For me much of the freshness and the insight which characterized a great deal of the earlier work in this field—exemplified by the quotation from Professor Roethlisberger which I cited in my introductory statement —has been lost as the effort has progressed to blow human relations up into a science—something to be explored and practiced for its own sake.

I realize that many people in the human relations field—Professor

Roethlisberger in particular—are also disturbed about this trend, and about its unintended repercussions. But it was almost inevitable that other people would run away with such a fruitful concept, and set it up as an idol with appropriate rituals of worship (usually called "techniques"). Once you throw yourself into trying to "listen," to "gain intuitive familiarity," to "think in terms of mutually independent relationship," and so on, you can easily forget that there is more to business— and life—than running around plying human relations "skill" to plumb the hidden thoughts of everybody with whom you come in contact, including yourself.

This is the same mistake that some consumer motivation researchers make, as Alfred Politz has pointed out—trying to find out the attitudes, opinions, and preferences in the consumer's mind *without regard* to whether these factors are what determine how he will act in a given buying situation.[5] In his words, the "truth" that such researchers seek— and he always puts the word in quotes—is not only of a lower order than the scientifically established facts of how consumers react in real life, but it is also of less use to managers in making marketing decisions.

The whole thing gets a little ridiculous when . . . foremen are assumed to have progressed when they have gained in "consideration" at the expense of something called "initiating structure"—yet such was the apparent objective of one company's training program.[6]

From the standpoint of developing really good human relations in a business context, to say nothing of the job of getting the world's work done, the kind of training just described seems to me in grave danger of bogging down in semantics and trivialities and dubious introspection. I am totally unable to associate the *conscious practice of human relations skill* (in the sense of making people happy in spite of themselves or getting them to do something they don't think they want to do) with the *dignity of an individual person created in God's image.*

Apparently this "skill" of the "human relations practitioner" consists to a considerable degree of what is called "listening." The basic importance of the ability to listen is not to be gainsaid; neither is it to be denied that people do not always reveal their inward feelings in words. But in the effort to blow human relations up into a science and develop a technique of communication, some of the enthusiasts have worked up such standard conversational gambits as "This is what I think I hear you saying," or "As I listen, this is what I think you mean."

No doubt there are times when a silent reaction of this kind is appropriate, but if the human relations practitioner makes such phrases part

[5] "Science and Truth in Marketing Research," HBR January-February 1957, p. 117.
[6] Kenneth R. Andrews, "Is Management Training Effective? II. Measurement, Objectives, and Policy," HBR, March-April 1957, p. 63.

of his conversational repertoire, there are times when these cute remarks may gain him a punch in the nose. Sometimes people damn well mean what they are saying and will rightly regard anything less than a man-to-man recognition of that fact as derogatory to their dignity.

That a group of foremen who were given a course emphasizing human relations and thereafter turned out to be distinctly poorer practitioners than they had been before taking the course, as in the above case, would not, to my mind, be simply an accident. I think it a result that might well be expected nine times out of ten. In other words, the overemphasis on human relations, with all its apparatus of courses, special vocabulary, and so on, tends to create the very problems that human relations deals with. It is a vicious circle. You encourage people to pick at the scabs of their psychic wounds.

In evaluating the place of human relations in business, a recent incident is in point:

> At a luncheon gathering Miss Else Herzberg, the highly successful educational director of a large chain of stores in Great Britain, Marks and Spencer, Ltd., described at some length the personnel management policies of that concern and the high state of employee morale that existed. Throughout her description I was listening for some reference to human relations. I did not hear it, and when she had finished I said, "But, Miss Herzberg, you haven't said anything about human relations." Immediately she flashed back, "We live it; we don't have to talk about it."

In point also is a recent remark of Earl Puckett, chairman of the board of Allied Stores Corporation, when in discussing a particular management problem he said, "Of course you treat people like people."

And so, although I concede that there is still too little awareness of human relations problems in many business organizations, I think that the present vogue for human relations and for executive development programs which strongly emphasize human relations holds some real dangers because it weakens the sense of responsibility, because it promotes conformity, because it too greatly subordinates the development of individuals, and because it conveys a one-sided concept of the executive job.

*

I turn now more specifically to the dangers to business education at the college level which seem to me inherent in the present overemphasis upon human relations. Business executives should have as much concern with this part of the subject as teachers—perhaps more, because they must use the young men we turn out; furthermore, they represent the demand of the market and so can have a real influence on what the educators do.

The dangers to the education of young men, in my opinion, are even more serious than the dangers to business executive development programs for mature men. After all, we are well aware that businessmen follow fads, and so fairly soon the human relations cult in business will begin to wane and operations research or something else will become the fashion. Also, as remarked earlier, there is still a substantial need in business for greater awareness of human relations, and more businessmen are sufficiently adult to separate the wheat from the chaff. Thus in advanced management training programs for experienced executives there is no doubt greater justification for courses in Human Relations than there is in collegiate and immediate graduate programs.

From the general educational standpoint perhaps the first question is whether human relations can be taught at all. I do not deny that something can be learned about human relations, but I do maintain that direct emphasis on human relations as subject matter defeats the purpose. When things must come from the heart, the Emily Post approach won't do; and if behavior does not come from the heart, it is phony. Clarence Budington Kelland, that popular writer of light fiction, in a recent *Saturday Evening Post* serial entitled "Counterfeit Cavalier," makes one of his characters says:

"A very nice person has to start by being nice inside and have an aptitude for it. . . . They don't have to learn. It comes natural. No trimmings, but spontaneous. . . . If you have to think about it, it is no good." [7]

Good human relations do not lend themselves to anatomical dissection with a scalpel. How do people normally acquire good human relations? Some of course never do. In the case of those who do enjoy success in human relations and at the same time retain their sincerity, the result, I am convinced, is a composite product of breeding, home, church, education, and experience generally, not of formal Human Relations courses.

Hence in my view it is a mistake in formal education to seek to do more than develop an awareness of human relations, preferably as an integral part of other problems. This does not mean, of course, that the results of research in human behavior should not be utilized in the teaching of business administration. Certainly such results should be utilized (with due circumspection to avoid going overboard on theories that are still mostly in the realm of speculation). To take account of human relations in marketing problems and in personnel management problems and in labor relations problems and industrial management problems, and so on, of course makes sense. What I am decrying is the effort to teach human relations as such. Thus, I applaud the training of personnel managers, but I am exceedingly skeptical of training human relations practitioners.

[7] May 26, 1956, p. 24.

I should like also to venture the personal opinion that human relations in its fairly heavy dependence on Freudian psychology is headed the wrong way. In the long history of mankind, the few centuries, dating perhaps from the Sumerian civilization, during which we have sought to apply an intellectual and moral veneer to man the animal are a very short period indeed as compared with the time that has elapsed since our ancestors first began to walk erect; and it seems to me that a large part of the job of education still must be to toughen and thicken this veneer, not to encourage people to crack it and peel it off, as seems to have been the fashion for much of the last half century. I suspect that modern psychiatry is in a vicious circle, that some of the principal causes of increased mental disease lie in morbid introspection, lack of strong moral convictions, and leisure that we have not yet learned how to use.

I believe that one of these days a newer school of thought in these matters will re-emphasize the importance of will power, self-control, and personal responsibility. I can well recall hearing Charles William Eliot, on the occasion of his ninetieth birthday, repeat his famous prescription for a happy life: "Look up, and not down, look forward and not backward, look out and not in."

Our present preoccupation with the emotional and nonlogical aspects of life seems to me in many ways responsible for the prevalent wishful thinking of the American people. As a higher and higher proportion of American youth goes to college, it might be supposed that intelligently realistic ways of looking at things would be on the increase, but the contrary seems to be true. As people we are more prone than ever to let our desires color our thinking. More and more the few people who have the courage to present realistic viewpoints on national and world affairs find that the public will not listen to what it does not wish to hear. Why isn't education bringing us a more intelligent outlook on life?

Can it be that one of the reasons is that education itself has surrendered so far to the ideas that are concerned primarily with the current fashionable interest in the emotional and nonlogical aspects of living? In reviewing Joan Dunn's book, *Why Teachers Can't Teach—A Case History*, E. Victor Milione remarks, "Our educational system has substituted training in life adjustment for education." [8] Obviously there are many analogies between the doctrines of the progressives in education and the overemphasis on human relations. Personally I prefer a more rigorous educational philosophy. I can well recall a remark of A. Lawrence Lowell that "the business of education is making people uncomfortable."

In any event, I think it is the job of education to push for more and not less emphasis on logics and morals in dealing with social problems.

[8] *The Freeman*, March 1956, p. 59.

The following quotation from C. C. Furnas, chancellor of the University of Buffalo, makes much sense to me:

We must recognize, of course, that it takes much more than pure intellect to answer social questions. Great problems involving many people are usually handled in an atmosphere of high emotion and the participants often show but little evidence of being rational human beings. But, even though it acts slowly, it is certainly true that intelligence can and does have some influence in shaping mass emotions. It is in this slow modification of mass emotional patterns that the average intelligent person can and should play a continuing role within his own sphere of influence.[9]

How can we do this if we encourage immature minds to regard the nonlogical aspects as the most important? Not that teachers necessarily intend it this way—though I am sure some have been carried so far—but simply that putting so much explicit emphasis on the emotional and irrational makes the student feel it is all-important. No protestation to the contrary can undo that impression—that perhaps *nonlogical* impression—which is exactly what an understanding of human behavior ought to lead us to expect in the first place.

*

But perhaps my principal quarrel with the teaching of human relations has to do with timing. Discussion of such problems as what men should learn, and how they should learn it, is probably as old as education itself, but much less attention has been given to the question, "When should men learn?"

The whole modern development of adult education has brought into disrepute the old adage that you can't teach an old dog new tricks. In fact, in the area of business administration it is quite plausible that teaching of certain managerial skills is best accomplished in later years, after men have gained considerable experience in business activities. William H. Whyte, Jr., the author of *Is Anybody Listening?* and *The Organization Man,* in discussing the Alfred P. Sloan Fellowship Program at the Massachusetts Institute of Technology, has this to say:

But on one point there is considerable agreement: to be valuable, such a course should be taken only when a man has had at least five years' business experience. The broad view can be a very illusory thing. Until a man has known the necessity—the zest—of mastering a specific skill, he may fall prey to the idea that the manager is a sort of neutralist expediter who concerns himself only with abstractions such as human relations and motivation. Those who study these subjects after ten years or so of job experience have already learned the basic importance of doing a piece of work; in the undergraduate business schools, however, the abstractions are instilled in impressionable minds before they are ready to read

[9] *Ibid.,* p. 24.

between the lines and to spot the vast amount of hot air and wishful thinking that is contained in the average business curriculum.[10]

Among those managerial skills the specific teaching of which had better be left to later years is the handling of human relations. Thus I should not only rewrite the old adage in the form, "There are some tricks you can teach only to an old dog," but I should go on to the important corollary, "There are some tricks that you had better not try to teach to young dogs." The dangers in trying to teach human relations as such at the collegiate or immediate graduate level are substantial. Indeed, by developing courses in human relations for college graduates in their early twenties without previous business experience we are essentially opening Pandora's box.

Such courses lead to a false concept of the executive's job. There is a de-emphasis of analysis, judgment, and decision making. Someone has said that the job of the modern executive is to be intelligently superficial. This statement is true in the sense that when a man reaches an important executive post, he does not have time to go to the bottom of every problem that is presented to him, and he certainly should not undertake himself to do the work of his subordinates. If he does these things, he is a poor executive. But if an executive has not learned at some stage to go to the bottom of problems in one or more particular areas, he will not in the long run be a successful manager.

Human relations expertise is not a substitute for administrative leadership, and there is danger in getting young men to think that business administration consists primarily of a battery of experts in operations research, mathematics, theory of games, and so on, equipped with a Univac and presided over by a smart human relations man. Undoubtedly many of the new techniques are substantial aids to *judgment,* but they do not fully replace that vital quality. One of the great dangers in teaching human relations as such at the collegiate or immediate graduate level is that the student is led to think that he can short-cut the process of becoming an executive.

The study of human relations as such also opens up a wonderful "escape" for the student in many of his other courses. Let's admit it: none of us is too much enamored of hard thinking, and when a student in class is asked to present an analysis of some such problem as buying a piece of equipment, or making a needed part instead of buying it, he frequently is prone to dodge hard thinking about facts in favor of speculation on the probable attitudes of workers toward the introduction of a new machine or new process.

For some students, as for some businessmen, the discussion of human relations aspects of business management problems can even lead to the

[10] *Fortune,* June 1956, p. 248.

development of the cynical "ad prac" point of view, which assumes that the chief end of studying human relations is to develop skill in manipulating people; this perhaps is the present-day version of high-pressure selling.

A different but equally dangerous result occurs in the case of the student who becomes so much interested in human relations that he turns himself into an amateur psychiatrist, appraises every problem he encounters in terms of human relations, and either reaches an unhealthy state of introspection or else develops a zeal for making converts to human relations and winds up with a passion for running other people's lives.

*

The sum of the matter is this. It is not that the human relations concept is wrong; it is simply that we have blown it up too big and have placed too much emphasis on teaching human relations as such at the collegiate and early graduate level. A sound program in business education, in my opinion, will of course envisage research in human behavior; it may, with some possible good results, venture on offering specific courses in Human Relations for mature executives; but for students in their twenties who have not yet become seasoned in practical business activities we should keep away from specific courses in Administrative Practices and Human Relations, while at the same time inculcating an awareness of human relations problems wherever they appropriately appear in other management courses. In other words, let us look closely enough at what we are doing so we can be sure that the gains we make in this area turn out to be *net* gains.

Finally, to express a personal conviction on a somewhat deeper note, I should like to refer again to Dean Teele's comments, cited earlier, on "inner serenity." The attainment of that all-important goal, in my opinion, is not to be sought through the present vogue of interest in human relations. Inner serenity is an individual matter, not a group product. As Cameron Hawley puts it, "A man finds happiness only by walking his own path across the earth." [11]

Let's treat people like people, but let's not make a big production of it.

[11] "Walk Your Own Path!" *This Week Magazine*, December 11, 1955.

Part Five
PLANNING

A. OBJECTIVES

The Essential Nature of Objectives *

John F. Mee

Interest in management philosophy and practice has steadily increased during the present century. Since World War II, students of business and public administration have joined efforts with administrators in business and government to formulate an acceptable philosophy of management as a guide both for modern management practice and for the education of those who aspire to a career in the field. Professor Ralph C. Davis [1] offers the following comment concerning the problem of management philosophy.

The problem of greatest importance in the field of management is and probably will continue to be the further development of the philosophy of management. A philosophy is a system of thought. It is based on some orderly, logical statements of objectives, principles, policies and general methods of approach to the solution of some set of problems. . . .

Business objectives involve the public interest as well as the interests of customers, dealers, bankers, owners and employees. They affect everyone in an industrial economy. A managerial philosophy cannot supply a basis of effective thinking for the solution of business problems, if it is satisfactory only to owners and employees. A managerial philosophy that is commonly accepted is a requisite for a common scale of values in an economy. It is necessary, therefore, for unity of thought and action in the accomplishment of economic objectives. We cannot have an effective industrial economy without effective industrial leadership. We cannot have an effective leadership without a sound managerial philosophy.

Industrial leaders without such a philosophy are business mechanics rather than professional executives. . . . [2]

The main reasons for the continued interest in management philosophy among educators, public administrators, and progressive businessmen are:

1. The increasing trend toward decentralization of operating responsi-

* Reprinted by permission of the publisher from "Management Philosophy for Professional Executives," *Business Horizons* (December, 1956), pp. 5–7. Mr. Mee is Professor of Management and head of the Department of Management of the School of Business at the University of Indiana.

[1] Dr. R. C. Davis is Professor of Management at The Ohio State University.

[2] "Research in Management During the '50s," in Arthur E. Warner, ed., *Research Needs in Business During the '50s* (Indiana Business Report No. 13; Bloomington: School of Business, Indiana University, 1950), p. 32.

bilities and decision-making in business and governmental organizations.

2. The increasing numbers of professional executives required in business and government for growth and decentralization of operations.

3. The necessity for a logical framework of management philosophy and practice as a basis for training in executive-development programs and college curricula.

OBJECTIVES

In current thinking and writing, the starting point for either a philosophy or the practice of management seems to center around predetermined objectives. The entire management process concerns itself with ways and means to realize predetermined results and with the intelligent use of people whose efforts must be properly motivated and guided. Objectives may be general or specific; they may concern the organization as a whole, a segment of it within a decentralized unit, or even a particular function such as production, sales, or personnel.

What are or should be the objectives of management in our industrial economy? A study of current management literature and the published objectives of business firms provides some revealing and interesting concepts from recognized authorities. Here are some selected statements:

¶ The goal of the organization must be this—to make a better and better product to be sold at a lower and lower price. Profit cannot be the goal. Profit must be a by-product. This is a state of mind and a philosophy. Actually an organization doing this job as it can be done will make large profits which must be properly divided between user, worker and stockholder. This takes ability and character.[3]

¶ If we were to isolate the one factor, above all others, that transformed the tiny company of 1902 into the industrial giant of 1952, while hundreds of competitors failed and are forgotten, I should say that it has been Texaco's settled policy of thinking first of quality of product and service to the customer, and only second to the size of its profit. To some of you, this may sound somewhat trite. But it is the starkest kind of business realism. In a highly competitive industry such as ours, the highest rewards are reserved for those who render the greatest service.[4]

¶ To make and sell quality products competitively and to perform those functions at the lowest attainable cost consistent with sound management policies, so as to return an adequate profit after taxes for services rendered. As a corollary objective, the corporation must be the low-cost producer of the product it offers for sale. (United States Steel Corporation statement of general company objectives.)

[3] James F. Lincoln, *Intelligent Selfishness and Manufacturing* (Bulletin 434; New York: Lincoln Electric Co.).

[4] Harry T. Klein, *The Way Ahead* (New York: The Texas Co., 1952), p. 14.

¶ The mission of the business organization is to acquire, produce and distribute certain values. The business objective, therefore, is the starting point for business thinking. The primary objectives of a business organization are always those economic values with which we serve the customer. The principal objective of a businessman, naturally, is a profit. And a profit is merely an academic consideration, nevertheless, until we get the customer's dollar.[5]

Numerous further examples of published and stated objectives of modern business management could be presented. However, all of them could be summarized with the conclusion that: (1) *Profit* is the motivating force for managers. (2) *Service* to customers by the provision of desired economic values (goods and services) justifies the existence of the business. (3) *Social responsibilities* do exist for managers in accordance with ethical and moral codes established by the society in which the industry resides. The economic values with which customers are served include increased values at lower costs through innovation and creativity over a period of time.

In formulating and developing a modern management philosophy for successful practice, a combination of the above objectives in the correct proportion is required. Every decentralized organization unit and essential function must contribute to the realization of the general objectives by attaining the organizational, functional, and operational objectives. Unless predetermined objectives are set and accepted, little or no basis exists for measuring the success and effectiveness of those who perform the management functions.

The importance of predetermining the objectives desired has resulted in the formulation of the management principle of the objective. This principle may be stated as follows: Before initiating any course of action, the objectives in view must be clearly determined, understood, and stated.

[5] Ralph C. Davis, "What the Staff Function Actually Is," *Advanced Management*, XIX (May, 1954), p. 13.

The Objectives of a Business *

Peter F. Drucker

Most of today's lively discussion of management by objectives is concerned with the search for the one right objective. This search is not only
likely to be as unproductive as the quest for the philosopher's stone; it is
certain to do harm and to misdirect.

To emphasize only profit, for instance, misdirects managers to the
point where they may endanger the survival of the business. To obtain
profit today they tend to undermine the future. They may push the
most easily saleable product lines and slight those that are the market of
tomorrow. They tend to short-change research, promotion and other
postponable investments. Above all, they shy away from any capital expenditure that may increase the invested-capital base against which profits
are measured; and the result is dangerous obsolescence of equipment.
In other words, they are directed into the worst practices of management.

To manage a business is to balance a variety of needs and goals. This
requires judgment. The search for the one objective is essentially a
search for a magic formula that will make judgment unnecessary. But
the attempt to replace judgment by formula is always irrational; all that
can be done is to make judgment possible by narrowing its range and the
available alternatives, giving it clear focus, a sound foundation in facts
and reliable measurements of the effects and validity of actions and
decisions. And this, by the very nature of business enterprise, requires
multiple objectives.

What should these objectives be, then? There is only one answer:
*Objectives are needed in every area where performance and results
directly and vitally affect the survival and prosperity of the business.* These
are the areas which are affected by every management decision and which
therefore have to be considered in every management decision. They
decide what it means concretely to manage the business. They spell out
what results the business must aim at and what is needed to work effectively toward these targets.

* Reprinted by permission of the publisher from *The Practice of Management*
(New York: Harper & Brothers, 1954), pp. 62–65, 126–129. Mr. Drucker is Professor of
Management at New York University and is also a well-known management consultant,
lecturer, and author.

Objectives in these key areas should enable us to do five things: to organize and explain the whole range of business phenomena in a small number of general statements; to test these statements in actual experience; to predict behavior; to appraise the soundness of decisions when they are still being made; and to enable practicing businessmen to analyze their own experience and, as a result, improve their performance. It is precisely because the traditional theorem of the maximization of profits cannot meet any of these tests—let alone all of them—that it has to be discarded.

At first sight it might seem that different businesses would have entirely different key areas—so different as to make impossible any general theory. It is indeed true that different key areas require different emphasis in different businesses—and different emphasis at different stages of the development of each business. But the areas are the same, whatever the business, whatever the economic conditions, whatever the business's size or stage of growth.

There are eight areas in which objectives of performance and results have to be set:

Market standing; innovation; productivity; physical and financial resources; profitability; manager performance and development; worker performance and attitude; public responsibility.

There should be little dispute over the first five objectives. But there will be real protest against the inclusion of the intangibles: manager performance and development; worker performance and attitude; and public responsibility.

Yet, even if managing were merely the application of economics, we would have to include these three areas and would have to demand that objectives be set for them. They belong in the most purely formal economic theory of the business enterprise. For neglect of manager performance and development, worker performance and public responsibility soon results in the most practical and tangible loss of market standing, technological leadership, productivity and profit—and ultimately in the loss of business life. That they look so different from anything the economist—especially the modern economic analyst—is wont to deal with, that they do not readily submit to quantification and mathematical treatment, is the economist's bad luck; but it is no argument against their consideration.

The very reason for which economist and accountant consider these areas impractical—that they deal with principles and values rather than solely with dollars and cents—makes them central to the management of the enterprise, as tangible, as practical—and indeed as measurable—as dollars and cents.

For the enterprise is a community of human beings. Its performance is the performance of human beings. And a human community must be founded on common beliefs, must symbolize its cohesion in common principles. Otherwise it becomes paralyzed, unable to act, unable to demand and to obtain effort and performance from its members.

If such considerations are intangible, it is management's job to make them tangible by its deeds. To neglect them is to risk not only business incompetence but labor trouble or at least loss of worker productivity, and public restrictions on business provoked by irresponsible business conduct. It also means risking lack-luster, mediocre, time-serving managers—managers who are being conditioned to "look out for themselves" instead of for the common good of the enterprise, managers who become mean, narrow and blind for lack of challenge, leadership and vision.

How To Set Objectives

The real difficulty lies indeed not in determining what objectives we need, but in deciding how to set them.

There is only one fruitful way to make this decision: by determining what shall be measured in each area and what the yardstick of measurement should be. For the measurement used determines what one pays attention to. It makes things visible and tangible. The things included in the measurement become relevant; the things omitted are out of sight and out of mind. "Intelligence is what the Intelligence Test measures"—that well-worn quip is used by the psychologist to disclaim omniscience and infallibility for his gadget. Parents or teachers, however, including those well aware of the shakiness of its theory and its mode of calculation, sometimes tend to see that precise-looking measurement of the "I.Q." every time they look at little Susie—to the point where they may no longer see little Susie at all.

Unfortunately the measurements available to us in the key area of business enterprise are, by and large, even shakier than the I.Q. We have adequate concepts only for measuring market standing. For something as obvious as profitability we have only a rubber yardstick, and we have no real tools at all to determine how much profitability is necessary. In respect to innovation and, even more, to productivity, we hardly know more than what ought to be done. And in the other areas—including physical and financial resources—we are reduced to statements of intentions rather than goals and measurements for their attainment.

For the subject is brand new. It is one of the most active frontiers of thought, research and invention in American business today. Company after company is working on the definition of the key areas, on thinking through what should be measured and on fashioning the tools of measurement.

Within a few years our knowledge of what to measure and our ability to do so should therefore be greatly increased. After all, twenty-five years ago we knew less about the basic problems in market standing than we know today about productivity or even about the efficiency and attitudes of workers. Today's relative clarity concerning market standing is the result not of anything inherent in the field, but of hard, concentrated and imaginative work.

WHAT SHOULD THE OBJECTIVES OF A MANAGER BE?

Each manager, from the "big boss" down to the production foreman or the chief clerk, needs clearly spelled-out objectives. These objectives should lay out what performance the man's own managerial unit is supposed to produce. They should lay out what contribution he and his unit are expected to make to help other units obtain their objectives. Finally, they should spell out what contribution the manager can expect from other units toward the attainment of his own objectives. Right from the start, in other words, emphasis should be on teamwork and team results.

These objectives should always derive from the goals of the business enterprise. In one company, I have found it practicable and effective to provide even a foreman with a detailed statement of not only his own objectives but those of the company and of the manufacturing department. Even though the company is so large as to make the distance between the individual foreman's production and the company's total output all but astronomical, the result has been a significant increase in production. Indeed, this must follow if we mean it when we say that the foreman is "part of management." For it is the definition of a manager that in what he does he takes responsibility for the whole—that, in cutting stone, he "builds the cathedral."

The objectives of every manager should spell out his contribution to the attainment of company goals in *all areas* of the business. Obviously, not every manager has a direct contribution to make in every area. The contribution which marketing makes to productivity, for example, may be very small. But if a manager and his unit are not expected to contribute toward any one of the areas that significantly affect prosperity and survival of the business, this fact should be clearly brought out. For managers must understand that business results depend on a balance of efforts and results in a number of areas. This is necessary both to give full scope to the craftsmanship of each function and specialty, and to prevent the empire-building and clannish jealousies of the various functions and specialties. It is necessary also to avoid overemphasis on any one key area.

To obtain balanced efforts the objectives of all managers on all levels and in all areas should also be keyed to both short-range and long-range considerations. And, of course, all objectives should always contain both the tangible business objectives and the intangible objectives for manager organization and development, worker performance and attitude and public responsibility. Anything else is shortsighted and impractical.

MANAGEMENT BY "DRIVES"

Proper management requires balanced stress on objectives, especially by top management. It rules out the common and pernicious business malpractice: management by "crisis" and "drives."

There may be companies in which management people do not say: "The only way we ever get anything done around here is by making a drive on it." Yet, "management by drive" is the rule rather than the exception. That things always collapse into the *status quo ante* three weeks after the drive is over, everybody knows and apparently expects. The only result of an "economy drive" is likely to be that messengers and typists get fired, and that $15,000 executives are forced to do $50-a-week work typing their own letters. And yet many managements have not drawn the obvious conclusion that drives are, after all, not the way to get things done.

But over and above its ineffectiveness, management by drive misdirects. It puts all emphasis on one phase of the job to the inevitable detriment of everything else. "For four weeks we cut inventories," a case-hardened veteran of management by crisis once summed it up. "Then we have four weeks of cost-cutting, followed by four weeks of human relations. We have just time to push customer service and courtesy for a month. And then the inventory is back where it was when we started. We don't even try to do our job. All management talks about, thinks about, preaches about, is last week's inventory figure or this week's customer complaints. How we do the rest of the job they don't even want to know."

In an organization which manages by drives people either neglect their job to get on with the current drive, or silently organize for collective sabotage of the drive to get their work done. In either event they become deaf to the cry of "wolf." And when the real crisis comes, when all hands should drop everything and pitch in, they treat it as just another case of management-created hysteria.

Management by drive, like management by "bellows and meat ax," is a sure sign of confusion. It is an admission of incompetence. It is a sign that management does not know how to plan. But above all, it is a sign that the company does not know what to expect of its managers—that, not knowing how to direct them, it misdirects them.

HOW SHOULD MANAGERS' OBJECTIVES BE SET AND BY WHOM?

By definition, a manager is responsible for the contribution that his component makes to the larger unit above him and eventually to the enterprise. His performance aims upward rather than downward. This means that the goals of each manager's job must be defined by the contribution he has to make to the success of the larger unit of which he is a part. The objectives of the district sales manager's job should be defined by the contribution he and his district sales force have to make to the sales department, the objectives of the project engineer's job by the contribution he, his engineers and draftsmen make to the engineering department. The objectives of the general manager of a decentralized division should be defined by the contribution his division has to make to the objectives of the parent company.

This requires each manager to develop and set the objectives of his unit himself. Higher management must, of course, reserve the power to approve or disapprove these objectives. But their development is part of a manager's responsibility; indeed, it is his first responsibility. It means, too, that every manager should responsibly participate in the development of the objectives of the higher unit of which his is a part. To "give him a sense of participation" (to use a neat phrase of the "human relations" jargon) is not enough. Being a manager demands the assumption of a genuine responsibility. Precisely because his aims should reflect the objective needs of the business, rather than merely what the individual manager wants, he must commit himself to them with a positive act of assent. He must know and understand the ultimate business goals, what is expected of him and why, what he will be measured against and how. There must be a "meeting of minds" within the entire management of each unit. This can be achieved only when each of the contributing managers is expected to think through what the unit objectives are, is led, in other words, to participate actively and responsibility in the work of defining them. And only if his lower managers participate in this way can the higher manager know what to expect of them and can make exacting demands.

Setting Corporate Objectives*

C. L. Huston, Jr.

In the Summer of 1954, the Lukens Steel Company found it advisable to set forth its objectives and its means of accomplishing them. The project, spearheaded by the president, received the full cooperation of all company officers.

The initial step was to develop down-to-earth fundamentals, called *Lukens bedrock objectives,* representing objectives for the company as a whole. Armed with them, organization heads—in consultation with the chief executive and with each other—developed basic objectives for their respective organizations and plans by which it was believed they could be achieved in the years ahead.

LUKENS BEDROCK OBJECTIVES FOR THE SHORT AND LONG TERM

The two Lukens bedrock objectives developed for the short and long term are as follows:

First, to promote reasonable and improving corporate earnings through productive effort applied primarily but not limited to the manufacture of steel plate, steel plate specialties, fabricated parts, and partially or fully assembled units.

Second, to conduct the business in a manner that earns for the company recognition as a constructive and honorable corporate citizen in its relations, designed to be mutually profitable, with stockholders, employees, customers, suppliers, community, and government.

In respect to these bedrock objectives, two points should be noted which we consider to be important philosophies influencing the conduct of our business. One is the emphasis on the "profit motive." The other is emphasis on "good relations" based on mutual profitability. We believe these to be fundamental to the long-term success of our business.

The initial bedrock objective not only stresses reasonable and improving corporate earnings to be derived from our established lines of business but also declares our determination to move as justified by

* Reprinted by permission of the publisher from *Targets for Management,* General Management Series, no. 177 (New York: American Management Association, 1955), pp. 3–14. Mr. Huston is President of the Lukens Steel Company.

market and earning potentials into areas of business apart from our traditional base.

Bedrock objective No. 2 underscores our belief that business relations, in order to be considered "good," require "mutual profitability," in which both parties benefit. Moreover, it points up our company's commitment, as a part of the American enterprise system, to uphold its share of responsibility in achieving public recognition of American business for constructive and honorable corporate citizenship.

LUKENS CORPORATE OBJECTIVES FOR THE ADMINISTRATIVE ORGANIZATION

Now let us turn from the bedrock objectives to the corporate objectives of each organization ("organization" is the term Lukens uses for each of its major units):

A. To establish and periodically re-evaluate broad basic objectives for corporate guidance.

B. To develop and maintain sound, clearly understood organization structure and personnel designed to meet the needs of the business.

Corporate Objective "A" and Its Basic Objectives. Each of the corporate objectives breaks down into basic objectives. Under "A," our broad objectives for corporate guidance, it is our aim:

1. To plan, direct, and coordinate the various company organizations, programs, and activities for comprehensive balanced accomplishment.

2. To secure a reasonable return on company investments in markets, plants, facilities, products, and manpower.

3. To build good, mutually profitable relations with all who help to make the company a constructive and successful enterprise.

In brief, how does the Administrative Organization go about accomplishing its objectives?

To direct and coordinate the company's various organizations, it is definitely in order to have carefully prepared plans, plans which originate from a recognition of market needs, followed by plans to direct the over-all abilities of the company toward finding a solution for the market needs. The Sales, Operating, Engineering, Research, Finance, and other organizations all may be involved in making the plans and certainly are involved in the execution of them. We count on the Administrative Organization to insure comprehensive balanced accomplishment, being alert to institute corrective measures when accomplishment is perceived to be out of balance.

To secure a reasonable return on company investments, it is our intention to develop expanded standards, to evaluate our earnings performance not alone by perusal of the monthly profit and loss and balance sheet reports but by detailed evaluation of product returns, equipment contribution to earnings, and the most effective use of human resources.

Over the long term we are firmly convinced that good and constructive relations have an important influence on the success of our business. It is our aim to promote good relations in support of the second bedrock objective as an earnest and continuing activity. Good relations come from sound and effective corporate performance and from well-rounded, positive communications to interpret their performance. We accept the premise that it takes recognized mutual profitability and not simply curiosity or casual circumstances to build good relations in business.

Corporate Objective "B" and Its Basic Objectives. The "B" section of our corporate administrative objectives also breaks down into basic objectives. In their development we recognize them to apply to all company organizations, though, for brevity's sake, we shall mention them only in connection with the Administrative Organization.

1. To design and maintain an organization structure capable of meeting the increasing standards of modern business requirements. ("Organization structure" means the establishment of clear lines of authority and responsibility *plus* appropriate compensation levels.)

2. To select and appropriately place qualified personnel in the organization structure.

3. To develop personnel in advance for future corporate needs. (It is often said that a man is known by the company he keeps. It is equally true that a company is known by the men it keeps. As we do a good job in this area, we sow seeds today for a harvest of new markets and facilities beyond present imagination.)

4. To build a climate of constructive cooperation within the organization.

5. To promote sales-mindedness (and awareness) among all employees. (One of our industrial friends has this motto: "The sales department is *not* the whole company, but the whole company *is* the sales department." We at Lukens feel that this is a good motto for us to follow, too, so that constantly before us is the principle that before we can profit from our efforts we must sell our products.)

6. To protect the health and safety of employees at their work.

As will be noted, the second half of our corporate objectives has to do with developing and maintaining the right organization and personnel to meet the needs of our business now and in the future. As the company progresses and the nature of Lukens' business changes, our organization structure must change too. To provide us with the best organization structure appropriate to our business, a separate department in the Industrial Relations Organization studies this subject constantly, both within and without the company, and assists in the setting up of new units as well as in the periodic appraisal of established ones.

For the proper placement of qualified personnel, it is our constant effort to learn more clearly the comprehensive requirements of a given job, and then to fill the position with the man or woman who, through his or her talents and interests, gives promise of better than average performance. So important is the development of personnel in advance for corporate needs that a member of the president's staff has been assigned to work with Industrial Relations, considering the promotion of *supervisory personnel development* as his major responsibility.

Setting the climate for cooperation occurs when a business relationship promises to be mutually profitable and is clearly understood. "Objective evaluation" and "communications" are the tools upon which we count to produce the cooperative climate. Sales-mindedness will be expanded through improved communications, looking toward broader knowledge, throughout the organization, of our relationship with customers.

The implementation of health and safety goals requires a comprehensive program starting with and incorporated with the engineering and planning stage for equipment and processes, and continuing with individual indoctrination and with day-to-day supervisory-employee relationships. It will be supported by educational and promotional media. Our own lost-time accident-reduction program began to be really effective only when top-level management evidenced sincere determination for results, and itself participated in carrying out the effort.

CORPORATE OBJECTIVES OF THE SALES-MARKETING ORGANIZATION

Sales-Marketing is another of Lukens' major organizations. Its broad objectives are to set sales and marketing objectives, within broad corporate aims, for improvement of company earnings and acceptance. We feel that these goals can best be approached through three distinct channels:

1. To search out and develop satisfactory markets for products and services with special attention to more lucrative and stable markets than are traditional for the steel industry in general and for Lukens in particular.

2. To sell company products and services at prices which will yield a reasonable and improving return over costs.

3. To assist customers to develop and service their own markets to the benefit of Lukens.

How do we go about achieving those goals:

Market Development. Lukens believes that the best way to develop new markets and new products is to recognize and to remedy the unmet needs of our customers and the industries they serve. (We refer, of course, to established products and services plus new and improved products and services closely allied to them.) Obviously, the field sales force, in its daily contact with customers, can provide the primary means of transmitting those needs to us. Marketing, engineering, and service personnel who travel frequently are additional aids to sensing out interesting market needs.

We must lean heavily in another direction, however, to secure more lucrative and stable markets than are traditional to the steel industry and to Lukens. To that end, a commercial development unit has just been established as an addition to the Market Development Organization. The new unit is considered a "business diversification operation." It will be the job of this group to go possibly far afield of recognized steel markets in quest of desirable markets to be served. A carefully-thought-out, comprehensive checklist will be followed to evaluate specific markets and the products which show growth prospects in such markets.

We intend to iron out in some measure the valleys that occur periodically in our sales and income results owing to almost complete current dependence upon heavy capital-goods markets. Improved return on investment and faster capital appreciation are specific goals.

Improved Return. To sell company products and services at prices which will yield a reasonable and improving return over costs will require more comprehensive sales standards and controls to guide the field sales force for efficient performance of its work. The use of such controls will tend to minimize actual sales costs, insure adequate attention to prospective purchasers of our products, and focus a critical light on various expenses such as entertainment, travel, telephone, and telegraph.

Customer Service. With reference to the No. 3 basic objective—to assist customers to develop and service their own markets to the benefit of Lukens—the vast majority of Lukens' existing products reach end-use markets only after fabrication and assembly by customers. The company's cause is believed to be well served to the extent that a portion of our merchandising efforts is directed to the customer's customer. This, we trust, will tie customers closer to us as a source of supply.

In addition, we intend to step up the program to encourage customers to visit and see at first hand Lukens' production facilities. Special inducements—such as plane service at our expense—will be employed. Furthermore, we plan to participate to a larger degree in the activities of trade associations whose membership includes our customers and our potential customers.

Corporate Objectives of the Operating Organization

Next let us consider Lukens' Operating Organization, whose mission it is to set operating objectives, within broad corporate objectives, for improvement of the business. This corporate goal falls in three areas:

1. To manufacture company products with qualities, costs, and delivery schedules attractive to existing and new markets.

2. To strive for both major and minor economies in operations and

procedures, within the limit of company resources, for increased savings and improved earnings.

3. To be aware of and to undertake developments such as give promise of new and improved products, together with appropriate facilities for their manufacture.

In order to accomplish the first basic operating objective, more detailed standards and controls will be developed to aid improvement and quality of our products, reduce the costs of their manufacture, and provide added insurance for on-time deliveries.

A medium-sized producer in the industry, such as Lukens, develops ready acceptance of its products and services in competition with larger companies which have a greater variety of products to sell only to the extent that it can be counted upon for superior quality, service, and delivery. The use of expanded statistical quality controls is a relatively new technique in our company which is expected to indicate where method changes can be made resulting in improved quality. Of course, it can result in decreased costs, too, which carries us into one of the means of helping to accomplish the second basic objective—to strive for both major and minor economies in operations and procedures, within the limit of company resources, for increased savings and improved earnings.

Specific cost-reduction goals for each operating department, the application of industrial engineering to methods and procedures, new or improved operating facilities, and the wider use of incentives will be additional aids to the development of major and minor operating economies.

In regard to objective No. 3, contributing ideas from sales representatives, outside consultants, customer contacts, and our own research and engineering departments will be cultivated. A long-established suggestion system is producing a larger and increasingly promising number of improvement recommendations. Capital expenditures for new plant and equipment will be evaluated more thoroughly on a return-on-investment basis prior to their authorization. Existing equipment will be appraised regularly and individually for improvement possibilities and replacement justification.

CORPORATE OBJECTIVES OF THE CONTROLLER'S ORGANIZATION

All this is equally true in the Controller's Organization, where the corporate objective is to set objectives, within broad corporate objectives, for adequate recording and control of costs. The basic objectives are:

1. To gather, record, analyze, and report cost and financial information for effective use by the corporation itself, stockholders, the government, and financial institutions.

2. To develop financial forecasts and organizational budgets for comprehensive planning and guidance of the entire company.

3. To review and improve clerical methods and procedures on a regular basis for better service and lower unit costs.

4. To investigate and develop better methods of presenting financial information.

Basic objective No. 1 is nothing spectacular or unusual, yet the company's management depends on the effective attainment of this goal to know where we have been and where we are going.

Periodically, it is well to take inventory of how efficient an organization has been, either by a self-audit or with the assistance of competent consulting firms. Just recently Lukens completed a year's exhaustive review and appraisal of the Controller's Organization, its functions and its facilities against the standard of the most modern practices appropriate to our operations. An outside firm was employed to assist. Innumerable recommendations for improvement are being employed progressively to implement more effectively not only the first but all the specific objectives set forth for the Controller's Organization. Budgeting, for example, is being raised to full department status, and a Systems and Procedures Department is being established to search out and develop economies in office work and procedures throughout the company.

Profit goals will be assigned on the assets used in the business, and management responsibility for income, cost, and profit will be defined more clearly. Recognizing that the Controller's Organization is essentially a service unit, research is being undertaken for the most effective presentation of financial information, presentation which will promote prompt and appropriate action by management. Expanded use of electronic statistical and accounting equipment is under active investigation.

CORPORATE OBJECTIVES OF THE INDUSTRIAL RELATIONS ORGANIZATION

It is the responsibility of the Industrial Relations Organization to set industrial relations objectives, within broad corporate objectives, for most effective development and application of human resources by the company. These fall into four categories:

1. To promote a climate of constructive cooperation throughout the company.

2. To maintain and improve human relations, relations with employees' bargaining agents, and public relations.

3. To conduct such programs and activities as will supply adequate and qualified additional manpower as required, and develop further the human resources existing within the company.

4. To assist in developing the organization structure for the entire company.

Expected achievement of the industrial relations objectives lies in six principal areas:

1. *Stimulating effective communication that will promote cooperative understanding among management, employees, and the people of the community.* Some of the more readily recognized tools of communication include our annual report to stockholders and employees, the company magazine, and interpretative publicity as released to the radio and press.

2. *Encouraging and assisting employees to prepare for advancement in the organization to their individual capacities.* Such stimulation includes determining interests and capabilities, defining job requirements, and planning programs for individual development.

3. *Promoting the development and maintenance of appropriate standards for the safety, health, and well-being of employees.* Programs in which the company assumes responsibility for employee security are subject to constant review and change. Lukens' performance in accident prevention now has national attention. From an accident frequency twice the average of our industry only 12 years ago, we have risen to a position of safety prominence, having received from the National Safety Council its Award of Honor—the highest that is presented by the Council to an individual concern.

4. *Promoting the development and maintenance of adequate wage and salary standards in equitable relationship,* considering job difference and individual performance.

5. *Recognizing the right of employees to collective bargaining, genuinely settling grievances and causes of grievances.* The labor agreement is a living document. We accept the challenge of a literal interpretation of the opening statements of our current agreement, which read in part:

> The company and the union agree to cooperate fully to achieve harmonious industrial relations and efficient production. The company and the union recognize that maximum production can be attained only through genuine creative cooperation.
>
> It is the intent and purpose of the parties hereto that this agreement will promote and improve industrial and economic relationships between the employees and the company. . . .

6. *Stimulating recognition of every employee as an individual—*his dignity, his status and service in the organization, and his contribution to the success of the enterprise.

CORPORATE OBJECTIVES OF THE PURCHASING ORGANIZATION

The basic objectives of the Purchasing Organization, within the broad corporate objectives, are as follows:

1. To develop and maintain an adequate supply of materials, services, and equipment as required and authorized for the needs of the business.

2. To give due consideration in procurement to ethical and quality standards, and also to the real value obtained rather than simply price alone.

3. To establish and maintain close liaison and cooperation between Purchasing and the users of procured material.

4. To build good relations with suppliers.

5. To keep abreast of both domestic and foreign economic trends that may affect our purchases for volume and price.

To develop and maintain an adequate supply of materials, services, and equipment with which to carry on the business, Lukens must deal with thousands of suppliers. Whatever we buy and however we find it, Purchasing will be expected to maintain a continuity of satisfactory supply with a minimum of investment.

The second objective is all-important in our purchasing activities because it encompasses the standards by which the purchasing job is accomplished. Price alone is not the final or all-important criterion. Many facets must be examined to determine true value-dependability, ethics, and quality being highest among them.

The third objective—to establish and maintain close liaison and co-operation between Purchasing and the users of procured material—is simply common sense. Salesmen with new or good ideas on products that are capable of filling our requirements, at less cost to Lukens, are to be put into contact with those in our company who are in a position to evaluate the products' worth. We are requesting our buyers to familiarize themselves with the ultimate uses of our purchases and with those instituting the orders.

To meet our fourth objective, that of building good relations with suppliers, buyers will need to have a thorough knowledge of a supplier's abilities to supply, his problems of supply, and—very important—his performance record versus his promises. Constantly stressed within the Purchasing Organization is the practical importance of a friendly hand and hearing for all callers.

Finally, it is our objective to keep abreast of both domestic and foreign economic trends which may affect our purchases for volume or price. Discussions with importers and domestic suppliers, and studies of business building and industrial trade papers, will be effective aids in this effort. Consultants in industrial economics and trends will help supplement our own observations.

Corporate Objectives of the Secretary's Organization

In developing and establishing objectives for the Secretary's Organization, within broad corporate objectives, we have four principal goals.

1. To collect and preserve corporate records and agreements of long-term value.

2. To guide, protect, and advance the company from a legal standpoint.

3. To develop mutually constructive and satisfactory relations with corporate stockholders.

4. To develop the company's contribution practices from the standpoints of public and community relations and the technical and personnel objectives of the company.

Boiled down, these objectives might be considered as giving to the Secretary's Organization a four-way personality: it is, first, the company's "memory"; second, its "watchdog"; third, its "family ambassador"; and, finally, a sort of "philanthropist."

1. As the company's "memory," the Secretary's Organization will have the responsibility which goes far beyond the mere collection of records and documents in a lifeless archive. These records are to become living instruments of the business—to protect it, advance it, and document its day-to-day history.

2. Our "watchdog"—that is, legal—efforts are to be geared to positive aid to the company after examining the existing pitfalls, and will be concerned more with how best to get things done than with the consideration of insurmountable obstacles.

3. "Family ambassadorship" is to be related to the friendly understanding and close relationship with stockholders which the company maintains on a *mutually profitable* basis by keeping them informed, answering their questions, and soliciting their views.

4. "Philanthropy" is undoubtedly a misnomer for our company contribution program. Lukens expects that its corporate contributions, carefully studied and directed, will work to the mutual advantage of the company and its employees, its trade relations, and the community it serves.

Corporate Objectives of the Treasurer's Organization

The basic aims of the Treasurer's Organization in setting goals, within broad corporate objectives, as they pertain to corporate financing and the receipt and disbursement of funds, are these:

1. To arrange both short- and long-term financing as required on advantageous terms.

2. To safeguard adequately our investment in plant and property through a comprehensive insurance program.

3. To conduct credit and service relations with the trade in such a way as to build business and avoid losses.

4. To acquire real estate on advantageous terms for current and future business development.

In regard to the first objective, we believe it can best be accomplished by building good relations with the borrowing agencies. To that end, a schedule of personal contacts is to be maintained and followed carefully. It is our practice to keep these agencies informed periodically so that when the need arises they will understand our situation.

Effective credit and service relations stem from readiness at all times to cooperate with customers. In other words, wherever credit is questionable, everything will be done to see how the sale can be made. Even high-volume customers occasionally need credit assistance.

To safeguard our investment in plant and property adequately through comprehensive insurance, it is necessary to maintain a complete fire, casualty, marine, and liability insurance program. An insurance committee within the company, and frequent discussions with insurance brokers, will be counted upon to keep protection in line with changing values.

As to the fourth objective, current and future business developments will depend partly on acquisition of desirable real estate at favorable terms. The Treasurer's Organization will be expected to maintain liaison with other company organizations for advance information on corporate expansion programs involving real estate needs. . . .

B. PURPOSE AND NATURE OF PLANNING

Planning *

Henri Fayol

The maxim, "managing means looking ahead," gives some idea of the importance attached to planning in the business world, and it is true that if foresight is not the whole of management at least it is an essential part of it. To foresee, in this context, means both to assess the future and make provision for it; that is, foreseeing is itself action already. Planning is manifested on a variety of occasions and in a variety of ways, its chief manifestation, apparent sign and most effective instrument being the plan of action. The plan of action is, at one and the same time, the result envisaged, the line of action to be followed, the stages to go through, and methods to use. It is a kind of future picture wherein proximate events are outlined with some distinctness, whilst remote events appear progressively less distinct, and it entails the running of the business as foreseen and provided against over a definite period.

The plan of action rests: (1) On the firm's resources (buildings, tools, raw materials, personnel, productive capacity, sales outlets, public relations, etc.). (2) On the nature and importance of work in progress. (3) On future trends which depend partly on technical, commercial, financial and other conditions, all subject to change, whose importance and occurrence cannot be pre-determined. The preparation of the plan of action is one of the most difficult and most important matters of every business and brings into play all departments and all functions, especially the management function. It is, in effect, in order to carry out his managerial function that the manager takes the initiative for the plan of action, that he indicates its objective and scope, fixes the share of each department in the communal task, co-ordinates the parts and harmonizes the whole; that he decides, in fine, the line of conduct to be followed. In this line of conduct it is not only imperative that nothing should clash with principles and rules of good management, but also that the arrangement adopted should facilitate application of these principles and rules. Therefore, to the divers technical, commercial, financial and other abilities

* Reprinted by permission of the publisher from *General and Industrial Administration* (New York: Pitman Publishing Corporation, 1949), pp. 43–52. Henri Fayol was a French industrialist who probably earlier than anyone else saw management as a universal, pervasive task based upon principles. His book, based largely on lectures made in 1900 and 1908, first appeared in French in 1916

necessary on the part of a business head and his assistants, there must be added considerable managerial ability.

GENERAL FEATURES OF A GOOD PLAN OF ACTION

No one disputes the usefulness of a plan of action. Before taking action it is most necessary to know what is possible and what is wanted. It is known that absence of plan entails hesitation, false steps, untimely changes of direction, which are so many causes of weakness, if not of disaster, in business. The question of and necessity for a plan of action, then, does not arise and I think that I am voicing the general opinion in saying that a plan of action is indispensable. But there are plans and plans, there are simple ones, complex ones, concise ones, detailed ones, long- or short-term ones; there are those studied with meticulous attention, those treated lightly; there are good, bad, and indifferent ones. How are the good ones to be singled out from among the others? Experience is the only thing that finally determines the true value of a plan, i.e., on the services it can render to the firm, and even then the manner of its application must be taken into account. There is both instrument and player. Nevertheless, there are certain broad characteristics on which general agreement may be reached beforehand without waiting for the verdict of experience.

Unity of plan is an instance. Only one plan can be put into operation at a time; two different plans would mean duality, confusion, disorder. But a plan may be divided into several parts. In large concerns, there is found alongside the general plan a technical, commercial, and a financial one, or else an overall one with a specific one for each department. But all these plans are linked, welded, so as to make up one only, and every modification brought to bear on any one of them is given expression in the whole plan. The guiding action of the plan must be continuous. Now the limitations of human foresight necessarily set bounds to the duration of plans, so, in order to have no break in the guiding action, a second plan must follow immediately upon the first, a third upon the second, and so on. In large businesses the annual plan is more or less in current use. Other plans of shorter or longer term, always in close accord with the annual plan, operate simultaneously with this latter. The plan should be flexible enough to bend before such adjustments, as it is considered well to introduce, whether from pressure or circumstances or from any other reason. First as last, it is the law to which one bows. Another good point about a plan is to have as much accuracy as is compatible with the unknown factors bearing on the fate of the concern. Usually it is possible to mark out the line of proximate action fairly accurately, while a simple general indication does for remote activities, for before the moment for their execution has arrived sufficient enlightenment will have been forthcoming to settle the line of action more precisely. When the unknown factor occupies a relatively very large place there can be no preciseness in the plan, and then the concern takes on the name of venture.

Unity, continuity, flexibility, precision: such are the broad features of a good plan of action.

As for other specific points which it should have, and which turn on the nature, importance and condition of the business for which the plan is drawn up, there could be no possibility of settling them beforehand save by comparison with other plans already recognized as effective in similar businesses. In each case, then, comparable elements and models must be sought in business practice, after the fashion of the architect with a building to construct. But the architect, better served than the manager, can call upon books, courses in architecture, whereas there are no books on plans of action, no lessons in foresight, for management theory has yet to be formulated.

There is no lack of good plans, they can be guessed at from the externals of a business but not seen at sufficiently close quarters to be known and judged. Nevertheless, it would be most useful for those whose concern is management to know how experienced managers go about drawing up their plans. By way of information or sample, I am going to set out the method which has long been followed in a great mining and metallurgical concern with which I am well acquainted.

Method of Drawing up the Plan of Action in a Large Mining and Metallurgical Firm

This company includes several separate establishments and employs about ten thousand personnel. The entire plan is made up of a series of separate plans called forecasts; and there are yearly forecasts, ten-yearly forecasts, monthly, weekly, daily forecasts, long-term forecasts, special forecasts, and all merge into a single programme which operates as a guide for the whole concern.

(i) *Yearly Forecasts.* Each year, two months after the end of the budgetary period, a general report is drawn up of the work and results of this period. The report deals especially with production, sales, technical, commercial, financial position, personnel, economic consequences, etc. The report is accompanied by forecasts dealing with those same matters, the forecasts being a kind of anticipatory summary of the activities and results of the new budgetary period. The two months of the new plan which have elapsed are not left without plan, because of provisional forecasts drawn up fifteen days before the end of the previous period. In a large mining and metallurgical firm not many activities are quite completed during the course of one year. Co-operative projects of a technical, commercial, and financial nature, which provide the business

Contents

Technical Section

Mining rights. Premises. Plant.
Extraction. Manufacture. Output.
New workings. Improvements.
Maintenance of plant and buildings.
Production costs.

Commercial Section

Sales outlets.
Marketable goods.
Agencies. Contracts.
Customer importance. Credit standing.
Selling price.

Financial Section

Capital. Loans. Deposits.

Circulating assets $\begin{cases} \text{Supplies in hand.} \\ \text{Finished goods.} \\ \text{Debtors.} \\ \text{Liquid assets.} \end{cases}$

Available assets.
Reserves and sundry appropriations.

Creditors $\begin{cases} \text{Wages.} \\ \text{Suppliers.} \\ \text{Sundry.} \end{cases}$

Sinking funds. Dividends. Bankers.

Accounting

Balance sheet. Profit and Loss account. Statistics.

Security

Accident precautions.
Works police. Claims. Health service.
Insurance.

Management

Plan of action.
Organization of personnel. Selection.
Command.
Co-ordination. Conferences.
Control.

311

with its activities, need more time for their preparation and execution. From another aspect, account must be taken of the repercussions which proximate activities must have on ultimate ones and of the obligation to prepare far ahead sometimes for a requisite state of affairs.

Finally, thought must be given to constant modifications operating on the technical, commercial, financial and social condition of the industrial world in general and of the business in particular, to avoid being overtaken by circumstances. These various circumstances come outside the framework of yearly forecasts and lead on to longer-term ones.

(ii) *Ten-yearly Forecasts.* Ten-yearly forecasts deal with the same matters as yearly ones. At the outset these two types of forecast are identical, the yearly forecast merging into the first year of the ten-yearly one, but from the second year onwards notable divergences make their appearance. To maintain unity of plan each year the ten-yearly forecasts must be reconciled with annual ones so that at the end of some years the ten-yearly forecasts are generally so modified and transformed as to be no longer clear and need re-drafting. In effect the custom of re-drafting every five years has become established. It is the rule that ten-yearly forecasts always embrace a decade, and that they are revised every five years. Thus there is always a line of action marked out in advance for five years at least.

(iii) *Special Forecasts.* There are some activities whose full cycle exceeds one or even several ten-yearly periods, there are others which, occurring suddenly, must sensibly affect the conditions of the business. Both the one and the other are the object of special forecasts whose findings necessarily have a place in the yearly and ten-yearly forecasts. But it must never be lost sight of that there is one plan only.

These three sorts of forecasts, yearly, ten-yearly, and special, merged and harmonized, constitute the firm's general plan.

So, having been prepared with meticulous care by each regional management, with the help of departmental management, and then revised, modified, and completed by general management and then submitted for scrutiny and approval to the Board of Directors, these forecasts become the plan which, so long as no other has been put in its place, shall serve as guide, directive, and law for the whole staff.

Fifty years ago I began to use this system of forecasts, when I was engaged in managing a colliery, and it rendered me such good service that I had no hesitation in subsequently applying it to various industries whose running was entrusted to me. I look upon it as a precious managerial instrument and have no hesitation in recommending its use to those who have no better instrument available. It has necessarily some shortcomings, but its shortcomings are very slight compared with the advantages it offers. Let us glance at these advantages and shortcomings.

Advantages and Shortcomings of Forecasts

(a) The study of resources, future possibilities, and means to be used for attaining the objective call for contributions from all departmental heads within the framework of their mandate, each one brings to this study the contribution of his experience together with recognition of the responsibility which will fall upon him in executing the plan.

Those are excellent conditions for ensuring that no resource shall be neglected and that future possibilities shall be prudently and courageously assessed and that means shall be appropriate to ends. Knowing what are its capabilities and its intentions, the concern goes boldly on, confidently tackles current problems and is prepared to align all its forces against accidents and surprises of all kinds which may occur.

(b) Compiling the annual plan is always a delicate operation and especially lengthy and laborious when done for the first time, but each repetition brings some simplification and when the plan has become a habit the toil and difficulties are largely reduced. Conversely, the interest it offers increases. The attention demanded for executing the plan, the indispensable comparison between predicted and actual facts, the recognition of mistakes made and successes attained, the search for means of repeating the one and avoiding the other—all go to make the new plan a work of increasing interest and increasing usefulness.

Also, by doing this work the personnel increases in usefulness from year to year, and at the end is considerably superior to what it was in the beginning. In truth, this result is not due solely to the use of planning but everything goes together; a well-thought-out plan is rarely found apart from sound organizational, command, co-ordination, and control practices. This management element exerts an influence on all the rest.

(c) Lack of sequence in activity and unwarranted changes of course are dangers constantly threatening businesses without a plan. The slightest contrary wind can turn from its course a boat which is unfitted to resist. When serious happenings occur, regrettable changes of course may be decided upon under the influence of profound but transitory disturbance. Only a programme carefully pondered at an undisturbed time permits of maintaining a clear view of the future and of concentrating maximum possible intellectual ability and material resources upon the danger.

It is in difficult moments above all that a plan is necessary. The best of plans cannot anticipate all unexpected occurrences which may arise, but it does include a place for these events and prepare the weapons which may be needed at the moment of being surprised. The plan protects the business not only against undesirable changes of course which may be produced by grave events, but also against those arising simply from changes on the part of higher authority. Also, it protects against deviations, imperceptible at first, which end by deflecting it from its objective.

CONDITIONS AND QUALITIES ESSENTIAL FOR DRAWING UP A GOOD PLAN OF ACTION

To sum up: the plan of action facilitates the utilization of the firm's resources and the choice of best methods to use for attaining the objective. It suppresses or reduces hesitancy, false steps, unwarranted changes of course, and helps to improve personnel. It is a precious managerial instrument.

The question may be asked as to why such an instrument is not in general use and everywhere developed to the farthest extent. The reason is that its compilation demands of managerial personnel a certain number of qualities and conditions rarely to be found in combination. The compilation of a good plan demands for the personnel in charge—

1. The art of handling men.
2. Considerable energy.
3. A measure of moral courage.
4. Some continuity of tenure.
5. A given degree of competence in the specialized requirements of the business.
6. A certain general business experience.

(i) *The Art of Handling Men.* In a large firm the majority of departmental managers take part in the compiling of the working arrangements. The execution of this task from time to time is in addition to ordinary everyday work and includes a certain responsibility and does not normally carry any special remuneration. So, to have in such conditions loyal and active co-operation from departmental heads an able manager of men is needed who fears neither trouble nor responsibility. The art of handling men is apparent from keenness of subordinates and confidence of superiors.

(ii) *Energy.* Yearly and ten-yearly forecasts and special forecasts demand constant vigilance on the part of management.

(iii) *Moral Courage.* It is well known that the best-thought-out plan is never exactly carried out. Forecasts are not prophecies, their function is to minimize the unknown factor. Nevertheless, the public generally, and even shareholders best informed about the running of a business, are not kindly disposed towards a manager who has raised unfulfilled hopes, or allowed them to be raised. Whence the need for a certain prudence which has to be reconciled with the obligation of making every preparation and seeking out optimum possible results.

The timid are tempted to suppress the plan or else whittle it down to nothing in order not to expose themselves to criticism, but it is a bad policy even from the point of view of self-interest. Lack of plan, which compromises smooth running, also exposes the manager to infinitely graver charges than that of having to explain away imperfectly executed forecasts.

(iv) *Continuity of Tenure.* Some time goes by before a new manager is able to take sufficient cognizance of the course of affairs, its general set-up and future possibilities, so as usefully to undertake the compiling of the plan. If, at such a moment, he feels that he will not have enough time to complete the work or only enough to start putting it into execution, or if, on the other hand, he is convinced that such work, condemned to bear no fruit, will only draw criticism upon him, is it to be thought that he will carry it out enthusiastically or even undertake it unless obliged? Human nature must be reckoned with. Without continuity of tenure on the part of management personnel there can be no good plan of action.

(v and vi) *Professional Competence and General Business Knowledge.* These are abilities just as necessary for drawing up a plan as for carrying it out.

Such are the conditions essential for compiling a good plan. They presuppose intelligent and experienced management. Lack of plan or a bad plan is a sign of managerial incompetence. To safeguard business against such incompetence—

1. A plan must be compulsory.

2. Good specimen plans must be made generally available. (Successful businesses could be asked to furnish such specimens. Experience and general discussion would single out the best.)

3. Planning (as a subject) must be introduced into education. Thus could general opinion be better informed and react upon management personnel, so that the latter's inefficiency would be less to be feared—a state of affairs which would in no wise detract from the importance of men of proven worth.

Managerial Planning*

Billy E. Goetz

Plans alone cannot make an enterprise successful. Action is required; the enterprise must operate. Plans can, however, focus action on purposes. They can forecast which actions will tend toward the ultimate objective of economic efficiency, which tend away, which will likely offset one another, and which are merely irrelevant. Managerial planning attempts to achieve a consistent, coordinated structure of operations focused on desired ends. Without plans, action must become merely random activity, producing nothing but chaos.

Various segments of an enterprise have repeated contacts with the same other economic and social units. Each of these other units also has managers who plan its operations in terms of its environment. These managers are inconvenienced and antagonized and their cooperation lost if the enterprise's contacts lack consistency, either through lack of coordination among its personnel or through vacillation. All points of contact should be coordinated; e.g., advertising, salesmen, product design and quality, packaging, credit arrangements, repair service, and delivery should all be fused into a team conveying a unified impression of quality and service.

The sequence and timing of events are parts of the master plan formulated by management. Failure in timing may mean congested shop departments, shutdowns, delayed deliveries, excessive carrying charges. Even the managerial activity of planning is itself subject to planning in which sequence and timing are important. For example, a company decided to formalize its compensation structure. Its management analyzed each position as to job content and as to knowledge, skill, responsibility, judgment, and experience required of the job incumbent. The study incidentally revealed much duplication of effort and some activities directed at cross-purposes. A complete procedural analysis was undertaken, which resulted in major changes in assignment of duties to departments and persons. Many job descriptions and analyses were rendered obsolete, and the job analysis and evaluation study has to be repeated.

* Reprinted by permission of the publisher from *Managerial Planning and Control* (New York: McGraw-Hill Book Company, Inc., 1949), pp. 63–68, 83–89. Mr. Goetz is Professor of Management at the Massachusetts Institute of Technology.

The broader and more permanent plans, i.e., policies and procedures, reduce management cost by eliminating recurrent decisions. Once a policy or procedure is adopted, recurrent problems are met by automatic, routine application of the rule adopted. For example, a company may work out the economic lot to purchase for each separate item needed. It may later discover that economic purchase lots for castings tend strongly to be approximately 3 months' usage while those for screw machine parts approximate a 6 months' supply. Starting from these facts, investigation may show that the cost of calculating each purchase lot separately is not justified by the minor savings resulting from the precision of separate calculations. A policy of buying 3 months' supply of castings and 6 of screw machine parts loses the minor savings of precision but avoids the costs of recurrent analyses and decisions.

Interdependence of Plans

The plans of an enterprise should constitute an integrated program. Necessarily all current plans of a single management share a common environment. They should all be directed toward a single consistent pattern of objectives. The plans should reinforce one another; they should mesh in an articulated sequence.

Perhaps the best illustration of a complete program of plans, internally consistent and properly articulated, is the budget produced by a well-conceived budgetary procedure. Typically, the sales department furnishes estimates of sales volumes and selling expenses, both broken down to show component elements. On the basis of these sales estimates, the planning department plans inventories and production. These plans serve as a basis for estimates of purchases of materials, of employment of labor, and of needs for machinery and equipment. These estimates, in turn, supply a basis for forecasting purchasing and employment department activities and thus for estimating the expenses of these two departments. Data concerning machinery needs and aggregate personnel requirements furnish the starting point for calculations of floor space, locker- and washroom facilities, heating, electricity, etc., required to maintain over-all operations. All these plans are reduced to anticipated cash revenues and expenditures, leads and lags are estimated, and a cash budget calculated. Finally, estimated financial statements are prepared. The whole procedure provides a complete, internally consistent, integrated program of enterprise operations.

Structure of Managerial Plans

We have assumed that the ultimate objective of management is economic efficiency, i.e., maximization of the ratio of output to input. This objective is implemented by major policies formulated by stockholders or board of directors. These major policies largely determine the general form of the operating organization, i.e., the division of the enterprise into major departments. Each department head, with some collaboration by his colleagues, with some assistance from his subordinates, and subject to review by president and board of directors, formulates departmental policies directed at carrying out the major policies imposed from above. These departmental policies largely determine departmental organization. Both the processes of policy formulation and of organizational design are repeated on the division level and so on down to the terminal operational level.[1] The number, elaborateness, and specific detail of these plans increase rapidly as the operation level is approached. This terminus is represented by a mass of specifications, drawings, dimensions, and standard-practice instructions. Perhaps the penultimate is reached in motion studies, such as those of surgical operations wherein every motion of each finger is planned and prescribed.

In a large enterprise, the activities of thousands of employees are directed and coordinated by this elaborate hierarchy of plans. A few broad plans are implemented by policies of several levels, and these are supported by a multitude of almost as permanent procedures. The whole governs almost numberless specific detailed decisions. For example, a company is formed to manufacture and sell road machinery (stockholder-level decision). Policies are formulated by the board of directors as to the scope to be given this general plan: Will the company manufacture road scrapers, steam shovels, ditchers, pavement finishers, rollers, snowplows, or sweepers? These decisions are implemented at the departmental level by policies governing the sizes and styles of each line included in the program, materials to be purchased, processes to be performed, and items to be subcontracted. Many procedures for handling customers' orders, for routing and scheduling production, for keeping the score of the profit-seeking game. Finally, a multitude of detailed decisions are made within the permanent general frame: should a specific customer order be accepted? Should a particular part be a casting or a forging? Should the company buy a turret lathe or an engine lathe?

POLICIES

Major Policies

Some policies are considered important enough to be imbedded in the corporate charter or in its by-laws. These can be changed only by vote of its stockholders and are the broadest and most fundamental of

---

[1] In a sense, policies are sometimes generated at the operating and first-line supervisory levels and imposed upward. If certain matters are not recognized or provided for by the set of policies adopted, or if regularly adopted policies are not enforced, customs may gradually emerge and achieve the generality, permanence, and authority of true policies.

corporate policies. Typically, the choice of industry is stated in the purpose clause, and the scale of operations vaguely fixed by the authorized capital structure. The composition and organization of the board of directors is usually stated in the by-laws. Many companies refer other matters to annual stockholders' meetings, e.g., pension plans, plans for major financing operations, and profit-sharing plans.

Somewhat less significant (or more urgent) plans and choices are made by the board of directors. These policies tend to be company-wide in scope, crossing departmental lines, although a few departmental matters may reach the board through financial importance alone. Choice of industry is perhaps the most fundamental of company policies, underlying and limiting all departmental policies. In its broadest sense, this choice is usually written into the corporate charter and thereby reserved to the stockholders' discretion. However, within these broad limits the board may decide to take on a new line or to discontinue an old one. For example, the board of directors of a manufacturer of plastic firebrick may decide to bring out a line of air-setting materials or a manufacturer of thermostatic controls may add a line of recording thermometers. The new line presents new problems to sales, production, and finance departments. Prospect lists must be revised with the new products in mind; new sales stories must sing the praises of the new line; perhaps additional sales force will have to be recruited and trained to give the new line effective representation. The engineering department will have to prepare new formulas or designs. The factory will have to buy new tools, dies, and fixtures and possibly new machinery; radical changes may become necessary in the system of production scheduling and cost control. New financing may be necessary, and credit policies may need revising, as the new line is sold to new types of customers. Both the importance and the interdepartmental character of the change make it a subject for consideration by the board of directors. After its decision is made, all departments will have to revise their policies to conform.

Selection of the competitive level is a similarly all-pervasive issue, properly the prerogative of the board. If the board decides to seek the quality market, the engineering department must specify close tolerances and fine finishes, the purchasing department must buy good materials from dependable sources, the personnel department must hire and train workmen able to produce the desired quality product, the production department must acquire high-grade equipment and provide adequate inspection, the sales department must stress a quality appeal in its advertising copy and in the type of salesperson employed, and the financial department should arrange credit terms appropriate for the quality trade. Every department must orientate its plans and operations with regard to this major policy imposed by the board of directors.

A third all-pervasive basic set of decisions fixes the company's policy as to venturesomeness, aggressiveness, and expansion. Closely related are policies regarding dilution of stockholders' equity and disposition of earnings. Aggressive expansion suggests extensive borrowing and plowing back of profits. Implications of these policies with respect to departmental plans are too obvious to require detailed comment.

In addition to formulating such fundamental policies, the board co-ordinates departmental plans through review and approval of the master budgets. This gives the board an opportunity to review departmental plans and ascertain that such plans are designed to implement the broader policies set by the board. Also, the board reviews and approves major expenditures before departments are allowed to proceed with their plans. Later the board compares performance with plans and passes on explanations and new plans growing out of experience with the old.

Within the frame imposed by the board of directors, all departments of whatever type formulate more specific policies to give effect to those set by the board. This will be true whether the major departments follow commodity or functional lines. Thus Chevrolet policies may differ substantially from Cadillac, and both will necessarily differ widely from Frigidaire or Electromotive: the variety of styles and sizes offered, the financing of sales, the channels of distribution will all differ profoundly. General Foods can appeal to coffee lovers with Maxwell House, to coffee haters with Postum, and to limbo with Sanka. Since no two enterprises have the same commodity divisions, commodity departmental policies must be discussed with reference to a specific company. However, many enterprises are divided into substantially similar functional departments, and commodity departments themselves are divided into similar patterns of functional divisions. This affords opportunity to investigate and partially catalogue the wide range of policies formulated by functional departments.

PROCEDURES

Nature of Procedures

Procedures are a species of managerial planning. As such, they share with policies and organizational configuration the objectives and techniques of managerial planning. Procedures, in common with other forms of planning, seek to avoid the chaos of random activity by directing, coordinating, and articulating the operations of an enterprise. They help direct all enterprise activities toward common goals, they help impose consistency across the organization and through time, and they seek economy by enabling management to avoid the costs of recurrent investigations and to delegate authority to subordinates to make decisions within a frame of policies and procedures devised by management.

Procedures also share the techniques of managerial planning. Many alternate procedures may implement the same policy complex. The managerial technique for devising procedures, as for all other planning, is one of analysis of alternate possibilities and selection of the most desirable. For example, professional firms are jealous of the accuracy of their reports. The final copy must be carefully checked to eliminate errors of typing. Columns of figures may be checked by reading back, figure by figure, to check against the original, or they may be checked by footing and comparing the total with that of the original column. The two procedures can be checked for effectiveness in catching errors and for cost.

Policies are relatively general, reasonably permanent managerial plans. Procedures are less general but comparably permanent. A policy maps out a field of action. It determines objectives and limits the area of action. Procedures are stipulated sequences of definite acts. Procedures mark a path through the area of policy. They may fork, generally with adequate clues to determine clerical choice of path; they may contain trivial gaps to be filled in at the discretion of a clerk; but there is little that resembles the extension of a policy. Procedures are not multidimensional; they do not cover areas of behavior; they have only chronological sequence.

Procedures implement policies. Specific routings of salesmen embody a policy concerning territories within which sales shall be sought. Scheduling of work through the shop gives effect to policies regarding size of inventories and balancing of load factors. As already noted production planning procedures may, as a matter of policy, be based on estimated shipping requirements, on stock limits, or on customer orders. Similarly, purchasing procedures may implement a policy of shopping the market for bargains or one of selecting a few reliable sources. Policy always sets an objective or delimits an area of action, while procedures fix a path toward the objective or through the area. Sequence is the *sine qua non* of procedure.

Structure of Procedures

Since a great objective can be analyzed into partial objectives or a large area divided into smaller areas, a major policy can be sub-divided into a number of minor policies. Thus policy has structure—usually paralleling the organizational configuration. Procedures also have structure. Many important procedures cross departmental lines, binding the activities of all into a common effort. Thus, a typical sales order procedure is initiated by receipt of an order from a customer. The sales department interprets the order and prepares multiple copies on the company's own standard forms. One copy may be sent to the engineering department as instructions covering necessary designs and estimates. Another may later be sent to the factory as an order directing the factory to produce the articles required for shipment to the customer. A third may be sent to the shipping department directing it to make shipment of the goods when received from the factory. A fourth may be sent to the bookkeeping department as an original evidence to be journalized and posted. A fifth may be sent to the customer as an invoice. These procedures obviously supply an important part of the connective tissue that holds the enterprise together.

Such all-pervasive procedures are main arteries tying together a great many branch paths. Many of these subordinate procedures are intradepartmental in character, but not necessarily so. Thus a complete sequence of cues and acts touched off by receipt of a customer's order could include all details of interpretation and write-up of the order by the sales department, origin and issuance of a series of shop orders with all their supporting documents and posting of production control records by the planning department, origin and return of reports of shop performance with more posting of production control and cost records, and all billing and collection procedures in the accounting department. Automatically instigated ramifications may lead through virtually all purchasing and disbursing procedures, into all pay-roll procedures, etc.

There are also a large number of relatively independent procedures tending to be largely intradepartmental in nature. Among these are procedures governing assignment and payment of second or swing shifts, employee bidding on job vacancies, the settling of employee grievances, seniority rights, handling of customer complaints, taking physical inventory counts, and many more. Though adding little to the coordinative machinery of the enterprise, these procedures are of great importance in achieving the objectives of consistency and economy.

All these procedures are implemented by a great mass of detailed procedures pertaining to single operations—often called "standard-practice instructions." For example, the operation sheet charts a series of acts by a number of employees necessary to production of articles ordered by a customer or needed for stock. Each operation listed is defined and described by blueprints and standard-practice instructions detailing setup, tooling, fixtures, feeds and speeds, and motion patterns. Standard-practice instructions govern such activities as issuance of new telephone directories, the routes of plant messengers, follow-up of delayed purchase orders, the posting of journal entries to the ledgers. Some companies produce "manuals of style" to govern preparation of letters, reports, and other written documents used by the company.[2] Similar manuals may regulate various accounting or tabulating procedures.

---

[2] For example, among a multiplicity of other procedures governing its educational processes, e.g., matriculation, registration, the University of Chicago issues a 61-page booklet of detailed rules governing the physical appearance of dissertations submitted by candidates for higher degreees. A typical detail is the insistence on the use of Roman numerals to designate chapters.

Recurrent Procedural Problems

A number of problems recur persistently in the course of procedural design. Among the most common are (1) relevance of the procedure, (2) duplication of effort, and (3) use of clerical substitutes.

Relevance of Procedure. Perhaps most frequent and most important of recurrent procedural problems is the problem of relevance. Does the procedure do a useful job? Is it worth what it costs? There are several major sources of useless procedures. Clerks and minor supervisors may attempt to build up their prestige and bolster their security by devising intricate and obscure rituals. Or procedures may become obsolete without being discontinued. For example, material shortages may plague a company. Reports may be instituted to inform a number of executives as to condition of inventories and probable delivery dates on outstanding purchase orders. Later the supply situation eases. One by one the executives no longer need or use the report. None orders it discontinued, as each believes that others use it. But the law of clerical procedures inexorably produces and submits the report until positive orders are issued to discontinue it.

Many procedures are traditional or copied from other enterprises where they may or may not be useful. Perhaps many cost procedures illustrate this possibility. Some costs are computed because "all businesses should figure costs," not because someone is going to use the figures obtained. It is customary for cost accounts to "tie in" with general ledger controls, but many cost systems have gradually been converted to standard cost systems in which clerical errors and deviations of performance from standard are merged in the variance accounts. Yet extra clerical costs are incurred to figure costs on trivial nonrepetitive jobs or to obtain redundant data on repetitive work to secure the tie-in that no longer serves its prime purpose of proving arithmetic accuracy.

Procedures may lose relevancy by getting hopelessly behind. Data produced may be altogether obsolete, and yet reports continue. For example, one cost department was reporting costs of producing tools some 9 months after tools were completed and in use. By the time facts regarding excessive costs of tool production became known, it was much too late for the superintendent to take remedial action. Finally, the superintendent issued instructions to skip 9 months of figuring tool costs and so got on a current and useful basis. Had he worshipped the tie-in with general ledger controls, he would have put on extra clerical help to produce useless cost data at an accelerated rate until the data were brought to a current basis.

Duplication of Effort. Many procedures are needlessly duplicated because of a desire for secrecy or through ignorance. Foremen often keep private records of departmental production because they have no access to or knowledge of duplicate records kept by the planning department. The cost department may keep records of material prices charged by different vendors that duplicate records kept by the purchasing department. Stock-room records, cost records, and planning department records may maintain a useless triple watch over inventory balances. Avoidance of such duplication is one major reason for centralizing responsibility for design of forms and procedures and for conducting periodic reviews of procedural configurations.

Duplication often stems from a desire for "protection." Private, duplicate records are maintained to protect individuals rather than through mere ignorance of existing similar records. Forms may be routed to a long succession of persons or duplicate copies sent each for the legitimate purpose of informing each of certain activities or to provide each with expensive but useless protection. The game may be played to the extent of requiring virtually every person touching a form to initial it to prove he has seen it. He may be required to date his initials to protect himself from a charge of delaying vital procedures.

Skillful design of procedures may eliminate clerical copy work by provision of duplicate forms. For example, copies of sales invoices filed chronologically may serve as the sales journal, eliminating traditional methods of journalizing. In some instances, another copy filed alphabetically may serve as customer's ledger, substituting filing for more expensive forms of posting. Such multiple use has resulted in many companies producing tens or even hundreds of copies of basic documents. So many companies are requesting duplicate or triplicate copies of invoices that provision of such copies is becoming standard practice. Some procurement divisions of the federal government require as many as 21 copies of invoices. The principle involved is sound. Why should clerks in one company copy documents prepared by clerks in another if the first can produce the required number of forms with little or no extra effort?

Sometimes accuracy is sought through verification by duplication. Thus, extensions may be computed on the customer's order and recomputed on the sales invoice to prove the accuracy of the original computation and of the subsequent typing. When possible, it is usually cheaper and better to verify by juncture rather than by duplication. An illustration is the checking of total hours reported on job time tickets against the total shown on employees' gate cards. Another illustration is verification of detail carried in subsidiary ledgers by comparison of trial balances of such ledgers with the balances of corresponding general ledger controls.

Use of Clerical Substitutes. Taylor and his disciples revolted against the rule of tradition. Trade mysteries, long carried in the memories of skilled craftsmen, were subjected to scientific test, standardized, and made a matter of record. Policies and procedures were reviewed and reduced to writing. Routing and scheduling were taken from foremen and made subjects of elaborate clerical rituals. Taylor's functional foremen became whole departments: planning, personnel, cost, toolroom, maintenance, stock room, and materials handling. The ratio of indirect to direct labor rose spectacularly.

In general, the new technique proved amazingly effective. Clerical work became important and hence the subject of inventive activity and intensive development. Clerical aids of all kinds were vastly improved. Duplicating devices, calculating machines, visible records, and tabulating equipment were invented or improved to conserve clerical time and reduce clerical errors. Today, determination of the extent to which clerical procedures should be mechanized and selection of the most effective types of equipment are major problems of the procedural analyst.

At times, paper work has been overelaborated. Too many managers at all levels have attempted to use reports to the exclusion of direct observation. For example, a shop superintendent attempted to install planning procedures that would virtually be automatic. Provision was made for reporting all irregularities. There appeared to be no remaining reasons why the man should ever leave his comfortable office. Two disadvantages gradually emerged. The superintendent lost all feeling for intangibles, which resulted in foolish decisions and the antagonism of all foremen, and several clerks were required to keep all records posted currently and to originate the multitude of required reports. A successor superintendent found that one planning clerk armed with a simple memorandum record of shop orders could visit every machine in the shop and ascertain progress of every order in less than 2 hours. The simple memorandum served adequately both as progress record and as report to the superintendent.

Dependence on paper work and the accounting fetish of a tie-in with general ledger controls often produce needlessly elaborate inventory records. There is seldom sufficient reason for carrying extensions and dollar values in such records. Receipts and withdrawals can be entered in physical units, and balances priced and extended whenever financial statements are to be prepared. Furthermore, trivial items can be controlled by physical means rather than by paper procedures. Stock limits can be set, and minimum quantities separately packaged. Each minimum package is thrown into the corresponding bin of parts. When the bin is emptied, the minimum package is broken, and an attached tag bearing the part number is sent to the purchasing or planning department as an indication that a new order should be released for the part.

C. FORECASTING FOR PLANNING

Elements of Forecasting*

J. S. Redfield

The businessman who said, "I'd like a copy of next Thursday's newspaper," when he was asked what he'd like most in the world to have, expressed a universal wish. Who wouldn't like to know what is coming, particularly in business? Who wouldn't like to know what is going to happen in his business during the next year, or in the next five years—with the assurance of at least reasonable accuracy?

In business, a great deal of time and energy are spent in trying to figure out what is likely to happen next. It is always the first step in budgeting, scheduling, and planning; and every businessman does it at least to some extent, either consciously or subconsciously, either systematically or otherwise. There simply has to be *some* basis for setting up future financial, production, and sales requirements and objectives. However, although estimating future business by one means or another is an essential and regular practice, the way it is done often leaves much to be desired from the standpoint of the reliability and dependability of the resulting forecasts. Many executives, consequently, have only loose estimates to use as the basis for business planning—estimates that often reflect the sales manager's optimism, on the one hand, or the controller's or production manager's conservatism, on the other. In either case these estimates are likely to be highly subjective and, as a result, biased by the distinctly human tendencies toward caution, self-protection, or the desire to please.

As a matter of fact, also, many businessmen, even in large companies where forecasting is an organized staff function, tend to distrust formalized forecasting. They are inclined either to discount or reject it as a "crystal-ball" activity or, once having given it a trial, mistakenly to expect a great deal more from it than it is intended to achieve. This is not only unfortunate, but it is also unnecessary. Business forecasting, done properly on a formalized basis, minimizes overenthusiastic as well as unduly conservative estimates, and the results can be rational, realistic, and believable.

The purpose, here, is to throw some light on systematic business fore-

* Reprinted by permission of the publisher from the *Harvard Business Review*, vol. 2, no. 6 (November, 1951), pp. 81–91. Mr. Redfield is associated with the management consultant firm of Cresap, McCormick, and Paget and is a well-known lecturer and instructor in management.

casting in the hope that this highly useful activity will be better under-stood and more widely used. Rather than focusing on statistical proce-dures, which do play an important part in certain of its phases, the ap-proach will be to discuss in simple but down-to-earth terms: (1) what a formal business forecasting program can contribute to management, (2) how it should be carried out, and (3) what its inherent limitations are.

ACCEPTING BUSINESS FORECASTING

Let it be noted immediately that the value of establishing a formal forecasting program is not limited to the assistance it provides in future planning. There are a number of important subsidiary advantages that should not be overlooked. Some of them are likely to have far-reaching effects on the operation of the business and can lead to a better control over and evaluation of the key functions of the company.

Such corollary benefits come automatically, as a consequence of setting up a logical basis for looking ahead. These preparations (particularly if the activities involved are not already established as regular procedures in the company), while producing information needed for the forecast, are likely also to bring to light the lack of control information on certain operations of the business or the need for improving some of the existing control reports. Not least important are the opportunities a formal fore-casting program presents for encouraging teamwork among the key executives and for allocating accountability for actual results where these differ from earlier estimates.

Add these advantages to the more immediate gains in the form of sounder procurement and production schedules, firmer budgets and appropriations for sales, advertising, and so forth, and it becomes plain common sense to approach the question of business forecasting with an open mind.

Actually, the crystal-ball tag has become attached to forecasting pri-marily because the process has not been fully understood. In particular, one limitation of forecasting has not been brought out into the open, recognized, and accepted: no one can foretell the future *exactly,* and all forecasting must include some elements of *guesswork.*

Once that fact is recognized, one can go on to ask himself, "Since no business can operate successfully without planning ahead, is it not sen-sible to make sure we obtain the best possible and most logical estimates of what will occur?" Certainly the best possible guess is infinitely better and more reliable than any substitute—including the "rule of thumb" or "feel" methods that are still used by many otherwise astute businessmen.

Guesswork being inescapable, the idea is simply to reduce the limits of error to a minimum. This can be done by following a procedure for combining mathematical analysis with the best business judgment available and then using the resulting estimates as the basis for future planning.

THE FORECASTING PROCEDURE

The forecasting process itself is approached on the premise that a general understanding of what is done and of how sound future estimates can be obtained is prerequisite to a full utilization of this activity as a practical business tool.

There are four essential elements in the process. Whether the forecast is to cover a short period (of several months to a year) or a longer period, the steps are as follows:

(1) *Developing the groundwork*—that is, carrying out an orderly investigation of products, company, and industry, in order to determine generally how each of these has progressed in the past, separately and in relation to each other. In short, the aim is to build a structure on which future estimates can be based.

(2) *Estimating future business*—that is, following a clear-cut plan for working out future expectancies in the form of a *mutual* undertaking with key executives and, after future business has been estimated in accordance with the predetermined step-by-step procedure, issuing an official statement of the resultant forecast. The key executives, by mutually developing the forecast, automatically assume co-responsibility and individual accountability for such later deviations of actual from estimated results as may occur.

(3) *Comparing actual with estimated results*—that is, checking the attained with the anticipated status of the business periodically, and tracking down reasons for any major differences. The forecast provides bench marks for measuring unanticipated gains or losses. Once measured, the reasons for important variations can be investigated on the spot.

(4) *Refining the forecast process*—that is, once familiarity with estimating the future of the business is gained through practice, sharpening the approach and refining the procedure. One must be reasonably tolerant with early forecasts, recognizing that proficiency with a new tool is not acquired overnight, and at the same time insist on constant improvement as experience with the process is gained.

Each one of these elements of the process is described below in some detail—(a) to show the part it plays in the development of the forecast and (b) to point out the subsidiary benefits which management can reasonably expect as by-products of proper forecasting procedure.

But, first, a word of warning: the accuracy and dependability of any forecast depend to a great extent on the care and analytical astuteness with which the early steps of the process are carried out. The results of the early steps become the foundation for later steps. Therefore, careful planning and a thorough job are essential. For example, the initial step, analyzing historical data, often is a lengthy operation. However, enough time must be allowed for its proper accomplishment. The common tendency of management to "hurry things along," particularly in the preparatory stages of a project involving statistical analyses, should be curbed. Putting the pressure on at this point can only lead to hastily done and poorly planned work that is likely to distort the picture later on.

DEVELOPING THE GROUNDWORK

The logical starting point is to find out everything possible about the past activities of the business and of the industry. A familiar principle is involved: that you cannot figure out where you are *going* unless you know where you *have been*.

Some of the questions about the business and industry for which answers will be wanted are presented below. Answers to such questions on the past and present situation will tell you where you have been going and will establish the basis for judging the future. In addition, unless this sort of historical analysis has already been carried out in a company, some highly interesting and pertinent information is likely to come to light that will contribute to an even better understanding of the business. This could well become subsidiary benefit No. 1.

In this initial step of the forecast process, it is wise to try to find out:

(1) Did the trend of company sales return to its pre-1929 level, or did a new era at a different level set in after 1932?

(2) What was the trend of the *company's* sales (by products, product lines, total, etc.) *before* and *after* World War II—through a sufficiently long period prior to the war for the trend to be significant? Has this trend been generally the same postwar as it was prewar, or has a significant change occurred?

(3) What has been the trend of sales in the *industry* through the same periods?

(4) Has the industry trend remained the same or has it, also, changed significantly?

(5) What has been the relationship between the company trend and the industry trend? Has the company been losing or gaining ground in the industry; that is, has the company's share of the total market been increasing or decreasing?

(6) Is there evidence that the market for the company's particular type of product is or may soon become saturated and, therefore, that the replacement market is likely to be the principal source of business in the future?

(7) From an internal standpoint, how do the trends of the several product lines compare, one with the other? Have some shown consistent gains

while others have dropped off? Have some gained more rapidly than others and consequently carried more than their share of the load?

Analyzing Company Historical Records. Now, how does one get the answers to these questions? First of all, the old company records are brought out and appropriate tabulations made showing the company's monthly and yearly sales, by products and totals, for an extended period before World War II and for the postwar years. As many prewar years as possible should be included, even going back beyond the early 1930's. Comparing the general direction of sales prior to and after 1930–1932 and before and after World War II may be revealing. In any event, the longer the period studied, the better.

It is important at this stage to plan ahead, having in mind that later comparisons based on the historical data about to be developed can be valid only if the data are set forth in comparable terms. For example, unit sales prewar and postwar are likely to be capable of direct comparison. Dollars of sales prewar, however, are less likely to be comparable because selling prices probably have been increased. In the latter case, it would be necessary to devalue the postwar dollar figures using the prewar prices as the base in order to achieve comparability.

The chances are that the best procedure will be to tabulate the monthly and yearly sales of individual products or product lines in units, and thus avoid the necessity of reducing the more recent figures to a comparable dollar base. It will be possible later to convert units to dollars for budget purposes. When it comes to over-all company sales, however, perhaps the dollar basis will be better. Part of the process is comparing company sales over the period being studied with industry sales and other figures (to be discussed) for the same period, and these are most likely to be stated in dollars. The principal idea is to look ahead, now, to the future uses for the tabulations and thus avoid the need for redoing them later on.

Tabulating sales over the selected past period by month and year for each product or line separately will be helpful. In this way each product can be studied individually. A "total" sheet for over-all company sales should also be included in order to develop a picture of the past trend of the company as a whole. (Large columnar sheets are useful for such tabulations.)

Of course, the initial going may not be so smooth as one would like. For example, the company sales records may be buried deep in the archives and have to be "dug out." Again, record-keeping methods may have changed over the years; sales may be listed only in total and not by type of product; or cancellations of orders, returned goods, and the like may not be properly accounted for. Regret that the company's record keeping has not been all it should have been and realization that more accurate records are needed will naturally result in making improve-

ments in the record-keeping methods—and this could be subsidiary benefit No. 2.

Developing Information on the Industry. Historical data on the industry as a whole are usually fairly easy to obtain. Dollar (and/or sometimes unit) figures for an increasing number of industries are being published or are available from the proper sources, now that managements
are beginning to recognize the importance of having current figures on
the industries they work in. One good source is the standard government
publications of the Census Bureau, the Federal Reserve Board, the Department of Labor, or other government agencies; also, industry associations may have previous studies or may currently publish data that will be
helpful. A little searching will probably turn up figures that can be tabulated on the same basis as the company figures and therefore can be used
to good advantage.

Here, again, the important thing is to achieve comparability. Industry
sales data which are later to be compared with company sales must be
stated in the same terms—units or dollars—and they must cover all or the
greater part of the same period of years selected for study.

It may happen, however, that only broad breakdowns of the industry
figures are available from published sources. Though these may be used,
it soon becomes obvious that finer breakdowns would be even more
helpful, not only to the particular company but also to others in the same
general field. Management may decide, therefore, to arouse interest
among members of the industry association in having it, or some other
impartial body, currently assemble and circulate more detailed industry
information on a controlled basis. Setting up the mechanics for this
exchange of industry information, if there is no provision for it now,
certainly would lead to subsidiary benefit No. 3.

Developing Information on Competitors. Once company and industry
figures have been whipped into shape for the forecast, the job of accumulating historical information on the company's chief competitors must be
tackled. Of course, competitive data are not easy to obtain. Competitors
are notoriously cagey about publishing their sales figures in convenient
form for others' analysis. In fact, marketing analysis or field research is
often needed to fill in this gap. But by digging in the right places much
helpful information can be obtained.

For example, the company may be able to size up competitors fairly
well through its own salesmen's knowledge of what goes on in their territories. A review of the salesmen's reports, particularly reports of business
lost if they are available, and similar records will be helpful. In addition,
it may be desirable to talk to the salesmen in person or send them a
carefully worked-out questionnaire designed to get as many facts as
possible about competitive activities. Questions such as these will be
appropriate: "Are our competitors making any greater inroads on our

customers than in the past?" "How does our company stand alongside our chief competitors in the market now and as compared with past years?" "What are competitors' plans as reflected in their field activities?"

Information of this sort, obtained from all corners of the market and from the men right on the ground, and boiled down to its essentials, can be of considerable help in providing an understanding of competitive activities and of the company's status in the trade. To be most meaningful, however, such a search for information should be thought through and carefully planned. If this is done first, then all of the salesmen will understand thoroughly what they are expected to do, will answer the same questions on the competitive and company situation, and will comment on the same aspects of the market; and, of utmost importance, the questions asked will go directly to the core of the situations being explored and will cover the subject completely.

Such a tussle with past company figures sharpens the attention to other operational weaknesses that may exist. Perhaps in talking to the salesmen, reviewing sales reports, and so on, areas of information on characteristics of the market or on competitive aspects wherein some, or maybe all, of the salesmen are weak may come to notice. Perhaps it will become clear that the salesmen would sell better if they knew more about these things. If such is the case, the decision may be made to look into ways of educating them as soon as the forecast project has been completed—subsidiary benefit No. 4.

(All along, the exploratory work is likely to touch upon activities of the business which are related to, even though they may not be specifically a part of, the forecasting project—activities which perhaps could, and should, be strengthened. Once these are brought to light, corrective measures can be applied promptly and systematically, whereas these activities might otherwise have continued to limp along. Thus, there may be possibilities all the way through for additional subsidiary benefits.)

The executives should be questioned too. One or several probably have wide acquaintance with and special knowledge of competitors. This suggests making a systematic effort to find out what information these men can add about the company's competition, about competitors' progress over the years, and about their future intentions. Even though a great deal of what will be contributed may already be known, pertinent bits of added information are very likely to come to light. Perhaps Company A, for instance, has a new product in mind that could hurt the company's sales if it is marketed; or Company B may be thinking of changing its method of distribution; and so on. All of this additional information adds to the detailed background.

In addition, during this questioning the executives obviously will want to know the "why" of the interrogation. This provides the opportunity to get *them* interested in the forecast project. They are going to be brought into the proceedings later on anyway, and this is a good time to get started. Let them have a brief "run-down" on the forecast project and on the way in which any information they can supply is to be used. A little "selling" of the forecast project now will help just that much toward obtaining the cooperation of all of these interested executives during the steps to come later.

Developing Trends and Relationships

By this time a lot of information on what the company and industry have done over the past years will have been assembled. Now the job is to find out what the various figures mean. There is nothing mysterious or difficult about this, and nothing basically complicated. What is necessary is merely knowing how to figure percentages and the like and being alert to detect relationships and trends. Native curiosity and good business judgment are two very useful aids at this stage.

The objective is to show how the sales of each product and of the company as a whole have varied throughout the period, but in such a way as to avoid the picture's being confused by individual monthly or annual variations.

Trends. For this purpose, company and industry trends are developed from the historical figures already assembled. These trends are part of the basic forecast structure, now beginning to shape up, on which the forecast itself will later be based. So long as they truly represent a broad past period, they will be highly useful as the starting point for working out the future estimates.

Once sales for each product and for the company as a whole have been tabulated by months and years for a period extending from, say, around 1920 up through the current year, it is a simple matter to plot these figures on separate cross-ruled charts. Then curves are drawn on these charts to represent the general direction taken by the plotted points and thus show the trends of individual product and company sales over the selected period of years.

A trend curve is nothing more than a simple way to show the predominant, over-all characteristics of a series of figures. Its principal advantages lie in its ability to reconcile the wide variations in magnitude that usually occur in untreated historical figures and in its facility for showing the net effect of these variations.

These curves can be drawn by hand, or they can be developed mathematically. The latter method, of course, is preferred, but freehand curves, if drawn carefully, will serve the purpose. Whether drawn freehand or computed mathematically, the curves will not pass through all of the plotted points but will take a "middle course" leaving about as many plotted points above as below the curve, thus in essence "averaging out" the variation in magnitude of the plotted points. The purpose, remember, is to show the *general* direction of sales. Exhibit I provides a rough—and admittedly oversimplified—illustration.

EXHIBIT I

TREND CURVES FOR ANNUAL SALES, IN UNITS, OVER A PERIOD OF 13 YEARS, OF COMPANY A (DRAWN FREEHAND) AND COMPANY B (COMPUTED BY THE LEAST SQUARES METHOD)

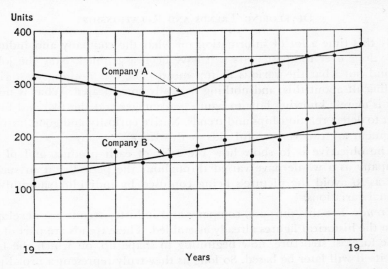

At this point we must take notice of a rather common objection. It is often said that trend curves are coldly impartial and will reflect unusual as well as usual conditions with equal unconcern. How, then, can historical trend curves be used as a valid basis for future estimates? The solution is simply to make sure, in developing them, that they represent *only* the *usual* conditions: (1) The monthly or yearly historical figures are examined to discover unusual variations; (2) the cause of these variations is located; (3) the original figures are corrected as required; and then (4) the trends are developed from the *corrected* data. Almost invariably unusual past conditions are reflected unmistakably by wide variations in the historical figures, and it is not difficult to identify and find explanations for these abnormalities in corollary company and other records or in the memories of company executives.

For example, suppose the sales curve for product "X" looks something like that in Exhibit II. Only the year 1936 is shown in order to illustrate the point. It is unmistakable that all was rational until July, when for no apparent reason the bottom dropped out. Such a variation would be patently atypical.

In the actual case from which this example was taken, it was found after considerable digging that someone way back there in 1936 had "charged off" a large number of backlogged orders that had been accumulating on the books and had reduced the record of July's sales accordingly. (Perhaps it should not have been done, but it was.) It is logical, therefore, to synthesize a July figure that conforms generally with the figures for the preceding and succeeding months. This correction is indicated by the dotted line. Other such unusual variations can be adjusted in the same way once the reasons have been ascertained.

EXHIBIT II

TREND CURVE OF MONTHLY SALES, IN UNITS, 1936, SHOWING ABNORMAL VARIATION FOR JULY AND CORRECTION MADE ON BASIS OF PREVIOUS AND SUCCEEDING MONTH

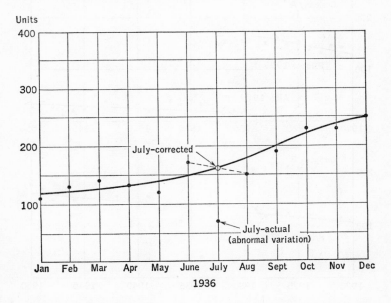

Charts showing plotted sales and trends for each product or line, for the company, and for the industry should be set up, more or less as in Exhibit III. For this example two possible company situations have been hypothecated and their sales curves shown.

Curve A is patterned after the sales curve of a large manufacturer in the midwest. Two points become apparent: (1) a decided drop in business occurred *prior* to the general business decline that followed 1929; and (2) the sales curve did not return to its previous level. In the actual case from which this example was taken it was found that the market for the products involved had become saturated along about 1927, and a decline in sales had already started by the time 1929 came along. Significantly, it was apparent that during the succeeding years a new "era" had set in. Since about 1932 replacement business had accounted for most of the company's sales. The entirely new and lower level of the sales curve did not necessarily reflect successful competitive inroads.

Curve B, on the other hand, reflects a less exciting situation. This sales curve shows that ground lost after 1929 has been regained and that the trend has been generally the same throughout the whole period.

EXHIBIT III

TREND CURVES OF ANNUAL SALES, IN UNITS, 1920 TO 1950, SHOWING RADICAL CHANGE IN COMPANY A'S LEVEL AND RECOVERY OF COMPANY B AFTER 1929

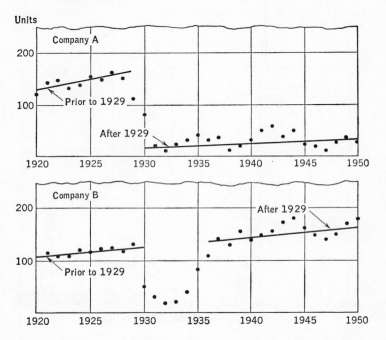

Close examination of any company's charts will reveal similar or other equally interesting information about total company sales during the period before and after 1929 and the years before and after World War II.

Relationships. In addition to charting product, company, and industry sales and developing trend curves for these, it is desirable also to compute and tabulate percentages representing the relationship of each one to the other throughout the past period selected for study. In doing this, it is best to determine for each month and year: (1) the per cent, or share, of the industry's sales accounted for by the company; and (2) the per cent, or share, of total company sales accounted for by each of the products or lines. Then, the resulting percentage figures for each of these can be plotted on charts and trend curves developed for them.

These relationships and their trends tell their own very interesting stories. For example, examining this record of the share the company has obtained of the total market over the years will tell where the company has been heading *in relation to the industry*—that is, whether the business has increased at a greater rate than competition (which is always good to see) or whether it has been losing ground in the industry over the years. Although an increasing trend would reflect company progress compared with past years, one that has increased at a rate less than that of the industry would indicate that the competition has progressed even more rapidly. In other words, a company could have been gaining, on the one hand, and (without realizing it) losing, on the other. A little study along these lines can easily lead to subsidiary benefit No. 5.

It may appear desirable to examine the past sales of individual products or product lines the same way as total company and industry sales. Comparing the trends of the products' sales will show how successful each one has been *in relation to the others*. The fact may be uncovered that one or another of the products or lines, while showing some gains over the years, has actually lagged behind the others so far as its contribution to total company sales is concerned. To know such facts about the company's products or lines could be subsidiary benefit No. 6.

These percentage relationships and trends also will help later on in the forecast process in determining the share of industry sales that the company is likely to obtain, and the share of company sales that each product or line is likely to account for in the period ahead.

Short-term Characteristics. The next step is to determine whether seasonal or other repetitive variations have been characteristic of the past sales of individual products, the company, or the industry. Preferably this is done mathematically, in order to obtain precise measures of whatever periodic swings in sales there may be. However, the same results can be obtained roughly by visually comparing the charts. If up-surges or valleys occur every year during the same season or month, the percentage of the annual total that each month of the year characteristically accounts for can be figured out.

Such a measure of past seasonal, or similar, variations will help to make the forthcoming forecast realistic. Later on future annual sales will be estimated without regard to these periodic increases or decreases, and then the annual expectancy can be distributed over the months of the year in accordance with the characteristic monthly proportions.

A National Index. Finally, it is necessary to have a series of figures representing activities up to the present in some broad segment of the national economy—a series whose trend over the past period being studied closely approximates the trend of the industry.

Nationally published indexes on production or on the financial aspects of the nation's industrial activity are commonly used for this purpose, and there are often several to choose from among the many now compiled by various governmental agencies. Here the personnel of the local Federal Reserve or Department of Commerce field office should be consulted; these people are universally helpful and cooperative and are qualified to suggest still other sources.

Reflecting, as they do, activities for large segments of the nation's total economy, such indexes are not likely to be affected materially by activities within most single businesses or industries. Moreover, they will tend to maintain a relatively even course over the years, except in the event of drastic economic changes. Because this sort of index is relatively stable, the trend of the selected national series, developed for the past years and up to the present and extended out through the future period of the forecast, is particularly useful as the backbone of the forecast structure being built.

Progress to This Point. Most of the preliminary work has now been done. The past activities of the individual products, of the company, and of the industry have been "boiled down"; and a related national index has been found and adapted. As a result, these things can now be seen:

(1) *Trends*—that is, where the individual products, the company, the industry, and a related large segment of the national economy are heading, as of today.

(2) *Relationships*—that is, how the company's progress has compared with that of the industry, and how the individual products or lines have fared in relation to each other.

(3) *Inherent characteristics*—that is, whatever seasonal variations are characteristic of the company and in the industry.

In addition, certain of the control aspects of the business have had a close scrutiny. Possible improvements in these and in other control and reporting activities, particularly those that heretofore have been conducted too loosely to be relied upon as the basis for future planning, have probably been considered, if not actually initiated.

As far as the groundwork of the project is concerned, all that remains now is to extend (on the chart) the trend curve of the selected national index out through the future period to be forecast, and to extend the trend curve of the industry out through the same period in such a way as to parallel the national index curve.

ESTIMATING FUTURE BUSINESS

Actually working out the forecast from this point on should be a mutual undertaking participated in by all of the company's key executives whose knowledge and experience qualify them to contribute opinions on the future of the company and the industry.

In the first place, each of the key executives has a definite stake in the company's progress. Each one, therefore, not only should contribute to the best of his ability toward planning for its future, but also should be placed in a position of joint accountability for the accuracy of the estimates on which these plans are to be based. In the second place, a group approach avoids the mistake of placing the whole responsibility for the forecast on one head. Too often the findings of that one executive about the future of the business become the target of the remaining executives or provide them with a ready-made defensive position when future sales do not stack up with what was expected. Unless they are brought into it, these other executives, not having contributed to the forecast, can (and will) deny with impunity any responsibility and accountability for deviations of actual from forecast results.

Developing the Forecast Plans. The next step, therefore, is to bring the best brains available in the company to bear on the forecast problem. This requires planning and a spelled-out approach. These men should do some concentrated thinking about the forecast, but they are also going to be busy with other problems. The easier it is made for them to grasp and understand the forecast aims and procedures, and their individual responsibilities in connection with the project, the better chance there will be of getting their full cooperation.

Accordingly, the forecast program should be described briefly in writing, and the plan circulated among the key executives. This write-up should have the overt approval of the chief executive and should explain the purpose of the forecast project, stating what it is intended specifically to do. Above all, it should stress the cooperative part and responsibilities the key executives are to have in it. This description should also cover the mechanics of the process and should include charts and tables as required.

These points should be made and emphasized:

(1) That the trend curves, the percentage relationships, and the charted historical characteristics of the business and industry, while revealing past activities, are also capable of indicating what is *likely* to happen in the future, *"all other things being equal"*;

(2) That the best collective judgment and knowledge of the company's executives with respect to the business and industry is now to be called into action in order to form a *composite company opinion* on (a) whether all things *will* be "equal" in the future period as compared with the past period or (b) whether things will be different; and, if different, in what ways and to what extent.

The stage is set in this way so that the forecast will be the product of: (1) precise mathematical or at least reasonably accurate measures of known facts—measures that are both objective and impersonal; and (2) a consensus of considered executive judgment—judgment that is based on a variety of experience in the business and the industry. The stage is also set so that a group executive meeting (or meetings, if necessary) may be held for working out the forecast, and so that executives included can come in fully prepared for the discussions.

Working Out the Forecast. In the executive meeting the forecast should be worked out systematically. The chief executive of the company, or another executive of adequate standing, should direct this activity. Strong leadership will be desirable because differences of opinion will need ironing out; overoptimistic and overpessimisitic opinions will have to be reconciled; and a clear, hardheaded, and realistic view of the company's future must be maintained throughout. The actual working out involves two steps:

(1) Determining how much business there is likely to be for the *industry* as a whole during the forecast period by (a) observing the out-and-out mechanical extensions of the past trends of the industry and of the related national index through the forecast period, and (b) adjusting this rough industry forecast upwards or downwards until it conforms with the executive group's consensus of opinion of anticipated general business conditions and the future outlook for the industry.

(2) Reaching a consensus of realistic opinions concerning the trends which the company's own total business and its several products or lines are likely to take during the forecast period, based on considerations of (a) the products' and the company's past trends as shown on the charts; (b) the trends which, it is anticipated, the products, the company, and the industry will follow; and (c) the share of the industry's total business that the company has obtained in the past and is likely to obtain in the future.

These joint opinions, obviously, should take into consideration the company's own plans and what is known of competitors' plans for the future. Any unusual internal conditions of backlog, shortage of materials, and the like which threaten to affect the forecast should also be considered.

Applying the Forecast. It is a simple matter to translate this consensus of executive opinion into formal chart form showing the anticipated trends of the industry, of the company, and of the individual company products or lines throughout the forecast period. At this point the company forecasts should be adjusted according to whatever predetermined seasonal or similar variations may have been characteristic of the business in the past.

It is now time to write up a brief, final statement of the official company forecast, including a full description of the assumptions on which the forecast was based. Here is an example of the way it might go:

In the official opinion of the company, the trend of general business, of the industry, and of the company is expected to continue to rise [or to decline, as the case may be]. The company's plans for expanding its distribution are to be implemented shortly and are expected to produce $x\%$ of additional business. On the other hand, new [or improved] competitive products, now about ready for the market, are expected to account for a loss of $y\%$ of the company's business during the forecast period. On the basis of these assumptions, such-and-such an amount of business is forecast for each product and for the company during the forecast period.

In such a forecast, developed mutually by all of the key executives of the company from a sound base of historical facts, no one executive opinion is likely to be predominant, and each participant has had free opportunity to contribute his opinions. It follows, then, that each of these executives can be expected to accept the forecast, without personal reservation, as the basis for planning his own segment of company operations. Consequently, the controller, sales manager, advertising manager, production chief, and any other of these executives can plan his respective operation with the assurance that management *as a whole* has taken into full account all major contingencies that can reasonably be anticipated.

Using an official forecast like this as the starting point for company planning is likely to produce another important subsidiary benefit. Inasmuch as the group method of developing the forecast discourages individual hedging with an eye to a later accounting and particularly because it provides a mutually developed starting point for planning, certain executives begin to operate more from an aggressive and less from a defensive position with respect to their own segments of the company's operations.

COMPARING ACTUAL WITH ESTIMATED RESULTS

It would be a mistake to drop the forecast project at this point. To regard any business forecast as static and unchanging and, once having worked it out, to file it away and forget it, or, on the other hand, to accept it without a further look as the year proceeds, is the surest possible road to disappointment. Disappointments need not occur, however, if the forecast is looked on not only as the very best estimate possible at the time of its inception but also as a means of bringing to light, throughout the entire forecast period, any major variations from what has been forecast when and as such variations occur.

To avoid disappointment, and to use the forecast for all it is worth, arrangements must be made to compare actual with anticipated sales results periodically. It must be understood that minor variations from the forecast are bound to occur; so, as the months (or weeks or quarters) unfold, no one should worry about small interim swings. But major variations and also lesser deviations which begin consistently to repeat should be scrutinized closely.

These are the danger signals. As soon as a significant variation appears, and regardless of whether the actual performance is greater or less than was expected, it is important to try to determine what lies behind the difference.

Tracking Down Causes for Variations. Suppose actual sales results are appreciably less than were forecast. The immediate reaction is: "Let's get to the bottom of this." The first move is to call in the sales manager and ask him why sales, apparently, have gone sour. Things begin to happen! Developing the forecast has accustomed executives to looking at sales results from the vantage point of specific measurements; so now they want facts.

Probably one of these two situations will be revealed:

(1) If the sales control and analysis function is operating properly, it is probable that the sales manager has anticipated this action and has taken steps to find out why sales have slipped. In that case he will already have analyzed current reports and identified the sales territories, the products, or the product lines that are responsible. Perhaps he already has made a move to find out directly from the field what is happening.

(2) On the other hand, perhaps what develops is that the sales control and analysis function needs strengthening; that current analysis of sales is not being carried out effectively; and that, as a result, it is proving difficult to isolate the specific reasons for the decline promptly enough to take effective remedial action.

In cases such as the former, it is usually easy to provide a logical follow-through—that is, to establish the facts and take direct and speedy action on the adverse situation. In the latter case, the need for establishing adequate sales controls or for improving the present function becomes apparent, and the required steps for improvement can be taken. Subsidiary benefits of the forecast project like this may continue to crop up.

It might be, for example, that as various problems of this nature arise, more information is needed, say, on markets or distribution methods than is regularly available in the company. A detailed study of these factors may be highly desirable. In that case, the market research department can be put to work on this specific project. Or, if no formal market research function is established in the company, expert assistance can be obtained from the outside either on a project basis or to aid in establishing a permanent market research activity within the company.

Adjusting the Forecast. Perhaps the reasons found for a major deviation from the forecast may strongly indicate that a new situation has developed that could not reasonably have been foreseen. Competitive activity may have changed radically; or there may have been some other serious alteration of the basic assumptions of the initial forecast. In that case, either the company's competitive tactics must be altered so as to counteract the change; or, if that is not possible, the forecast must be adjusted to conformity with this new situation. Significant variations of actual from forecast results, like these, can happen at any time and must be taken care of "on the spot."

It would be foolhardy, however, to limit re-examination of the forecast to the times when these danger signals appear. If it is to reflect accurately company and industry-wide influences and activities—which are always changing and are never static—the forecast, perforce, must be periodically rechecked and, if necessary, adjusted. Company plans may change, not necessarily radically but enough to have an effect on future expectancies; the trend of the industry or the national economy may shift. Of particular importance is the fact that conditions affecting the forecast in the third or fourth quarter of a year can be foreseen and evaluated with much greater accuracy at the beginnings of these quarters than at the beginning of the year, the time the initial forecast ordinarily is completed.

It should be a regular and unchanging procedure in the company at the beginning of each quarter (1) to restudy the principal measurable factors affecting the forecast and to re-evaluate the extent of their change since the last recheck, and (2) to assemble the executive group as was done for the initial forecast and mutually reaffirm or adjust the forecast as it will apply to the period then ahead. This should be done in the light of whatever changes may have occurred in the measurable factors and on the basis of the then current opinions of the executives. If a change in the forecast seems indicated, it is also advisable to repeat the procedure used initially of issuing a new official forecast statement showing and explaining the changes.

REFINING THE FORECAST PROCESS

The foregoing description of the forecasting process undoubtedly is something of an oversimplification. The primary objective, however, has been to point up the basic principles, procedures, and benefits that are involved. Some difficult problems are bound to be encountered; and, particularly at first, mistakes may be made. But it should be realized that forecasting, like anything else, gets better and more accurate with practice. One can learn only by experience how to gauge with accuracy the sensitivity of products and industry to changing company, industry, and economic conditions.

With learning will come more and more precise evaluations of the extent to which products, company, and industry are likely to react to various stimuli. Moreover, the method adopted initially for developing a forecast almost invariably is subject to some later refinements of application to the particular characteristics of the business, based on experience gained with the selected method in actual use.

For these reasons a certain latitude should be allowed the forecast when evaluating its effectiveness during its early years in the company—but not to the extent of being complacent. There is always opportunity to improve not only the mathematical but also the judgment aspects of the forecast method in use. In that way it will become more and more helpful, in fact more and more indispensable.

Fitting the Sales Forecast to the Firm *

James B. Boulden

Although the preparation of the sales forecast is difficult, the alternative to sales forecasting may be the economic failure of the firm. Unfortunately, no single source of information, technique, or type of forecasting can be suggested as most suitable for all firms. Businessmen must analyze their own products and market to determine what methodology of forecasting is most applicable to them. To make this choice intelligently, it is necessary that they be aware of the various alternatives which are available, and this will be the objective of the following discussion.

Figure 1 illustrates the process of sales forecasting: Briefly, information is drawn from the several sources and processed by one or more of the forecasting techniques. Each of these techniques may be used in several different ways depending on the type of forecasting being done. These types are not mutually exclusive but are often combined, so that one firm may draw from several information sources, utilize more than one technique and apply them in several ways. All sales forecasts end at the stage of executive decision where they are modified and adjusted. The remainder of this paper will be devoted to defining and clarifying this intricate process.

SOURCES OF INFORMATION

The business firm has three general sources of forecasting information: national and industry sources, the firm's own records, and its market channel. The national and industry information may be historical, as are the U.S. Department of Commerce National Income Statistics; or it may be expectational data, for example the Survey of Consumer Finances prepared for the Federal Reserve by the University of Michigan. Many firms also purchase national or industrial forecasts prepared by professional forecasters (although some large firms prepare their own national forecasts). These broad forecasts provide information from which the sales forecast of the firm may be prepared.

* Reprinted by permission of the publisher from *Business Horizons,* vol. 1, no. 1 (Winter, 1958), pp. 65–72. Mr. Boulden is Assistant Professor of Business Administration, University of California, Los Angeles.

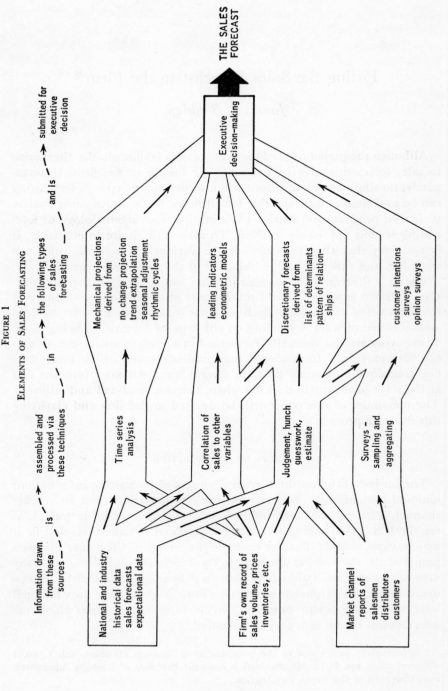

FIGURE 1

ELEMENTS OF SALES FORECASTING

Information drawn from these sources --- is --- assembled and processed via these techniques --- in --- the following types of sales forecasting --- and is --- submitted for executive decision

National and industry
historical data
sales forecasts
expectational data

Firm's own record of
sales volume, prices
inventories, etc.

Market channel
reports of
salesmen
distributors
customers

Time series analysis

Correlation of sales to other variables

Judgement, hunch guesswork, estimate

Surveys – sampling and aggregating

Mechanical projections derived from
no change projection
trend extrapolation
seasonal adjustment
rhythmic cycles

leading indicators
econometric models

Discretionary forecasts derived from
list of determinants
pattern of relation–ships

customer intentions
surveys
opinion surveys

Executive decision-making

THE SALES FORECAST

Almost every sales forecast makes some use of the historical records of the firm. Past sales volume, product prices, inventory levels, etc., are often important in predicting future sales. In addition, the firm may call on the salesmen, customers, or distributors of the firm for information useful in forecasting sales. The same firm may use all of these general sources as is illustrated by the following example of sales forecasting as performed by the New Departure Division of General Motors.

Two independent forecasts are prepared by separate company groups to determine the future sales of ball bearings, the major product of this division.

This first forecast is prepared by the sales engineers, who determine their customers' future requirements through direct interviews during regular service calls. These customer forecasts are then sent by the sales engineers to the home office where they are combined and summarized by individual product.

The second forecast originates with an economic forecast using a national index as forecasted by available consulting services. The relationship of sales to the indicators is determined by using the historical data of the firm. The forecast is then prepared from the projected national index and the established sales-index relationship. It may be modified by executive decision according to anticipated changes in prices, competitive position, and other determinants.[1]

The information is not useful until it is assembled and processed by one or more of the available techniques applied in the proper type of sales forecasting.

Techniques of Sales Forecasting

Prior to a discussion of the various types of sales forecasts, it may be helpful to identify and classify the techniques available to the forecaster for use in gathering and analyzing information.

By "technique" I mean the method of handling the forecasting information while preparing the forecast—that is, the manner of performance. The same technique can be applied in different ways according to the type of forecasting being done. For instance, the time-series analysis technique can be used to identify seasonal variations, cyclical fluctuations, and trends that may be projected through time. Each of these applications is a specific type of sales forecast, which may be used separately or in conjunction with the other types.

The four general techniques of sales forecasting are: time-series analysis, correlation analysis, judgment or guessing, and sampling. Time-series analysis consists of relating sales to time; it can be performed either graphically or mathematically. According to an American Management

[1] Robert E. Randel [General Supervisor of Finish Operations, New Departure Division, General Motors Corporation], "Variations in Forecasting Techniques at New Departure," in *Sales Forecasting, Uses, Techniques and Trends* (Special Report No. 16; New York: American Management Association, Inc., 1956), pp. 132–38.

Association survey of forecasting practices in 1956, this is the most common forecasting technique used by business firms. It is also one of the simplest and most easily utilized. An example of the use of this technique of forecasting is provided by the production-planning department of the Eli Lilly Company, which prepares a forecast for individual items by projecting historical sales data for the previous four years into the future using a 12-months moving-total sales figure. This trend is then reviewed by market research, where influences affecting the trend are considered.[2]

Sales of the firm may also be forecasted by correlating their movement to that of other variables in the firm, the industry, or the economy. For example, many firms have found that their sales are closely related to the level of disposable personal income in the economy. This relationship may be so loose that only general shifts can be detected (lead series), or it may be so close that a mathematical relationship can be established (econometric models).

Another very common technique of forecasting used by businessmen places reliance on the use of judgment, informed estimates, hunches, and guesswork. This technique assumes that the analyst is capable of identifying the major determinants of sales and of weighting them according to their relative importance. The success of this technique depends largely upon the ability of the forecaster. It has the advantage of flexibility because it can be quickly adapted to changes in the economy— but it requires a very capable forecaster. Broadly speaking, all techniques of forecasting involve some judgment and/or guesswork, but some forecasters are able to produce excellent forecasts by relying on this technique alone.

In recent years, various types of sales forecasting that utilize sampling techniques have become popular. The basic proposition here is that effective sales forecasts can be prepared by directly or indirectly surveying the intentions of buyers. If this technique is to be valid, it must be ascertained that buyers plan in advance what and when they will buy and that they have the financial means to make the purchase. In addition, the forecaster must be able to conduct the survey effectively and interpret the results accurately.

There seems to be no one "best" technique of forecasting, although professional forecasters often have favorites. In each instance, the nature of the product and the market must be analyzed carefully to determine which technique (or combination of techniques) is the most suitable. Once this decision is made, the businessman has to determine how the technique will be used. The following classification of sales-forecasting types may assist him in making this decision.

[2] *Practical Techniques of Forecasting, Planning, and Control* (Manufacturing Series No. 216; New York: American Management Association, Inc., 1954), I.

MECHANICAL FORECASTING

Sales forecasts may be broadly classified as "mechanical" or "discretionary"; these classifications are not mutually exclusive. The mechanical forecasts are all based on the premise that past relationships or performance will continue into the future. James Meredith of the Standard Oil Company of New Jersey states:

. . . The basic premise in forecasting is that, by and large, the forces which operated in the past to produce certain results will continue to be associated with those results in the future . . . the real difficulty lies in timing.[3]

It is possible to prepare mechanical forecasts objectively because past performance or conditions are relatively fixed and measurable. Of course, the distinction between mechanical and discretionary forecasts is relative rather than absolute because *all* forecasts involve some discretion. For example, even in the use of the time-series technique in trend projection, it is necessary to use discretion in determining whether to apply the technique graphically or mathematically, and in deciding what to project. Finally, executive decision concerning acceptance or modification of the forecast is always involved. However, having made this qualification, it is still useful to distinguish between the forecasts that are predominantly mechanical and those that rely primarily on the use of discretion by the forecaster.

Mechanical forecasts utilize the techniques of time-series analysis and correlation analysis—in "no-change projection," "trend extrapolation," "seasonal adjustments," and "rhythmic cycles"—in "lead series" and "econometric models."

No-change Projection

The simplest method of forecasting is projecting the current level of sales into the next period on the assumption that volume will not change. Unfortunately, this is the elementary stage at which the majority of small- and medium-sized firms are stranded. One purpose of this article is to inform these firms of the excellent forecasting tools available so that they may be motivated to develop their own forecasting process. In fact, the firm that makes no forecast is actually anticipating that no change will occur in sales; this is certain to be an error for all but the most stable and mature firms.

[3] James B. Meredith [Division Head, U.S. Division, General Economics Department, Standard Oil Company of New Jersey], "Short, Medium, and Long-Range Forecasting," *Sales Forecasting*, p. 88.

Trend Extrapolation

This method projects the past trend of sales into the future. An example of this type of forecasting is the sales forecast of Pyrex cooking ware; the trend is extrapolated by the Corning Glass Company because the record of sales growth is fairly constant.[4] This basic theme can be expanded into a number of variations, such as projecting the percentage change in the previous period, the trend in percentage changes in sales, or the past trend in the level of sales. This technique may, in some instances, be the same as a no-change projection.

Seasonal Adjustments

One of the most widely accepted types of forecasting for less than one year is making a seasonal adjustment to "normal" sales. Many industries such as clothing, gasoline, and electric power experience seasonal variations. The basic reason for using this type of forecast is the certainty that physical changes will occur each year in the climatic environment with sufficient regularity to be predictable. Also, many business influences such as Christmas occur on specific calendar dates. This technique is often used to adjust seasonally a forecast made by other methods.

Rhythmic Cycles

Economists and businessmen have attempted (without much success) to isolate and identify uniform rhythmic cycles in sales of certain products, such as producers' durable equipment; and for certain types of activity, such as construction. An example of this type of forecasting is that of the Dodge Manufacturing Company, which produces equipment for the mechanical transmission of power.[5] The company forecasts, in part, by assuming that an upward movement in sales will last approximately 18 months and the downward movement around 12 months. Certain other firms have been able to identify regular replacement cycles such as the three-year automobile replacement cycles. Unfortunately, the cycles change frequently.

Lead Series

Recent improvements in lead-series techniques have brought increased recognition and use of this method of forecasting. This technique consists of selecting economic series in the economy that precede sales in changing direction. Once the sequence and the lead have been established,

---

[4] Richard L. Patey, "Preparation of Coordination of Forecasting at Corning Glass Works," *Sales Forecasting*, pp. 111–20.

[5] Donald E. Gates [Director, Marketing Research, Dodge Manufacturing Company], "Reliable Forecasting in the Smaller Company, Dodge Manufacturing Company," *Sales Forecasting*, pp. 121–31.

the forecaster can quickly forecast future changes in the direction of sales by observing the lead series.

Lead series are widely used, especially in the area of industrial goods. The demand for industrial products is derived from the sale of end products, and changes in sales may lag behind the demand for the end product. Many firms find it possible to identify events or variables that logically precede changes in product sales and that can be used to predict future turning points in sales. The early-moving economic indicators of the National Bureau of Economic Research provide a valuable tool for some firms.

Econometric Models

The econometric model consists of a mathematical equation(s) expressing a historical, fixed relationship between sales and other variables. The model represents a "line of best fit" to historical data. The model technique may be used as a device for converting predictions of independent variables into a forecast of sales (the dependent variable), or a lead series may be used for the independent variable. In the former case, the forecaster is still forced to rely on other methods of forecasting to estimate the independent variables, and this may be as difficult as forecasting sales directly. The following method utilized by the Eli Lilly Company is an example of the use of a *simple* econometric model.[6]

The first step of the forecast consists of an intensive study of the past records of the company sales and the size of the total market in which they occurred, for the purpose of determining the historical share of the market obtained by the company. The total industry volume is then forecasted from an estimate of disposable personal income which is purchased from an independent agency. This forecast is multiplied by the estimate of the company share of the market to obtain a forecast of company sales.

$$V = (I)^n(t) \qquad S = (V)(\%) \qquad S = (\%)(I)^n(t)$$

Sales volume of pharmaceutical industry $= V$
Disposable personal income $= I$
Weighted $= n$
Company share of the market $= \%$
Time trend $= t$
Total company sales for the forecasted period $= S$

A very similar approach is used by the Upjohn Company, which is also in the pharmaceutical industry. However, this latter firm prepares two alternative forecasts. In addition to the forecast obtained from a forecast of the industry as described above, another forecast is prepared from

[6] Kenneth F. Griffith [Director, Market Research Division], "Sales Forecasting at Eli Lilly," *Practical Techniques*, I, pp. 3–35.

sales estimates submitted by branch sales managers for their respective sales areas. Executive judgment is then used to reconcile these two forecasts into a final sales forecast.[7]

DISCRETIONARY FORECASTING

Discretionary forecasting assumes that past relationships will not necessarily continue in the future. Thus, the forecaster must rely primarily on discretion in forecasting rather than on mechanical reference to past relationships.

One of the major advantages of discretionary forecasting is that both qualitative and quantitative factors can be considered, whereas pure mechanical forecasts are limited to quantifiable data. New methods of quantifying data are becoming available, particularly through the application of probability theory; however, many factors affecting the sales of a company still defy quantification—for example, the death of the company president or a major change in national politics. Because discretionary forecasts require the extensive use of judgment in interpreting information, highly trained forecasting personnel are usually necessary to produce satisfactory forecasts. This type of forecasting is well illustrated by the following discussion of sales forecasting by the Bell and Howell Company.[8]

". . . There is no substitute yet developed for executive judgment and this is the essential basis for our forecasts." Top executives hold monthly forecasting meetings to consider past forecasts and compare them with actual sales. Other factors are also considered, such as the current manufacturing schedule, the projected inventory position, competitors' activities, price changes, and special promotions. The treasurer also presents for consideration a long-range forecast covering general economic facts and summarizing the predictions of business analysts. The sales forecast is then prepared by executive judgment after consideration of these important variables.

List of Determinants

This type of discretionary forecasting is accomplished by listing the important variables that affect the sales of the firm and by considering the nature and importance of each. This is essentially the method used by the Bell and Howell Company in the earlier discussion, where the forecast is the result of executive judgment after consideration of important factors affecting sales.

The businessman often performs this type of analysis when he infor-

[7] Alfred C. Scott [General Sales Staff Manager, The Upjohn Company], "Finding and Evaluating Basic Data for Sales Forecasting," *Practical Techniques*, I, pp. 41–51.

[8] Harold F. Driscoll [Director of Advertising and Market Research, Bell and Howell Company], "Sales Forecasting at Bell and Howell," *Practical Techniques*, II, pp. 38–39.

mally notes his impressions of important factors mentally or on scratch paper in order to arrive at a considered conclusion about future sales. Since it is extremely difficult to select the pertinent variables and to weight them according to their relative importance, the success of the technique depends to a very great extent on the ability of the forecaster.

Pattern of Relationships

This technique has almost as many adaptations as there are forecasters who believe in the use of judgment and flexibility in making forecasts. It is exemplified on the national scale by forecasting through the use of the nation's economic budget. The basic approach is to forecast important elements separately and then combine them into some pattern in which their relationship can be re-evaluated with respect to each other until the system is internally consistent. An example is provided by the producer of a large variety of products who divides his total production into principal product lines and establishes patterns in the composition of sales within the line and between lines. A forecast of principal classes of products can then be cross-checked and expanded into specific forecasts of each individual product.

Customer-intention Surveys

"The most direct method of estimating sales in the near future is to ask customers what they are planning to buy." [9] This type of forecasting is illustrated by the General Motors example given at the beginning of this paper. Here, the sales engineers directly interview customers during their regular service calls.

In evaluating the usefulness of intention surveys, it may be helpful to define two extremes of customer classification. At one extreme are the industrial buyers of large mechanical installations and production facilities, who plan far in advance of expenditure and who often follow through with their plans. At the other extreme is the consumer-goods field, in which planning and expenditures are practically instantaneous. The customer-intention survey is much more useful in the first instance than in the latter. An example of the use of customer-intention surveys is that of the Dodge Manufacturing Company.

This company found that its sales are closely related to the producers durable equipment component of the gross national product. Therefore, the firm has found it useful to refer to the survey of intentions to invest in plant and equipment which is made quarterly by the Securities Exchange Commission and the Department of Commerce. The sales forecast is prepared, in part, by utilizing the established relationship of company sales to the forecasted producers durable equipment expenditures for the economy.[10]

[9] Joel Dean, *Managerial Economics* (New York: Prentice-Hall, Inc., 1951), p. 167.
[10] Gates, "Reliable Forecasting in the Smaller Company," pp. 121–31.

The firm may determine customer intentions even more directly by personally contacting the specific customers of the firm. However, this often proves to be so expensive for firms serving large market areas, that it may be more practical to rely on surveys of consumers in general such as those performed by the Survey Research Center of the University of Michigan.

Opinion Surveys

The business firm may obtain some measure of future sales by surveying the opinions of persons likely to know what and how much customers will buy. Examples of opinion surveys include the annual survey of economists' opinions published by the F. W. Dodge Corporation and also the Survey of Bankers' Opinions published by the Credit Policy Commission of the American Bankers Association. These opinion surveys are an indirect means of determining how consumers will behave in a future period by asking a particularly qualified group what they *think* the consumers are intending to do in the forecasting period. This may be contrasted with the consumer-intention surveys that ask the consumers directly what they intend to do.

The firm may wish to supplement these national opinion surveys with private-opinion surveys through the regular distribution channels of the firm. This may be accomplished by polling wholesalers and retailers who are in close association with the ultimate consumer. Surveys or panels of experts may also be utilized by the firm in preparing the sales forecast.

THE FINAL COMBINATION

It would be very misleading if this discussion were to conclude without re-emphasizing the fact that many business firms draw their information from more than one source and apply more than one forecasting technique for assembling and analyzing the information in several types of forecasts. An improved forecast is often prepared by comparing several independent forecasts. This is illustrated by the following example of sales forecasting performed by a prominent midwestern bank.

This bank draws information from national and industry sources, the firm's historical records, and from customers of the firm. Two independent forecasts are prepared, the first of which is formulated by the bank economist who forecasts the course of the national economy through the use of leading indicators. Using this information, he then prepares an "ideal" forecast for the various loan divisions and the deposit division with major consideration to maximizing the return on net worth in a manner consistent with approved banking practices and legal restrictions. The concept of what is "ideal" is extremely complex and involves consideration of the most effective distribution of bank funds as established by banking theory and law.

The various loan division heads also independently forecast loans and deposits

for their specific accounts. (The bank is organized around classifications of accounts.) These forecasts are prepared through projection of past trends and by
personal discussion with major customers of the bank.

The economist and the division heads then combine their judgment to reach
an agreement on a reasonable forecast. This involves the use of judgment and
detailed explanation on both sides to determine the proper integration of the
two forecasts. The combined judgment is then presented to the comptroller,
who prepares projections of the profit and loss statement and the balance sheet
for future periods using past records to determine pertinent ratios. The forecast
is prepared by months for the first quarter and by quarters for the year; it is
revised each quarter. The final product is submitted to the president and the
board of directors (they had also participated to some extent in formulating the
forecasts) for executive decision and approval.

This illustration may be compared to a similar-sized bank also in the
Midwest that relies on its loan division heads alone to prepare the
forecast. The result is that the bank always surpasses the forecast because
the responsible officers purposely, by their own admission, forecast low
to make their "showing" better and relieve future pressure.

Sales forecasting then is a basic tool for anticipating the nature of
future business operations. Future personnel requirements, purchasing
commitments, production schedules, inventory plans, and financial
budgets are based upon it. It is vital that businessmen be informed
about the available alternative forecasting techniques, methods, and
sources of information. The very success or failure of the firm depends
upon selecting forecasting elements properly and fitting them to the
needs of the business.

D. POLICY FORMULATION

Product-line Policy*

Joel Dean

A company's conscious competitive actions have three facets: (1) product policy, (2) promotion policy, and (3) pricing policy. Product policy commands not only managerial attention, because of rapid changes in technology and demand; it is also significant for the entire economy, since it is the mainspring of economic progress and hence an important test of a company's social contribution.[1]

The purpose of this article is to examine, from an economic standpoint, the managerial problems of product coverage in a multiple-product firm. We are concerned with only one phase of product policy, namely, product coverage—that is, decisions on what end products the company will make and sell. Product improvement—the other phase of product policy—is not examined here. We shall attempt to sketch a framework for a policy approach to product coverage, that is, a set of standing answers to recurring product proposals.

The term "product" in this discussion will mean an end product offered for sale by the firm. Intermediate products produced as a consequence of vertical integration and parts and components purchased for inclusion in final products are excluded from this analysis.

The term "product line" will be used here in a broad sense to include all the products manufactured by the firm. The term can be used in a narrower sense to refer to groups of products that are related either on the marketing side as being complements or substitutes or on the production side as being made from the same materials or by similar processes.

* Reprinted by permission of the publisher from the *Journal of Business*, vol. 23, no. 4 (October, 1950), pp. 248–258. Copyright, 1950, University of Chicago. Mr. Dean is Professor of Business Economics in the School of Business at Columbia University and senior partner in Joel Dean and Associates, Management Economic Consultants.

[1] Although most modern firms make several products, economic theory has been developed on the premise that each firm makes only one product. The reasons for such an inadequate premise are to be found partly in the historical origins of theory and partly in the simplicity of theoretical analysis when it is confined to single-product output. Determination of the costs of individual products in a multiple-product company is both conceptually and empirically difficult. The neglect of these problems may also be due to the notion that management views each product as a separate business activity with the characteristics of a single-product firm, but this approach has little theoretical and no practical support.

In a dynamic economy, where product monopolies are characteristically transient and where product development is a major facet of competitive rivalry, economically sound decisions on additions to the company's product coverage are obviously of great importance. Three important problems encountered by top management in formulating policy on adding new products are: (1) scouting out potential product additions, (2) appraising these proposals and making the product selection, and (3) launching each new product venture in a way that gives it a maximum chance of success.

The first, development of a flow of promising proposals for candidate additions to the company's product line, is fundamental to sound product additions. For many companies product research is the main instrument. Others license new product inventions or buy them directly from independent inventors and corporate research departments or through professional "product-finders." Product proposals also come from customers, from the company's marketing staff, from small companies that want to sell out, and from independent inventors.

The third top management problem—launching the new venture—involves questions of refinement of the product design, selection of market targets, methods of distribution, pricing the new product, and making capital expenditures for production and marketing facilities.

Top management's second problem—the appraisal of candidate product additions—is the central concern of this article. Even in large, well-managed companies the methods used in selecting product additions leave much to be desired. A survey of the experience of two hundred leading packaged-goods manufacturers in the postwar development of new products revealed that only 20 per cent of the products put on the market actually turned out to be money-makers.[2] For most of these products, expectations had been far too optimistic. This dismal experience showed that product innovation required more careful selection and more deliberate planning than these companies had anticipated. A rich mixture of market research, product testing, adequate financial resources, and persistence was needed.

POLICY PROPOSALS

Management needs a rational routine for this appraisal in the form of a set of criteria to guide its analysis. In this section we consider what questions management should ask and what criteria it should establish. The discussion has three parts: (a) Standards of prospective profits from the candidate product; (b) considerations of product-line strategy; and (c) specific criteria of acceptability of new products.

[2] "The Introduction of New Products," a survey made by Ross Federal Research Corporation, for Peter Hilton, Inc.

(a) Standards of Profitability

Usually the most important question about a new product is its prospective profitability. If the sole objective of the enterprise were to maximize profits in a strict sense, all considerations affecting additions to the product line could be subsumed under profitability; to a degree, the nonprofit considerations are merely indicators of long-run profit prospects. Yet, business motivations are more complex than has been assumed in economic theory. They encompass objectives such as external corporate life, market share, volume growth, comfortable cash reserves, assured tenure for management, and pleasant employee relationships. These purposes can be forced into a concept of long-range profit maximization; but, when this is done, the concept evaporates for analytical applications.

Prospective profitability, in the narrow, cash-return sense, is nevertheless the key consideration. Candidates for addition to the product line should be ranked in a priority ladder according to profitability and should be selected from the top down, except in unusual strategic circumstances. But a profitability ladder raises four questions: (1) What concept of profits is relevant? (2) What form of profit standard should be used? (3) How should profit prospects be measured? (4) What rejection level should be established?

1. *Profit Concepts.* The relevant concept of profits for product-line additions is not always clear; it depends on circumstances. The basic choice lies between some notion of incremental profits and the concept of net profits over full cost. Incremental profits refer to the difference in the firm's profits with and without the addition of the product in question. It thus credits the new product with the whole increase in profitablity of existing facilites that its introduction produces. In contrast, the use of net profits means that some of the fixed overheads are loaded onto the new product, and cost burdens of existing products are correspondingly lightened.

If they are extended over a long enough period to encompass the probable life-cycle of the new addition, incremental profits are the relevant concept. Sometimes product additions are so short lived that incremental profits are the difference between price and short-run marginal cost. Examples are sub-contracting work, war work, and production of specially designed products in a job shop. In this special case the usual strategic considerations that enter into product-line additions are rather unimportant. But here, as in a longer-range setting, incremental profits must be measured against the profits that could come from the best alternative use of money, time, and facilities. If the alternative is idleness, then presumably any incremental profits will justify the addition of the product. If, as is more common, the alternative is to use resources on some other product, the alternative return sets the standard of minimum incremental profits.

For more durable additions to the product line, short-run marginal cost is not the correct concept for estimating the added profitability of the new product. The adoption of a new product carries with it explicitly or tacitly the commitment to stay with the new venture at least until it has had a fair trial, and possibly longer. Additions to common costs that are often unforeseen at the time of the introduction of the new product are likely to occur, so that the businessman's rule of thumb of loading on the new product its full share of common overhead is often the most appropriate method after all.[3]

2. *Form of Profit Standard.* In order to compare the profitability of alternative uses of facilities, profit standards must be stated in a form that is relevant for ranking them. What form should a profit estimate take—unit margins, return on investment, aggregate dollar profits? The most general form is the total dollar income over the whole life of the product minus the total outlay to produce it. But in cases where the new product is a permanent addition, it may be easier to measure the profit return per unit of some fixed, bottleneck factor of production absorbed by the new product. Such a bottleneck factor might be executive time, machine time, or materials (e.g., steel during the postwar period of shortage and private rationing by producers). In the most usual case it is strictly limited funds for capital outlays on the new product (e.g., those available from retained earnings). In this case, return on incremental investment is the best measure. This form of profit measures the income-producing efficiency of the product relative to alternatives uses.[4]

3. *Measuring Profit Prospects.* The major problem in estimating profitability is to make decent projections of revenues and costs. Ideally, these should cover the expected life-span of the product; in practice, three to five years is the limit of visibility. Forecasts of demand and costs are extremely speculative for new products; indeed, they are much more so than many firms realize. In explaining the failure of new products, the two hundred companies mentioned at the beginning of this section put particular emphasis on (a) inadequate market research and (b) under-estimated selling-cost requirements.

The hardest cost estimates to make are estimates of development and selling expenses. Pressure to get the product onto the market may cut short the research that is needed to work all the bugs out of the product.

[3] The experience of many business organizations is that new products added to mop up overhead actually produce new overheads and, in addition, incur untraceable costs, such as added drain on executive time and energy. These costs make their incremental profits quite different from those indicated by short-run marginal cost estimates.

[4] In the extreme case, where all resources are idle and there is just one candidate product which itself cannot absorb any resource completely, the rate-of-return form is inapplicable, since inefficiency is not a consideration in production.

This can be an expensive short cut, since the bad impressions made on the first venturesome customers may cause delays and perhaps foreclose market acceptance.

Products vary widely in forecastability; for some products no refined calculations are possible at all. Consequently, any use of profit standards for appraising the candidate product is precluded. Going into some products is like making a bet on the horses. Decisions then must rest more completely on grand strategy and on criteria of acceptance like those discussed later in this section.

4. *Level of Profit Standards.* To determine how large an incremental profit should be to justify the addition of the product to the line requires some standard of adequate return. Ideally, the market cost of new capital should always be the criterion, but is not widely used. One alternative standard is supplied by the competition of rival product additions and rival internal investments of all sorts for the company's limited resources. Under such a plan, a candidate product will be rejected unless it promises a rate of return that exceeds the next best use for funds. Another standard (where resources are not limited) is in terms of some historical return on investment. Thus some companies require a minimum return equal to the company's ten-year average; others develop an arbitrary standard of adequate profits of this type that is not specifically related to anything. For example, a large automobile manufacturer, for unknown reasons, has adopted 30 per cent before taxes as a standard. Sometimes the standard is formulated in terms of unit net profit margins at some normal output rate. One company, for example, in the drug field, has a minimum 50 per cent margin. Presumably, such a high standard reflects competition of highly profitable alternative products; thus it is likely to be an opportunity cost standard.

5. *Summary.* The pivotal test for the addition of a new product is its profitability. If profit maximization were the sole goal of the enterprise, this test would encompass all others, but pluralistic motivation makes the other goals relevant as well. The relevant concept of profits is incremental returns over the appropriate time period, that is, what addition the product makes to enterprise profits over its life-span. The profit prospects must be expressed in a form that allows significant comparison with alternative uses of labor, plant, and time. It is common practice to establish some standard of minimum acceptable earnings, but this floor should really be determined by profitability of alternative opportunities, that is, by external conditions.

(b) Product Strategy

Supplementing tests of profit prospects are general considerations of strategy. These are to a degree composed of the specific acceptance criteria discussed in the next subsection.

Multiple-product "strategy" is a shorthand name for the company's long-run purposes in product diversity. Although strategy is usually focused on profits in the long run and is confined by economic limitations, it is also affected by the technical abilities and personal preferences of management. It is a position consciously taken to simplify decision-making at crucial points. Presumably, under an enterprise system, the purpose of strategy is to make money, in the long run at least. Yet, as we have seen, this is not the whole story. In a going concern, product-line strategy usually has historical roots—sometimes in the company's original purposes but often later in a basic merger or an empire-builder's dream.

Companies with no clear product-line strategy have been conspicuously profitable, and many mergers have grown in spite of the seeming lack of kinship among the products of the merging companies. Other companies say that they have a product-line policy, although they are simply rationalizing a product that grew without pattern. Yet considerable evidence indicates that many well-managed, mature, multiproduct enterprises do have a logical product line that serves as a real guide to action, as is demonstrated by both product surgery and acquisitions that are constant with announced product policies.

A few examples will show the general character of product-line strategy. A leading electrical manufacturer conceives of its broad product-line policy as a beneficent circle. Its apparatus line generates and transmits electricity; its industrial products and its lamps and home appliances build up the demand for power and help lower the public utility companies' costs; as a result, the price of current is reduced and the demand for its industrial apparatus to produce more current is expanded.

A large producer of insulating materials views its product-line strategy in terms of a complete coverage of the full thermal range, with adequate alternatives throughout the range. The company wants to be considered a specialist in insulation, able to deal with any insulation problem impartially. It assumes that if it sells various alternative devices itself, customers will rely on it to select the most effective technique or material for their particular uses. The product line is an implement for selling a complete insulation service.

Product lines are sometimes conceived in terms of a framework of know-how. Thus one company views its know-how as essentially paper-making techniques. The pivotal machine converts wet pulp into dry, flat products. The company refuses to add products that depart significantly from this framework of know-how (e.g., products that involve intricate metal stamping or assembly operation). A leading automobile manufacturer looks upon its product line as essentially motive-power units and incidentally produces the bodies and wheels that use the power. Chemical companies sometimes conceive their product-line boundaries in terms of the equipment and processes that have been peculiar to the chemical industry. But the constant stream of discoveries in by-products and methods has recently made these borders quite elastic. Chemical companies have been led toward textile and paper processes, and oil companies into chemical industry research and processes.

Sometimes product-line strategy is strictly defensive. One of the building material companies, for example, has in the last twenty years been guided in its product acquisitions by the broad line of building materials offered by the two giants in the industry, whose coverage of building materials was formerly far more comprehensive than the company's own. This policy was in part based on the belief that basic distribution economies were possible in selling a broad and related line of products all handled by the building materials dealer.

The outer limits of a product line (like the outer limits of an industry) are typically framed in terms of common raw materials, production processes, distribution channels, or final uses. These criteria—which are alternative and occasionally contradictory—are often less fundamental for determining product-line strategy than are the competitive relationships in terms of tactics for increasing profits and rivals' reactions to these tactics. Thus considerations of product-line strategy reflect technical as well as competitive limitations on management. They thus become the groundwork for that nebulous but real part of the company—"grand strategy."

(c) Acceptance Criteria for New Products

Because estimates of probable profits from new products have wide margins of error and cannot be projected far into the future, and because maximizing financial profits is not the only strategic objective of the company, supplemental standards of acceptability for new products are needed. In theory, these standards are not so fundamental as are direct estimates of profits. They rest on empirical characteristics of the firm. Nevertheless, since they are frequently easier to appraise than are profitability standards, they have much value in themselves. A candidate product can be compared with the existing product line in terms of:

1. Interrelation of demand characteristics with the existing product line.

2. Use of the company's distinctive know-how.

3. Use made of common production facilities.

4. Use of common distribution channels.

5. Use of common raw materials.

6. Benefits to existing products.

These criteria can supplement estimates of the direct profits from adding the product.

1. *Interrelation of Demand Characteristics.* An important factor in considering new products for the product line is the relation of their

demand characteristics to the characteristics of the existing group of products. Since the right combination of products in the product line has powerful promotional value, this interrelation is a primary criterion of acceptable product additions.

What are the kinds of demand relationships between the candidate product and the existing product that will improve its chances of success? Two kinds may be distinguished: the new product may be a substitute, or it may be a complement. Rigorously speaking, the distinction may be framed in terms of cross-elasticity of demand. The candidate product is a substitute if its sales fall when the price of an existing product is reduced (other things equal). If its sales gain, then it is a complement.

There are various kinds of substitute relationships in demand that favor admission of the candidate product. Sometimes the new product, by extending the range of coverage, acts as a hedge against uncertainties and shifts in consumer demand. The garment industry provides many examples of product diversity to reduce risks that stem from buyers' ignorance and style change. Addition of paper, glass, and plastic containers to the product line of manufacturers of tin cans is probably partly a hedge against a revolution in container materials. Another type has to do with innovations. The acceptance of a new product which makes obsolete the company's existing product is justifiable, primarily because obsolescence is inevitable. The present product would be displaced by new ones in any event—by competitors, if not by the company itself.

Complementarity is the other general kind of demand relationship that is important in testing product additions. Typically, the question is whether the new product can fit into the pattern of demand so that the company's name established by the present products can help to sell the new one. In a sense, this condition shows excess capacity in advertising. Occasionally, another type of complementarity exists when a spectacular new product adds prestige to the existing line. Closely related to the promotional assistance of a new product, and more fundamental and common in most businesses, is the ability of a new product to make the present product line either operate or sell better. Thus the addition of fine-grain film to the product line of a camera manufacturer who sold high-speed lenses brought out the full usefulness of the high-speed lens.[5]

A second demand characteristic is the entity of the product group as a whole. The promotional advantages of a full line often make the whole greater than the sum of its parts. The tactical advantage of a full line of sizes, grades, and supplementary products in getting good dealers and in

[5] Accessories and extras, particularly in the early days of the automobile industry, served both as promotional balloons and as functional improvements. For example, the roof of the 1905 Stanley Steamer was an extra, and the self-starter remained an extra in cars for years.

merchandising high-margin specialties makes this kind of interrelationship of demand a commonly used basis for product-line policy. Some
would go so far as to deny the validity of analyzing sales performance for
any individual member of a product group, because each member contributes to the sales and profits of the other members and because the
economic unit of merchandising activities is the whole group of products.

A "full line" may be defined as the broadest coverage of related products successfully sold by a rival manufacturer. This concept brings out
the defensive nature of a full line policy. By carrying a broad product
line (relative to rivals), a manufacturer has advantages in getting good
dealers and in efficiently aiding in their merchandising activities by
training, co-operative advertising, and "point-of-sale" materials. Consequently, whether the candidate product is needed to match a competitor's breadth of line is an important criterion.

2. *Distinctive Know-how*. Sometimes the determining consideration in
making product-line decisions is that new products must make use of
the company's distinctive and almost personal source of differential advantage. An example is the M. W. Kellogg Company, which sells engineering skill in the design of giant processing equipment for chemical
and petroleum industries. Fabrication and construction are carried on
but are subsidiary to the principal product—technical pioneering skill.
One of the company's product-line specifications is that products must
fully utilize this asset and must be suitable vehicles for the sale of this
service.

One of the large electrical manufacturers uses this same test in an
indirect fashion. Only products that are highly engineered and that call
for intricate manufacture and assembly methods are regarded as suitable, partly because the market that is developed for such products will
be protected from easy invasion by these know-how requirements.

Sometimes the distinctive asset is research power. It is a fairly conscious
policy of one of the large chemical companies to choose only those new
products that have been developed by its product research organization
and that are distinctive enough in both chemical and manufacturing
requirements to be protected for some time to come. The counterpart of
this policy is to abandon products when they have degenerated to the
status of commonly produced commodities. The company advances to new
monopoly positions as fast as economic progress wears down the walls of
the old.

For many companies, research capacity and experience is the major
phase of its distinctive know-how. In such a case an admissibility standard
should be framed in terms of whether the candidate product is susceptible to the kind of improvement that will put the research capacity of the
company to its highest and noblest use.

Another test that may fall into this category is the volume potential test. Many large companies scorn product additions that would meet other tests but that do not promise a sufficiently large volume of sales to use the powers of a large company fully or to overcome its disadvantages of inflexibility. They look upon small-volume new products as requiring an organization that is quicker on its feet than a large company can expect to be.[6]

3. *Common Production Facilities.* The requirement that the candidate product use existing or highly similar production facilities is a widely used test of admissibility. When applied strictly to the use of existing facilities, it depends on economies of mopping up excess capacity, which are short lived. Hence, to this extent, the test has perils of using short-run incremental cost when long-run increments are involved.

When the test is framed in terms of requiring similar production facilities, it does not run these risks, since it is not then short run in concept. In this form it bears a close resemblance to the test of distinctive know-how. Similar production facilities are, in large part, a monopoly return on specialized knowledge and concentrated effort.

Most product additions fall somewhere between the extremes of idle capacity and familiar production methods. They normally make use of unused capacity of some facilities, at least common overheads, but often require additional facilities that, though different, have much in common with those for existing products.

4. *Common Distribution Channels.* Another popular test of the admissibility of a new product is that it must permit effective marketing through the same distribution facilities used by the company's existing products. In economic terms this criterion is sometimes used to mop up unused capacity. More often, the economies result from savings of specialization or of large scale.[7]

The test is most applicable when the company has a single or a clearly dominant distribution mechanism. A company whose only channel is direct sales to retail stationers might require that a new product be the kind that could be handled by stationery stores and sold by the sales force that serves them. Manufacturers' postwar experience with new products traveling through unfamiliar distribution channels and requiring a different sales organization was, on the whole, quite disappointing.

Even though a product meets this distribution test, there are limits

[6] A systematic search for products developed by large research organizations whose volume prospects were too small for the developing company to commercialize was made recently by an outfit which has shown considerable success in developing fairly diverse small businesses. Professional "product-finders" also prospect here for their 5 per cents.

[7] A special case of distribution mechanism economies is the savings of carload mixed-shipment rates for products that come under common freight classifications. This economy has been an important one in inducing building materials manufacturers to broaden their product lines.

to the number and variety of products that can be efficiently sold by a salesman if he is to be more than a mere order-taker.

Sometimes the selling power rests on no more than a blanket brand name. Products that can be sold compatibly under a well-known company label are sometimes added even though they are sold through different channels and require a specialized sales force.

In addition to savings of specialization and scale, established marketing organizations of salesmen and distributors constitute a source of monopoly advantage. Frequently the dealer organization is the company's most valuable and hardest to duplicate asset. Development of adequate distribution is sometimes a major barrier to entry. Hence the selection of products that will most happily utilize this facet of monopoly power is an important element in successful product-line development.[8]

5. *Common Raw Materials.* Many companies look for product additions that use the same basic raw material or its by-products. The rubber industry's product lines exemplify the application of this test. A company with extensive asbestos mining properties has directed its product research toward developing new products that will use not only asbestos but also the short fibers and other wastes that are left after the regular asbestos products have been manufactured.

The economic rationale for this test rests on two points: First, the basic source of raw material is controlled by the company (e.g., asbestos mines or bauxite deposits); the addition of products that use the common raw material may help develop the market for that material. They can also put the company in a position to exploit differentials between the prices of raw materials and finished products. Second, important savings result from intimate familiarity with intricate processing methods. For this reason the petroleum companies rely heavily upon the common-material test.

6. *Benefits to Present Product Line.* The foregoing tests depend largely on the contributions that existing products and facilities can make to candidate new products. This "benefits" test, in contrast, asks what the new product can offer to existing products. Contributions through interrelationship to demand have already been mentioned; contributions through experience in new types of production methods which have applicability to old products have received much attention as a result of the peacetime lessons of war production. Similarly, postwar "defense" research and pilot production supported by the military organization illustrate this educational contribution of some new products. Private ventures into new products simply for educational benefits in producing

---

[8] The question is not whether the new product can be distributed at all through the company's marketing organization but rather whether it can be distributed economically, both as compared with alternative candidate products, which might otherwise use these limited distribution facilities, and as compared with selling the product to other distributing organizations, while itself manufacturing it.

old products are long bets which few companies can take. Old products are a generic class subject to continual evolution. The educational benefits from an added product, either in research, production methods, or even demand interdependence, apply not only to the present products. Often, more importantly, these benefits apply to the projected path of development of these existing products. Remington Rand's recent acquisition of a company making a new type of "electronic brain" computing machine may illustrate this kind of contribution along the paths of projected development of existing Remington equipment.

(d) Dropping Old Products

The problem of determining what products should be dropped is, in general, the converse of the problem of selecting products for additions. There are, nevertheless, certain differences.

Broadly speaking, when a product's profit or sales behavior is absolutely or relatively unsatisfactory, there are four choices: (1) improve the present operation and keep the product; (2) keep on making it but sell it in bulk for others to market; (3) keep on selling it but buy it from others who can produce it more advantageously, and (4) stop manufacturing it and stop selling it.

The first three are outside our present discussion. The criteria for eliminating a product altogether are substantially the opposite of those for product additions. One approach, therefore, is to screen products that look sick enough to be candidates for deletion through the same kinds of suitability tests discussed above. Another approach is to appraise the product in terms of profits and sales results, such as whether it accounts for a trifling percentage of the company's sales, and whether its net or incremental profits are satisfactory as compared with other products or with products that might be produced if it were eliminated. A product that fails the suitability tests and also shows up badly in profit results is more clearly a candidate for total elimination than one that is inherently suitable but temporarily sick.

In applying the profit tests, a distinction must be made between the long-run and the short-run profits. Products that show comparatively low or negative net profits may still have incremental profits, that is, they may make contributions to general overhead that would not be made if the product were dropped. This sort of short-run consideration can lead to serious errors if it is projected too far into the future. Presumably, the growth of more profitable products should soak up the excess capacity that produces these incremental profits, and the continual stream of candidate products may in the long run produce a greater contribution to overhead than the old product that is retained because of its incremental showing.

The main economic difference between dropping and adding a product is, of course, sunk costs. Deletions that are decided upon solely on the basis of net profit, with no consideration given to the fact that costs are sunk, can lead to short-run losses. But, again, it may be that this is a more valid criterion than it appears to the economist, because executive time squandered on the squeaky wheel and on passed-up opportunities to substitute new and better products overbalances the sunk-cost element.

Product Planning for Future Profits*

Richard D. Crisp

As of March 1958, anyone's list of the half-dozen most worrisome problems of top management would have to include two items that quite a few of today's executives have never before encountered at first hand. Once is a continuing softening of sales volume, often showing up in a shrinkage of back orders and a swelling of inventories. The other is the mounting pressure on profits, resulting from the unpleasant combination of lower-than-capacity operating levels and higher break-even points.

Serious as these two problems can be, in the long run they're far from insoluble. Many management people have learned that there is one area of constructive action that promises to contribute to the solution of both. That area, of course, is new-product development.

If management attention today is more intensely concentrated on the development of new products than ever before, the reason is simply the tremendous potential profit and volume in new products. The nature of this potential shows up in the results of a recent study by an industrial publisher. In ten different industrial classifications new products were expected to contribute from 30 per cent to 80 per cent of total volume over a period of five years—that is, from 1955 to 1960.

FIGURING THE ODDS

But while the development and marketing of new products promise important volume and profits to those who succeed, the odds against the success of a new product today are higher than most business men realize. In fact, a frequently quoted observation, that four out of five new products fail, greatly underestimates the odds. There are three reasons for this.

First, the observation was based on the experience of 200 large manufacturers of consumer products, all of whom have substantial experience and skilled, specialized personnel. If four out of five of *their* new products fail, the odds for all companies are certain much higher. Second, the

* Reprinted with permission of the publisher from *Dun's Review and Modern Industry*, vol. 71, no. 3 (March, 1958), pp. 34ff. Mr. Crisp is Director of Marketing for Guild, Bascom, and Bonfigli, Inc., of Chicago, Illinois, and also Lecturer in Marketing, Northwestern University.

study was made in 1945. The competitive pressures against a new product in 1958 are unquestionably much heavier, and the chances of success correspondingly lower. Third, the estimate was based on the performance record of products actually placed on the market. It didn't take into consideration cases of product-mortality before launching but *after* substantial investments of time, effort, and money.

Long experience in the marketing-management field has convinced me that there are few areas of management practice today where the gap between the most effective and the least effective performance is as wide as in new-product activities.

What does this mean for companies whose experience in new-product activities has been less satisfactory? Simply this: If your company is like most others, a marked improvement in your new-product batting average can be achieved rather quickly and easily, by introducing into your operation certain approaches and principles distilled from the experience of companies outstandingly effective in new-product marketing.

How to Look for Trouble

To help you identify the areas in your new-product program where the greatest opportunities for improvement exist, here is a rundown of the chief trouble spots.

1. *What are the objectives of your new-product activities?*

The single difference that most commonly distinguishes the successful from the unsuccessful company in the new-product area lies in the answer to this question: Do you have the specific objectives of your new-product program in writing so that they can be clearly understood by all? Failure to crystallize the objectives of a new-product program before making substantial commitments of time, money, and effort is a major source of new-product failure.

Crystallizing the objectives of a new product is essential for increasing efficiency and minimizing wasted effort. The search for a promising new product often involves considerable wasted motion. Sharply defined objectives can greatly reduce that waste by (1) narrowing the search to those products that will contribute to the attainment of the predetermined objectives and (2) insuring the early abandonment of projects inconsistent with those objectives. Dropping a product at a lower and hence less expensive point on the developmental curve results in marked savings.

An example will help to show how successful new-product marketers use objectives as a tool. The Toni Company was once actively seeking new products. The objective of the search was to find and develop products with a Winter consumption peak to offset the Summer peaks of existing products. But an important subsidiary objective was to find products that could share the cost of some of the company's expensive television commitments during the Winter months.

One product that was considered, evaluated, developed, and even carried into the test-market stage was a hand lotion. But research disclosed that hand lotion as a product class has a consumption peak in small town and rural areas. At that time, television audiences peaked sharply in larger cities. The lack of fit between the shape of the market for the product and the company's objectives counted heavily in the decision to drop the product.

A similar lack of fit was disclosed when S. C. Johnson & Sons, Inc., makers of wax products, was considering adding shoe polishes to its line. One prime objective of the company's new-product program at that time was to find products that could be sold by the consumer-product sales organization through the same distribution channels used for its other summer products. Shoe polish sells in substantial volume. Much of that volume, however, involves specialized distribution channels to reach shoe-repair and shoe-supply retailers. The company lost interest in the product when it found it would have to set up a separate sales organization or else divert a considerable amount of the present sales department's time from its regular customers. Again it was the predetermined objective that led to an early recognition that there was a serious lack of fit.

2. *How similar are the new products you are considering to those you now make?*

Getting the answer to this question can be vital to success or failure and hence should be considered as early as possible in the planning of a new product. For the experience of countless companies has led to the distillation of this principle: *The more a proposed product differs from those you are now making and know thoroughly, the greater are the odds that it will never contribute a dollar of profit.*

The explanation lies in what we might call a buried assumption. (In new-product situations, there is usually an intrinsic and implicit assumption.) That is, it is assumed that the new product can be added to the line and marketed without much more drain on the time and effort of the management team, per sales or profit dollar, than existing products require.

In the case of variations of products with which the management team is already familiar—like a new cake-mix flavor or a new industrial lubricant added to an existing line—this assumption is likely to be valid. But when management has to learn an entirely new business to produce a new product, the assumption most emphatically does not apply.

The millions of dollars that have been poured down the rathole before management faced the facts and asked, "What are we doing here?" would make a large dent in the Federal deficit.

Two factors are present in this kind of situation. The first is the high cost of the time and effort necessarily expended by a company's top management team. This added burden might be taken on without difficulty if a team began the job with time on its hands. Such a starting point is mighty unusual. The second factor is the effect that this diversion of a large share of management's time and attention will have on a company's existing products and product lines. Such a diversion is often an important contributing factor to a decline in sales and share-of-market for existing products. When management concentrates attention on new-product activities, it's important to be sure that someone is watching the store. For it is a rare new product indeed that can contribute enough to a company's volume and profit to offset fully a significant decline in the company's established products. Such a decline is often an unanticipated and unidentified "cost" of a new product.

Incidentally, there is a big opportunity here for many companies to improve their new-product planning. An aggressive new-product program often requires the commitment of a significant share of a company's total assets, including the important if intangible one of top-management time and attention. Companies doing the best job in new products rarely lose sight of this fact. In evaluating a proposed new product, they always ask, "Would the same amount of time, effort, and money devoted to our existing products pay us a larger return on our investment?" If the answer is "yes"—and it often is—the new product is dropped.

These comments do not mean that emphasis on new-product development is being overdone. Rather, they are intended to underline this fact: A new-product program is likely to be fully effective only if it is first planned and then executed with a full awareness of its probable impact on the company's total situation.

3. *Does your new-product planning proceed from factory to consumer, or does it work in reverse?*

An accurate and objective answer to this question will do much to reveal exactly how up-to-date your company's marketing management is in its approach to the new-product area. At one time production-minded managements decided what they were going to make and proceeded to make it. The sales department was then given the task of selling the product. Often the market was restricted, or the product was unsuited to the needs of the market. Extraordinarily high sales costs were the result.

Today well-managed companies accept beyond question that it is easier and cheaper to make what customers want to buy than to sell them what you want to make. As a result, management tends to be customer-oriented. It is this shift in emphasis, more and more widely recognized, that is largely responsible for what is sometimes described as the "new marketing concept."

In new-product development and marketing, a consumer-oriented approach prevails in those companies with the most impressive new-product record. Perhaps you think these comments are too obvious. The sad fact is that they are not. The proportion of companies devoting expensive developmental time to "getting the bugs out" of products for which there is no customer need or desire is shockingly high.

This comment isn't meant to apply to products that are too new for consumers to be aware of their need for them. I am thinking of those products with "advantages" that the customer can enjoy only by sacrificing other values more important *to the customer*.

For example, not so many years ago, Servel developed an automatic ice-cube maker that fitted inside the frozen-food storage section of the Servel refrigerator. The device, introduced with considerable fanfare, jolted other refrigerator manufacturers, one of whom quickly conducted a small-scale consumer study. When the results were laid before him, he told his design department to scrap plans for trying to top the Servel innovation. What did the research show? It disclosed that housewives, being reasonable creatures, would much prefer to have the space taken up by the device given to additional frozen-food storage, which they use every day, rather than have the convenience of automatic ice cubes, which they need in quantity only on special occasions.

To determine how your company stacks up in this respect, study a list of the new products you have done major work on over the last several years. Ask yourself where the basic suggestion or idea came from that started the work on a project. What evidence was there of a real and important need for such a product among the customers you hoped to sell it to?

In the case of the industrial and consumer durable goods market, it is often difficult to secure a customer's-eye-view of a proposed product. But don't let the high costs of tooling up or the difficulties of working with a heavy or bulky product persuade you to rely on guesswork alone. Techniques for pre-evaluating proposed products, even of such kinds, are widely and inexpensively available.

4. *Have all basic assumptions underlying new-product work been exhaustively studied and tested?*

Often the initial decision to assign a high priority to a proposed new product is based on a preliminary (and sometimes superficial) appraisal of the problems involved. It is extremely important to subject such a decision to careful review, *before* committing sizable funds to the project. In particular all basic assumptions should be reviewed.

Many a new-product failure can be traced to using unsound premises as a basis for its development. Those premises may involve scale of demand, price, nature of competition, distribution channels, or almost any other element of marketing. You should be especially on guard against wishful thinking in this key area.

As an illustration of how it could happen to you, here is the experience of a well-managed company, an industry leader in a field that sells largely, although by no means exclusively, through jewelry channels. The objective of the new-product program was to expand volume by adding products similar to the company's existing line in terms both of manufacturing skills required and of distribution channels used. One product under consideration was a camera about as large as a pack of cigarettes. The analysis that led the company to embark on research and development of the camera simply stated that a product with such-and-such characteristics could be sold in volume through jewelry outlets. Hundreds of thousands of R&D dollars later, the company perfected the product. At that point they found that cameras in the same price class as theirs were sold almost exclusively through photographic outlets. The product was quietly interred.

5. *When products have been in development over a period of time, is the marketing picture periodically and routinely re-examined for new or changed factors that affect the volume outlook?*

It often takes considerable time to move a new product from the idea to the ready-for-production stage. A further lag is caused by the varying lead-times required for tooling and production. In effective new-product programs, provision is made for a periodic and routine, but far from perfunctory, re-examination of the marketing situation. Today the marketing picture changes with often breath-taking rapidity. A soundly conceived product, created to fill an unquestioned need, may fail because some other product aimed at the same need-target beat it to the marketplace.

Careful attention to trends affecting basic market factors is also essential. The hazards of basic market changes are illustrated by the case of Ford's new Edsel car. When the plans to launch the Edsel were made, the middle-price automotive market was a large and expanding segment of the total. But it took three years to translate the plans for the Edsel into a product-in-being with a going dealer organization to sell it. Early Edsel sales were below expectations—partly because the middle-price share of the auto market was far smaller in 1957 when the car was introduced than it had been when plans were frozen for production.

You are unlikely to have to cope with the hazards that a three-year lead-time adds to the always risky business of developing and marketing new products. Even so, the Edsel experience is one to remember. A major competitive innovation or a sharp change in import competition may make it desirable for you to re-examine your plans. Often it is far less expensive to put the brakes on a product and "eat" the research and development costs than to market a product when the odds against its success have changed materially.

6. Have the differences between your new products and your basic business—and especially the marketing differences—been fully recognized?

A company's failure (especially in the planning stages of the program) to recognize the basic and striking differences between the business it is in and the business it proposes to enter spells doom for many new products even before they see the light of competition.

This problem is particuluarly acute in the case of companies that dominate their industry. They tend to enter new-product marketing with a rather strong "we are a leader" bias. Despite the new-product actuarial tables, they are confident of success. Often they stumble and fall, tripped by overconfidence.

Their new product goes into a market where it is often a "me, too" or "just another" product, rather than a leader. Competitors ignore (as they should) the company's acts. They fail to follow—which can be disconcerting to those who think in terms of leadership. As a result, the company finds that its appraisals of "what will happen when we do such-and-such" are grossly in error.

This is an extremely important problem area, partly because of its great and inescapable complexity. Differences between your established product and your new product may exist in almost any section of the marketing picture. They may exist in the area of product differentiation, for example. You are a leader in your basic industry because your products are clearly superior in ways that are important to the customers who use them. Your new product may be insufficiently differentiated, or differentiated in ways that are considered unimportant by the customers you're selling. What happens then? All the experience you have developed in your basic business becomes either irrelevant or obsolete. You have no basis for judging the extent to which, for example, your conversion of "triers" to users is good, fair, or poor. Besides, your estimate of the influence of price strategy on volume is unlikely to apply to this new, strange situation.

Or consider service. Perhaps the basic products you have been selling have required very little service. Your new product takes you into an industry or product area in which prompt service is more important to your customers than what seem to you to be basic differences in the qualities of the products themselves. What do you do now? To keep the situation simple, let's assume that you anticipated this problem. But it would be far more realistic to assume that you had failed to do so and only found out about it when you tried to diagnose your disappointingly low rate of sales.

Another problem might well develop in trade practices and terms. As a newcomer in an industry, you will have to offer distributors all the attractions and advantages they have been getting from other companies.

To break in, you may have to offer more. What will you do if the existing concerns equal or exceed your offers? How far are you prepared to go to "buy your way in"?

The answer to that last question can be vital. It certainly was in the case of one of the most spectacular financial flops in the new-product area. When Lever Brothers introduced Swan soap as a challenge to Procter & Gamble's Ivory, initial plans called for an advertising expenditure rate three times that of Ivory's going rate *in the planning period*. But by the time Swan was actually launched, P&G's expenditure rate for Ivory had been tripled. Published estimates of Lever Brothers' loss on Swan have run as high as $20 million.

7. *Is the scheduling of your new-product development realistically established and reasonably maintained?*

There can be no question of the difficulties implicit in establishing and maintaining an "on time" schedule in research and developmental work, particularly where that work is primarily creative. But eventually, in the development of every product, a point is reached when it is possible to predict with reasonable certainty how soon the product can be launched. It is in the scheduling of activities during this interval that the most marked differences between the practices of successful companies and average concerns appear.

Traditionally, delays in research and development are allowed to soak up a larger and larger part of the total time before introduction day. As an almost inescapable consequence, vital elements in marketing planning are telescoped or eliminated. The new product slides down the ways and sinks with only a few bubbles to mark the spot.

In contrast, those companies that make something close to a fine art of new-product activities generally enforce a carefully predetermined time schedule throughout the new product's developmental period. They have written lists of all key elements and decisions that must be made and adequate time allocated for each. That kind of detailed schedule—which might run to more than 150 different major decisions in marketing alone—is a potent planning tool, which minimizes many of the serious risks that might handicap the new product.

There are two ways to enforce such a schedule on a research-and-development team. First, successful companies often have no research and development team. Instead, they have a new-product team, on which both research-and-development and marketing management viewpoints are represented and closely integrated. Second, commercially acceptable standards of product performance are provided as a guide to research and development efforts. This eliminates the time problem, with which most executives experienced with new products are familiar. The technical research group wants "just a little more time." In return, they promise a "much better" product.

In some ways, producing a new product is like a pregnancy. A point is reached when more time in the womb contributes little to the baby, and it can be mighty hard on the mother.

8. *Is your new-product marketing routinely begun either on a test-market or on a controlled, limited area basis?*

New-product marketing is fraught with risk. It is only plain common sense to minimize that risk by reducing the scale of its introduction. Experienced companies try to do this by using a carefully pre-planned test market or a limited geographical introduction, which is also a test of sorts.

There are two important advantages in this limited-risk approach. First, when the product is a dud, the small-scale introduction demonstrates that fact, usually unmistakably, with a minimum investment of time, effort, and money. Second, almost all test-market or limited-scale introductions reveal "bugs" in the marketing plan or ways to improve its effectiveness substantially. By using a market test as the production management team uses a pilot plant, both the likelihood of success and the scale of that success if achieved can be increased.

9. *Is nonrepetitive or stock-building volume carefully considered in evaluating the limited-scale test or introduction?*

One of the most frequent mistakes is the strong (often, it seems, irresistible) tendency of management to underestimate the length of time and the volume required to build up distributors' supplies of a new product. As a result, some of this stock-building volume is incorrectly translated into actual consumer sales, thus causing estimates of the new product's market potential to be ridiculously exaggerated.

10. *Do you carefully compare the sales volume and the cost of achieving it with the pre-introduction budgets and forecasts?*

Careful and continuing attention to whether the sales achieved and the costs of securing those sales match, exceed, or run under pre-introduction budgets and forecasts is standard operating procedure in effective new-product programs. It is important to watch the vital early results so that appropriate action can be taken. The definition of "appropriate action" depends on how actual volume and expenses compare to the forecast. If the product is destined for failure, minimize losses and trip the trap on it at the earliest possible moment. If the product is running ahead of forecasts, then carefully controlled experiments to see how high volume can be pushed, perhaps with additional promotion or sales force, are indicated.

It is impossible to cover new-product development completely in a single article. But these questions and answers represent a comprehensive checklist for setting up an effective new-product program. No one can hit the ball out of the park on every new product, but if you follow these tips you'll make fewer strike-outs.

E. DECISION MAKING

The Environment of Decision *

Chester I. Barnard

The acts of individuals may be distinguished in principal as those which are the result of deliberation, calculation, thought, and those which are unconscious, automatic, responsive, the results of internal or external conditions present or past. In general, whatever processes precede the first class of acts culminate in what may be termed "decision." Involved in acts which are ascribed to decision are many subsidiary acts which are themselves automatic, the processes of which are usually unknown to the actor.

When decision is involved there are consciously present two terms—the end to be accomplished and the means to be used. The end itself may be the result of logical processes in which the end is in turn a means to some broader or more remote end; or the immediate end, and generally the ultimate end, may not be a result of logical processes, but "given"—that is, unconsciously impressed—by conditions, including social conditions past or present, including orders or organizations. But whenever the end has been determined, by whatever process, the decision as to means is itself a logical process of discrimination, analysis, choice—however defective either the factual basis for choice or the reasoning related to these facts. . . .

I. THE OCCASIONS OF DECISION

The making of decisions, as everyone knows from personal experience, is a burdensome task. Offsetting the exhilaration that may result from correct and successful decision and the relief that follows the terminating of a struggle to determine issues is the depression that comes from failure or error of decision and the frustration which ensues from uncertainty. Accordingly, it will be observed that men generally try to avoid making decisions, beyond a limited degree when they are rather uncritical responses to conditions. The capacity of most men to make decisions is

* Reprinted by permission of the publisher from *The Functions of the Executive* (Cambridge, Mass.: Harvard University Press, 1938), pp. 185, 189–198, 201–205. Mr. Barnard was formerly President of the New Jersey Bell Telephone Company and the Rockefeller Foundation; currently retired, he is a member of the New York City Board of Education and a director of several business corporations and foundations.

quite narrow, although it is a capacity that may be considerably developed by training and especially by experience.

The executive is under the obligation of making decisions usually within approximately defined limits related to the position he has accepted; and is under the necessity of keeping within the limits of his capacity if he is continuously to discharge this obligation. He must, therefore, to be successful, distinguish between ths occasions of decision in order to avoid the acceptance of more than he can undertake without neglecting the fields to which his position relates. For the natural reluctance of other men to decide, their persistent disposition to avoid responsibility, and their fear of criticism, will lead them to overwhelm the executive who does not protect himself from excessive burdens of decisions if he is not already protected by a well regulated and habitual distribution of responsibilities.

It is for this reason necessary in the making of decisions to maintain a balance between the fields from which the occasions of them arise. I suppose this is rarely a matter of conscious selection, and is probably subject to no general rules. It involves in itself important decisions. For our purposes, however, it may be helpful to note that the occasions for decision originate in three distinct fields: (a) from authoritative communications from superiors; (b) from cases referred for decision by subordinates; (c) from cases originating in the initiative of the executive concerned.

(a) Occasions for decision are frequently furnished by instructions or by general requirements of superior authority. Such decisions relate to the interpretation, application, and distribution of instructions. These occasions cannot be avoided, though the burden may be reduced by delegation of responsibility to subordinates. They involve serious decisions when the instructions seem morally wrong, harmful to the organization, or impossible of execution.

(b) The cases referred for decision may be called appellate cases. They arise from incapacity of subordinates, uncertainty of instructions, novelty of conditions, conflict of jurisdiction or conflicts of orders, or failure of subjective authority. The control of the number of appellate cases lies in adequacy of executive organization, of personnel, of previous decision; and the development of the processes of informal organization. The test of executive action is to make these decisions when they are important, or when they cannot be delegated reasonably, and to decline the others.

(c) The occasions of decision on the initiative of the executive are the most important test of his capacity. Out of his understanding of the situation, which depends upon his ability and initiative, and on the character of the communication system of his organization, it is to be determined whether something needs to be done or corrected. To decide that question involves not merely the ordinary elements but the executive's specific justification for deciding. For when the occasions for decision arise from above or below the position of the executive, others have in advance granted him authority; but when made on his own initiative, this always may be (and generally is) questioned, at least tacitly (in the form whether decision was necessary, or related to scope of obligations, etc.). Moreover, failure to decide is usually not specifically subject to attack, except under extreme conditions. Hence there is much incentive to avoid decision. Pressure of other work is the usual self-justification. Yet it is clear that the most important obligation is to raise and decide those issues which no one else is in a position to raise effectively.

From the point of view of the *relative* importance of specific decisions, those of executives properly call for first attention. From the point of view of *aggregate* importance, it is not decisions of executives but of non-executive participants in organization which should enlist major interest. Indeed it is precisely for this reason that many executive decisions are necessary—they relate to the facilitation of correct action involving appropriate decisions among others. In large measure this is a process of providing for the clear presentment of the issues or choices. At any event, it is easily evident merely from the inspection of the action of the non-executive participants in organization that coordination of action requires repeated organization decisions "on the spot" where the effective action of organization takes place. It is here that the final and most concrete objectives of purposes are found, with the maximum of definiteness. There is no further stage of organization action. The final selection of means takes place at this point.

It should be noted, however, that the types of decisions as well as the conditions change in character as we descend from the major executive to the non-executive positions in organization. At the upper limit decisions relating to ends to be pursued generally require the major attention, those relating to means being secondary, rather general, and especially concerned with personnel, that is, the development and protection of organization itself. At intermediate levels the breaking of broad purposes into more specific ends and the technical and technological problems, including economic problems, of action become prominent. At the low levels decisions characteristically relate to technologically correct conduct, so far as the action is organization action. But it is at these low levels, where ultimate authority resides, that the *personal* decisions determining willingness to contribute become of relatively greatest aggregate importance.

II. The Evidences of Decision

Not the least of the difficulties of appraising the executive functions or the relative merits of executives lies in the fact that there is little direct opportunity to observe the essential operations of decision. It is a perplexing fact that most executive decisions produce no direct evidence of themselves and that knowledge of them can only be derived from the cumulation of indirect evidence. They must largely be inferred from general results in which they are merely one factor, and from symptomatic indications of roundabout character.

Those decisions which are most directly known result in the emission of authoritative communications, that is, orders. Something is or is not to be done. Even in such cases the basic decision may not be evidence; for the decision to attempt to achieve a certain result or condition may require several communications to different persons which appear to be complete in themselves but in which the controlling general decision may not be disclosed.

Again, a firm decision may be taken that does not result in any communication whatever for the time being. A decision properly timed must be made in advance of communicating it, either because the action involved must wait anticipated developments or because it cannot be authoritative without educational or persuasive preparation.

Finally, the decision may be not to decide. This is a most frequent decision, and from some points of view probably the most important. For every alert executive continually raises in his own mind questions for determination. As a result of his consideration he may determine that the question is not pertinent. He may determine that it is not now pertinent. He may determine that it is pertinent now but that there are lacking adequate data upon which to base a final decision. He may determine that the question is pertinent, can be decided, will not be decided except by himself, and yet it would be better that it be not decided because his competence is insufficient.

The fine art of executive decision consists in not deciding questions that are not now pertinent, in not deciding prematurely, in not making decisions that cannot be made effective, and in not making decisions that others should make. Not to decide questions that are not pertinent at the time is uncommon good sense, though to raise them may be uncommon perspicacity. Not to decide questions prematurely is to refuse commitment or attitude or the development of prejudice. Not to make decisions that cannot be made effective is to refrain from destroying authority. Not to make decisions that others should make is to preserve morale, to develop competence, to fix responsibility, and to preserve authority.

From this it may be seen that decisions fall into two major classes, positive decisions—to do something, to direct action, to cease action, to prevent action; and negative decisions, which are decisions not to decide. Both are inescapable; but the negative decisions are often largely unconscious, relatively non-logical, "instinctive," "good sense." It is because of the rejections that the selection is good. The best of moves may be offset by a false move. This is why time is usually necessary to appraise the executive. There is no current evidence of the all-important negative decisions. The absence of effective moves indicates failure of initiative in decision, but error of action probably often means absence of good negative decisions. The success of action through a period of time denotes excellence of selection and of rejection of possible actions.

III. THE NATURE OF THE ENVIRONMENT

Whatever the occasions or the evidences of decision, it is clear that decisions are constantly being made. What is the nature of the environment of decisions, the materials with which they deal, the field to which they relate? It consists of two parts: (a) purpose; and (b) the physical world, the social world, the external things and forces and circumstances of the moment. All of these, including purpose, constitute the objective field of decision; but the two parts are of radically different nature and origin. The function of decision is to regulate the relations between these two parts. This regulation is accomplished either by changing the purpose or by changing the remainder of the environment.

(a) We may consider purpose first. It may seem strange perhaps that purpose should be included in the objective environment, since purpose of all things seems personal, subjective, internal, the expression of desire. This is true; but *at the moment of a new decision,* an existing purpose, the result of a previous decision under previous conditions, is an objective fact, and it is so treated at that moment in so far as it is a factor in new decision.

This is especially true because organization decisions do not relate to personal purposes, but to organization purposes. The purpose which concerns an organization decision may have been given as a fact to and accepted as such by the person who is responsible for making a new decision. But no matter how arrived at, when decision is in point, the purpose is fact already determined; its making is a matter of history; it may be as objective as another man's emotions may be to an observer.

We must next note, however, that purpose is essential to give any meaning to the rest of the environment.[1] The environment must be looked at from *some* point of view to be intelligible. A mere mass of things, atoms, movements, forces, noises, lights, could produce some response from a sensitive creature or certainly would have some effect on it, or on other things, but the reduction of this mass of everything to something significant requires a basis for discrimination, for picking

[1] I am under the impression that in a general way both the form of expression and the concepts stated in the next several paragraphs were derived from or influenced by A. N. Whitehead's *Process and Reality.*

out this and that as pertinent, relevant, and interesting. This basis is that in *this* situation something is or is not to be done. The situation aids, obstructs, or is neutral from *this* point of view. The basis for this discrimination is a purpose, an end, an object to be accomplished.

Purpose itself has no meaning, however, except in an environment. It can only be defined in terms of an environment.[2] Even to want to go somewhere, anywhere, supposes some kind of environment. A very general purpose supposes a very general undifferentiated environment; and if the purpose is stated or thought of it must be in terms of that general environment. But when formed, it immediately (if it is not in suspense or dormant, so to speak) serves for reducing that environment to more definite features; and the immediate result is to change purpose into a more specific purpose. Thus when I decide I want to go from A to B my idea of terrain is vague. But as soon as I have decided, the terrain becomes less vague; I immediately see paths, rocks, obstacles that are significant; and this finer discrimination results in detailed and smaller purposes. I not only want to go from A to B, but I want to go this way, that way, etc. This constant refinement of purpose is the effect of repeated decisions, in finer and finer detail, until eventually detailed purpose is contemporaneous accomplishment. But similarly with each new edition of purposes, a new discrimination of the environment is involved, until finally the last obstacle of progressive action represents a breaking up of a general purpose into many concrete purposes, each as it is made almost simultaneously associated with the action. The thing is done as soon as decided; it becomes a matter of history; it constitutes a single step in the process of experience.

Thus back and forth purpose and environment react in successive steps through successive decisions in greater and greater detail. A series of final decisions, each apparently trivial, is largely accomplished unconsciously and sums up into an effected general purpose and a route of experience.

(b) We may now consider the environment of decision exclusive of purpose. It consists of atoms and molecules, agglomerations of things in motion, alive; of men and emotions; of physical laws and social laws; social ideas; norms of actions, of forces and resistances. Their number is infinite and they are all always present. They are also always changing. They are meaningless in their variety and changes except as discrimi-

[2] Care should be taken to keep in mind that environment throughout does not mean merely physical aspects of the environment, but explicitly includes social aspects, although physical rather than other aspects are used for illustration as simpler. In many organizations, however, the physical aspects are constant and it is the social aspects which are pertinent. This is the case especially when the purpose is a concrete expression of social ideas or attitudes, as, for example, in ritualistic types of action whether religious or political.

nated in the light of purpose. They are viewed as static facts, if the change is not significant from the viewpoint of the purpose, or as both static and dynamic facts.

This discrimination divides the world into two parts; the facts that are immaterial, irrelevant, mere background; and the part that contains the facts that apparently aid or prevent the accomplishment of purpose. As soon as that discrimination takes place, decision is in bud. It is in the state of selecting among alternatives. These alternatives are either to utilize favorable factors, to eliminate or circumvent unfavorable ones, or to change the purpose. Note that if the decision is to deal with the environment, this automatically introduces new but more detailed purposes, the progeny, as it were, of the parent purpose; but if the decision is to change the purpose rather than deal with the environment, the parent is sterile. It is abandoned, and a new purpose is selected, thereby creating a *new* environment in the light of *that* purpose.

This looks like metaphysical speculation if one thinks of it as individual and personal—undemonstrable assumptions, speculative reasoning. But it can be observed in an organization, at least sufficiently to corroborate it roughly. Thus if the president of a telephone company for good reasons orders [3] two poles carrying a cable removed from the north side of First Street between A and B Streets to the opposite side of First Street, it can, I think, be approximately demonstrated that carrying out that order involves perhaps 10,000 decisions of 100 men located at 15 points, requiring successive analyses of several environments, including social, moral, legal, economic, and physical facts of the environment, and requiring 9000 redefinitions and refinements of purpose, and 1000 changes of purpose. If inquiry be made of those responsible, probably not more than a half-a-dozen decisions will be recalled or deemed worthy of mention—those that seemed at the moment difficult or momentous, or that were subject to question or proved erroneous. The others will be "taken for granted," all a part of the business or knowing one's business. However, a large part of the decisions, purposes, and descriptions and analyses of the various environments will be a matter of record—short-cut, abbreviated, to be sure, but marking the routes of decisions with fair definiteness. Only in the case of individual workmen shall we be almost completely reduced to speculation as to the number and character of the decisions required, because many of them certainly will relate to physiological action. . . .

[3] Partly to illustrate several statements in this essay I may say that it is necessary to imagine extreme conditions to suppose he would issue such an order. Ordinarily what he would do would be to inquire whether it would be feasible to take the action suggested, or what would be involved in doing so, or he would state the problem and ask for its solution, etc. The executive art is nine-tenths inducing those who have authority to use it in taking pertinent action.

[IV.] The Theory of Opportunism

The opportunistic element refers to the objective field within which action must take place. The process of decision so far as it relates to this objective field is essentially one of analysis, even though in practice much of the process will be intuitive or not conscious. The analysis of present circumstances is in part the definition of purpose in immediate terms; but it is also the process of finding what present circumstances are significant with reference to that purpose. What events, what objects, what conditions aid, what prevent, the attainment of purpose?

This analysis will lead to the rejection from present interest or attention of most of the innumerable events, objects, details, circumstances of the situation, since under the conditions they are irrelevant to the purpose. This, of course, is sometimes an easy, sometimes a difficult task. It is easy if it has been done before for similar circumstances, if it yields to an established technique of analysis, if it is a solved scientific problem. It is difficult if it is novel, if there is no technique, or no science. For then the analysis is in effect partly unaided surmise, hypothesis, assumption. This fact, even when the decider is aware of it, does not permit escape from decision, though it may lead to negative decision, that is, to decision not to decide the question for the present. Hence, there is no escape from *some* decision once the process of setting up purpose against environment has begun.

The analysis required for decision is in effect a search for the "strategic factors." The notion of the "strategic factor," a term I borrow from Professor John R. Commons,[4] is related to the term "limiting factor" which is common in scientific work. Professor Commons' use of the word is restricted to certain aspects of managerial and bargaining operations in economic systems, but the restriction to this field is unnecessary; the principle involved is the same in whatever circumstances decision is required. The theory of the strategic factor is necessary to an appreciation of the process of decision, and therefore to the understanding of organization and the executive functions as well as, perhaps, individual purposive conduct. As generally as I can state it, this theory is as follows:

If we take any system, or set of conditions, or conglomeration of circumstances existing at a given time, we recognize that it consists of elements, or parts, or factors, which together make up the whole system, set of conditions, or circumstances. Now, if we approach this system or set of circumstances, with a view to the accomplishment of a purpose (and only when we so approach it), the elements or parts become dis-

[4] John R. Commons, *Institutional Economics* (New York: The Macmillan Co., 1934), *passim*, but especially chapter ix at pp. 627–633.

tinguished into two classes: those which if absent or changed would accomplish the desired purpose, provided the others remain unchanged; and these others. The first kind are often called limiting factors, the second, complementary factors. Moreover, when we concentrate our attention upon a *restricted* or subsidiary system or set of circumstances, we often find, on the basis of previous experience or knowledge, that the circumstances fail to satisfy the requirements of purpose because they lack an additional element or elements, that is, elements which are known to exist in the *larger* environment. These are likewise limiting factors.

The limiting (strategic) factor is the one whose control, in the right form, at the right place and time, will establish a new system or set of conditions which meets the purpose. Thus if we wish to increase the yield of grain in a certain field and on analysis it appears that the soil lacks potash, potash may be said to be the strategic (or limiting) factor. If a tank of water is to be used for cleaning purposes, and is found to contain sediment, the sediment is the strategic (limiting) factor in the use of the water for cleaning. If a machine is not operable because a screw is missing, the screw is the strategic (limiting) factor.[5]

Where the crucial element or part present or absent is a thing or physical element or compound or ingredient it is convenient to call it "limiting" factor; but when personal or organizational action is the crucial element, *as it ultimately is in all purposive effort,* the word "strategic" is preferable. This preference relates to a distinction in the use of the analysis. If its purpose is knowledge for its own sake, that is, if the purpose is immediately scientific, the term "limiting factor" conveys the relatively static situation of the analyst. If the purpose is not knowledge but decision as to action, "strategic factor" conveys the relatively changing position of the analyst, in which the subjective aspects of decision interact with the objective field in which it is developed.

The fact that a strategic factor is always involved is overlooked because the personal or organization action required often seems trivial; the necessary effort is less than that required to analyze the situation or system. For example, it may require great effort to determine that the land needs potash, but little effort to get the potash. Nevertheless, when the need has been determined, a new situation has arisen because of the fact of knowledge or the assumption that potash is the limiting factor; and instead of potash, the limiting factor *obtaining* potash then becomes the strategic factor; and this will change progressively into *obtaining* the money to *buy* potash, then *finding* John to *go* after potash, then *getting* machines and men to *spread* potash, etc., etc. Thus the determination of the strategic factor is itself the decision which at once reduces purpose to

[5] There may be more than one limiting factor, in which they may all be taken as a limiting set, or broken down to single factors for action in some order.

a new level, compelling search for a new strategic factor in the new situation. Says Commons:

But the limiting and complementary factors are continually changing places. What was the limiting factor becomes complementary, when once it has come under control; then another factor is the limiting one. The limiting factor, in the operation of an automobile, at one time may be the electric spark; at another the gasoline; at another the man at the wheel. This is the meaning of efficiency— the control of the changeable limiting factors at the right time, right place, right amount, and right form in order to enlarge the total output by the expected operation of complementary factors.[6]

If we rephrase this last sentence to accord with our terminology and our broader subject, it will read: "This is the meaning of effective deci- sion—the control of the changeable strategic factors, that is, the exercise of control at the right time, right place, right amount, and right form so that purpose is properly redefined and accomplished."

Professor Commons continues:

But out of the complex happenings, man selects the limiting factors for his purposes. If he can control these, then the other factors work out the effects intended. The "cause" is volitional control of the limiting or strategic factors. . . . The "effects" are the operations of the complementary factors. . . .

With the distinctions in phraseology which Commons makes for his purposes we are not concerned. I think it sound to say that the strategic factor always determines the *action* that is controlling, even in the case of what he calls the limiting factor. It is not the element that is missing but the action that could procure the missing element that is the controlling factor. To determine what element should be changed or is missing is the first step in defining the *action* required. Decision relates to *action,* whether it be in the field of business transactions, political transactions, mechanical operations, chemical combinations, scientific experimentation, or whatever relates to accomplishment of intention.

The strategic factor is, then, the center of the environment of deci- sion. It is the point at which choice applies. To *do* or not to do *this,* that is the question. Often there are tentatively several strategic factors, any one of which meets the immediate situation or satisfies the necessity of immediate purpose. This expands the horizon into the less immediate future, increases the objective field. The final strategic selection will be made on the basis of the estimate of less immediate future consequences.

[6] *Institutional Economics,* p. 629.

F. OPERATIONS RESEARCH AND DECISION MAKING

"Operations Research" for Management *

C. C. Herrmann and J. F. Magee

There is a new concept in management. It is called operations research. It has helped companies to solve such diverse business problems as directing salesmen to the right accounts at the right time, dividing the advertising budget in the most effective way, establishing equitable bonus systems, improving inventory and reordering policies, planning minimum-cost production schedules, and estimating the amount of clerical help needed for a new operation.

Operations research makes possible accomplishments like these and many others because (a) it helps to single out the critical issues which require executive appraisal and analysis, and (b) it provides factual bases to support and guide executive judgment. Thus, it eases the burden of effort and time on executives but intensifies the potential of their decision-making role. In this sense operations research contributes toward better management.

What is this thing called operations research? How does it work? How does it differ from other services to management? Where can it be used? How should management get it organized and under way? What are its limitations and potentials? These are all questions that we shall try to answer in the following pages.

ESSENTIAL FEATURES

Operations research apparently means different things to different people. To some businessmen and scientists it means only the application of statistics and common sense to business problems. Indeed, one vice president of a leading company remarked that if his division heads did not practice it every day, they would not last long. To others it is just another and perhaps more comprehensive term for existing activities like market research, quality control, or industrial engineering. Some

* Reprinted by permission of the publishers from *Harvard Business Review*, vol. 31, no. 4 (July-August, 1953), pp. 100–103, 106–107, 111–112. Mr. Herrmann is Associate Professor of Industrial Management at Massachusetts Institute of Technology and Associate Director of the Institute's Executive Development Program. Mr. Magee is an operations research consultant with Arthur D. Little, Inc.

businessmen consider it a new sales or production gimmick; some, a product of academic people interfering in the practical world. In truth, operations research is none of these things, as we shall soon see.

It should not be surprising that there has been this confusion. Operations research is not an explicit, easily identifiable concept that developed to meet the specific needs of industry. It was first applied in World War II by groups of scientists who were engaged by the government to help frame recommendations for the improvement of military activities. After the war a few soundly managed companies experimented with it and found that it worked successfully in business operations as well; and it has since gained a secure foothold in industry.

Early attempts by operations analysts to describe their activities, based on the objective of arriving at a precise and comprehensive definition of operations research, tended to be overly generalized, broad, and self-conscious, and suffered from emphasis on military applications. Some of the confusion surrounding the meaning of the term, operations research, has resulted from attempts at identification with special techniques or unnecessarily rigid distinctions between operations research and other management service activities.

Now, let us see if we can cut through some of this confusion.

The first point to grasp is that operations research *is* what its name implies, research on operations. However, it involves a *particular* view of operations and, even more important, a *particular* kind of research.

Operations are considered as an entity. The subject matter studied is not the equipment used, nor the morale of the participants, nor the physical properties of the output; it is the combination of these in total, as an economic process. And operations so conceived are subject to analysis by the mental processes and the methodologies which we have come to associate with the research work of the physicist, the chemist, and the biologist—what has come to be called "the scientific method."

The Scientific Method

The basic premise underlying the scientific method is a simple and abiding faith in the rationality of nature, leading to the belief that phenomena have a cause. If phenomena do have a cause, it is the scientist's contention that by hard work the mechanism or system underlying the observed facts can be discovered. Once the mechanism is known, nature's secrets are known and can be used to the investigator's own best advantage.

The scientist knows that his analogue to nature will never be entirely perfect. But it must be *sufficiently* accurate to suit the particular purposes at hand; and, until it is, he must repeat the processes of observation, induction, and theory construction—again and again. Note that a satisfactory solution must be in quantitative terms in order that it can be predictive—the only accepted fundamental test of being physically meaningful.

The scientific method, in its ideal form, calls for a rather special mental attitude, foremost in which is a reverence for facts. Of course all modern executives are accustomed to using figures to control their operations. But they are primarily concerned with results and only secondarily with causes; they interpret their facts in the light of company objectives. This is a much different attitude from seeking out the relationships underlying the facts.

Thus, when an executive looks at sales figures, he looks at them primarily in terms of the success of his sales campaign and its effect on profits. By contrast, when the scientist looks at these same figures, he seeks in them a clue to the fundamental behavior pattern of the customers. By the process of induction he tentatively formulates a theoretical system or mechanism; then by the inverse process of deduction he determines what phenomena should take place and checks these against the observed facts. His test is simple: Does the assumed mechanism act enough like nature—or, more specifically in this case, does it produce quantitative data such as can be used for predicting how the customers will in fact behave? For example:

In a company manufacturing specialty products, examination of account records showed that customer behavior could be accurately described as a time-dependent Poisson process—a type of phenomenon found widely in nature, from problems in biology to nuclear physics. This concept yielded the key to establishing measures of the efficiency of the salesmen's work and of the effect of the promotion in building sales. On this basis a new method of directing promotional salesmen to appropriate accounts was constructed—and then tested by careful experiments, to see if sales increases resulted at less than proportionate increases in cost. (The results in this case were spectacular: an over-all sales rise in six figures, and a corresponding gain in net profits.)

Implementation

Through the years mathematical and experimental techniques have been developed to implement this attitude. The application of the scientific attitude and the associated techniques to the study of operations, whether business, government, or military, is what is meant by operations research.

Newton was able to explain the apparently totally unrelated phenomena of planetary motion and objects falling on the earth by the simple unifying concept of gravity. This represented a tremendous step forward in helping men to understand and control the world about them. Again, more recently, the power of the scientific method was demonstrated by the ability of the nuclear physicists to predict the tremendous energy potential lying within the atom.

Here are a few summary examples of the way this same kind of approach has been applied to down-to-earth business problems.

¶ A company with a number of products made at three different locations was concerned about the items to be produced at each location and the points at which the items would be warehoused. Freight costs constituted a substantial part of the delivered cost of the material. Operations research showed that what appeared to be a complex and involved problem could be broken into a series of rather simple components. Adaptations of linear programing methods were used to find the warehousing schedule which would minimize freight costs. The study is now being extended to determine the best distribution of products among manufacturing plants and warehouse locations in order to minimize net delivered cost in relation to return on investment.

¶ A manufacturer of chemical products, with a wide and varied line, sought more rational or logical bases than the customary percentage of sales for distributing his limited advertising budget among products, some of which were growing, some stable, and others declining. An operations research study showed that advertising effectiveness was related to three simple characteristics, each of which could be estimated from existing sales data with satisfactory reliability: (a) the total market potential; (b) the rate of growth of sales; (c) the customer loss rate. A mathematical formulation of these three characteristics provided a rational basis for distributing advertising and promotional effort.

¶ In a company making a line of light machines, the executive board questioned the amount of money spent for missionary salesmen calling on customers. Studies yielded explicit mathematical statements of (a) the relation between the number of accounts called on and the resulting sales volume and (b) the relation between sales costs and manufacturing and distribution costs. These were combined by the methods of differential calculus to set up simple tables for picking the level of promotion in each area which would maximize company net profits. The results showed that nearly a 50% increase in promotional activity was economically feasible and would yield substantial profits.

¶ An industrial products manufacturer wanted to set time standards as a basis for costs and labor efficiency controls. The operations research group studied several complex operations; expressed the effect of the physical characteristics of products and equipment and the time required to produce a given amount of output in the form of mathematical equations; and then, without further extensive time study or special data collection, set up tables of production time standards according to product characteristics, equipment used, and worker efficiency, which could be applied to any or all of the production operations.

¶ A company carrying an inventory of a large number of finished items had trouble maintaining sound and balanced stock levels. Despite careful attention and continued modification of reorder points in the light of experience, the stock of many individual items turned out to be either too high for sales or inadequate to meet demand. The problem was solved by a physical chemist who first collected data on the variables, such as size and frequency of order, length of production and delivery time, etc.; then set up an assumed system, which he tried out against extreme sales situations, continually changing its characteristics slightly until it met the necessary conditions—all on paper (a technique well known to physical scientists); and thus was able to determine a workable system without cost of installation and risk of possible failure.

These examples should serve to give some idea of how the scientific method can be applied. But they represent only a few of the many scientific techniques available (as we shall see when we examine further cases in more detail). Some practitioners even take the rather broad point of view that operations research should include the rather indefinite and qualitative methods of the social fields. Most professional opinion, however, favors the view that operations research is more restricted in meaning, limited to the quantitative methods and experimentally verifiable results of the physical sciences.

Basic Concepts

There are four concepts of fundamental importance to the practice of operations research: (a) the model, (b) the measure of effectiveness, (c) the necessity for decision, and (d) the role of experimentation.

The Model

The most frequently encountered concept in operations research is that of the model—the simplified representation of an operation, containing only those aspects which are of primary importance to the problem under study. It has been of great use in facilitating the investigation of operations. To illustrate with some familiar types of "models" from other fields:

(1) In aeronautical engineering the model of an aeroplane is used to investigate the aerodynamic properties in a wind tunnel. While perfectly adequate for this purpose, it would hardly do for practical use. It has no seats; it may not even be hollow. It is, however, a satisfactory physical model for studying the flight characteristics of the ship.

(2) Another, quite different kind of model, with which we are all familiar, is the accounting model. This is essentially a simplified representation on paper, in the form of accounts and ledgers, of the flow of goods and services through a business enterprise. It provides measures of the rate of flow, the values produced, and the performances achieved, and to that extent is useful (though it is hardly a realistic representation of *operations*).

(3) Many models are used in physics. Three-dimensional models of complex molecules are probably most familiar to laymen, but the most powerful models in this field are sets of mathematical equations.

There are several different types of operations research models. Most of them are mathematical in form, being a set of equations relating significant variables in the operation to the outcome. . . .

Another type of model frequently used is the punched-card model, where components of the operation are represented by individual punched cards; masses of these are manipulated on standard punched-card equipment. For example, in a study of a sales distribution problem, each customer, of thousands served by the company, was represented by a punched card containing significant information about his location, type of business, frequency of purchase, and average rate of business. The punched cards representing the customers could then be subjected to assumed promotional treatments, with the effects of the promotions punched into the cards. The resulting business could be calculated and an evaluation made of alternative sales-promotion campaigns.

Occasionally a model is physical like the ones often used by engineers. For example, the use of a hydrokinetic model has been proposed in the study of a mass advertising problem. The fluid flowing through the model would represent business of various types going to the company or to competitors as a result of various forms of the company's own and competitive promotional efforts (represented in the model by forces acting on the fluids).

Operations research models can also be distinguished as exact or probabilistic:

(1) An *exact* model is used in operations or processes where chance plays a small role, where the effect of a given action will be reasonably closely determined. Exact models can be used, for example, in long-range production scheduling problems in the face of known or committed demand. The exact model is sufficiently accurate since it can be assumed that, barring a major catastrophe, over the long run planned and actual production will be reasonably close.

(2) The *probabilistic* model, on the other hand, contains explicit recognition of uncertainty. Such models are of great use in the analysis of advertising problems, where the unpredictability of consumers plays a great role. . . . They make extensive use of the highly developed theory of probability, which has come to be of such great value in the physical science. One customarily thinks of a physicist as dealing with rather exact concepts and highly predictable experiments. Yet physicists faced a problem equivalent to the advertising problem in predicting atomic activity. Methods developed for physical problems involving mass behavior under random conditions can be applied with great facility and value to operations.

The model is a major goal of the operations research analyst. In one sense, the construction of the model, or a faithful representation of the operation, is the scientist's primary job. In doing it he develops a theory to explain the observed characteristics of the operation. . . . The remaining task is to interpret this theory through the manipulation of the model, whether mathematical or physical.

Measure of Effectiveness

Related to the concept of a model or theory of operation is the measure of effectiveness, whereby the extent to which the operation is attaining its goal can be explicitly determined. One common over-all measure of effectiveness in industrial operations is return on investment; another is net dollar profit. Measures of effectiveness down the scale might be the number of customers serviced per hour, the ratio of productive to total hours of a machine operation, etc.

A *consistent* statement of the fundamental goals of the operation is essential to the mathematical logic of the model. (It does not matter if the goals are complex.) Just as the model cannot make 2 and 2 add up to 5, so it is impossible to relate fundamentally inconsistent objectives and produce consistent and meaningful results.

Operations research has frequently brought to light inconsistencies in company goals. Take production scheduling, for instance. Very often its object has been stated as scheduling production to meet sales forecasts with minimum production costs, with minimum inventory investment, and without customer-service failure. Yet minimizing inventory investment typically requires the use of start-and-stop or at best uneven production plans, resulting in excessive production costs; and eliminating the risk of not being able to ship every customer order immediately requires huge inventories, in the face of fluctuating and at least partially unpredictable demand.

The solution is to combine and sublimate such otherwise inconsistent goals to a higher unified and consistent goal. To illustrate:

The diverse goals of customer service, production economy, and investment minimization can be expressed in terms of costs—the cost of inefficient production (hiring, training, overtime, etc.), the cost of investment in inventory (the rate of interest the treasurer wishes to charge to conserve his funds or perhaps the return on investment which can be earned through alternative uses of the available funds), and the cost of inability to meet a customer's demand (estimated loss of goodwill and future business). While the latter two costs are primarily policy costs, experience has shown that they are sufficiently determinable and realistic to afford a basis for management decision.

The three component costs can then be cast in an algebraic equation expressing their interrelationships in terms of total scheduling cost;

and the minimum total scheduling cost becomes the one, consistent goal.

Note that, once set up, the algebraic equation can be worked in reverse. Thus, the sales manager might be told how much the company can *afford* to pay for an inventory large enough to avoid varying risks of failure to meet consumer demand.

This kind of clarification of goals is particularly important in relating subordinate and over-all company goals—as in the case of a department run efficiently at the expense of other departments or of a promotion budget based on a fixed percentage of sales without regard to the adverse effects on manufacturing budgets.

The statement of a complete and wholly consistent goal of company operations must be recognized as an ideal. Business goals are very complex, and to catch the full flavor of the objectives of an intricate business operation in any simple, explicit statement is difficult. Many business goals remain, and probable ever will remain, at least in part intangible—e.g., efforts to improve employee morale or contribute to the public welfare. To that extent, the objective of operations research must be more modest than the construction of a complete model and the measurement of the extent to which the operation is attaining the complete set of goals established for it. But it still can serve to clarify the interdependency of those intangibles with the company goals which in fact are measurable, thus providing a guide to executive decision.

Necessity for Decision

The third concept inherent in operations research is that of decision and decision making. An essential element in all true operations research problems is the existence of alternative courses of action, with a choice to be made among them; otherwise the study of an operation becomes academic or theoretical. This should be clear from the cases already cited.

In sum, the objective of operations research is to clarify the relation between the several courses of action, determine their outcomes, and indicate which measures up best in terms of the company goal. But note that, while this should be of assistance to the executive in making his decision intelligently, in every case the ultimate responsibility still lies with him.

Role of Experimentation

The fourth significant concept concerns the role of experimentation. Operations research is the application of experimental science to the study of operations. The theory, or model, is generally built up from observed data or experience, although in some cases the model development may depend heavily on external or a priori information. In any event, the theory describing the operation must always be verifiable experimentally.

Two kinds of experiments are important in this connection:

(1) The first kind is designed simply to get information. Thus, it often takes the form of an apparently rather impractical test. In one case the operations analysts directed advertising toward potential customers the company knew were not worth addressing, and refrained from addressing customers the company typically sought—and for a very simple reason. There was plenty of evidence indicating what happened when advertising was directed toward those normally addressed but not enough about its effects upon those *not* normally addressed. To evaluate the effectiveness of the advertising, therefore, it was necessary to find out what happened to those normally promoted when they were not promoted, and what happened to those normally not promoted when they were.

(2) The other type of experiment is the critical type; it is designed to test the validity of conclusions. Again, what appear to be rather impractical forms of experimentation are sometimes used. Thus, in the most sensitive experiments of this type, the validity of the theory or model can often be tested most revealingly in terms of the results of extreme policies rather than in terms of the more normal policy likely to be put into practice. . . .

EVALUATION

In perspective, what is the current status of operations research? What are its contributions, its limitations, its future?

Contributions

Case histories show that operations research provides a basis for arriving at an integrated and objective analysis of operating problems. Characteristically, operations research tends to force an expansion in viewpoint and a more critical, questioning attitude. It also stimulates objective thinking, partly because it emphasizes broad purposes and partly because the mathematical nature of the model and techniques limits the influence of personal bias.

The results of operations research studies are quantitative. They provide an opportunity for sound estimates in terms of requirements, objectives, and goals, and a basis for more precise planning and decision making.

The contributions of operations research to business analysis and planning have been important and substantial. Here are two worth singling out:

1. *The application of organized thinking to data already existing within the company*—Frequently a major contribution has been the location, collection, and classification of existing data scattered through widely separated branches of the company. In one recent study, an opera-

tions research team found the same fundamental problem cropping up under various guises in a number of different parts of the company. Each division or section had its own point of view toward the problem, and each had significant information bearing on it that was unavailable to the others. This sort of thing happens despite the most sound and progressive management; operations research tends to rectify it.

2. *The introduction of new concepts and new methods of analysis—* Some of these concepts, such as information theory, control theory, and certain aspects of statistical mechanics have been carried over from other fields; the physical sciences, and in particular modern physics, have been a very fruitful source of transplanted analytical techniques. But there are also certain original contributions, such as the newborn theories of clerical organization and consumer behavior, which suggest the possibility of developing further tools for attacking important business problems. All these techniques make it possible to explore the effects of alternate courses of action before management becomes committed to one of them.

Limitations

Operations research is hardly a cure-all for every business ill; neither is it a source of automatic decisions. It is limited to the study of tangible, measureable factors. The many important factors affecting business decisions that remain intangible or qualitative must continue to be evaluated on the basis of executive judgment and intuition. Often they make it necessary to adjust or modify the conclusions drawn from the quantitative analysis of the researchers. Professional personnel in operations research strongly emphasize this distinction between the operations research responsibility for analysis and the executive responsibility for decision. They point with approval to cases like this one:

In a recent series of conferences called to implement the results of a long and major operations research investigation, the analysts emphasized that their conclusions were based in part on the assumption that the output of a plant in question could be increased substantially at the existing level of efficiency. The executive responsible for the operation of the plant felt that this assumption was a sound one. The official responsible for the ultimate decision, however, decided to follow a more conservative course of action than the one indicated by the study, primarily because of his estimate of the psychological effect that increases in volume would have on the plant personnel.

The fact that operations research is scientific in character rather than expert means that more time is required to achieve useful conclusions than in the case of normal engineering analyses. As an applied science, the work is torn between two objectives: as "applied" it strives for practical and useful work; as "science" it seeks increasing understanding of the basic operation, even when the usefulness of this information is not immediately clear. The executive who plans to support research work of this character must be fairly warned of the need for restraint. The natural tendency to require that the studies or analyses be "practical" can, if enforced too rigidly, result in the loss of substantial benefits. Also, the results of studies of this type are necessarily somewhat speculative. When operations research is purchased, neither the specific program to be followed, the precise questions to be answered, nor the successful achievement of results can be guaranteed.

Recognition of this difference between operations research and more conventional engineering methods is essential to the satisfaction of both the controlling executive and the analyst.

Problems Ahead

Thinking ahead about the future of operations research, the principal internal problem which it faces is the development of a reserve of manpower adequately trained and motivated. There is a serious need at the present time for trained personnel to carry forward even the present limited level of activity. Lack of manpower, even now, threatens the quality of the work. The insufficient supply of adequately trained and experienced men to meet the demand can create a vacuum, drawing in poorly trained persons and making maintenance of standards difficult. The growing interest among mathematicians, physicists, and others is easing this problem somewhat, however, and colleges and universities have taken the first steps in training young men to fill the gap. The problem the academic institutions face is primarily lack of sound case material and the current amorphous state of a subject with uncertain acceptance in industry generally. Industrial support of educational efforts by providing realistic case material and opportunities for field investigations would be of tremendous help.

The most serious problem in external relationships is probably the need to develop efficient means for communicating ideas and results of research to executive users. The more experienced operations research groups have come to realize that explaining or "selling" conclusions is just as important as arriving at conclusions, if they are in fact to be useful. The communication needs are simple: in short, an ability to express clearly and concisely conclusions based on lengthy studies, to organize results in terms of interest to the reader and user, and to recognize that executives' interests are more practical than the researchers'. . . .

New Horizons

In conclusion, the future of operations research appears reasonably bright at the present time. Successful applications in industry are fulfilling the hopes of its early supporters, and the skepticism of businessmen is tending to break down as successful case histories pile up and become available for publication.

The areas of potential application of operations research appear broad. The future holds possible extensions such as the development of strategic concepts through the applications of the much heralded (but as yet largely untested) theory of games and by the development of a fundamental understanding of the impact of advertising and merchandising methods.

How will operations research help in the future to clarify the role of the executive? Present indications are that it will live up to its expectations of helping executives to make decisions more intelligently, but the decisions will always remain to be made. The possibility of removing all subjective and qualitative factors must be deemed at the present time to be more a hope than a real possibility, and the construction of completely consistent and logical goals, while a reasonable objective in decision making, is probably unattainable. The balancing of the responsibilities to society, consumers, owners, and employees will therefore still be the fundamental task of executives.

G. MAKING PLANS OPERATIONAL

The Mechanics of Implementation *

George A. Peck

In launching a program of expansion, we believe that sound forward planning is absolutely essential to achieve efficiency and show a profit in such a competitive industry as ours. Intelligent planning, coupled with our present cost-reduction program, should:
1. Pave the way for a more effective sales program.
2. Improve the procurement of purchased materials.
3. Smooth out production peaks and valleys.
4. Simplify labor problems.
5. Provide a systematic basis for sound budgeting.

In our case, some definite period over which to plan had to be chosen. As stated, we think that a five-year span is the optimum period of time, since anything else is insufficient for long-range engineering, real estate, and capital assets planning, while a longer period would involve too much "crystal balling." A new year is added to the plan on December 15th, and the plan is adjusted and revised at the divisional level every June 15th. This frequency of adjustment maintains the plan as a current guide but prevents it from fluctuating to the point of confusion.

Except where specifically indicated, the following discussion will deal with those phases of the planning work carried out at the divisional or operating level.

THE SALES FORECAST

The backbone of any long-range planning, of course, is the sales forecast which is prepared by the Sales Department of each division in cooperation with the Business Research, Market Analysis, Engineering, Research, and Production Departments of the company. This forecast is broken down into individual product lines.

Exhibit 1 is a typical flow chart outlining the group effort and individual department responsibility for furnishing various phases of information to the Sales Department for sales forecast purposes. As shown, the

* Reprinted by permission of the publishers from *Launching a Company Expansion Program*, Financial Management Series, no. 112 (New York: American Management Association, 1956), pp. 23–34. Mr. Peck is Vice-President–Manufacturing, Stromberg-Carlson Company, a division of the General Dynamics Corporation.

Production Committee is responsible for furnishing the preliminary cost estimates to the Research and Development group as well as furnishing preliminary cost details to the Sales Forecasting group (see dotted lines on chart). This happens in advance of the preparation of the divisional sales forecast. The information is used by Research and Development and Sales Forecasting to arrive at their final forecast. Then, once the sales forecast has become final for budget, it becomes the responsibility of the Production Committee to prepare final figures on manpower, space, and machinery needed to fulfill the forecast.

EXHIBIT 1

FLOW CHART

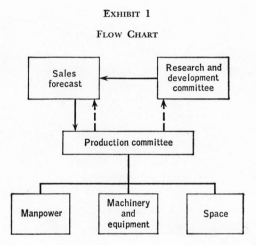

One of our recent sales forecasts (Exhibit 2) indicates a steady increase of commercial and government dollar volume for a particular division. The rate of increase was decided by our top management in the manner that has previously been described. In the case of equipment manufactured for the government, Exhibit 3 shows a sales forecast giving information upon which each prediction is based. This involves classifying the sales figures as (a) signed contracts, (b) good possibilities, and (c) hopeful guesses. The five-year forecast of sales is considered as relatively firm for its first two years, while the last three years are regarded as "preliminary."

While the Production Committee has done much preliminary estimating for the Research and Development Committee, it has also worked very closely with the Sales Department in preparing the sales forecast by estimating the cost of new developments and revising costs on present production contracts. These revised cost data serve as a guide for the Sales Department to predict selling prices of the same equipment on future contract production runs.

Once a sales forecast becomes final, the Production Committee swings into a very important phase of its work. The production manager of each division heads up the Production Committees; and, with the aid of production engineers, test equipment engineers, and inspection, purchasing, and production control personnel, he prepares the requirements for manpower, space, and equipment.

Exhibit 2

TYPICAL DIVISIONAL 5-YEAR SALES FORECAST

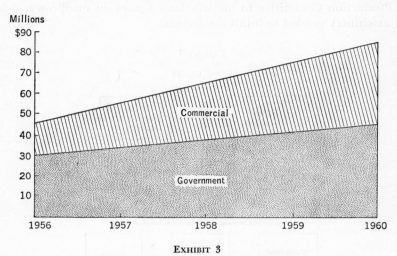

Exhibit 3

GOVERNMENT CONTRACTS—5-YEAR SALES FORECAST

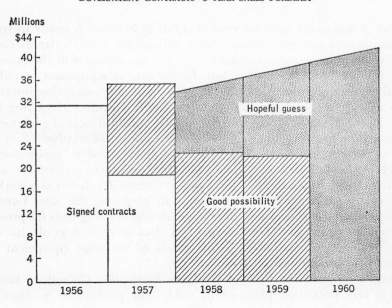

MANPOWER REQUIREMENTS

Each production manager prepares for his operational vice president manpower requirements estimated from the size and rate of production indicated by the sales forecast. These requirements are scheduled for each product line on a monthly basis for the first year and on an annual basis thereafter. The various charts are combined into two schedules: one which shows the monthly schedule for the first year and another which shows the yearly fluctuations in the divisional personnel requirements for the next five years. Because it is a well-known fact that a steady or gradually increasing workforce is the most efficient, considerable effort is expended to achieve this condition.

EXHIBIT 4

TYPICAL DIVISIONAL FORECAST OF MANPOWER REQUIREMENTS

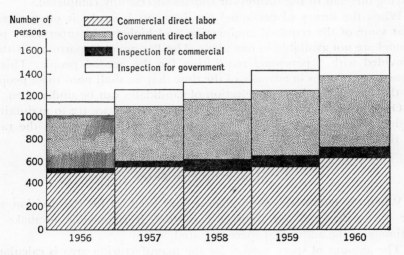

Exhibit 4 shows a typical manpower chart for a division. To achieve a smooth-looking chart of this nature, the production rates are juggled and rearranged for the various product lines—within reason, of course— so that an over-all manpower requirement schedule is obtained. From this schedule of direct labor personnel, needs for supervisory and indirect personnel are predicted by using ratios developed for individual departments at Stromberg-Carlson. Although these ratios vary from job to job, we have developed fairly practical estimates for the commercial and government production lines. Requirements for supervisory personnel, as well as such indirect labor as production engineers, expediters, maintenance men, janitors, and stock clerks, are estimated in this way.

Plans are made to fill these personnel needs, first, by transferring surplus personnel from other departments and, second, by hiring. The president of our local union is advised at this time of our anticipated personnel requirements and of the plans which we intend to use to meet
them. This policy has met with the wholehearted approval of both the
union members and the officers, and we have never experienced any
difficulty in selling our plans and policies to them. The absence of job
seniority in our plants allows us to transfer workers from job to job for
the mutual advantage of both employee and company.

If the requirements for supervisory and indirect personnel exceed the
present supply, the direct labor payroll is examined by the responsible
supervisors for persons who might qualify for promotion to these better
jobs. If there are sufficient numbers of such persons involved, a formal
in-plant training program is initiated; and, in addition, these persons
might also be enrolled in appropriate technical schools in the area. With
regard to these outside courses, our company follows the practice of
paying one-half of the tuition for courses successfully completed.

When the survey of personnel requirements is made, it often reveals
that some of the required engineering and higher-paid supervisory personnel are not available in our plant. The Personnel Department is then
provided with a personnel requisition for the needed people. This is
done some months in advance of the time that we shall need these people,
so that careful testing and selection of candidates can be undertaken.

Once the various manpower schedules are set up, we try to maintain a
ratio of direct labor personnel to indirect labor personnel in the ratio
of three direct to one indirect.

MANUFACTURING SPACE

When the manpower requirements have been set for the division and
we have calculated our indirect personnel, it is possible to make an
estimate of the additional space required.

The amount of space needed for the manufacturing area is calculated
by multiplying the number of production and inspection workers by our
standard square-foot allowance per employee. The space requirements for
engineering, production engineering, and office can all be estimated in a
similar manner. The requirements of all departments are then totaled
and compared to the amount of space available. The difference, of course,
is the amount of additional engineering office and production space
required to fulfill the demands of the growth and expansion program.

Exhibit 5 shows the total manufacturing area required by one of our
divisions. The dotted figures represent the existing space, and those
crosshatched represent the space which must be added. Space requirements cannot be fully determined without considering the type and

amount of production machinery and equipment that will be required for the planned rate of production as well as the type of assembly. Past history proves a very important aid in determining some of these factors for future production.

EXHIBIT 5

REQUIRED MANUFACTURING FLOOR SPACE

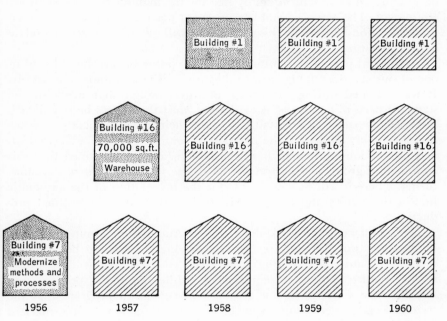

| 1956 | 1957 | 1958 | 1959 | 1960 |

After the exact space requirements have been determined, it is necessary to convert this information into monetary terms to determine how much the space is going to cost us; whether we are going to build or lease; and, also, the type of building that we are going to put up. Will it be single-story or double-story? Will we have available parking space? What about heating in our central plant, materials handling in the new space, and so forth?

NECESSARY EQUIPMENT

Once these questions have been answered and space requirements have been settled, we can move to the last and probably the most important of the functions—the determination of how much equipment is necessary to carry on our program.

Automation. Automatic assembly, dip soldering machines, materials handling systems, and automatic packers are only a few of the large and expensive tools which must be planned for. To determine the full impact of these and other automatic machines upon the company, Stromberg-Carlson formed an Automation group two years ago. It soon realized that automatic assembly machines would be an absolute necessity for survival in an industry as competitive as ours. Accordingly, this group was transferred to the Research Department and given the responsibility of developing an automatic assembly line for the manufacture of electronic equipment. The actual assembly equipment has recently been purchased to specifications written by this group, who will modify it to accommodate our various products.

An integral part of this automation study program was the redesign of one of our standard table-model radios to facilitate automatic assembly. It was revealed during the course of this redesign that many of the standard parts of a radio or television set must themselves be redesigned, reshaped, or packaged differently to allow their use in automatic production machinery. Now that the redesign of component parts, end product, and production equipment has been established, it is planned that this Automation group will be transferred to the vice president of manufacturing. There it will be responsible for the installation of the automatic line in the factory and for supervising the pilot run on scheduled production.

To complement the work done by the Automation group on assembly methods, our Test Equipment Engineering Department began investigation of automatic testing techniques and equipment that would further reduce manpower requirements while improving product uniformity. It is essential to our growth and expansion program that the technical manpower requirements be lessened, as there are not a sufficient number of technically trained persons available to meet even the present requirements.

The equipment developed by this department enables us to conserve technical manpower and thereby realize cost reductions in the manufacture of commercial equipment as well as government electronic gear. As to product uniformity, one of the prime virtues of automatic production equipment, to the government inspector, is the much higher degree of control that is possible. With automatic testing equipment, aligning and testing are less subject to human error, thus making statistical analysis a more potent and meaningful tool.

Standard Tools and Machinery. Funds also have to be provided for additional tools and machinery of a standard nature and for replacement of tools and machinery which are wearing out. Historically in our shop, over a period of years, insufficient funds were appropriated to maintain our machine departments properly; therefore, we have been, and are, faced with "catching up" as well as planning normal replacement and expansion. The Production Engineering Department is responsible for this program.

There are many areas where a need for replacement is apparent simply because available equipment is not capable of producing satisfactory parts within specification. It is not only a question of old and worn machinery; we are constantly faced with changes in design concept which require tolerances that were not considered feasible when the present equipment was manufactured 20 or 30 years ago. This then means that much equipment cannot be used for certain parts. For scheduling work, and for considering replacements, we have graded all machines into three classifications which indicate their condition.

It is not necessary that all equipment be of the latest design and in top condition. But a great amount of desirable efficiency and flexibility is lost if a foreman can use only a small percentage of his equipment on high-precision work. Since an increasing percentage of our requirements call for very close tolerances, he is forced to schedule more and more of his work on fewer machines. This means shorter, uneconomic runs in order to free the machines for other urgent requirements, with the resulting increases in setup time and costs.

Replacement or Redesign? Because the older equipment is also subject to higher maintenance cost, a program has been established to provide for accumulating maintenance and repair labor and the cost of major parts by machine number. Although these are general overhead charges against the department, this statistical accumulation by machine will provide factual data which can be used to good effect in determining when a machine should be replaced. Moreover, a tabulated report of machine utilization gives us information which is increasingly useful. This shows the per cent of the normal 40 hours each week during which a machine is actually used, and also reflects certain major items, such as down time for repair. Other reasons for non-use—for example, "no requirement," or machine inadequacy—must likewise be studied.

In an increasing number of cases, we therefore have such factual data as (1) grading of the machine, (2) maintenance and repair costs, and (3) per cent of utilization, as indications that perhaps a machine should be replaced. The next step is examination of the requirements for the type of work done by the machine. Are the parts produced part of a continuing sales requirement, or is this requirement only temporary? Is Design Engineering reasonably satisfied with the product, or is a redesign under way, and would the concept of the redesign be changed if there were a possibility of using a new and different machine? Perhaps Design Engineering is partially restricted in its work by its knowledge of the equipment presently available, and its thinking might change if this restriction were removed and different equipment were available for manufacturing the part.

Choice of New Machines. Assume that as a result of these considerations a new machine is suggested. It then becomes necessary to forecast accurately production costs for the appropriate parts on the new machine. A comparison of production costs for the old and new machines provides a basis for determining the "return on investment," which is the current measuring stick being used.

It may be necessary, of course, to compare several possible new machines to determine which is the most profitable replacement. In this area, we encounter a need to anticipate future development in the field. A machine may wear out or be obsoleted by new developments in machine design. New equipment in a competitor's factory can obsolete our equipment much more rapidly than the passing years. Therefore, although it is impossible to predict many new machine developments, it is necessary for our production engineers to stay abreast of all new machines and processes. An example of this type of planning is the fact that certain equipment recommended for the 1956 program was specifically chosen because it will fit into possible automated assembly lines now in the very early planning stages.

Analysis of Results Obtained. Another very important phase of Production Engineering's responsibility is the investigation and analysis of results actually obtained by new equipment which has been purchased and installed. This continuous check is essential if we are to be certain of our approach to the problems. We must "discover if we were right"—this must not be a case of "proving we were right."

Our initial results in this type of investigation are encouraging. An example is the Stokes automatic molding machine which has recently been installed in one of our departments. The original justification contained a cost analysis indicating an annual cost saving of approximately $19,600. To date, 130,000 parts of one type have been run on this new machine with a saving of $2,600. Extended to an annual rate, our experience thus far indicates a continuing annual saving of $18,500 per year for this machine which cost $10,500.

Justifying Expenditures. Our concept of planning and itemizing a capital budget has changed considerably in recent years, and much more detailed analyses to provide proper justification of new acquisitions are now required. The limiting factor, of course, will always be the funds available, and there will be the problem of comparing the relative merits of many possible expenditures, all of which are justified, to determine which ones will produce the greatest return for the company.

The budget for capital equipment is presented in both written and graphic form. Exhibit 6 shows a typical capital expenditures budget for a division over a five-year span. It indicates the machinery necessary to maintain production at forecast levels.

We find that capital equipment expenditures vary considerably between the divisions and that it is necessary to do juggling to provide ample protection across the years. Exhibit 6, it must be remembered,

EXHIBIT 6

PROJECTED FIXED CAPITAL EXPENDITURES

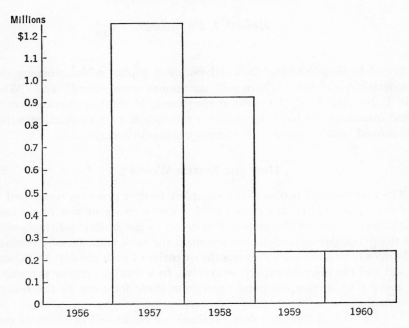

represents just one of the divisions. When all divisional requirements are added together, we show a more constant level of annual expenditures.

*

In these few pages, we have tried to show how our formal growth and expansion plan is handled at the operating level. The important point to keep in mind is that it takes a great deal of coordinated effort and constant attention to keep a program of this nature on the track. Needless to say, we feel that the amount of effort involved is more than justified by the results.

Forecasting of Cash *

Robert I. Phemister

Stated in simple terms, financial policy is a plan which answers two important questions: "Where will the money come from?" and "What will it be used for?" To assist management in finding the answers to these questions, we have developed a method of cash forecasting which has proved reliable under many changing conditions. . . .

How the System Works

The cash forecast is based on a complete budget program comprised of a series of individual forecasts covering every phase of our operations. Each forecast is carefully prepared in detail by the individual responsible for the particular operation. For example, the sales manager of a division submits a forecast of sales showing the quantity of each product he expects to sell and the price he expects to receive. In a similar manner executives in every part of our company contribute their forecasts to the budget program.

The individual forecasts thus obtained are translated in terms of cash and set down in a way which shows clearly their relationship to each other. The resulting cash forecast then becomes the framework from which definite financial policies can be developed. This forecast is prepared each month for the Board of Directors and covers a period of 24 months in advance. It shows the cash position of the company in terms of long-range planning.

The first of the two statements which comprise the cash forecast shows the estimated change in cash position for the two-year period (Figure 3). This statement is divided into two sections, the first showing the estimated sources of cash. "Estimated Earnings" as given in this section are based on information furnished by the division general managers and include new earnings from the proposed expansion of plant facilities in addition to forecasted earnings from present facilities. Since the estimated earnings have been reduced by the estimated amount of depreciation

* Reprinted by permission of the publishers from *A Program of Financial Planning and Controls: The Monsanto Chemical Company*, Financial Management Series, no. 103 (New York: American Management Association, 1953), pp. 10–13. Mr. Phemister is Comptroller, Phosphate Division, Monsanto Chemical Company.

and provision for income taxes, these items are added back to arrive at the cash earnings.

The second section of the form shows the estimated disbursements of cash. "Expenditures for Construction" are obtained from the construction budget, which lists every construction project that is seriously contemplated during the next two or more years. These budgets are submitted by each plant manager and approved by his division manager. They contain a brief description of each project, its estimated cost, and the quarterly periods in which funds will be required for construction. Here again we work from the smallest element toward the total result.

FIGURE 3

MONSANTO CHEMICAL COMPANY AND CONSOLIDATED SUBSIDIARIES
ESTIMATED CHANGE IN CASH POSITION FOR THE TWO YEARS
ENDING SEPTEMBER 30, 1952
(In thousands of dollars)

| | Year ending September 30 | |
	1951	1952
Cash balance at beginning of period..................	$ 56,263	$ 27,113
Sources of cash:		
Earnings	25,622	30,461
Depreciation	13,510	15,956
Provision for income taxes...........................	40,627	46,559
Total	$136,022	$120,089
Disbursement of cash:		
Expenditures for construction	$ 44,789	$ 79,620
Working capital, etc.:		
For new construction projects......................	8,920	13,200
Other	200	452
Investment in associated companies...................	1,000	7,000
Dividends paid	12,400	12,400
Purchase of tax notes................................	41,600	47,650
Total disbursements	$108,909	$160,322
Cash balance at end of period........................	$ 27,113	($ 40,233)

Notes:

"Working Capital," as we use the term, is the money which we need to finance operations from the time raw material is purchased until the cash from the sale of finished goods is collected from customers. In addition to the funds required for regular operations, we provide for the additional working capital which will be required for the expanded facilities. This amount is determined from the estimates of construction projects which show the new working capital required in addition to the construction cost of the project.

"Investment in Associated Companies" as used on this form represents funds which these companies expect to require for construction or other purposes. "Dividends Paid" is based on the common and preference shares outstanding at that time. It is assumed that the existing quarterly rate on common shares will be maintained. Since income taxes represent a major disbursement and it is our policy to carry a balance of tax notes on hand equal to our federal income tax liability, we include in the estimated disbursements the amount of tax notes we expect to purchase.

DETERMINING FUNDS REQUIRED

On this statement the estimated disbursements of cash may well exceed the estimated cash that will be available. For example, if we have planned a large expansion program, this statement will show the need for additional funds.

FIGURE 4

MONSANTO CHEMICAL COMPANY AND CONSOLIDATED SUBSIDIARIES
ESTIMATED MONTHLY CASH POSITION FOR THE TWO YEARS
ENDING SEPTEMBER 30, 1952
(In thousands of dollars)

1950	Month end cash balance	Tax notes on hand
October	$54,676	$23,741
November	51,594	27,092
December	50,210	27,879
1951		
January	46,767	31,025
February	42,061	34,248
March	37,166	29,826
April	32,403	32,060
May	31,628	35,297
June	29,405	30,533
July	28,287	33,761
August	28,359	36,904
September	27,113	34,221
October	27,287	37,552
November	26,593	40,808
December	26,887	37,865
1952		
January	25,344	41,726
February	12,066	45,694
March	(2,106)	36,530
April	(17,405)	40,434
May	(34,913)	44,391
June	(49,022)	35,324
July	(60,095)	39,519
August	(52,898)	43,769
September	(40,233)	41,663

The second statement (Figure 4) of the cash forecast shows the estimated balance of cash and tax notes at the end of each month during the two-year period covered by the forecast. Information for this statement is obtained by spreading each of the factors on the previous statement and computing the month-by-month change in cash. From the monthly cash balances, the Directors can determine how much and at what time additional cash will be required. Armed with the information shown in these statements, the Directors can appraise the situation and determine a course of action.

I might mention an actual forecast which we furnished our Directors in September, 1950. It was evident from this forecast that funds would be required early in 1952 and that the cash deficiency would reach a maximum of about $60,000,000 in July, 1952. As early as 1949, when our construction program began to take shape, the monthly cash forecast indicated that additional funds would be required to carry out the program. Therefore, the Directors were advised of the estimated financial picture well in advance.

In this particular instance, the Directors secured additional funds in 1951. In January, 1952, we sold $104,000,000 worth of common stock and debentures. That is one illustration of the value of our cash forecast as an aid to financial planning. Without a forecast the needs for additional funds would have become apparent eventually. It is very unlikely, however, that the requirements could have been estimated accurately either as to time or amount. Financial planning under these conditions would have been reduced to expediency, which is both risky and expensive.

*

The success of our cash-forecasting procedure lies in the fact that we gather together and coordinate all the individual forecasts covering each phase of our operations. Each responsible executive in our company contributes a carefully prepared forecast covering those operations for which he is responsible. We believe this method yields more accurate results than one based on a few general estimates of future conditions. Because it has been reliable under many changing conditions, it has earned the confidence of management.

Profit Planning for the Operating Man *

W. T. Seney

Successful operation of a budgetary control system depends in the final analysis on how well the operating organization understands and accepts it. It is therefore worth the expenditure of considerable time and effort on the part of the controller to see that the top executives and key personnel of his company are well and favorably acquainted with the basic concepts of profit planning and budgetary control.

Is It the Controller's Job?

Is it the controller's job to inform management about budgetary control? Customarily this responsibility is included among the controller's responsibilities. However, some plans of organization locate elsewhere the responsibilities for profit planning and for interpreting results against plans. For instance, there is the widely known financial control plan of Koppers Company, Inc. At Koppers, this function reports to the president. In other companies, a budget director may report directly to the president; or in still other companies, an assistant to the president may supervise planning activities and the presentation and interpretation of reports showing actual results against plans. So we see a real diversity in placement of responsibility for budgetary control. This dilemma need not concern us here. In the first place, we can discuss the basic structure of profit planning itself without regard to the specific organization of responsibility for its over-all coordination. In the second place, a solution to the organizational problem will never be achieved by articles in magazines. Rather, the solution will be worked out in actual practice in American companies by men who act judiciously or foolishly and who either provide or fail to provide to all levels of management the planning and control services that management so honestly requires.

* Reprinted by permission of the publishers from *The Controller*, vol. 22 (May, 1954), pp. 211–214. Mr. Seney is a management consultant of McKinsey & Company, New York. He was formerly Controller of Univis Lens Co. before joining McKinsey & Company.

A Tool for Creating Understanding

Visual presentation has a well-earned reputation as a teaching technique. The schematic chart presented in this article is designed to serve as a common meeting ground for accounting and nonaccounting executives. It is often difficult for the nonaccounting executive to understand how the profit and loss statement reflects operations, and how the balance sheet reflects the results of operations on the financial status of the company. Even if the operating man understands the after-the-fact effect of operations on financial statements, he may not appreciate the advantages of forecasting the results of operating plans on the financial statements. The chart is intended as a tool to help in describing how planning for profits increases profits.

Planning for Profits Increases Profits

The visual presentation may be used to spell out four fundamental points:

First, the basic plans of a business must be measured in terms of money if there is to be any assurance that money will be available for the needs of the business.

Second, it is possible to plan for the future of a business in a comprehensive way, coordinating every aspect of the business with every other aspect to establish optimum profit goals.

Third, profit planning is preplanning what to do in terms of choosing an optimum profit course of action from among several alternatives.

Fourth, profit planning is preplanning not merely what to do if things work out as forecasted, but also what to do if things work out differently from the forecast.

The chart may be used in discussing the above points because it visually presents the interdependence and the interrelationships of the various activities of a business. Therefore, it makes it easy to show how any change in one area of the business can be traced through for its effects on other areas, on the balance sheet, and on the profit and loss statement.

The Flow of Profit Planning

In sound profit planning, key forecasts form the bases for operating plans. Operating plans, when translated into budgets, tie directly into the forecast balance sheet and profit and loss statement. These forecast financial statements provide information for financial planning. And the financial requirements in turn react upon the key forecasts and plans. The individual steps in this figure flow are discussed briefly below.

BASIC STRUCTURE OF PROFIT PLANNING IN A MAKE AND SELL COMPANY

1. *Forecast and Plan.* The distinction between forecasting and planning is not an easy one. Webster gives "to plan ahead" as the leading definition for "forecast." However, there is a practical distinction.

Forecasting is our best thinking about what will happen to us in the future. Planning is our best thinking about what we can cause or want to happen in the future. In forecasting, we define situations, and recognize problems and opportunities. In planning, we develop our objectives in practical detail, and we correspondingly develop schemes of action to achieve these objectives.

Forecast and plan react upon each other. For example, suppose that we are interested in a company that makes and sells an item used in residential construction. The sales of such an item should, other things being equal, follow closely the curve of residential building activity. Therefore, we could forecast sales by using a forecast of building activity. However, when we come to plan the sales of this item, we may contemplate actions which lead us to alter our original forecast. For instance, we may consider doubling the number of our distributors. Or we may plan to concentrate additional sales effort in selected key areas where major construction activity is likely to occur. These or any similar plans would change the forecast, and the sales plan would thus have reacted upon the forecast.

Sound management practice includes forecasting future probabilities affecting all major aspects of the business. Forecasts are required not only of long- and short-range sales outlooks, but also of the outlooks for availability of management talent and labor force; for availability and prices of raw materials; for favorable governmental and community relations; for developments of new scientific and industrial techniques bearing on the business; and for many other possible influences upon the direction and rate of company growth.

All forecasted events of significance to the company will pertain to one or more of the five key forecasts—long-term sales, short-term sales, going concern activities, future development activities, and fixed investment. When you think about what the future course of events may be, and then define what the future problems and opportunities of the company may be, you can classify all your findings under one or another of the five headings. Thus, these key forecasts are the logical starting point of the profit planning procedure.

2. *Sales Forecasting and Planning.* The short-term sales forecast provides the basis for the current year's sales plan and finished goods inventory plan. At the same time, the influence of the long-term sales forecast is reflected in the capital expenditure plan and in the finished goods inventory plan.

The long-term forecast serves as what might be called the anchor-end of the finished goods inventory plan. Since inventory at the end of this year is the beginning inventory for next year's business, it is necessarily influenced by the longer-term sales thinking as well as by the current year's short-term forecast. The long-term sales forecast also provides the basis for developing, in rough outline, the capital expenditure plan. That portion of the plan falling within the current year is reflected in the capital expenditure budget.

The short-term sales forecast and resulting sales plan look in two directions. On the one hand, they look outside the company to define the sales income budget and the variable selling expense budget required to obtain sales income. On the other hand, they look inside the company to serve as the basis for the production plan. The planning is not complete until it meets the requirements in both directions.

The sales plan should be worked out on a sound and reasonably detailed basis. It should reflect seasonal influences and any anticipated irregularities in sales. It should be broken down not only into time periods but also into geographical or responsibility areas by the use of sales quotas. A well-developed sales plan is generally built up on a quota basis in the first place, so that the double-check by individual quota on total plan is inherent in the building. In a multiplant situation, where there is a choice of manufacturing product items in more than one plant, the geographical distribution of sales is of special importance for production planning.

Adequate sales planning is fundamental to profit planning. In spite of this, some companies base operating budgets on a sales plan which is "same as last year," or "normal sales volume." These companies, if they use standard costs and flexible budgets, do exercise budgetary control over their plant operations. However, they do not obtain the full advantages of profit planning by costing out alternative sales plans and finding out which plan offers the optimum profit opportunities.

3. *Production Plan.* Once sales and inventory requirements have been established, the logical first step in the production area is a facilities survey. This survey should determine that all planned products can be produced on existing or contemplated equipment (including subcontracting facilities where necessary), and that they can be made in the volumes required. In this initial stage, availability of labor supply and the necessary skills is considered. Bottlenecks caused by lack of skills or equipment are frequently uncovered. At this point decisions must be made either to eliminate bottlenecks or to reduce planned volume.

The coordination of sales and inventory requirements with productive capacity provides the groundwork for spelling out the production plan. This plan should be sufficiently detailed to establish the material purchasing plan and budget and also plans and budgets covering plant variable costs. The definition of variable costs will of course differ in accordance with the nature of the industrial operations involved and with management policies governing operations.

The production plan is reflected on the balance sheet through the planned inventory control procedure. Material purchases on a planned basis are charged to the raw material inventory budget, which in turn is cleared to the work-in-process budget. Plant variable costs incurred per the production plan are reflected in the plant variable budget covering labor and burden items. This budget is also cleared to the work-in-process budget. Work-in-process inventory is cleared to finished goods inventory in accordance with production plan.

The use of finished goods inventory for sales is charged on the planned profit and loss statement by transferring from the finished goods inventory budget to the cost of goods sold budget. (Please note again that cost of goods sold is on a direct costing basis and therefore includes only variable elements of cost.)

At this point, planned operations have been reflected in the profit and loss statement to the extent of a sales income, variable selling expense, variable cost of goods sold, and a resulting budgeted profit after variable cost.

4. *Fixed Costs.* There remains, then, to reflect fixed costs in the profit planning of the business. The planning of fixed costs, like the planning of variable costs, should be based on forecasts of what the future holds in store.

Forecasts may be said to affect management thinking about three classes of management commitments. These three classes are *going concern activities, future development activities,* and *fixed investment.* In spite of detailed differences between one company and another, the general concepts represented by these terms are fairly straightforward.

Going concern activities are those activities required "to keep the doors open," as our British cousins say. Rentals and some taxes and insurance premiums; expenses of the permanent staff of a company, including sales force and sales office salaries and expenses; advertising; plant supervisory staff, minimum administrative staff, and all their related expenses—these are generally included in going concern activities.

Future development activities include such things as research and development program expense; possibly some advertising and promotion expense; and the like. In addition, if a company plans to open new sales offices or plants, the expense portion of the expansion program would be a future development expense unrelated to current sales. Also, the training of staff for future use in the business (as for instance an executive development program, or the expenses of training a new crop of business school graduates) would be future development expense.

Fixed investment is defined by the balance sheet. Those expenses associated with fixed investment such as depreciation, taxes, insurance, and the like are recognized as part of the fixed cost load which the business must carry.

Fixed expenses are for the most part fixed by management definition. They are usually (with the exception of fixed investment expense) fixed only for the year that is being forecast; and they may be for less than that period in the event of a radical change in the level of business activity.

The fixed expense forecasts underlie the fixed operating plan. This plan includes the organization structure of the company, the amount of administrative and clerical assistance which will be provided to management, and the authorized expenditures in the fixed areas for which managers will be held accountable. The fixed operating plan is spelled out in the fixed selling, general, and administrative expense budgets and in the fixed plant expense budget, all of which are integral parts of the master profit and loss budget.

The subtraction of planned fixed expenses from the planned profit after variable cost results in the planned net profit. This completes the planning of the company's income and profit performance.

5. *Capital Expenditure Plan.* The capital expenditure plan, as mentioned previously, stems in the final analysis from the long-term sales outlook. Management necessarily plans as a minimum to maintain its productive capacity and its competitive position by replacing worn out and obsolescent facilities. The assumption lying behind this minimum plan is that long-term sales will remain equal to current sales. If, on the other hand, management assumes long-term sales increases, then logically management plans for capital investment to increase facilities. A sound capital plan runs for considerably more than a year. However, for purposes of current year budgeting, only that part of the capital expenditure plan on which expenditures are to be made during the current year is reflected in the capital expenditure budget.

Part Six

CONTROL

A. THE CONTROL PROCESS

The Meaning of Control *

Douglas S. Sherwin

"What exactly do you mean by management control?" When this question was asked of a number of managers, in both Government and industry, the answers showed a surprising lack of agreement—surprising, since in a field for which theory has been developed to the extent it has in business management, terms should be precise, specific, and unambiguous. The literature, as one might expect, reflects about the same variety of views as entertained by management men themselves, and so does little to clarify the situation.

Is it important that managers have a clear understanding of this concept? The question almost answers itself. A manager who does not understand management control cannot be expected to exercise it in the most efficient and effective manner. Nor can staff men whose duty it is to design systems and procedures for their organizations design efficient systems unless they possess a clear understanding of management control. And certainly (though the truth of this is seldom sufficiently appreciated) anyone who is subject to control by others has to understand clearly what that means if he is to be contented in that relationship.

Indeed, when management control is *not* understood, good management is a very improbable result. This is especially true when—as frequently it is—control is identified with management, or is confused with certain devices of management, such as objectives, plans, organization charts, policy statements, delegations of authority, procedures, and the like. The manager who believes managing and controlling are the same thing has wasted one word and needs a second to be invented. And one who believes he has provided for control when he has established objectives, plans, policies, organization charts, and so forth, has made himself vulnerable to really serious consequences. A clear understanding of control is therefore indispensable in an effective manager.

Understanding control really means understanding three principal things about it: What is control? What is controlled? And who controls? By proposing answers to these questions, I will try to frame a concept of control that will be useful to practitioners of the managerial art.

* Reprinted by permission of the publishers from *Dun's Review and Modern Industry* (January, 1956), pp. 45ff. Mr. Sherwin is Assistant Coordinator, Rubber Chemicals Division, Phillips Chemical Company.

The conception of control which I advocate can be simply and briefly stated as follows:

The essence of control is action which adjusts operations to predetermined standards, and its basis is information in the hands of managers.

We have a ready-made model for this concept of control in the automatic systems which are widely used for process control in the chemical and petroleum industries. A process control system works this way. Suppose, for example, it is desired to maintain a constant rate of flow of oil through a pipe at a predetermined, or set-point value. A signal, whose strength represents the rate of flow, can be produced in a measuring device and transmitted to a control mechanism. The control mechanism, when it detects any deviation of the actual from the set-point signal, will reposition the valve regulating flow rate.

BASIS FOR CONTROL

A process control mechanism thus acts to adjust operations to predetermined standards and does so on the basis of information it receives. In a parallel way, information reaching a manager gives him the opportunity for corrective action and is his basis for control. He cannot exercise control without such information. And he cannot do a complete job of managing without controlling.

As mentioned earlier, some students of management have defined control as what results from having objectives, plans, policies, organization charts, procedures, and so forth; and they refer to these elements of the management system, consequently, as controls or means of control. It is not difficult to understand why these devices of managing are so described by proponents of this point of view. Without objectives, for example, we all know results are likely to be other than desired, so it is assumed they function to control the results. And so it is with the other elements of the system.

Nevertheless, these elements are neither controls nor means of control. They do have, however, as we shall see later, an important role to play in a control *system,* and we can therefore examine them now in a little detail.

Certainly, to accomplish a task except through accident, people must know what they are trying to do. Objectives fulfill this need. Without them, people may work quite industriously yet, working aimlessly, accomplish little. Plans and programs complement objectives, since they propose how and according to what time schedule the objectives are to be reached.

But though objectives, and plans and programs are indispensable to the efficient management of a business (or, for that matter, to the management of almost any human endeavor) they are not means of control.

Control is checking to determine whether plans are being observed and suitable progress toward the objectives is being made, and acting, if necessary, to correct any deviations.

Policy is simply a statement of an organization's intention to act in certain ways when specified types of circumstances arise. It represents a general decision, predetermined and expressed as a principle or rule, establishing a normal pattern of conduct for dealing with given types of business events—usually recurrent. A statement of policy is therefore useful in economizing the time of managers and in assisting them to discharge their responsibilities equitably and consistently.

POLICY VERIFICATION

Nothing in these advantages, however, makes policy a means of control. Indeed, by their very nature, policies generate the need for control; they do not fulfill that need. Adherence to policies is not guaranteed, nor can it be taken on faith. It has to be verified. Without verification, there is no basis for control, no control, and incomplete managing.

Organization is often cited as a means of control. This detracts both from its own significance and from the concept of control.

Organization is part of the giving of an assignment. The organization chart, for example, is a first crude step in the defining of assignments. It gives to each individual, in his title, a first approximation to the nature of his assignment, and it orients him as accountable to a certain individual. But it is not in a fruitful sense a means of control. Control is checking to ascertain whether the assignment is being executed as intended—and acting on the basis of that information.

The relation between 'internal check' and 'internal control' is likewise not well understood. The two terms refer to quite different aspects of the managerial system. 'Internal check' provides in practise for the principle that the same person should not have responsibility for all phases of a transaction. This makes it clearly an aspect of organization, rather than of control. For how do we provide for internal check? We provide for it through segregating the duties of recording and those of custodianship and assigning them to different employees or groups of employees.

Assigning duties is, of course, the very essence of organizing, and thus internal check is simply organizing in a special way in order to realize special objectives. Internal control, on the other hand, observes the actual performance of duties as against the assigned duties and acts, where necessary, to correct deviations of the actual from the assigned.

Internal check and internal control are obviously both very necessary in an enterprise. But they operate differently. The objective of internal check is to reduce the opportunity for fraud or error to occur. The objective of internal control is to restore operations to predetermined standards. Internal check is thus static or built-in; it is provided before-the-fact; and its operation is preventive in its effect. Internal control, in contrast, is active and continual; it is exercised after-the-fact; and its operation is corrective in its effect.

Assignments are far from defined, however, by the preparation of an organization chart. Among the ways we have for supplementing the titles and lines of authority of an organization chart are delegations of authority. Delegations of authority clarify the extent of authority of individuals and in that way serve to define assignments. That they are not means of control is apparent from the very fact that wherever there has been a delegation of authority the need for control increases, and this could hardly be expected to happen if delegations of authority were themselves means of control.

MANAGER'S RESPONSIBILITY

Control becomes necessary whenever a manager delegates authority to a subordinate, because he cannot delegate, then simply sit back and forget all about it. A manager's accountability to his own superior has not diminished one whit as a result of delegating part of his authority to a subordinate. It is therefore incumbent upon managers who delegate authority to exercise control over actions taken under the authority so delegated. That means checking results as a basis for possible corrective action.

The question whether budgets are a means of control does not yield a straightforward answer because budgets perform more than one function. They perform three: they present the objectives, plans, and programs of the organization and express them in financial terms; they report the progress of actual performance against these predetermined objectives, plans, and programs; and, like organization charts, delegations of authority, procedures, and job descriptions, they define the assignments which have flowed down from the chief executive.

In expressing the objectives and plans of the organization, budgets are of course not means of control, for reasons examined earlier when objectives and plans were considered. Nor do budgets qualify as means of control in their function of defining assignments. Though this service of budgets is frequently overlooked, defining an assignment, as I have suggested previously, is neither a means of control nor the exercise of control.

Budgets are a means of control only in the respect that they report progress of actual performance against the program,—information which enables managers to take action directed toward bringing actual results into conformity with the program.

In the previous paragraphs I have tried to show that objectives, plans and programs, organization charts, and other elements of the managerial system are not fruitfully regarded as either 'controls' or 'means of control.' They nevertheless do bear a very important relationship to the control function. They are the pre-established standards to which operations are adjusted by the exercise of management control.

It may seem unfamiliar to some to view these devices of management in that light. Perhaps 'standards' is not the very best word. Yet these elements of the system are standards in a very real sense, for they have been laid down by competent authority as models or standards of desired performance.

These standards are, of course, dynamic in character, for they are constantly altered, modified, or revised. But for a moment let us give our attention to their static quality.

An objective is static until revised; a plan or program is static until it is abandoned. They possess a kind of temporary durability or limited permanence. They are in force until superseded. This same static quality inheres also in the other elements of the managerial system we spoke of. Policies, organizational set-up, procedures, delegations, job descriptions, and so forth, are, of course, constantly altered and added to. But, like objectives and plans, they retain their force until they are either abandoned or revised.

Suppose, for convenience, we use the phrase 'framework of management' to mean all the elements of the managerial system taken together—objectives, plans and programs, policies, organization, and the like. Doubtless, a more descriptive phrase could be invented, but this one at least suggests the notion that there is something of a semi-permanent nature in the managerial system. Now we can in a new way identify what is controlled. Managers control adherence to the objectives, plans, policies, organizational structure, procedures, and so forth, which have been laid down. In brief, managers control adherence to a predetermined 'framework of management.'

Now we can turn to the very important question that must be answered: "Who should act?"

It has become almost axiomatic as a management principle (which is unfortunately not always given effect in practise) that that person should act who is responsible for the results. 'Results' has to be interpreted here in a broad sense. For results include not only profits and costs—obvious items—but the conformity of all operations with all standards. Hence, whoever had responsibility for specifying and establishing a particular standard has to be ultimately responsible for controlling adherence to it and responsible, therefore, for such corrective action as is necessary. Of course, those below him in the chain of command may help him, but they cannot relieve him of final responsibility for control. Therefore, authority for managers to establish standards should be delegated as far down in the organization as practical wisdom permits. It then becomes their responsibility to control adherence of operations to the system they establish.

It is not only a responsibility, but a right; and it is asking for trouble to place in anyone else's hands the responsibility for controlling results in the operating manager's sphere of responsibility.

If the basis of control is information in the hands of managers, 'reporting' is elevated to a level of very considerable importance. Used here in a broad sense, 'reporting' includes special reports and routine reports; written, oral, and graphic reports; staff meetings, conferences, television screens, and any other means whereby information is transmitted to a manager as a basis for control action. Even the non-receipt of information, as where management is by exception, can be informational and imply the existence of control.

We are often told that reports should be timely and designed to meet the needs of managers. We are in a better position to appreciate this when we realize the important role that reporting plays in the control function. Certainly if it is to be the basis for control, information should be assembled with that objective in view. It should exclude material extraneous to the problem of control and must be placed at the disposal of managers quickly so that operations do not deviate any further from the desired norm—or for a longer period—than can be avoided.

That control occurs after the fact is a point that sometimes troubles managers. It should not—since this is simply part of the nature of the concept. The situation is entirely comparable in the process control system described earlier. In that system the detecting device continuously evaluates results and transmits them back to the control mechanism, which, sensing the difference between the actual and the desired results, acts to restore results to the desired value. The results, just as in management control, precede the exercise of control. Control systems, human or mechanical, deal with transfers of energy and a transfer of energy takes time. We learn from this—and it underscores the importance of speed in reporting—that all we can do for the management problem is to minimize the time lag between results and action.

CONTROL SPECTRUM

There is another sometimes troublesome aspect of control, namely, that control over some things must be relinquished as successively higher echelons of management are reached. This again we must simply face. Managers in the first echelon require certain information as their basis for controlling. But in the next higher echelon, the character of required information changes; some information is dropped, some is added. There is thus a kind of 'control spectrum.' For the process of fading out and shading in of information is continued as you move up the pyramid

CONTROL

until, just as in the visible spectrum the colors at one end are wholly unlike those at the other, the information reported to the top is wholly different from the information reported to first line managers.

This would hardly be worth pointing out except that some managers are burdened with a persistent sense of insecurity which undermines their self-confidence and ability to do the job, because they are unable to keep track of all the details under their management. Of course, they should not be able to keep track of all the results, or more accurately, should not allow themselves to do so. Relinquishing control over some operations is a calculated risk, taken so that managers can assume more important tasks.

It will bear mentioning that information serves other purposes than as the basis for control. The notion of a 'framework of management,' which we suggested earlier, is helpful in describing one of these purposes. This 'framework,' we said, is constantly undergoing change in one or another of its aspects. Such change takes place, not accidentally, but following conscious decisions for change by those responsible for such decisions. And decisions for changes in the framework are based on information that is conceptually different from information used for controlling adherence to the framework.

Where Forecasts Fit

Forecasts and projections, for example, have no place in the problem of control (since control is after-the-fact while forecasts are before) but they are very important for setting objectives and formulating plans. Of course, information for aiming and for planning does not have to be before-the-fact. It may be an after-the-fact analysis proving that a certain policy has been impolitic in its effect on the relations of the company with customer, employee, or stockholder; or that a certain plan is no longer practical; or that a certain procedure is unworkable. The prescription here certainly would not be 'control' (since in these cases control would simply bring operations into conformity with obsolete standards), but the establishment of new standards—a new policy, a new plan, and a new procedure—to be controlled to.

Besides furnishing evidence of a need for reconstructing the managerial framework, information is, of course, the basis of all communication. But since that subject is one of the most discussed in the management field to-day, there is no need to discuss it further here.

Control, we have seen, means something quite specific in the managerial art. This is certainly as it should be in an area of thought as well developed as business management. For in any field for which theory has been developed to an appreciable extent, terms should be precise and unambiguous. Control, when used in a management context, should mean one thing and one thing only. I have suggested that it means action directed toward bringing operations into conformity with predetermined standards and goals; that it is exercised by managers; and that its basis is information in their hands after-the-fact.

In addition to being a specific part of managing, control is also, quite evidently, an extremely important part of managing. In organizations, therefore, where the responsibility for control is not placed in the hands of managers, or not accepted by them, difficulties are certain to arise. Managers must control. Staff members of the organization may, by furnishing information, help a manager discharge this responsibility, but may not share in it. Where this philosophy is adopted by top management as the policy of the organization, the probability is enhanced that the energies of the organization will be channeled in fruitful directions.

TERMINOLOGY

Control is admittedly a term with emotional connotations. The denotation of the term, however, suffers from no such objection. Control is not supervision. Experienced managers perceive that as their authority is broadened, their superiors must place increased reliance on control as

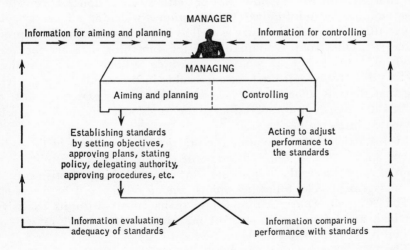

a means of safeguarding their own accountability. But at the same time, supervision of their activities by superiors becomes less close. There seems every reason to believe, therefore, that as the real nature of control becomes better understood, managers will come to recognize that their being subject to it in increasing measure is as sure a sign as any of their progress in the organization and in the fulfillment of their position.

Control Means Action *

Arnold F. Emch

In today's competitive economy there is a tremendous premium on
initiative in management. Although intelligent policy making and planning are, as always, of decisive importance, top-level planners feel more
dependent than ever on those "centers of initiative" down the line. Many
companies have greatly increased in size; more important, new techniques, processes, and products are changing industry patterns. Unless
the management organization is alert and alive to these changing conditions, the most intelligent efforts of top planners may be futile in the
face of shrewd competitors exploiting new ideas and approaches.

How does the concept of "control" fit into this picture, particularly
with respect to the problem of initiative on the part of executives who
are charged with the responsibility of getting things done? Is control a
boon or a barrier to initiative? This question is widening a four-way split
of executive opinion in industry as well as in governmental and nonprofit
enterprise. One group is unqualifiedly for something or other they call
"control"; a second group looks on the whole business with a jaundiced
eye; a third group finds itself uncomfortably in the middle with the feeling that there is something wrong with each of the extreme points of
view; and a fourth group subscribes to the functional concept that will be
presented in the following pages.

In this article I shall examine the practical consequences of these different approaches, highlighting some of the abuses and the misconceptions of control as well as suggesting ways of establishing effective control
in management. The following points, among others, will be discussed:
¶ The "Captain Queeg" approach to management—with its excessive,
detailed, and often useless control measures—is ineffectual as well as
as highly repugnant to red-blooded executives.
¶ The "Will Rogers" top executive—the antithesis of Captain Queeg—
usually finds himself engaged in a weird performance of subterfuge as he
tries to run his business with some semblance of order and direction without recognizing or acknowledging that it is a "controlled" situation.
¶ A common mistake is to treat control systems and plans of organization

* Reprinted by permission of the publisher from *Harvard Business Review*, vol. 32,
no. 4 (July-August, 1954), pp. 92–98. Mr. Emch is a partner in the management consulting firm of Booz, Allen & Hamilton.

independently of each other. Control must not only provide measures for adequate planning and for performance evaluation, but also stimulate initiative on the part of executives and employees.

¶ The controller should not try to control in the sense of encroaching on the authority of those who have been charged with the responsibility of getting something done.

¶ Planning and budgeting are only devices to assure correlated and consistent actions in the future.

¶ Control techniques can be better understood and applied if control is equated with action. And action should be taken only by those having authority and responsibility for the activities which are affected.

¶ Information can be tailored effectively to executive needs for taking imaginative action by following certain definite criteria (which will be spelled out). Neither a famine nor a surplus of data is necessary.

INEFFECTIVENESS AT THE TOP

The bewildering difference of opinion and practice in this area makes no sense at all until we remember that control—perhaps more than any other major management function—reflects the personalities and attitudes of those at the top. Let us see what some of these executives look like.

Captain Queeg: Excessive Control

At one extreme is the Captain Queeg type of *Caine Mutiny* fame, who insists on the letter of the law to such an extent that war can rage all around him while he is trying to find out who ate the quart of strawberries. From the standpoint of management, what was the matter with Captain Queeg? Two things—one psychological, the other methodological.

As Herman Wouk, the author of the book, painted him, Captain Queeg was fundamentally so insecure and suspicious that he had to know every last detail of what every last tar aboard the U.S.S. Caine was doing in order to protect himself and to assure himself that all policies, rules, and regulations of the Navy were observed down to the last minutia. What he forgot in this preoccupation with detail was (a) that he and his kind might lose the war, and (b) that he was stifling all initiative, interest, and enthusiasm on the part of his men. In short, he was, through his interpretation of control, forgetting the strategic objectives of the war and, at the same time, creating a serious morale problem in his crew.

The situation on Captain Queeg's ship was a typical example of the stultifying effect of rigidly confining strait-jacket "control procedures" on the imagination and intellect of men. In the words of Keefer, one of the principals of the story, it was a situation in which "the work has been fragmentized by a few excellent brains at the top, on the assumption that near-morons will be responsible for each fragment."

In business this type of control does not of course bring about mutiny in the usual sense. What it does instead is to create (a) an undertone of frustration and a sense of futility; (b) a pattern of alibis, truth-slantings, and downright dishonesty; (c) outright conflicts among executives, due to exercise of control by some who have no corresponding responsibility for action; (d) a gradual diminution of the use of initiative and judgment to the point where executives are absorbed in clerical detail and meticulous line-by-line paper-pushing practices; and (e) an increase in executive turnover as a result of the more intelligent and courageous personnel looking elsewhere for a more favorable condition for the exercise of their real talents.

I have cited a fictitious character as an example; but actually, in business, government, and nonprofit enterprises, there are literally hundreds of Captain Queeg's counterparts. These men build up a system of control that in the end defeats the purposes for which it was originally intended. The paper, the personnel, the money, and the time expended on forms, reports, manuals, bulletins, and statistics in support of these misbegotten control systems are enough to stagger the most eager imagination. As pointed out in the *ACME Reporter* (bulletin of the Association of Consulting Management Engineers):

> It often develops to the point where mere following of procedures becomes more important than carrying out policies and striving toward objectives. The result is a creeping, self-propagating bureaucracy.

Do these burdensome control systems ever accomplish their original purpose? Do they not have some merit? All I can say is that in my experience as a management consultant to different kinds of businesses over the past 20 years, I have never seen such a setup or such an operation pay off.

Quite the contrary! I have found all the shortcomings of the usual dictatorial and all-embracing regime, including the inevitably weak, insecure, or overambitious executive at the top; mountains of forms, reports, manuals, directives, and interpretative bulletins which nobody reads or which, if they are read, require special staffs to pore over them to keep executives abreast; bad morale in the second and third layers of management; and, believe it or not, usually poor planning and lack of significant management information when and where it is needed—the very things you would think *could* be accomplished by these immense, involved, and demanding systems of control,

Will Rogers: Insufficient Control

Now let us look at Captain Queeg's opposite, the executive who is pretty sure of himself and who inclines to be a "good egg" with democratic impulses. He does not like control and he does not want any part of it. It is repugnant to him. His philosophy of management is to shove his men off the dock and make them swim. That is the way they can learn best. "Sure, they'll make mistakes," he says with a confident, genial grin; "that's good for them; that's the way they'll learn the facts of life." His is the freedom-of-enterprise point of view in the extreme.

But despite his rodeo-bronco-swim-for-your-life approach to management, this Will Rogers sooner or later will want to know where his business is going and how well it is doing on its way. Instead of having a "controller" in any usual sense—this of course he would not tolerate—he sets out to find himself a bright, young, likable, willing fellow, and without much ado appoints him "assistant to the president."

There are all kinds of things that Mr. Rogers will want to know—usually pronto—and no ready information will be available to supply this need. So he will call in his assistant, throw him the ball without concern or premeditation, and let it go at that.

It takes no genius to figure out what this apparently simple practice will lead to. The assistant is eager, able, and willing; and he goes about these repeated assignments with energy and dispatch. It does not take long for him to realize that he does not have certain information at hand. He begins to build up a little system all his own. His desk drawers and filing cases fill up with special data. He takes an increasing interest in the budget and begins to question department heads as to the justification of certain items. He even has misgivings on just how he ought to go about getting some of the information that he knows he will eventually need.

But the rest of the staff soon comes to realize that, although the newcomer is only the assistant to the president whereas they are vice presidents or managers, this young fellow has the ear of the boss and is beginning to analyze things and increasingly make judgments for the president. Perhaps they had better play ball with the young man, they think, if they are to stay in the good graces of Mr. Rogers. And so it goes. A roundabout way of control is devised—never direct, never through channels, never through organization objectives, or policies, or clear-cut statements of basic procedure. Nobody quite knows any more what he should or should not do, but everyone is quite certain that "cooperation" with the assistant is the order of the day.

Functional Control

Now what is the matter with all this? What is the matter with Captain Queeg's or Mr. Rogers' approach to control? It boils down to this: Each approach shows a complete lack of understanding or appreciation of what control is trying to accomplish in an enterprise, and of how to get executives to assume and carry out effectively their proper responsibilities. Put

very simply, there can be too much control and there can be too little
control; in both cases there is a misunderstanding or a corruption of
control in the necessary and sound sense.

Let us look at it in another way. What is the problem we are dealing
with when we talk of "control"? Actually it is simple: We have a job
to do—a line of services or products to make and sell at a profit. There are
a number of persons involved in the doing of that job. Hence we organize
ourselves in some fashion so that each one of us has specific, assigned
tasks, all more or less related to one another. And we try to see that
each key individual has a clear understanding of his functions, of his
lines of authority downward, and of his line of responsibility upward.

But if we should go only this far, we would not go far enough. We
must also determine what each of these individuals needs in the way of
facts and figures in order to perform his job effectively. This, then, is the
problem of control: to match the responsibilities of every key position
with the management information necessary for the effective and efficient execution of those responsibilities. Control itself can be defined as
the making of decisions and taking of actions required by the responsibilities of each position, i.e., the proper performance of each executive
according to the requirements of his position.

Now, some readers may object to this concept on the ground that it
does not even mention the familiar rudiments of control, traditionally
conceived. You may be prompted to say: "Control means making sure
that actual results conform to desired results, and this involves three
basic functions: (a) setting standards of satisfactory performance; (b)
checking results to see how they compare with the standards; and (c) taking corrective action where actual results do not meet the standards."

I have no quarrel with this concept, except that these functions ought
to be, and in fact must be, built *into* the organization structure as part
and parcel of the responsibilities and authorities of every key position.
They should not be segregated and put on a list of functions under the
heading "control."

This brings us to the basic flaw of most control systems as well as of
most plans of organization. Control and organization have generally been
treated independently of each other, thus missing the point of how the
organization is to work in practice, or of what the executives are trying
to control in the operations. Actually organization and control are inseparable when there is effective management; they cannot function properly
without each other.

How many times have you pored over an organization plan only to
find yourself saying: "In general I think it is good, but how do I do this
particular job; how can I carry out the responsibilities entrusted to me?"
The answer here to a very large extent is in the informational and control system that is established. What are the "management dials" neces-

sary for you to do your job? What are the significant management factors you should have before you in order to make executive judgment, and what is it you do when certain things take place? Do you know what you should do, and why, and what are the probable consequences of your decisions?

This is the problem of control in every executive position in the enterprise, up and down the various levels in the organization. In short, the answer to the effective operation of the plan of organization is primarily through a system of control which is part and parcel of it.

An effective system of control, in turn, depends on the plan of organization. If you tried to look at your control problem without considering the plan of organization, you would soon find yourself asking, "Who gives me this information? Why do I get it? What do I do with it?" Obviously you could not answer until you knew who was responsible for what in the scheme of things—in other words, the organization again.

Relating control to the specific responsibilities and authorities of each executive position is what I have chosen to call "functional control." In this sense control is an integral element of every function in the organization, and every function will then be truly under control.

Rules and Guides

If management accepts the concept of control just described, it will find that a number of challenging corollaries follow in consequence. I should like to discuss them now, with particular attention to their implications for the everyday realities of company operations.

Controllers Don't Control

First, the new concept of control will require some reorientation in the traditional or prevailing practices and tendencies of controllers or control offices. It will require recognition of the fact that a controller does not actually control, and that any effort on his part to take over the function of control from the operating personnel will lead inevitably to the abuses and misunderstandings I have already mentioned.

The word "control" itself has no doubt led to the misconception that the control function of an enterprise is a highly centralized activity in the office of a controller; that management reports, statistics, and information generally are not only collected by the controller but are also specifically for his use; and, finally, that he has the authority to bring about executive actions throughout the organization without assuming corresponding responsibility for those actions.

Nothing of course could be farther from the application of effective control in a well-managed enterprise. Although the controller is or should be a major executive at the same level as the other divisional executives of an enterprise, and hence is or should be a part of the top-management team, it should be noted that, apart from his usual departmental activities such as keeping records, paying bills, receiving cash, preparing invoices, maintaining the office and routine accounting, he has no direct operating responsibilities.

In fact, the more important and delicate tasks the controller must perform have to do with advising the president and other executives on the broad, over-all picture of the enterprise; coordinating basic plans and budgets; preparing and issuing special control reports; and standardizing methods of accounting and other procedures. Note the predominantly *informational* character of each of these responsibilities.

Let me illustrate what can happen when this is forgotten and the controller is allowed to get out of hand.

I recall the case of a large city administration which had the usual bureau of the budget with a controller in charge. The extent to which the powers of this office had been stretched to make decisions or to stop decisions in the actual operations of the various city departments was beyond belief. No powers of a foreign monarchy were ever exercised with greater authoritarian finality.

Yet the end result scarcely justified the appellation "control." Instead there were phony figures, tampered statistics, and endless ingenious manipulations on the part of department and division heads in order to accomplish some degree of operating effectiveness within the restrictive patterns and requirements of the controller—and in order to conceal the true facts from the authorities above. The result was more nearly the *opposite* of control!

Here, for example, is what happened when the controller decreed that new personnel for a newly constructed establishment would have to be employed at the lowest end of the salary ranges. (Staffing patterns had been worked out for various types of city establishments, with the usual minimum-maximum salary ranges for each kind of position.) The operating heads soon found that they could not employ this lower and inexperienced level of talent and expect any degree of competence in running the new plant. Appeals to the controller were of no avail.

So they embarked on a weird set of thimblerigging operations, whereby they hired employees for the new plant at the lowest level decreed by the controller and forthwith began to distribute these to various other installations, and in turn quietly "loaned" some of the more experienced and competent personnel from these other installations to the new plant to get it under way.

Of course the records and the statistics and the payrolls never reflected what went on, and the subsequent budgets and staffing patterns were continued year after year without ever revealing the true state of affairs.

The budget actually turned out to be a device for the concealment of the facts.

The operating personnel chuckled with cynical satisfaction; the controller's pride and vanity were assuaged through "compliance" with his rules and regulations; the files of the bureau of the budget were replete with dubious reports, figures, and statistics. But there was no real, honest, or effective control in the best sense of modern management.

If, instead of these attitudes and practices, the controller had been motivated by a deep sense of service and had realized that most of what he did had value only insofar as it was *helpful* to someone else in doing his job, there would have been a much more effective and efficient operation.

Lest executives in business react to this example from government by thinking, "It can't happen here," let me add that, in my observation at least, it *does* happen in industry—and oftener than we think! In fact, many of those unexciting profit statements that are being written today are a direct result.

Planning Is the Basis

The misuse of the control function has far-reaching consequences in the planning and budgeting process. The budget is a primary means of assuring that actions conform to basic plans. It is a device for measuring the actions taken and for determining the actions required. But it does not, *of itself,* control.

Almost as important as the budget itself is the planning of the operation that is finally translated into the budget. In the planning phase, as we all know, actions are proposed, opposing points of view are resolved, and a consistent course of action is set. Conditions expected are appraised, and proposed actions to meet these conditions are devised. To the extent that planning determines the actions that need to be taken and stimulates thinking ahead about those actions, it is a most effective basis for control—but, again, it is not control itself.

Thus, plans and budgets together provide a picture, in common related terms, of what is intended and expected and the means by which the goals are to be achieved. They provide a means for reporting back the progress made against the goals, and a general framework for new decisions and actions in an integrated pattern of development. A good example of a planning and budgeting basis for control is provided by the postwar experience of a company that was producing large, expensive precision equipment.

The management of this company decided to prepare a report called a "production forecast." It was based on an estimate of sales and was adjusted for both engineering and manufacturing loads. When finally approved by the executive committee, it became an 18-month plan which was to be adjusted periodically in accordance with manufacturing lead times and in terms of what the company expected to make (the rate and volume of production).

The plan was eminently successful and, even to this day, is eagerly awaited each quarter by all operating executives, since it has become the basis for many decisions throughout the company. From it can be calculated such figures as number of direct workers required, number of workers needed in service areas (payroll and accounting), adjustments in the level of inventory, and adjustments in purchasing loads and selling programs.

Prior to adoption of this plan the company was continually faced with unexplained increases in inventories, with serious imbalances between number of production workers and actual requirements, and with the sales department and the manufacturing department working at cross purposes. For instance, it was found that the sales department was selling custom designs for delivery at times when the manufacturing department was unable to produce even its normal load of standard lines.

Properly conceived and used, such plans and budgets can become important elements in implementing effective control. Rather than impeding judgment, they should contribute to initiative in avoiding undesirable conditions and in meeting such conditions when they do arise.

Action Is the Essence

Control is being exercised when the operations of the enterprise are guided within the plans adopted, are held in line in the face of varying conditions, or are returned to an in-line state after deviations are located. Note that action is implied in each case. This is important. In a very real sense, control means action—action to correct a condition found to be in error, or action to prevent such a condition from arising—and is never achieved without having action as an essential step.

Thus, in the case of the precision equipment company whose planning procedure was just described, control was actually achieved through a series of specific steps taken by the various department heads acting in response to the production forecast:

(1) Idle workers, approximating 10% of the total number, were reassigned to other areas.

(2) Personnel requirements in all service and staff areas were recalculated.

(3) Personnel were added in the sales area in order to step up sales effort.

(4) Order points and ordering quantities on two major product lines were reset.

(5) Deliveries on open orders with vendors were extended.

(6) For the near future, purchasing requirements were frozen at minimum levels.

(7) Sufficient cause was found to re-examine the company's entire inventory, which resulted in scrapping $500,000 in materials and using materials on hand in lieu of ordering new materials.

Note that management had first made a cooperative planning and budgeting effort; then came control in the form of action.

Delegation Is the Key

But control action can be taken only by the individual executives who hold delegated responsibility and authority for the operations affected. Certainly it makes little sense to assign someone the "responsibility" for a specific operation; set the achievement of certain results as a goal; and then, though a series of denials, restrictions, limitations, specifications, and decisions, allow him no initiative.

In such instances, the wise, loyal, and experienced executive will try to conform and to achieve the desired results. If he succeeds, it will probably be because of his own ingenuity, patience, flexibility, and doggedness, rather than because of any superimposed decisions coming from above. If he fails, however, there is a real question of accountability, since many of the decisions and actions will have been precipitated by others not directly responsible for the operation. This of course is a perfect setting for alibis and for passing the buck when the going gets rough; someone has to be the scapegoat for miscalculations or poor performance.

To sum up, merely discovering out-of-line conditions, or having detailed information about a situation, does not achieve control. Control is exercised by taking action, and action must be taken within the authority delegated. And just as no person can be said to control directly the activities assigned to another's jurisdiction, so the only person who can directly control activities is the one directly responsible for them. This is fundamental to the healthy and successful operation of any enterprise; at the same time it is probably one of the least observed principles of management. There are a great many more instances of its violation than there are of its wholehearted acceptance and practice.

Information Is the Guide

Now we can see more clearly where information, such as provided by the controller, fits into the picture. Many enterprises have grown beyond the size where they can be managed by decisions arrived at through direct observation alone. So there must be control; and control requires a system of information tailored to the specific management needs of every key executive—information that is *timely* and *adequate*.

Let us take the timeliness factor first. While information *as such* does not control, it is needed by executives as a guide to actions which do control. Because they overlook this, controllers frequently miss the mark in being of real service to operating personnel. In general, they submit too many historical reports which merely relate what has taken place. Management would rather have approximate information that is prompt than highly accurate information after it is too late to be of value in decision making.

Turning now to the second factor, what is the criterion of "adequate" information? What *kind* of information is adequate, and how *much?* Frequently controllers solve this problem by giving the line executives everything there is to know—by virtually swamping them in facts and figures. But the effect of too much is likely to be almost as bad as too little or too late.

A system of control should require no more than is absolutely necessary in the way of reports, data, and statistics. The determination of what is "necessary" should conform to this simple dictum: In accord with your responsibilities and authority, can you or should you do anything about the information that is presented to you and, if so, what? This is the final criterion of management or control information. If you can do nothing about the material that is presented, then it is purely informative and not strictly necessary for you for management purposes.

For example, I recall the instance of a very successful insurance company whose president was far ahead of most chief executives in wanting to renovate the company operations and to introduce modern management practices. He was completely sold on the idea of decentralization, with a small central headquarters and a top policy and planning level.

But in his attempt to supply the necessary information to all key executives throughout the country, he embarked on a colossal and expensive statistical program that included computations on all manner of items. He distributed this information routinely and at frequent, regular intervals to all concerned. There was a thick, 18-inch by 30-inch book of these tabulations, statistics, and data on the desk of every executive throughout the land. It was so voluminous that each executive had to have an assistant or "analyst" who devoted himself almost exclusively to the problem of keeping up with the most recent data supplied. It became a byword in the company that "wherever there is an executive, you will also find an analyst."

The data were there in generous quantity, and the figures were accurately reported and fairly up to date. But it was standard information for all alike. What was missing was the specific bit of significant management information that each key executive needed in order to watch and control his own particular operation or department. What each of these executives could use to advantage might have been put on one page, but what they got instead was 200 large pages of involved, mechanically tabulated statistics which were largely academic and irrelevant from the point of view of any given executive.

Every key position in an enterprise is or should be related to some objective or set of objectives. These, in turn, should be translated into specific goals for specific calendar periods. The executive in charge of any operation or department, in order to achieve these specific goals within certain time limits, should have before him specific performance data—"management dials"—so he can known how well his operation is progressing and, if significantly out of line, what he individually must do to correct the situation.

CONCLUSION

What is needed is an understanding that the functions of planning and performance evaluation are part and parcel of the entire organization, and must therefore be distributed to each and every appropriate level of responsibility—instead of being concentrated in a highly centralized office that usually carries the name of "the controller." Every key executive, in fulfilling his responsibilities, is or should be his own "controller." In this sense, control can be as much an energizing as a steering function. So conceived it should no longer be a barrier but a tremendous boon to initiative.

If controllers, in turn, will recognize that real control is achieved only through actions taken by executives other than themselves, they will be well on the way to realizing that theirs is basically a service to render and that, however difficult this role, its sole value is to assist the key executives in the proper performance of their functions. A very wise man once said: "Control is primarily a state of mind." Let us make certain that it is a *healthy* state of mind.

B. DEVICES OF CONTROL

The Budget Comes of Age *

James L. Pierce

Any technique of management reaches maturity when, after its earlier mistakes have antagonized human beings sufficiently, it emerges with a new outlook and practice that is in harmony with the basic motivations of people. Budgeting now seems to be undergoing this metamorphosis. Out of the disturbance it has created is appearing a calmer, more orderly, more positive approach.

It is my purpose in this article to add weight to the spreading view that budgeting rests on principles which have more in common with concepts of human relationship than with rules of accounting; and that, if these principles are applied, successful practice is inevitable.

DEFENSIVENESS—THE TROUBLE

There is no doubt that thousands of management people are well grounded in constructive budget practice and derive from it a sense of balance and direction in their business affairs. No businessman who has had extensive experience with an ably managed budget system appears to doubt its value. But there are many more thousands who are so confused on the subject that it might indeed be better for them to discard their budgets entirely than to continue as they are. Surveys have shown that in some quarters budgeting is about as popular among foremen as a layoff, and analyses stress the damage that results from the misuse of budgeting procedures.

Some executives freely admit the shortcomings of their budget practices and acknowledge that they could be remedied by the application of more intelligent human relations. If it is as simple as that, then why cannot budgets be made a welcome and productive feature of all business operation without delay? The answer, I think, is that the problem is not such a simple one—just as human beings are not simple, just as the science of human relationships is not simple, as witness the many failures to apply it effectively.

* Reprinted by permission of the publisher from *Harvard Business Review*, vol. 32, no. 3 (May-June, 1954), pp. 58–66. Mr. Pierce is Vice-President and Controller of the A. B. Dick Company.

How shall we go about the task of instilling revitalized ideas in place of negative or shortsighted attitudes?

We can accomplish nothing until we face up to the fact that many of us have acquired a defensive approach to the subject through painful experience. Here we must dig deep into the recesses of thought—not omitting the realm of emotional misconception that colors our word associations. Why do the two words "budgets" and "people" repel each other? Why should they, when taken together, suggest the image of a problem? Why, in fact, should it even be necessary to discuss a positive approach to the matter of budgets and people?

This unhappy reaction comes from the fact that people generally do not like budgets. We must remember that foremen are people first and supervisors second; so are department managers and top executives. Budgets represent restriction. They are in the same category as school bells and Monday mornings. Each of us has entered business life with a primitive aversion to restraint, only thinly veneered by academic training.

Someone should have presented the budget idea to us very constructively in order for us to accept it, must less to enjoy it. If from the very beginning of our careers we have been told, with accompanying evidence, that budgets were a help to us, affording us guidance, stability, and strength, as well as keeping us out of innumerable troubles, our responses would by now be quite different.

But what was our actual experience? Have not many of us been introduced to budgets in business when the budget was blamed, rightly or wrongly, for our failure to get a raise in pay? Have not many of us become acquainted with the budget only as a barrier to spending what we felt were necessary amounts of money for better equipment or performance? Is it surprising, then, that budgets are associated in many people's minds with paucity and niggardliness rather than with planning and direction?

Fortunately, it is not too late to effect a correction in the thinking of the current generation of managers.

ATTITUDES—THE KEY

In probing further, it quickly becomes evident that good attitudes are the key to successful budgeting. When the attitudes of people toward each other are generous, understanding, and based on mutual respect, any technique adopted by management to further effective performance is apt to be successful. When human attitudes are dominated by distrust, criticism, and recrimination, any technique designed to improve performance is likely to fail miserably. In such cases, by a strange twist of human nature, the budgets and those who defend them bear the brunt of the blame for more fundamental errors which are entirely unconnected with budgets.

Budgeting is a trained, disciplined approach to all problems, which recognizes the need for standards of performance in order to achieve a result. Hence it must be built on a base of good organization; otherwise, favorable attitudes have no chance to operate. But at the same time it lives in an atmosphere of perpetual adjustment to the needs and capacities of people. It thrives on such fundamentals as recognition of accomplishment, consideration for the rights of individuals, fair play— in other words, enlightened relationships among people.

Motivation for Budgeting

In exploring budgeting principles as they relate to people, the first consideration should be the motivation for the budget system. Why have one at all? Is the budget a part of a system of over-all planning, in order that all concerned may have a measure of the amounts to be spent, and in order that action may be by design rather than by expediency? Or is the budget a pressure device designed to goad people into greater efforts? It takes a little soul-searching to determine honestly which of these concepts represents the position of a particular management.

Both concepts are prevalent. They may be symbolized by two wooden sticks—one neatly divided into thirty-six one-inch spaces, and the other sharply pointed at one end. The yardstick, symbolizing the planning concept of budgets, may be used, for example, by a foreman to establish standards of performance and cost and to measure actual results in relation thereto; in this sense, it is a tool used by the foreman and his boss in partnership. The pointed stick, a symbol of the pressure type of budget, is always found in the hand of the superior, turned menacingly toward his foremen or workers. The yardstick concept elicits the voluntary effort of men to do their best work. The pointed stick forces a reluctant and minimal performance.

There is plenty of evidence that the choice of the yardstick concept will not diminish the yield from the budget tool in terms of cost reduction. It has been shown again and again that high costs which stubbornly resist all efforts of the pressure type will melt away under the warmth of an approach which is attuned to the basic responses of humanity. The attitude to be adopted here is an enlistment of all concerned in a common effort, with a complete explanation of objectives and methods.

PLANNING—THE FOUNDATION

Next in the line of exploration of principles is the dependence of budgets on general company planning. Although budgeting can be separately applied to any unit of the business, it is far more effective when it rests on a foundation of integrated planning for the entire operation. In the proper sense, it is only one phase of planning. When the planning concept has been adopted, budgets emerge of necessity—budgets with a purpose as deep as the stream of ideas giving direction and drive to the business itself.

The presence or absence of intelligent planning is reflected to a surprising degree in the effectiveness of the people who are asked to operate with a budget system. And this means all the people—from top executives to production-line workers. Individuals are usually more intuitive than we realize. When a budget is built on sound business planning, they respond to that fact without always knowing why.

Meaning of Planning

As used in this discussion, *planning* refers to the predetermination of a course of action in such detail that every responsible unit of the company may be guided thereby. It includes sales forecasting, production scheduling, expense budgeting, and estimating of manufacturing costs and inventory levels. It involves making advance decisions concerning new product development and introduction, merchandising methods, material procurement, and labor rates. In short, planning implies anticipating all the knotty problems to be met by a business during the planning period—usually a year so far as operations are concerned, longer for financial and developmental activities—in other words, facing the problems and making decisions about them *ahead of time* (subject to later revision if necessary).

These decisions are frequently so hard to make in advance that they border on the impossible. Yet they insure a reasonable net profit as no other method can. And on this planned net profit figure—the apex of the planning structure—depends our ability to attract new capital as needed and to compensate management and shareholders.

I need not elaborate the importance of profit planning. I am only concerned here that it be recognized that when budgeting has a hard core of deliberate planning, adhered to by the company's top, middle, and all other management, the budget idea takes on real meaning for all concerned. Without this basis, it can never be completely palatable to those who do not understand how it can benefit them.

Effect on People

Let us examine the effect of the planning process on the people involved in it. In particular, we might first consider the impact on administrative people, for their outlook in the long run determines the attitudes of the larger non-administrative group. What is the planning technique doing to foremen, department managers, division heads? Is it building up or tearing down their confidence in their company's future?

Is it affecting favorably or adversely their independence of thought, their self-assurance, their capacity to understand and rely on those around them?

It seems self-evident that planning alone does not afford the entire answer. If a company's administrative personnel are exhibiting what is called "good morale" before the installation of a planning system, the chances are that turning their eyes to the future and asking them to construct together a plan for better achievement can do them no harm, but can do them untold good. With proper explanations, the management can hold forth the legitimate promise of better accomplishment, greater satisfaction, more confident operating, and, ultimately, opportunity for increased compensation.

If, on the other hand, the management is struggling with a discordant staff, perhaps suffering from the blight of fuzzy organization lines or any of the other impediments to good work resulting from a mediocre job of personnel administration, it might be better off to defer trying the planning and control idea until it has put its house in order. Too frequently a well-designed budget system has collapsed after being superimposed on a faulty base of administrative personnel policy. Then the budget is discarded and all concerned return to their familiar bad habits.

CONTROL—THE COMPLEMENT

But there is another phase of budgeting which tests the fiber of men even more than planning. I am referring to control, which is the eternal complement of planning. Neither one is useful without the other, and to budget even the smallest unit of a business implies the presence of control also.

Budget Abuses

It is in the control area that the colossal mistakes of budgeting are made. It is here that the amateurs have censured their subordinates for exceeding budgets, without realizing that they themselves were to blame for inadequate training. It is here that men have become so frustrated under maladministered budgets that they have resorted to all sorts of tricks to conceal the actual results and have padded their budgets to give themselves breathing room. It is here that staff men have usurped authority, merited pay increases have been denied because of budget limitations, and tales have been carried around supervision and up to the top under the guise of budget reporting.

The list of abuses could be prolonged indefinitely. There are many wrong ways to exercise budget control. There is only one right way. Let us then discard the negative approach, since the assertion of an affirmative truth will dissolve all counterfeits.

Control might be quickly and simply defined as a disciplined effort to follow a plan or explain deviations from it. The effort referred to takes the form of self-discipline—voluntary, unified, and cooperative. The deviations from plan are deliberate, foreknown, and authorized. If they are apparently beyond anyone's ability to prevent—as for instance a failure to reach budgeted sales volume—at least they are spotlighted as early as possible, and management has the chance to take whatever action is indicated. Control is simply the modern form of the old formula, "management by exception."

It is, of course, at the point of deviation from the budget that most of the human problems are born. This is, by design, the central point in the entire system—the moment which demands explanation, instruction, decision, argument, or even discipline, as the case warrants—the flash point for management in action.

Common-sense Departures

It should be evident that the effect of control on people is commensurate with their training and conditioning for it. If they understand thoroughly the meaning and uses of control, they will view it in the light of common sense. They will neither resent it nor be awed by it. They will turn it to the constructive use for which it is intended, and it will become an aid rather than an obstacle.

Perhaps the best way to clarify this common-sense approach is to examine a typical situation in which a manager wishes to make what he believes to be a desirable expenditure not covered in his budget. This problem is encountered daily and solved without friction by management people equipped with knowledge of budget principles and skill in their application—in other words, by the trained minority which shows the same attitudes-in-action of a manager grounded in good budget practice as illustrated in the following case.

The case of a sales promotion manager who is also responsible for advertising—Having been instructed to prepare a budget, he has first carefully completed his sales promotion and advertising plans for the coming period, basing them on discussions with the sales vice president and others responsible for policy and sales objectives. After constructing an acceptable plan, he has converted it into dollars in the form of a budget, which has been approved.

Because he has prepared this budget himself, he is thoroughly familiar with it. It is supported with adequate detail, including schedules of space insertions, estimates of costs of mailings, salary lists, and so on. He has reached an understanding with his "boss" concerning all of these items as a preliminary to approval of the budget. He feels confident that the plan and budget are as nearly right as he can make them.

Furthermore, he knows the implications of accepting this budget as his guide to operations. It is not to be exceeded without approval. It is a commitment that must be honored, and he well understands its importance to the company, his associates, and himself.

Nevertheless, he senses in the attitudes surrounding his budget an element of flexibility. If conditions change, the budget will have to be altered, either upward or downward. The sales promotion manager is not uneasy about this prospect. He is simply alert to recognize such a situation if it should develop.

Now let us suppose that an opportunity is presented to exert extra pressure on a certain market, and it appears that a special direct-mail campaign, supplemented by some local newspaper advertising, will yield good sales results. He knows enough not to throw the whole idea aside simply because it is not provided for in his budget. He has already had a clear understanding with the top sales executive about what to do in such cases. So he goes about preparing a report, including proposed action, cost, and anticipated results; and he presents this report, knowing that it will be given proper consideration, even though it represents an expenditure in excess of budget limits.

The important point here is that this man, as manager of sales promotion, will not be subjected to injustice, censure, or negative treatment of any sort in advancing his ideas. He is fully aware of having a plan and a commitment to abide by it; yet he has assurance that if the interests of the company will be best served by breaking the budget, permission to do so will be forthcoming. All concerned will have an opportunity to evaluate the proposal and to weigh the desirability of deviating from the adopted plan.

How simple this miniature study in budget attitudes! How mature the responses governed by common sense! And yet how often common sense is violated! Is there any reason not to extend this frank approach to the foreman who sees a need for maintenance expenses or a merit increase not embraced in his budget? The frictions, frustrations, and other evils supposed to be inherent in budgets must all be susceptible to eradication in the same sensible manner.

Essential Prerequisites

All this presupposes, of course, that the supervisor in question—regardless of which division of the business he may be in—enjoys a satisfactory working relationship with his immediate superior. It also rests on clearcut organization lines and the disposition to delegate authority along with responsibility.

Further, the accounting principles used must be well tested, and the accounting administration of high caliber. Strict honesty must govern the determination of the content of budget accounts and of the charges made thereto. Nothing confuses budget operation more quickly than the charging of costs over which the supervisor has no control, unless such items are set out separately and so labeled.

A last important requisite is understanding of the make-up of the budget. Flexible factory budgets especially can be complicated and subject to dispute. The factors used must be clearly explained, with full recognition of their weaknesses. If an item—such as machine repairs, for example—is neither wholly fixed nor wholly variable, but must be treated one way or the other for budget purposes, the shortcomings of the resulting budget figure should be conceded frankly. If scrap and rework costs are subject to dispute between foremen, the situation must be talked out in an air of give-and-take. No plant management should encourage or permit embittered arguments between foremen on such a matter. If all concerned have a clear understanding of the function of the budget and a reasonable attitude toward each other in the framework of modern industrial organization, such disputes will not occur.

Cost Reduction—The Goal

The attitudes we have been discussing should add to, rather than detract from, the effectiveness of budgets in the field of cost control. Most companies operate continuously, in good times and bad, under the pressure of relentless competition, which forces them in turn to devote ceaseless effort to cost reduction. It is perhaps this circumstance more than any other that has given impetus to the spread of budgeting. And it has doubtless given rise to the abuses falling under the general heading of "pressure."

The usual tone of the complaints in this category is to the effect that budgets are used only as a hammer on costs (and at the same time on people), and particularly that the budgets are constantly being tightened and compliance with them enforced indiscriminately. The impression received by a supervisor in this situation is one of constant insistence on better and better performance, continuous blame for failure to meet the budget, and complete absence of credit for his good work. The budget becomes purely a pressure device, against which he must defend himself or lose his job.

The only really effective cure for such a distorted outlook is to substitute, as rapidly as possible, a "let's do it together" attitude for the shortsighted "you do it or else" attitude. The latter may have gained more ground in a plant or office than the management realizes. To correct this attitude may take time and patience, but it is never impossible to blank out negatives and substitute positives in human thinking.

Cost reduction drive is a feature of the American competitive system and is admittedly responsible in large measure for our high living standard. Budgets can be used for such stimulation without enslaving people. They furnish the standard from which to explore cost-savings possibilities.

They provide the measure of yield from improved methods. But the attitude surrounding the practice must be right.

Incentives, True and False

This line of thought runs directly into the question of incentive. What incentive does a production supervisor have to reduce costs? Certainly the incentive supplied by threat is negative and, in the long run, ineffective. Direct money incentives, correlated to budget factors, claim some merit but, as we shall see, are fraught with problems. The true incentives, becoming clear after generations of management experiment, are those usually referred to as "intangible," supplemented by wages carefully determined and sympathetically explained.

But as an alternative let us examine for a moment the possibilities of direct money incentives. Some companies use and defend them—and we can have no quarrel with success. The line of reasoning on which they are based runs something like this: "If simple piecework can be an effective incentive for the workman, then the same principle can be applied to the foreman. We will provide a supervisory bonus and include in its computation a factor measuring success in complying with the budget. Savings against the budget will benefit the company and, at the same time, will provide funds for rewarding the foreman."

The fallacies in this reasoning begin to appear early in the process. They arise from two sources: (a) from the almost insurmountable difficulty of setting a completely fair and acceptable budget for this purpose, especially in the light of unforeseeable changes in operating conditions, and (b) from the tendency for the foreman to emphasize budget performance to the detriment of necessary action. It is a distinct temptation to defer maintenance when the need is not urgent and the expenditure would reduce one's own pay check.

As the foreman grows to the stature of a responsible manager, as he becomes more and more able to carry added responsibilities independently (and this is the goal of enlightened management today), the problems of basing incentive pay on budget factors become progressively tougher to handle. The experienced foreman is conscious of the importance of cost reduction, both by training and by virtue of the understanding of the job which his company has given him. He is also conscious of the need to spend money. He is likely to resent being rewarded for unwise penny-pinching as much as being penalized for exceeding his budget when the need for it is evident to everyone.

To a supervisor properly informed and aware of his role as a part of the management team, the real incentive is the satisfaction that comes from knowing that he has given his best effort, evidenced by suitable recognition both financial and in the manner and words of the superior. There is no substitute for the positive kind of understanding that can be developed between a supervisor and the rest of management if all concerned resolve to cultivate it.

By the same token, there is nothing better to assure the success of a cost-reduction program than a foreman with an inspired attitude and a real comprehension of the company's objectives, needs, and policies. To such a man, the budget will be a tool used to measure common achievements, rather than an irritant to the men and women entrusted to his leadership.

MANAGEMENT SUPPORT—THE NEED

One of the rocks on which many systems founder is the lack of top-management support. This is a strange commentary on a management group which, in this country, is generally supposed to have reached the acme of sophistication in the motivation of people. Nevertheless, examine any limping, halfhearted budget system, and note how the "chickens come home to roost" in the president's office.

Even more surprising, it frequently turns out that the top man does not really understand the planning and control concept and the simple interplay of attitudes that make it work. Consequently his allegiance to it is tentative and lukewarm. He constantly questions the methods used and is instinctively distrustful of results. This frame of mind permeates the organization. It bolsters opposition to the budget idea and weakens its proponents.

No budget system can realize its potential value without the unqualified support and understanding of top management. The solution, of course, lies in a process usually known as "education." Actually, it is even deeper than that. The budget idea is an expanding, growing concept —usually pioneered by one man with vision in a company. Little by little, this man—be he president or controller—patiently inculcates the advancing idea on his associates, until it is tested and accepted by all.

Controllers' Mistakes

There is another enemy of successful budget practice which may well be the cause of more of the friction between budgets and people than all the other errors put together. I refer to the misconception on the part of controllers, budget managers, accountants, and other staff people concerning their part in the process.

When a controller takes operating personnel to task for exceeding the budget, he is inviting trouble of the worst kind. His correct course is to report the situation to responsible operating management and, if necessary, to the president, using the same figures and terms in each case. The problem then rests with the president and his operating subordinate, which is exactly where it belongs. It should be discussed and action determined in the direct line organization. No controller should permit himself to be placed in the position of representing the president in such matters—of giving approval to budgets or disapproval to results.

The same principle applies to all staff people concerned with coordinating the budget system, whether they report to a controller, treasurer, or factory accountant. There is impressive evidence that overzealous budget people have caused a great deal of mischief in this field, practically all of it unnecessary. They cannot be blamed individually, of course, for the failure of management to provide the principles needed for good budget practice. The remedy is in the eradication of a vicious set of faulty notions concerning the relationships of staff and line.

One of the first steps is to insist that each manager or foreman establish his own budget. He knows best his potential performance and the extent to which he can commit himself. He may enlist expert help, of course, from the budget man, but under no circumstances should the budget man or controller establish the budget, nor should the foreman be permitted to feel that this is happening. The penalty for violating this rule is the sacrifice of the sense of responsibility that locks a man securely to his budget when he knows it is his own.

Another misconception sometimes indulged by budget men is that they are almost solely responsible for cost reduction; that they alone are expected to seek and find opportunities for cost savings, such as excessive waste, dispensable overtime, carelessness in handling tools, and so on. In some cases, they have apparently been instructed to report such instances to a factory superintendent or even to top management rather than to the responsible first-line supervisor. It is difficult to conceive of a practice that violates more completely the basic principles of good human relations.

Line Organization

This medieval mess will clear itself up once management has established the fact that the line organization is responsible for cost control—fully and absolutely. Using a familiar type of organization, let it be clear that the vice president of manufacturing is charged with the duty of conducting the manufacturing cost reduction campaign; he delegates this work as he sees fit to plant managers, and they in turn to factory superintendents, who then look to the front-line men, the foremen, for control of costs.

The controller and budget men still fit into this picture importantly:

(1) They are equipped to establish and coordinate the budget system, with all of the tools of accounting and cost analysis.

(2) They should be able to teach the operating people how to use it.

(3) They should provide timely and intelligible reporting on performance against budget. (This reporting should of course be tailored to the

organization level to which it is addressed. For instance, at the top, the controller is obligated to report that which is pertinent to the president of the company.)

The attitude which should govern the staff people in this field, as in all other staff assignments, is one of maximum helpfulness to the line personnel. Only in this way can the budget man gain the foreman's confidence. If he finds cost-saving ideas, they should be volunteered promptly to the foreman for what use the latter can make of them. Personal credit is not the primary consideration. The budget man's own superior should be adept enough in detecting a skillful job to accord it the recognition it deserves—and one primary evidence of such performance will be a satisfactory relationship with the operating personnel. It is a preposterous notion that a budget man vaults to success on the failures and errors of the line.

CONCLUSION

The specific steps to be taken to improve budgeting practice depend, of course, on the mistakes an organization has been making. A searching self-examination in the light of the known principles of budgeting would seem to be the first move. Having identified the practices in an organization which most clearly abuse these principles, management will find that the corrective steps will present themselves. Courage and patience are needed to follow them.

Summary of Principles

Here, for your convenience, is a summary of points to be considered by any management wishing to establish its budget practice on a sound foundation:

(1) Establish your budget system on the highest possible level of motivation. To be specific, this means using it as a means for setting standards of performance, for measuring actual results, and for guiding management to satisfactory achievement. It means rejecting the use of budgets primarily as a pressure device to goad people into greater efforts. Accept this as a part of the philosophy of your company. Think about it, talk about it, make it a reality. And give more than lip service, even if it is difficult at first to separate the two conflicting motives. A budget program cannot be advanced to the stage of maximum fruition without this step.

(2) Anchor your budgeting firmly in a foundation of company planning. Do not permit it to float unattached—a technique without a clearly thought-out reason for being. The budget is not the plan; it is merely the statement of the plan in the language of figures. First turn the thinking of your organization to basic planning; then ask your people to prepare

budgets to effectuate their plans. Plan sales by markets and products, plan development, plan methods of manufacturing, purchasing, and merchandising. Determine the performance required of each department of the business; then budgets become simply the standard of dollars needed to do the job. This is the approach that makes managers out of men.

(3) Establish the meaning of control, and then put it into practice. In particular this requires the manager of each department to establish his own budget, based on his understanding of the job to be done. Top management may not be able to approve as high a figure as he asks for, but it can reach agreement with him as to what he is expected to accomplish and what it will cost. Having done this, he is responsible for planned performance. If he finds it necessary to exceed the budget, he should discuss this action with his superior and ask for advance approval. A budget is neither to be considered sacred nor to be taken lightly. Managers will respond with better attitudes when they understand that the use of the budget is to permit them to control their own operations.

(4) Insist on a clear-cut organization structure. A budget system cannot thrive without it. Each department should have a responsible manager, vested with authority commensurate with his responsibilities. He should have a clear understanding both as to the individual to whom he reports and as to the people who report to him. These are well-known precepts. A searching organization audit may be needed to determine whether they are being followed. The limitations on budget success are precisely marked by the degree of organization soundness.

(5) Arrange for good, common-sense accounting and complete, simple, and prompt explanations of the content of the items. This requires an accounting staff that is more concerned with the operating facts than with the techniques of balancing the books. Extreme care should be devoted to seeing that no supervisor has in his budget any item over which he does not have control. This area is fraught with debatable items and unending technical complications. If your house is not in order in this respect, almost any amount of effort is justified to put it in shape. And unless you are the exception to the rule, it will cost more money initially than you expect to pay, in terms of staff salaries and, perhaps, outside consulting services. The cost is usually well justified, however, in the end result.

(6) In the field of cost control, use your budget as a tool to be placed in your foremen's hands—not as a club to be held over their heads. To implement this rule, it may be a good idea to design an educational program. Meetings attended by line and staff supervisors may prove an effective vehicle. Cost reduction must be placed on the basis of mutual effort toward a common aim. The creation of this atmosphere is an essential, definitive step in budget practice.

(7) Insure the active participation of top management. The budget

program cannot succeed otherwise. The way of going about this step depends on your organizational status. If you are the president and question how well you measure up to this requirement, examine your thinking critically and ascertain which of the points in this article, if any, arouse resistance in your thought. Discussion with a controller other than your own may afford a fresh view. In any case, set aside the time to explore and understand the subject fully and to practice budgetary control in your daily affairs. If, however, you are a controller, your course in enlisting top-management support is one of patient, untiring teaching, until your case is won and the planning and control idea is in the warp and woof of your company's thinking.

(8) See that the controller and his staff express the correct attitude for the responsibility they undertake with respect to budgets. It is the controller's job to establish, maintain, and coordinate a budgetary system—in fact, a complete system of planning and control. But this work must be accomplished through authorized management. He must not enforce his instructions nor issue orders. He and his staff must be devoted to producing, reporting, and interpreting information—to making the planning and control machinery run. He is wholly a staff executive, and his only honors stem from the confidence of his associates. This he earns by honestly providing the control service and refraining from making operating decisions. Perhaps the cultivation of this attitude is the most productive single step of all, because from it the impetus to take the other steps may flow.

I have refrained from specifying the manner in which these ideas might be made known, or "sold," to the administrative groups. The task is essentially one for controllership. It is the most challenging project the controller is privileged to conduct, and it gains momentum as he enlists the support of top management and of supervision at all levels.

The actual method of carrying on this unremitting campaign varies from company to company, but there is a predominant tendency to rely largely on daily contacts. The controller and his staff—all the budget men and cost accountants—spread the idea in their working conversations. Meanwhile, special attention is continuously given the top echelon by the controller himself. Relatively few companies appear to hold regular educational or discussion meetings for this purpose.

It is interesting that all of the eight steps listed have their roots deep in personnel administration—that each one is, in the final analysis, the reflection of a problem involving people.

Deeper Significance

The present era demands a new appraisal of our daily work. The symptoms of budget irritations may point to deeper meanings in the spiritual emancipation of mankind. We are beginning to learn that no tool can be used effectively unless the hand that guides it is rightly motivated. Like all other techniques of business, the budget should be a door open to more satisfying and profitable work—not an instrument of torture.

Then it will be known that what you can do without a budget you can do better with one. It will be seen that the entire planning and control procedure, under whatever name, is a device for freeing men to do their best work—not a machine of restriction and condemnation. This better view is within our grasp today.

Planning is but another word for the vision that sees a creative achievement before it is manifest. Control is but a name for direction. The genius of management cannot fail to turn the budget idea finally into positive channels, so that people individually, as well as business leadership generally, will reap the harvest that it promises.

The Breakeven Concept *

Fred V. Gardner

Introduction. An inquiring reporter with the knack of getting to the heart of a subject would find that those who manage business affairs and who are responsible either for guiding profit performance or for measuring it know very little about what breakevens are, why they are what they are, or what to do about them when they show eccentric characteristics.

Do You Know Your Breakeven Point? It is true that when the question is first put to management men they are prone to say, "Of course I know what breakevens are. They are the place where profits turn to losses or losses to profits, depending upon whether you are going up or down." It is surprising how many first-class, high-ranking executives shrug off the whole problem with this type of comment.

A *Business Week* magazine article made three important points: "Most management men talk about breakeven points, but they often mean a lot of different things." "A few companies really figure the points closely—and swear by the results." "Most companies know—or guess—that their breakeven points have risen little in terms of capacity." [1] These statements agree with our findings. The 19th hole on the breakeven point is played in about the same vein as on the golf course. The poorer the performance, the louder the excuses.

Breakevens and Capacity. It is true that the breakeven point is that point of capacity at which operations pass from profits to losses or vice versa. The only trouble with this concept is that this point in terms of either capacity or income is not rigid or static. It changes with every decision of management. It changes when selling prices change and when operating efficiency rises or falls. It changes as the relationship between product lines varies even for short periods of time. These and many other reasons cause a breakeven point to move in a definable orbit. Unless the path of this orbit can be measured, conclusions reached about breakevens may be as dangerous as a bottle marked "Poison" if not used correctly.

* Reprinted by permission of the publisher from *Profit Management and Control* (New York: McGraw-Hill Book Company, Inc., 1955), pp. 19–26. Mr. Gardner is senior partner of Fred V. Gardner and Associates, Management Consultants.
[1] *Business Week*, December 13, 1952, p. 158.

Resistance to Breakeven Control. Because the postwar years were so lucrative that management energy was concentrated on the problem of keeping up production, many executives have built up "straw men" of resistance in their minds against the breakeven concepts without thinking of the consequences.

Most management men have adopted the term "breakeven" as a part of their vernacular and the word bobs up everywhere. Yet most of those in authority who toss the word around in conversation have little concrete knowledge about the structure of a breakeven point, its habits, or its characteristics, and know even less how to harness the breakeven concept in guiding their operations. To offset these shortcomings in advanced management thinking, alibis and excuses have developed.

The major excuses run about as follows: "Why worry about the breakeven point today? We will get it down when we have to." Or, "It will work all right for others perhaps, but it just won't work in our company," or, "It's all theory and not very practical."

These are but a few of the hundreds of defensive comments used daily in explaining all types of performance to all kinds of people who are interested in these problems. Were we to attempt cataloguing the variations and ramifications of the statements above, they would range from the ridiculous to the sublime. Many of them, if put together in proper sequence, would be as interesting and entertaining as the proverbial three-ring circus.

Today's Breakeven Too Easy to Attain. To answer broadly . . . the foregoing comments, . . . the following observations are appropriate. Why worry about the breakeven point today if we can get it down when we have to? We did not bring it down from 1929 to 1932, when it was a fight for survival. To be sure, that was over 20 years ago, and we have learned much in management techniques since then. Nor did many industries demonstrate ability to hold on to their breakeven-point positions in the 1937–1938 recession. And breakeven-point control was widely lacking in 1949–1950. The truth is that each faltering and falling-off business, however slight the hiatus, again demonstrates the need for better control mechanisms to protect against the "close-haul" years.

The average company today will find it difficult even to maintain its existing breakeven point when volume falls off, let alone attempt to reduce or improve its breakeven picture. Inflexible labor contracts, sheer size and diversity, multiplicity of operating locations, and unstreamlined methods of selling are just a few of the present conditions leading to less cost flexibility and greater difficulty of control.

Companies that have run contra to the pattern of constant growth which has been so typical of industry in recent years are living monuments to attest to the fact that breakeven reduction is not a "sleight-of-hand" process. It requires hard work to build techniques based on dynamic and forceful controls, controls which tell why profits vary as well as what profits are.

"Breakeven Concepts Won't Work for Our Company." Holding that breakevens may work all right in other companies but not in your own runs counter to experience in retailing, service, and manufacturing, from capital goods to soft goods, from technical to highly competitive lines. Whether it be the airline industry with its peculiarities (including people who think you can be good only if you are a flyer) or a chain of lumber yards or a chemical plant, breakeven concepts will work, provided the idea has executive support, the controls are honestly built, and the findings honestly followed. Of course they will not work for you if you do not want them to.

Are Breakevens Theory? Some say breakevens are all theory. If you think breakevens are simply theoretical, it is because you are theoretical. The breakeven point does not harness you. It records what you harness. If it appears to be unrealistic, if it presents conditions which you do not believe, that is not the fault of the breakeven point. Like the thermometer which measures the temperature in your office or home, it measures facts. If the thermometer tells you it is cold, that is not the fault of the thermometer but of the temperature being measured.

Breakevens are the mirror of your business, nothing less, nothing more. Their application and use will tell you how your business looks and will help you decide whether it is "time for a change."

Delving deeply into the objections to breakeven-point analysis and control, one finds but few real bases for opposing application of this scientific and sensitive aid to business operation. Plain lack of understanding can be cured, but more disturbing are the resistances rooted in downright indifference and in personal ego.

Indifference arises in prosperous periods during which profits are easy to come by. Simple evolution will jar lethargy of this kind because it is inevitable that the going will be more difficult in some years than in others. In the meantime both employees and owners suffer. Personal ego objections are more difficult to meet. In such cases the chief executive is proud of his ability, likes to run by the seat of his pants, and despite protestations to the contrary, enjoys the role of local god and crystal-ball gazer extraordinary. He does not want science in management if he will lose the zest of his mysterious maneuvering. Even such a manager will find breakeven control useful in lightening his load. Apart from the better performance his executives will register, his own life will be more free of ulcers, hardening of the arteries, and frightening heart disturbances.

The *Business Week* article cited earlier gives a clue which is worthy of note: "Relatively few companies make explicit operational use of breakeven points, or even figure them very closely. The companies that do use breakeven points frequently build intricate systems out of them, and swear by their usefulness."

To refresh our thinking of what a breakeven point is, how it is determined, and how it gives dynamics to static information, an illustration from a section of the history of Caterpillar Tractor will be helpful.

Caterpillar Tractor Company Breakeven Chart. For illustration, a simple breakeven chart of the Caterpillar Tractor Company is shown for the most recent years (Chart 2).

CHART 2

BREAKEVEN CHART, CATERPILLAR TRACTOR COMPANY

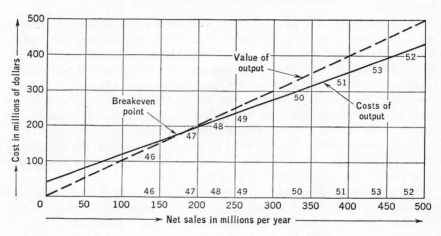

The base scale of the chart is the reason for incurring cost—therefore we have plotted the annual net sales in millions of dollars horizontally. The vertical scale is assigned to the value to be compared with the reason for incurring cost. Since we are concerned with the behavior of costs in relation to sales income, the vertical scale is assigned to annual costs (before income taxes) in millions of dollars.

It is axiomatic that "breakeven" means balance of sales income with cost outgo. Therefore we draw a "sales" line (really a line of 100 per cent correlation between costs and sales income) from the zero point at the left to Point B on the chart. At that point the line indicates, according to our scales, that there is a "breakeven" condition if sales and costs are both 500 million dollars; and the breakeven condition will be shown if costs fall on any point of the broken "sales" line down to zero.

Then we take the adjusted costs from Table II and plot the costs for each year, measuring up on the cost scale, and recording its point directly over the sales value plotted for that year along the base line. It is apparent that in the years 1946, 1947, 1948, and 1950 cost and sales relationships were such that a straight line could be drawn through them. But we are dealing with the record through 1953. A straight line drawn through the 1949 and 1953 points falls through an approximate average of the 1950 and 1951 points. Furthermore such a line closely imitates the slope of the 1946–1948 points. Therefore, for illustrative purposes it is a fair assumption that this higher line, marked "costs of output" on the chart, is fairly representative of the more recent cost-value-income relationships realized by the Caterpillar management.

TABLE II

CATERPILLAR TRACTOR COMPANY SALES AND COSTS
1946–1953

Year	Net sales	Adjusted costs *
1946	$128,437	$126,069
1947	189,120	172,816
1948	218,037	193,686
1949	254,872	228,482
1950	337,285	276,727
1951	393,756	356,903
1952	477,600	406,106
1953	433,800	371,465

* Depreciation for all years restated to that used in 1951 to eliminate effect of changed plant capacity and accelerated amortization. Income share not included in costs.

It is evident that the slopes of the sales line and of the cost line are substantially different. Running the cost line down to the zero net-sales axis (extreme left) we find that this "cost pattern" indicates a substantial remainder of cost even though sales income were zero. This remainder is the standby or constant relationship common to certain kinds of costs in every business. There would be no such thing as a breakeven point (point of crossover between the cost and sales lines) unless this were true. Accounting statements do not suggest the presence of this kind of costs nor afford any means of estimating the relative importance of the variable and standby costs.

We are not concerned here with the specific value of Caterpillar's breakeven point. Rather, using data which can be checked with public sources, we seek only to demonstrate that the slopes of the cost and sales lines for Caterpillars, and, indeed, for every company no matter what the nature of its business, will disclose two kinds of costs.

As we have drawn the line, the cost line rises from the standby constant at a rate of approximately $79 for each $100 of sales. This was the rate at which Caterpillar added costs (as sales volume rose from some 228 million dollars in 1949 to 406 million dollars in 1952), a little more or a little less, year by year. Over the term of years as the adjusted years are plotted, this could be said to represent Caterpillar's quality of control on the upside. But should sales volume decline, we could not attribute the same quality of control *unless Caterpillar also removes $79 of cost for each $100 of sales decline.* That kind of cost control is necessary to hold the breakeven point at the indicated 150 million dollars of sales.

CHART 3

THE IMPORTANT POINTS OF BREAKEVEN ANALYSIS

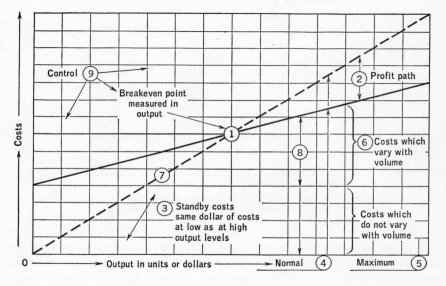

To control costs and their resultant profits, the problem of management is one of understanding how the two elements—standby and variable time factors—are affected by specific decisions. So long as there is no means of separating them, as in the conventional accounting statement, management cannot but confuse its people and confuse itself in its efforts to "do something about the breakeven point."

Why Fly Blind? Fly blind if you are happy, but if you prefer instruments to control your course, they must be used correctly and with sufficient knowledge to bring you out of the overcast and land you safely at some selected objective. The breakeven chart is an excellent instrument panel for your guidance in controlling your business. The ten salient points of the breakeven-point chart are so many gauges for checking out your management decisions. Study Chart 3 carefully. Let your imagination take hold. With good understanding of these points you can appraise your own breakeven point and can interpret the signals for important management action. The ten points of significance in a breakeven chart are:

1. The breakeven point itself
2. The profit path above the breakeven point as an indication of inherent profitability
3. The standby cost relationship to other costs and sales values at the breakeven point and at other capacity levels
4. The breakeven point as a percentage of normal output capacity—the margin-of-safety index
5. Point of maximum output as measured by existing plant or organization capacity, or point at which diminishing returns appear as a higher rate of variable costs because of major productive inefficiencies
6. Variable cost rate, an approximation of true "direct" or out-of-pocket costs
7. Selling price per unit
8. Relationship of variable and standby costs at any level of activity
9. Tie-in with profit and loss statement as a test of validity
10. Competitive comparison with other companies . . .

Conclusion. As with any control-instrument panel, much is needed behind the breakeven chart to make it work and to make it the reliable, ever-ready management aid that it can and should be. Take warning: we have but started on the road to dynamic business control and costing; there is much hard work ahead.

There must, however, be a basic understanding and acceptance of the breakeven concept. Remember that you are trying to bring order out of the chaos of the conflicting *time* effects of different kinds of business cost. Unproved promises and "guesstimates" will be more harmful than helpful. Your breakeven chart must be thoroughly supported with detailed cost planning and structuring, carrying the concept down into each phase, department, and account within your business.

Internal Auditing Control *

E. A. Lamperti and J. B. Thurston

INTERNAL AUDITING CONTROL

Modern internal auditing is one of the essential means for establishing and maintaining management control of a business. It rounds out all of the basic elements of management control and is in itself the main element of the appraisal, measurement, and evaluation control.

The rapid growth and widespread acceptance of modern internal auditing results primarily from the fact that it has provided executives with an important control which was lacking before its development and use. The acceptance of this function as a medium of control was accelerated by World War II, not only through specifications in governmental regulations and the requirements of war contracts, but also through the sheer necessity on the part of owners and managers to maintain close supervision over rapidly expanding companies and large industrial organizations.

Since the war, a variety of factors have contributed to its continuing growth, among them being the further development and perfection of internal auditing itself; the postwar growth of many relatively new as well as older companies to a size where internal auditing is required to establish adequate coordination; and, finally, management's increasing familiarity with, and recognition of, the importance of this new control technique.

RESPONSIBILITIES OF THE INTERNAL AUDITOR

In 1947, the Institute [of Internal Auditors] published a statement outlining the responsibilities of the internal auditor. . . . The following paragraph, captioned "Nature of Internal Auditing," summarizes the highlights of the statement:

Internal auditing is the independent appraisal activity within an organization for the review of the accounting, financial, and other operations as a basis for

* Reprinted by permission of the publisher from *Internal Auditing for Management* (New York: Prentice-Hall, Inc., 1953), pp. 83–84, 86, 89–92. Mr. Lamperti is an internal auditor and organization consultant, and Mr. Thurston, now deceased, was the first president of the Institute of Internal Auditors and a consulting management engineer

protective and constructive service to management. It is a type of control which functions by measuring and evaluating the effectiveness of other types of control. It deals primarily with accounting and financial matters but it may also properly deal with matters of an operating nature.

RELATIONSHIP BETWEEN CORPORATE ACCOUNTING AND INTERNAL AUDITING

It is important to recognize at the outset that internal auditing is not just another accounting function. In fact, it is not an accounting function at all but a management-control function.

A great many executives, however, still consider internal auditing as a branch of accounting, with its activities limited to the verification of accounting and financial transactions. This is no doubt a result of the close historical association that has existed between the two functions. Internal auditing was born of accounting. It came into being as soon as the need for establishing accountability developed. The need for someone besides the owner to handle revenues and transactions brought with it the need for someone to verify these revenues and transactions objectively. The association has been close for centuries and is still close.

New interests have come into the life of internal auditing until it has reached a point where it is time to leave the parental shelter and branch out into an independent life. It is associated closely but objectively with every activity and every transaction which contributes to its company's profit dollar. It issues no orders, originates no transactions, but is everywhere as a searching, appraising, and open evaluating function, with the object of helping those who do issue orders or originate transactions.

In many instances accounting data are limited in scope. Consequently, management decisions based on them alone may be faulty if the actual conditions behind the statements are not known. Because the limitations of accounting have been recognized, increasing attention is being paid by management to internal auditing and other control techniques.

Aside from the statement of responsibilities, the internal auditing function is difficult to define in precise terms. It varies materially with the size and type of each organization and with other contributing circumstances. Many smaller companies do not have an internal auditor; the public accountant's services include the responsibilities usually given him. On the other hand, larger companies and corporate entities which have expanded materially have found a definite need for a management representative who could replace the personal contact which formerly existed between management and personnel. This need is being filled today by the internal auditor.

Larger companies have found it necessary also to develop a system of administration which may be called *management by exception*. Under this system, top management determines and provides the policies and procedures best suited to meet the objectives of the company. It assumes then that these policies are being carried out effectively and that the only items which come to its attention thereafter represent exceptions from established policy and procedures or suggestions for improvement.

This form of management technique calls for extensive reliance on reports covering all phases of operations. If properly designed and compiled, these reports should reflect the effectiveness of management's policies and the thoroughness with which they are observed. It is the internal auditor's responsibility, and one he is particularly fitted to carry out, to see that the operations are in accordance with the policies and that the reports reflect these operations properly. In so doing, he is in a position to keep management informed of how effectively it discharges its responsibilities. The very nature of the auditor's examination discloses also the propriety and effectiveness of the procedures and the results obtained through them.

This brings us to another contribution of the internal auditing function, namely the determination of the adequacy of the procedures in force, as well as the recommendation of improved procedures wherever necessary. As a result of the examination of records and procedures throughout all organizations of the company, the internal auditor is in a good position to (a) recommend improvements in existing procedures, (b) suggest new ones which will serve management objectives better, and (c) makes available to other divisions any particularly effective practice developed in a specific unit of the company. Conversely, where an undesirable change has been made in established procedures in a particular unit, the auditor can point out its disadvantages from an over-all point of view and bring about necessary corrections.

There is a marked difference between the establishment of well-defined controls and their day-to-day use. Variances are bound to creep in as a result of any number of reasons. Someone may believe that he has found a shortcut, another person misinterprets a directive, others may willfully desire to see certain steps circumvented. Only periodical objective examination and appraisal can maintain the efficiency of these controls. The internal auditor provides these examinations. Internal auditing is the inspection unit of the system, constantly on the alert for any weakness or breakdown of controls. It challenges every feature examined from a multiplicity of angles, determining particularly whether:

1. It conforms with company policies.

2. Controls are adequate, effective, and efficient as a transaction flows through company processes.

3. Accounting and operating procedures are proper.

4. External regulations are complied with.

5. All records are prepared and stored with adequate care.

6. Controls provide necessary safeguards against fraud, removing all sources of temptation as much as possible.

What are the means available to the internal auditor for determining compliance with management directives? The fundamental source of information is to be found in instruction manuals. Most companies have manuals covering each of the major functions. For example, the accounting manual will delineate the accounting procedures for the home office, or a branch sales office, or a factory, or any other unit of the company. The manual contains an expression of accounting management's policies as well as applicable procedures. This is essential in fostering uniformity of practice and coordination of operations. It is the internal auditor's duty to see that performance is in accordance with the manual. Consequently, his first job is to be thoroughly versed in its contents. The same is true of any other function to be audited.

In addition to the question of compliance and effectiveness of procedures, the auditor must be able to assure management of the accuracy of records and reports. This can result only from thorough checking. He must always determine the facts, note all exceptions, and follow every avenue of investigation before he can be satisfied as to the accuracy of the work and the effectiveness or desirability of existing practices.

What is true of accounting is true also of other service departments such as purchasing, traffic, advertising, personnel and others. Management establishes policies in respect to each one. Large sums of money are expended by each of these groups and the internal auditor must determine whether these funds are spent in accordance with management policies. Again, the auditor's examination and appraisal of results should indicate whether these monies are being expended to the best interests of the company. Frequently such departments, most of which are directly under management supervision, are audited only indirectly, if at all. There have been instances of serious misapplication of company funds in some of these areas which might have been avoided or lessened through proper coverage by internal auditing.

Obviously it is difficult to define the functions of the internal auditor except in general terms, since his duties are prescribed by specific companies and vary substantially from firm to firm. However, there is a basic pattern which runs through most established auditing units, namely, the function of continuously measuring and evaluating all other controls. It is the inspection department of management controls, necessitated by the ever-increasing complexity of business administrative problems associated with the increasing decentralization of authority, with corresponding realignment of responsibilities. Other general areas of responsibility would include the following:

1. Examination of the financial transactions of the business, such as cash balances, customers' accounts, and adherence to credit terms; investigation into suppliers' accounts, into expense accounts, and so on.

2. Examination of the administrative procedures of the company to insure that the policies laid down by the management are adhered to, particularly in connection with the exercise of authority and the adherence to limits of expenditures.

3. Examination of methods with a view to the elimination of unnecessary and repetitive work, reduction of paper work, and the clearing of channels of communication.

4. An examination of procedures, both mechanical and otherwise, throughout the business with a view to suggesting improvements.

5. Checks upon the investment policy of the company with particular regard to the building up of stocks and their relation to the scale of the business; maintenance of a proper relation between the size of each department and the scale of its activities.

6. Investigation into the management functions of branches and subsidiaries, and comparison between such sections of the company with a view to improving administrative and other techniques in general.

Business Reports: How to Get Facts You Need *

Philip Gustafson

New and dynamic forms of management control are being worked out and applied today throughout the business world.

As business becomes increasingly decentralized and complex, more and more does today's executive need a sensitive instrument panel to keep from flying blind, to see what's going on and whether people are doing what they're supposed to be doing.

Today's instrument panel is management control, and this is a highlight report on what some of the leaders are doing in the field.

Control is bound up with planning and, taken together, the process consists essentially of three basic steps:

1. Deciding in advance what should be accomplished and what will constitute good performance. These decisions frequently take the form of budgets, cost standards, operating programs and the like.

2. Finding out actual performance, then measuring and evaluating it.

3. Taking corrective action.

There are many ways to check actual performance. A few of the commonest include direct observation by a line supervisor, consultation through informal contacts with subordinates, regular operations or financial audits, special investigations or analyses and the formal management control report, which is the most commonly used type of control in medium to large-scale business organizations.

All of these forms of control are used in the average business today. However, as business has grown in size and complexity, informal and intermittent methods of keeping in touch with what's going on, such as personal contact, have diminished in value. The method of growing importance in large-scale business is the written or graphic management report. This is today's instrument panel.

A growing number of managements, however, are finding that the instrument panel in the front office hasn't kept pace with the complex instrumentation they have built into the factories. Thus, many companies are overhauling their formal reports—statistical, accounting, narrative

* Reprinted by permission of the publisher and author from *Nation's Business*, vol. 44, no. 8 (August, 1956), pp. 78–82. Mr. Gustafson is now a professional journalist and was a public relations consultant in New York.

and graphic. A survey of what some of these companies are doing has produced the following guides.

1. GIVE STANDARDS FOR COMPARISON

Since the object of control is to see that everything is carried out according to decisions already made, every control report should facilitate the evaluation of actual results by comparing them with what they should have been.

"Your report must have built-in standards as a basis of comparison," say Paul Hamman, partner in Touche, Niven, Bailey and Smart, Certified Public Accountants, of Detroit, Mich.

"One manufacturing company used to get out a report on scrap losses that was a horrible example of what not to do. In the first place it had no basis of comparison.

"The vice president wanted to know 'Is one per cent of the material going through, or 10 per cent?' He wanted an area of tolerance, let's say below three per cent. If they got out of this area, he wanted to raise Cain. As it was, he was left without a bogey."

Since control can be exercised only by people, management control reports must follow the structure of the organization and be set up by individual responsibilities.

"Operating reports rest on a cornerstone of well-defined responsibility," says Mr. Hamman. "You must give a man a goal and then measure his progress against this goal."

2. POINT OUT DANGER AREAS

A good report focuses attention on matters requiring action by accenting the significant trends or out-of-line performance. This is known as reporting by exception. Such reports highlight the exceptions which require management attention. You want your reports to tell you:

What is good?

What is bad?

Who is responsible?

The man making the report should report on the pertinent areas of his own responsibility. The recipient should be able to tell where he should go for more information if he wants it.

3. BE TIMELY

Reports should be issued promptly and at appropriate intervals. Operating information is perishable and must be made available in sufficient time for necessary action. Besides, the report must reflect current operating conditions.

4. Cover Critical Areas

"There are two major areas of need that are not covered by the structure of management reports that exist in most companies today," says Richard Neuschel of McKinsey and Company, management consultants. "The first of these includes those elements of performance that can be expressed quantitatively but which are not covered by the accounting system nor by budgets or standard costs. These might include such factors as facilities utilization, customer turnover, market penetration, delivery performance and the like.

"Second, there is a need for some kind of reporting on elements of performance that cannot be expressed either quantitatively or in terms of contribution to short-term profits. This category includes practically all important performance factors comprising such functions as engineering, research and development, industrial relations, controllership, etc."

"The structure of formal management reports in many companies today is a pretty sorry thing," Mr. Neuschel adds. "The typical approach to improving the reports has three basic weaknesses:

"It is self-limiting because it ties the mind to the make-up of existing reports.

"It provides no reasoned basis for determining what information is needed. The principal criteria for cutting or keeping existing reports are personal preference and preconceptions.

"It is not dynamic. It does not go deeply enough in trying to rebuild the structure of management information into a real profit-making tool. It is a negative approach aimed primarily at cutting office expense through the elimination of unnecessary or duplicate information.

"Furthermore, no system of management control or of management reports is anywhere near complete if it is limited to the elements of performance covered by the accounting system—that is, income, cost and expense . . . those elements which have a direct and measurable effect on short-term profits."

5. Aim for Simplicity

"A lot of companies don't realize how old fashioned their top management reports have become," says Mr. Hamman. "The reports of most companies have the atmosphere of the middle '20's. One company used a page full of close-packed figures that looked like a bookkeeper's summary of the year's work. It was a transcription of a bookkeeper talking to himself.

"The company directors couldn't have been helped less if a bushel basket full of figures had been poured out on the table in front of them."

"One of the big problems is that posed by electronics equipment," says another consultant. "We've gone through an era of office mechanization and automation to such an extent that the capacity to produce management information has outstripped the capacity to assimilate it and use it intelligently in running the business."

6. CLARITY IS ESSENTIAL

Make sure your reports are easy for a non-figure-minded executive to understand and use. Few top management executives today come up through the accounting department, though most reports are prepared as if they did.

The real object of reports is to get them used. If they are not in a form in which they can be used, they're no good. They simply lie around. The report should not only be expressed in the language of the report user but it should report only the essential facts so the reader can learn the whole story without becoming confused.

A good report should have eye appeal. Eye appeal requires that the report should be readable, with information organized to lead the eye through a well-aligned format rather than through a labyrinth of words and figures.

Graphs, charts and other visual presentation techniques are becoming increasingly popular in business.

"We design a report not to be read," says one consultant. "We don't want the reader wasting time reading reports. We want him just to look at the paper and say, 'Here's what I wanted to know'—then not have to read any farther. The real test is whether a stranger to the business can read a report effectively."

7. FOCUS ON THE FUTURE

"Management reports should include a liberal number of predictions and predictors rather than aim solely at a meticulous reporting of historical data," says Mr. Hamman. "Indicated trends are far more useful to management than determination of so-called exact profits for a short-time period."

8. INTEGRATE YOUR REPORT SYSTEM

Instead of being a coherent, understandable whole, a report structure often tends to be a hodgepodge of unrelated bits and pieces—some overlapping, or conflicting, some clear, some confusing. It is not difficult to see why this condition develops. In most companies, the structure of management information is neither the product of one mind nor one time. Its parts are seldom developed according to any conceptual scheme. Each came into being without any thought as to how that part related to the whole.

The report structure as a whole should represent an integrated plan of control under which the information given to all levels of management is tied together and simply becomes more condensed as higher levels of management are reached.

This means that the reporting system must have unity. One should be able to follow logically step by step from one report to another and from summary to supplementary or subsidiary reports.

A well-designed structure of reports should:

1. Provide each executive with the planning information necessary to make the decisions for which he is responsible.

2. Provide each executive with the control information necessary to relate performance with the planned goals covering the activities for which he is responsible.

A number of progressive corporations, usually those with facilities spread throughout the country, have worked out highly successful systems of management reporting.

Two of these are taken up here in detail.

The Du Pont System

The whole structure of top management information at E. I. du Pont de Nemours & Company, Inc., is based on graphic presentation. It is centered around the chart room, an amphitheater on the ninth floor of the company's offices at Wilmington, Del. The charts are mounted on 30 by 40 inch metal frames suspended by wheels from an overhead network of trolleys, specially designed and constructed so that, in a matter of seconds, any series can be brought to a central display room for review. There are more than 400 of these charts and they carry a running account of the operations of Du Pont's 10 manufacturing departments and of the company as a whole. This is the nerve center of the business.

When an executive at Wilmington wants to review any division, he comes to the chartroom and says,

"I want the facts of life about X Department."

A member of a special reports and charting staff from the treasurer's department, constantly at work on these reports, brings him the information he wants.

The Du Pont company believes that effective reporting of internal data is fully as important to the company as good public reporting. Its chart system was conceived as a means of enabling the company financial staff to report to executive management the financial results of an operation in a manner at once simple and yet complete. The basic concept emphasizes return on investment and the factors contributing to it.

Return on investment is shown on the charts as the financial end result of operations; it is the product of two percentages—turnover multiplied by earnings as per cent of sales. Turnover is obtained by dividing sales by total investment; it reflects the rapidity with which plant and working capital is being employed. The separate effects of these two percentages on return on investment may be determined through an analysis of charts showing sales, elements of cost of sales, earnings and the details of plant inventories, accounts receivable and cash.

The principal advantage of the chart system is to point up immediately the places where further analysis, review and attention may be desirable or necessary. The charts are intended to show what happened in terms of profit return on investment, and to put the finger on the broad underlying factors which caused the results to be what they were. They do not displace the customary financial statements such as forecasts, budgets or historical reports.

On the fourth Wednesday of each month, the executive committee reviews the operations of a group of departments, so that each department averages about four reviews a year.

A member of Du Pont's treasurer's department presides at the session, moving each chart or series of charts in place before the executive committee. He is prepared to give background reasons for normal variations in current data against past performance or against forecasts.

If an unusual variation shows up, however, the general manager of the department under review is on hand to explain, and the reason is traced back to its source through the chart system.

The charts used for review by the executive committee in general show the results of departmental operations for the current year against a background of exactly the same data for the ten preceding years and a forecast for the next 12 months.

Similar chart series are employed to some extent by all levels of departmental management. The company has a thoroughly developed method for following up on one-shot decisions. It has, for example, a hard-headed system for following up on capital expenditure results.

Each one of the major departments, when seeking to expand, must submit to the executive committee an appropriation request spelling out the facility it wants to build, then give a complete long-term evaluation on:

Anticipated sales volume
Price projections
Competitive outlook
Profit prospects
Prospects for return on investment

After the authorized facility has been in operation one year, the general manager submits a "Report of Accomplishment," which is a statement of actual sales volume and earnings contrasted with expectations at the time the appropriation request was initiated.

If the over-all picture is not entirely favorable, the executive committee may request another accomplishment report at the end of the second year.

Sometimes the series of reports for a particular project is continued for three or four years. Meanwhile, the departmental management gets interim reports more frequently.

Such reporting has become so much a part of the procedure that it's part of the thinking and working habits of the people who do it.

Plans for the Du Pont people are something to be carried out, not predictions of probability. For them, good planning plus good follow-up equals a programmed decision.

This process of follow-up, company executives say, has forced people to be a lot more hard-headed and realistic in the estimates on which they base their decisions. They know they are going to be followed up. Also, it forces them to be more realistic in programming their efforts to make sure the results are going to be achieved.

Decision-making and planning complement each other. The better the plan, the more effective the control—the more realistic the goals.

The United Airlines System

One of the fastest and most dynamic reporting systems in business is operated by United Airlines with the aid of electronic machines. It produces a profit and loss statement which is laid on the desk of President W. A. Patterson in Chicago every 24 hours.

The statement has its birth every day in the statistical production room at United's Denver operating base. Passenger and cargo volumes, collected from each flight, are combined at the end of the day. The results are wired to United's Chicago offices ready for processing at 8:30 A.M. Economic research employees apply revenue rates predetermined by experience and expense rates based on current operating budget requirements to the previous day's volume appearing on the wire. Within an hour, an operating profit or loss is estimated and passed on to top management.

The daily report shows the day's operating profit or loss along with a month and year to date accumulation. Also, daily revenue passenger miles and the passenger load factor are given. Data are broken down in such a way as to give the passenger department information on which to decide whether to put more planes on the Chicago to San Francisco run or advertise to get additional passengers.

An intrinsic part of United's reporting system is what company executives like to call "the room with the 14,000-mile view." This is an information and planning center at Denver which is the business world's equivalent of the military briefing room. Facts funneled daily into this center present a clear picture of operations throughout United's 80-city system.

In keeping with the idea of expansive vision, the room has glass walls on one side. Modern white plastic chairs are grouped before a map of the United States, eight feet high and 20 feet wide, on which United's routes are outlined. Colored lights (red for weather, green for maintenance and white for passengers) at major terminals show current operating conditions. If the red light glows steadily, for example, it means adverse weather; if it is flashing, the weather is marginal. Electric clocks above the map show the time in each zone through which United operates.

The room is designed to provide management with operational facts in the most convenient form. Data, such as mileage flown, delays at terminals by type of plane and total number of departures, are posted on lucite panels, flanking the map. Dozens of supplementary charts deal with payload volumes and load factors, weather, actual performance as compared with schedule and related information.

Daily at 8:30 A.M., MST, United's operations executives meet in the room for a 14,000-mile view. Four briefing specialists review operations of the past 24 hours and outline what the next 24 are expected to bring. The opening summary is presented by a meteorologist who analyzes the decisive factors in yesterday's weather conditions from the Atlantic seaboard to the Hawaiian Islands. He then gives his forecast for the next 24 hours, accenting developments which may affect operations.

A mechanical specialist follows with information on the status of the company's fleet. He reports the number and types of aircraft withdrawn from service for overhaul and comments on the progress of various engineering projects at the San Francisco base.

A traffic specialist then gives a resume of the previous day's performance in terms of any customer service problems which arose. Approximately 750 plane departures are scheduled daily. Those which deviate from schedule are spotlighted for management study to prevent possible recurrence.

The remaining gaps in the 14,000-mile view are filled in by a flight operations specialist who discusses the availability of equipment, and weather outlook on the line. The session then adjourns. Immediately afterwards, some department chiefs may call their staffs together to act on particular facets of the day's operating plan.

No matter how highly-developed a management report system may be, it's only as good as the action management takes. So once a good reporting system is set up and all the information is in, what does management do to improve the situation?

Here are ten possibilities, depending on conditions:

1. It supplies additional skills.

2. It provides more guidance or training to improve the ability to meet the goal.

3. It sets up a new program.

4. It obtains new finances.

5. It procures more facilities.

6. It finds a better product.

7. It supplies better incentives.

8. It replaces people not functioning properly.

9. It changes the program by which the objective is to be achieved (perhaps by adding more facilities, money, etc.).

10. Or, it might change the goal itself.

No business can be run by formula nor can any system of control replace the need for perception, vision, imagination, inventiveness, leadership or executive qualities.

The Control Section as an Aid to Management*

T. S. McGinnis

THE EXECUTIVE JOB

The basic problems of management present themselves in the operation of any enterprise. While they are subject to variation in degree, depending on the nature, size and complexity of the undertaking, fundamentally they are the same.

In the case of a small business of proprietary nature, the exercise of management is more or less a personal responsibility, since limited size makes it possible for one individual to control the business and to supervise and direct its operations. When the elements of size and complexity are such as to place the job of management beyond the physical capacity of one individual there arises the necessity of developing suitable means of sharing the overall responsibility. The latter condition is typical of modern industry, particularly those businesses which are conducted under a corporate ownership. The impersonal association of the stockholder with the business itself leads to the necessity of vesting trusteeship in the hands of a Board of Directors, and in turn, in some one Chief Executive.

It has been said that the executive job is to "Organize, Deputize, Supervise, and Energize." Upon the Chief Executive falls the overall responsibility for the success of the business, and for direction of the many functions which will make success possible. His job may be further described as including these seven essential duties:

1. To divide the total responsibility into logical assignments.
2. To select, train and develop competent people.
3. To establish measures of accountability.
4. To determine or agree on plans and programs for attainment.
5. To guide and coordinate performance.
6. To appraise results.
7. To take steps to correct unsatisfactory conditions.

The first three duties listed are the type which require personal performance by the Chief Executive. He alone can develop or approve the basic organization plan, and only he can assign primary responsibility to

* Reprinted by permission of the Koppers Company from a brochure of the same title published by the Koppers Company. Mr. McGinnis is head of the Control Section of the Koppers Company.

the components of the organization for carrying out specific parts of the overall enterprise. Likewise, the selection or approval of the men who are to carry out these responsibilities must rest with the Chief Executive, and he must, through daily contacts and supervision, train and develop his immediate subordinates. They become accountable to him alone for the manner in which they carry out their assignments, through whatever measures he may choose.

The remaining four duties are such as to be beyond performance by the Chief Executive himself. They involve direction and control of each individual activity and the coordination of all. A working balance must be maintained between production and sales on the one hand, and between these and the supporting functions of finance, law, research, personnel, traffic and transportation, procurement, public relations, and others. Without this balance, the variation in aggressiveness and effectiveness between individuals might result in any one of these functions bearing a greater or lesser influence on the overall business than would be desirable.

Obviously the Chief Executive requires assistance in order to perform these last four duties. He needs more hands, more eyes and ears, and more hours per day. Also, this assistance can be most effective if it can operate with his own, overall, impartial viewpoint—with no special or primary interest in any one phase or function.

This need is the basis of the Control Section concept. A Control Section can provide the assistance needed, can operate from an impartial overall position, and can perform the detailed analysis and coordination work, leaving the Chief Executive free to concentrate on only the most important matters.

THE CONTROL SECTION

It is possible to draw a rather basic line of distinction between the work of the Chief Executive and that of his Control Section, by employing the words "what" and "how." It is the task of the Chief Executive to determine "what" the company shall do—to set its objectives and goals. The Control Section is concerned with "how" the company shall do these things, as well as how effectively it *is* doing them. Specific examples of the work carried on by the section will serve to illustrate further the manner in which it assists the Chief Executive in carrying out his management responsibility.

1. *Determining or Agreeing on Plans and Programs for Attainment.* It is considered essential to the success of the enterprise that definite objectives be set forth as goals, and that definite plans and programs be developed which will allow attainment of these goals. This is clearly a job of top management, yet one which requires detailed work beyond the

capacity of an individual. The Control Section coordinates the development of plans and programs by drawing together the forecasts and plans of each operating unit and staff agency. In cooperation with the finance group it analyzes these plans in terms of the sources of and requirements for working capital, and develops plans to obtain necessary funds. The desires of operating units to expand production capacity are reconciled with the prospective ability to provide funds for this work.

A detailed program is secured from each operating unit covering sales, costs, profits, inventories, receivables, payables, and many other elements. These are reviewed carefully in the light of historical results, independent forecasts of the general trend of business and other factors. This review is of particular value to the Chief Executive, since it tends to offset the over-cautiousness or over-zealousness of individual operating managements.

The supporting staff units are required to program their activities, as well as their expenses, these being consolidated and reviewed in the interest of obtaining a reasonable balance between staff activity and operating volume. Programs are prepared to cover research, advertising, and other major types of expenditures.

These programs are prepared to cover the coming calendar year, by months, in considerable detail. A longer range program is concurrently developed covering five years, by year, for long range planning purposes. When finally consolidated and reviewed, they are recommended to the various management committees and to the Chief Executive. After approval, they are reproduced and distributed to management.

The Control Section maintains a continuing watch over the program throughout the year, in order that revisions may be recommended where conditions have substantially changed, or where for other reasons a revised plan is necessary.

2. *Guiding and Coordinating Performance.* As a means of assisting the Chief Executive, the Control Section performs a constant review of the organization of the company, as well as of the organizational plans of its various divisions and departments. It is responsible for the preparation and maintenance of the Organization Manual, which includes charts, limits of authority for key positions, and job specifications covering the duties, responsibilities and relationships of each key position.

Studies are made of the organization of individual divisions and departments, consisting of interviews and conferences with the successive levels of organization, in order to obtain the ideas and views of a cross section of management. Reports of these studies are presented to the division or department executive, containing all facts, findings and recommendations. Only when an agreement cannot be obtained on the correction of a deficiency, does the matter require consideration of the Chief Executive of the company.

The conditions under which business is conducted, and the frequent change in these conditions, make necessary the development and modification of company policies. Matters which affect the company generally, rather than one specific part of its work, channel through the Control Section for study, appraisal and recommendation to the Chief Executive. Where directives or orders are necessary, this section coordinates their preparation and distribution.

Another function of the Control Section concerns procedures, or the preparation of orderly and efficient methods by which the work will be performed. Any routine act that is performed repeatedly is a worthy subject for procedure study. Consequently, coverage of all procedure work for the company would require a large force. The Control Section therefore confines its direct work on procedures to those involving actions between operating divisions and staff departments, or between staff departments, and publishes such material in a General Management Procedures Manual. Procedure work with respect to the internal activities of these units is performed locally, but generally supervised and coordinated by the Control Section.

3. *Appraising Results.* In order to exercise intelligent direction of the business, the Chief Executive must provide some adequate means of being informed of the results which are being experienced and the special problems being met. General practice has consisted of the preparation of reports and financial statements, usually by the Finance Department. Because a Finance Department is more statistical than analytical in nature, such reports have tended to be mere statements of operating results, sometimes supplemented by comparisons with past periods, but lacking an analysis of why the results are what they are, and whether the results are as good as they should have been. This analysis would therefore be an additional task of the Chief Executive to whom the reports were addressed.

Reporting is a fundamental and logical function of the Control Section. In the first place, it has prepared the company's operating program, which serves as the measuring stick to judge the actual performance during each program period. With a supply of statistical data from the Finance Department, plus a narrative report from the operating units, the Control Section constructs a monthly Progress Report which relates not only what has occurred, but explains *why* it has occurred. Further, it relates all actual results to the programmed goals and clearly shows the current prospects of attaining these goals.

The impartial and objective viewpoint of the Control Section is of particular value in this work, for it can detect and correct rationalization, over or under-emphasis and other faults in the basic reports which may be due to a conscious or unconscious influence on the part of the operating units. The report also covers the activities of staff units, including progress made against programmed projects and general information in their respective functional fields. A section of the report is also devoted to an analysis of current economic factors and their probable effect on the company's business.

The monthly Progress Report is collected, consolidated, edited, and finally arranged by the Control Section, reproduced in the company's multilith unit under Control Section supervision, and distributed by it to the Chief Executive and to division and department management. It is the basis of a discussion of the business at monthly committee meetings, and is supplied to each director for review prior to monthly board meetings. The arrangement of the report, and the use of text, charts and tables make it a flexible and valuable source of information for use by each level of management.

In addition to this monthly report, the Control Section prepares and furnishes special reports on items of current interest, either on its initiative, as requested by the divisions or departments, or on assignment by the Chief Executive. It also furnishes advice and assistance to the company in general on problems of internal reporting.

As an additional way of assisting the Chief Executive to appraise results, the Control Section conducts audits of the progress being made by staff departments, particularly those whose operations are not measurable in terms of dollars, volume or other definite units. These audits are made to determine, where possible, the benefits being realized through the staff unit's operations, and if possible, the value of these benefits as related to the cost of the activity. Results of these studies are made available to the Chief Executive after having been reviewed with the staff unit concerned.

4. *Correcting Unsatisfactory Conditions.* The correction of unsatisfactory conditions must, of course, rest with the Chief Executive himself. However, he may be assisted by the Control Section in the location and analysis of troublesome conditions, and by its preparation of recommendations on a course of remedial action. In many cases the condition may thus be self-correcting, due to the analysis itself. In others, the problem may be referred to one of the staff units, where the trouble lies in a specific functional field.

ORGANIZATIONAL RELATIONSHIP OF THE CONTROL SECTION

The effectiveness of a Control Section, and in fact its very existence, depends on a thorough understanding of its relation to the company, both within the section and among the operating and staff units. In all of its work, the Control Section assists the Chief Executive, but exercises *no authority* over any other part of the organization. Should the attitude be taken, on either side, that it is a super-management agency with power to control and direct in itself, its value is lost and it will very likely become a liability rather than an asset.

It may request information, give advice and assistance, coordinate and report, but it must under no circumstances issue directions or orders. Its findings and recommendations are supplied to the Chief Executive, are subject to his approval, and are put into effect by him, over his name only.

Properly applied, the control concept will minimize the need for executive action and orders. Recommendations, advice and persuasive action on the part of the Control Section will generally result in cooperative action on the part of other units, especially when confidence in its work has been well established.

OTHER FUNCTIONS OF THE CONTROL SECTION

In addition to the routine, repetitive tasks which it performs, the Control Section is constantly at the disposal of the Chief Executive for the pursual of whatever problem may arise. Subject only to the demands of the Chief Executive, it is available to any division or department for assistance in management problems.

It keeps constant watch over the company's activities in order to observe instances of difference, dissension, lack of cooperation and jurisdictional dispute. It serves in the capacity of arbitrator and mediator in many such matters, thereby relieving the Chief Executive of many problems which may be petty, but which would otherwise represent demands on his time and patience. Confidence in the impartial attitude of the Control Section leads to voluntary submission of such matters to it by the units concerned.

THE CONTROL FUNCTION AT OTHER LEVELS

The concept of a Control Section is equally applicable at lower levels of organization, providing the division or department is of sufficient size to require internal control activity. A control unit can do for the division or department executive what it does for the Chief Executive at company level. Further, there arises an effective functional relationship between those units at various levels which expedites and improves the quality of information, reports, studies and other control work.

For those units too small to require internal control activities, the services of a control unit at some higher level should be available.

CONTROL PERSONNEL

As in the case of any job, selection of personnel for control work must be based on personal characteristics and ability to do the job. It is highly desirable that control personnel be selected from a standpoint of their prospective future in the company, for service in this capacity is a most excellent form of training for future management material. The ability to get along with others is an essential characteristic, for the success of the group will depend greatly on the tact and good judgment of its men.

ORGANIZATION OF THE CONTROL SECTION

The section need not be large, and in fact may be limited to five or less key men, depending on the scope and volume of work to be handled. Supplementing these, the required amount of stenographic assistance will be necessary. It may also be advisable to provide a draftsman for the design and preparation of charts and other such material, to be included in reports and studies. A Control Manager should report to the Chief Executive, and other Control Section personnel to the Manager. Specialization within the unit should not be attempted in too rigid a manner, as the volume and nature of assignments can vary greatly from time to time.

CONCLUSION

Whether or not assigned to a Control Section as described herein, the functions of programming, planning, coordinating, reporting, etc., are management tools which contribute greatly to successful direction of business. Experience has shown that when these functions are assigned as secondary duties, to a unit or individual having additional responsibilities, they are either performed less effectively or not at all. The Control Section concept has been successful and is therefore recommended for adoption wherever management problems such as described herein exist.

C. OVER-ALL CONTROL OF PERFORMANCE

How the Du Pont Organization Appraises
Its Performance *

T. C. Davis

Once again our attention has been directed to the function of the profit incentive in holding an industrial enterprise to a successful course and one which will best serve the whole economy. Because the profit system is misunderstood by a considerable segment of our population and is actually under attack from some quarters, no effort should be spared to present at every opportunity a clear picture of the function of profits. Certain principles cannot be ignored if capital and manpower are to be successfully utilized in the production of goods, stimulated on the one hand by the incentive reward of profits and on the other hand by the prospect of a rising standard of living.

As far back as I can remember, both the measuring and reporting of profits have been controversial subjects. Although they have been debated at great length by business men, economists, bankers, accountants, lawyers, labor leaders, legislators, educators, and even statesmen, nothing definitive seems to have emerged. We appear to have made very small progress in this particular field during the past two decades. While this is discouraging, certainly we cannot abandon effort to bring about public understanding that the profit incentive is both the carrot and the stick which prods an industrial enterprise to its best performance, and that from this relationship the entire population benefits.

The stock market crash of 1929 seems in retrospect to have been the flare that set off an economic depression of great magnitude. Business management was quickly made the whipping boy. One of the charges hurled with great frequency and vigor was that the public had been misled by the information made available to it concerning corporate business operations. Some said these data were incomplete; some said they were presented in a manner which was misleading; and some even made charges that trickery in accounting had been employed which resulted in false reports. Out of this great clamor emerged the Securities and Ex-

* Reprinted by permission of the publisher from *How the Du Pont Organization Appraises Its Performance*, Financial Management Series, no. 94 (New York: American Management Association, 1950), pp. 3–4, 6–7, 20–22. Mr. Davis was formerly Treasurer of the E. I. du Pont de Nemours & Company.

change acts, with an ever-growing body of law and regulation concerning the disclosures to be made upon the public sale of securities, and the manner of reporting to stockholders by companies with listed securities.

Under the impetus of these requirements, and because of the natural desire of business men and accountants to present to stockholders all the data they want which is at once meaningful and yet not unduly helpful to competitors, much study has been given the so-called public reporting by corporate business. And I think we may say that some improvement has been made in public reporting, although there still exists a widespread belief that all financial reporting is double talk. We haven't yet solved the problem of making a public statement of the financial results of an operation which is so simple yet so complete that it can withstand attack from every quarter. Perhaps this is a great deal to hope for, but, as I said before, we simply cannot relax in our effort to achieve this goal.

These remarks with respect to external reporting have only an indirect bearing upon my subject, but they serve as background for an important observation: Unfortunately, financial management probably has had no greater degree of success in solving the problem of reporting financial data to executive management (i.e., internal reporting) than can be claimed for financial reporting to stockholders and other public interests. My assignment has to do with internal reporting as distinguished from external reporting—in fact, it is to say something about one important part of the system of internal reporting actually in use in the duPont Company.

FUNCTION OF THE CHART SYSTEM

Any system of financial control, to be of maximum usefulness, should include a forecast of sales and profits, a forecast of working capital requirements and cash resources, and capital-expenditure budgets and working-capital standards, together with statements which show the actual operating performance and balance-sheet condition promptly after the close of an accounting period. It is the duty and responsibility of the financial staff to make these data available to executive management when required, and in a form which will reveal the operating results of each particular product line. The complexity of operations and/or the diversity of product lines complicate the financial accounting problems, and clarity in the presentation of operating results should be the objective through which solutions to specific financial and accounting problems are worked out.

At duPont one of my predecessors saw one phase of this problem of internal reporting in clear perspective. Slightly more than 30 years ago he conceived and guided the design of what we have come to call *the chart system*. This system utilizes charts and tabulations for presenting to the Executive Committee data pertinent to the performance of each operating investment. We maintain approximately 350 individual charts, a number of which are presented to the Executive Committee each month, so that in a year's time, all charts have been reviewed several times. . . .

THE EXECUTIVE COMMITTEE CHARTS

The charts [discussed] here are of the kind utilized by the Executive Committee in its direction of the business. While these or similar chart series are employed to some extent by all levels of departmental management, our considerations will here be directed toward the charts which the Treasurer's department maintains for the Executive Committee. These charts and tabulations do not displace the customary financial statements—whether forecasts, budgets or historical reports. They are used by the Executive Committee in reviewing with a general manager the operations of his department.

Once each month the Executive Committee reviews charts, the schedule being so arranged that the charts for each department are reviewed no less frequently than once every three months. At least one set or series of charts and tabulations is set up for each department. In some cases the operations of a particular department are sufficiently diverse that it has been found necessary to set up several sets of charts and tabulations, each set bracketing a portion of the department's activities which it is desired to treat as a separate unit. Thus, for our nine industrial departments we have 20 separate operating investment chart series, representing approximately 350 charts.

For each of these series the results of operations for the current year are shown against a background of exactly the same data for the 10 preceding years and a forecast for the ensuing 12 months.

We place primary emphasis upon *return on investment*, and the central theme around which the chart series is built is to focus attention upon this end result, without neglecting the factors that produce return on investment—*gross profit on sales* and *turnover*. It might be helpful if at this point we examine an outline of the formula (Figure B) which is controlling in the chart concept. . . . From this formula you will see that we wish to present *return on investment* through the factors of *earnings as a per cent of sales* (which is the gross profit margin) and *turnover*.

The return on investment responds to movement in these two factors. If there has been no change in selling price, an improvement in turnover indicates that capital is being worked harder, i.e., *the business is getting increased sales out of the same plant and working capital*. Again, if there is no change in selling prices an improvement in gross profit margin indicates that the cost in proportion to sales dollar is being reduced.

The figures used in these charts are hypothetical; they do not depict the operating results of any one of duPont's investments. However, the chart series is complete and we have borrowed from actual experiences in deciding upon what trends to present through the medium of these hypothetical figures. We have used our own experience merely as a starting point, and where it was felt that a point could be more forcefully illustrated, have exaggerated the figures in order to accomplish this. . . .

FIGURE B

RELATIONSHIP OF FACTORS AFFECTING RETURN ON INVESTMENT

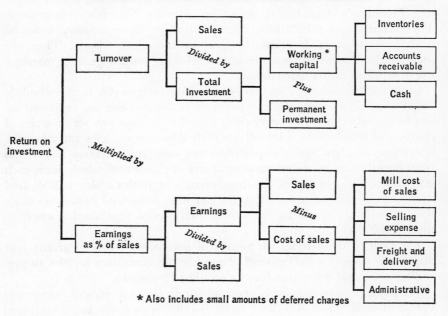

Also includes small amounts of deferred charges

SPECIAL ADVANTAGES OF THE CHART SYSTEM

If you have concluded that there is nothing new in these charts, you are right. Our chart series and tabulations present nothing which cannot be portrayed in a score of ways, and perhaps with even greater clarity. Not by way of defense, but rather by way of explanation, then, I want to call your attention to several points which in our opinion give this particular method of presenting the financial results of operations special merit and appeal.

First, you will note the complete absence of narrative. There is no opportunity for one reviewing the figures to bog down under the weight of particular words or phrases which may be chosen by an individual to explain a given variation in operating results. In the course of presenting the charts to our Executive Committee, the chart supervisor is always prepared to answer questions, or even to propose an answer without question, giving the background reasons for sharp variations in current data against the past or against forecasts. However, the primary purpose of reviewing data presented on the charts is to point up the places where further analysis, review and attention may be desirable or necessary. The charts are intended to show what happened in terms of *profit return on investment,* and to put the finger on the broad underlying factors which caused the results to be what they were. This identification of broad factors leading to a particular result enables the Executive Committee to raise questions with a general manager regarding possible trouble spots and, of course, may lead to further analysis and presentation.

Second, note the comparative ease with which the attention of an entire group can be held to one item at the same time. I imagine most of us have had some experience in analyzing schedules, tabulations, charts and the like with a group of men, each of whom has the data in hand, on a table or elsewhere, and have had to deal with the perplexing problem presented by the proneness of each individual comprising the group to pursue his own analysis in his own way. The manner in which we use these charts minimizes this problem. You can be pretty well assured that each member of the group is giving attention to the same item at the same time.

Third, more or less rigid rules govern the assembly of data for the presentation. To the maximum extent possible the data for all periods shown on the charts are on a uniform basis and afford common measurement of performance for all investment lines. If we find that changing conditions require a new approach to presenting any one or more of the chart series, then all the data for the current year and the 10 preceding years are re-set on the new basis. We all know the loss of confidence in financial presentations that can be experienced when those using the data are able to allege, and perhaps to show, that a lack of uniformity or comparability has destroyed their value. To a very large extent we avoid that pitfall by keeping our charts comparable throughout.

Fourth, strict adherence to format is observed until such time as it becomes clear that a change would substantially improve the presentation. Then a new format is brought into use, complete at one time, including a re-set for the entire 10-year period. Admittedly, this means slow progress at times in improvement of format, because a helpful minor change brought to light by experience must be held on the shelf until an important change or an aggregate of minor changes makes it worthwhile to modify the whole format.

This chart series was inaugurated more than 30 years ago—in 1919, to be exact. We consider it a tribute to the foresight of those who designed and installed it that whereas the format has been changed and perhaps improved several times, *the basic concept which emphasizes return on investment, supported by the factors contributing to it, has not given way to any other.*

Fifth, the Executive Committee, for whose use these charts are primarily maintained, makes the rules governing the division of lines of business into chart series; and the classification of financial data into the several items which are set forth in the presentation. To be sure, the Executive Committee requests and receives the recommendations of the Treasurer, but in the final analysis it is the Committee's decision, after full consideration of all the pros and cons presented by the Treasurer, which is final.

This approach to data presentation, i.e., as a rule by decision of the executive management group—the group by which the data are to be used—serves to remove a potentially wide area for possible disagreement on the classification of the basic data to be presented. Disagreement in these matters dissipates energies and dilutes the value-in-use of internal financial reporting. We are disposed to think our approach to this phase of the problem goes a long way toward getting the maximum value out of presentation of the financial results of our operations.

CALCULATION OF RETURN ON INVESTMENT

You will note that on this chart series we calculate the return on investment on the gross value of plant and working capital rather than on stockholder-invested capital. Calculations based on stockholder-invested capital would require the deduction of reserves and liabilities from the cost of plant and working capital. The general managers of the Company are responsible for the production and sale of the products assigned to them, and for the necessary investment in plant facilities and working capital. The charts are uniform and are designed to afford a comparison of past and current performance for the same operating investment, as well as a comparison with the performance of other operating investments made in corresponding periods.

In this chart series we are seeking a clear portrayal of the profitableness of the employment of plant property and working capital. Funds provided by reserves and liabilities are invested for varying periods of time in operating properties upon which a profit must be earned if a business is to be successful, but these funds are not reflected in stockholder-invested capital. You will readily appreciate, therefore, that a deduction for liabilities and reserves from the amount invested in operating properties would show a fluctuation in operating investment due to growth of reserves and change in amount of liabilities, which, in turn, would produce such a distortion in the return on investment as to render meaningless the very figures intended to disclose the profitableness of employment of plant property and working capital.

It is entirely proper, in some instances and under some conditions, to measure corporate-entity profit performance against stockholder-invested capital, and we do it ourselves for many purposes. But it would not serve our purpose in the chart series. I am sure you will agree, upon brief reflection, that for all purposes of securing an indication of the profitableness of dollars devoted to plant and working capital—which dollars must at some time be returned intact to the corporate entity—the dollar profits made during each and every period of the use of the property must be related to the total dollars dedicated to the particular operation.

CONSTRUCTION OF THE CHARTS

The charts and tabulations which we show to our Executive Committee in Wilmington are hand-drawn on cardboard measuring 30 by 40 inches. The letters, numerals, and arrows are purchased from a supplier of such items. They come coated with an adhesive and are pasted on the boards by our chart clerks. Each chart or tabulation is mounted in a metal frame suspended on wheels so that it can be moved from one place to another in the chart room on specially designed and constructed overhead track. The network of track is so arranged that in a matter of seconds any series of charts can be brought to the central display point for review.

We are aware that presentation of this type of data is more and more being made by means of projection on a screen. The projection method enjoys some flexibility over our method but we have not yet found that a clear visual presentation of our charts can be obtained by projection in the physical setup presently at our disposal. In addition, we find that the preparation of material for screen projection requires time, skills and processing equipment which we are not yet prepared to devote to it. There has been some improvement in projection equipment and methods since the end of the war, and no doubt still further improvements are in the offing. We do not intend to lag behind where progress is being made, and it is entirely possible that we shall at some future date abandon the hand-drawn charts conveyed on overhead track in favor of some projection method.

CONCLUSION

In closing, permit me to say that we who are charged with varying degrees of responsibility for the financial and accounting matters of our respective companies must remain alert, must continue in our determination to find and employ the most effective means of presenting financial data to executive management. Our success in doing this is so closely linked with the effective application of executive management talent that it is not out of order to say that effective internal reporting is quite as important to a business organization as good external reporting.

Return on Investment *

Earl J. Wipfler

In judging the management of a company, the stockholders' primary interest is in the relationship of earnings and dividends to the cost of their investment. This relationship is also most significant to prospective investors interested in purchasing additional securities issued by the company.

It is only natural that this stockholder and investor interest is reflected by management. Accordingly, its policies and plans are directed toward the goal of realizing the maximum net income on the capital invested in the business. This basic ratio is the yardstick for measurement of financial success.

RETURN ON INVESTMENT DEFINED

For Monsanto, "return on investment" means the relationship of net income for a period of time to the average dollars of capital invested in a specific activity at the beginning and end of a period. The accompanying table shows the calculation of return on investment for the year 1951. Note that "investment" is composed of the gross assets.

The reserve for depreciation is not deducted from the gross asset value of property since it represents the retention in the business of the funds required to keep intact the original investment by the stockholders. Actually, the fixed assets are used to produce net income during their entire life, and therefore the full cost value is considered a part of investment until they are retired from use. Current liabilities, reserve for pensions and employees' bonuses, and the minority interests of our subsidiary companies are deducted from the gross assets to obtain the net investment.

"Net income," as used in the calculation, is the net income after all costs and expenses. The percentage of return on investment based on net income after taxes is the principal yardstick. However, we also determine

* Reprinted by permission of the publisher from *A Program of Financial Planning and Control: The Monsanto Chemical Company*, Financial Management Series, no. 103 (New York: American Management Association, 1953), pp. 6–10. Mr. Wipfler is Assistant Comptroller of the Monsanto Chemical Company.

the return of net income before taxes in order to make comparisons which eliminate the effect of changes in tax rates.

MONSANTO CHEMICAL COMPANY AND CONSOLIDATED SUBSIDIARIES
CALCULATION OF RETURN ON INVESTMENT
FOR THE YEAR 1951
(In thousands of dollars)

| | As of December 31 | |
	1951	1950
Investment:		
Current assets	$116,141	$111,375
Investments and miscellaneous assets	12,636	4,655
Property (gross)	201,240	166,299
Deferred charges	2,152	1,379
Total	$332,169	$283,708
Deduct:		
Current liabilities	$ 52,303	$ 23,230
Employees' bonus awards payable beyond one year	1,608	1,036
Reserves for pensions and employees' bonus— unawarded	9,045	8,781
Minority interests in subsidiary companies	2,083	1,936
Total deductions	$ 65,039	$ 34,983
Net investment	$267,130	$248,725

Average of investments at December 31, 1951 and 1950	$257,928
Net income for the year 1951:	
Before income taxes	$ 62,121
After income taxes	23,478
Return on investment:	
On net income before taxes	24.1%
On net income after taxes	9.1

In addition to the capital investment just described, it is necessary to make adjustments for comparative purposes, such as:

1. Eliminating large excess cash and securities balances over normal requirements. This condition usually occurs for a short period of time after obtaining funds to finance periodic construction programs.

2. Elimination of the cost of fixed assets for major projects which are uncompleted and not in operation. Since there can be no income on such projects, this elimination provides a more comparable rate of return.

We feel that this concept of "return on investment" is a better yardstick for measurement of financial success than the concept of "return on net worth." With the passing of time a company may change its fiscal program, establish or reverse special reserves, or revise its depreciation policy. Changes of this nature have no effect on our concept of investment, and therefore we obtain a reliable and consistent base for measuring the rate of return.

USE OF RETURN ON INVESTMENT BY MANAGEMENT

While management is particularly interested in the rate of return on investment for the company, including its consolidated subsidiaries, there are other uses of this ratio—for example, return realized on:

1. Each operating division and subsidiary company.
2. Individual products.
3. Proposed projects covering new or expanded facilities.

Among the reports we issue in which reference is made to return on investment are:

1. The monthly directors' report, which contains a statement setting forth the percentage of return on investment based on net income and net income before taxes. The return for each operating division and subsidiary company is shown, as well as that for the consolidated picture.

2. A report covering our income budget for the coming year, which is received in December of each year by the Executive Committee and the Directors. The budgeted return on net income before and after taxes is shown on these statements along with the actual return for the previous seven years. In addition to this report a presentation of the budget is made in chart form.

3. The monthly financial reports, furnished by the Comptroller, in which the various division managers are advised of the rate of return for the month and year to date. Our top management can readily determine from these reports the trend of the company's progress in achieving the goal of obtaining the maximum return on the capital invested and can use it as a basis for determining which divisions or subsidiary companies need corrective investigation.

APPLICATION TO INDIVIDUAL PRODUCTS

Another important use of the per cent of return on investment is for the individual products of the company. Space will not permit a discussion of the methods used in determining the investment and net income for each product. However, our definition of net income and investment previously described is also applicable to individual products.

The rate of return on investment for each product is of great value to management. It gives the information necessary to appraise properly the divisional and company rates of return. The investment in those products which are not showing adequate returns as well as unprofitable products, can readily be determined. Studies can be made for these products to determine what corrective measures are required.

Further, it may be determined that rates of return on investment not economically justifiable are being made on some products. In such cases, a reduction in sales prices may result in greater volume, thereby enhancing the over-all profit of the company.

ESTIMATING RETURN ON NEW PROJECTS

This gauge is also used most effectively as a basis for evaluating appropriation requests covering projects requiring new fixed capital. In order to determine the return on investment for each of these projects, it is necessary to estimate capital requirements and annual new earnings.

FIGURE 2

FACTORS USED IN DETERMINING RETURN ON INVESTMENT FOR NEW PROJECTS

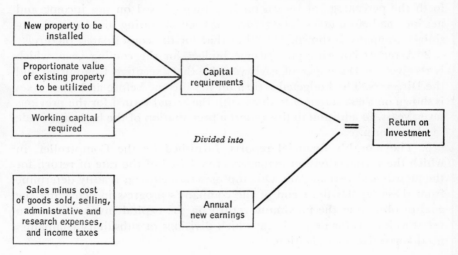

The formula for determining return on investment on such new projects (Figure 2) is divided into two parts, which are: (1) estimated capital requirements and (2) estimated annual new earnings.

1. The three factors taken into consideration in arriving at the capital requirements are:

    a. New property to be installed.

    b. Proportionate value of existing property to be utilized.

    c. Working capital required.

2. Estimated annual new earnings, the second part of the formula, are based on sales quantities and prices determined by the sales department, less all costs and expenses.

The resulting estimated return on investment is one of the primary considerations of our Executive Committee and Board of Directors in determining whether these new projects will be approved. When approved projects are completed and have been in operation for six months, a report is made showing a comparison of the actual investment, earnings, and return with the estimates.

It is generally known that the chemical industry is a "growth industry" —that huge sums are constantly needed for plant expansion. A company such as ours may double its plant investment within a few years. The investment of large sums in projects which fail to produce an adequate return could mean the difference between success and failure. It is imperative, therefore, that all estimates of new capital requirements and their estimated return should be most realistic. It has been our experience that the actual returns are as much or more than the estimates.

*

In conclusion, let me summarize the use of return on investment as a basic factor in planning the operations of the company:

First, as a guide to the efficiency of current operations as compared to past periods on a division and company-wide basis.

Second, as a yardstick for measuring our budgeted performance for the coming year against past years, again on a division and company-wide basis.

Third, as a basis for determining planning to increase returns on individual products.

Finally, as a means for appraising the adequacy of expected return on contemplated new and expanded facilities.

Return on Invested Capital*

T. G. Mackensen

As men advance to positions of responsibility in management, it is only natural that their judgments remain heavily weighted with their specialty training and background.

Yet, across the collective judgments of management, runs a certain age-old fundamental principle around which all business enterprise revolves, and which was the original and primary reason for forming the business—to earn a profit on the capital employed.

I shall first endeavor to show how in our company we attempt to rally the diverse talents and capacities of management around this principle, and then discuss some of the techniques we employ in applying it.

THE SUCCESSFUL COMPANY

Among the characteristics of a successful business enterprise are expanding sales, increased employment and production, respected name, dollars of profit, acceptable products and services, and many others. All of these are unquestionably desirable, yet separately or together they are not enough to guarantee continued existence or growth. One other important characteristic is needed—the ability to earn a satisfactory return on the capital employed.

Increased sales volume is at best a short-term indication of successful growth and, without additional information, must be viewed as such. In the long run, it may prove to be a misleading guidepost if there is not a proper return on the capital necessary to support those sales. True growth comes from the ability of management to employ successfully additional capital at a satisfactory rate of return. This is the final criterion of the soundness and strength of a company's growth, for in a free competitive economy capital gravitates toward the more profitable enterprises. The company that is merely expanding at declining rates of return

* Reprinted by permission of the publisher from *How H. J. Heinz Manages Its Financial Planning and Controls*, Financial Management Series, no. 106 (New York: American Management Association, 1953), pp. 37–45. Mr. Mackensen is Coordinator, Special Accounting Studies, of the H. J. Heinz Company.

on investment will eventually be brought to a stop for lack of expansion capital.

Thus any appraisal of a company's effectiveness must be based on the successful employment of capital. Proposed projects and activities should be evaluated in the final analysis in the light of their demands on company assets and their probability of earning a satisfactory return on those assets. Projects that fail to meet this standard have an exhausting effect that tends to neutralize the value of other projects and may seriously limit the company's ability to press advantages in more promising areas. The over-all ability of a company to employ its present assets profitably and to develop opportunities for the successful employment of additional capital is dependent upon the individual contributions of its various activities and products and their opportunities for true growth.

THREE CATEGORIES OF PROFIT POTENTIAL

The 57 Varieties, over the many years, have undergone extensive changes in so far as the composition of the line is concerned. This continuing evolution is, of course, characteristic of any long-established business. In view of the ever-changing nature of things, we find it very helpful in keeping our long-range sights in focus to have an awareness that, as of any given time, our entire line is divisible into three categories of profit potential. These are:

1. *The Strong and Established Items of the Line.* These are the products on which the company depends for adequate dollar profits to meet dividend requirements and to provide capital for expansion. They are capable of further growth and produce a satisfactory return on their investment. Normally, these are the products that should constitute the major portion of sales volume and command the major portion of capital investment. They are entitled to priority in day-to-day managerial attention to assure that they remain strong and flourish in accordance with their possibilities for as many years into the future as possible.

2. *Products That Are New and As Yet Unproved.* These are the products that management believes to have extraordinary growth possibilities and is willing to subsidize during their development period. Since their justification lies in the expectation of future profits, they require specialized attention and frequent review and re-appraisal as experience and knowledge are aquired. To assure an adequate flow of such promising new products, there should be an effective research and development program.

3. *Products That Have Passed Their Peak in Growth and Profitability.* These products can justify little consideration for increased capital investment, since they offer no reasonable prospect for future growth and improved profit contribution. Many are logical items for pruning so that

their capital requirements and managerial demands can be diverted to more profitable products.

We endeavor to maintain a sound financial balance among these three groups of products. The company's strength today is dependent upon Group 1, the predominant items of the line producing a satisfactory return on the capital they employ. The future depends on Group 2, the flow of new products that is needed to perpetuate the vitality of the line. Group 3, the products that have passed their peak in growth and profitability, can seriously sap the company's strength, both present and future, unless eliminations are made from time to time.

RECORDS FOR EACH PRODUCT LINE

Experience has shown us, also, that no class of expense or investment remains fixed in amount over a period of continuing expansion in volume, even though it may be called fixed during a specific limited interval within the growth period. Accordingly, since we cannot expect profits to improve automatically with volume increases, we have adopted the view that management must have an effective program for the employment of capital if it is to realize an adequate rate of return on the assets it employs.

In order that our management will have the necessary facts and figures to aid in making its decisions, we augment the usual operating income statements, wherein profits are measured against sales, with records of capital employed and rates of return on investment for each of our product lines. These records are kept on a consistent basis, and comparative figures for a long term of years, including the current year's budget, are in handy form for ready reference. We group *The 57 Varieties* into a lesser number of related product lines, and we strive to make our allocations accurate and realistic, so that the resulting figures will represent as nearly as possible the results for each product line as if it were a separate business.

I shall try by means of four simplified exhibits to show the methods employed by our company in allocating capital to product lines and in making the rate of return on investment determinations. All the figures used are purely hypothetical, but they have been set up in such a way as to show the unfavorable results that can easily accrue over a period of time if the rate of return on investment is not carefully controlled and steps are not taken to correct adverse trends.

These exhibits will illustrate four product lines—A, B, C, and D—and will show comparative figures for two years, designated as "base year" and "current year." These are not successive years, but embrace a longer interval for purposes of this presentation in order better to emphasize the changes that can take place over several years.

OPERATING INCOME COMPARED

Chart 19 is a comparative income statement showing sales, costs, and operating income for the four products mentioned earlier for the base year and the current year.

CHART 19

MULTI-PRODUCT COMPANY
COMPARATIVE OPERATING INCOME STATEMENT
(In thousands)

	Total Sales		Costs				Operating income *	
			Direct		Prorated			
Base year:	Amount	% of total	Amount	% of sales	16.1% of sales		Amount	% of sales
Product A....	$ 39,300	40	$ 28,200	71.7	$ 6,300		$ 4,800	12.2
Product B....	29,500	30	21,900	74.5	4,800		2,800	9.4
Product C....	19,600	20	14,400	73.1	3,100		2,100	10.8
Product D....	9,800	10	7,700	78.3	1,600		500	5.1
Total....	$ 98,200	100	$ 72,220	73.5	$15,800		$10,200	10.4
					17% of sales			
Current year:								
Product A....	48,100	25	34,300	71.4	8,200		5,600	11.6
Product B....	96,200	50	71,400	74.2	16,300		8,500	8.8
Product C....	38,500	20	28,000	72.8	6,600		3,900	10.2
Product D....	9,600	5	7,500	78.0	1,600		500	5.2
Total....	$192,400	100	$141,200	73.4	$32,700		$18,500	9.6

* Before interest on borrowed money and federal income taxes.

Operating income is defined as the profit from operations before deduction of interest on borrowed capital employed and before federal income taxes. Sales dollars are analyzed by product lines, and changes in product mix are disclosed by showing the percentage that each line bears to total company sales. Cost of product, transportation from factory to sales warehouses, and product advertising are charged directly to each product line on an actual basis. Sales branch operating expense is prorated on the basis of sales, since *The 57 Varieties* are sold in mixtures. Institutional advertising and general administrative expenses are also prorated on the sales basis. The objective is to charge as many of the costs as practical on an actual basis, in order that a minimum need be prorated. Operating income is shown in dollar amount and as a per cent of sales.

The example reflects a considerable increase in dollar sales for the current year over the base year. Similarly, a handsome increase in dollars of operating income is shown. While a slight decline in rate of return

on sales is indicated (10.4 per cent to 9.6 per cent), it is nevertheless understandable that the performance shown could appear quite acceptable
in the absence of any statement showing the return in terms of assets
employed.

THE BALANCE SHEET AS A BASIS

Chart 20 is a comparative statement of total assets employed. It
represents the asset side of the balance sheet averaged for the four quarters
of each year shown.

CHART 20

MULTI-PRODUCT COMPANY
COMPARATIVE STATEMENT OF ASSETS EMPLOYED
(Four-quarter average, in thousands)

	Base year			Current year		
	Total	Prorated to all sales	Analyzed by product	Total	Prorated to all sales	Analyzed by product
Cash	$ 6,100	$ 6,100	$	$ 12,100	$12,100	$
Accounts receivable...	4,800	4,800		10,000	10,000	
Inventories	20,100		20,100	55,700		55,700
Other current assets ..	600	600		1,700	1,700	
Total current assets.	$31,600	$11,500	$20,100	$ 79,500	$23,800	$55,700
Investments	excluded			excluded		
Plant & equipment net	17,200	2,100	15,100	45,000	4,600	40,800
Construction in progress	excluded			excluded		
Other fixed assets	400	400		1,200	1,200	
Total fixed assets...	$17,600	$ 2,500	$15,100	$ 46,600	$ 5,800	$40,800
Total assets employed	$49,200	$14,000	$35,200	$126,100	$29,600	$96,500

In order to determine the assets by product lines, it is first necessary
to exclude certain items appearing on the balance sheet, because they were
not used in the production of operating income. Investments that represent outside financial holdings are thus excluded, as is the income from
such investments. Similarly, construction in progress is excluded until
such time as the facility under construction comes into use. Funds obtained to finance such construction programs would also be excluded
from the cash allocated to current operations.

The treatment accorded depreciation might well be mentioned. We
have elected to show fixed assets at net depreciated values. We take the
position that the depreciation reserve represents that portion of the initial
investment which has been recovered through charge-offs against opera-

tions and is re-invested in other fixed assets, or is being used as working capital. To the extent that recovery and re-investment have been made, we relieve the old asset of the obligation of earning a return. Instead, we look to the new asset in which the value is now lodged for such earnings. Eliminating depreciation from the base gives a realistic investment figure which our operating people can accept without raising the question of duplication of asset values. At the same time, this treatment places a relatively greater demand for earnings on the new, modern installations than on the old, worn, and partially obsolete ones.

Management is charged with the responsibility of earning a rate of return on all the capital it employs, whether it be equity capital or borrowed money. The risks to financial security from the use of borrowed capital justify the requirement that such funds be placed at least on a par with equity capital in so far as earnings requirements are concerned. Accordingly, we do not deduct liabilities; and, in compensation, rate of return is computed before deduction of interest paid for the use of outside capital.

DETERMINATION OF INVESTMENT BY PRODUCT LINES

The next step is to determine asset usage by product lines.

Cash. We prorate cash to product lines on the basis of sales. Total cash requirements of each product line for costs, equipment replacements, interest, income taxes, and dividends approximate sales income from each product line. Therefore, sales is an appropriate basis for allocation of cash.

Accounts Receivable. We prorate accounts receivable on a sales basis. In our company, credit terms on all our varieties are identical; and, therefore, every dollar of sales is regarded to be outstanding for the same average length of time.

Inventories. We analyze inventories by product lines. Finished goods are readily identifiable, while work in process and raw materials require somewhat more detailed analysis to trace them to the end products.

Other Current Assets. This is a small item with us, and we prorate it on the basis of sales.

Factory Plant and Equipment. We analyze this important item by product. Where an entire factory is devoted to one product, the allocation is, of course, simple. Where more than one product is produced at a factory, departmental breakdowns are made, and from these we arrive at allocations by product lines.

Administrative and Sales Facilities. This item includes general offices, sales warehouses, etc., and is prorated on the basis of sales.

Other Fixed Assets. This is another small item with us, and we prorate it on the basis of sales.

The resulting analysis is Chart 21, where the applicable balance sheet values appear by the product lines. Inventory, factory plant and equipment, the prorated assets (cash, receivables, etc.), and the total assets are shown for each product line both in total amount and in usage per dollar of sales. Such a statement is indispensable in measuring the efficiency with which capital is employed. This is particularly true with respect to inventories. When all other methods of controlling inventories fail, it discloses when a need for tightening of purse strings is indicated.

This record is valuable, also, for projecting capital requirements when changes in volume levels or in product mix are contemplated.

CHART 21

MULTI-PRODUCT COMPANY
ALLOCATION OF INVESTMENT BY PRODUCT LINE
(In thousands)

	Net sales	Analyzed by product					Prorated	Total assets employed	
		Inventories		Factory plant & equipment		Cash accts. rec., etc.			
Base year:	Amount	Amount	per $ sales	Amount	per $ sales	14.3¢ per $ sales		Amount	Per $ sales
Product A	$ 39,300	$ 8,000	20.4¢	$ 7,100	18.2¢	$ 5,600		$ 20,700	52.9¢
Product B	29,500	7,500	25.3	5,200	17.7	4,200		16,900	57.3
Product C	19,600	3,300	16.7	2,800	14.1	2,800		8,900	45.1
Product D	9,800	1,300	13.2	....	...	1,400		2,700	27.5
Total	$ 98,200	$20,100	20.4	$15,100	15.4	$14,000		$ 49,200	50.1
Current year:						15.4¢ per $ sales			
Product A	48,100	11,800	24.5	9,200	19.1	7,400		28,400	59.0
Product B	96,200	35,400	36.8	25,100	26.1	14,800		75,300	78.3
Product C	38,500	7,100	18.4	6,500	16.9	5,900		19,500	50.7
Product D	9,600	1,400	14.5	....	...	1,500		2,900	29.9
Total	$192,400	$55,700	28.9	$40,800	21.2	$29,600		$126,100	65.5

COMPARATIVE RATES OF RETURN

Thus we arrive at the all-important exhibit (Chart 22) which shows —for each product line—sales, assets employed, and operating income expressed as an amount and as a per cent return on sales and on assets employed.

It is to this statement that we look for the results earlier discussed. It will be recalled from Chart 19 that, while the amount of operating income practically doubled, the rate of return on sales showed an apparently minor decline from 10.4 per cent to 9.6 per cent. When the same dollars of operating income are measured against the assets employed, it will be seen that the rate of return on investment decreased from 20.8 per cent to 14.6 per cent, a substantial reduction in profitability. Thus the conventional profit and loss statement measuring profit in terms of sales dollars gives way to the more relevant comparison wherein profit is measured in terms of assets employed.

CHART 22

MULTI-PRODUCT COMPANY
COMPARATIVE RATES OF RETURN
(In thousands)

	Total sales		Assets employed		Operating income *		
Base year:	Amount	% of total	Amount	Per $ sales	Amount	Per cent return On sales	on assets
Product A....	$ 39,300	40	$ 20,700	52.9	$ 4,800	12.2%	23.1%
Product B....	29,500	30	16,900	57.3	2,800	9.4	16.4
Product C....	19,600	20	8,900	45.1	2,100	10.8	23.9
Product D....	9,800	10	2,700	27.5	500	5.1	18.5
Total	$ 98,200	100	$ 49,200	50.1	$10,200	10.4	20.8
Current year:							
Product A....	48,100	25	28,400	59.0	5,600	11.6	19.7
Product B....	96,200	50	75,300	78.3	8,500	8.8	11.2
Product C....	38,500	20	19,500	50.7	3,900	10.2	20.1
Product D....	9,600	5	2,900	29.9	500	5.2	17.2
Total	$192,400	100	$126,100	65.5	$18,500	9.6	14.6

* Before interest on borrowed money and federal income taxes.

This statement makes possible investigation into at least four major areas, and in each of them there are questions to which satisfactory answers must be found.

1. *Increases in Investment.* What has happened to the promised rates of return on the appropriations approved during the period? Were they overstated? Mythical? Unattainable? Were costs understated? Why was so much approved for Product B when its profits were subnormal? Is Product A suffering from lack of capital expenditure? Are we employing existing assets at capacity and most profitably? Are we deploying available capital to its most useful purpose?

2. *Product Mix.* The threefold increase in sales for Product B is accompanied by a fivefold increase in assets for that line, and its profits were below normal, measured both as per cent of sales and per cent of assets employed. Increases in profitability did not come automatically with volume. What must be done to bring this important product into a better earnings position? Are we penetrating a market that is saturated?

While Product A has had a modest increase in sales, are we developing a sufficient market share? Are we keeping pace with industry growth? Is sufficient management attention being given to this important product?

Are we alerted to possible deterioration of some varieties? What provisions are we making to replace them? Are we holding on to unprofitable varieties too long?

Is the unsatisfactory showing of a product line due to problems involving particular items within the line?

3. *Volume of Sales.* While a large increase is apparent, we must ask ourselves what per cent of total market we have. Have we lost ground in any of our lines, particularly Product A? Have we gained ground in any of our lines, particularly Product B? How have we fared in relation to our competitors in regard to share of the market?

4. *Operating Costs.* We notice a consistent drop in profit per dollar of sales. In what areas of expense has this occurred? Is our pricing policy achieving our purposes? Is our budget holding in check both our manufacturing costs and commercial expenses?

These and many other areas of investigation are opened. Through the answers we seek for them, we attempt to outline a balanced program for management, alerting the members to the most profitable employment of capital and helping them understand the meaning of even minor shifts which might be compounded into major situations which would hamper future earning power.

Leasing versus Owning

The subject of leasing versus owning is no more than a specialized application of capital management. In determining the most productive means of putting capital to work, we are faced with such questions as whether to make or buy, to lease or own, etc. In seeking the basis for decision, many considerations will appear, such as the availability of funds, the stability of demand, the reliability of outside sources, and the seasonality of requirements, to name a few.

In those cases where the decision is not forced by some obvious consideration, and where alternative choices are open to management, the ultimate criterion for decision is the adequacy of the rate of return on the capital involved.

In our manufacturing operations, we own practically all the land, buildings, and equipment we require. We do, however, supplement our outright ownership in this area with short-term leases for facilities such as temporary warehouse space for peak-load, seasonal requirements. At the same time, in our selling and distribution areas, we acquire most of our branch warehouses on long-term leases. We find that outside investors have funds for such purposes on which they are willing to accept lower rates of return than we must demand from our working capital.

In all cases, however, the final test applied is the best use of capital measured by the rate of return it provides.

D. MANAGEMENT AUDITS

Outline for a Management Audit *

Metropolitan Life Insurance Company

How productive is your management. Does it measure up to present day requirements?

Most progressive companies make it a point to audit their accounts at least once a year in order to establish the adequacy and accuracy of such accounts and to reveal fiscal weaknesses that may need correction. The periodic inventorying and appraising of physical assets is also an accepted practice.

There is need for the same sort of stock-taking as applied to the management of business. This can be accomplished through the medium of a management audit. Through this device, a business executive undertakes, in effect, to back off and survey his company critically and objectively. A comprehensive management check-list is helpful in this connection.

PROBLEMS OF THE SMALL ORGANIZATION

The smaller organization has essentially the same management problems as a large concern. Naturally, the emphasis on specific problems is different in the small company because of the close personal contact between management and employees and because the executive must necessarily be a jack of all trades. However, these differences are primarily superficial and they should not blind the small company's management to the real nature of their job.

The check list shown in this report raises a wide variety of questions on basic management problems. The importance of each problem will naturally vary with the individual concern, depending on its size or its field of operations. Some of the questions are more important to large organizations than to small ones, and vice versa. However, all companies, irrespective of their size or industry, will find in these questions an outline of their basic management problems.

To use the check list effectively, attention should be paid to the sub-

* Taken from *Outline for a Management Audit,* A Report for Metropolitan Group Policyholders (New York: Metropolitan Life Insurance Company, 1947). It should be noted that the original outline had an interesting check list of questions in the functional fields of finance, procurement, inventories, traffic and transportation, insurance, office management, business research, personnel management, production management, marketing management, and public relations.

stance rather than to the exact wording of each question, because the wording may seem to be directed at the problems of the large company. Conversely, the wording will be pointed toward the small company if the problem involved is of greater importance to it.

Organization

1. Is your organization set up in accordance with a definite plan, or has it developed in a "hit-or-miss" fashion with little or no recognition of basic functions or logical groupings of activities?

(a) Have you conducted organization surveys to correct wartime distortions or to adjust to postwar changes in the volume or nature of operations?

2. Are the functions and responsibilities clearly defined for each department and division of your business and for individual executives?

(a) Are lines of authority clear-cut and direct?

(b) Does every individual know to whom he reports and who reports to him?

3. Has the organization been put on paper in the form of carefully prepared organization charts or written outlines of duties?

(a) Is there some provision for keeping these up to date?

4. Has your policy of centralizing the administration of various functions or activities been such as to get the maximum benefits from the specialization of personnel—at the same time, have you had in mind the possible value of some decentralization of management as a means of executive development and of encouraging initiative?

5. Do you follow the principle of an understudy for every executive position to provide for contingencies and to insure continuity?

(a) Have you some means of locating and developing potential executive ability?

(b) Have you some plan for rewarding executives in proportion to results secured?

6. Do you employ committees or some other practical means of coordinating all the different phases or activities of your company so that the organization operates as a team and not as a collection of individuals and independent departments or divisions?

7. Are you making the best use of the "line and staff" organization plan as a means of providing specialized staff assistance at various organization levels?

(a) Are line and staff relationships and authorities clearly established?

Executive Control

1. Are you making the most effective use of control techniques, i.e., the establishment of practical standards or yardsticks, the measurement and reporting of performance, and the initiation of corrective action?

   (a) Does your control procedure serve to spotlight conditions requiring action in time for such action to be taken?

2. Is your accounting system designed to furnish significant control information both by functions and by departments?

3. Do you get current and reliable information on the costs of individual products or services, processes, customers, and localities?

4. Do you operate under a budget?

   (a) Are budget allowances and classifications designed to reflect individual executive responsibilities? Is there provision for frequent comparison of budgeted with actual performance?

5. Have you taken steps to develop or to reinstill a spirit of cost consciousness throughout your organization so that each action will be weighed in terms of the costs involved?

   (a) Do you hold regular cost analysis meetings of operating executives and supervisors for this purpose?

6. Have you examined and appraised all your control reports and records from the standpoints of (a) the value, adequacy, and timeliness of the information furnished; (b) economy of executive time; (c) cost of preparation? Do you check this at least once a year?

   (a) Do you require that those submitting reports include a brief interpretation of the significant points revealed?

7. Is there provision for acquainting executive and supervisory personnel with the company's basic policies?

Management Audits Simplified *

Jackson Martindell

Intimate knowledge of the corporate history of an organization and of the attainments, personalities and capacities of a company's officers must be assembled before any sense of the degree of team spirit imbuing an organization can be grasped. This is the first indispensable step to management appraisal.

There is no way whereby this part of an audit can be simplified. A comprehensive study of the personalities involved is required because the activities and modes of conduct of the individual corporation are determined by the character of the men who lead it and the relationship between them.

Intimate knowledge, in this sense, does not require personal intimacy. The career of the average corporate officer is well documented. The viewpoints of his associates, colleagues, customers, suppliers and rivals regarding his abilities and characteristics are readily enough obtainable for sound appraisal of each man to be possible by any trained inquirer. In fact, the Institute's attempt at simplification of corporate analysis demonstrates that the best judgments regarding the personalities involved are usually obtainable from outside sources.

Requisite information concerning the management personnel of a corporation is obtainable in many quarters. Retired executives and employees are among the valuable sources of such information. The opinions of these men are usually unbiased, or, if biased, are usually swayed only by concern for the welfare of the organization in which they spent their business lives. Their philosophy of management may be outmoded, their grasp of production or marketing may be that of a past generation, but their sense of the devotion to duty of individual corporate officers is uncannily accurate.

Other, and equally important informative sources as to the qualities of men in management are labor unions, credit agencies, banks, investment brokers, officials of insurance companies, auditors, executives of advertising agencies, and the company's own competitors and main suppliers.

* Reprinted by permission of the publisher from *The Corporate Director*, Special Issue no. 15 (December, 1951), pp. 1–6. Mr. Martindell is President of the American Institute of Management.

The latter are particularly important. The company's customers are an obvious source of sound judgment.

In simplifying the process of evolution, the Institute has found that a cooperative management willing to undertake evaluation of itself, upon the basis of the Institute's 10 Functional Categories of the Rating System, is of great value. This does not mean that if the management rates itself, the Institute need not thereafter rate it. On the contrary, the weighting given by the management to the various functional subdivisions of its own organization is evidence of the relative importance placed by the executive group upon the separate phases of its activities. It indicates the quality which men in management ascribe to the functions which they are called upon to carry out.

Under the Institute's simplified procedure, companies are now asked to appraise themselves under each of the ten categorial subdivisions, to give the reasons for the weightings they award themselves, and to supply supplementary information in substantiation of their findings.

The attempt at justification of a self-rating compels the officers to re-examine the findings it has arrayed, and assists toward better understanding of the varying degrees of importance and excellence of its several operations.

It is the Institute's experience that only after such self-appraisal has been supplied by the company, individual officers and directors need be approached directly. This is because management evaluation must not at first be concerned with broad generalities as to what a company's officers claim to have achieved in the past or hope to achieve in the future, but in discovering whatever special traits may exist within the management group.

Simultaneously, the 10 largest stockholders are consulted as to what influence they believe themselves to have upon the board of directors and as to their opinion of the directorate as a whole. It does not matter whether these 10 largest stockholders are themselves members of the board. It is not in their capacity as board members that we consult them, but as representative stockholders.

Finally, a list of prepared questions is submitted to the officers and directors. The answers to these questions are intended to supplement information already gathered, or to provide information otherwise unobtainable.

SUBDIVIDING THE MANAGEMENT ANALYSIS

The American Institute of Management has subjected over 3000 corporate managements to comparative examination. In doing so, it has discovered that the basic categories of the managerial function resolve themselves to ten, no matter what the industry. These ten categories are functional subdivisions of the management process. They do not coincide with the formal structure or organization of any single corporation. They represent the functions performed by the corporation as a whole and not the form of organization adopted to carry out that function. As such, they cut across the nominal business structure. By so doing, they bring into visible relief the separate activities carried on by the several divisions of the corporation and its officers.

Economic Function

Corporations, like individuals, develop distinctive characteristics over the years. These characteristics derive from the purposes which the corporation—like the individual—attempts to accomplish, and by its habitual way of doing so. Over the span of time, each company develops its own tradition. These traditions are truly important. They express the moral quality of the whole organization; a quality which in turn depends upon the relative importance of the company's purposes.

In evaluating this, it is important to discover:

1. When, why, where and by whom the present company was founded?
2. What changes have occurred in the fundamental nature of the business? When, why and how did these occur?
3. Has the competitive standing of the company in its industry risen since the company was founded?
4. What important changes have occurred in management since the company's inception and why did these occur?
5. Has the company always enjoyed a reputation for fair dealing with all who come in contact with it?
6. What important changes have occurred in the ownership of the corporation during its life span?
7. What contribution do the company's operations make to the national economy, regardless of the size of the company?

Among leading companies which meet the Institute's rigid tests to qualify as excellent under "Economic Function" are the following: American Telephone and Telegraph Corporation; Great Atlantic and Pacific Tea Company of America; Merck and Company; National Steel Corporation; B. F. Goodrich Company; and Procter & Gamble Company. A number of smaller companies also qualify for top rating. We mention the foregoing companies mainly because their names are familiar to almost every person in the United States—perhaps because their devotion to worthy purposes has become synonymous with their names themselves.

Corporate Structure

In any continuing organization, an established way of doing things must ultimately result in a formal organizational structure. In terms of the corporation, this amounts to saying that, with the passing of time, distinct lines of communication develop within the enterprise. The way these lines of communication intersect determines how decisions are arrived at, how they are put into effect, and how and by whom their results are appraised. In certain corporations, the making of fundamental decisions is often untimely. On occasion, fundamental decisions are not even arrived at. Instead, problems are allowed to "sort themselves out." In other corporations, basic policy decisions are made but are not followed through or, too frequently, are carried out half-heartedly. In still other companies, no attempt is ever made to evaluate the results of policy decisions and the way that they have been carried out. It is astonishing that perhaps in the majority of corporations, job evaluation and merit rating has not been extended systematically up to the top executive levels.

The essential questions in corporate structure are:

1. Who exercises the principal authority?
2. How many individuals report directly to this principal authority?
3. Is the president also the general manager?
4. Is the business decentralized geographically, or is control exercised over all functions from a central point?
5. To what extent does the company operate on product-division lines?
6. Is the structure such that profitableness or unprofitableness of each product is at all times apparent to the men responsible for its supervision, and to the principal executive officers?
7. Is there a system of job evaluation and merit rating reaching up to the president himself?

In terms of corporate structure, the Institute is particularly impressed by the soundness of internal procedures and lines of communication in General Motors Corporation, General Foods Corporation, National Dairy Products Corporation, Bethlehem Steel Corporation, E. I. Du Pont de Nemours & Company, and Sears, Roebuck & Company.

Health of Earnings Growth

Because corporate taxes bear unequally upon corporations during periods of excess profits tax levies, the essential measure of the growth of earnings must be the net profit after prior charges but before taxes. Nevertheless, such earnings must be translated into dollars available to the outstanding common stock. This is particularly true in terms of growth. The Institute's studies have uncovered many examples of corporations with large apparent growth in net earnings but with virtually no growth of earnings expressed in terms of earnings available for the payment of dividends to the common stockholder.

Size of earnings is not in itself a criterion of health of earnings growth. The earnings record during years of general prosperity or of unusual temporary demand for a company's main products is no criterion whatever. Most emphatically, earnings which derive from a natural or artificial monopoly cannot be regarded as basically healthy, no matter what their size. Therefore, it is not the size of earnings alone which determines the health of earnings growth, but the conditions under which that growth has come about, its continuousness, and its ability to be sustained, at least moderately, even during depression years.

The best corporate managements pursue policies intended to prepare the company for unforeseen contingencies. As a result, the most efficiently managed corporations show satisfactory profits even during times of bad trade. How these profits are earned, whether they result largely from the sale of new products continuously generated by development and research work, or whether they merely bear a statistical relationship to the growth of population and national income, cannot be left out of account. Merck & Company, for example, now gains more than three-quarters of its profit from products—and from methods of producing them—unknown a decade ago. In numerous other companies, Procter and Gamble and the Du Pont Company being prime examples, substantially the same is true.

To arrive at a decision as to whether the growth in a corporation's earnings has been healthy, the Institute seeks to know:

1. What growth in earnings does a study of a 10, 20, and 30 year record reveal?

2. How has the company fared in all the significant trade cycles of the past 10, 20, and 30 years?

3. How have its operating ratios compared with those of its leading competitors?

4. What percentage of the company has been owned by the common stock at the close of each year since its inception?

5. Over an extended period, what has been net before taxes in % of sales?

6. Over an extended period, what has been net before taxes in % of gross fixed assets?

7. Over an extended period, what has been net before taxes in % of net investment?

Among outstanding examples of corporations whose growth of earnings has been pronouncedly healthy, the Institute regards the following companies as exemplary: U.S. Plywood Corporation; Merck & Company; E. I. Du Pont de Nemours & Company; B. F. Goodrich Company; Grand Union Company; Minnesota Mining and Manufacturing Company; Minneapolis Honeywell Regulator Company; Standard Oil Company (New Jersey); International Paper Company; Union Carbide and Carbon Corporation; Cities Service Company; Formica Company; and Marathon Corporation.

Fairness to Stockholders

So far, we have concerned ourselves with the basic factors of the company's economic function, the reputation for probity which it has earned over the years, its form of executive organization which determines whether the business will be conducted smoothly and efficiently, and the health of its earnings growth. These three points are closely interrelated and lead to the next point to be examined: What benefits the proprietors of the company have received from their investment in it, directly in the form of dividends, and indirectly in the form of growth in their equity value.

The individual investor gains no benefit from a corporation whose own advance has been at the expense of exposing the stockholder to undue risks or of failing to pay him an adequate return for the risks he has voluntarily assumed. In the course of its researches, the Institute has uncovered numerous instances of companies well-run in other respects, but whose officers have disregarded both the private interest of the shareholders and the general interest of the public. Such companies are not well conducted; their operations are out of harmony with the needs and trends of our time.

Fairness to stockholders is perhaps the most difficult category of evaluation to define. There can be few, if any, hard and fast rules whereby quality under this heading may be measured. However, comparative study within an industry gives strong evidence of managerial quality in this respect.

The questions most carefully examined by the Institute are the following:

1. What percentage of earnings available for dividends has been paid out of dividends in each of the past thirty years?

2. Is there an established dividend policy and how long has it been established?

3. Have the dividends paid out by the individual company borne the same percental relationship to earnings as in the industry as a whole?

4. Have dividends consistently been so large as to prevent an adequate rate of growth in earned surplus?

5. Has the company shown a consistent effort to deal fairly with stockholders in all respects?

The stockholder attitudes of the following corporations appear particularly impressive to the Institute: Pennsylvania Salt Manufacturing Company; Container Corporation of America; Grand Union Company; National Cash Register Corporation; CIT Financial Corporation; General Electric Company; and American Telephone and Telegraph Company.

Research and Development

It is by now an axiom of management quality that increasing attention must be paid to research and development work as the years go by. Top management which fails to give adequate attention to ground-breaking experiments is simply failing its managerial purpose.

Unfortunately, the term "experiment" is misunderstood in the average corporation. Perhaps because the chemical and petroleum industries have done an outstanding job of research, most businessmen seem to feel that unless this specific type of work is undertaken, no research worthy of the name is being done. With this attitude is coupled the apparent belief that research can stop at this point and yet prove wholly adequate. The fact is, however, that the areas in which profitable research can be undertaken are co-extensive with every activity of the corporation, no matter what the nature of its products or the scope of its operation.

The neglected areas of research, even in companies aggressive in the development of new products, are usually the following: market research is neglected or underemphasized; few companies have properly developed research as to the most fruitful forms of advertising; inquiries into economical handling, packaging, shipping, and many other individual phases of manufacturing and distribution are given insufficient attention.

Opportunities for profitable research exist even in commercial banking, although the bank's main functions are the safekeeping and employment of money. Almost every department of the average bank would benefit from the installation of new and more efficient methods. The markets available to some banks have been extended by the development and employment of new forms of the banking business. The National City Bank of New York is a case in point. As a result of investigating the potential profitableness of the small loan business, it now has more than 800,000 clients in this category and does more than 80 per cent of this type of business in the territory it serves.

Under the category "research and development" the broadest questions the Institute attempts to have answered are:

1. What research activities are conducted and how long have they been established?

2. Who is the executive head of research and what role does he play in the top management?

3. Are research budgets established by projects, or is there an over-all research allotment?

4. What has been the history of research expenditures and what results were achieved?

5. Have research activities been concentrated in one direction or do they embrace the whole scope of the company's activity?

6. What annual procedure is followed in determining the results

achieved by individual research projects and by the over-all research activity?

Self-evident examples of companies whose research and development activities have proved particularly fruitful are: Merck & Company; E. I. Du Pont de Nemours & Company; B. F. Goodrich Company; General Electric Corporation; Grand Union Company; Procter & Gamble Company; Standard Oil Company (New Jersey); Phillips Petroleum Company; Union Carbide & Carbon Corporation; and Minnesota Mining and Manufacturing Company.

Directorate Analysis

The Institute, after studying thousands of corporations, is convinced the greatest single weakness in American business organization lies in the composition of the average board of directors. Less effort is devoted towards improving this phase of the organization than to any other. Until two years ago, this was true beyond question. Since then, however, increasingly critical expressions by stockholders have led to some improvement. In fact, more than one-half of the correspondence of the American Institute of Management, in answer to inquiries from the outside, is now concerned with matters regarding directors.

In evaluating the board of directors, the crucial questions are:

1. Is the board an inside board or an outside board?

2. Who are the members of the board, and when and why was each added to the board?

3. What civic activities is each board member engaged in and what is his military record?

4. To what extent does the chief executive dominate the board of directors?

5. What percentage of the directors consists of lawyers, bankers, customers, suppliers, or competitors?

6. Which directors exercise the greatest influence over the board, and what form does that influence take?

Companies characterized by first-rate boards of directors are none too common. Certain paramount examples of excellence in this respect include the following companies: Procter & Gamble Company; General Foods Corporation; National Gypsum Company; Travelers Insurance Company; National City Bank of New York; National Cash Register Company; Pittsburgh Consolidation Coal Company; and Owens-Illinois Glass Company.

Fiscal Policies

The studies pursued by the Institute indicated that most of the financial difficulties experienced by corporations during the past thirty years have originated less in the development of an adverse economic environment than in defective fiscal policies pursued by managements. There is remarkable variance in the fiscal policies of companies, even within the same industry. During periods of general refinancing, one company may be selling preferred stock in order to retire bonds, while its competitor may be selling bonds to retire preferred stock. The former is sacrificing an immediate tax advantage in the search for long-term safety; the latter, sacrificing long-term safety in return for the temporary tax advantage.

It is astonishing that dividends being paid at the present time by many corporations are not proportioned to current additions to earned surplus, but actually constitute a liquidation of capital, without top management being aware of the fact. This is caused by the inflation from which we are suffering and by the fact that more than one management seems unaware that the cash it will ultimately require in order to replace its plant facilities at increasing costs may prove higher than the whole current depreciation charge and earnings combined. Management with a sound concept of fiscal conduct should be aware of this fact. It should be especially aware—and no difficulties prevent such awareness—that, perhaps within a decade, significant fluctuations in earnings and in the replacement cost of plant assets may occur. Proper fiscal procedures would deter management from dissipating liquid assets which may be needed to make up for the deficiency between annual depreciation charges and the replacement cost of annual wear and tear.

Sound fiscal policy must at all times be consistent, must be coordinated with the over-all needs of the enterprise, and must have the main purpose in view of preserving the corporation from perhaps unforeseeable stresses whose effects could be disastrous if the unforeseen were unprepared for.

The following questions are particularly weighty in this regard:

1. What has been the history of operating and financial ratios over an extended number of years?

2. Are daily financial reports made to the top executives?

3. What form of budgetary control is exercised?

4. Are reserves being established to cover the increased replacement cost of plant facilities over and above the depreciation charge against earnings?

5. How has expansion been financed in the past and what changes have occurred in the company's capital structure in recent years?

Financial administration is particularly laudable in the following corporations: E. I. Du Pont de Nemours and Company; Procter and Gamble Company; General Electric Company; Minneapolis-Moline Company; Electric Auto-Lite Company; National Dairy Products Corporation;

American Telephone and Telegraph Company; Hooker Electrochemical Company; Archer-Daniels-Midland Company; National Steel Corporation; St. Regis Paper Company; and International Paper Company.

Production Efficiency

Production efficiency is the outstanding contribution made to world progress by American business. The larger markets of America, and the resulting possibility of long-line productions, are in part the cause of our increasing superiority over European production methods. In turn, the vast potentialities of the American market have spurred us to surprising competitive efforts. Our competitive standing is paramount throughout the world in all mass production items.

Nevertheless, there is discernible need on the part of management to re-appraise its plant locations, the relative advantages of horizontal or vertical integration, the efficiency which might be achieved by discarding multiple product operations within one plant or vice versa; and the advantages to be gained by permitting greater autonomy at separate production centers. Labor management relations are the primary management concern today. This is certainly true of the larger corporation. Friction is less apt to develop in smaller companies between workmen and top management but the distressing effects of the employment of untrained department heads, due to a smaller area of selection, and of incompetent direction by unsatisfactory foremen are more likely to be felt.

In general, a corporation becomes successful because of the competitive superiority resulting from its lower cost methods of production. No matter what the product, this is a basic axiom of corporate progress. Therefore, production efficiency must be gauged otherwise than by mere volume of output.

The Institute, in examining a company's past record, seeks to determine:

1. What has been the growth in productivity per capita of production employees?

2. Are the company's production costs competitive with, similar to, or higher than those of the rest of the industry?

3. Do the production executives operate mainly on the floor or from behind their office desks?

4. What machinery exists for the handling of employee grievances?

5. What labor disputes have occurred in the company in recent years?

6. What percentage of the plants now in use were built for the specific operations now performed?

7. Is production [segregated so] that the profitability of each product is at all times apparent?

8. How important is the engineering division to the over-all operation?

9. What procedures are followed in job evaluation and merit rating?

Companies with outstanding production records include: Bethlehem Steel Corporation; Standard Oil Company (New Jersey); Interchemical Corporation; Fruehauf Trailer Company; A. O. Smith; Procter & Gamble Company; Olin Industries, Incorporated; E. I. Du Pont de Nemours and Company; Chrysler Corporation; Humble Oil and Refining Company; Standard Oil Company of California; Johnson and Johnson (N.J.); Borg-Warner Corporation; Signode Steel Strapping Company; Marathon Corporation; Scott Paper Company; and Dow Chemical Company.

Sales Analysis

More expressions of concern are presently being made by managements over the inadequacy of their sales division than over any other single aspect of business administration. For more than a decade, the problem of competitive selling has affected but few companies for more than a few months at a time. Some companies, because production is on an allocation basis, are now channelling their sales activity into the building of good will, a unique variant of institutional advertising. This is especially true of the General Electric Company.

In the past, the contrary has been the case. The greatest single achievement of American business has been sales promotion, exceeding even our production efficiency to the need for which it has contributed markedly. The aggressive search for markets is an American characteristic, compared with the European attitude of waiting for the purchaser to materialize. In most European companies, sales executives are not regarded as top level officers. In a number of languages, indeed, there is no phrase meaning sales manager.

The Institute gives greater weight to the sales effort than to any other single departmental activity of the corporation. The ultimate purpose of every corporation working for profit is to transform a stated sum of cash into a larger sum of cash. The incidental cost of labor, materials, and overhead are necessary expenses in this expanding transformation. They would be of no value whatever were the final product not translated into money through sales. Consequently, selling is the main single activity of any business organization. The vigor with which markets are exploited and the wisdom with which items are priced are therefore paramount evidences of managerial excellence.

In the modern world, sales are more closely related to advertising in all its forms than to direct salesman-customer contact. The supermarket has become the leading medium for distribution to the consumer. Major sales of appliances are now made through dealers who display the items in salesrooms and stores instead of by door-to-door selling as in the past. Because of this, the Institute pays increasing attention to the effectiveness of advertising policies pursued, since such policies both get the goods into the hands of dealers and out of their hands into those of the ultimate user.

The following information is sought when the Institute evaluates a sales organization:

1. How is the sales personnel selected?

2. What sales-training programs exist, and how do they operate?

3. What is the nature of the distributing organization?

4. What facilities are maintained for quick delivery and speedy repairs or replacement?

5. To what extent, and in what form, is market research conducted?

6. What routine reports are required from each segment of the sales division?

7. How are sales quotas established?

8. How does the company price its goods?

9. What is the company's advertising policy?

10. What structural link exists between advertising, selling and production?

Exceptional sales vigor is evident in the following companies: Grand Union Company; General Electric Company; Procter & Gamble Company; General Mills, Incorporated; Sun Oil Company; Eastman Kodak Company; Carrier Corporation; CIT Financial Corporation; Studebaker Corporation; International Business Machines Corporation; Marathon Corporation; Sylvania Electric Products, Incorporated; and Cluett Peabody & Company.

Executive Evaluation

Excellent management demands that men work together in harmony, each pursuing his own special task within the general effort, conscious that he is participating in a joint endeavor with men who command his respect. This unity of command is the central question to be sought in any management audit. It exists only where a qualified top executive is able to surround himself with other qualified men who will operate with him as co-executives and not as henchmen.

It is essential to learn whether the executive group actually operates as a team, and whether each man is already grooming one or more possible successors to take over his task when the day comes for his retirement. In no case should such possible successors be chosen from among an executive's relatives! Nepotism, indeed, is the antithesis of sound management. It renders a team spirit impossible of achievement and turns a public corporation into a private preserve. Many of our largest enterprises suffer in this respect.

Executive evaluation is by far the most important of the ten functional divisions of the management audit. The other nine categories, in fact, are no more than expressions of the thinking and actions of the executive group. They are examined separately in order that the effective results of the human qualities of the men in management may be measured. Analysis of the individual officers is therefore indispensable to management appraisal.

The attitude of the public towards the individual company is a prime expression of the state of public knowledge regarding the calibre of the men in top management. This means: The good will of the communities in which plants, offices, and sales organizations are located; the expressed confidence of stockholders in the ability and integrity of the officers; the quality of the mutual relations existing between the company and its suppliers and customers; the extent to which relations with the public authorities are honest, forthright and healthful. Good will is earned not by advertising but by the daily actions of men of the proper type conducting the affairs of responsible corporations.

Analysis of the executive personnel requires knowledge regarding:

1. What changes have occurred in executive personnel in recent years and why?

2. Is there, or has there ever been, nepotism in the organization?

3. Are there any rules, written or unwritten, which forbid employment of two or more members of the same family in executive position?

4. In what way are executives selected?

5. What procedures are followed in training promising executives?

6. Have any training programs been established on the top management level? If so, what are they?

7. In what public activities do the top executives engage?

8. What is the company's attitude towards the importance of public relations regarding the entire executive group?

9. How do executives' salaries compare within the industry?

Companies with especially fine executive personnel characterized by unity of command, sound programs for the training of executives, and with a general spirit of competent harmony which has resulted in an over-all excellence of management performance, include: Procter and Gamble Company; Merck and Company; E. I. Du Pont de Nemours; General Foods Corporation; National Cash Register Company; Standard Oil Company (New Jersey); B. F. Goodrich Company; General Motors Corporation; Sears, Roebuck & Company; National Gypsum Company; Union Carbide and Carbon Corporation; Electric Boat Company; Gillette Safety Razor Company; J. C. Penny Company; and American Telephone and Telegraph Company.

SUMMARY AND CONCLUSIONS

The foregoing résumé has been presented in order to make both investors and executives more familiar with the Institute's thinking regarding a simplified approach to the Management Audit.

In order to justify the system of corporate enterprise, it must be demonstrable that it is increasing in efficiency, and it must offer sound evidence of its progressive improvement. Progressive development of the profession of management, based upon rational self-analysis, contributes to increasing the strength of private enterprise itself. The investor's greatest safety lies in the comforting knowledge of good management.